Current issues: future scenarios

John Edwards • Peter Webber
Series Consultant: Simon Ross

Text © John Edwards and Peter Webber 2001

Original illustrations © Nelson Thornes Ltd 2001

The rights of John Edwards and Peter Webber to be identified as authors of this work have been asserted by them in accordance with the Copyright, Designs and Patents Act 1988.

All rights reserved. No part of this publication may be reproduced or transmitted in any form or by any means, electronic or mechanical, including photocopy, recording or any information storage and retrieval system, without permission in writing from the publisher or under licence from the Copyright Licensing Agency Limited, of 90 Tottenham Court Road, London W1T 4LP.

Any person who commits any unauthorised act in relation to this publication may be liable to criminal prosecution and civil claims for damages.

Published in 2001 by:
Nelson Thornes Ltd
Delta Place
27 Bath Road
CHELTENHAM
GL53 7TH
United Kingdom

01 02 03 04 05 / 10 9 8 7 6 5 4 3 2 1

A catalogue record for this book is available from the British Library

ISBN 0 7487 6040 7

Illustrations by Multiplex Techniques, Angela Lumley and Francis Bacon
Page make-up by Multiplex Techniques

Printed and bound in Spain by Graficas Estella

Essential GCSE Geography Website

The activities in this book are supported by a website, the address of which is:

HYPERLINK
http://www.nelsonthornes.com/essential_gcse

The user should be aware that URLs or web addresses change quite often. Although every effort will be made to provide accurate addresses, it is inevitable that some will change. We will maintain the site to ensure this frustration is an infrequent event.

Remember to bookmark this address within your browser. You may even wish to create a separate folder in which to deposit downloaded materials. We trust that the information and activities we have provided will enable you to make the most of your course in GCSE level Geography

Contents

1 Planning for Population Change — 4
- A How many people? The world's rising population — 4
- B People on the move — 11

2 Providing for Future Settlements — 19
- A Growth of the mega-city — 19
- B Improving quality of life — 28
- C Urban-rural interaction — 32

3 Changing Employment Patterns — 42
- A Changing employment structures — 42
- B Primary industry: farming — 63
- C Secondary industry: car making — 69
- D Tertiary industry: tourism — 73
- E Employment and development — 78

4 Using and Abusing the Environment — 92
- A Resources — 92
- B Water supply and management — 112
- C Pressures on the environment — 124

5 What You Need to Succeed — 142
- A Why are issues important in Geography? — 142
- B Using and interpreting photographs — 144
- C Using and drawing maps — 152
- D Drawing and interpreting graphs — 158
- E Using ICT — 163
- F Undertaking a coursework enquiry for GCSE — 165
- G Taking notes and researching — 169
- H Revision and exam preparation — 173

6 Coping with Hazards — 177
- A What is a hazard? — 177
- B Earthquakes — 184
- C Floods — 191
- D Fire — 196

7 Changing Environments — 199
- A Coastline management — 199
- B Weather and climate — 214
- C Environmental issues — 227

8 Towards a Sustainable Future — 240
- A What is sustainable development? — 240
- B Managing the desert environment — 246
- C The cleaned-up Thames — 251
- D Managing fragile environments — 255
- E Managing the coastline — 261
- F Towards sustainable cities — 267
- G Towards sustainable industry — 274
- H Reducing world poverty — 280

Section 1 Planning for Population Change

A How many people? The world's rising population

Towards the end of 1999 a young mother in eastern Europe became world famous for a brief period of time. Helac Fatima's son was officially declared the world's six billionth inhabitant, although around the world several other babies would have been born at exactly the same time. By the time of his first birthday, the human population would have grown by another 100 million.

Since 1950 the population of the world has been growing at a faster rate than ever before. This dramatic recent rate of growth is shown in Figure 1A.1.

World population did not pass the one billion mark until 1801. It took over 100 years to grow by another billion, yet a similar increase only took 12 years towards the end of the 20th century. What has caused such a spectacular rise in population? How does this affect people in different parts of the world? What is being done?

Why is population growing?

The rate of growth of population *varies through time*. During the 19th century, for example, population changed at a similar rate in many countries with the growth of towns and industries. Based on population growth in wealthy countries, a model of population change was developed called the **demographic transition model**. This identifies four stages of growth (see Figure 1A.2). Like other models in Geography, the demographic transition model shows general patterns, but it also has limitations.

Countries in **Stage 1** have a fairly stable population. The main factors affecting the rate of population change at this stage are the **birth** and **death rates**. In Stage 1, these are both high. Modern medicine has not yet developed techniques to help people live longer, and standards of personal hygiene are low. With poor healthcare and education, **infant mortality rates** (deaths before one year old) are high. Most people live in villages, with farming being the main employer. The need for a large workforce and lack of contraception means that families are large. This is known as the **pre-industrial stage**.

By **Stage 2**, population is growing quickly. Notice that this is not due to a rise in the birth rate, but rather to a sharp fall in the death rate. More modern medical techniques reduce the number of deaths, while birth rates remain high. This second stage is called the **transition stage**.

Stage 3 is marked by the growth of towns and cities, usually as a result of industrial growth. The cost of keeping a family living in towns, together with discouragement from government, results in fewer children being born. This brings the birth rate down, often to little higher than the death rate. This stage is characterised by a decline in the rate of growth of population, together with migration to other countries when there are not enough jobs. This is the **industrial stage** of the model.

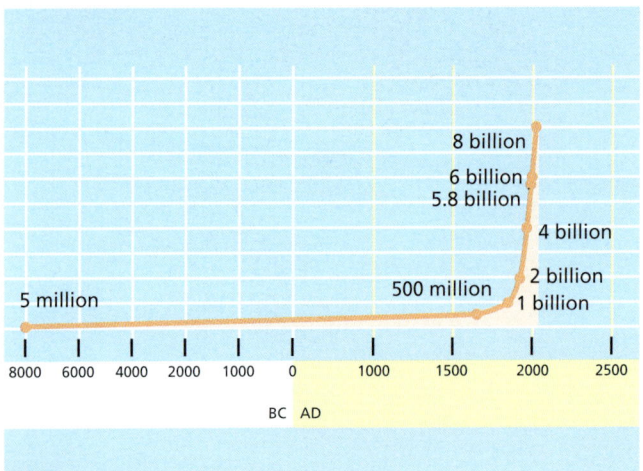

1A.1 The world's rapidly rising population

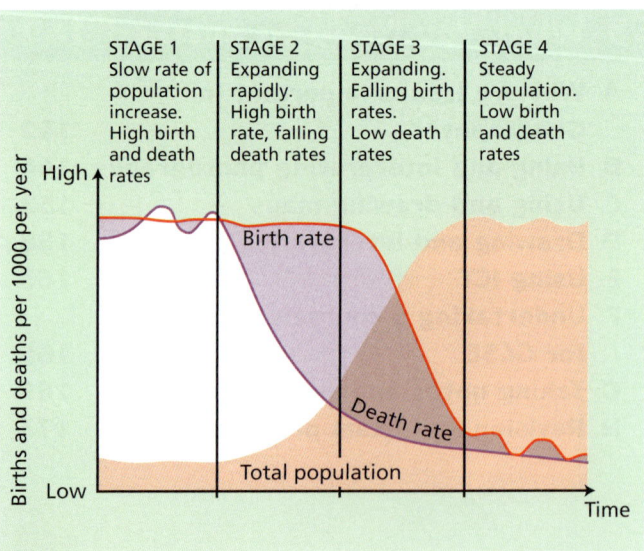

1A.2 The demographic transition model

A How many people? The world's rising population

The final part of the model, **Stage 4**, represents a period of relative population stability. Unlike Stage 1, this is due to low rates of both birth and death. Standards of living are higher, families smaller and life expectancy longer. This is the **post-industrial stage**.

How well does the model explain worldwide population growth? It is possible to compare the four stages with population figures for individual countries. Figure 1A.3 shows population change for Sweden, which has passed through each stage of the model. A similar pattern is apparent in many other European countries, as well as in the USA and Japan. In other parts of the world, however, the growth and development of population may follow a different pattern. The demographic transition model was developed using only **MEDCs** (More Economically Developed Countries) as examples, and so is unlikely to be appropriate for parts of the world such as Africa and Asia. Many **LEDCs** (Less Economically Developed Countries) have experienced rapid growth, and missed out at least one stage of the model. Others seem stuck in the transitional stage (Stage 2).

These problems with the demographic transition model highlight the fact that population growth rates *vary throughout the world* (see Figure 1A.4). The population of Sweden is

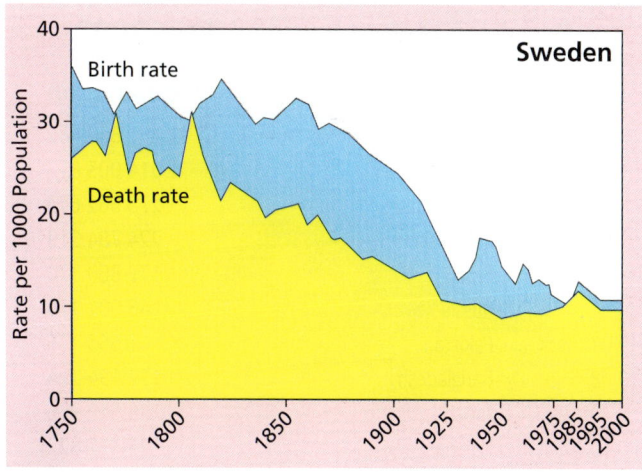

1A.3 *Sweden's birth and death rates*

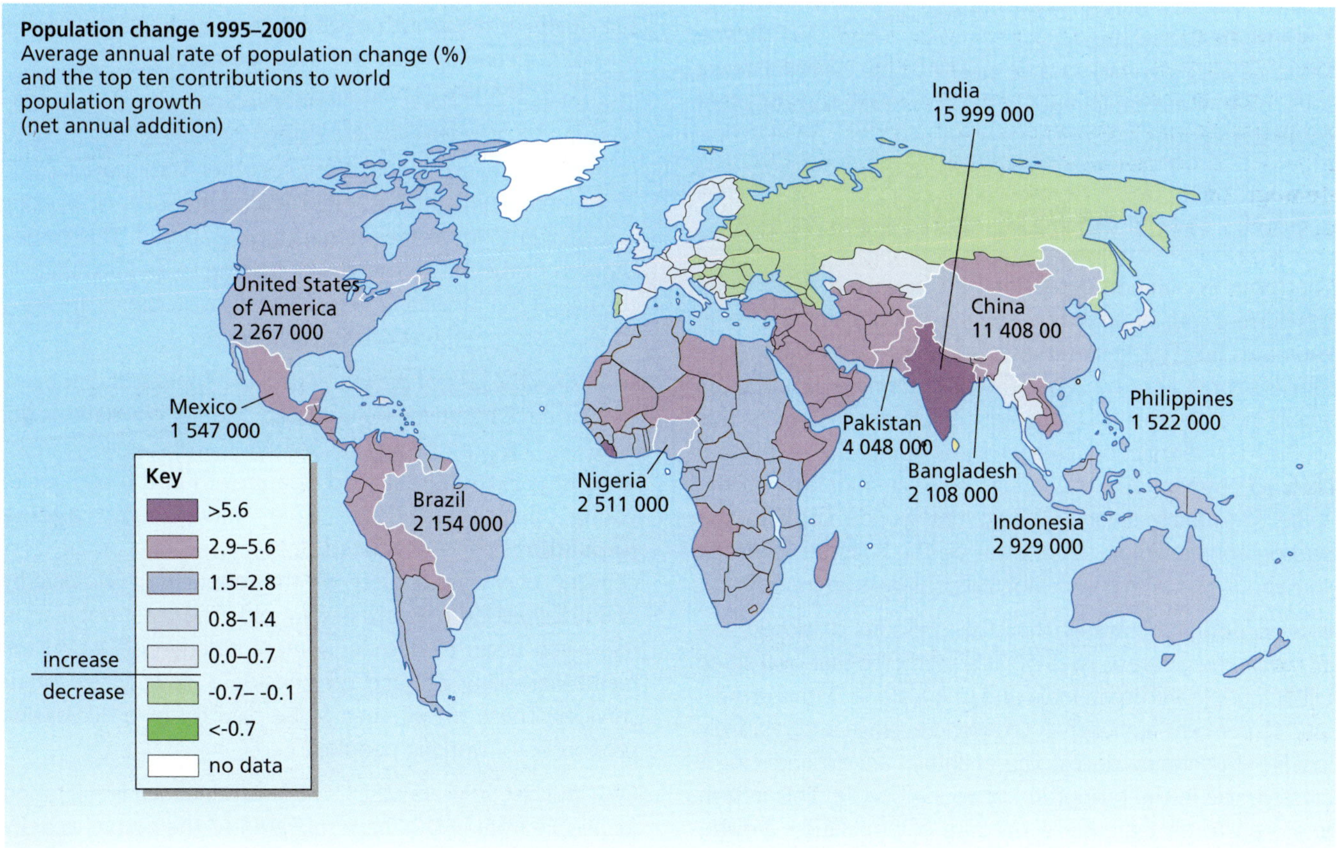

clearly quite stable, with only a very slight increase. This is the case in most MEDCs, with some countries such as Italy actually having a slight decline in population. Elsewhere in the world, the situation is very different. Since 1950, nearly 90 per cent of population growth has taken place in LEDCs,

1A.4 *The rate of population change varies greatly throughout the world*

Section 1 Planning for Population Change

Countries ranked by population: 2000		
Rank	Country	Population
1	China	1 261 832 482
2	India	1 014 003 817
3	United States	275 562 673
4	Indonesia	224 784 210
5	Brazil	172 860 370
6	Russia	146 001 176
7	Pakistan	141 553 775
8	Bangladesh	129 194 224
9	Japan	126 549 976
10	Nigeria	123 337 822

Countries ranked by population in 2050		
Rank	Country	Population (estimate)
1	India	1 619 582 271
2	China	1 470 468 924
3	United States	403 943 147
4	Indonesia	337 807 011
5	Nigeria	303 586 770
6	Pakistan	267 813 495
7	Brazil	206 751 477
8	Bangladesh	205 093 861
9	Ethiopia	187 892 174
10	Congo (Kinshasa)	181 922 656

1A.5 *The world's most populated countries*

which in total now account for 80 per cent of the world's total population. The fastest growth is in India and China, with these two countries alone being responsible for one-third of current world population growth (see Figure 1A.5).

Many poorer countries are experiencing rapid population growth due to falling death rates. This is because of improvements in medical technology and healthcare. Diseases such as cholera and measles now claim far fewer lives. Birth rates remain high, often due to religious or other cultural traditions.

LEDC and MEDC differences

The term 'population explosion' is often used to describe the current rate of growth of the world's population. Some estimates have suggested that there could be as many as 14 billion people alive by 2060. The planet's natural resources would not be able to cope with such expansion. Is this 'doomsday' prediction caused by a population explosion likely to happen? Are the effects of population growth the same for people everywhere in the world? Look at the photographs in Figure 1A.6. What do the images suggest to you about stages in the demographic transition model?

It is in poorer countries that the pressure of population growth is the greatest. By 2050, it is predicted that over three billion people will live in India and China alone. With a growth rate 40 per cent higher than the world average and relatively low life expectancy, developing countries are experiencing a massive rise in the proportion of young people. This in turn may lead to an increase in the rate of population growth; some fear that India's population, already over one billion, is in danger of growing out of control.

A rapidly increasing population has many effects. The pressure of a growing population may lead to the destruction of natural environments, for example through deforestation and soil erosion. This may also cause other problems, such as flooding and desertification. Millions of people move to cities in the hope of a better quality of life. This leads to the growth of cities, causing urban sprawl, the loss of farmland, and air and water pollution.

There have also been conflicts, revolutions, and starvation in some LEDCs where governments have been unstable or corrupt. Increased population, together with poverty and high unemployment, has caused large numbers of working age people to leave their homes to live abroad. This causes the loss of the 16–40 age group, leading to an imbalance in the age of the remaining population. The problems are likely to increase as populations become larger.

In MEDCs the lack of growth of population means that many of the above problems do not exist. The wealthy nations do, however, face problems caused by a very slow or non-existent growth rate. Instead of a growth in the number of young people, MEDCs have increasingly **ageing populations**. It is estimated that, by the end of the 21st century, over one-quarter of the population in wealthy countries will be over sixty years old. The total population may even begin to decline. A more elderly population will mean increasing demand on pensions, medical and other services. These will all need to be paid for by a decreasing proportion of working people.

Over the last 50 years MEDCs have experienced immigration as people from LEDCs have migrated to their more wealthy economies. Migration is another part of population change and is studied later.

A How many people? The world's rising population

Average family sizes are largest in Africa

MEDC family sizes have steadily reduced

Death rates have fallen in many LEDCs

Longer life expectancy has many effects upon the population of a country

1A.6 *Population change is not the same everywhere in the world*

Too many people? Coping with population change

Is the population of the world growing out of control, to a stage where the limited resources of the planet cannot cope? While this may appear to be the case according to many predictions, experts disagree.

An 'MEDC viewpoint' is that people in poorer countries are having too many children, and it is the growth of their population that is putting the future of the planet at risk. People in LEDCs say that the Earth has enough resources to support a larger population, but that resources need to be more evenly spread. The rich nations, while having only one-fifth of the world's population, use 85 per cent of its resources. It takes about twenty times as much of the world's resources, for example, to raise a child in the USA as it does in Asia.

Recent world population growth may be faster than at any time in the past, yet forecasts predict it will soon begin to slow down. By the middle of the 21st century, it is likely that the world's population will have stopped growing at all (see Figure 1A.7). A maximum figure of about 9 billion is predicted by 2050, after which the total number is likely to decline. What is it that controls the rate of population growth?

1. **Economic development** As nations grow more wealthy, family sizes become smaller. In many South American countries where industrial development has taken place quickly, the decline in the birth rate has been sudden.
2. **Equality for women** More equal opportunity for jobs and education in developing countries has led to women having fewer children, and at an older age.
3. **Family planning** The key to falling growth rates is a reduction in the birth rate. Women are having fewer

Section 1 Planning for Population Change

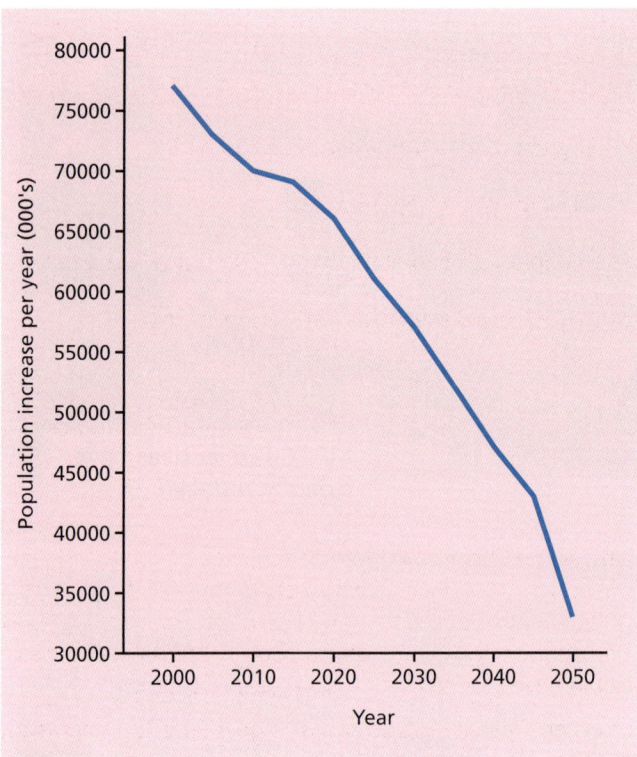

1A.7 *The rate of increase in world population is slowing down*

NOTING ACTIVITIES

1. Describe how the population of the world has changed since 1950.
2. On a copy of Figure 1A.3, label the four stages of the demographic transition model.
3. What are the main features of each stage of the model?
4. Why does the demographic transition model not apply to every country in the world?
5. What are the main differences in population change between MEDCs and LEDCs?
6. Do you think the photographs in Figure 1A.6 are stereotypes? Would it be possible to find similar photographs of the LEDCs from Europe?

children: the average fertility rate is falling faster than predicted. Contraception is becoming more widely available, and improvements in healthcare have greatly reduced worldwide infant mortality rates.

4 **Government policies** Where population growth has been a major problem, governments have stepped in to offer rewards for those who have small families, and penalties for those who do not. China's one-child policy is an example.

Population control in China

China has a larger population than any other country in the world. At the start of the 21st century, more than one-fifth of the world's people were Chinese. The population of the country has more than doubled since 1950, reaching 1.3 billion by the millennium. Although China is the third largest country by area in the world, such a rapid rate of increase has put great pressure on the nation's natural resources. Millions of people have moved away from the countryside, which is home for most Chinese people. China's urban areas have been placed under increasing strain, while improved overall living standards have increased life expectancy.

Faced with the danger of population growth becoming out of control, the Chinese government decided to take action to control future expansion. People were encouraged to marry at an older age, making it likely that they would have fewer children. The most drastic measure, however, was the **one-**

1A.8 *Although nearly 80 per cent of Chinese people live in villages, the most rapid population growth has taken place in large cities such as Shanghai*

child policy. Introduced in 1979, families with one child received benefits and allowances that were unavailable to those with more children. People with larger families were penalised (see Figure 1A.9).

A How many people? The world's rising population

WAYS TO ENCOURAGE PEOPLE TO HAVE ONE CHILD	WAYS TO DISCOURAGE PEOPLE FROM HAVING MORE THAN ONE CHILD
• couples with one child get a 10% wage bonus • one-child families get priority in education and housing • families receive a certificate • free contraceptives and birth control education	• no grain rations if there is a second child • poor education opportunities • a couple with two children pay a fine and more tax • compulsory sterilisation of all couples with two children

1A.9 *China's one-child policy*

Successes and failures

Even with the policy, China's population reached 1.3 billion in 2000. Those in favour of the policy say it would have been even higher without the policy and that 300 million births have been prevented. There are also many Chinese families better off because they have only one child.

The policy has worked better in the towns and cities than in the countryside. In China baby boys are often preferred to girls. The medical ultrasound equipment that helps to predict the gender of babies is widely used and some girl babies are aborted. Some girls are even abandoned after birth. The result is there that are 113 boys born for every 100 girls. Some Chinese boys are pampered and spoilt and many will never find women to marry. Opponents of the policy call it cruel. Maybe if China had allowed the demographic transition to follow its natural course, the natural increase would have reduced, as it has in other countries.

Another difficulty China faces in planning for population change is knowing exactly how many people there are in the country. Even without the one-child policy, it is difficult to count all of the people living in China. With unpopular population control measures in place, it is thought that millions of children are born secretly throughout the country (see Figure 1A.10).

China prepares for huge census

BEIJING – China is preparing to conduct the world's largest census in November, with more than five million census takers expected to work on getting an accurate picture of how many people live in the most populous country in the world, state media said on Friday.

Beginning on 1 November 2000, census takers throughout the country will try to find out exactly how many people there are in China and for the first time they will try to count the number of children born who break the 'one-child' policy, the *China Daily* said. China officially has a population of 1.26 billion people, but since the government began implementing a one-child policy in 1979, many families have broken the rule.

Despite forced abortions and severe financial penalties, many couples still get around the law by sending the pregnant woman to stay with relatives until the baby is born or claiming the newborn baby was adopted or belongs to a friend or relative.

China claims the one-child policy is succeeding and has estimated its population will rise to 1.4 billion people by 2010, peak at 1.6 billion by 2050 and then decrease, with India then replacing China as the most populous country in the world.

1A.10 *From the* China Daily *newspaper 1 October 2000*

Section 1 Planning for Population Change

NOTING ACTIVITIES

1 Why were the Chinese authorities keen to adopt a one-child policy in 1979?
2 What were the measures used to make the policy work?
3 How do the Chinese authorities argue that the policy has been successful?
4 Do you think it is a cruel policy? Give reasons for your answer.
5 Using Figure 1A.10, describe the problems faced by the Chinese government in controlling population growth.

STRUCTURED QUESTION

Study Figure 1A.4, which shows how the world's population is changing.

1 Describe the pattern of population change shown on the map. (2)
2 Why does the rate of growth vary throughout the world? (2)
3 Study Figure 1A.11, showing population change in Germany and Kenya.
   a Draw a graph to show population change in Kenya. (4)
4 a Describe the main differences between population change in Sweden (Figure 1A.3) and Kenya as shown by the graphs. (5)
   b Suggest reasons for the pattern of population change in **either** Germany **or** Kenya. (5)
5 With reference to one named country you have studied,
   a what population issues are there?
   b how have people tried to deal with these issues? (7)

Population change in Kenya

Year	Population	Year	Population
1950	6 121	1997	28 644
1960	8 157	1998	29 277
1970	11 272	1999	29 842
1980	16 685	2000	30 340
1990	23 767	2010	33 068
1991	24 627	2020	34 001
1992	25 592	2030	34 836
1993	26 312	2040	36 247
1994	26 806	2050	38 660
1995	27 315		
1996	27 957		

(figures in thousands)

1A.11 *Population change in Germany and Kenya*

Section 1 Planning for Population Change

B People on the move

Migration is the movement of people between two places for a long period of time. Although it is difficult to be exact about this time span, there is clearly a difference between people going on holiday for a few weeks, and others seeking a permanent move (Figure 1B.1). Migration usually involves people moving in search of somewhere to live. Has your family ever moved home? Who do you know who has moved home? People may move within a country, or from one country to another. They may choose to move, or have no choice but to move. There are four main types of migration.

1 Internal voluntary migration This is the movement of people by choice from one place to another within a country, often for economic or social reasons. Moving for school or work are examples of this type of migration. Within the United Kingdom many people have moved to London and the south-east of England in search of jobs.

2 Internal forced migration This is the movement of people within a country in which they have no choice. This may be caused by civil war or forced by the government, such as in the former Yugoslavia in eastern Europe.

3 International voluntary migration This is the movement of people across national boundaries, often in search of better jobs. The United States, for example, receives migrants across the border from Mexico in search of employment.

4 International forced migration People forced to leave their country because of war or famine, such as in Ethiopia, are forced migrants.

CASE STUDY

Migration into western Europe

The movement of people from one place to another has always made a big contribution to population change in Europe. Migration has become an increasingly important issue for governments throughout the world attempting to cope with population change in the 21st century. Since 1960, over 35 million people have moved away from LEDCs, where standards of living are poor and growth rates high. Western Europe is an attractive destination for migrants.

With slow or zero growth rates, western European countries have fewer people of working age and an increasingly elderly population. Some governments began to encourage the temporary migration of workers from other parts of Europe and beyond. Nearly three million 'guest workers' moved to Germany, for example, the largest proportion of them from Turkey. Migration is changing the make up of European populations. In France, over one million people are

1B.1 *People may choose to migrate, or be forced to move ...*

1B.2 *People forced to leave their country by war or famine are called* **refugees**

Section 1 Planning for Population Change

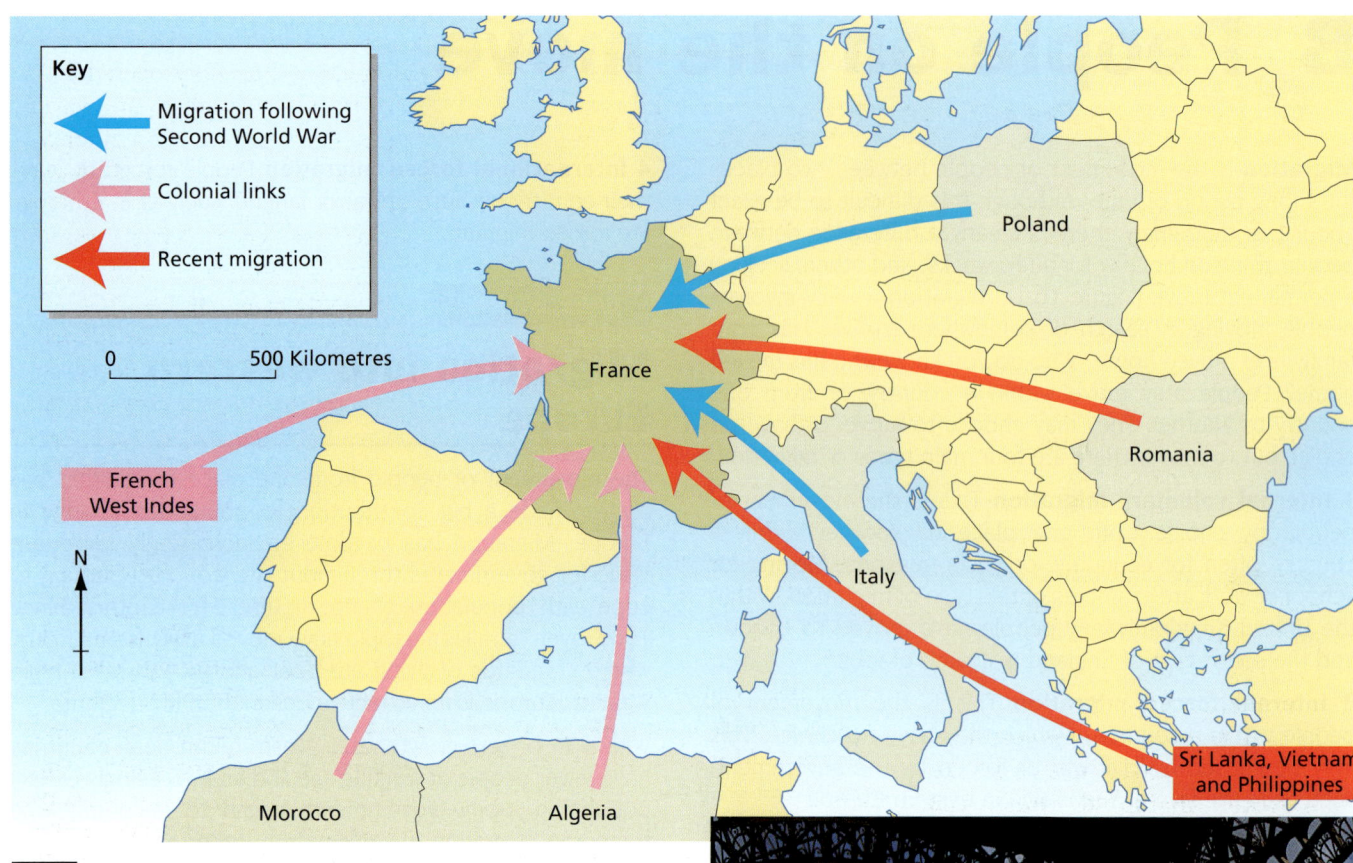

1B.3 *Origin of migrants to France*

descendants of north African migrant labourers, the majority of whom are under 25 years old. Nearly one-quarter of French people have a parent or grandparent who was a migrant into the country (see Figure 1B.3). Since the beginning of the 1990s there has also been an increase in the number of migrants within Europe, mainly to the west from countries such as the former Yugoslavia. The collapse of communism together with civil wars forced many people to leave their homes.

Fortress Europe?

The governments of western Europe have tried to limit the number of people migrating to their countries. Many refugees, people who have been forced to leave their own country, have been refused entry to countries such as France, Spain and the United Kingdom. What benefits and problems are caused by refugees? Figure 1B.4 examines some of these issues with reference to migrants attempting to enter Spain.

B People on the move

Refugees arrive on Spanish beaches

From our Europe correspondent

At one time the illegal immigrants from north Africa landed on Spanish beaches at night and were quickly smuggled away to the mountains. But this summer refugees have been landing on beaches where holidaymakers are sunbathing and surfing. These are the beaches of the Canary Islands which are a part of Spain. There is a 100 kilometre unguarded stretch of water between the African mainland and the Canaries and boatloads of people from countries such as Nigeria, Sierra Leone, Senegal and Cameroon are willing to risk the journey.

The final boat ride to the Canary Islands is not the hardest part of the refugees' migration journey. To get to the African coast many people travel overland through countries foreign to them and through the Sahara desert.

However, once in the Canary Islands the refugees are in Europe. As Spain is a member of the European Union they see themselves as having reached a part of the EU.

Still, only a few people arrive via the Canaries. Thousands continue to risk the short journey between Morocco and southern Spain around Gibraltar. In the last ten days police around the town of Tarifa have intercepted 600 people. A sports stadium is being used to accommodate the African refugees.

Spain has spent £80 million on a radar system which will detect illegal immigrants along 550 kilometres of the Mediterranean Sea. This will be fully operational in 2004; until then there are ways of entering Spain – as this summer has shown – via the Canary Islands.

And yet recent reports show that Spain needs people to work in its booming economy. By 2030 12 million immigrants will be needed to work in the factories and on the farms. Throughout western Europe natural population increase has declined. Countries no longer reach the population replacement rate. The whole of Europe will need massive immigration to sustain its economy.

Against these demographic facts how does making Spain a 'fortress' help? How does halting the influx of refugees help the future of Europe's economy? The answer is complex. Too many Europeans do not understand the need for immigrants and see their continent as a white European one which needs protecting from those who would like to come to work in it.

1B.4 *From the* Guardian *31 August 2000*

NOTING ACTIVITIES

1 What are the four main types of migration?

2 Why do people want to enter Europe from African countries?

3 a Why do the Spanish authorities want to keep illegal immigrants out of their country?

   b Are there arguments for more immigrants being accepted into Spain?

4 'Fortress Europe' is a term relating to the strict immigration controls that have been set up.

   a From what other directions do you think illegal immigrants arrive in Europe?

   b Why do you think some people get so angry about new arrivals to Europe?

   c If Europe needs more immigrants how do you think it should try to attract them?

   d How could the European authorities change people's attitudes towards new immigrants?

5 What is a refugee and how is one different from an asylum seeker?

6 Write down some of the issues about refugees that have interested you.

Section 1 Planning for Population Change

How accurate are people's impressions of the effect of migrants upon the countries to which they move? In November 1999, there were 7100 people who applied to enter the United Kingdom to live. Figure 1B.5 shows where they came from together with some statements about refugees. Read through the quotes. What do you think?

Refugees: some myths and facts

Asylum seekers to UK November 1999	
Federal Republic of Yugoslavia	795
Sri Lanka	755
China	385
Somalia	385
Afghanistan	380
Poland	350

'Refugees are an economic burden.'
Some might be but most will work hard in their new country.

'Refugees are uneducated.'
Some might be but some are well educated and have been forced to leave their country.

'Refugees are those people made homeless by floods, famine and earthquakes.'
These people cannot be called refugees under the UN definition; they are migrants.

'Refugees come from very poor countries and homes.'
Certainly this may be true for some but others would have been comfortably well off. When they arrive in their new country they may be much poorer. Of refugees coming to the UK, 90% go to London where there is a housing shortage. Many live in very poor conditions to start with.

'Refugees always seem to come to rich countries.'
This is definitely wrong; 83% of the world's refugees live in poor countries.

1B.5 *Who are refugees?*

NOTING ACTIVITIES

1 Using Figure 1B.5, draw a map to show the origin of applicants to enter the United Kingdom in November 1999. Make the width of your lines proportional to the number of people from each country.

2 Why do you think that people have migrated to the United Kingdom from these countries?

3 What advantages and problems might be caused by migrants moving to another country?

B People on the move

STRUCTURED QUESTION

Study Figure 1B.6 which shows some information about migration in Europe.

1 Describe the pattern of migration shown on the map. (3)
2 Why do rates of migration vary within as well as between countries? (4)
3 Give reasons for migration in one named area on Figure 1B.6. (5)

Key
- Immigration area
- Emigration area
- ← Major migration

1B.6 *Migration in Europe*

15

Section 1 Planning for Population Change

STRUCTURED QUESTION

Study Figure 1B.7 which shows unemployment rates in the European Union.

4 a Describe the pattern of unemployment shown on the map. *(4)*

b What similarities and differences are there between the patterns on this map and Figure 1B.6? *(4)*

5 Do the maps support the idea that there is an economic **core** and **periphery** in Europe? (See Figure 3A.9 on page 47.) *(5)*

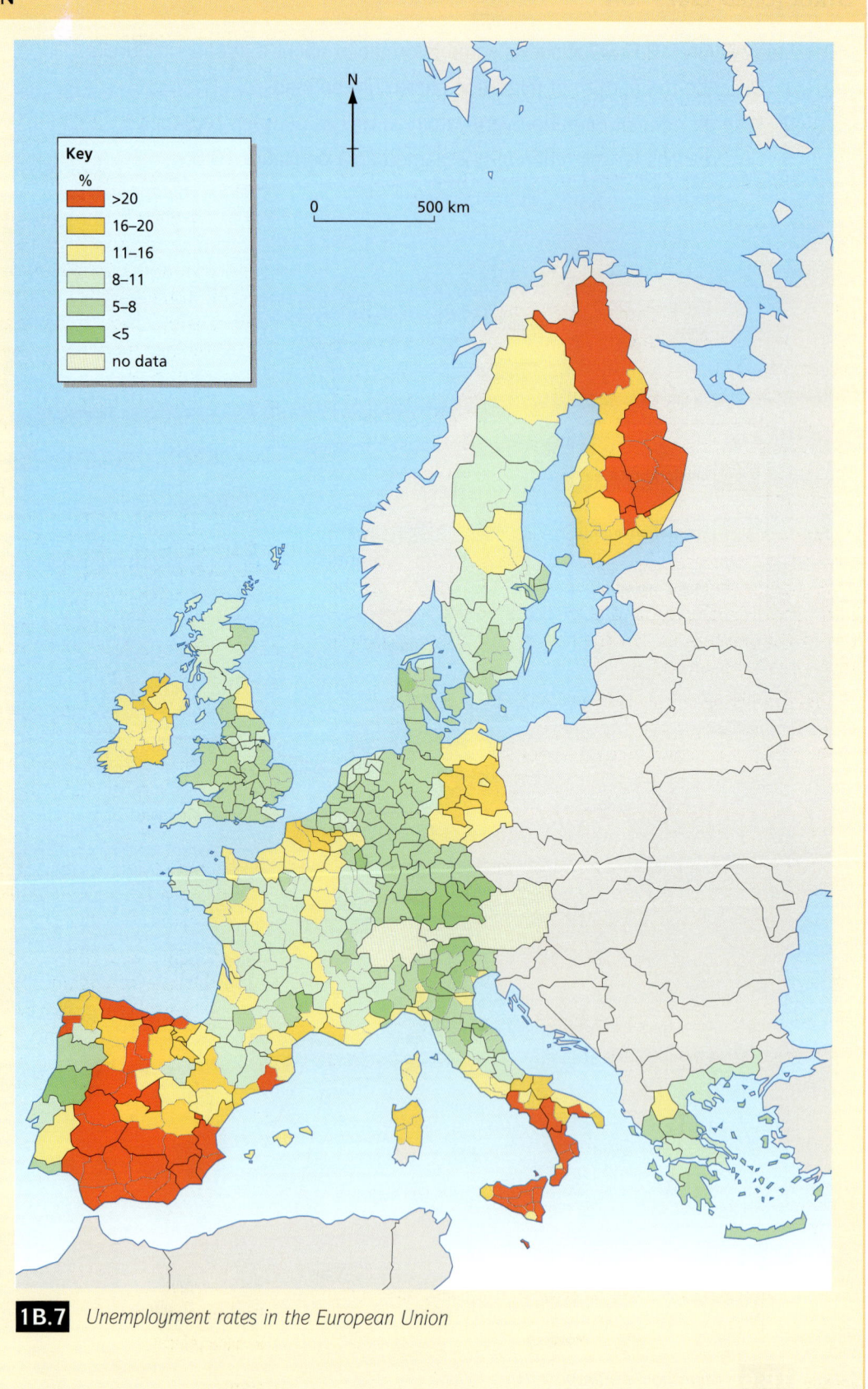

1B.7 *Unemployment rates in the European Union*

B People on the move

CASE STUDY

Population change in Italy

With an advanced economy and high GNP, why is population an issue for Italy at the start of the 21st century? How is the population of the country changing, and what effects are these changes likely to have? How important is migration, within Italy as well as to and from other countries?

How is population changing?

Italy only became a country in 1861. Until then it had been a series of individual states. Population grew quickly during the second half of the 19th century, even though many people moved out of Italy. Population growth slowed down steadily during the 20th century, with both birth and death rates falling. Following the Second World War, most of the increase in Italy's population was due to people moving in from abroad.

In common with many other European countries, there were not enough workers after years of conflict, and migrants were encouraged to come to live in Italy. By the end of the 20th century, birth rates had fallen so sharply that they were lower than death rates. For the first time, the population of Italy actually began to fall.

The **fertility rate** in Italy is lower than anywhere else in the world. On average, women only have 1.2 children (see Figure 1B.9). If this trend continues, the population of Italy is likely to fall greatly during the 21st century. The structure of the population will also alter. The number of elderly people will rise, representing a higher proportion of the country's population. Using these estimated figures, it is possible that the single most common age group in Italy by 2050 will be women aged 85 and over.

How important is migration for Italy?

Since 1861, about 25 million people have left Italy in search of a new home. Nearly half of these joined 40 million other Europeans by crossing the Atlantic and living in the United States. The majority of people moved from the poorer south of Italy. By the second half of the 20th century, most Italian migrants moved to places within Europe. Many stayed abroad for a short period of time, especially in countries allowing entry only to males of working age.

By the 1970s more people returned to Italy than left. In addition to Italians returning home, migrants freely entered Italy taking advantage of the few controls on immigration. By 2000, over one million foreigners lived in Italy, 90 per cent of them coming from beyond Europe. The number of migrants to Italy has recently grown because of people moving from eastern Europe following the collapse of communism in countries such as Yugoslavia.

Migration within Italy has contributed much to population structure and distribution. Movement of people has generally been from the south to the north, and from east to west. The south of Italy, the *Mezzorgiorno*, has long been poorer than the north, especially with the growing wealth of the northern cities of Milan, Turin and Genoa. The dry and remote mountainous areas of the south of Italy offered too few jobs for the 6 million people who moved to the north in search of work.

In recent years, despite the continued relative poverty of the south, the rate of migration to the north-western cities of Italy has slowed. Unemployment has risen in many parts of the north, and the large cities suffer from problems such as overcrowding and pollution. Many people have returned to live in rural communities, while the fastest recent economic growth has taken place in the small towns of the north-east or 'Third Italy'.

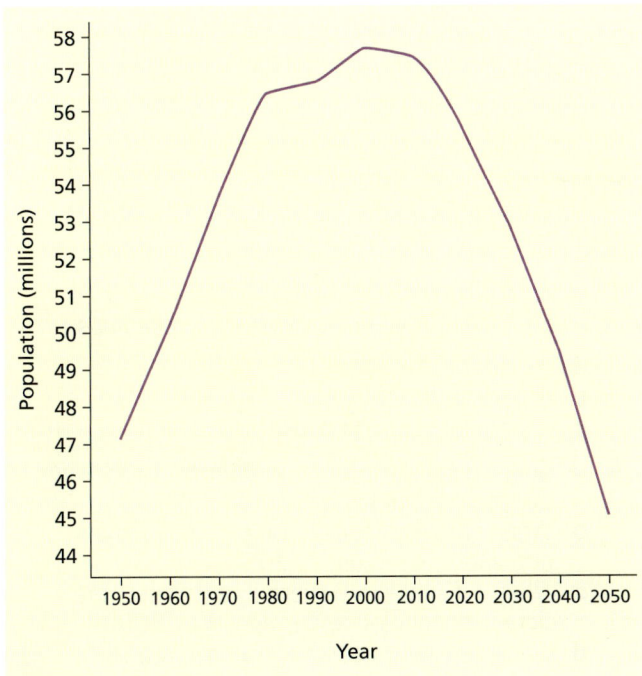

1B.8 *Italy is predicted to experience one of the sharpest rates of population decline in the world*

1B.9 *Total fertility rates, per woman*

Italy	1.2
USA	2.1
World average	3.3
Developing countries	2.6
Rwanda (Africa)	8.5

Section 1 Planning for Population Change

1B.10 *People have moved to smaller settlements in the north-west of Italy away from the largest urban centres such as Milan and Turin*

Why is population an issue in Italy?

Although having low birth and death rates has solved many problems, a zero rate of population increase also has disadvantages. With increasing life expectancy, more people may be expected to live beyond working age. These people will need to be supported by the working population of the country, which at the same time is becoming smaller. More elderly people will put a greater strain on Italy's health and other services, all of which need to be paid for.

Italy will need more workers in the 21st century to meet the demands of its people. With such a low birth rate and small number of young people, Italians will not be able to provide the necessary workforce. At a time when European countries have looked to tighten immigration laws, Italy may have to look abroad again to strengthen its economy.

NOTING ACTIVITIES

1 Describe the growth of Italy's population since 1861.

2 Outline the pattern of international migration that has affected Italy.

3 Which parts of Italy have benefited most from migration within the country? Why is this?

4 What problems does Italy face because of a low rate of population growth?

STRUCTURED QUESTION

1 a What is migration? *(1)*
  b What are the four main groups of migrants? *(4)*
  c What is a refugee? *(1)*

2 Why have governments encouraged migrants to move to western European countries? *(2)*

Study Figure 1B.11, which shows the age–gender pyramids for Denmark and Nigeria for 2050.

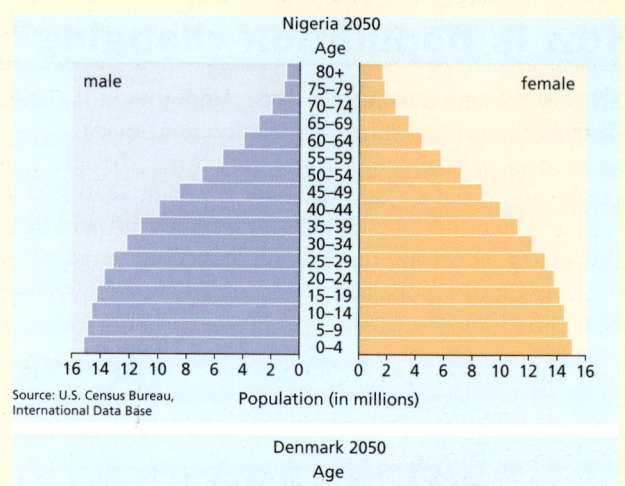

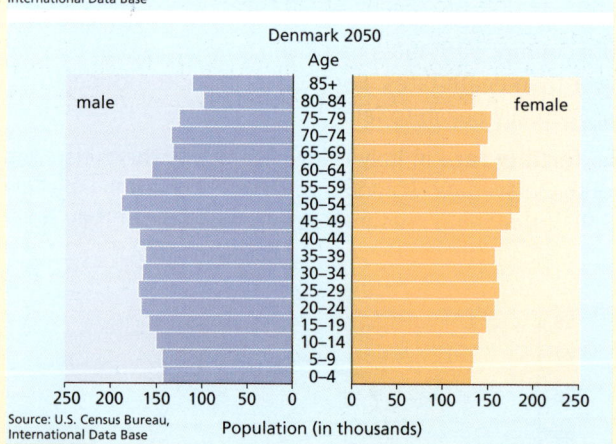

1B.11 *Age–gender pyramids showing the predicted population structure of Denmark and Nigeria in 2050*

3 Describe the structure of the population of each country under each of the following headings:
  a dependants (under 16)
  b working age (17–65)
  c retirement (66 and over) *(6)*

4 a Give reasons for the main differences between the two pyramids. *(4)*
  b What problems could result from Nigeria's population structure in 2050? *(3)*
  c What difficulties are there in accurately predicting population as far ahead as 2050? *(3)*
  d Using a named country you have studied, explain how migration has contributed to the population structure. *(6)*

Section 2 Providing for Future Settlements

A Growth of the mega-city

The growth of cities is called **urbanisation**. In developed countries (MEDCs) urbanisation has been taking place since the 19th century, often linked to the growth of industry in towns and cities. As a result, most people in MEDCs now live in urban areas. In poorer countries of the world (LEDCs), urbanisation has taken place much more recently, and often more rapidly. A smaller proportion of people live in urban areas in LEDCs, yet in some countries a small number of cities have grown very quickly. These are the world's **mega-cities**.

The ten largest cities in the world are shown in Figure 2A.1. Notice how many of them are in poorer parts of the world such as South America, Africa and Asia. Cities in Europe, North America and Australia are not growing at anything like the same rate. Why are cities in LEDCs growing so quickly? What are the effects of such rapid urban growth?

Cities in LEDCs are growing rapidly for two main reasons.

1 More people are being born in the cities. This is called the **natural growth** of a city. In some countries, this is the main reason for the growth of cities. In São Paulo for example, the largest city in Brazil, a child is born every two minutes. This means that the natural increase of the population of the city is 260 000 every year.

2 People **migrate** to cities from the countryside. In many poor countries, this is the main reason for the rapid growth of cities. It is generally people of working age who migrate to cities. These are people who are most likely to have children, causing the natural increase of a city's population to rise even further. People may move to cities because they are 'pushed' from the countryside, or 'pulled' to the city.

Most migrants are well aware that life in the city will not be much better than in the countryside. Conditions in rural areas are often so difficult that they are left with little alternative but to move, and a large city is the most common destination. They know that their chances of surviving are only slightly better in the city. Most migrants are pushed from the countryside rather than pulled to the city.

Rapid urban growth has led to many problems in urban areas in poor countries. Cities do not have the housing or service facilities to cope with the huge number of people moving from the countryside. People have to build their own

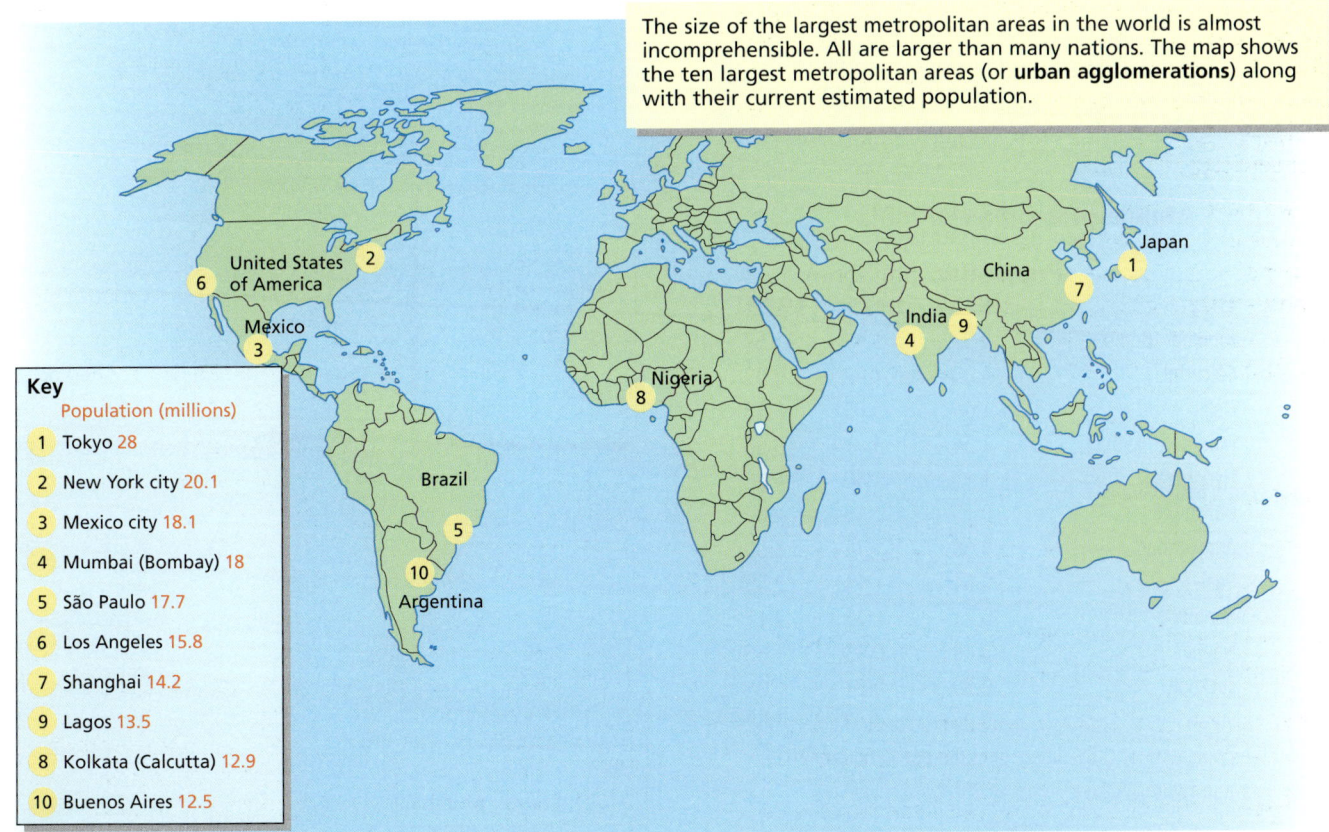

The size of the largest metropolitan areas in the world is almost incomprehensible. All are larger than many nations. The map shows the ten largest metropolitan areas (or **urban agglomerations**) along with their current estimated population.

Key
Population (millions)
1 Tokyo 28
2 New York city 20.1
3 Mexico city 18.1
4 Mumbai (Bombay) 18
5 São Paulo 17.7
6 Los Angeles 15.8
7 Shanghai 14.2
9 Lagos 13.5
8 Kolkata (Calcutta) 12.9
10 Buenos Aires 12.5

2A.1 *The world's largest urban areas*

Section 2 Providing for Future Settlements

houses on the edge of cities, the only place where space is available. Life is hard for newcomers in these **squatter settlements**. Most migrants are young, have few skills, and take jobs that are very poorly paid. There is rarely access to safe water or sanitation, and conditions are often very crowded. With little money to spend on food, many people go hungry. Without fresh water or toilets, disease spreads easily and there is a high death rate especially among young children.

A study of any LEDC city will show these characteristics and a poor quality of life for many. But LEDC cities also have rich people living in them and areas of great wealth. There are often grand old buildings from former colonial times and many cities also have modern buildings and monuments, which some people call 'prestige developments'. In the following case study the gap between the rich and poor is certainly a large one.

Distribution of urban population by size class of towns

Size of towns	Population range	No. of towns	Share of urban population (%)
I	>1 000 000	300	65.20
II	50 000–99 999	345	10.95
III	20 000–49 999	947	13.19
IV	10 000–19 999	1 167	7.77
V	5 000–9 999	740	2.60
VI	<5 000	197	0.29
All classes		3 696	

Million-plus cities of India

		Population (millions)		
Rank	City	1951	1971	1991
1	Mumbai (Bombay)	2.97	5.97	12.57
2	Calcutta	4.67	7.42	10.92
3	Delhi	1.44	3.65	8.38
4	Madras (Chennai)	1.54	3.17	5.36
5	Hyderabad	1.13	1.80	4.28
6	Bangalore	0.79	1.66	4.09
7	Ahmedabad	0.88	1.75	3.30
8	Pune	0.61	1.14	2.49
9	Kanpur	0.71	1.28	2.11
10	Nagpur	0.48	0.93	1.66
11	Lucknow	0.50	0.81	1.64
12	Surat	0.24	0.49	1.52

(Note: the population of cities differs from the population of urban areas shown in Figure 2A.1.)

2A.2 India's largest cities

CASE STUDY

Mumbai (Bombay): an LEDC city

Mumbai is the capital city of the Indian state of Maharashtra and India's largest commercial city (see Figure 2A.2). The city has recently changed its name from Bombay back to its older name. It is now one of India's mega-cities with a population of nearly 13 million. Yet at the start of the 18th century, the area now occupied by Mumbai was a cluster of seven isolated islands. What caused Mumbai to grow into one of the world's largest cities? What are the effects of this growth? How can the quality of life of people living in Mumbai be improved?

Mumbai developed as a settlement when English colonists used the area for industry, and as a seaport (Figure 2A.3). More recently, the city has grown rapidly for reasons that are typical throughout the poorer world (Figure 2A.4). Figure 2A.5 shows how both push and pull factors have contributed to the rural-to-urban migration that has swelled Mumbai's population. Migrants make up over 60 per cent of the population of the present-day city. Birth rates in Mumbai are high, and so natural growth also contributes to the city's expansion.

2A.3 The location of Mumbai

Population (millions)
13
12
11
10
9
8
7
6
5
4
3
2
1
0
very fast growth
steady growth
stable population
1911
1921
1931
1941
1951
1961
1971
1981
1991
Year

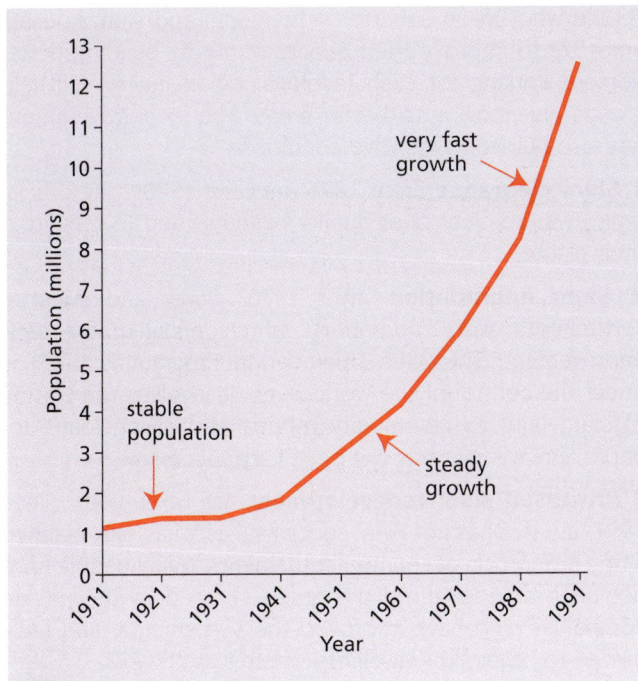

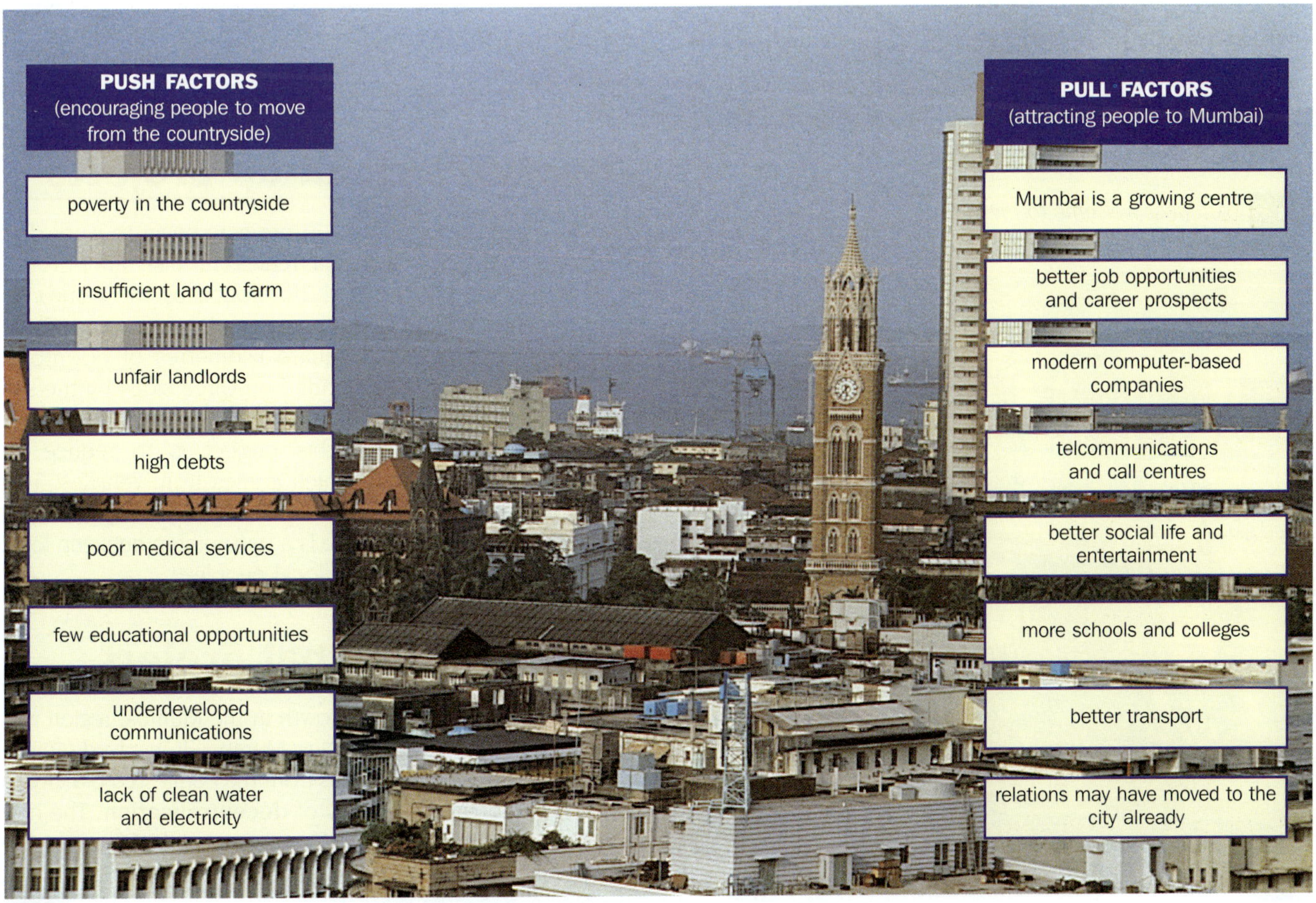

2A.4 *The growth of Mumbai's population*

What are the effects of fast urban growth?

The rapid expansion of Mumbai has brought many problems to the city, but there have also been benefits. The economy is expanding rapidly, with a range of new industries. Almost all of India's major companies have offices in the city, which today is known as the Gateway to India. International hotels attract business people and tourists from all over the world. Figure 2A.6 describes a busy and pleasant city.

The booming economy and creation of wealth has benefited millions of Indian people. Yet there are also many disadvantages of Mumbai's rapid expansion. Many migrants cannot find work in the city, or are underemployed. The majority find work in the **informal sector** of the economy, for example washing cars or selling small amounts of goods such as sweets or tobacco. The fast expansion of the city has also caused environmental problems. The natural mangrove swamps of the area have been destroyed, the sea has been polluted and there are no efficient systems to dispose of the city's waste and rubbish.

PUSH FACTORS
(encouraging people to move from the countryside)
poverty in the countryside
insufficient land to farm
unfair landlords
high debts
poor medical services
few educational opportunities
underdeveloped communications
lack of clean water and electricity
PULL FACTORS
(attracting people to Mumbai)
Mumbai is a growing centre
better job opportunities and career prospects
modern computer-based companies
telcommunications and call centres
better social life and entertainment
more schools and colleges
better transport
relations may have moved to the city already

2A.5 *Reasons for the growth of Mumbai*

Section 2 Providing for Future Settlements

Housing problems lead to social problems. The gap between rich and poor has widened. The middle classes live in new areas such as New Mumbai, while as much as 60 per cent of the city's population live in squatter settlements like those in Figure 2A.7.

> ## Tourist information describes a busy and pleasant city
>
> **Malabar Hill and Marine Drive.** *The visitor cannot do better than to start off his or her visit with a view of Mumbai from Malabar Hill which, together with Cumballa Hills, comprises the most fashionable residential area. There are many large houses with lovely gardens. Going up Marine Drive, a modern promenade by the sea, the jostling crowds in the cool of the evening can be so great that the newcomer may well imagine that an important festival is being celebrated.*

2A.6 A tourist welcome to the city

2A.7 Despite improvements, the majority of Mumbai's population live in squatter settlements

People who live in squatter settlements and slum housing areas try to improve their quality of life by building better homes, working for cash incomes, belonging to self-help groups and moving to better areas. The local government has also helped to improve conditions.

1 Slum clearance From 1896 until the 1970s, the official policy was to clear poor quality buildings and to rebuild in their place.

2 Slum upgradation After 1976, slums and squatter settlements were upgraded, which allowed for self-improvement. The Slum Upgradation Programme (SUP) is under the control of the World Bank. It involves the leasing of slum land to community groups and giving loans for improvements, but has not been very successful.

3 Privatised slum redevelopment has taken place since 1991, but this has not been successful as it has only reached a tiny proportion of squatter settlements. Many people have not been able to afford the prices charged by the private companies who have improved the settlements, and have moved to other slum dwellings where it is cheaper.

4 Community action has taken place since the 1980s. This is known as **bottom up** development, where local people decide what is needed and work with local organisations. Unfortunately, even these schemes have had difficulties because of corruption among some organisations; the poorest miss out again.

Mumbai's clean-up projects

Death rates fall when clean-up projects begin to work. The Mahim Nature Park was once a treeless rubbish dump. Today it is a 15-hectare green park developed by the Worldwide Fund for Nature (WWF). Another project is known as 'Clean Air Island' and covers 5 square kilometres of downtown Mumbai. This area is surrounded on three sides by the sea and is home to 200 000 people with a million daily commuters. The goal of this project is to reduce air pollution, 70 per cent of which comes from vehicles. This area suffers from smog at least 120 days a year. Such projects can work when there is a partnership between local government, businesses and local people.

The New Mumbai project

One way to accommodate growth in the Mumbai region was to build up a new city called New Mumbai. It involved moving industries, markets and offices from the congested old city to the new area. This is a policy of **decentralisation**. The new planned urban area should be more sustainable than the congested and polluted older city. Unfortunately it is becoming a middle class residential area and the poorer people are moving away.

A Growth of the mega-city

The future

Some people have said that Mumbai is an 'unintended' city. It has not been planned and it has grown with no overall structure. Where there is water, electricity, sewerage and rubbish clearance, it is not reliable. The city authorities claim everyone is near to a water tap. The truth is that one-third of the general population does not have a tap on their premises; when there is one it is often broken or not connected. Maybe for millions of people Mumbai's future will be as bleak as its past.

NOTING ACTIVITIES

1. Look at Figure 2A.2 and use your atlas. Find the six largest cities in India and locate them on a simple sketch map.
2. What percentage of the urban population lives in cities of over 50 000?
3. What is a squatter settlement?
4. What are conditions like in the squatter settlements of Mumbai?
5. Why have squatter settlements grown up in Mumbai?
6. Outline the attempts to improve the quality of the urban environment in Mumbai.

STRUCTURED QUESTION

1. a Why has Mumbai grown? (2)
   b How has the growth of Mumbai affected:
      i   better-off inhabitants (2)
      ii the very poorest people? (2)
   c How have housing conditions been improved? (3)
   d What difficulties have there been with attempts to improve the slum housing in Mumbai? (3)

Study Figure 2A.1, which shows the location of the world's largest cities.

2. What is a 'millionaire city'? (1)
3. Describe the trends shown on the graph (Figure 2A.8). (4)
4. Give reasons for the distribution of millionaire cities in 2000. (4)
5. For a named city in a LEDC, describe three problems for the authorities which have resulted from rapid growth. (5)
6. What have people done to try to solve these problems? (4)

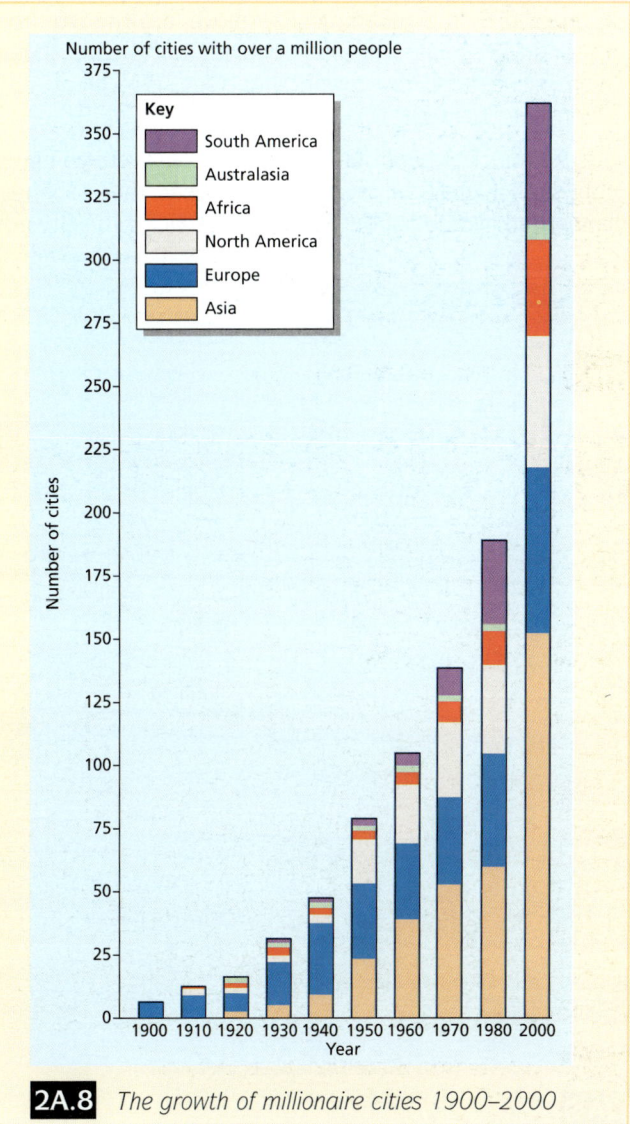

2A.8 *The growth of millionaire cities 1900–2000*

Section 2 **Providing for Future Settlements**

CASE STUDY

Tokyo: success and challenge

The population of Japan is nearly 130 million. Almost two-thirds of these people live in the three largest urban centres of Tokyo, Osaka and Nagoya. There are many other large cities in Japan such as Kobe and Kyoto, but Tokyo is easily the largest city as well as having been the capital since 1603. Japan has the second wealthiest economy in the world behind the United States, and Tokyo has grown to be one of the world's richest cities. It is even wealthier than some countries!

Tokyo has overcome many difficulties in its history. It was devastated by an earthquake in 1923 when over 300 000 houses and other buildings were destroyed. It was rebuilt but destroyed again by bombing during the Second World War, during which the population fell to half its pre-war level. The city was quickly rebuilt again after the war, people being encouraged by the government to move into the city from surrounding regions. The total population of Greater Tokyo, which includes nearby towns and cities, is now over 33 million (see Figure 2A.10).

With so much wealth and a history of overcoming its problems, it may be surprising to hear that Japanese planners are worried about the problems facing the city now and in the future. Despite its successes, the rapid growth and popularity of the city have brought difficulties that must be solved if Tokyo is to remain a prosperous city in the 21st century. What are these problems, and what is being done to solve them?

Why so much success?

Tokyo is located in the centre of Honshu, Japan's largest island. It is sited on a sheltered bay surrounded by flat land and land that has recently been reclaimed from the sea. This area has developed as a centre for industries and port activities. After the Second World War Japan received investment from the USA and there was a policy to concentrate on heavy industry. This was followed by the development of the motor vehicle and engineering industries, and more recently the growth of hi-tech industries. Tokyo was also at the centre of the growth in service industries. The city is easily accessible to other centres in Honshu and throughout Japan, particularly by means of the high-speed bullet train.

In addition to becoming the nerve centre of the Japanese economy, Tokyo has become an important part of global economic development. It held the Olympic Games in 1964, and has become the world centre for 'consumer and leisure' industries such as electronic games machines. Tokyo's

2A.9 *The location of Tokyo*

2A.10 *Population of the Tokyo metropolitan area*

A Growth of the mega-city

2A.11 *Tokyo is one of the world's largest consumer centres*

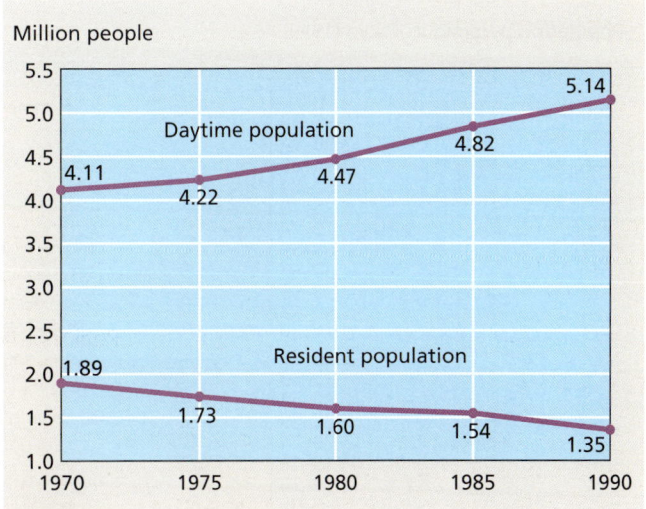

2A.13 *Daytime and resident population of central Tokyo*

inhabitants have high incomes, but the cost of living in the city is very high. The city boasts advanced technology, information, culture and fashion, together with a high degree of public safety and low crime rates. It is an expensive city to visit and therefore has not become a popular holiday destination for foreign tourists.

Tokyo has become successful using Japanese rather than foreign labour and investment. Only 2.4 per cent of the city's residents are foreign. It does, however, need a large workforce of commuters who live in areas surrounding Tokyo (see Figure 2A.12). Commuting times are high, and increasing. Trains are very crowded, making the journey to and from work uncomfortable as well as lengthy. There is a great difference between the number of people present in the city during the day and the night, as shown in Figure 2A.13.

The challenges facing Tokyo

Fast economic growth has brought a range of problems to Tokyo. Perhaps the city has grown too fast. In the 1990s the economy slumped, and people began talking about Tokyo being 'a city in crisis'. Economic growth slowed, and unemployment became a major problem. As with many other parts of the industrialised world, Tokyo started to have an increasingly aged population (see Figure 2A.14).

Some of the problems facing Tokyo today are:

- high land prices
- shortage of homes
- long commuter journeys
- lack of open space
- air and noise pollution
- river and sea pollution
- traffic congestion
- waste disposal problems.

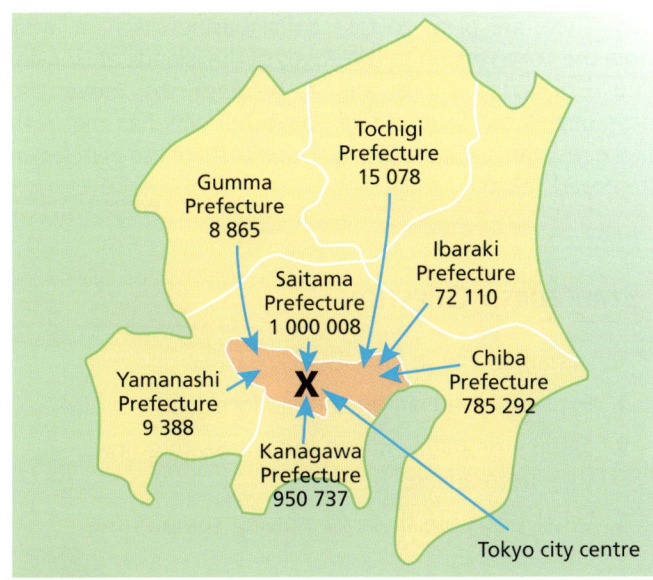

2A.12 *Commuters add greatly to the daytime population of Tokyo*

Section 2 Providing for Future Settlements

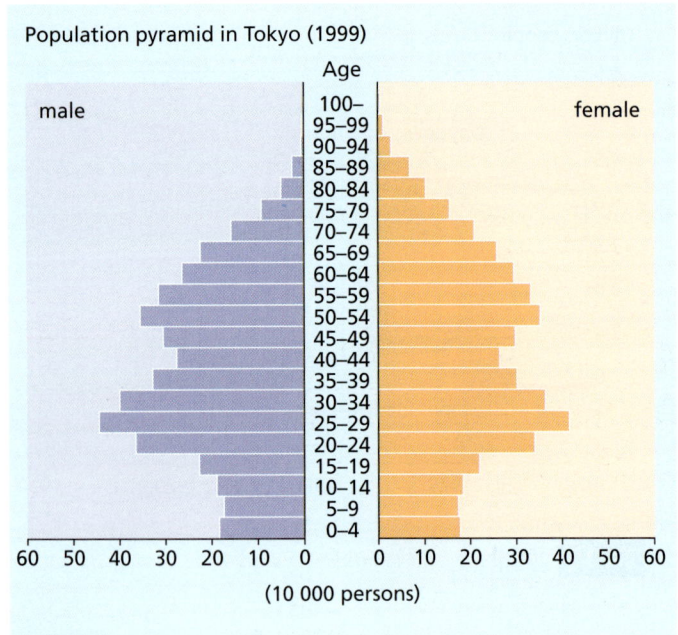
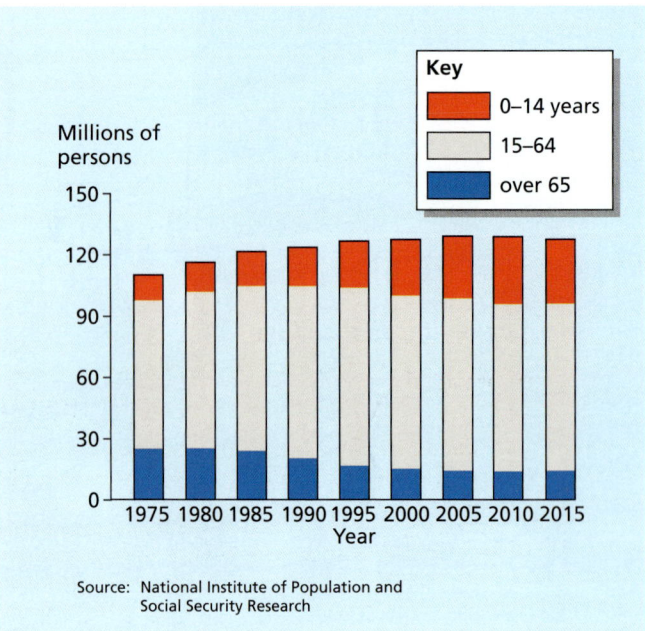

2A.14 Tokyo's population structure

What is the future for Tokyo?

Several solutions to the problems of Tokyo have already been put in place, with others being developed for the future. The city has started to **decentralise**, meaning it is encouraging businesses and people to leave the centre. In an attempt to reduce crowding, congestion and pollution, an increasing number of its functions are no longer located right in the city centre. Many **sub-centres** (minor centres), have developed around railway stations away from the city centre. Each sub-centre has its own commercial centre and offices, which are often linked by underground trains. The layout of each sub-centre is similar, as shown in Figure 2A.15. Each location has its own speciality or focus; Shibuya to the west of Tokyo, for example, has become a fashion centre for the region. More than twenty sub-centres are being developed.

Further away from the city of Tokyo is the Tsukuba **science city**. There are plans to take some businesses right away from the Tokyo region to the edges of the islands of Honshu and Hokkaido. There was a proposal to move the government buildings out of Tokyo but this has met with fierce resistance. Figure 2A.16 shows parts of the plan for an improved Tokyo.

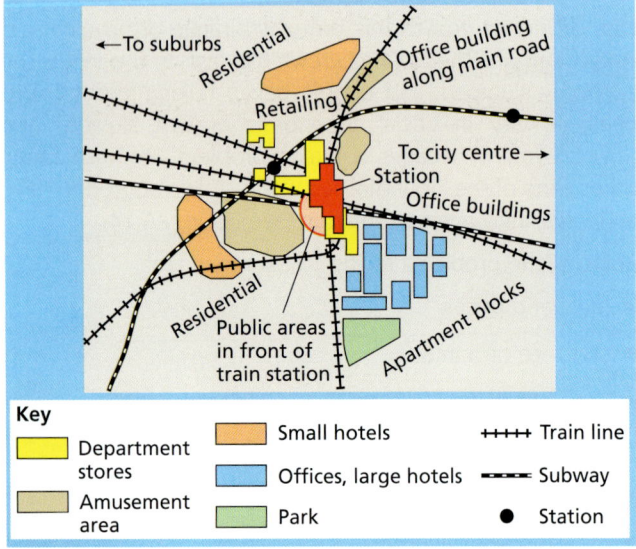

2A.15 A typical Tokyo sub-centre

STRUCTURED QUESTION

For a named city in an MEDC,
1. Explain the advantages of its location. (4)
2. Outline problems facing the city stating how they have arisen. (5)
3. What plans are there for solving some of the city's problems? (6)

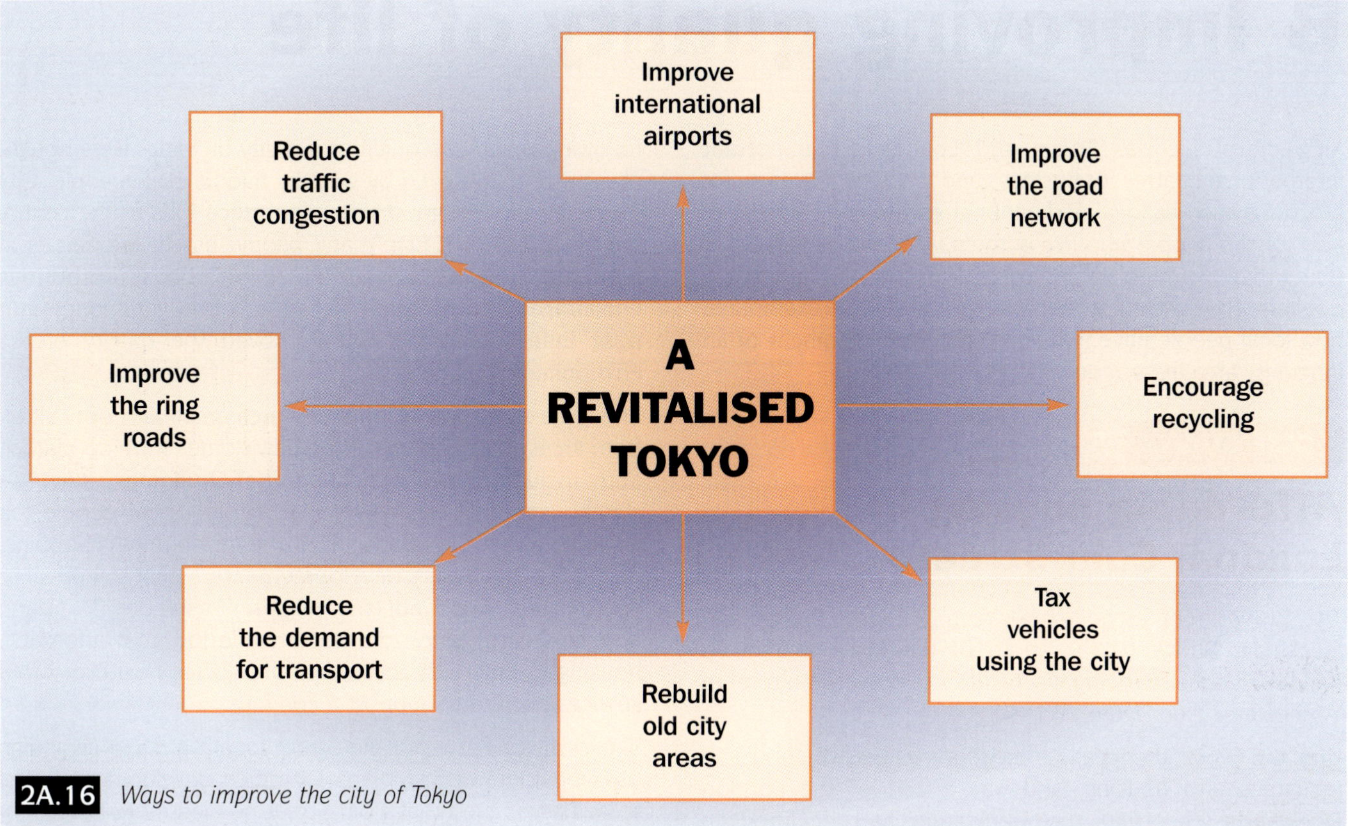

A Growth of the mega-city

2A.16 *Ways to improve the city of Tokyo*

A REVITALISED TOKYO
- Improve international airports
- Reduce traffic congestion
- Improve the road network
- Improve the ring roads
- Encourage recycling
- Reduce the demand for transport
- Tax vehicles using the city
- Rebuild old city areas

"As the city has grown, so have its problems."

2A.17

NOTING ACTIVITIES

1. Draw a spray diagram similar to Figure 2A.16 to show the successes of Tokyo.

2. Make a list of the problems faced by Tokyo. For each item on your list, give reasons why it is a problem, and suggest possible solutions.

3. In what ways are the problems faced by Tokyo similar to or different from those faced by cities in LEDCs?

27

Section 2 Providing for Future Settlements

B Improving quality of life

Mega-cities such as Tokyo and London are important international centres for business and industry, as well as for functions such as local and national government. Cities are also for the people who live in them, and so it is important that urban planning improves the quality of life for city dwellers. The case study below is one small scale example of how local people have influenced the redevelopment of an inner city area in London.

CASE STUDY

Affordable housing in London: Coin Street

The Coin Street area lies between Waterloo Bridge and Blackfriars Bridge to the south of the River Thames in London. It consists of eight separate sites covering a total of 5.5 hectares (see Figure 2B.1).

Until the 1960s, the area was used for riverside warehousing, industries and housing, and was a part of the London Docklands. By 1970 the Docklands had declined in importance and much of the Coin Street area lay derelict. The Docklands became a centre of **gentrification** in the following years. Low quality inner city buildings were bought cheaply and improved by wealthy middle class people. City locations allowed good access to office jobs in the central business district (CBD), many people buying properties in inner London as a second home. Local authorities encouraged gentrification because it brought money into poor inner city areas and improved the quality of the environment.

The redevelopment of inner city areas met with opposition from local people. Many of the new homes were up-market, and included the conversion of buildings such as warehouses into expensive apartments. Local people felt left out as they could not afford the new homes. Shopping, restaurant and leisure developments were built to appeal to new residents and not the original 'Eastender' Dockland people. Gentrification did not provide low cost affordable housing in inner city areas, nor the social, health or other services needed to support a community.

The local residents of Coin Street fought a major campaign of opposition against plans for office development in the area. They argued that Coin Street needed more homes for local people, not offices for city workers. The local residents were victorious, and in 1984 the Coin Street Community Builders (CSCB) group was formed. It was a company set up to provide public services, not run for profit. All money made was to be used for future developments, and all members had to live in the area.

The company has been successful in providing low cost housing for local people. Six new developments house over

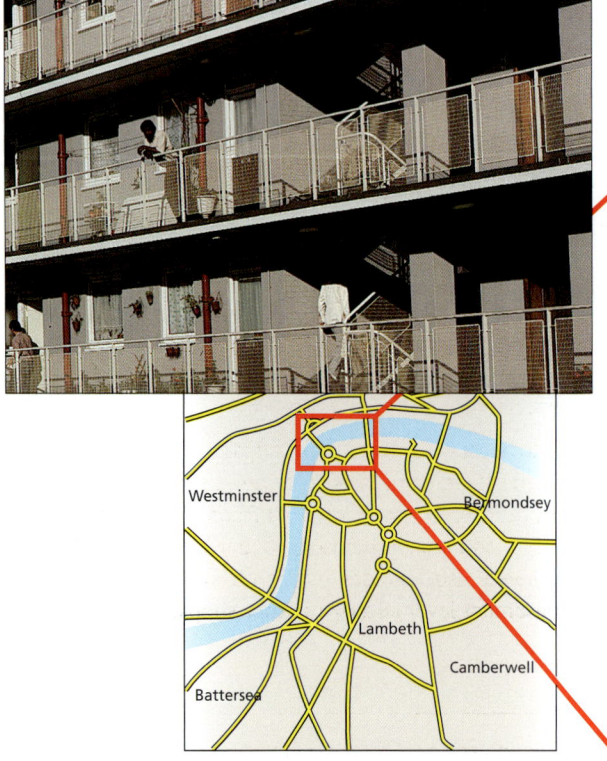

2B.1 The Coin Street redevelopment area

B Improving quality of life

1300. These houses are rented by local people, and are eventually available for them to buy. The first development, Mulberry, was occupied in 1988 and consisted of 46 houses and 10 flats. The greatest success of the CSBC was the saving of the OXO tower (Figure 2B.2). It was planned to knock it down to make way for office blocks. The Coin Street campaign 'Save the OXO Tower' stressed the need for more houses for the local area. In 1996 the tower re-opened with a mix of cafes and restaurants, retail design studios and shopping. There are five floors of affordable housing in flats with their own entrance, lifts and parking.

A new CSCB project is described in Figure 2B.3. As well as being a successful housing company, CSCB also runs the colourful Coin Street Festival each summer, attracting thousands of visitors.

2B.2 *The OXO tower*

NOTING ACTIVITIES

1. What is gentrification?
2. Why does gentrification not solve the problem of housing for poorer people?
3. Why is there such a need for low cost affordable housing in inner city areas?
4. How did local people achieve low cost housing in the Coin Street area?
5. Write about how CSCB have helped the social and economic regeneration of Coin Street.
6. Some people say there would have been more economic benefit by allowing the building of office blocks instead of houses. What is your opinion?

MINISTERS LAUNCH CONSTRUCTION OF AFFORDABLE HOMES ON LONDON'S SOUTH BANK

Another brownfield site gets the Coin Street treatment

Nick Raynsford MP, Minister for Housing, Planning and London, and local MP and Minister for Sport Kate Hoey, launched the latest development by Coin Street Community Builders (CSCB) on 12 October 1999. Not-for-profit CSCB has transformed this part of central London. Previous projects include the refurbishment of Oxo Tower Wharf, award-winning co-operative housing at Broadwall, the creation of the Bernie Spain Gardens and the completion of the South Bank Riverside Walkway.

Construction of the scheme of 59 flats, maisonettes and large family homes is under way on the old Coin Street car park site, opposite the London Television Studios, on the South Bank, London SE1. When completed in spring 2001 the development will provide homes for up to 350 people in housing need and, like all Coin Street's housing developments, will be run as a co-operative.

The homes – to be known as Iroko Housing – will be built on three sides of the site (Coin Street, Upper Ground and Cornwall Road) surrounding a large communal landscaped garden. The £14m scheme also includes public off-street parking at basement level and two corner shops.

2B.3 *The latest Coin Street development*

Section 2 **Providing for Future Settlements**

CASE STUDY

A new capital city for Nigeria: Abuja

The government of Nigeria wanted to provide a new settlement for the people who lived in the **capital** city of Lagos. The main problems of Lagos that contributed to a poor quality of life were:

- too many people lived in Lagos, the original capital
- too many people were moving to Lagos
- Lagos had become the **core** region of the country (the dominant region where economic activity and wealth are concentrated)
- the largest seaport, airport and communications centre was Lagos
- most of the country's growth and wealth was centred in Lagos
- Lagos was dominating Nigeria and the north felt left out
- Lagos was the centre of the Christian Yoruba people but the north was Muslim
- pollution and congestion were increasing in Lagos
- for many people the quality of life in Lagos was getting worse.

Nigeria had money from oil and in the 1970s it was decided to build a new capital and move the government from Lagos to Abuja (Figure 2B.4). In 1991 Abuja became the new Nigerian capital. By the late 1990s government ministries had moved to new buildings in the new city.

Were the issues resolved?

Figure 2B.5 shows the original plan for the city. When there has been money from oil there has been a building boom.

Unfortunately the plan has been changed over the years; building plots have been sold to private individuals and corrupt officials have sold land to friends and family. There has been little large scale private investment by large companies. There is an airport, and a road network radiates from the new city but it lacks the coastal trade enjoyed by Lagos.

The photographs (Figure 2B.6) show the new city which is not as luxurious to live in as they suggest. The city still has no proper sewerage system, beggars live on the streets and road traffic laws do not seem to be obeyed. Outsiders accuse Nigeria of building a **prestige** settlement, which impresses outsiders and acts as a symbol of wealth, rather than trying to improve the quality of life of the people who live there.

When the American president visited Abuja in 2000 he went to the small village of Ushafa, about 30 kilometres outside the city. The village chief wanted to tell the president that the village needed a bigger school, clean water and jobs for the local people. The gleaming government buildings and hotels of Abuja could not hide the poverty of the surrounding area.

Congestion remains in Lagos and its population continues to grow. Certainly moving the capital to a neutral zone between north and south was a positive step to unite Nigeria and relieve pressure on Lagos. In the future Abuja might help distribute the wealth of Nigeria away from the southern core of the country.

EXTENDED ACTIVITY

1. Draw a simple sketch map to show the shape of Abuja. Label one example of a residential area, a government area, industry, parkland, business area, transport and the airport. Around your sketch map highlight the problems experienced by the new capital and the surrounding areas.

2. Research which other countries have built a new capital city. Name them and write in detail about one of them.

3. What would the following people think about the new city?

    a. An unskilled worker in the village of Ushafa outside Abuja
    b. A government official working in Abuja
    c. The head of the Nigerian government industrial development agency
    d. The head of a large manufacturing company in Lagos
    e. A worker commuting a long distance to work in Lagos

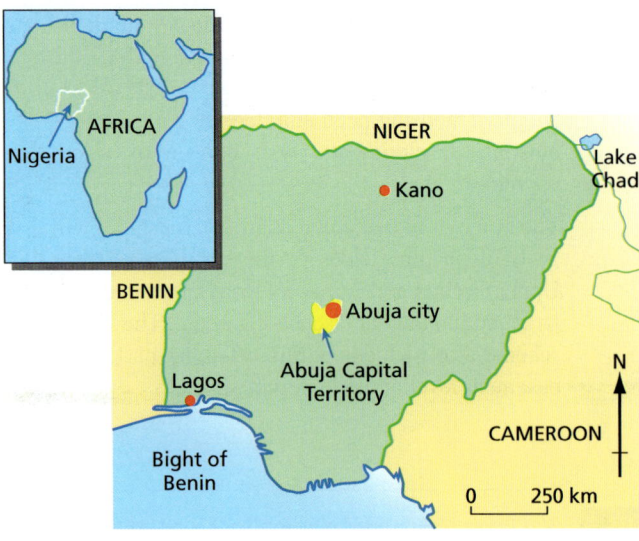

2B.4 *Abuja*

B Improving the quality of life

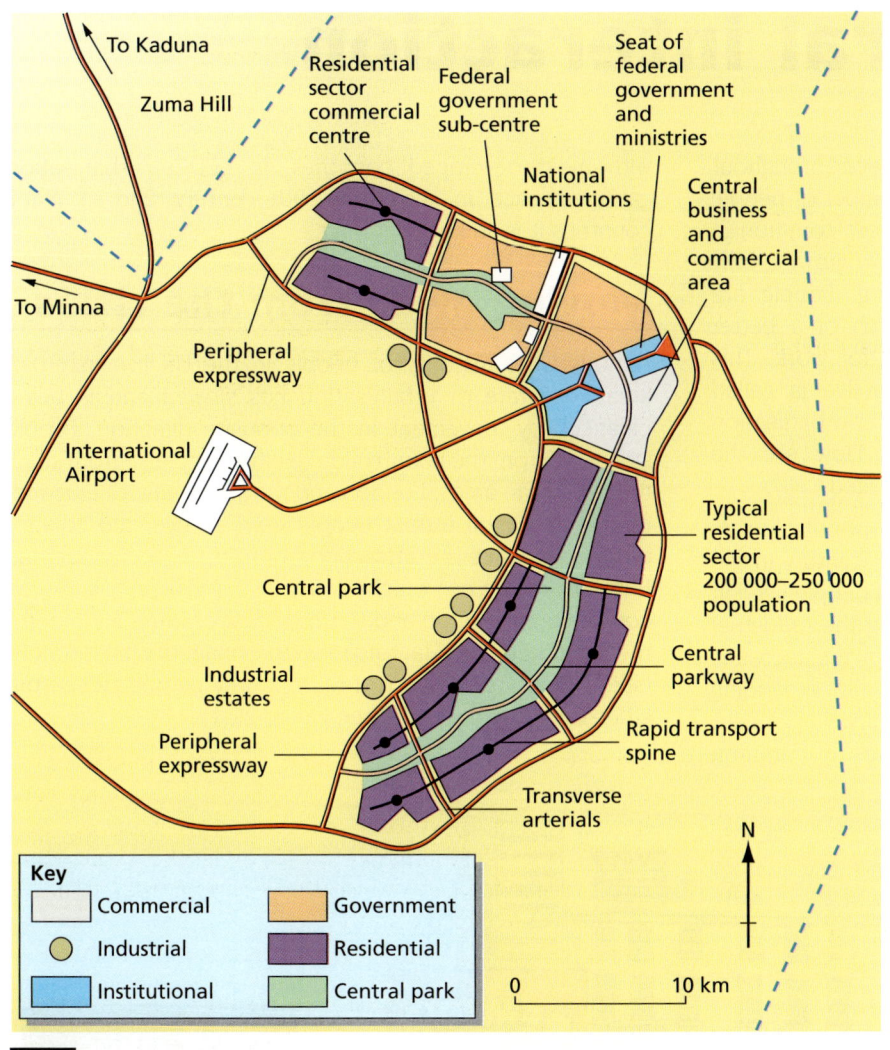

NOTING ACTIVITIES

1. What was the problem with Lagos as a capital city?
2. Why was Abuja built in the middle of Nigeria?
3. Why might Abuja *not* solve the problems of Lagos?

2B.5 *The original plan of Abuja*

2B.6 *Luxurious buildings in the new Nigerian capital city*

Section 2 Providing for Future Settlements

C Urban–rural interaction

Urbanisation is a process that has taken place throughout the world, leading to an explosion in the number of people living in towns and cities. This process is most common in LEDCs. Many cities in richer countries are now growing only slowly, or their populations are decreasing. People are moving beyond the city boundary in search of a better quality of life, often travelling to the city for work. This movement of people away from cities to live is called **counter-urbanisation**. What effect is counter-urbanisation having, on both urban and rural areas? How are the problems caused by this process being managed?

The balance between urban and rural population is constantly changing. At the start of the 19th century in the United Kingdom, for example, the majority of people lived in villages. The drift to the towns began during the Industrial Revolution, people being needed to work in the factories that were being built in the country's rapidly expanding industrial areas. By the end of the 20th century, 93 per cent of people in the UK lived in towns and cities, in common with most developed countries. In LEDCs, urbanisation gathered pace in the early 20th century, and in many countries it is still accelerating.

Moving away from the cities

Although the majority of people in the UK live in urban areas, the rate of urbanisation has slowed and is being balanced by movement in the opposite direction. People still move from the countryside to cities, and also from small to large urban areas. London and the south-east of England, for example, still attract people from all over the country and beyond. Yet the attractions of living in a city such as London must be weighed against problems such as congestion, pollution and the high cost of living. Rather like the 'push' and 'pull' factors used to explain the migration to cities, there are a variety of reasons why people move from cities to the countryside (see Figure 2C.1).

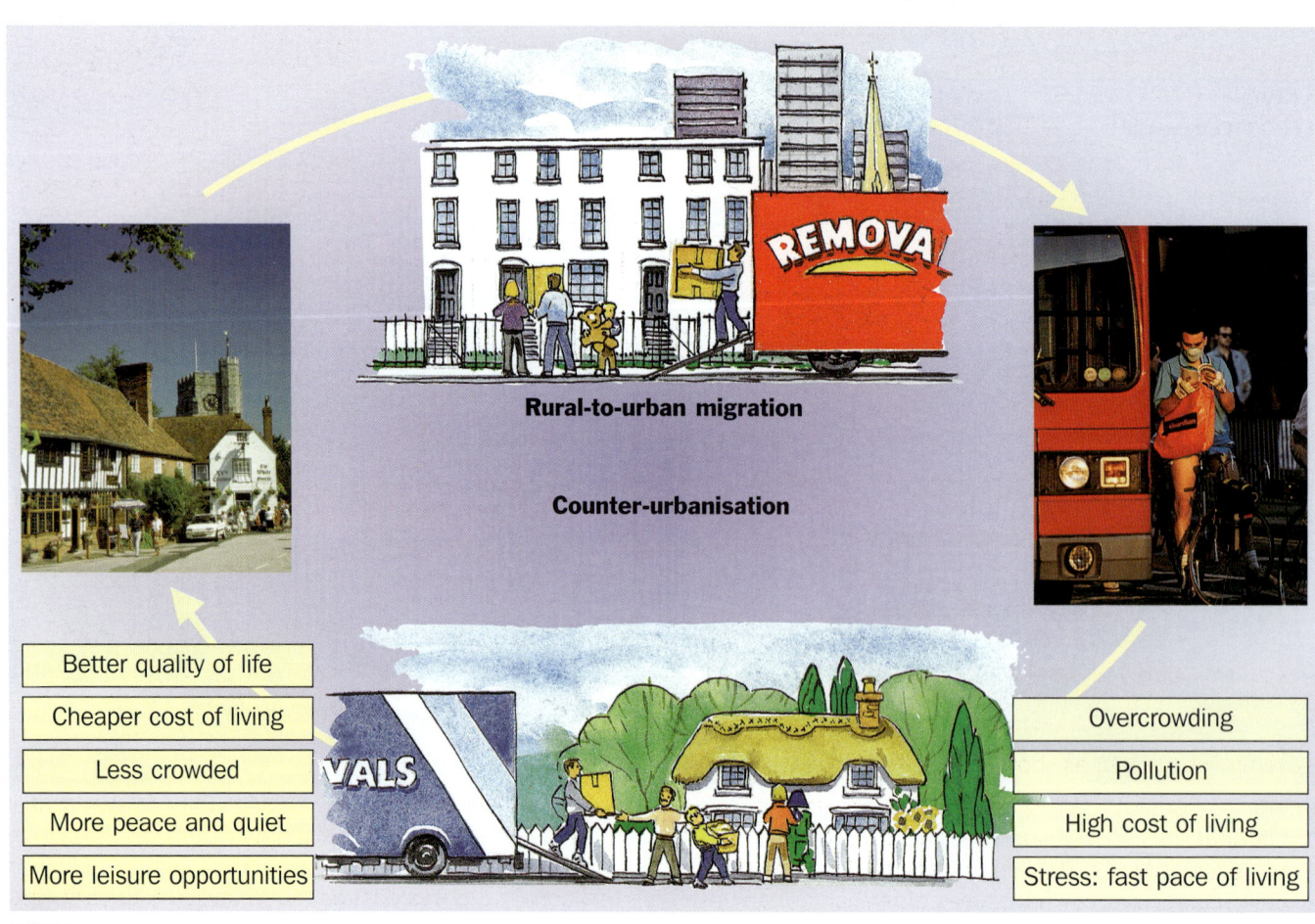

2C.1 Counter-urbanisation

C Urban–rural interaction

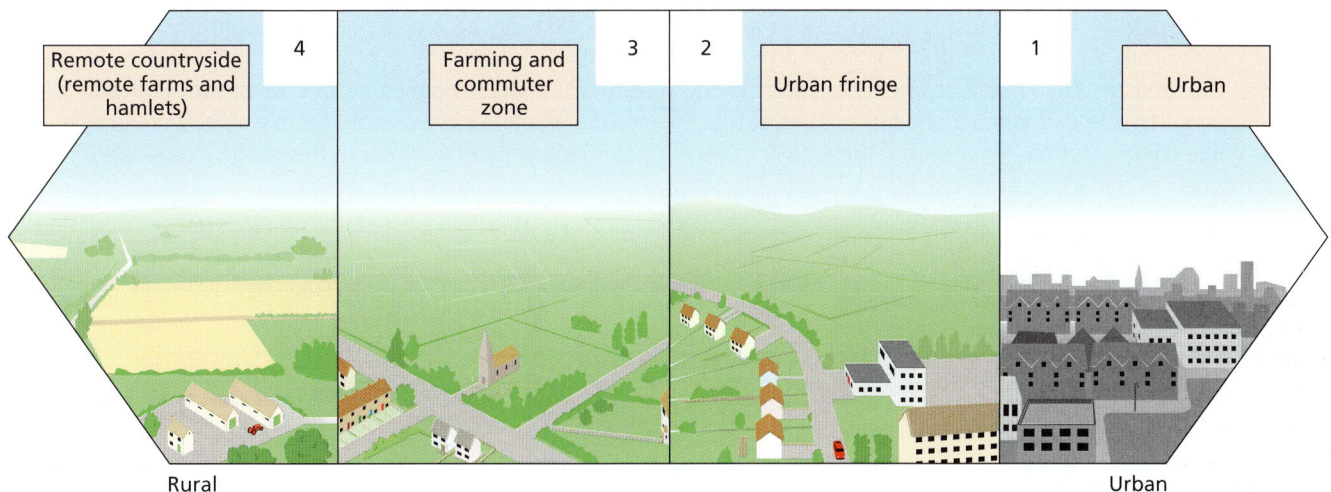

2C.2   *The rural–urban continuum*

This movement of people away from cities has led to a changing relationship between urban and rural areas. Although some people move to remote locations, many wish to live within travelling distance of large cities. The result is that small towns and villages surrounding cities grow to such an extent that they become a part of a larger urban area, or become swamped by the city. It is increasingly difficult to draw a boundary between rural and urban areas, as there is no obvious place where the city ends and countryside begins. Many people live in a part of this **rural–urban continuum**, rather than in city or countryside areas (see Figure 2C.2).

What are the effects of these changes on the nature of rural and urban areas in the United Kingdom? There is increasing pressure on the country's limited land resources as towns and cities spill their population into the surrounding areas. Conflict arises over whether land should be conserved, used for development, or managed to provide leisure resources for urban dwellers.

Urban sprawl

The government predicted in 2000 that 3.8 million new homes would be needed in the United Kingdom by 2021. Local councils are supposed to make sure that 60 per cent of new homes are built on **brownfield** sites, locations of previous building, which is often derelict land. The government wants a maximum of 1.5 million new houses to be built in the countryside. Their achievement is very different; only the South-west region so far is meeting the government's target, as shown in Figure 2C.3.

The urban sprawl caused by housing developments on **greenfield** sites will result in 70 square miles of countryside being bulldozed in London and the south-east alone. House building companies buy huge areas of farmland often years ahead of any possible planning permission. Since 1945,

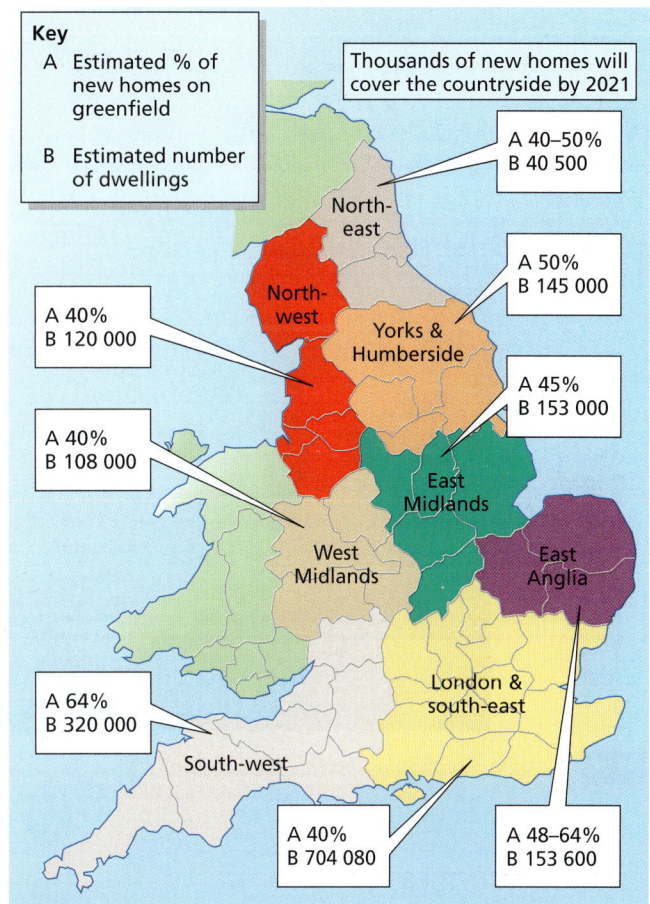

2C.3   *House building threats to the countryside*

there has been an increase of more than 50 per cent in urban space in the United Kingdom. The greatest pressure has been in London and the south-east of England, traditionally the area offering the greatest job opportunities and highest standard of living.

Section 2 Providing for Future Settlements

The space occupied by housing in the south-east is set to increase dramatically. An estimated 860 000 new homes are needed in the area by 2016, many of which are likely to be built in the countryside surrounding already existing towns. It is possible that by this time urban areas will have swamped much of the south-east, reaching in some places from London all the way to the south coast (see Figure 2C.4). New homes are often built on low density estates, providing larger houses as well as private and public open space. In inner city London, for example, there is an average of 80 houses per hectare. In the region as a whole, however, the figure is only 24 per hectare.

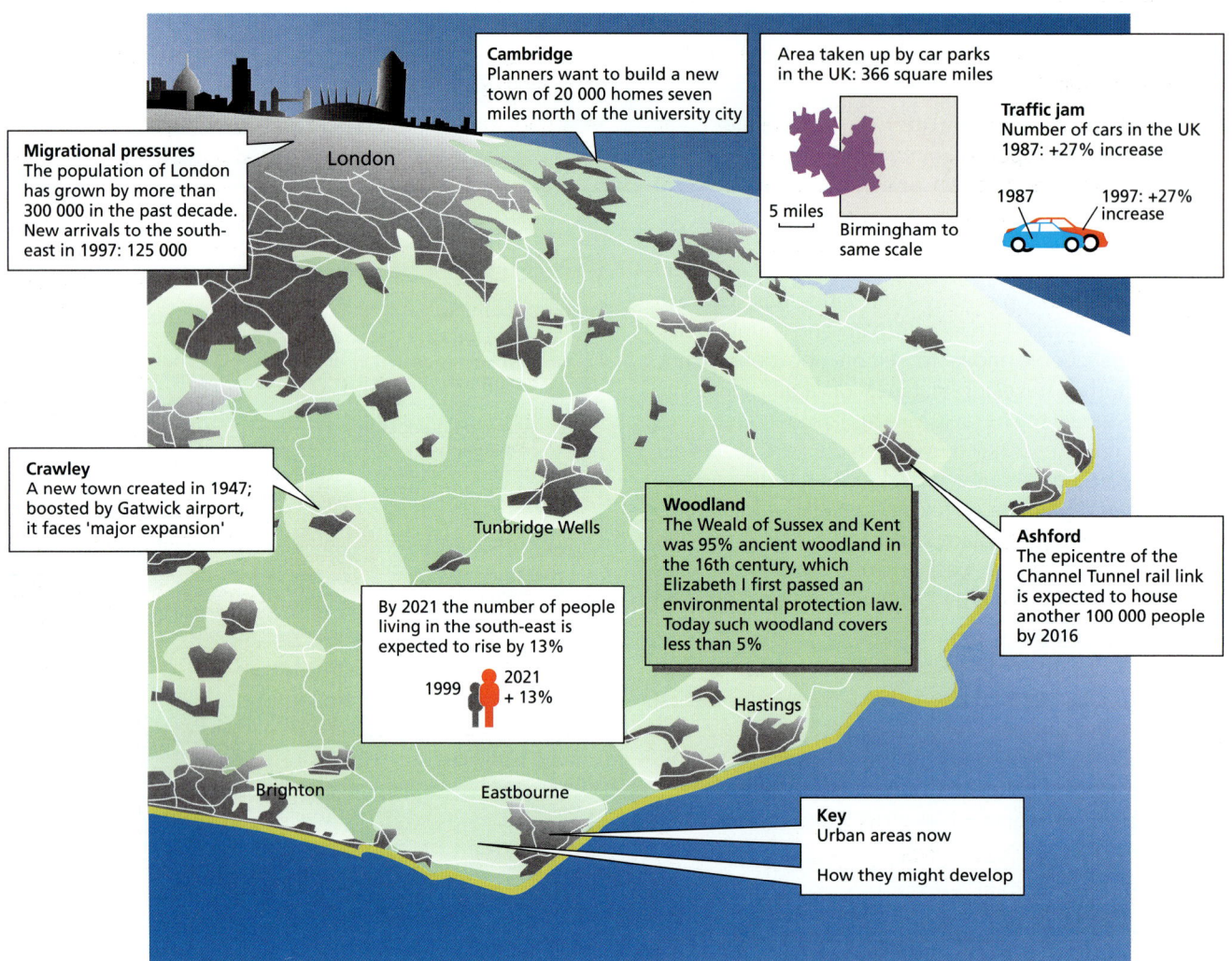

2C.4 *London: swallowing up the countryside?*

NOTING ACTIVITIES

1. What is meant by the term counter-urbanisation?
2. Give reasons why people have moved away from cities. List your answer as push and pull factors.
3. Draw a diagram to show the rural–urban continuum.
4. What are brownfield and greenfield sites?
5. Why do you think the government is keen to develop more brownfield sites?
6. Why is the south-east of England under particular pressure to build new houses?
7. Research an area where new housing is taking place. Describe the development, and its impact upon the surrounding area.

C Urban–rural interaction

Areas for development

Certain areas have been targeted for development.

1 Thames Gateway

This area contains over 2000 hectares of potential development land between the City airport in east London and the Thames estuary (Figure 2C.5). As many as 100 000 new homes could be built by 2010 in parts of London, Essex and Kent, making it the largest development site in the south-east of England.

The particular attraction of the Thames Gateway for planners is the high proportion of brownfield sites available. The east of London is a region of economic decline, and therefore development will help to **regenerate** the area. There are substantial problems; the Gateway has:

- the largest concentration of unemployment in the United Kingdom. Over 10 per cent of people have no job, the figure reaching 25 per cent in some areas
- over 6 per cent of all the unemployed in the UK
- highest unemployment in the 25–34 age group. Many of these people have not had a job for years
- income per person less than half that for London as a whole. The boroughs of Newham and Tower Hamlets are among the most deprived in western Europe
- lost manufacturing jobs at a rate of over 3000 per year
- a high crime rate that has prevented both economic and community development
- derelict land that is often polluted and costly to redevelop
- a poor and unattractive environmental quality.

Faced with these problems, the government in 1991 produced a report that outlined the need for development and the location of potential sites. Development needed to be undertaken both by councils and businesses, to ensure that the requirements of housing, industry and transport were all taken into account. Despite its problems, the Thames Gateway had advantages. These included:

- land being available for development at over 40 different locations, more than anywhere else in the south-east of England

2C.5 *The Thames Gateway*

Section 2 Providing for Future Settlements

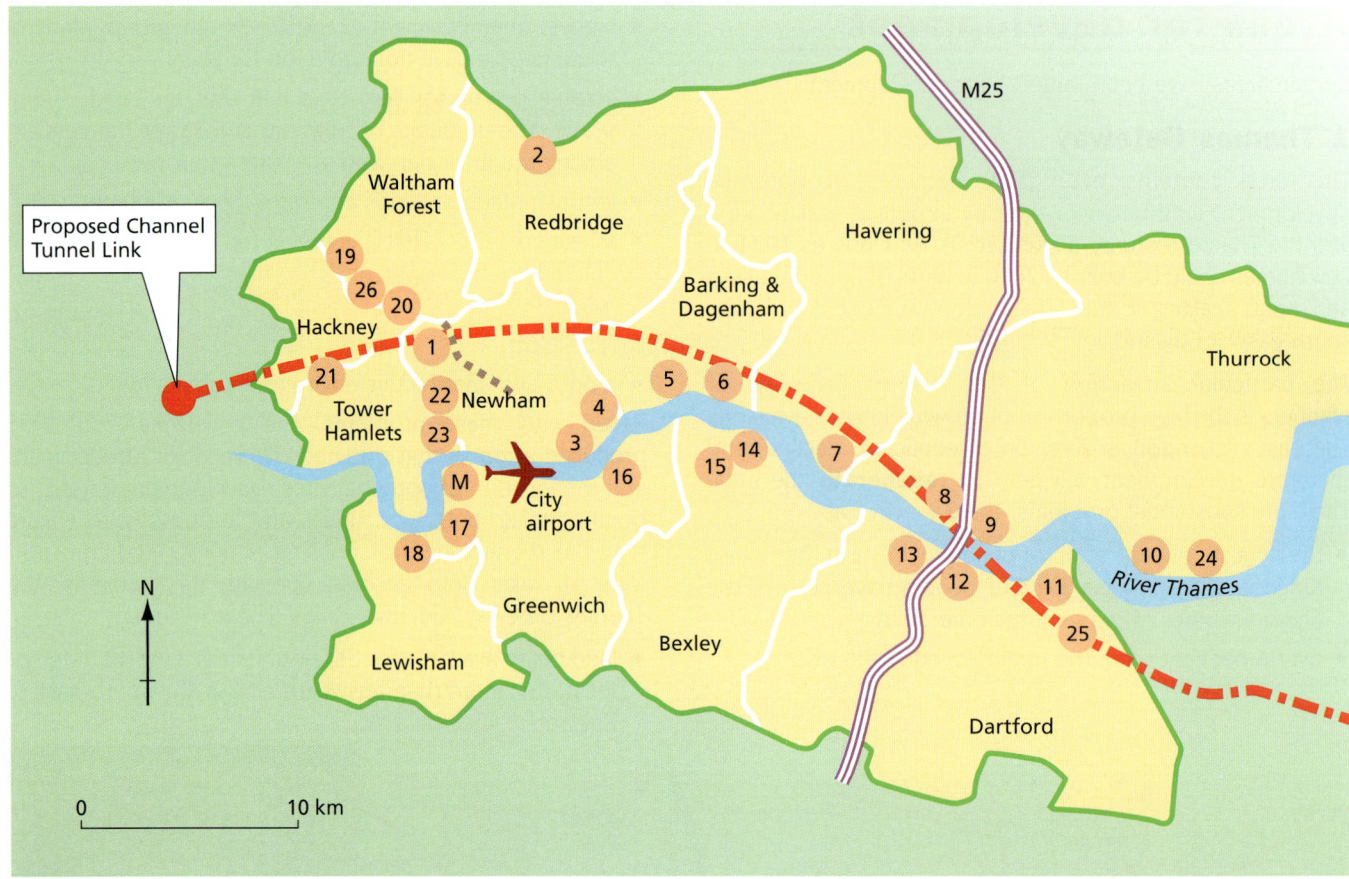

2C.6 *Development sites in the Thames Gateway*

- an airport (City) in the middle of the area
- two planned international railway stations on the proposed Channel Tunnel link for 2003. This would provide direct links to Europe and the rest of the UK
- improvements to the Underground network providing fast access to the City of London
- government grants and loans.

The Thames Gateway Partnership is to manage the area. They have to decide which locations should be developed, and in what order. Some of the proposed locations are shown in Figure 2C.6. Which do you think are likely to be the best locations for new housing and industry in the next decade? The decision making exercise below examines some of the issues that face the planners.

The Thames Gateway London Partnership aims to:
- create new jobs, helping to improve London's position as a city of world importance
- improve transport links to Europe
- use brownfield sites for development wherever possible
- preserve the natural and human environments. All new buildings must meet strict environmental standards.

2C.7 *The Thames Gateway London Partnership*

Decision making exercise

For the purpose of this activity, imagine that you are a student studying for a course at a college in London. As part of your course, you spend time working for the Thames Gateway London Partnership, the group in charge of developing the Gateway area. The Partnership's aims are shown in Figure 2C.7.

In addition to providing housing, the Partnership also needs to encourage industry to the area in order to provide employment for the local people. The Thames Gateway currently has the highest concentration of unemployment in the United Kingdom.

C Urban–rural interaction

You are required to assess five locations as potential sites for development, which are shown in Figure 2C.8. You need to provide a report for the managing directors of the Partnership, recommending which sites should be developed. Your report will be used to persuade local and national organisations to fund the developments, and should contain the following information.

- An introduction to the area: what is the current situation?
- A background to the proposed Thames Gateway Development. What does the Partnership aim to achieve?
- Advantages and disadvantages of each of the five potential development sites.
- Your chosen site or sites for development, in order of priority. Clearly state reasons for your first choice.
- An advertisement suitable for a national newspaper to attract businesses to locate at one of your chosen sites.

Bishopsgate Yard
Located a short distance from Liverpool Street Station, up to 13 acres could be made available for development. The site is owned by Railtrack and is adjacent to a proposed new underground station on the East London Line Extension.

Redevelopment of the Goods Yard would require demolition of the existing structure for which public sector grants may be available.

Ebbsfleet
The government has decided that the Ebbsfleet International and Domestic Railway Station together will be built in the Ebbsfleet Valley. This historic decision will bring benefits to an area which is currently underdeveloped. Blue Circle Properties is proposing a large mixed use scheme on the site which is an old quarry and landfill area between Northfleet and Swanscombe in the Boroughs of Dartford and Gravesham.

The scheme is centred on Union Railways Ltd's proposal to contract an Intermediate International and Domestic Passenger Station (IPS) at Ebbsfleet on the Channel Tunnel Rail Link (CTRL) which passes through the Ebbsfleet Valley.

The Ebbsfleet Valley has been subject to extensive chalk quarrying, cement works and waste land filling since the 1890s. The area is in urgent need of regeneration and the major purpose of locating the IPS in this location is to act as a focus for economic regeneration. In this respect there is a huge potential as the area is within 60 minutes drive time for 9.6 million people.

Hearn Street
On the northern edge of Broadgate in the City of London, up to 3 acres of Council owned land is available for employment based uses. Liverpool Street and Old Street stations are nearby.

Section 2 Providing for Future Settlements

Tilbury Power Station
A major development opportunity adjacent to Tilbury Port and a short distance from the M25. Up to 70 acres are available with excellent access and no contamination. The site falls within the Port of London Authority area and port related uses as well as other industrial developments will be encouraged.

Dagenham Dock
Dagenham Dock is located on the north bank of the Thames at the southern end of Chequers Lane. It is served by a station of the London to Tilbury and Southend rail link and is approximately four miles from London City Airport. On completion of the A13 diversion directly to the north, Dagenham Dock will be within 7–8 minutes of the M25 by road.

Dagenham Dock consists of a large area of private dock hinterland. The area totals some 160 acres in multiple ownership. It is proposed that the site will be directly served from the re-aligned A13 by a new bridge across the existing railway.

Thamesmead Business Park
A range of development opportunities in Greenwich and Bexley with the largest single site totalling around 50 acres. The wider Thamesmead initiative is providing significant residential and business park opportunities close to the Blackwall Tunnel River Crossing. Major infrastructure improvements will further improve the area's location. The proposed mixed uses would include a variety of business uses, particularly offices and housing, schools, retail and other community facilities. In addition uses such as hotels, entertainment and leisure facilities would be required. The servicing of these facilities with car parking, open space, roads and transport infrastructure will be fundamental.

2C.8 *The five proposed development sites*

2 Silicon Gorge

The government plans to build 400 000 houses in the south-west of England to cope with expected demand (see Figure 2C.9). The pressure is greatest in the area between Swindon and Bristol. This is a region of rapid economic expansion at the west end of the M4 motorway, shown in Figure 2C.10. Like the M4 corridor to the east, 'Silicon Gorge' has developed as a centre of hi-tech information based industries. The area has the advantages of quick access via the motorway and rapid rail links to London and the south-east, as well as nearby universities in Bath in Bristol. Another major attraction for many investors is the quality of life, the region being close to National Parks and the coast, as well as larger towns and cities.

Silicon Gorge is the fastest growing area of **hi-tech industries** in the UK. Although nearly half of the demand for new jobs will be met by local people, many workers are moving in to the region from elsewhere in the country. Development is controversial because there are relatively few brownfield sites available. Most building will have to take place on greenfield sites, unlike elsewhere in the region. Small towns such as Bradley Stoke, to the north of Bristol, have grown because of their location next to the motorway (Figure 2C.11). The government's proposals for new house building are likely to see such settlements sprawl over the surrounding countryside in the near future.

C Urban–rural interaction

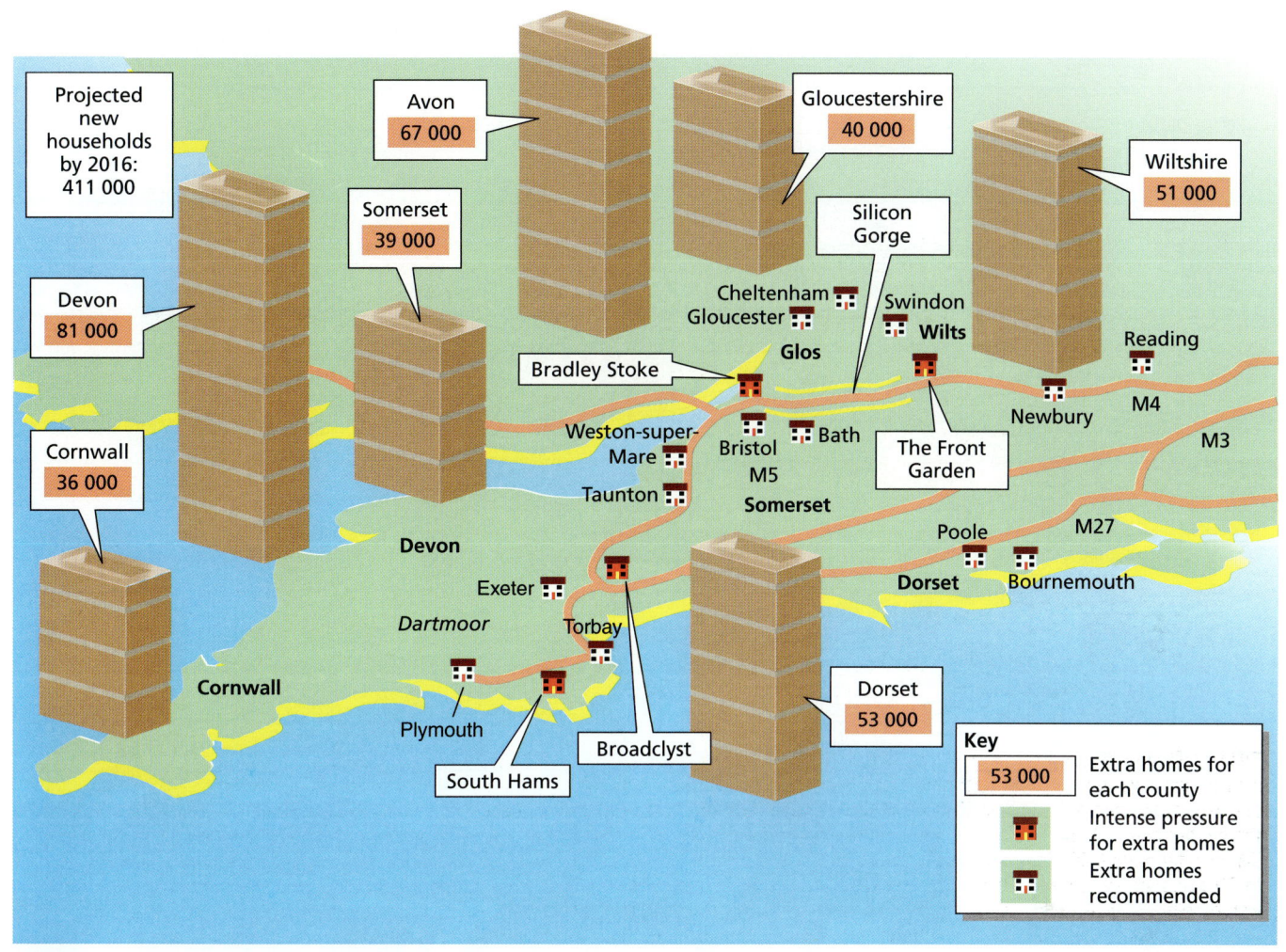

2C.9 Urban sprawl in the south-west of England

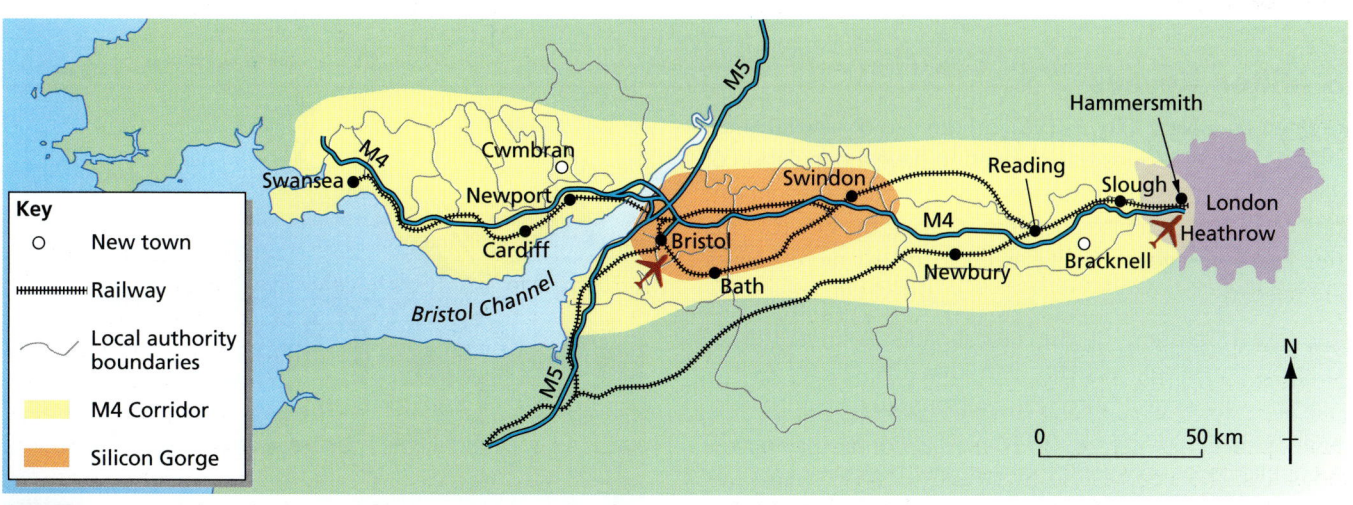

Projected new households by 2016: 411 000

- Devon 81 000
- Cornwall 36 000
- Somerset 39 000
- Avon 67 000
- Gloucestershire 40 000
- Wiltshire 51 000
- Dorset 53 000

Key:
- 53 000 Extra homes for each county
- Intense pressure for extra homes
- Extra homes recommended

Locations shown: Cheltenham, Gloucester, Glos, Bradley Stoke, Swindon, Wilts, Reading, Newbury, M4, M3, Weston-super-Mare, Bristol, Bath, The Front Garden, Taunton, M5, Somerset, Poole, M27, Bournemouth, Dorset, Exeter, Dartmoor, Torbay, Plymouth, Broadclyst, South Hams, Cornwall, Devon, Silicon Gorge

2C.10 Silicon Gorge

Key:
- ○ New town
- Railway
- Local authority boundaries
- M4 Corridor
- Silicon Gorge

Locations: Swansea, Cwmbran, Newport, Cardiff, Bristol Channel, M5, M4, Bristol, Bath, Swindon, Newbury, Reading, Bracknell, Slough, Hammersmith, London Heathrow

0 50 km   N

39

Section 2 Providing for Future Settlements

2C.11 *Bradley Stoke*

3 Milton Keynes

Created as a **New City** in 1967 on the site of several small villages, Milton Keynes was planned to have a population of 250 000 by the turn of the century. Although the present rate of 1700 new houses per year is taking the city towards this figure, the government has decided that more houses are needed.

The exact location of the new homes is a matter of controversy. Local residents fear that the city of Milton Keynes will sprawl into the surrounding countryside, swallowing up villages like Aspley Guise (Figure 2C.12). With a population of only 2500 the character of Aspley Guise as a peaceful village is under threat by the proposed developments. House building companies have already purchased land in the 2 kilometre-wide strip between the village and the motorway, ready for the go-ahead to develop the area.

2C.12 *Aspley Guise*

C Urban–rural interaction

The building of new houses in the area is also likely to bring other problems for local inhabitants. There is greatest demand for executive homes, particularly for people moving into the area and commuting to London. The building of such expensive housing is likely to push up prices throughout the area, making it more difficult for local people to purchase properties.

> **NOTING ACTIVITIES**
>
> 1 Draw a sketch map to show the location of Silicon Gorge.
>
> 2 Why are industries keen to locate in the area?
>
> 3 What problems may be caused by the expansion of settlements such as Bradley Stoke?
>
> 4 What are the likely possible effects of house building in the Milton Keynes area? Think about the environmental and economic impacts, both for people already living in the area and for newcomers.

2C.13 *How will housing developments affect local people?*

Section 3 Changing Employment Patterns

A Changing employment structures

Employment is an essential part of the economic development and wealth of a country. A job contributes to an individual's well-being and prosperity, as well as to the overall wealth of a nation. On a world scale, patterns of employment are controlled by a small number of rich nations; 20 per cent of the population control over 80 per cent of the world's wealth. Many poor countries are in debt to these rich nations. Child labour and unfair trading systems are also common problems for LEDCs.

The world situation is becoming more complicated with the rise of **transnational corporations** (TNCs), huge companies operating in more than one country. Several TNCs have grown to such a size that they are more wealthy and powerful than many nations. FIAT, the Italian based car company, has sales of over $50 billion per year, greater than the entire annual GNP of countries such as Hungary or Pakistan (Figure 3A.1).

The nature of employment is constantly changing. It is an important issue at all scales, from the individual to the global. How do employment structures vary across the globe? How is employment changing, and what are the reasons for these changes? What is the role of governments, transnationals and organisations such as the European Union in shaping future global employment? What can be done about trade and aid systems to help reduce the huge differences between the world's richer and poorer nations?

Employment structures

Economic activity is usually divided into four groups or sectors, shown in Figure 3A.2. An analysis of the percentage of people employed in each sector describes its **employment structure.** The economic development of a country can be determined according to its employment structure. Figure 3A.3 shows the stages of development of economies. In the least developed countries such as Gambia, agriculture is an important part of the employment structure. In many MEDCs such as the UK, manufacturing industries have declined as tertiary industries became more important. This process is called **de-industrialisation.**

FIAT: annual turnover 1999	= $50 billion
Pakistan GNP	= $43 billion
Hungary	= $30 billion
Bangladesh	= $23 billion
Sudan	= $11 billion

3A.1 *FIAT's turnover is greater than the wealth of many countries*

A Changing employment structures

Primary industries extract natural resources from the earth. These include jobs such as farming and forestry.

Secondary industries manufacture products. Examples include car assembly factories and furniture making.

Tertiary industries provide services for people. Service industries include schools and hospitals.

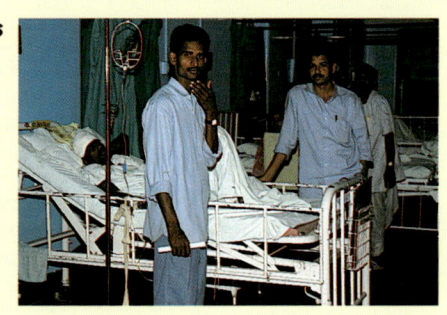

Quarternary industries provide information and expertise, and are sometimes included with tertiary industries. Examples of quarternary industries include universities and research laboratories.

3A.2 *Classification of industry*

3A.3 *The stages of economic development*

CASE STUDY

How does employment structure change?

The UK's new electronics economy

The balance of employment between sectors changes through time. Until the 19th century, for example, the majority of people in the United Kingdom lived and worked in the countryside. The Industrial Revolution saw a growth in manufacturing industries, and people moved to towns and cities to work in factories. As these industries became more productive, so more people worked in service industries. With the rise of these service industries, traditional manufacturing industries such as steel and shipbuilding became less important. Many manufactured goods were imported from other countries more cheaply than they could be made in the UK. Towards the end of the 20th century, new hi-tech industries grew rapidly, once again changing the nature and location of industry in the United Kingdom.

The growth of new industries resulted in employment moving from old industrial areas and inner cities to new industrial estates. These were generally greenfield sites on

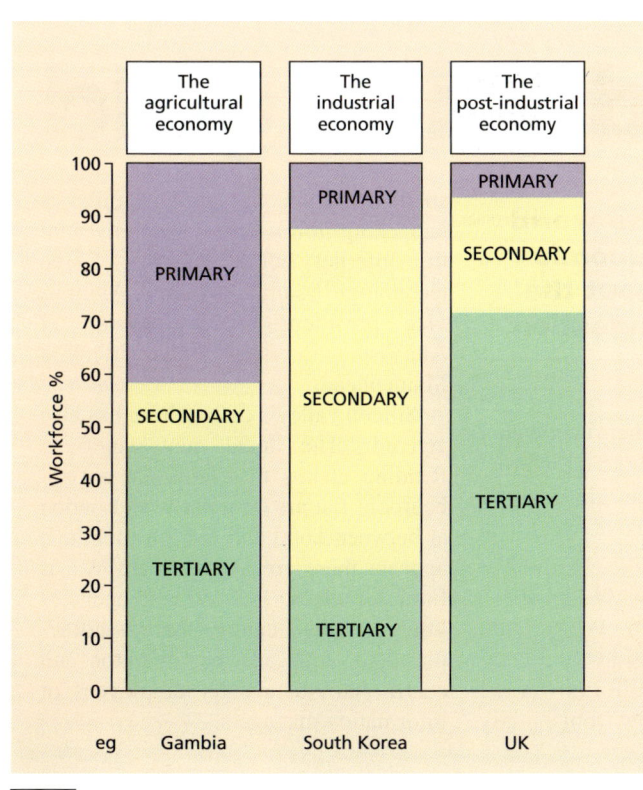

Section 3 Changing Employment Patterns

the edge of urban areas, near to motorways or fast main road links. Built on cheap land with room for expansion, industrial estates included offices and warehouses as well as factories. They provided a pleasant working environment with landscaped areas that contrasted greatly with old industrial areas in cities (see Figure 3A.4).

Many companies locating on industrial estates were **footloose.** This means that they did not have to be located near to either raw materials or markets. In the case of companies relying on telecommunications and internet links, the location did not matter so long as there were enough workers living locally. In addition to locating near to motorways, industrial estates also developed near to towns and cities with universities, providing well educated and qualified workers. New electronics industries have transformed the economy of parts of the UK.

Who has benefited from the electronics revolution?

The M4 corridor to the west of London is a well established centre for hi-tech industries. As Figure 3A.5 shows, the area has continued to grow by attracting investment from abroad, particularly the United States. The region around Cambridge has also benefited. More recently, other parts of the UK have gained as a result of the electronics revolution.

Central Scotland provides 25 per cent of Europe's personal computers. The electronics industry employs nearly 100 000 people, including in the manufacture of computer software. Local universities have become centres of excellence in electronics and engineering.

Liverpool has attracted hi-tech industries with the aid of £1 billion investment from the EU Development Fund. The area had depended on manufacturing and port industries, many of which had closed down. The growth in hi-tech computer industries has helped to reduce unemployment in Liverpool from 20 per cent in 1990 to 9.5 per cent by 2000.

3A.4 *A planned working environment: Cambridge Science Park*

Corridor lined with gold

Anne Hyland

Along the M4 corridor construction cranes fight for space against the billboard size names of trail-blazing multinationals such as Microsoft, Oracle and Motorola.

Technology companies and internet start-ups have spread west from Slough to Swindon, sweeping up Reading, Maidenhead and Newbury to create England's silicon corridor.

The emergence of the new economy has seen US companies flock to the Berkshire countryside. More than 40% of the technology companies along the

'Nowhere in the world achieves economic success without the problem of congestion'

M4 have US roots and their investment in the area has given rise to an internet gold rush. The region ranks only behind London in terms of wealth in England, with a gross domestic product of £25bn for a population of just 2m.

Even diehard valley types from California has been lured here. "I lived in silicon valley in California for 22 years and watched it grow from a pretty small operation. Something similar is happening in this area, especially with the internet boom on top of the technology boom," says Jim Ambras, vice president of engineering at AltaVista's European headquarters in Maidenhead.

Silicon valley's cash culture has also arrived. The local newspaper in Reading claims that rents for a two-bedroom flat are on a par with London at between £600 and £900 a month. It appears there are as many BMWs as Ford Mondeos. Recruitment agencies litter the town centre, their windows plastered with ads begging for call centre staff, data entry employees or information managers.

3A.5 *From the* Guardian, *13 June 2000*

A Changing employment structures

One example is Psygnosis, a computer games company that has specialised in developing games for Playstation 2. The company has created 220 new jobs in Liverpool.

Leeds is rapidly becoming an internet capital, with 30 per cent of all UK internet traffic passing through the city. Much of the 'dot.com' activity has come from Freeserve, a company that was founded in Leeds. The city is also home of First Direct, the UK's first telephone bank. Call centres, warehouses and distribution centres for internet-based businesses have replaced the coalfields and steelworks of the area.

Who has missed out?

Not all of the United Kingdom has gained from the electronics revolution. In 1999 Tony Blair, the Prime Minister, warned against a society divided into 'computer haves and have-nots'. By 2000, 25 per cent of UK households were connected to the internet, with London and the South-east leading the way. Elsewhere in the country the picture is rather different.

- Only 11 per cent of the population in Northern Ireland have access to the internet.
- Computer ownership and access is lower in remote parts of the UK.
- Fewer retired and elderly people have computers.
- Computer use is least in lower income groups.

3A.6 *There is a growing market for hi-tech goods*

CASE STUDY

Changing employment in Europe

Levels of economic development vary within richer parts of the world as well as on a global scale. The world map of GNP (Figure 3A.7) shows all of the countries in western Europe grouped together as high income countries. A more detailed map of the wealth of European nations (Figure 3A.8) shows that there is great variation across the continent. The relative wealth of nations also changes through time. There is economic growth in some areas of Europe, while others are in decline.

The area of greatest wealth is the European **core** region. Countries such as Germany and France are in the core. Moving away from this central region, there is a decrease in GNP in countries on the limits of Europe. These countries form the European **periphery**.

The core region is like a magnet, attracting more jobs and increasing wealth and prosperity. Countries in the core are easily accessible from all over Europe owing to their central location. Regions on the periphery of Europe find it hard to attract jobs. Many people migrate from these areas to find better jobs and living conditions elsewhere. The difference in wealth between the core and periphery is likely to increase, despite economic growth and development in some of Europe's outer regions.

Differences also exist within the countries of Europe. There is a central zone where most development has taken place, which is shown in Figure 3A.9. Rather than being dominated by national economies, it is regions and cities that make this area wealthy. France is at the edge of this zone of development, and has recently experienced both economic growth and decline.

Section 3 Changing Employment Patterns

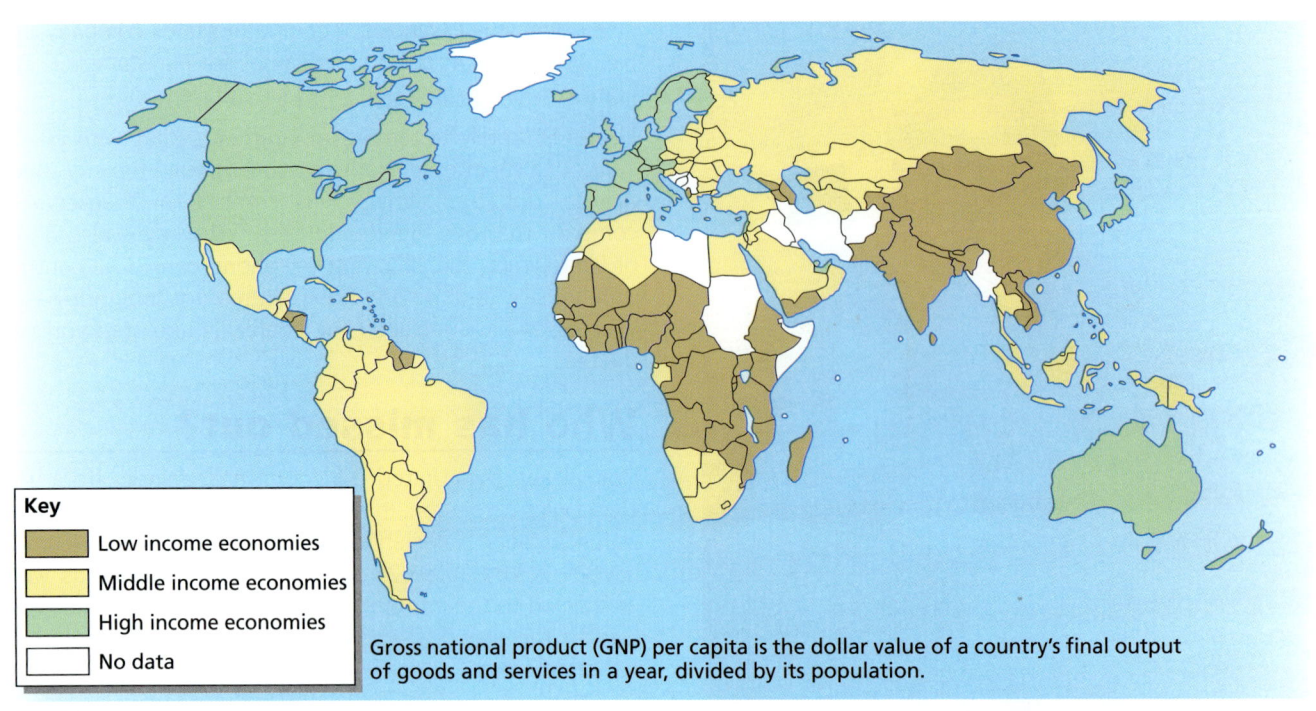

Key
- Low income economies
- Middle income economies
- High income economies
- No data

Gross national product (GNP) per capita is the dollar value of a country's final output of goods and services in a year, divided by its population.

3A.7 *World GNP per capita, 1998*

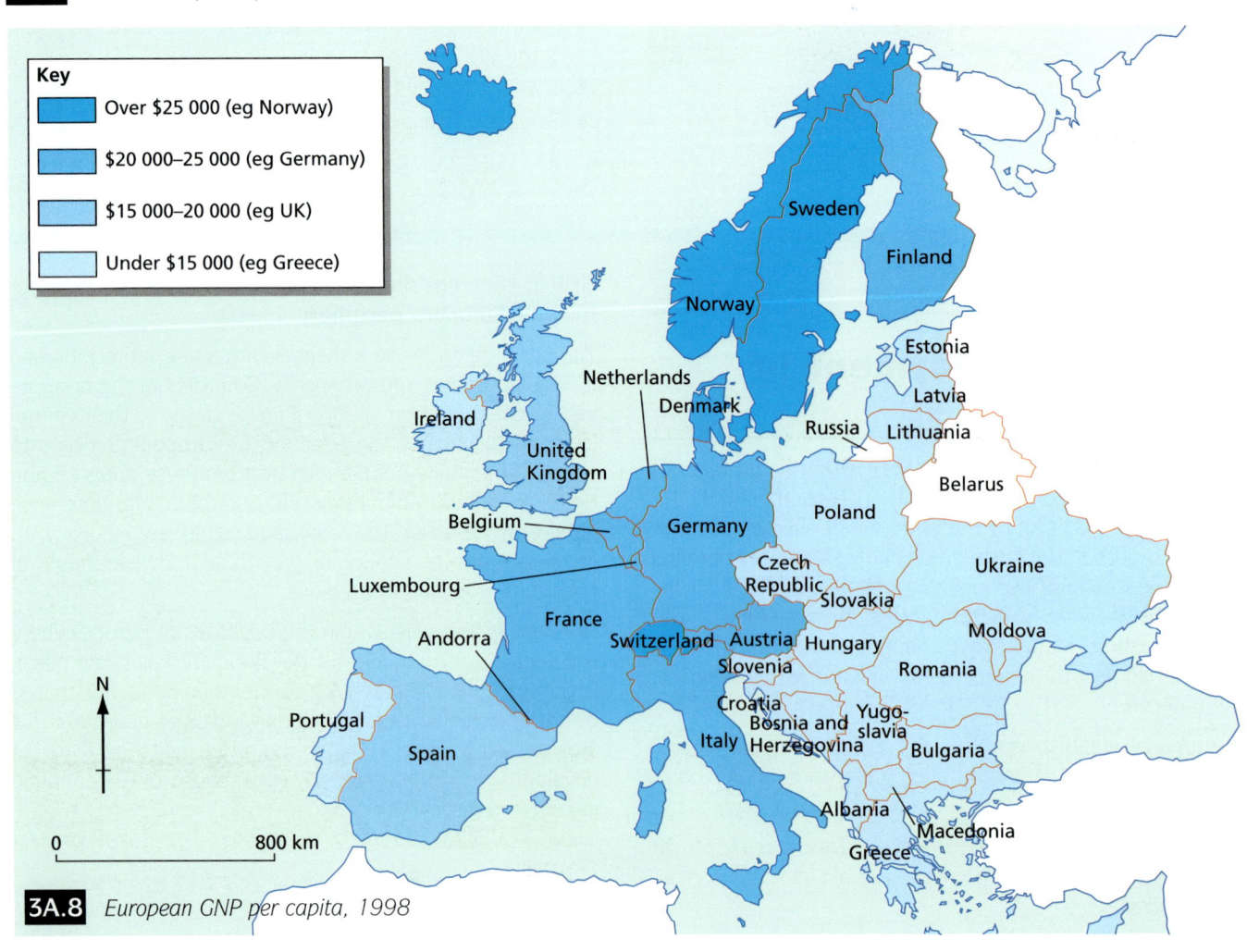

Key
- Over $25 000 (eg Norway)
- $20 000–25 000 (eg Germany)
- $15 000–20 000 (eg UK)
- Under $15 000 (eg Greece)

3A.8 *European GNP per capita, 1998*

A Changing employment structures

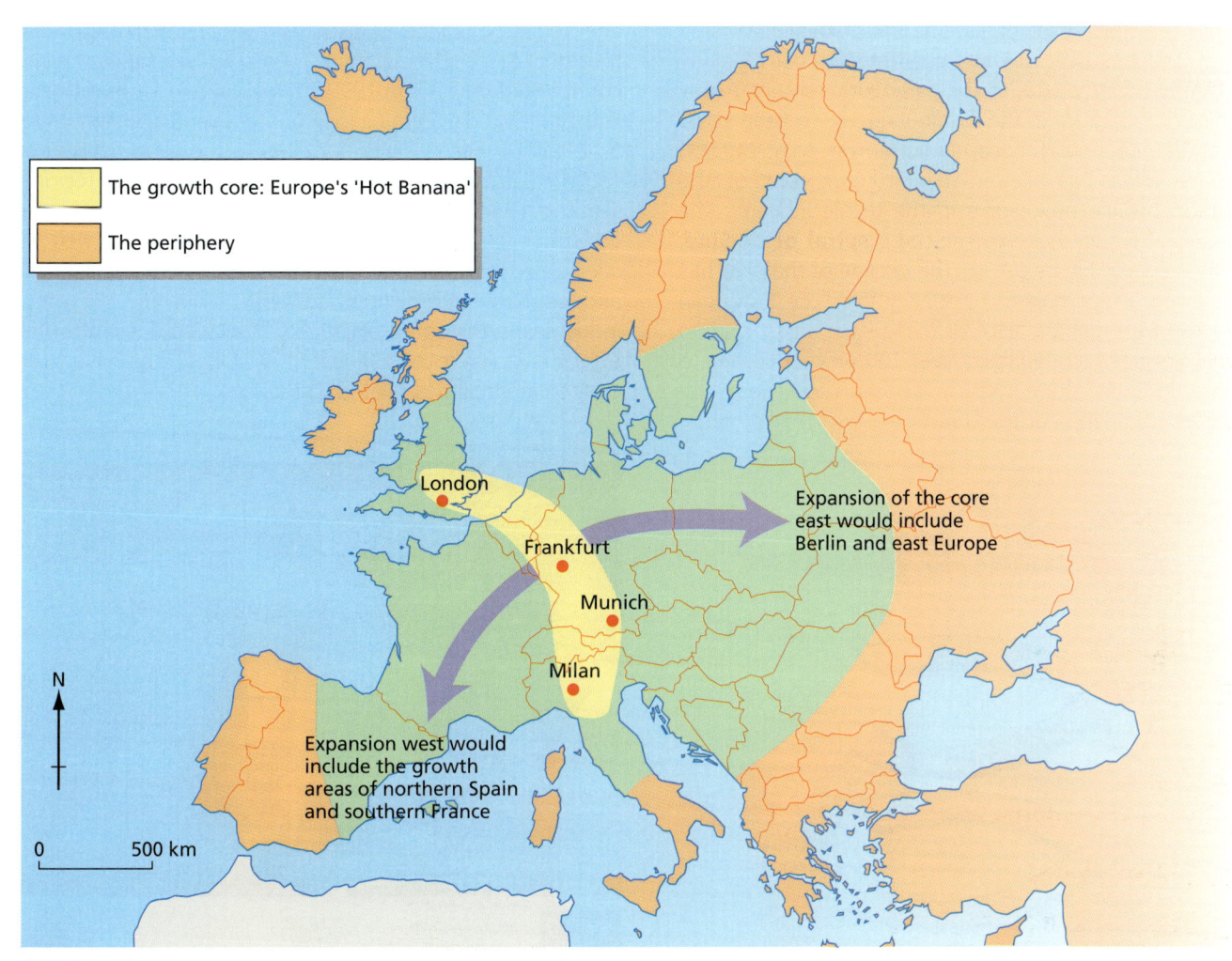

3A.9 *The European core region*

Map legend:
- The growth core: Europe's 'Hot Banana'
- The periphery

Map labels: London, Frankfurt, Munich, Milan; "Expansion of the core east would include Berlin and east Europe"; "Expansion west would include the growth areas of northern Spain and southern France"

France is the world's fourth largest industrial power, behind the USA, Japan and Germany. Like many other MEDCs, traditional manufacturing industries have declined, and been replaced by newer hi-tech and service industries. Some regions of France have gained from these changes, while others have lost out. The north-east of France was once dominated by industries such as coalmining, steelworks and textile manufacturing. These industries made the area wealthy. Faced with recent competition from goods that were produced more cheaply abroad, many factories and mines have closed. Coalmining once dominated the Nord region of the country, but the coal could not compete with cheap imports of oil. By 1990, every mine in the region had closed. There were few other industries to fall back on, and much of the area became derelict. The quality of the environment was poor, and many people moved to other areas of France.

3A.10 *The decline of traditional industries in northern France has left derelict land and a poor quality of environment*

Section 3 Changing Employment Patterns

Although the north-east of France has managed to keep some of its industries, this has been at the cost of many jobs. Lille is a city where, in the early 20th century, nearly one-third of jobs were in the textile industry. To keep costs down and compete with cheap imports from Asia, 240 000 jobs have been lost. Fewer than 10 per cent of the population of Lille now works in the textile industry. The north-east of France has experienced a **spiral of decline**, like that shown in Figure 3A.11. The decline of the area has been slowed, if not halted, by money from the European Union. The EU provides help for many such areas, and its Regional Policies have enabled over 100 new industries to start up in Lille alone. Nearly one-fifth of these are companies from Japan or the USA.

The south of France is also the major growth region for tourism. France attracts more foreign tourists than any other country in the world. In 1999, 70 million people travelled to France on holiday, earning the country over $10 billion. More than half of these visitors travelled to the south of France. Tourism has also created other jobs in some coastal regions, like the Languedoc and Les Landes. These include the construction and civil engineering sectors, as well as specialised industries such as sailing and boating equipment and clothing and cultural activities. Tourism, like other industries in the south of France, has created a **multiplier effect** (see Figure 3A.13). Over 1.5 million jobs have been created in industries related to tourism.

3A.12 *Hi-tech industry has helped increase industrial growth in the south of France*

3A.11 *The spiral of decline*

Today, the greatest growth in industry is to be found in the country's southern regions. The cities of Toulouse and Bordeaux, for example, have become centres for the defence and weapons industries. Overall, hi-tech industries now employ over 20 per cent of French workers. New centres have developed throughout the south, for example at Montpellier and Sophia-Antipolis. Companies are attracted to the south by the environment and climate, as well as good transport and communications.

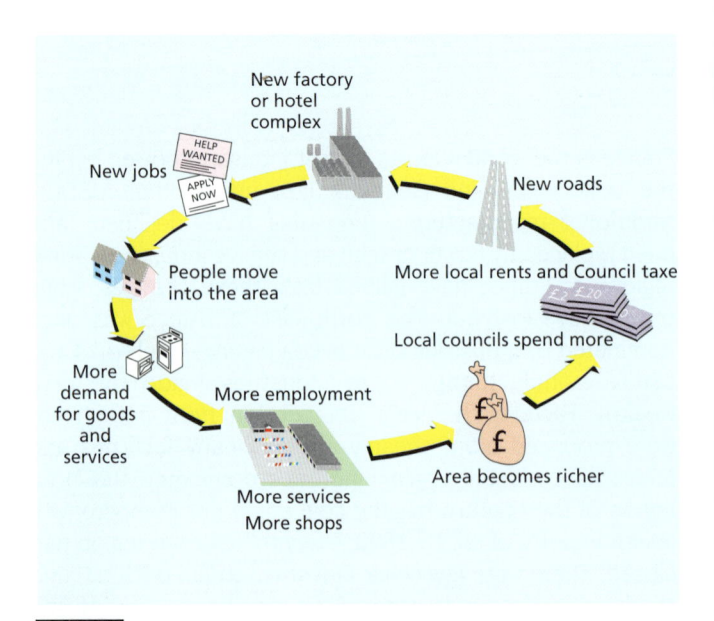

3A.13 *The multiplier effect*

48

A Changing employment structures

NOTING ACTIVITIES

1. What are the four sectors of industry? Give examples of two jobs in each sector.
2. How does employment structure vary throughout the world?
3. Figure 3A.3 uses the United Kingdom as an example of a post-industrial economy. Using Figure 3A.2 to help you, explain what you think this means.
4. Make a copy of Figure 3A.11. Add labels to show how the north of France has been affected by industrial decline.
5. Using Figure 3A.13, draw a diagram to show how the Millennium Dome in London has affected the economy of the area.

CASE STUDY

Employment and development in Gambia

Although there are differences in wealth within Europe, these are not as great as the gap between Europe and the world's LEDCs. Some of the poorest countries are to be found in Africa, having GNP rates much lower than even the poorest countries in Europe. What is the economic situation in Gambia, one of Africa's poorest nations? How is the country developing?

What is Gambia's employment structure?

Gambia is a very poor country in West Africa (see Figure 3A.14). In terms of its stage of economic development, Gambia is an 'agricultural economy' as defined by Figure 3A.3.

Although contributing less than one-quarter of the country's wealth, primary industries are Gambia's main employer. In the region around Gunjur, for example (see Figure 3A.15) such work is typical of that undertaken throughout Gambia.

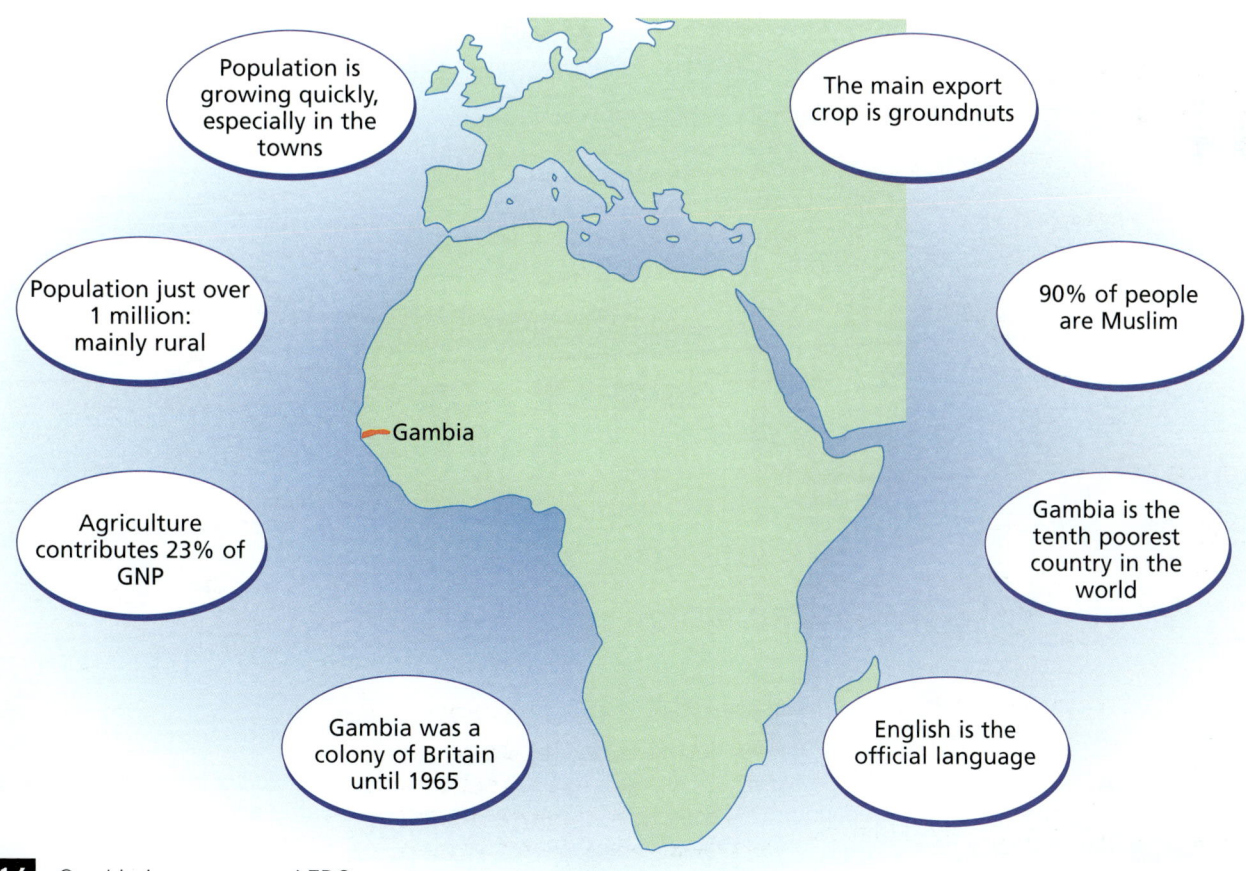

- Population is growing quickly, especially in the towns
- The main export crop is groundnuts
- Population just over 1 million: mainly rural
- 90% of people are Muslim
- Agriculture contributes 23% of GNP
- Gambia is the tenth poorest country in the world
- Gambia was a colony of Britain until 1965
- English is the official language

3A.14 *Gambia is a very poor LEDC*

Section 3 Changing Employment Patterns

3A.15 The Atlantic coastal region of Gambia

The photographs in Figure 3A.16 show people and their livelihoods in the Gunjur area. Many people do not work full time. They may help on the farm at harvest time and for clearing the scrub but may be unemployed for the rest of the time. This situation is known as **underemployment**. Although Gambians are involved in the fishing industry indirectly they do not go out in the fishing boats. Direct employment in fishing is by people from Senegal.

Development in Gunjur

In 1982 a community link began between the English town of Marlborough and the fishing and agricultural village of Gunjur in Gambia. The link was established on mutual respect, learning and development. Since 1990 small development projects have been set up. In 1998 a local non-governmental organisation (NGO) was established. It was called TARUD: Trust Agency for Rural Development. It has 28 workers who use computer technology powered by their own generator. Women have been at the centre of the development projects (see Figure 3A.17).

3A.16 Employment in the Gunjur region

A This woman working on her vegetable garden is preparing the land for a new crop.

B *Fulani* herdsmen take their cattle across the beach at Gunjur.

A Changing employment structures

C The local bonga fish, which is an important source of food, is being transported from Tanji beach.

D These women are at an uncovered well in Gunjur. The wells have not been a clean source of water and children fall down them.

E Children are keen to learn as they see education as a way forward.

F This handful of groundnuts and sorghum were grown in the same field.

Section 3 Changing Employment Patterns

business education **health education**

small loans scheme **mango orchard**

vegetable gardens

literacy and numeracy **water project**

carpentry co-operative **pre-school education**

3A.17 *Development projects in Gunjur have improved the role of women in the economy*

EXTENDED ACTIVITY

A new development project for a Gambian village

Imagine that you work for a British development organisation. As part of your work in Gambia, you are to work with TARUD to advise them on the best choice for a new development project for a village near to Gunjur which has set up an NGO. The NGO has £50 000 to spend on a development project. There are six projects to choose from, which are outlined below. Study Figure 3A.18 as well.

1 Water project

The people of the village have no access to clean, piped water. Their water comes from open, unprotected wells. Many of the local people become ill with water-borne diseases. The women draw the water by hand with a bucket and rope. A clean water supply is needed. Surveys have been made; it would cost £2 million to dig deep boreholes and to put in piped water. The village cannot afford this. The £50 000 would enable them to cover 12 of the existing wells and to install pumps on each of them to raise the water.

2 Women's literacy programme

Only 25 per cent of women and 53 per cent of men can read and write in Gambia. It is difficult for development projects such as health education and business education to work properly until the people become more literate and numerate. This money will set up a literacy project in the village. Women will go to evening classes, after they have returned from the fields. The classes will be held in family compounds; the project aims to reach one woman from every compound in the village. The women will then be able to use a telephone, write down prices, write letters, and read instructions on medicines. At present they can do none of these things.

A Changing employment structures

3 Small loans scheme and business education

Many people in the Gambian village are very poor. They would like to be able to start up small businesses in their backyards such as fish-smoking and tie-dying, or having a market stall, but they cannot as they have no money at all with which to start up the business.

The £50 000 would start a project to loan small amounts of money to very poor people. They will start small businesses and the loans will be paid back with interest within 2 years. The project will be run by the NGO with help from a business adviser, who will also run courses in business management.

4 Health education project

In Gambia, 9 per cent of the children die before they are 5 years old. They die mainly from preventable diseases like diarrhoea resulting from polluted water and bad hygiene, and also respiratory infections which could be cured with better healthcare. Most of the women are illiterate and it is difficult for them to read labels on medicines. The £50 000 would start a popular education project with the women. Puppet shows would visit each compound, in which puppets act out a story, for example of a sick baby with a cough; the mother says the doctor is too busy to see her but her friends tell her she must take him.

5 Marketing mangoes

Women grow most of the vegetables in the village, for their family to eat and also to sell in the local market if there is a surplus. A local farmer proposes to purchase land to grow a mango orchard. He needs to prepare the ground, put up fences, sink a well and plant the mango trees. The mangoes would be transported to Banjul for sale in the hotels or for export to Europe. He has asked for a grant of £50 000 to enable him to buy the land and begin his business. Village women would be able to use the land for their crops as the trees are growing.

6 A carpentry project

There is very little manufacturing employment in Gambia and in the village there is only a fishing boat builder who operates on the beach. There is a supply of tropical hardwood from nearby Senegal. As people have more cash to spend there will be a demand for furniture such as tables and chairs. Some craftsmen could be employed making items for tourists such as drums, carved animals and small decorated tables. A carpentry teacher would have to be paid for. It would give some men work and a cash income to help their families.

Your task is to advise TARUD on the best choice from the six projects for the local community. In addition to the information about each project, it is important that you consider the views of people who live in the area. Some viewpoints are shown in Figure 3A.18. Present a report which includes the following information.

1 A summary of each of the six projects.
2 The advantages of each of the projects.
3 Your choice of projects in order of preference.
4 For your chosen project, state clearly why it was your first choice.
5 For each of the other projects, outline why it was not your first choice.
6 An information leaflet designed for local people to explain your choice of project. Remember that many people will not be able to read or write.

Your report could be produced on a wordprocessor.

Section 3 Changing Employment Patterns

A nurse

My name is Isatou Touray, age 28. I have just returned to the village from the UK where I have been studying health education for two years, and before that I trained as a nurse. Although I am a citizen of the village I have not lived there for 6 years. I am shocked on returning to the village to see the level of poverty, the large number of children being born, and the general level of illness.

A mother of six children

I'm Kaddy Ceesay, age 30. Altogether I have had seven children, one died of malaria. I have lived in the village all of my life. My children benefit from the pre-school and junior school. I would like to be able to read and write. I would love to be able to read the papers which come into the village. Now some people have TV and I would like to be able to read the words which come up on screen.

A woman market stall holder

I am Fatou Bojang, age 28. I cannot read or write, having left school aged 10. I have had 5 children, one of whom died. I spend most of my day in my vegetable garden where I grow a lot of food for my family. If I have some spare, I sell it in the market. I really struggle to make ends meet. My husband is unemployed; I can only afford to send two children to school; the 12 year old has had to leave school to help in the gardens.

A young unemployed person

My name is Lamin Jammeh, age 20. I have been to primary and secondary school in the village but my family could not afford for me to go to High School in Banjul to take my 'O' levels. I have been unemployed for the past six months and can see no prospect of employment. My only skill is playing football, but I am not good enough to get into any good team. I would really like to go to the UK but see no way to get there. I have no money at all as there is no unemployment benefit.

A fisherman

I am Momodou Darboe, age 38. I have been a fisherman all my life. I have two wives and six children but an extended family of 22 people depend on me. I own a boat, and every day I spend 8 hours at sea, filling my boat with fish. I sell my fish to the women on the beach or to people who export them to other west African countries, but it's long, hard work and I don't make much money. I would like to buy a new outboard motor as my present one is getting very old.

3A.18 *Some local viewpoints*

Tourism: a way forward

Gambia is a popular country for tourists from the UK and northern Europe. Tourism is concentrated in the Bakau area west of Banjul (see Figure 3A.15). In recent years about 100 000 people have visited the country each year. Tourism employs up to 10 000 Gambians and it is estimated that ten times that figure are indirectly dependent on the earnings of tourism. Most tourists are on package holidays paid for in their home countries. Even the hotels are foreign owned so little is spent in Gambia itself.

Eco-tourism is an alternative to the all-inclusive package, whereby the host community is in control of and benefits directly from local tourism. Gambia Tourism Concern (GTC) is trying to promote eco-tourism to ensure that tourism contributes to the overall development of Gambia. GTC was set up by a Gambian in 1994. It is establishing small tourist initiatives which will benefit local people.

One such example is in Tumanitenda, a small village on a tributary of the River Gambia (see Figure 3A.15). The villagers have developed a tourist camp next to their village consisting of four traditional-style houses designed to

A Changing employment structures

accommodate sixteen tourists. The houses were built by local people using mud blocks, wood and thatch (see Figure 3A.19). The bedrooms have mattresses sunk into platforms and are furnished with tie-dyed fabrics made by local craft workers. Mosquito nets, sitting areas and a shower block are provided. Tourists can canoe on the river, watch birds, meet local people and learn traditional craft and music skills.

As a tourist on arrival you meet the village elders who welcome you and explain the background to their camp. The income you bring to the village, eg paying for water for a shower, goes to the villagers who manage the camp. This enables the villagers to use any profit to benefit and develop their own community. The women of the village cook meals for the tourists. The villagers know it is important that everyone from the village feels part of the development of the camp. They know they must remain united, but they are excited and proud of what they have achieved so far.

3A.19 *Part of the eco-tourist approach to development*

NOTING ACTIVITIES

1. Why is tourism a 'way forward' for Gambia?
2. How does eco-tourism benefit the local people and the environment more than traditional forms of tourism?
3. The new road from Banjul to Gunjur is being built (see Figure 3A.15). Write in detail about the possible impact of tourism on the village of Gunjur. Include the economic impact, the social changes that might take place, and the effects on the environment. Conclude with a paragraph about whether you think tourism will be good or bad for Gunjur.

Why is Gambia poor?

It is easy to say that:

- Gambia is poor because it has a high percentage of its population in primary employment
- it has a high natural population increase which causes pressure on its limited resources
- there is no oil, gas or coal
- mineral resources such as diamonds and iron ore do not exist
- people have a low level of literacy.

While these things are true, they are not the real answers to the question.

Why has Gambia remained poor and why does it have low income, poor health, low life expectancy and low levels of literacy?

Gambia is similar to many other LEDCs in Africa and they are also desperately poor compared to the MEDCs. It is at a different level of development compared to MEDCs. It has little manufacturing industry and does not seem to be attracting much. It is still only in the second stage of the Demographic Transition Model (see Figure 1A.2).

The country was exploited as a colony by Britain. Slaves were taken from Gambia to the West Indies. The character in the popular novel *Roots* by Alex Hailey was from Gambia. Gambia did not start to develop while it was a colony. As an independent African state it is short of money for investment. Foreign companies do not invest in a big way in the country. When they do, much of the profit leaves the country. Many of the best educated people in Gambia leave to live in the UK or USA; their skills are lost to Gambia's development.

Gambia does not earn much for its groundnuts or its fish. It has to import food and has to borrow money from abroad. It has a large debt which it cannot pay off. Its government has not been very stable and after a military coup in 1994 the British government advised tourists not to go to Gambia, and its small tourist income collapsed (although it has now risen again).

Section 3 Changing Employment Patterns

> **NOTING ACTIVITIES**
>
> 1 Write in your own words why Gambia has not developed at the same rate as the countries of Western Europe. Include the following: primary products, colony, slave trade, emigration, early stage of the demographic transition model, an agricultural economy.
>
> 2 What stages of economic development and population transition will Gambia have to go through before it can be called a developed country? Do you think that it might become rich or do you imagine that it will always be poor?

Changing regional employment structures: Yorkshire

Employment structures vary within and between regions of a country. They also change through time. Sheffield is an example of a city in England that has experienced many changes in its employment structure since the Industrial Revolution. How has employment changed in Sheffield? To what extent has the city and surrounding region experienced the spiral of decline and multiplier effect in employment?

Sheffield is in the Yorkshire and Humberside economic region. The United Kingdom is divided into eleven regions for planning purposes, which are shown in Figure 3A.20.

Yorkshire and Humberside is an economic region of great variety with National Parks, farming areas and important industrial regions (Figure 3A.21)

West Yorkshire was traditionally famous for woollen manufacturing. In 1950, 170,000 people were employed in the Yorkshire woollen and other textile industries. Since then the industry has been steadily in decline. There are many reasons for this decline:

1 out-dated machinery
2 old-fashioned processes
3 high production costs compared with other countries
4 competition from artificial fibres
5 competition from overseas producers eg India, the Far East and southern Europe
6 loss of overseas markets as the LEDCs started their own textile industries
7 slowness to adopt new fashions.

The Yorkshire Coalfield was Britain's most important coalfield stretching from Leeds to Nottingham. Coal from this coalfield powered the textile industry and the steel industry of the Sheffield area. The coalfields shut down for a variety of reasons, including the drop in demand for coal as industry turned to gas and electricity.

How did employment change?

Textile workers, steelworkers and miners were made redundant as the factories and mines shut down during the latter years of the 20th century. Unemployment was high and many new jobs appealed to women more than men. The factory areas became derelict and the mining landscapes were deserted. Inner city areas declined. People moved away from the most devastated areas. A spiral of decline set in. In many areas of Yorkshire the spiral of decline did not continue but was gradually reversed.

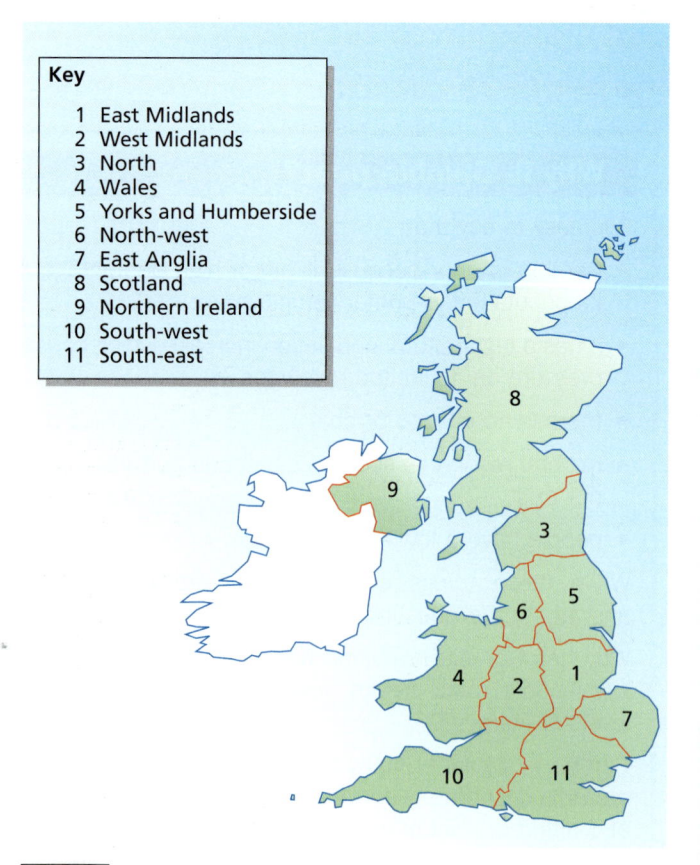

Key
1 East Midlands
2 West Midlands
3 North
4 Wales
5 Yorks and Humberside
6 North-west
7 East Anglia
8 Scotland
9 Northern Ireland
10 South-west
11 South-east

3A.20 *UK Standard Economic Regions*

A Changing employment structures

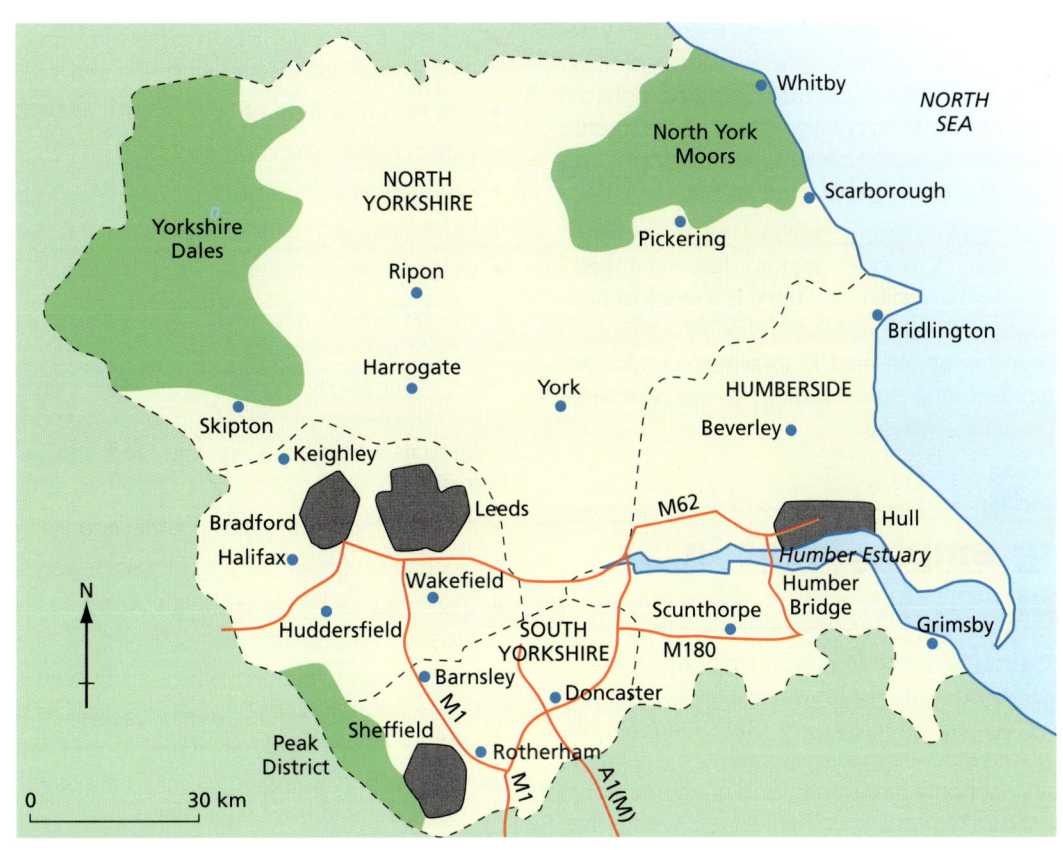

3A.21 *Yorkshire and Humberside*

Reversing the decline

A wide variety of measures have been taken to revitalise and energise the declining areas. Figure 3A.22 shows some of the major initiatives. The names of the initiatives have changed over the years; the level of grants and incentives change and different areas are included at different times. Policy has usually been to give aid to a declining region not to encourage people to move away.

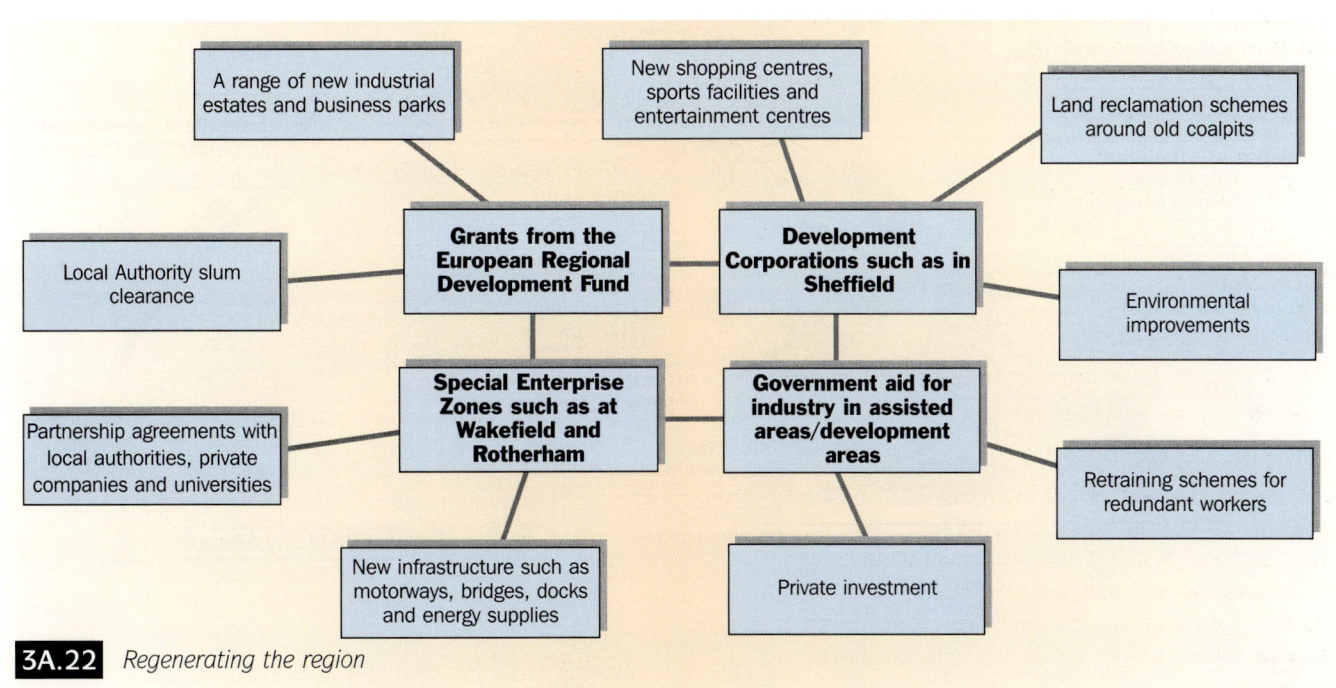

3A.22 *Regenerating the region*

57

Section 3 Changing Employment Patterns

Once the spiral of decline has been reversed then the **cycle of wealth** can begin. This is the opposite to the spiral of decline (see Figure 3A.11). When the area develops industry it will continue to attract other companies and investment, causing a multiplier effect. Services and component industries set up and the area gains a reputation.

Since the peak of textile working, steelmaking and mining, employment in the Yorkshire region has changed. Unemployment figures have fallen and there is a range of new jobs for men and women in the same variety of industries and services that occur throughout the UK. Yorkshire is no longer a region of manufacturing specialisation; it has *diversified*, *modernised* and has been *revitalised*.

CASE STUDY

Changing employment in Sheffield

Sheffield has been transformed from a steelmaking city to a modern regional centre. Its employment, land use and transport have changed. Sheffield, like other large British cities, is part of the post-industrial economy. The change from a secondary economy to a tertiary and quaternary one has not been without its problems. Sheffield has had to live with the issues of:

- industrial decline which affected male employment: 23 000 steel jobs were lost in five years in the 1980s
- new jobs that were often more attractive to women
- closed factories and derelict land
- sub-standard housing
- low attainment in its schools
- traffic congestion
- an unattractive city centre
- a poor national image.

The reasons for the decline of Sheffield's steel industry were similar to the reasons for de-industrialisation in other heavy industrial areas such as the Yorkshire woollen textile industry:

- low cost foreign imports of steel goods
- mechanisation and automation of processes
- inefficient methods and high labour costs compared to those of other countries
- new materials such as plastics being used instead of steel.

Since the 1980s Sheffield has tackled these social and economic issues. With government and European money the city has been transformed, but new issues have arisen as the new Sheffield has taken shape.

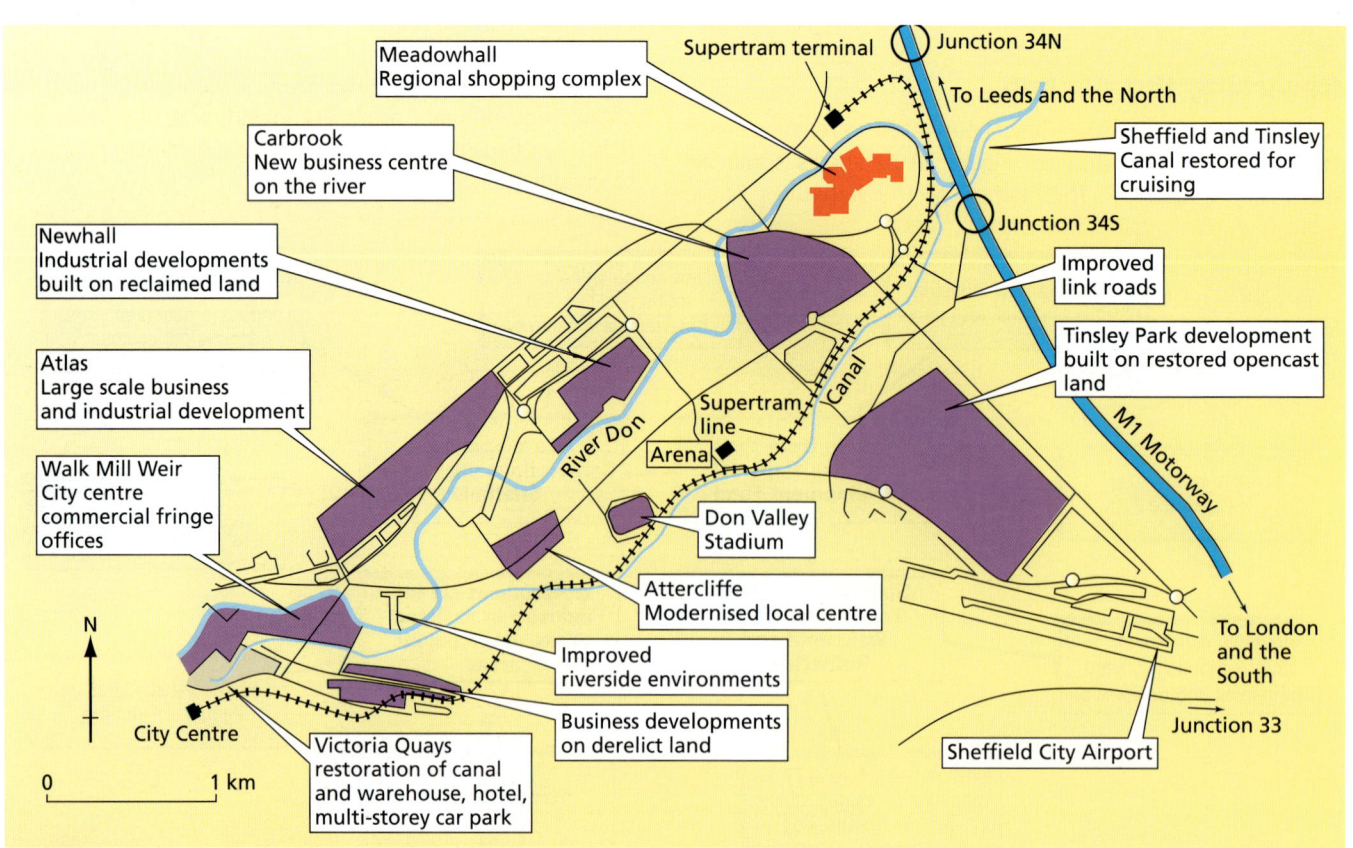

3A.23 *The new Don Valley*

58

A Changing employment structures

The Lower Don Valley

Sheffield's steel industry was centred in the Don Valley. Steel castings, railway carriages and heavy steel goods were produced. One-third of the land in the Don Valley was left derelict after terraced slum housing and steelworks had been cleared. In 1988 the Government set up the Sheffield Development Corporation to revitalise the valley and create new jobs. The Development Corporation was not as large as that in London Docklands and it only lasted 9 years, until 1997. The map (Figure 3A.23) shows the main characteristics of the new Don Valley.

Today the Lower Don Valley has over 900 employers employing 24 000 people. This includes the 7000 employees in the Meadowhall Shopping complex. Distribution industries now account for 50 per cent of the businesses in the valley. Other expanding employment is in transport, leisure and financial services. Figure 3A.24 shows two new developments.

Issues for local people

- What type of work could the male steelworkers expect?
- Does the Meadowhall employment give as much job satisfaction as the old manufacturing industries?
- Does the Victoria Quays (Figure 3A.25) redevelopment benefit local residents?
- Is the employment offered at the Abbey National Headquarters (Figure 3A.26) relevant to the local residents?

3A.24 *New industry in the Don Valley*

3A.25 *The Victoria Quays development*

3A.26 *The Abbey National Headquarters at Carbrook*

Section 3 **Changing Employment Patterns**

Understanding local issues

Each one of the above issues can be understood and analysed by asking the following series of questions.

- What is the issue?
- Who is involved?
- What are the important features of this issue?
- Why are they like this?
- How might this issue be resolved?
- What might be the consequences for different groups of people?
- What do you think should happen and why?

The Cultural Industries Quarter

The Cultural Industries Quarter (CIQ) was launched in 1980 when alternative jobs were needed in Sheffield. Development of this initiative took off after 1995. Cultural industries are defined as music, recording, film, video, radio, TV, photography and the performing arts. The area containing the CIQ is shown on the street map of Sheffield (Figure 3A.27). A more detailed map used for local fieldwork is shown as Figure 3A.30.

NOTING ACTIVITIES

1 Write a report on The Lower Don Valley using the following sub-headings:

   Sheffield's industrial past

   The steel industry declines

   New development in the lower Don Valley.

2 How do you think the following Sheffield people feel about the new Lower Don Valley?

   a A steel worker who lost his job in the valley in 1985
   b The family who lost their home in the valley when it was demolished
   c The businesswoman who is looking for a new office unit
   d The school children who live locally

3A.27 *The location of the Cultural Industries Quarter (CIQ) of Sheffield. Note the location of the Victoria Quays in the north-east corner which will help you link this map with Figure 3A.23*

A Changing employment structures

Funding has come from the National Lottery and the European Union. The aims of the CIQ are:

- to regenerate the local economy by developing new industries
- to provide opportunities for inward investment
- to provide entertainment
- to improve the city's image and bring in visitors
- to improve the appearance of the city.

By 1998 there were 1000 people working in the Quarter with 160 businesses. In 2000 building was still going on with new BBC Radio Sheffield and TV studios (Figure 3A.28).

The National Centre for Popular Music (Figure 3A.29) opened in 1998 but was not immediately successful in attracting visitors. In 2000 it was closed and later re-opened with the plan of attracting local people to use the centre.

3A.28 *Building in the Cultural Industries Quarter in 2000*

3A.29 *The National Centre for Popular Music with the Outdoor Music Venue in the foreground*

Figure 3A.30 is a land use map of the CIQ which was drawn by students in 1999. In 2000 the fieldwork area was revisited and photographs taken. Since 1999 there had been changes and it was clear that further changes were place taking during 2000–01.

What was learned from the fieldwork?

Before the fieldwork visit, information had been obtained on the CIQ from Sheffield City Council and internet research. The gathering of **primary data** from fieldwork added to the knowledge of the Quarter. It helped with:

- the exact location of the CIQ activities and nearby functions
- the building works and architecture of the area
- the atmosphere and 'feel' of the area
- the chance to see people moving in and out of the buildings
- data which was as up-to-date as possible
- an opportunity to take photographs of buildings
- data which could be analysed.

Visiting an area and observing its characteristics is an essential part of learning and appreciating the Geography of an area.

NOTING ACTIVITIES

1 Study the fieldwork map (Figure 3A.30). Link it to the street plan of the centre of Sheffield.

   a What are some of the advantages of collecting primary data compared to using secondary data?

   b What are 'cultural industries'? Why are they important in the modern economy?

   c Describe the location of the businesses associated with 'cultural industries'. (Are they distributed randomly, clustered or spread out in a pattern?)

   d What are the advantages of such industries locating together in a small area?

2 Using the information provided for Sheffield, undertake a fieldwork survey of an area near to where you live. What issues are involved in the area? How are people affected? What do you think could be done to improve the area or situation?

Section 3 Changing Employment Patterns

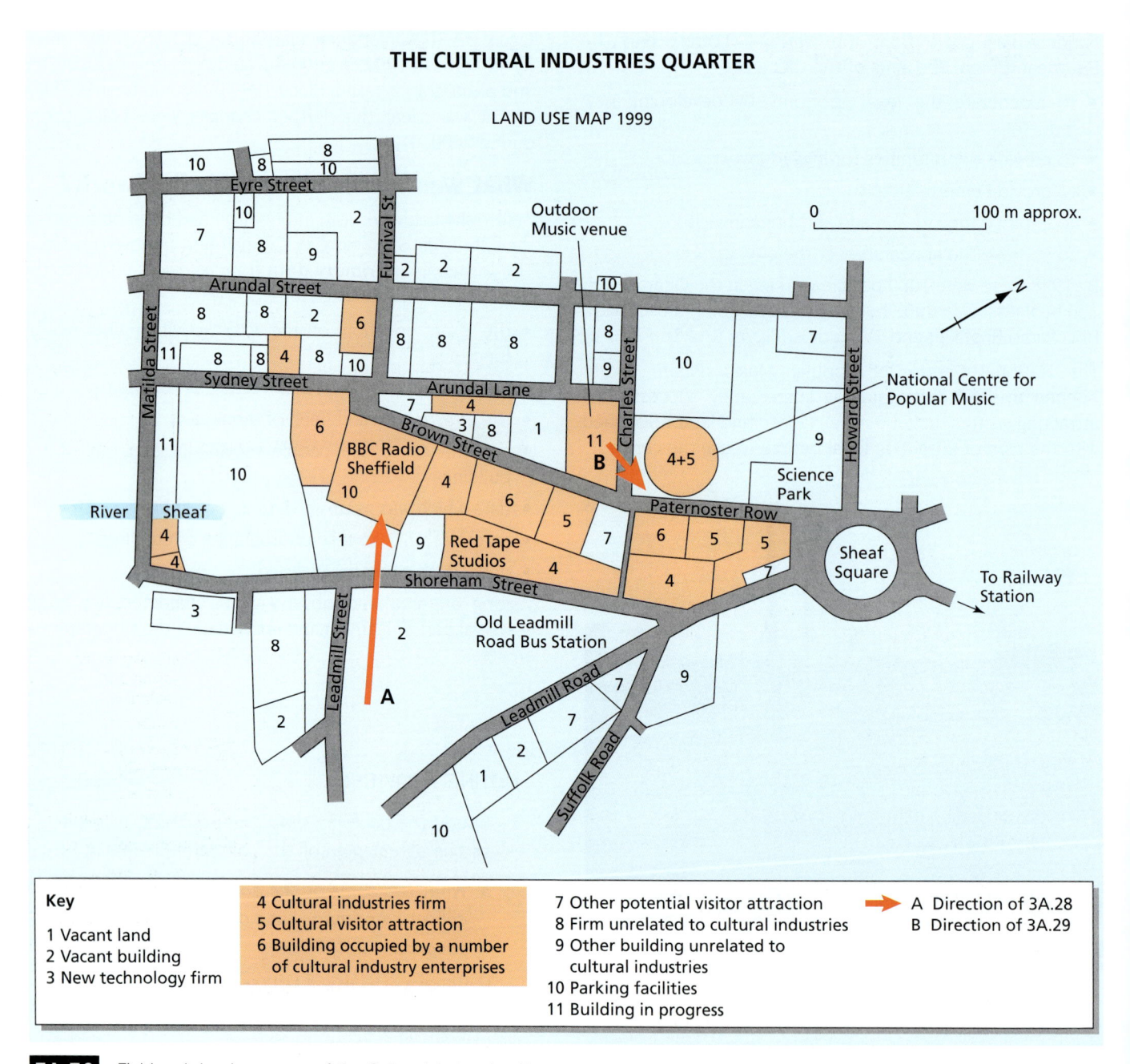

THE CULTURAL INDUSTRIES QUARTER
LAND USE MAP 1999

Key
1 Vacant land
2 Vacant building
3 New technology firm
4 Cultural industries firm
5 Cultural visitor attraction
6 Building occupied by a number of cultural industry enterprises
7 Other potential visitor attraction
8 Firm unrelated to cultural industries
9 Other building unrelated to cultural industries
10 Parking facilities
11 Building in progress

A Direction of 3A.28
B Direction of 3A.29

3A.30 *Fieldwork land use map of the Cultural Industries Quarter*

Section 3 Changing Employment Patterns

B Primary industry: farming

Farming in the UK

Farming in the United Kingdom has reached an all-time economic low. British agriculture earns a smaller part of the nation's wealth than ever before. Less than 1 per cent of the UK's GNP is earned by farming, and fewer than 1 per cent of the country's workforce are farmers. The situation is predicted to get even worse in the future. What has caused such a crisis in British farming?

Employment in farming in the UK has been declining for many years. The increased use of machinery has meant that fewer workers are needed to plough land and harvest crops, and to look after animals. Most people in villages once worked in jobs related to farming, but this is no longer the case. Many people left rural areas in search of better-paid jobs in towns and cities.

British farming has also faced tough competition from other countries. Much of the food we eat comes from abroad, even when there is a home grown alternative. Foreign produce such as fruit and meat are often bought in British supermarkets, either because of quality and taste, or because it is cheaper. British farmers find it difficult to compete against these imported goods. In recent years, the **exchange rate** in Britain has been very high. This means that the British pound is worth a lot abroad, which makes British goods very expensive to buy abroad. As a result, many farmers have been unable to sell their produce in other countries.

Farming has also been hit by fears surrounding food safety, most notably the BSE crisis. Infected food killed many cattle, and people have died from the human equivalent called CJD. As a result, sales of beef in the UK dropped dramatically, and the sale of British beef was banned in many other countries.

The value of farming to the British economy has fallen as a result of these changes. In 1999, farming contributed £7.2 billion to the nation's economy, having declined by 20 per cent since 1995. Farming now contributes slightly less to the British economy than sales of paint. The situation is even worse on a regional basis, as average national figures hide enormous differences throughout the country.

Traditionally, farming in Britain has been divided along the lines shown in Figure 3.B2. Arable farming dominated in the

3B.1 *Imported foods are often preferred to home grown produce*

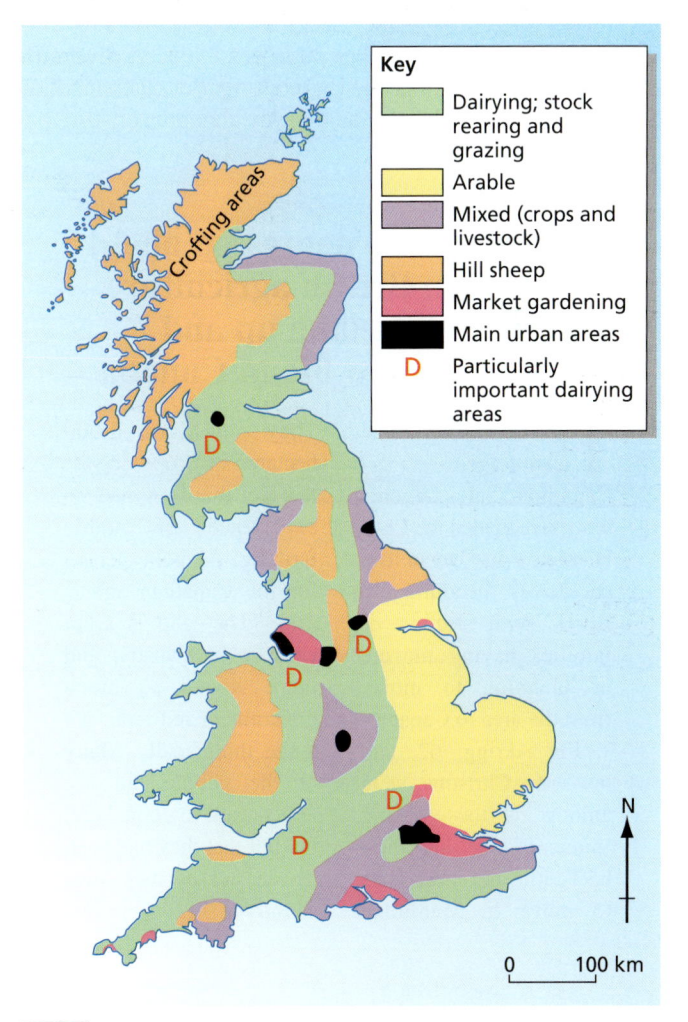

3B.2 *Farming in Britain*

Section 3 Changing Employment Patterns

low-lying fertile lands of the south and east. Hill farming, mostly of sheep, dominated in the harsher climate and relief of the north and west of the country. The economic problems facing farming have been greatest in the hill farming regions of Britain. Average incomes for sheep and cattle farmers in these areas have fallen as low as £2 000 per year. Farmers have only been able to survive as long as they have because of help they have received from the British government and from the European Union.

The situation has become so bad that many farmers have abandoned their way of life and moved away. In the Lake District, for example, farm incomes have become so low that farmers are leaving the area. Some who wish to continue farming for a living are even leaving the country, as shown in Figure 3B.3. Some farmers are turning to other means to earn more income. Over 60 per cent of Britain's farmers now have a source of income other than traditional farming businesses. In the Lake District, tourism has long been another source of income, as farmers have provided holiday accommodation for tourists. They know, however, that if more farmers leave the area and their fields are abandoned, the scenery that attracts visitors will disappear.

The use of farmland for other purposes is called **diversification.** In many parts of the United Kingdom diversification is big business, and is seen as the way ahead to ensure that farmers stay in business. As Figure 3B.4 shows, farmers have used their land in many ways to boost their incomes. In parts of the south-east of England, farmers have been keen to sell their land to developers for housing and roads. This is not surprising when figures of over £1 million per hectare of land have been suggested! The government has also supported some forms of diversification. Instead of giving money directly to help with the production of crops, farmers instead are given help with projects such as tourism. Much of this money actually comes from the European Union. It is intended to help preserve the countryside, by stopping farmers from abandoning their farms.

3B.4 *Farm diversification*

Farmers are so depressed about the crisis in British agriculture that they are selling up and moving to a new life in Canada

The trend has been encouraged by Canadian sales agents who have visited the Lake District. What began as a trickle is becoming a flood, with dozens of families having moved, or planning to move, from the area to Canada.

Jim Akrigg, 62, and his wife Christine were among the first 'pioneers', selling their beef cattle and sheep farm to move to Manitoba. They now farm 1,000 hectares of crops despite the fact that they had no experience of arable farming. A spokesperson for the Canadian agents said, 'The land is a lot cheaper in Canada, and there is not so much government red tape. It's a sad thing really. Many of the people did not really want to come here, but felt that they had been driven out of their own country.'

3B.3 *Adapted from the* Sunday Telegraph, *12 March 2000*

3B.5 *Some diversification receives grants from the European Union*

Organic farming

Until the mid-20th century, virtually all farming was organic. This means that food was produced without the use of artificially made chemicals. The use of these chemicals really started in the Second World War. Experiments developing chemical weapons showed that these chemicals killed insects. During the war, the use of chemicals in fertilisers and pesticides grew rapidly with the need to grow as much food as possible. After the war, these chemicals were widely promoted and used by farmers throughout the United Kingdom.

Organic farming has increased in recent years with greater public demand. This is mainly because many people are concerned about the safety of food grown using chemicals. The worry over BSE in cattle, concern over **genetically modified** (GM) food, and suggested links between pesticides and cancer are some of the main reasons.

Only 3 per cent of British farmland is organic, with fewer than 1000 farms producing organically grown food. Without the use of chemical pesticides and fertilisers, food is more expensive to produce. This extra cost is then passed on to the consumer. Despite this, more people are buying organic food. Sales in British supermarkets grew by 50 per cent from 1998 to 2000, and are set to continue rising at the same rate in the near future. British farmers are unlikely to be able to compete with other countries without help from the government. Over 80 per cent of organic food sold in the UK is grown abroad, including from as far away as South America and South Africa.

3B.6 *Supermarkets stock a wide range of organic foods, most of it imported*

NOTING ACTIVITIES

1. Why has farming declined in importance to the British economy?
2. What is farm diversification?
3. List some ways in which a farmer may diversify. In your opinion, which forms of diversification are most likely to be successful?
4. What is organic farming?
5. Why has organic produce become increasingly popular?
6. Research the following two issues. In each case, include a summary of the main facts relating to the issue, together with your own opinion.
    a. Should genetically modified (GM) crops be grown in Britain?
    b. Food safety, for example BSE in cattle.

CASE STUDY

West Lodge Farm

West Lodge is located in Northamptonshire, near to the town of Kettering (see Figure 3B.7). It is situated in the more prosperous farming areas of eastern England. Despite this, as with most farms, West Lodge has experienced a continued fall in its income. In 1999 alone, average farm incomes in eastern England fell by nearly 50 per cent. What is happening at West Lodge to ensure that the farm continues in business?

West Lodge is an arable farm of approximately 350 hectares. No animals are reared on the farm, as it was decided that they did not make enough money. Just over half of the farmland is used to grow wheat, much of which is bought by the nearby Weetabix factory. The next largest crop is of beans, most of which are exported to the Middle East.

Section 3 Changing Employment Patterns

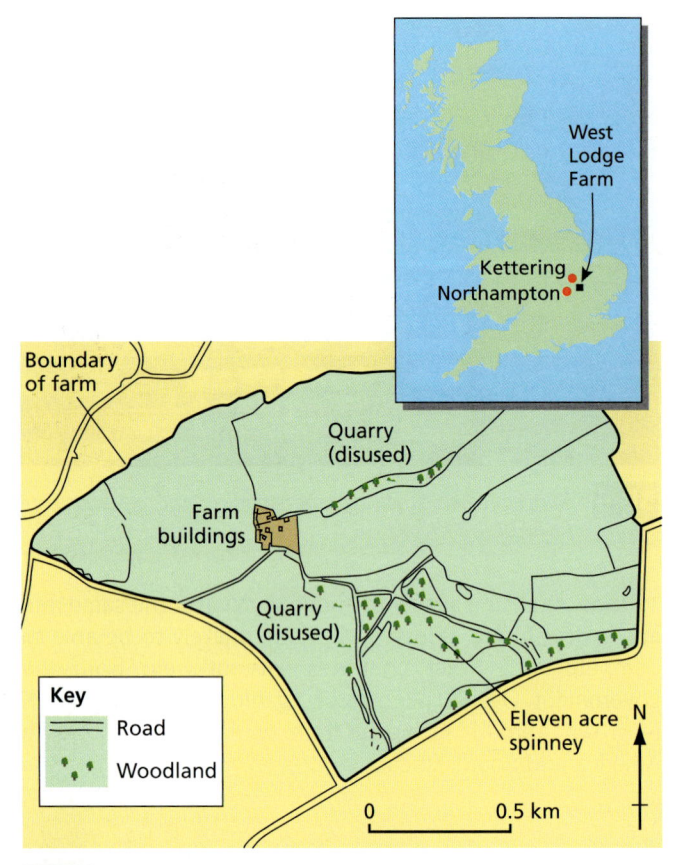

3B.7 West Lodge Farm

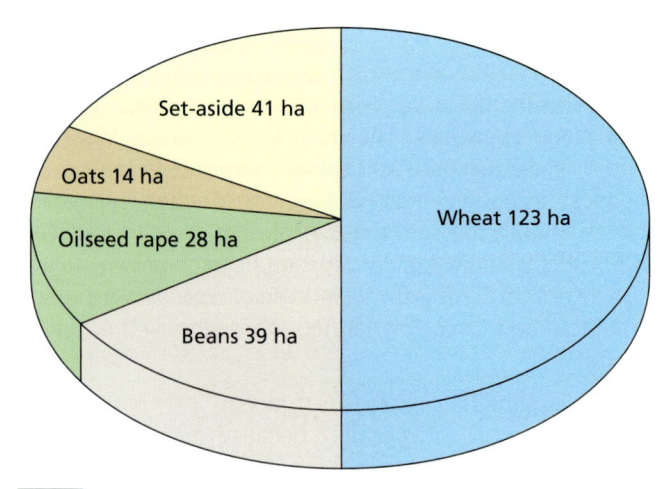

3B.8 How the land is used at West Lodge

Figure 3B.8 shows that some of the land at West Lodge is described as **set-aside**. This is a scheme whereby farmers are paid *not* to grow crops on their land. There are shortages of food in many parts of the world, but the United Kingdom actually produces too much. The British government pays farmers to leave some of their land and not grow crops or rear animals on it.

Since 1990, the Dee family who own West Lodge have tried to use their land in other ways to earn money. They realised that farm incomes were falling, and that they had to do something to prevent the farm from going out of business. The farm buildings have been put to other uses. Initially the farmhouse itself was used for Bed and Breakfast. While this made some money, it was not very much. Other buildings on the farm have since been used; for example, an old barn has been converted to a visitor centre. A large barn is even used for discos when it is not storing wheat!

Many of the building alterations are to support changes that the Dee family have made to how the land is used. Despite being in the more fertile east of England, the land is actually of quite poor quality for farming. It is on the edge of land that was once used by the large steelworks in Corby to extract iron ore. The rock may be rich in iron, but the soils are thin and poor. Some of the poorest land is covered by woodland, and was not really worth clearing for crop growing. The farmers decided to keep the land as forest and open it to visitors, providing nature trails and information signposts.

In order to get people to visit the farm, a range of attractions has been provided. These include:

- a pets corner
- animal and tractor rides
- facilities such as a café and shop
- guided tours and special event days
- activities for businesses, such as off-road driving and paintballing
- meeting rooms for companies to hire.

The farm has been renamed to highlight its changed land uses. It is now called West Lodge Rural Centre (Figure 3B.9).

The Dee family have invested heavily in providing these facilities. The profits are small, yet are likely to increase in the future while traditional farm incomes go down. There are likely to be further developments in the future at West Lodge. An area of land has been rented to the local cricket club for their pitch and pavilion, and there are plans to build a children's nursery and shops for rent.

Who is the countryside for?

The majority of Britain's countryside is owned by farmers. Even in a National Park such as the Lake District where there are many different landowners, over half of the land is privately owned by farmers. Yet less land than ever is needed to provide our food. Farming has become an efficient industry, but it is also losing money for many farmers. If in

B Primary industry: farming

3B.9 West Lodge Rural Centre

the future most of the food grown in the United Kingdom will come from East Anglia, what will happen to the rest of the countryside? Who is the countryside for?

Over 90 per cent of the population of the UK live in towns and cities. To most of them, the countryside is a place for leisure and recreation. Rural areas have become a place to escape to, rather than live in. Town dwellers want the countryside to be kept neat and tidy; but who is to do this? The countryside remains a place in which people live and work, in a variety of jobs. Many rural dwellers feel that the government does not pay enough attention to their needs. In 1998, for example, a mass demonstration highlighted some of the problems for people living in the countryside.

The needs of many people who want to use the countryside conflict with each other. Look at the opinions of the people in Figure 3B.11, all of whom were in a National Park one summer weekend.

3B.10 Do we pay enough attention to the needs of people living and working in the countryside?

67

Section 3 Changing Employment Patterns

Local MP It is important that farmers continue to work in the countryside. Farming is a vital industry. Britain will always need farmers to provide its food. We may be able to import food from abroad now, but who knows what could happen in the future – like another war? If we lose our farmers, we will never get them back.

Environmentalist The countryside may not be perfect, but it's all we have. It is important that the countryside is looked after, and farmers are the best people to do it. They should keep hedgerows, encourage wildlife, and use organic farming where possible. The use of GM crops should be banned.

Farmer It's no longer worth it. We lose so much money. Our costs keep going up, while the price we get for our produce is going down. If the government does not help us, most farmers will go out of business. I don't know what we would do then. My family have been farmers for hundreds of years, and I don't know any other trade.

Tourist We enjoy coming here, particularly for the pretty villages and the countryside. We bring money into the area, and would go somewhere else if the countryside was not looked after. Our farmhouse B & B is excellent, and I think farmers should do more things like this to make money.

Local resident This village is no longer a farming community. I work in a nearby town. I commute to work some days, and work from home on others. My business does not get help from the government. I don't see why farmers should be treated as a special case.

3B.11

EXTENDED ACTIVITY

You will need to work in a group of five for this activity.

1 Each person in your group should take the role of one of the people whose opinions appear above.
2 For your own role, write a summary of what you think should happen to the countryside.
3 Hold a meeting that is attended by each of the members of your group. Each person should give a short presentation to the others, lasting about two minutes. One member of the group should also chair the meeting. You should allow time for questions.
4 Write a summary of what happened in the meeting. How do you think the countryside of the future should be managed?

Section 3 Changing Employment Patterns

C Secondary industry: car making

3C.1 *Honda*

Honda the transnational

Honda is a Japanese car company that now has more than 100 manufacturing facilities in 33 countries. It is a **transnational company** manufacturing cars, engines, motorcycles and power equipment (see Figure 3C.2). The company was set up in 1948 and has become a **global company**. It has its headquarters in Tokyo and about 110 000 employees, all of whom are called 'associates'.

A transnational company (TNC) is one that operates in many countries. These companies are more wealthy than many individual nations, as shown in Figure 3A.1 on page 42.

Transnationals are now so dominant that they control the majority of the world's manufacturing industry. Most TNCs have their headquarters in rich developed countries. This means that, despite not being controlled by national governments, transnationals help to increase the gap in wealth between the world's richest and poorest nations. Over 60 per cent of TNCs are based in the USA and Japan, the two largest economies in the world.

Transnationals contribute to the **globalisation** of industry. They locate throughout the world, including some of the world's poorest LEDCs, in order to:

- move their production nearer to large markets. In addition to meeting local needs, this reduces the cost of transporting manufactured products
- reduce the cost of importing raw materials and component parts
- reduce the cost of labour; wage rates are often much lower in the LEDCs favoured by transnationals.

3C.2 *Transnational companies*

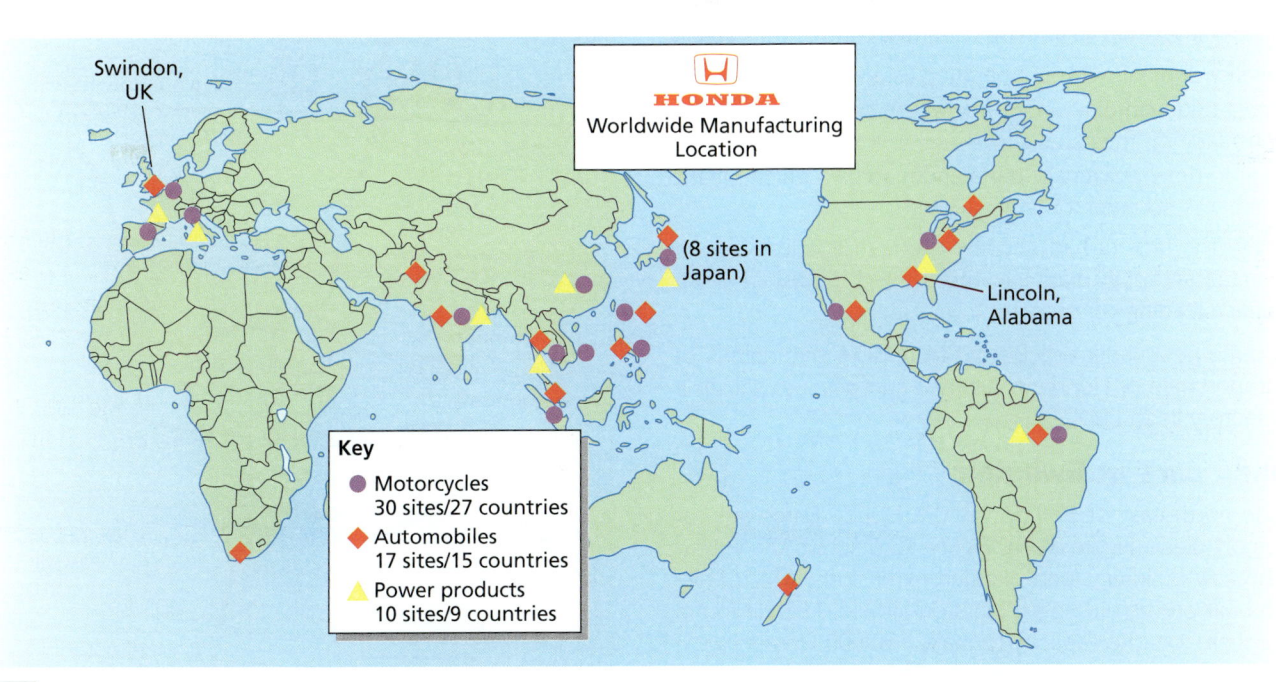

Key
- ● Motorcycles 30 sites/27 countries
- ◆ Automobiles 17 sites/15 countries
- ▲ Power products 10 sites/9 countries

3C.3 *Honda's worldwide manufacturing location*

Section 3 Changing Employment Patterns

11 February, 2000

HONDA ACCORD OUTPUT TOPS 5M UNITS IN US

According to Honda of America Mfg. Inc., output of the Accord passenger cars in the United States totalled 5,006,600 units as of the end of 1999, topping five million for the first time ever for a locally-produced single Japanese car model.

Ohio-based Honda of America Mfg. started producing the Accord in 1982.

HONDA BREAKS GROUND FOR NEW PLANT IN ALABAMA

LINCOLN, Ala. 25 April 2000 Honda broke ground on the new Lincoln facility in April of this year, and plans to begin production in late 2001. Honda will employ approximately 1,500 associates when it reaches its twin annual capacities of 120,000 vehicles and 120,000 engines in late 2002.

24 July, 2000

HONDA TO SET UP PRODUCTION PLANT IN MALAYSIA

The facility, with an initial production capacity of 15,000 and 20,000 vehicles annually, will be Honda's second manufacturing base in south-east Asia after Thailand.

3C.4 *Newspaper articles*

The company operates in four major regions: Japan; the Americas; Asia/Oceania; and Europe. Within these regions Honda has a local approach to manufacturing with a global outlook. It uses local suppliers and yet its philosophy and factory processes are global. The company has a well-developed environmental policy and is concerned to reduce the impact that it has upon the environment.

Figure 3C.3 shows the location of Honda's major manufacturing plants. In 1999 Honda of America celebrated its twentieth anniversary. The first factory was the Marysville Motorcycle Plant in Ohio. It was organised differently to the traditional assembly line factory. It featured:

- small groups of workers operating as a team
- integrated manufacturing where the whole motorcycle was made on the same site
- 'just-in-time' delivery of parts and materials which meant there was no need for large stores.

By 1982 the factory had become the first Japanese-owned car manufacturing plant in the United States. Honda became a leading car exporter from America.

The three newspaper articles in Figure 3C.4 give details of the importance of Honda in America and plans to set up a new factory in an LEDC.

Honda cars in Swindon

To the north-east of Swindon is the Honda European car assembly plant (Figure 3C.5). Figure 3C.6 shows the extent of the new buildings (and planned extensions) which have been built on the old South Marston airfield. At Swindon in 1999 there was the capacity to make 150 000 Honda cars a year, employing over 3000 people. This represents 50 per cent of all Honda cars sold in Europe. If Japanese companies were to sell cars within the EU, most components had to be made in the EU. Their only option was to manufacture in Europe. As with other Japanese firms they favour location in the UK because of the English language and lower costs than some other EU countries.

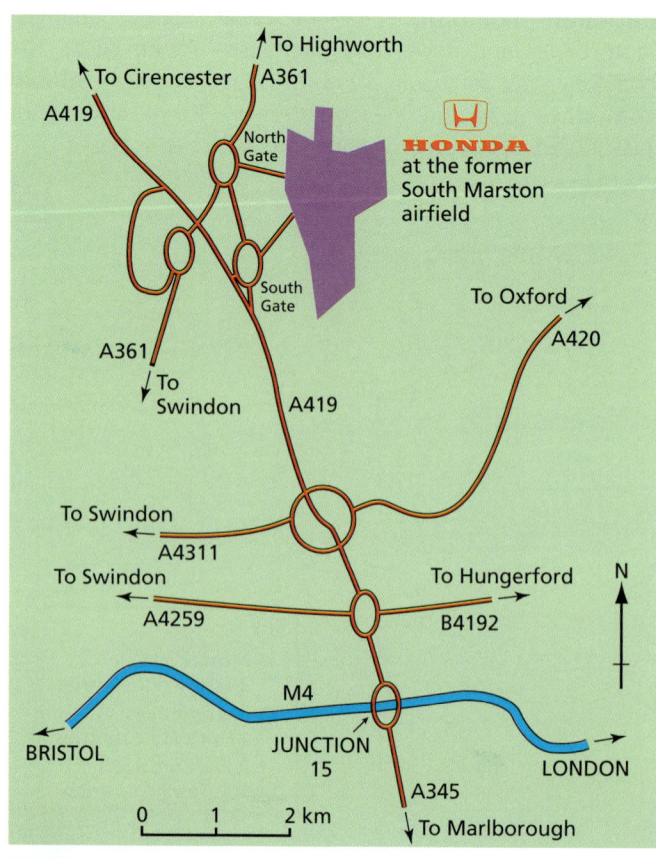

3C.5 *The location of the Swindon Honda car plant*

C Secondary industry: car making

3C.6 *The Honda car plant in Swindon showing the expansion area*

Honda was the third Japanese carmaker to base its European production in the UK. Nissan were the first choosing an old airfield site between Sunderland and Washington in north-east England. Toyota located near Derby and also chose an airfield site. Figure 3C.7 shows Honda's six reasons for choosing to locate in Swindon. Note that since establishing in Swindon, Honda and Rover have gone their separate ways after BMW took over Rover.

1 History of engineering in Swindon
- ex-workers from the British Rail works provided a high quality workforce

2 Access to the Rover group
- Rover's body and pressing plant already in Swindon
- Rover in Birmingham and Oxford

3 Good access to
- ports at Portbury and Southampton
- roads: see Figure 3C.5
- major rail links to Bristol and London
- proximity to Heathrow airport

4 Market
- well situated for the European market

5 Large site
- 148 hectares
- Vickers Supermarine previously owned the site; their old runway is used as a test track

6 The Borough Council
- welcomed Honda
- gave no cash incentives, however
- wanted a mix of manufacturing and service industries
- Swindon was already a very fast growing town

3C.7 *Why Honda chose Swindon*

Section 3 Changing Employment Patterns

3C.8 *Production at the Honda factory*

HONDA (UK) SUPPLIER MAP

- Netherlands 1
- Belgium 7
- UK 185
- Ireland 2
- France 20
- Portugal 2
- Spain 3
- Germany 21
- Austria 1
- Italy 5
- USA 1

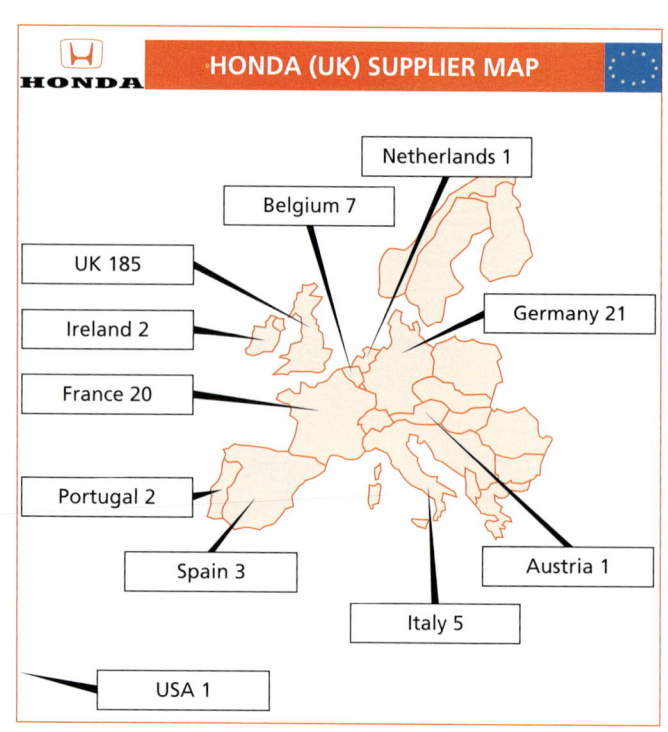

3C.9 Supplies to Swindon come from the UK and Europe

The total investment at Swindon was £340 million. This will generate much more wealth for the local area. Swindon and the M4 Corridor region is now a part of Britain's core region attracting more and more development. The expansion of the site in 2000 involved a second factory adding another 100 000 cars a year.

The manufacturing process at Swindon includes the same methods used by Honda worldwide. The factory needs a combination of skilled workers and modern hi-tech machinery including robot technology.

The Swindon Honda plant uses British and European component suppliers (Figure 3C.9). There is a big saving on transport costs compared to what they would be if the cars were made in Japan. The European customer has benefited with cheaper Honda cars. Honda's share of the European car market was 1.5 per cent in 1999 with a target of 2 per cent. Swindon will provide half the cars for European sales.

In 2000 it was announced that Honda at Swindon would step up its production of the CR-V sports vehicle. An extra 70 000 of these vehicles would be exported to the USA. Swindon had established itself as an **export-based** manufacturing plant.

NOTING ACTIVITIES

1. What is a transnational company?
2. Why do transnational companies locate throughout the world and especially in LEDCs?
3. List the important locations and activities of the Honda company.
4. Why have Japanese car companies located production plants in Europe?
5. Why was the site at Swindon suitable for Honda?
6. Draw a diagram to show the location advantages of Swindon for the Honda factory.
7. How similar are the sites of the three Japanese car companies manufacturing in the UK?
8. Describe the characteristics of the production and working methods at the Swindon factory.
9. What are the benefits to Swindon of the Honda factory?
10. What are the possible disadvantages of the Honda factory to Swindon? (Refer to pages 274–275 where the Honda environmental policy is discussed.)

Section 3 **Changing Employment Patterns**

D Tertiary industry: tourism

Tourism is a major global industry and source of **tertiary employment**. International tourism is growing very quickly. Over 700 million people took at least one foreign holiday in 2000, with the number predicted to increase by about 5 per cent each year. Europe is currently the world's major tourist region, as shown by Figure 3D.1. The Mediterranean coasts of France, Spain and Italy are the most popular destinations, attracting over 100 million visitors each year.

The global spread of tourism has seen the industry grow rapidly in areas such as the Middle East and South Asia. There is a growing number of people who travel both to and from LEDCs. Long haul holidays continue to increase at over 3 per cent per year. Such holidays represent a major source of potential for development in LEDCs.

Tourism is an **invisible export**; unlike selling goods to earn money, tourism is 'selling' the environment to tourists. There are three types of tourist environment, shown in Figure 3D.2.

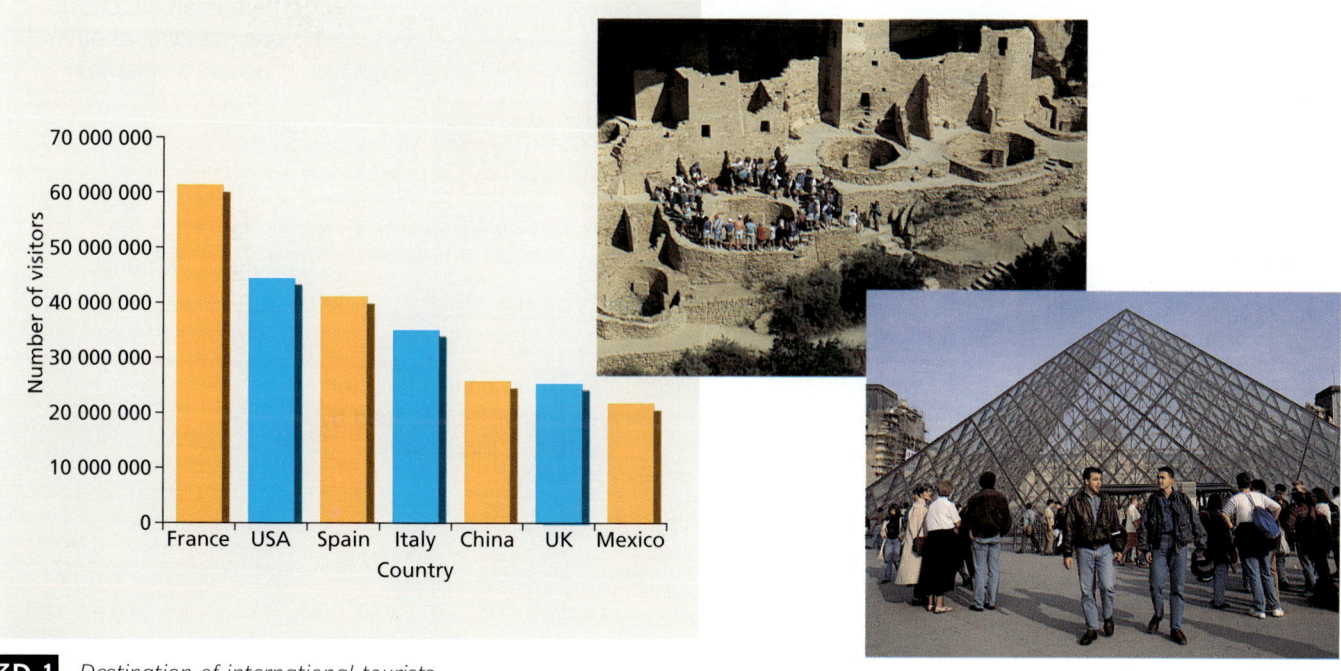

3D.1 *Destination of international tourists*

1 Natural Environments
Sea, beaches, mountains, lakes, wildlife

2 Cultural environments
Local foods, music, dancing, architecture

3 Amenities
Hotels, clubs, marinas, organised safaris, coach tours

3D.2 *Tourist environments*

Section 3 Changing Employment Patterns

LEDCs have been keen to develop tourism so that they can earn foreign exchange. They have used the tourist environments that are 'free' of high development costs. Their natural tourist environments have an instant appeal to tourists from the MEDCs. They are different, exciting and, with modern air travel, easily accessible. Figure 3D.3 shows the benefits of tourism to LEDCs.

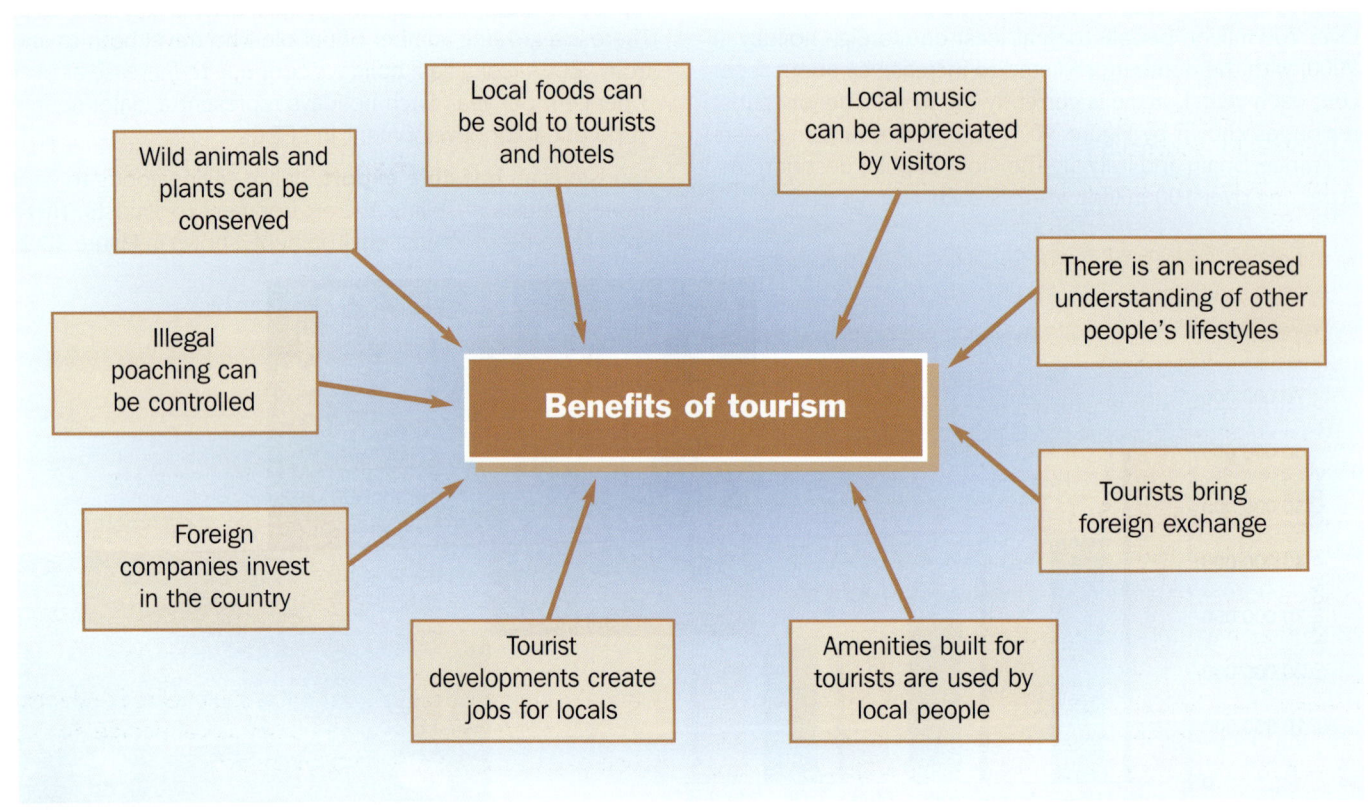

Benefits of tourism
- Wild animals and plants can be conserved
- Local foods can be sold to tourists and hotels
- Local music can be appreciated by visitors
- There is an increased understanding of other people's lifestyles
- Illegal poaching can be controlled
- Tourists bring foreign exchange
- Foreign companies invest in the country
- Tourist developments create jobs for locals
- Amenities built for tourists are used by local people

3D.3 *The benefits of tourism: a way forward*

- Goods have to be imported for the tourists
- Foreign workers are brought in to work in the tourist resorts: they send their money out of the country
- Most people pay for their holidays in their own country
- Foreign companies take profits from their investments
- Loans for tourist developments have to be paid back with interest

3D.4 *How tourist income can 'leak' out of a country*

D Tertiary industry: tourism

It's not all benefits

Money earned from tourism in an LEDC does not always remain in that country. Some of the income disappears through **leakage** (see Figure 3D.4). There are a range of issues associated with tourism. There are **economic problems**, and leakage is one of them.

There are social problems such as:

- local religious and cultural centres become shopping centres for souvenirs
- tourists introduce local people to gambling, alcohol and drugs
- imported food and drink become attractive to local people but they are expensive to buy
- young people are attracted to the resorts and leave their traditional ways of life
- local people may feel degraded if tourists do not take their traditions seriously.

There are also environmental problems:

- large hotels can be unsightly
- people's land may be taken over for tourist development
- large numbers of tourists can damage ancient sites
- tourists may put pressure on local resources, especially water and sewerage.

Tourism has brought advantages and disadvantages to LEDCs. Much of the tourist development in LEDCs is not sustainable. The environment is not being maintained in its natural state, the local cultures are being affected and local people are not receiving much money. Local people do not appear to be much involved or in control.

> **NOTING ACTIVITIES**
>
> 1 a Why is tourism an invisible export?
>
>   b Why do LEDCs need such exports?
>
> 2 Copy and complete the following table with at least two examples of each ADVANTAGE and DISADVANTAGE of tourism in an LEDC.
>
> | | Advantages | Disadvantages |
> |---|---|---|
> | Economic | | |
> | Social/Cultural | | |
> | Environmental | | |
>
> 3 Study the cartoon (Figure 3D.5) below.
>
>   List the good and the bad points from the local people's points of view. (Use the terms *economic*, *social* and *environmental*.)

3D.5 *The tensions of tourism*

Section 3   Changing Employment Patterns

Towards more sustainable tourism

Tumanitenda is a small village located on a tributary of the River Gambia. This is in the country of Gambia in West Africa (see Figure 3A.15). Tumanitenda is an example of local people trying to establish **eco-tourism**. This is an example of sustainable development that respects local people, their livelihoods and the environment. The village is described on pages 54–55.

CASE STUDY

Tourist development in Zimbabwe

Wildlife activities such as safari hunting, game cropping, 'safari' tourism, and live animal sales contribute more than $250 million annually to the national economy of Zimbabwe in southern Africa. Most wildlife is outside the system of National Parks on tribal or communally owned land (see Figure 3D.6). It was difficult to persuade local people that protecting wildlife could benefit them. Local people did not receive income from 'safari' tourists.

In 1988 the Zimbabwe government encouraged groups of communities to set up Communal Areas Management Programme for Indigenous Resources (CAMPFIRE) projects (Figure 3D.7). Under this scheme, it is the local people who control and manage tourism. It is now the local people who benefit from tourists. In the past the African elephant caused immense damage on farms and grazing lands. Today the local people derive more money from the wild elephants than they do from their farms.

The making of money out of killing elephants has not been without serious criticism. Some environmental groups cannot agree with the hunting of elephants. However, those groups supporting the CAMPFIRE projects say harvesting elephants is sustainable and appropriate wildlife management. Elephant damage has been reduced in some places by building solar powered fences around farmland. The fences have been paid for from money earned from foreign elephant hunters. The local people are now keen to conserve the elephants so more can be shot by rich tourists!

- CAMPFIRE generates profits for local communities through a number of different activities. Primarily, profits are generated through leasing trophy hunting concessions to foreign hunters.
- Profits also are generated through harvesting natural products such as antelope and crocodile eggs.
- CAMPFIRE is operated on communal lands, home to 42 per cent of Zimbabwe's poorest citizens.
- Revenues from the programme are used to provide schools, electricity, clean water, road building and mills for grinding maize.
- It has been estimated by the Worldwide Fund for Nature that households participating in CAMPFIRE increased their incomes by 15–25 per cent.

3D.6 *Land ownership in Zimbabwe and the location of CAMPFIRE projects*

3D.7 *How CAMPFIRE operates*

D Teritary industry: tourism

In 1980, before CAMPFIRE, the Binga district had only 13 primary schools and no secondary schools. By 1995 the district boasted some 56 primary schools and 9 secondary schools.

Chief Sinakatenge of the Binga district said, 'Up until 1985, we were a people without hope. Our children too were suffering as diseases took their toll. There were no schools, no wells and no clinics. Villagers continually sought help as they were engaged in a desperate struggle to survive. With CAMPFIRE, we now have rural health centres within easy reach'.

CAMPFIRE profits from eco-tourism

Sunungukai Camp is a few hours north-east of Harare, the capital of Zimbabwe. This eco-tourism enterprise is entirely managed by rural residents under CAMPFIRE. Visitors come to enjoy mountain hiking, try their luck at catching fish, enjoy the view, or watch birds, hippos, crocodiles and small game. Local guides take people to see nearby bushman paintings, or to consult the traditional healer.

Visitors camp or stay in traditional round huts and can make arrangements to share traditional meals with local residents. As well as receiving benefits from the revenues of the camp, some locals now work as guides. Others make handicrafts and souvenirs to sell at the camp. Community workshops and meetings are held to ensure that the locals can voice their opinions on the impacts of tourism in their area.

Figure 3D.8 shows the resources used by the tourists and the local people. Until the CAMPFIRE project the local people had not recognised their local 'tourist environment'. Now they make money from it and still have access to the resources they need.

If eco-tourism had not come to the Mazowe River Basin then the following might well have happened:

- trees cut down for fuelwood and construction
- increase in surface run-off
- soil erosion leading to the river silting up

> If we can manage the tourism in our area, then we will benefit from the income.

> As a tourist I would like the local people to receive what I pay out.

Tourists	Local people
Mountains covered with grass and trees	Wood for fuel and building
Picturesque Mazowe River	Broom and grass for thatching
Variety of fish species	Reeds for basket and hat weaving
Small and large game	Fish for food
Beautiful bird species	Land for cropping and grazing

3D.8 *Tourists and local people benefit from different resources in the same area*

- reduction in fish stocks
- lack of protein food for local people
- wild animals shot for food
- reduction in wild animal numbers.

As one local worker said, 'it is now true to say that the majority of our people have an increasing realisation of what the environment means to them and the future generations.'

NOTING ACTIVITIES

1 Draw a cartoon strip or a series of speech bubbles to show the following situation.

   A group of Zimbabwean villagers are discussing elephant damage to their crops. A visiting person from a CAMPFIRE project joins in and suggests they set up their own CAMPFIRE project and make money out of the elephant instead of moaning about it. The discussion turns into a list of improvements the villagers would like for their area.

2 Why is it so important that the local people control tourism and the revenues from it?

3 Explain why it is that killing elephants can be considered as sustainable development that will in the long term protect the environment.

Section 3 Changing Employment Patterns

E Employment and development

Transnational companies such as Honda are so powerful that they are able to control industry on a global scale. The poorer LEDCs often gain little by being host to these large companies. Labour is generally much cheaper in LEDCs, and the human rights of workers are often ignored. It is not uncommon to find young children being paid poor wages to make products that are eventually sold for high prices in rich countries. Have transnationals done anything about unfair trading and child labour? What part do national governments have to play in providing help for LEDCs?

CASE STUDY

Reebok

Reebok is a transnational company established in Britain in 1895. It makes sports footwear and clothing and competes with other companies such as Adidas and Nike. It is an example of a major company that is a part of **globalisation**. This is one of the most powerful economic forces in the world today. Globalisation brings threats and benefits to the world's people and nations.

Reebok's sales declined in the late 1990s but it remains a worldwide company supplying football kit and Olympic clothing (Figure 3E.1). Reebok makes its products in locations with low labour costs, such as Vietnam, China and Indonesia (Figure 3E.2). In such countries there is widespread use of child labour and human rights abuses of factory workers. Reebok has made a stand to improve working conditions in its Asian factories and the $67 per month wages are much higher than Nike's wages. Reebok made a stand on the production of footballs in Pakistan (Figure 3E.3) and set up its own 'Human Rights Foundation'. Even so a report in 1997 criticised the company for abuses in China (Figure 3E.4).

REEBOK OUTFITS 2500 IN SYDNEY FOR 2000 SUMMER GAMES

CANTON, MA (15 July, 2000) – Reebok will outfit 2500 athletes, coaches and officials head-to-toe in training apparel and footwear at the 2000 Summer Games in Sydney, Australia. Among the athletes who will train in Reebok footwear and apparel, and compete in Reebok footwear, are: Julie Foudy (USA, Soccer), Steve Smith (USA, Basketball), Stacy Dragila (USA, Pole Vault), Emma George (Australia, Pole Vault), Patrick Rafter (Australia, Tennis), Michellie Jones (Australia, Triathlon) and Christine Arron (France, Sprinter).

3E.1 *Reebok is an important supplier of equipment for Olympic athletes*

VIETNAM: HIEP HUNG GETS $20 m '97 ORDER FROM US REEBOK

Tuesday, 24 Dec 1996

The order is to produce 1.8 million pairs of shoes worth $20 million for Reebok International Ltd., a US footwear company, in 1997, said Le Thanh Phan, Hiep Hung's managing director. Phan said Vietnam's low wages and the relatively high skill level of its workers are the reasons Reebok and other shoemakers like to manufacture shoes in Vietnam, Phan said.

Hiep Hung's production for Reebok is sold in Europe, the US, Canada and Mexico, he added.

The company also produces for concerns such as Fila and Diadora.

The average monthly salary at Hiep Hung is 750,000 *dong* (about $67), the Newsreader said, adding this is the highest average salary in a shoe company under the Ministry of Industry.

3E.2 *LEDC locations are favoured by Reebok*

E Employment and development

We've drafted and implemented a *code of conduct for factories* manufacturing Reebok products, to ensure safe, healthy working conditions. We assess factory workplace conditions with the assistance of external monitors. We guarantee that *no child labour* is used in the production of Reebok soccer balls and have committed $1 million for the educational and vocational needs of former child workers in Pakistan's soccer industry. All these actions help build the infrastructures needed to guard against and eliminate human rights abuses in the workplace.

We will continue to honour our responsibilities to our consumers, employees and the global market place, and to use our assets to promote universal human rights.

'Guaranteed: Manufactured without child labour.'

3E.3 *Reebok's stand against child labour*

HONG KONG Wages below the legal minimum, forced overtime and dangerous factory conditions are among the labour violations revealed in a report released 21 September, 1997 on Chinese sweatshops that produce shoes for Nike and Reebok.

The following are among the violations documented.

- Both Nike and Reebok contracted factories consistently violate minimum wage laws, with workers paid as little as 25 cents an hour.
- Workers routinely work shifts of between 10 and 12 hours a day, and then have to work additional compulsory overtime of between two and four hours a day. This is in violation of China's labour law which requires a 44-hour week with voluntary overtime of no more than three hours a day. Those who refuse overtime can be fined, docked an entire day's pay, or even fired. Many workers surveyed received only two days off a month, and no days off at all during peak periods.
- Due to poor safety conditions, workers lose fingers and even hands in machinery and are exposed daily to dust, noise pollution and dangerous fumes from glues.
- Talking during work and refusal to perform compulsory morning exercises are punishable by fines, although deducting disciplinary fines from wages is illegal in China.

3E.4 *Poor working conditions still exist*

It seems that companies such as Reebok continually search for ways to keep costs down. Maybe they support human rights in theory, but they still continue to make shoes as cheaply as possible. Sometimes only 2 per cent of the cost of a pair of trainers actually goes to the workers.

NOTING ACTIVITIES

1. Why are Reebok such a well known company?
2. How does the company compete against its rivals?
3. Who are making complaints about the company?
4. How has Reebok responded to the criticism?
5. Suggest what might happen to the workers in the Asian factories if Reebok stopped making its products there.
6. Which other transnationals operate like Reebok?

Section 3 Changing Employment Patterns

The issues of trade

If you look around your home, school and community you will realise how many food products and goods have been **imported**. People in this country have paid other countries for these items. In contrast the UK sells a wide range of goods abroad; these goods have been **exported**. There is a complex 'language of trade' which you will come across in your studies of trade.

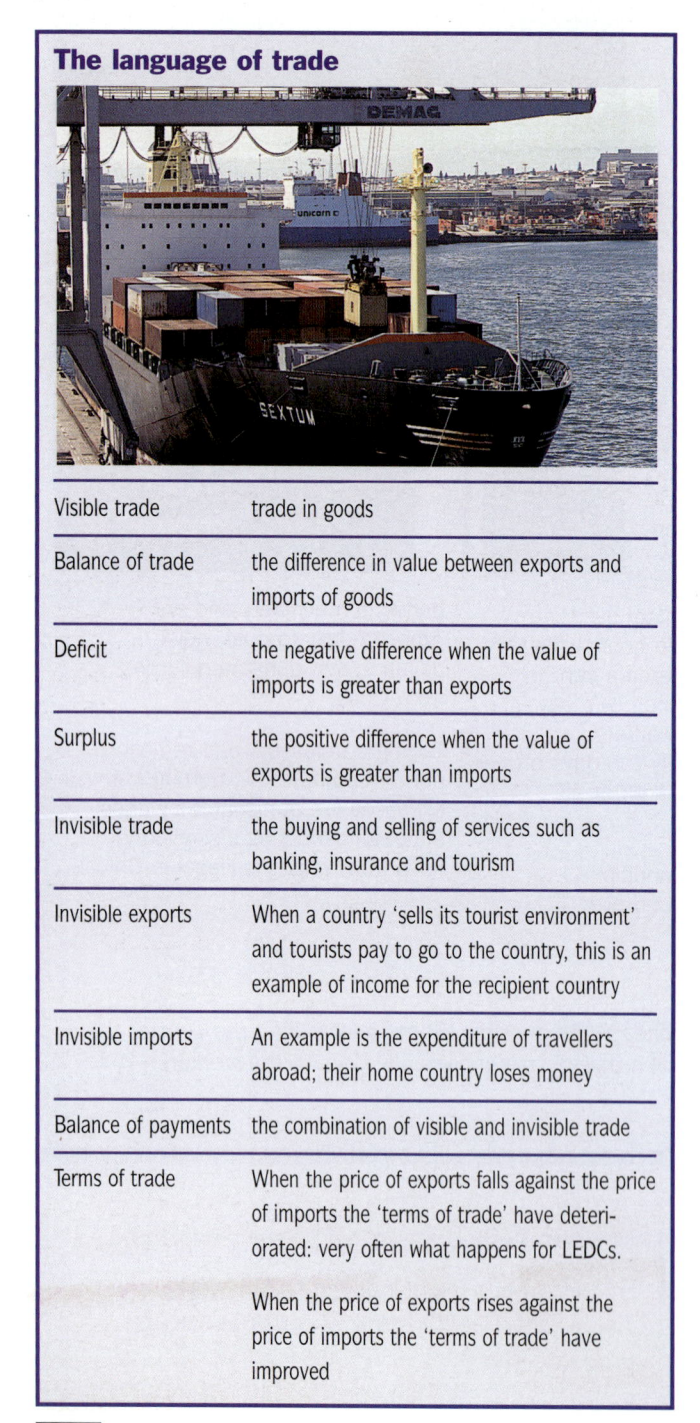

In order to buy what we want and are able to afford we need to trade. Trade seems to benefit the rich countries. They get what they want at prices they can afford. Trade exists because one country produces what another needs but cannot produce for itself.

The greatest issue associated with trade concerns *fairness*. How fair is the trade between the poor world and the rich world?

Who gets what?

Figure 3E.6 shows how the final price of jeans, coffee, chocolate and bananas is divided up between those who produce them. Study the diagrams and find the proportion of the price earned by the people making the jeans, and the farmers growing the coffee, cocoa and bananas. Next time you eat chocolate or bananas think about how much it cost and just how much the farmer may have received for it.

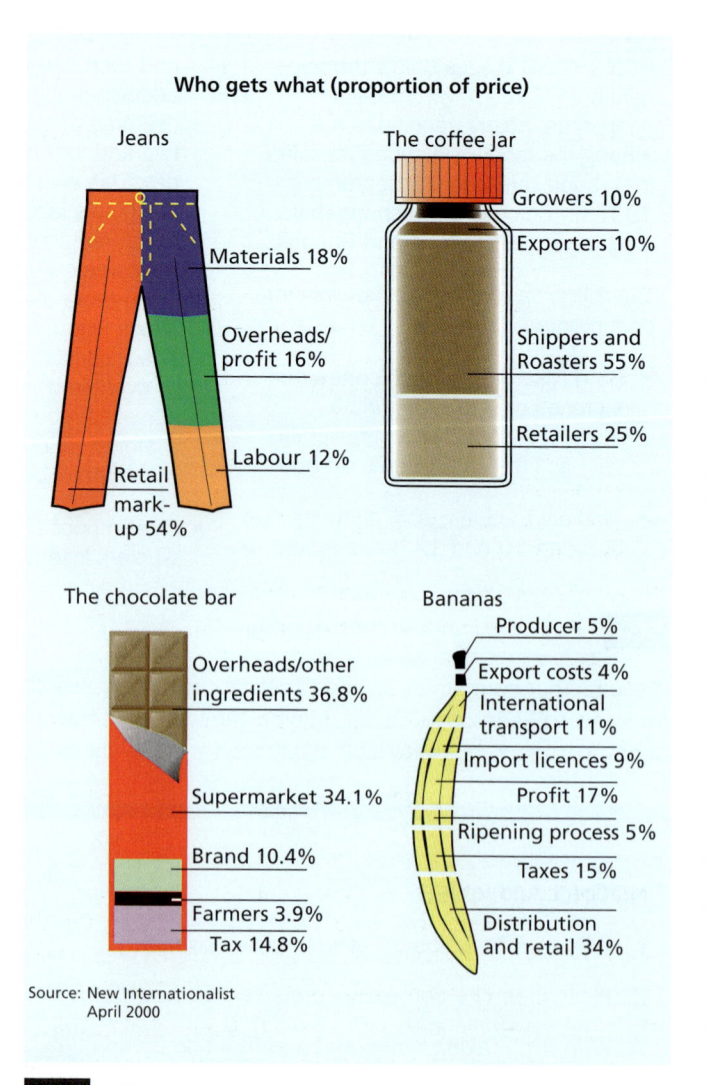

The language of trade

Visible trade	trade in goods
Balance of trade	the difference in value between exports and imports of goods
Deficit	the negative difference when the value of imports is greater than exports
Surplus	the positive difference when the value of exports is greater than imports
Invisible trade	the buying and selling of services such as banking, insurance and tourism
Invisible exports	When a country 'sells its tourist environment' and tourists pay to go to the country, this is an example of income for the recipient country
Invisible imports	An example is the expenditure of travellers abroad; their home country loses money
Balance of payments	the combination of visible and invisible trade
Terms of trade	When the price of exports falls against the price of imports the 'terms of trade' have deteriorated: very often what happens for LEDCs. When the price of exports rises against the price of imports the 'terms of trade' have improved

3E.5 *The language of trade*

Who gets what (proportion of price)

Jeans:
- Materials 18%
- Overheads/profit 16%
- Labour 12%
- Retail mark-up 54%

The coffee jar:
- Growers 10%
- Exporters 10%
- Shippers and Roasters 55%
- Retailers 25%

The chocolate bar:
- Overheads/other ingredients 36.8%
- Supermarket 34.1%
- Brand 10.4%
- Farmers 3.9%
- Tax 14.8%

Bananas:
- Producer 5%
- Export costs 4%
- International transport 11%
- Import licences 9%
- Profit 17%
- Ripening process 5%
- Taxes 15%
- Distribution and retail 34%

Source: New Internationalist April 2000

3E.6 *Who gets what*

E Employment and development

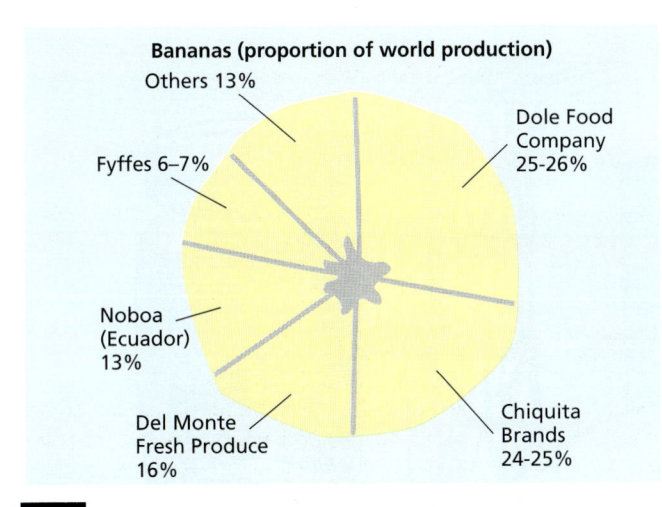

3E.7 *A few transnationals dominate world banana production*

Figure 3E.7 shows how the world production of bananas is controlled by various companies. Five companies dominate and control 87 per cent of world production. These large companies dictate the prices of bananas across the world. The situation with chocolate is similar. In the UK Cadbury, Nestlé and Mars account for 75 per cent of all chocolate sales.

Unfair trade

The LEDCs do not get a fair price for their exports and they have no control over the situation. Poor countries also:

- rely on only one or two **primary** products as their main exports
- cannot plan for the future as the value of their products changes frequently
- cannot increase the supply of their products as prices would fall.

When LEDCs begin to export their own manufactured products they find there are even more problems. The rich world has set up trading areas such as the European Union (EU). These control the imports that come in using **trade barriers**. The two types of 'barriers' that are used for trade are the **quota** and the **tariff**.

A quota is a limit on the amount of goods a country can export to another. For example, if Ecuador wanted to export clothes to the EU a limit would be set on the amount Ecuador could export. A tariff is a tax on imports. For example Ecuador might also have to pay taxes on the clothes it was trying to export to the EU. The clothes would therefore be more expensive and would not sell well.

The photographs in Figure 3E.8 and 3E.9 are other examples of problems faced by LEDCs. In Figure 3E.8 the Mexican worker is picking marigolds. These are exported to the USA

3E.8 *Marigolds to make egg yolks yellow*

to be fed to chickens in the winter months to make the egg yolks yellow. The community in the area of the marigold farming is a poor one. It would be of much greater value to this community to grow food for themselves rather than selling a product and then using the money to buy food. The value of the marigolds may change, and they may cease to be in demand by American farmers at any time.

Figure 3E.9 is a similar example. This photograph shows greenhouses on the outskirts of Bogotá, the capital city of Colombia. Here there is a flower export industry. The flowers are exported to the USA. There are benefits to the local community because many women have jobs in the flower industry. One issue is that of transport costs and the use of

3E.9 *Colombian flowers for the USA*

Section 3 Changing Employment Patterns

3E.10 A selection of fair trade products available in Europe

energy resources. Consider how much energy is consumed selling flowers to the USA when it would seem logical for the USA to grow its own flowers. Second, there is the issue that Colombia imports food (food comprises 7 per cent of its total imports). The principle of trade, however, is that if one country can produce a product more cheaply then trade will be beneficial. With the example of Colombia and the USA there are benefits to trade. The USA and Colombia are **interdependent**.

Fair trade

Sometimes trade is said to be 'free' when large amounts of cheap goods and food can be sold on the world markets. The large companies make big profits but the small producer earns little. Some people say that this type of trade is hardly 'free' and it is unfair. What is needed, some argue, is trade that is fair.

Fair trade is the alternative to free trade. In 1997 Fair Trade Labelling Organisations International (FLO) brought together Fair Trade organisations. Its members have common principles which include:

- no child labour
- environmental sustainability
- decent working conditions
- recognised trade unions
- prices that cover the costs of production.

Figure 3E.10 shows examples of some of the fair trade products available in European supermarkets.

The fair trade banana

Fair trade bananas are now bought in the UK by the Co-op and Sainsbury's from Ghana and Costa Rica. These two retailers are committed to selling fair trade products. In Switzerland as much as 20 per cent of all bananas sold are from fair trade suppliers.

On fair trade farms in Colombia the farmers receive a better reward for their hard work. Fertilisers have been cut down and animal manure is now used. Pesticides have been cut back and wildlife has increased. A nursery school has been built for the farmers in the community and piped drinking water is soon to be provided for the first time. The fair trade movement has helped a community to develop.

NOTING ACTIVITIES

1. **a** Write down the proportions that different people receive from the price of a jar of coffee.

   b Describe the life and work of a small coffee grower in a tropical country such as Colombia.

2. What is the difference between world trade controlled by the transnational companies and free trade?

3. Use the table (Figure 3E.11) to note down the possible advantages and disadvantages of the examples of trade.

E Employment and development

Example of trade	Advantages for the exporter	Disadvantages for the exporter
Exporting bananas from Ecuador to the USA		
Exporting cocoa from Ghana to the UK		
Exporting fair trade coffee from Colombia to the UK		
Exporting cut flowers from Colombia to the USA		
	Advantages for the importer	**Disadvantages for the importer**
Importing cheap bananas from Ecuador to the USA		
Importing fair trade bananas from The West Indies to the UK		
Importing cut flowers from Colombia to the USA		
Importing organic fair trade cocoa from Ghana to the UK		

3E.11 *Advantages and disadvantages of trading methods*

EXTENDED ACTIVITY

Study Figure 3E.12.

1 Describe and explain the composition of exports for four of the countries. Use phrases such as 'relying on primary products', 'vulnerable to price fluctuations', 'depending on the demand for their products from the MEDCs', 'unfavourable terms of trade', 'unfair trading practices'.

2 Suggest the problems for the four countries chosen if the price of the dominant export falls or if there is a production crisis in that product.

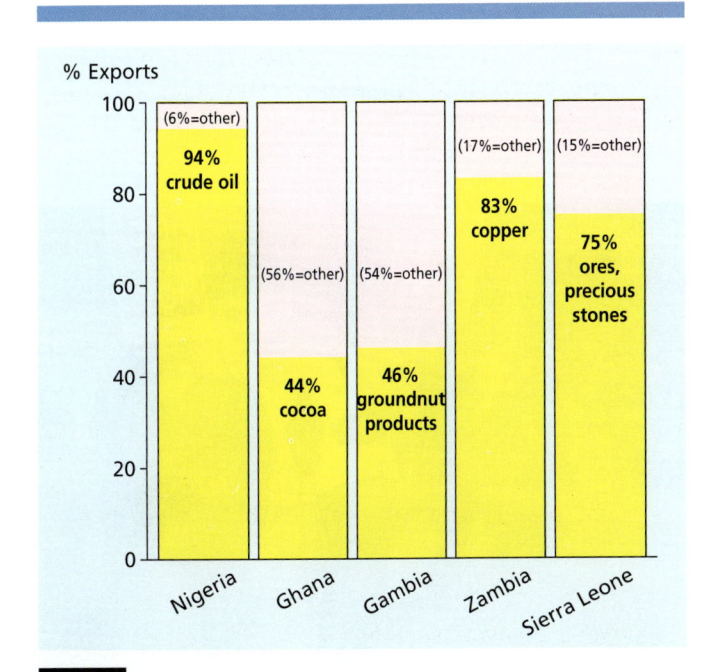

% Exports – bar chart:
- Nigeria: 94% crude oil (6%=other)
- Ghana: 44% cocoa (56%=other)
- Gambia: 46% groundnut products (54%=other)
- Zambia: 83% copper (17%=other)
- Sierra Leone: 75% ores, precious stones (15%=other)

3E.12 *Some countries depend heavily on single primary products for their exports*

The issue of debt

Although it is important to understand interdependence it is also important to realise that LEDCs are **dependen**t on the MEDCs. They are forced into dependency on the rich countries for trade and loans.

In the 1970s the income of the LEDCs fell as the prices of commodities dropped. Banks began to lend the LEDCs money. All the loans had to be repaid. interest rates rose and the LEDCs could not repay the money. Many LEDCs got caught in the 'debt trap' (Figure 3E.13)

Throughout the 1990s some LEDCs were paying a high proportion of their export income in debt repayments. Ecuador paid 22 per cent and Ghana 25 per cent; even Gambia with its small export earnings from groundnuts paid 14 per cent of its export earnings as loan repayments and interest.

In 1995 a campaign was launched to cancel the debt of the LEDCs. The campaign was called Jubilee 2000. It was very ambitious and was supported by famous people including pop personalities and politicians. Figure 3E.14 shows protesters at a World Leaders Summit in Birmingham. They are campaigning for debt relief for LEDCs.

The Trade game

This game (Figure 3E.17) may be played with one or more players. You will need one die and a counter for each player.
- Land on a square where the dollar signs begin and you advance to the square where the dollar signs stop.
- Land on a square with a downward spiral and you fall down to the square where the spiral stops.

Section 3 Changing Employment Patterns

The people of our country have always worked hard

Yes, I know, but the more we develop the more we seem to owe

We thought those loans were like aid

No, they were more like punishment

We will never pay them back at the rates they ask for

Have you ever thought ...they are getting richer at our expense!

3E.13 *How can we get out of this?*

NOTING ACTIVITIES

1 When you reach a square with the dollar sign or the spiral make a note of what happened to you.

2 When you reach the end write down some of your feelings about the game.

3 Devise your own game. Use the design of the Trade game to devise your own game about development and aid in an LEDC. Play the game with someone else and evaluate it. Here are some ideas to help you start:

Advances

an NGO sets up

small appropriate aid given

emergency aid sent

a small loans scheme set up

intermediate technology programme encouraged

Retreats

no money for fertilisers

commodity prices fall

foreign aid stops

big hydro-electric project agreed

debt repayments increase

3E.14 *Campaigning for debt relief: Birmingham, UK*

E Employment and development

Child labour

Millions of children around the world have to go to work, often for very low wages. There is a difference between children working – often helping the family and continuing their education – and child labour. Many children as young as eight are forced to work producing goods and receiving either little or no money for their efforts. They have little protection under national or international laws.

Child labour is one result of exploitation by MEDCs and transnationals of people in poorer countries. We have seen through the example of Reebok that workers making sports equipment are poorly paid, earning as little as 2 per cent of the final sale price of items such as trainers. Three-quarters of the world's hand stitched footballs are made in one small part of eastern Pakistan. Until recently, it was estimated that this industry relied on over 7000 children to make the footballs.

National governments around the world have tried to stop child labour. In Bangladesh, for example, an estimated 75 000 children worked in the clothing industry alone at the start of the 1990s. The United States threatened to ban imports of clothing from Bangladesh, resulting in the dismissal of over 50 000 children by employers from their factories. This did not solve the problem, however, as many of the children were forced into more hazardous jobs such as stone crushing or working on the streets.

Why is child labour such a difficult problem to solve? It is a complex issue.

- Child labour is not just a problem in poor countries. There are over 140 million child workers worldwide, many in MEDCs. In Italy, for example, over 90,000 children work in the region around the city of Naples alone.
- Very few child labourers are employed in export industries. Much publicity has been given to 'sweatshop' industries producing goods to be sold at great profit in MEDCs. In fact, this type of industry makes up only about 5 per cent of all child labourers. The vast majority may be found working in small factories, on farms, or on the streets.
- Child labour makes poverty worse. Children working up to fourteen hours a day have no time or energy for school. A working child therefore grows into an unskilled adult, usually working in badly paid jobs.
- Many MEDC governments have threatened to stop buying goods from countries employing child workers. While this can help, most children are not working in export industries.

What can be done to end child labour? The United Nations Children's Fund (UNICEF) suggests the following actions.

unicef

1 An end to all hazardous child labour, such as working in mines or in factories where conditions are dangerous.

2 Free education for all children, at least until the end of primary school.

3 Better legal protection, which should be the same throughout the world.

4 Birth registration of all children. Without being registered, children are not able to attend school. It is also easier for employers to use very young children if it is not possible to prove their age.

5 Better monitoring and publicity. Where child labour exists, authorities should be made aware and do something about it.

3E.15 *Large banana plantation supplying the world market with low-priced bananas*

3E.16 *Small farmer hoping to sell his banana crop at a fair price through a fair trade outlet*

Section 3 Changing Employment Patterns

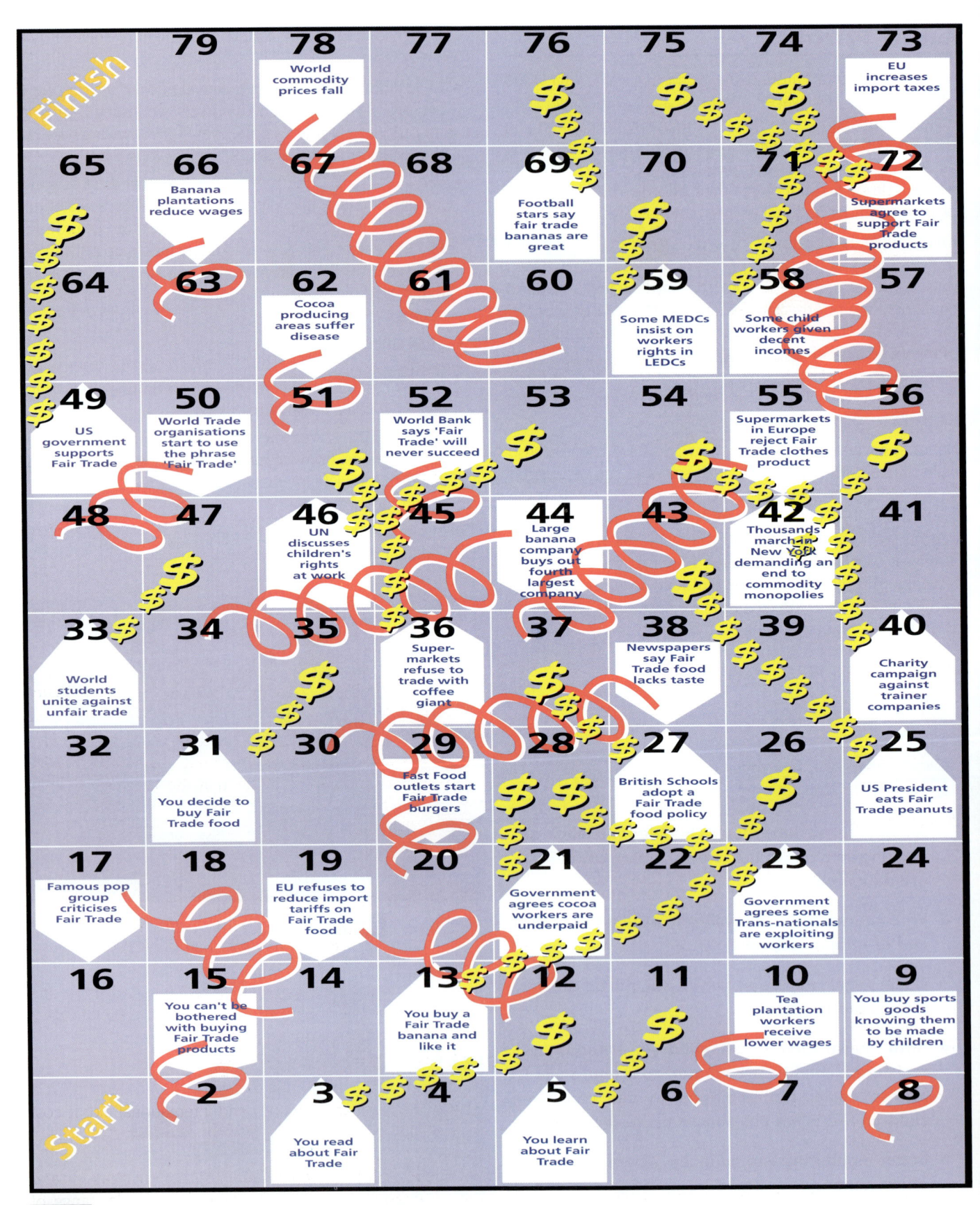

Finish

79	78 World commodity prices fall	77	76	75	74	73 EU increases import taxes
65	66 Banana plantations reduce wages	67	68	69 Football stars say fair trade bananas are great	70	71	72 Supermarkets agree to support Fair Trade products
64	63	62 Cocoa producing areas suffer disease	61	60	59 Some MEDCs insist on workers rights in LEDCs	58 Some child workers given decent incomes	57
49 US government supports Fair Trade	50 World Trade organisations start to use the phrase 'Fair Trade'	51	52 World Bank says 'Fair Trade' will never succeed	53	54	55 Supermarkets in Europe reject Fair Trade clothes product	56
48	47	46 UN discusses children's rights at work	45	44 Large banana company buys out fourth largest company	43	42 Thousands march in New York demanding an end to commodity monopolies	41
33 World students unite against unfair trade	34	35	36 Supermarkets refuse to trade with coffee giant	37	38 Newspapers say Fair Trade food lacks taste	39	40 Charity campaign against trainer companies
32	31 You decide to buy Fair Trade food	30	29 Fast Food outlets start Fair Trade burgers	28	27 British Schools adopt a Fair Trade food policy	26	25 US President eats Fair Trade peanuts
17 Famous pop group criticises Fair Trade	18	19 EU refuses to reduce import tariffs on Fair Trade food	20	21 Government agrees cocoa workers are underpaid	22	23 Government agrees some Trans-nationals are exploiting workers	24
16	15 You can't be bothered with buying Fair Trade products	14	13 You buy a Fair Trade banana and like it	12	11	10 Tea plantation workers receive lower wages	9 You buy sports goods knowing them to be made by children
Start	2	3 You read about Fair Trade	4	5 You learn about Fair Trade	6	7	8

3E.17 *The Trade game*

E Employment and development

3E.18 Child labour in Bangladesh

3E.19 Education: the best way to end child labour

> **NOTING ACTIVITY**
>
> Before you read further, write down anything you can under the heading **'Aid to the poor world'**. You could do this brainstorm activity on your own or in a group.

The issue of aid

What is aid?

You may have come up with ideas such as those in Figure 3E.20 which was the result of some students brainstorming the topic of aid.

The students who had brainstormed aid had based their ideas on charity aid. In fact, most of the world's aid is given by governments. Aid is a term used to describe any type of assistance given to a country. It can range from giving technical equipment to food and emergency supplies.

There are different types of aid.

- **Bilateral Aid** is given directly by one government to another
- **Multilateral aid** is government contributions to international organisations such as the United Nations Children's Fund (UNICEF)
- **Aid from charities**, **churches** and **schools** which are non-governmental organisations (NGOs)
- **Loans from commercial banks** which are direct loans from banks or other financial institutions

Aid sometimes comes 'with strings attached'. Some aid is **tied**. This means that the donor country (the country giving the aid) may impose conditions that the aid must be spent on goods the donor country exports. In fact the donor country benefits as the recipient buys goods back from the donor country!

Examples of aid

1 Big Projects

Dams for hydro-electricity production and irrigation schemes have been popular with some LEDCs. The dams are **prestige projects** carrying a great deal of publicity and promise but rarely fulfilling their aims.

The Kainji Dam on the River Niger in Nigeria was built in 1967 with Nigerian oil money and international aid. It cost £86 million of which the World Bank provided £34 million, Italy £9 million and the UK £5 million. It was a **multi-purpose** project which has both advantages and disadvantages (Figure 3E.21). There are a similar range of pros and cons for the Ilisu Dam, see page 113.

87

Section 3 **Changing Employment Patterns**

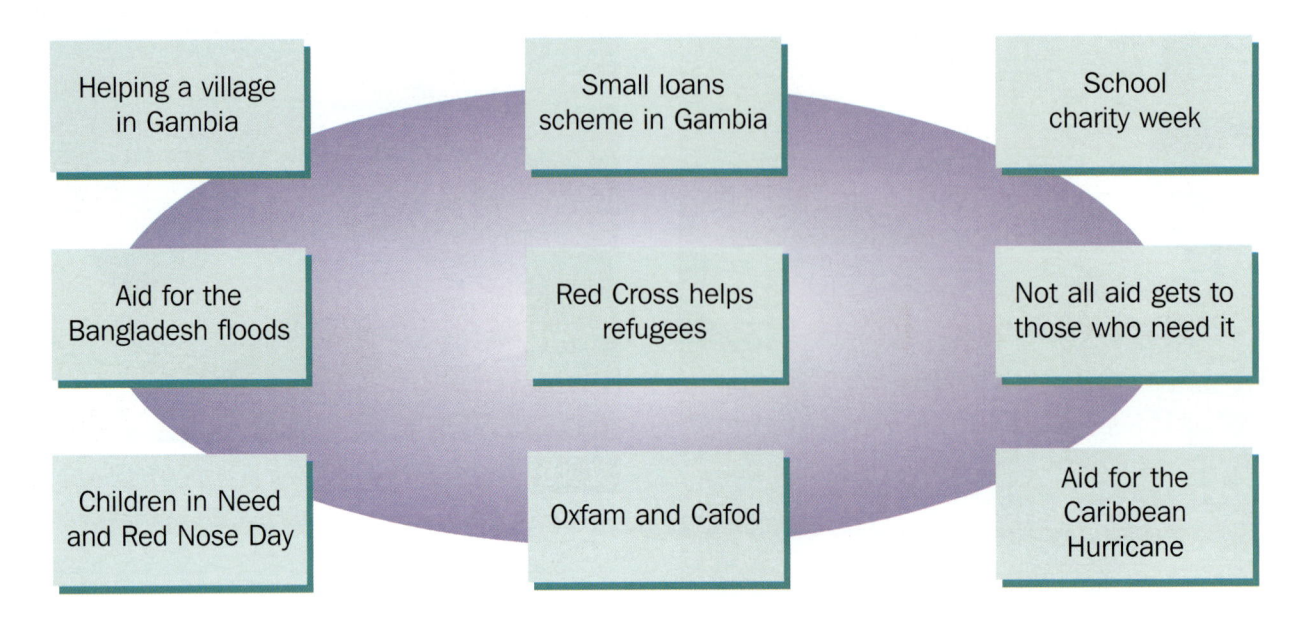

```
  Helping a village          Small loans                School
    in Gambia              scheme in Gambia          charity week

    Aid for the             Red Cross helps        Not all aid gets to
  Bangladesh floods            refugees             those who need it

                                                       Aid for the
  Children in Need           Oxfam and Cafod           Caribbean
  and Red Nose Day                                     Hurricane
```

3E.20 *Students' brainstorm of aid*

Advantages	Disadvantages
Hydro-electricity supplied to southern Nigeria and to an iron and steel works	High quality farmland flooded
Niger floods have been reduced	46 000 people were displaced
Irrigation water made available: rice and sugar cane grown	The HEP station has not worked at full capacity because of drought
Sugar cane factory set up	Malaria and river blindness were spread because of so much standing water
Lake Kainji became a fishing lake	Clean water was not provided
Top of dam used as a river crossing	Machinery breaks down and there is a lack of spare parts
River transport was improved	Interest on the loans has proved very expensive

3E.21 *The pros and cons of the Kainji Dam project*

3E.22 *The Carpentry Co-op in Gunjur, Gambia*

2 Appropriate, small scale projects

These usually meet the aims of development much better than the 'big projects'. They can involve **intermediate** or **appropriate technology** such as small workshop looms, education projects, farming improvements and renewable energy schemes.

Small scale projects can provide alternatives to large scale projects controlled by the transnational companies. They benefit local communities because they:

- use local materials
- employ local people
- train national experts
- do not rely on expensive imported raw materials
- do not need imported energy
- meet the needs of the local people
- enhance the quality of life of local people
- involve the local community.

E Employment and development

3E.23 *The small loans scheme in Gunjur, Gambia*

3E.24 *Flood defences in Bangladesh*

3 The Flood Action Plan in Bangladesh

The international aid community and the Bangladesh government designed a Flood Action Plan for the country after the very serious floods of 1987 and 1988. This is an example of large scale aid which will reduce devastation by floods in the future. Its plans included the development of early warning systems and the building of flood refuges in areas most at risk. In this case many international aid agencies joined together to plan for improvements in Bangladesh.

4 The Grameen Bank in Bangladesh

Sometimes aid comes from within an LEDC and it can be called **self help.** Examples include schools growing their own cash crops and communities building their own NGO centre, which happened in Gunjur in Gambia.

In 1976 a Bangladeshi set up the Grameen Bank or 'village bank'. He only lent money to people in extreme poverty. Most of the borrowers have no money and no education; they are organised into groups of five. If one member of the group fails to repay a loan, then no one in the group is allowed to borrow again. The borrowers have to keep to certain rules such as keeping their families small.

The Grameen Bank lends £20 million a month to 2 million borrowers and 98 per cent of all loans are repaid.

The case of Action Aid

Action Aid is a charity that works with over five million of the world's poorest people in more than 30 countries in Africa, Asia, Latin America and the Caribbean. The charity was founded in 1972 and Action Aid is now one of the UK's largest development agencies, with over 120 000 supporters.

Action Aid is helping families and communities hit by floods in south-west Bangladesh. Through its work many people are receiving vital food, shelter and safe drinking water. In 2000 the charity was seeking funds to rebuild homes, offer zero-interest loans and provide farming materials such as seeds to grow new crops.

Action Aid's income in 1999 rose by 10 per cent to £49.6m. Aid is channelled to several African and Asian countries such as Kenya, Tanzania, Ethiopia and Gambia. In Gunjur, Gambia, TARUD (Trust Agency for Rural Development) works closely with local Action Aid workers (see page 50).

CASE STUDY

Aid from Australia

Who does Australia give aid to?

Of the total aid budget, 65 per cent is given bilaterally to countries in Asia and the Pacific, with 29 per cent contributed to regional multilateral organisations and other agencies. This leaves just 6 per cent for Africa and the rest of the world. The country which benefits most from Australian aid is Papua New Guinea, Australia's largest bilateral partner.

What type of aid does Australia give?

One-third of Australia's bilateral overseas development aid (ODA) is tied. Students from developing countries receive scholarships for university studies in Australia. Indonesia, Malaysia, Thailand, the Philippines, Vietnam and Papua New Guinea send the most students.

Section 3 Changing Employment Patterns

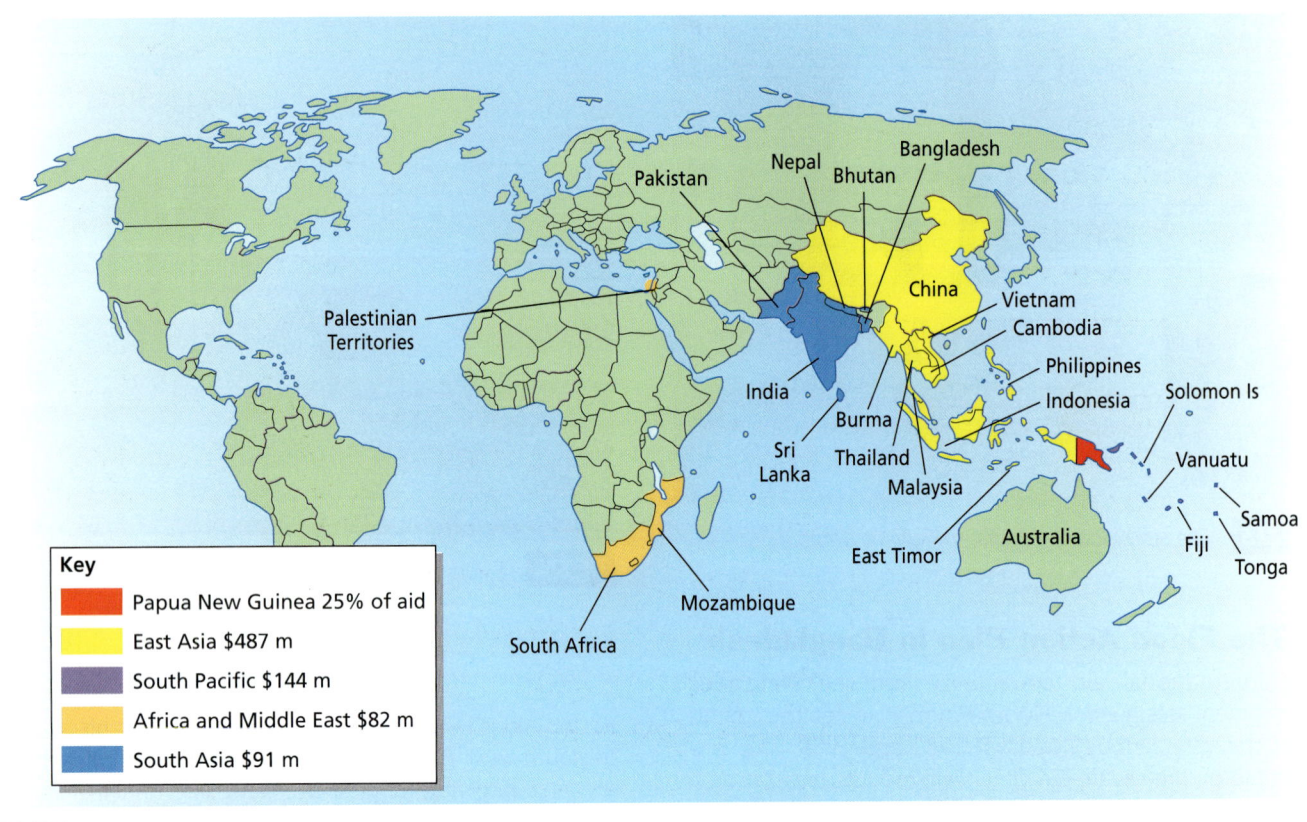

Key
- Papua New Guinea 25% of aid
- East Asia $487 m
- South Pacific $144 m
- Africa and Middle East $82 m
- South Asia $91 m

3E.25 *Aid from Australia*

Health, social service and education schemes have been set up in Asian and Pacific countries. Recently, special money has been given to relieve debt but this is not the primary aim of Australian aid.

Do Australians agree with their aid programme?

Although most Australians support the aid programme there is little real understanding of what it is aiming to do. Australia supports the United Nations' target for overseas aid of 0.7 per cent of GNP, though that target has not yet been reached. Aid has been used to increase support for Australia and promote Australian products.

Does Australian aid really make a difference?

Many NGOs in Papua New Guinea have expressed concern that Australian aid money is not reaching the rural areas, where health and education services are badly needed.

Sometimes logging companies working in Papua New Guinea promise assistance with the building of roads, bridges, schools and so on if local communities sell rights to the companies to cut down trees. Sadly, it is common for the companies to vanish as soon as the logs are removed, leaving villages with neither the rainforest nor the services that they were promised. This is an area where Australian aid could be more effective.

NOTING ACTIVITIES

1. Copy and complete the table to contrast aid for a large scale project with that for appropriate developments.

	Advantages	Disadvantages
1 Example and location		
2		
3		

2. Draw a simple spray diagram (or spider diagram) to show the main features of Australian aid.

E Employment and development

- How do I know that the money I give to charities reaches those who need it?
- Most of it does: although there are corrupt officials who take some aid resources.
- Of course it's not the charities who provide most aid. It's the world's governments.

3E.26

Section 4 Using and Abusing the Environment

A Resources

A **resource** is something that is of use to people. Natural resources arise from the natural environment, and people use them for their benefit. For example, wood is used for fuel, building and for papermaking. Some resources are **renewable**, meaning that they may be used continuously without running out. Power from water and wind are examples of renewable resources. Other resources may be used again, for example the metal components of a motor car. This is the **recycling** of resources. Other resources, once they have been used up cannot be replaced. These are **non-renewable** or **finite** resources. Examples of finite resources include coal, oil and gas.

At the start of the 21st century, the Earth's resources are being used up at an increasing rate. Renewable resources remain a small part of the world's resource use. What will happen if resources run out? One of the main uses of resources is to provide energy, for use in the home, in industry and for transport. What would happen if oil and gas ran out? On a global scale, over 40 per cent of energy used comes from oil. In September 2000, protestors objecting to the high cost of fuel stopped the supply of oil to industry throughout the United Kingdom (see Figure 4A.2). After only a few days, many industries and services were unable to continue, showing how much the country relied on supplies of oil. Some experts predict that the world's oil will run out in less than 25 years, and that the problems faced by the UK will be common throughout the world.

Most resources are limited, and they are not evenly distributed around the world. Many groups of people compete for resources, sometimes resulting in conflict. In the exploitation of resources the natural environment may be damaged and wildlife harmed. People may also suffer losses when a resource is developed, such as when farmland is lost when a dam is built. On the other hand people may benefit from the exploitation of resources.

4A.1 Types of resources

4A.2 The UK fuel protest, September 2000

A Resources

EXTENDED ACTIVITY

The oil enquiry

The purpose of this activity is to investigate issues facing the world's oil industry, and to suggest ways in which the industry may develop in the future.

You will investigate the following questions:

1 What are the issues facing the oil industry?
2 Are the world's oil resources running out?
3 What is likely to happen in the future?

The **Aim** of your enquiry is to present a report which should include the following:

1 Background information about the formation of oil, and the nature of reserves
2 The distribution of world supply and consumption of oil
3 How world oil supply is managed
4 How the demand for oil may be limited
5 The environmental impact of the oil industry
6 Issues facing the oil industry in the future

The **Method** of the enquiry is to:

1 Use the information on pages 93–97
2 Use your school's resource centre to research background information about the oil industry
3 Research the subject using the internet
4 Scan recent newspapers and CD-ROMs (eg the *Guardian* or the *Observer*) for issues relating to the oil industry.

4A.3 *The extraction of oil from the North Sea is a costly, hi-tech and dangerous industry*

The **Result** of your enquiry will be a report including the six sections outlined in the Aims. Use maps and diagrams to illustrate your work, and refer to case studies where appropriate.

Oil: the global fuel

Oil is a mixture of chemicals called *hydrocarbons*. The lightest hydrocarbons are gases, heavier ones are liquid (crude oil), and the heaviest are solid (tar). There are four stages in the production of oil: **exploration**, **production**, **transportation** and **refining.** Crude oil needs to be refined to make products such as petrol, diesel and aircraft fuel. Oil refineries have traditionally been located near to the market for oil, often a long way from areas of production.

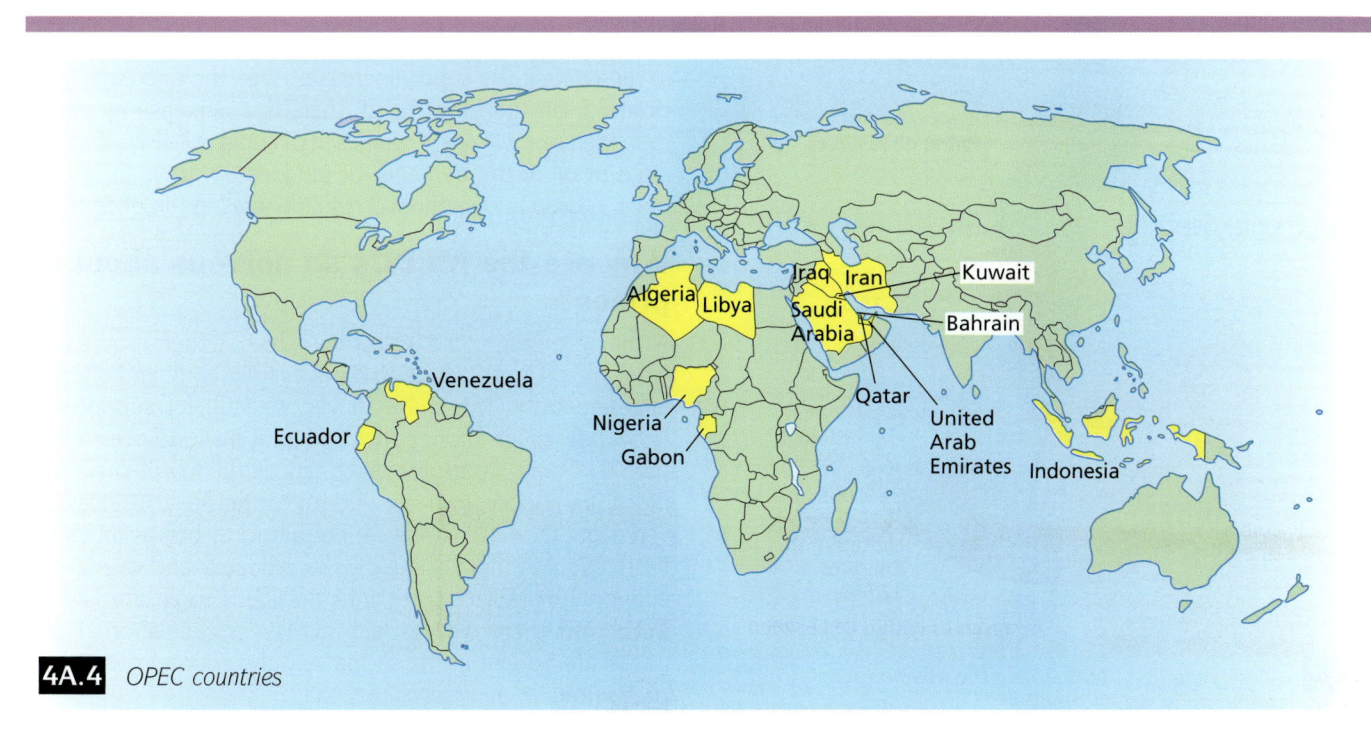

4A.4 *OPEC countries*

Section 4 Using and Abusing the Environment

It is difficult to measure the exact amount of oil that is available in the world. Some oil is very difficult and costly to reach, for example that in the North Sea. The **reserve** of oil is the amount that is known to exist and is obtainable. Statistics about reserves are very unreliable. In the 1960s it was thought that there were only 25 years of oil reserves remaining. Yet 25 years later, the amount has not actually decreased! Some countries and oil companies do not want the world to know the true situation. The smaller the reserve is thought to be, the higher the price for it.

Technology has also improved, meaning that oil may now be found in very difficult environments. Today there are more advanced techniques of oil drilling and oil extraction. Figure 4.A3 shows a modern oil drilling platform in the North Sea. In the future, it is possible that many new reserves of oil may be found, and that the life expectancy of oil reserves may actually increase rather than go down. Oil resources have been exploited in the Arctic wastelands of Alaska, and maybe oil will eventually come from Antarctica.

Oil production used to be dominated by the Oil Producing and Exporting Countries (OPEC), the members of which are shown on Figure 4A.4. Other countries outside the OPEC group now produce more oil, but OPEC are still very powerful in influencing world supply (see Figure 4A.5).

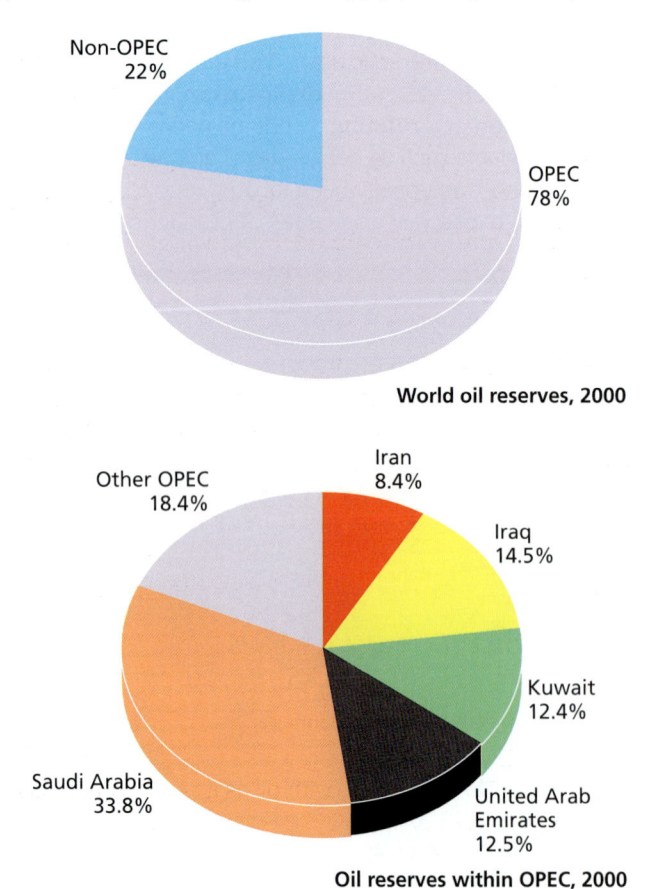

World oil reserves, 2000
- Non-OPEC 22%
- OPEC 78%

Oil reserves within OPEC, 2000
- Other OPEC 18.4%
- Iran 8.4%
- Iraq 14.5%
- Kuwait 12.4%
- United Arab Emirates 12.5%
- Saudi Arabia 33.8%

4A.5 *OPEC members, particularly the Middle East, dominate world oil supplies*

The market for oil has mainly been in the MEDCs but recently the newly industrialised countries of Asia have increased their consumption as they have developed. The Middle East, Africa and South America supply oil to Europe, North America and Japan. There is a great deal of potential for conflict between the countries that have the greatest quantities of oil and those that use the most.

The oil producing regions of the Middle East have become rich very quickly. Kuwait, Qatar, Saudi Arabia and Oman are among the world's top 40 nations in terms of Gross National Product. In some oil-rich countries, income from oil has been distributed to the people, whereas in others the wealth from oil has remained in the hands of a few.

4A.6 *The wealth of the Middle East depends almost entirely on oil*

Changes in the supply of and demand for oil lead to changes in the price. If the supply increases, then the price will come down. If, on the other hand, there is a decrease in supply, then the price will rise. Changes in demand will also affect the price of oil. If the demand for oil goes up, then so will the price. A drop in demand will result in a fall in the price of oil.

Why are the MEDCs so nervous about oil prices?

A major problem for countries which either produce or consume oil is that its price changes frequently, and often by large amounts. This makes it very difficult for suppliers to know how much money they will earn from oil over a long period of time. Countries which rely on oil do not know how much it will cost from one month to the next. If prices are very high, then industries cannot afford to buy as much oil. Production in many industries is reduced, and overall the economy of MEDCs goes into decline. People are laid off work, and there will be less money in circulation. Fewer goods are bought in the shops, and the country goes into a **recession**.

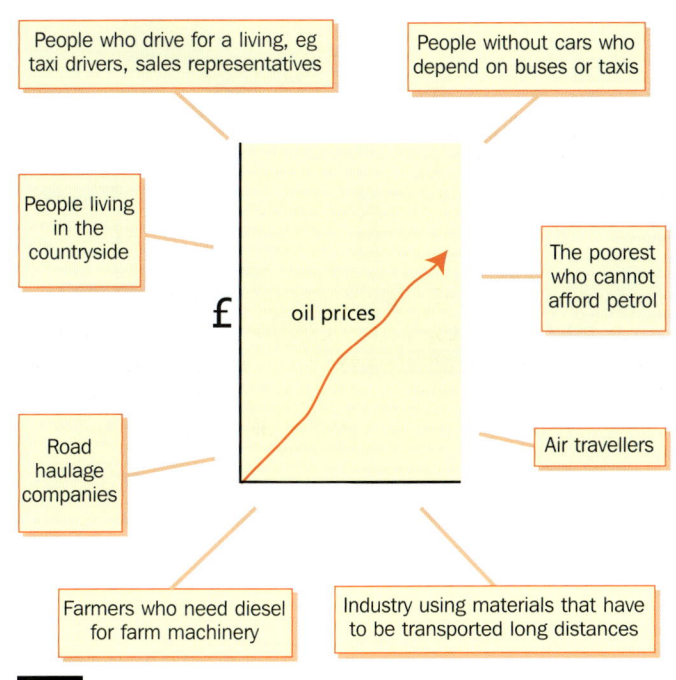

4A.7 Those affected by rises in oil prices

Boxes around the "oil prices" graph:
- People who drive for a living, eg taxi drivers, sales representatives
- People without cars who depend on buses or taxis
- People living in the countryside
- The poorest who cannot afford petrol
- Road haulage companies
- Air travellers
- Farmers who need diesel for farm machinery
- Industry using materials that have to be transported long distances

4A.8 Saving fuel and alternatives to oil-dependency have become an important part of the modern motor industry

There have been three major oil price rises in recent years, in 1973, 1979 and 1990. In each case, the economies of rich countries went into recession. The rich nations fear changes in oil prices because they depend so heavily upon oil for fuel. Because most of the world's oil is produced by a small number of countries, they can group together and control the world price of oil. This is what the OPECs have done in the past to increase prices. Within a rich nation like the United Kingdom, some people suffer the consequences of oil price rises more than others (see Figure 4A.7).

How is the world oil supply and demand managed?

In the 1970s when OPEC produced 75 per cent of the world's oil, they were very successful in controlling the amount of oil that was supplied. The supply of oil was restricted, and as a result the price of oil increased. Since then, the supply of oil has been more regular, and the price has become more stable. Saudi Arabia, the leading country within OPEC, has been befriended by the USA. In fact it is often the MEDCs that have tried to influence oil producing nations to control supplies.

It is possible that the years of greatest demand may have passed in the MEDCs. In some rich countries, the consumption of oil has started to fall. There are several reasons for this:

- modern hi-tech industries rely more on electricity than directly upon oil
- the growth of economies in MEDCs has included more people working from home, reducing oil-dependent transport
- cars have become more fuel efficient (see Figure 4A.8)
- people have become aware of the need to conserve fuel
- higher oil prices have made people look for cheaper alternatives.

The LEDCs need oil

As LEDCs develop, so their demand for fuel rises. Fuel is the major import of some of the poorest non-oil producing nations. Most of the extra demand for oil in the future will come from the LEDCs unless alternatives to oil are found. Sometimes vehicles in the poorest parts of the world are old and inefficient users of fuel. It is the rich in the MEDCs who are able to afford the modern fuel-efficient cars. Alternative fuels are perhaps needed more in the poorer nations than in the rich.

How does the oil industry affect the environment?

Using the Earth's resources has an effect upon the environment. This is the case with oil as it is with other fossil fuels such as coal and gas. There are often cases of oil pollution (see Figure 4A.9).

Section 4 Using and Abusing the Environment

Grounded off Milford Haven in 1996

Marine ecosystems destroyed

Fishing grounds polluted

Oil came ashore damaging holiday beaches

Bird life killed

4A.9 *The Sea Empress*

4A.10 *The trans-Alaska oil pipeline*

Oil tankers also deliberately discharge oil into the sea when they clean out their tanks. Occasionally oil wells or drilling rigs explode and oil is spilled. There have been serious cases of oil pollution in the Niger delta area of Nigeria where oil is pumped through pipelines. Local people accuse the oil companies of not repairing broken pipelines. The oil companies have accused some local people of sabotaging the pipes. Whatever the reason, oil has polluted local fishing waters and killed vegetation and wildlife.

CASE STUDY

More oil from Alaska?

Alaska, the USA's most northerly state, has a population of only 642 000. It is a remote wilderness that contains a complete range of arctic ecosystems. More than 200 species of animals, ranging from wolves to snow geese, live in Alaska. It also has Prudhoe Bay, centre of the oilfield that produces 20 per cent of the oil consumed in the USA. Oil production in the area has significant impacts on the environment and the people living there. The trans-Alaska pipeline taking oil away from the region stretches 800 kilometres across the countryside (Figure 4A.10). In 1989, a major environmental disaster was caused when the *Exxon Valdez* oil tanker spilled 230 000 barrels of oil into the sea, killing at least 300 000 seabirds.

As oil consumption in the USA has increased, it has become more difficult for the oil companies to meet growing demand. The cheapest oil, that which is easiest to reach, has been exploited, and production has started to decline. BP has recently been at the centre of a conflict over the proposed extension of oil production to the east of the Prudhoe Bay oilfields (see Figure 4A.11). This issue has not only caused a confrontation between local people and the oil company, but has also divided the local population.

The Arctic National Wildlife Refuge is an 8 million hectare wilderness bordering the Arctic Ocean. Although the whole refuge is protected from development, BP proposed to search for oil in the coastal plains. The area is home to the Gwich'in Indians, who have lived in the area for 20 000

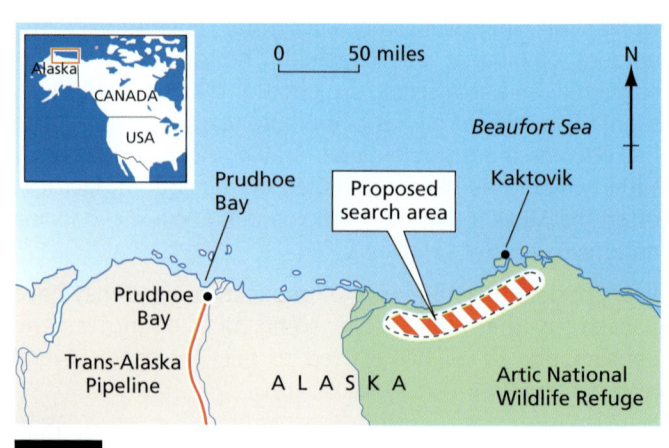

4A.11 *The proposed development area*

A Resources

years. They survive by hunting from the 130 000-strong herd of caribou that cross the coastal plains. Oil drilling and pipelines in the area would severely disrupt their livelihood. Environmentalists are appalled at the idea of the Gwich'in lands being invaded in the search for oil. A spokesperson for the Worldwide Fund for Nature (WWF) has estimated that there is probably only enough oil under the refuge to meet the USA's demands for 180 days. To provide that oil a traditional community could be wiped out forever. A spokesperson for one of the Indian villages said, 'why destroy one of the world's greatest animal migrations for oil? Our case against oil is a human rights issue. We need the caribou herd like the Amazon Indians need the rainforest. It is our lives and culture.'

4A.12 *The construction of more oil wells will disrupt the native Alaskan caribou*

To the west of the proposed development area, the local Inuit population have a different attitude. They have seen the benefits of oil money for years. Previously a poor region, the oil has helped pay for local facilities such as schools, transport and clinics. The average income of an Alaskan villager is less than $10 000 per year. The Inuit in the oil-rich north average nearly $50 000 per year, and are keen to see further development that will bring in more jobs. Alaskan politicians are also in favour of exploiting the region's oil reserves. They dispute the environmentalists' claims of how much oil there is in the refuge area, claiming it may be ten times as great. This would greatly reduce the amount of expensive oil that the USA had to import.

What are the issues facing the oil industry?

- Oil will eventually run out. Before it does, more supplies will be located and exploited in remote and fragile environments.
- People in various environments will have their livelihoods destroyed by oil.
- There will be oil spills at sea and on land.
- The oil producing nations could once again use their power to control supplies and cause oil shortages.
- There could be oil wars, similar to the Gulf War in 1990.
- Oil prices could rise and cause havoc to the world's economies.
- Developing alternatives to oil energy may take longer than the richer countries want to wait.

How energy is used

People living in MEDCs take energy supplies for granted. We switch on a light and do not think about where the electricity comes from. We get on a bus without having to consider where the fuel came from. This attitude towards energy is very different from that of most people who live in LEDCs. For many of the world's poorest people energy is sometimes a luxury and certainly a costly one. In rich countries, the issue is which energy source is the best to use. In the poor world, there is often no choice and energy supplies may be difficult to find at all.

> **NOTING ACTIVITIES**
>
> 1 As you read through this section make notes on the main issues related to energy use in the United Kingdom and in Africa.
>
> 2 Write down the main ways in which problems connected to energy are different in the UK and in Africa.

CASE STUDY

Energy in the United Kingdom

The UK needs most energy on cold winter days. Peak demand is during a major commercial TV event in the winter, when the nation goes for a cup of tea at a 'break'. There is a range of different types of **power station** that generate electricity. There is a **supergrid** of transmission cables that supplies the whole country with electricity.

Section 4 Using and Abusing the Environment

From energy supply to the consumer

Figure 4A.13 shows changes in the UK's **primary** energy sources. This is the direct use of a source of energy. Coal and oil (petroleum) dominated until 1970 when North Sea natural gas was produced. Nuclear power has been an important minority source but it seems that it will decline in the future. Figure 4A.14 is a similar *cumulative line graph* and shows how the nation's energy is used.

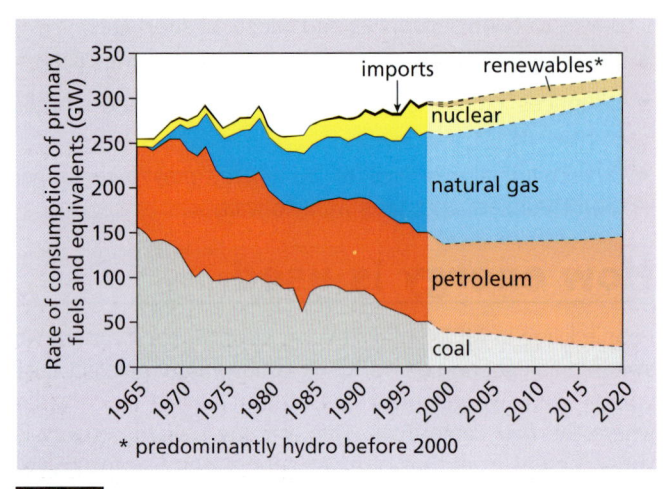

4A.13 UK primary energy sources

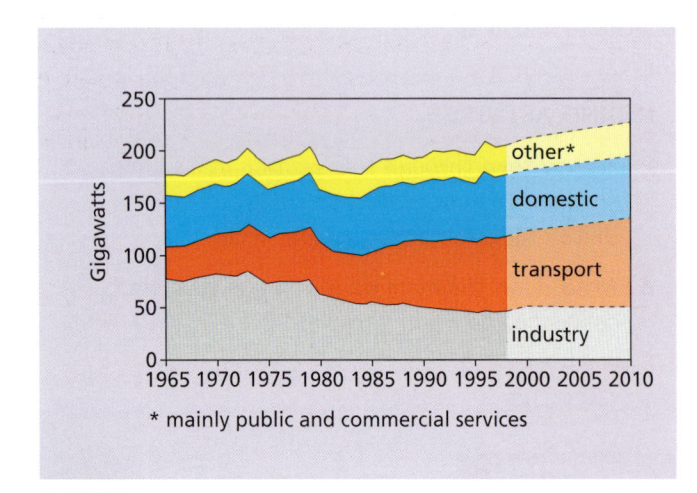

4A.14 UK energy consumption

4A.15 The North Sea has 24-hour production of oil and gas from platforms like this. There are 7 gas terminals in the UK being fed from 135 separate gas fields

4A.16 This Scottish oil refinery works 24 hours a day making oil products for transport and the petrochemical industry

4A.17 This coal-fired thermal power station produces electricity for the national supergrid. The use of coal has declined since 1990

Most of the primary energy sources are converted into electricity, which is therefore called **secondary** energy. Look through Figures 4A15–20. These show how energy is produced in the United Kingdom. Figure 4A.21 shows the location of the main supplies.

A Resources

4A.18 *This gas-fired power station produces electricity for the grid. Gas has been increasingly used to generate electricity since 1990. This power station is located at Illingholme close to supplies of North Sea gas*

4A.19 *Wind farm at Blyth Harbour, Northumberland. When the wind blows there is a capacity of 2.7 MW. This is small scale compared to the 24-hour working power stations with a capacity of over 2000 MW*

Changing electricity generation in the UK

The UK has for several centuries depended on power produced from **fossil fuels** such as coal, oil and gas. Electricity is generated by burning fuel to heat water which produces steam. This turns turbines which generate electricity. This is all **non-renewable** and the proportion of **renewable** supplies has been very low.

At the close of the 20th century the UK electricity industry was accused of polluting the air and causing acid rain which fell on other countries in Europe. This was an issue that had to be solved. Carbon dioxide emission levels had to be reduced, and cutting the use of coal was the solution. Between 1990 and 1997 CO_2 emission levels from power stations fell from 198 million tonnes to 147 million tonnes.

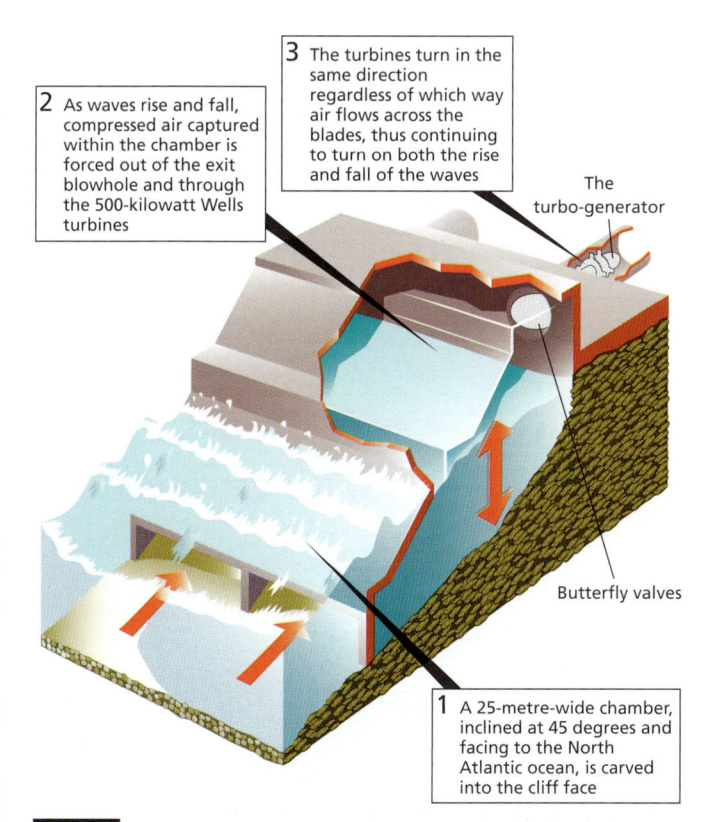

NOTING ACTIVITIES

1. **a** Describe the changes in the UK primary energy sources between 1965 and 2000.

   b How will the energy sources change between 2000 and 2020?

2. How has the use of energy changed since 1965? How will it continue to change in the future?

3. For each photograph in Figures 4A.15–20 state what is shown and whether it involves a primary energy source, a secondary source, a non-renewable resource or a renewable resource.

4. Figure 4A.21 shows the UK's main energy supplies.

   a State where the energy is produced.

   b Write briefly about its location.

4A.20 *Section through Limpet module built into the cliffs of Islay, Scotland, generating electricity from the tides*

Labels on diagram 4A.20:

1. A 25-metre-wide chamber, inclined at 45 degrees and facing to the North Atlantic ocean, is carved into the cliff face

2. As waves rise and fall, compressed air captured within the chamber is forced out of the exit blowhole and through the 500-kilowatt Wells turbines

3. The turbines turn in the same direction regardless of which way air flows across the blades, thus continuing to turn on both the rise and fall of the waves

The turbo-generator

Butterfly valves

Section 4 Using and Abusing the Environment

Figure 4A.22 shows how the fuel used in electricity production has changed since 1990. Since 1990 natural gas has been the major fuel in power stations.

Natural gas power stations:

- are highly mechanised
- employ small numbers of people
- make electricity more cheaply than coal
- waste less energy while making electricity
- produce about half the carbon dioxide compared to coal
- produce one-tenth of the nitrous oxides
- produce almost no sulphur dioxide.

There are some issues arising from the change-over to gas fired power stations:

- the demand for gas rose by 50 per cent between 1990 and 1997
- there are only 16 years of gas reserves in the UK. There will be more discovered but exploration will be very expensive

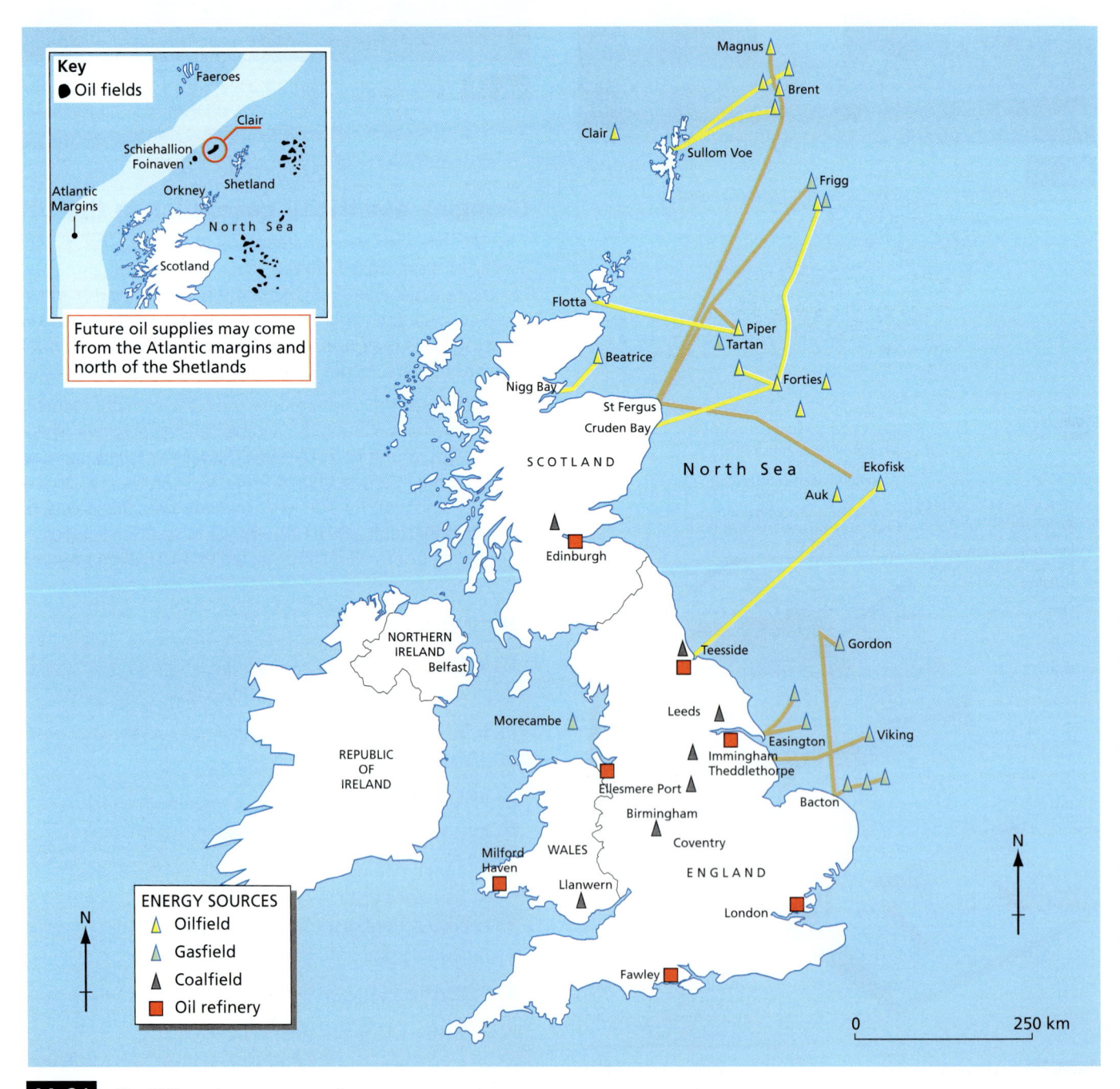

4A.21 *The UK's main energy supplies*

A Resources

Fuel used to generate energy, 1990

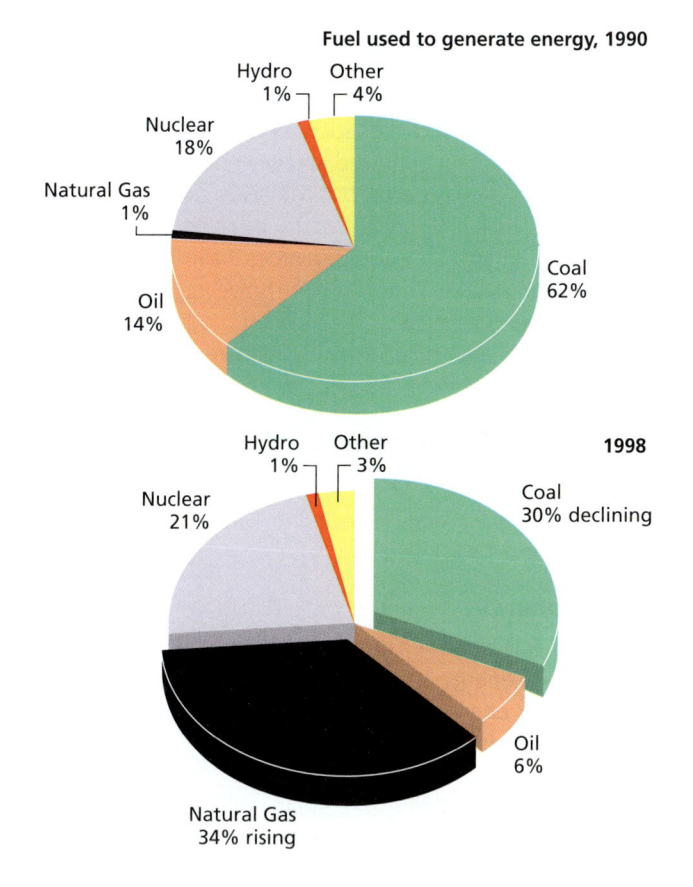

- Coal 62%
- Nuclear 18%
- Oil 14%
- Other 4%
- Hydro 1%
- Natural Gas 1%

1998

- Coal 30% declining
- Natural Gas 34% rising
- Nuclear 21%
- Oil 6%
- Other 3%
- Hydro 1%

4A.22 *Coal is no longer so important in generating the UK's electricity*

- gas may become more expensive if drilling for it takes place in more extreme areas such as the Atlantic margins
- imports of gas may be necessary which will be costly
- the country could become too dependent on gas especially if it is imported
- using more gas has caused unemployment in the country's coalmining areas.

More electricity needs to come from renewable energy sources. Targets are for 5 per cent of the UK's requirements to come from renewable sources by 2003, 10 per cent by 2010. Building up non-renewable electricity infrastructure is costly. **Tidal barrages** will be expensive and will have high environmental costs. **Wind farms** are not popular with local pressure groups, especially in the National Parks. **Solar panels** for houses are only just available and take-up rates will only increase if there are substantial government subsidies to householders.

There are other ways to make electricity and these will become more important this century. At Roves Farm near Swindon, for example, the farmer grows willow trees to provide **biomass** for electricity generation. The issue for the farmer is who will help him purchase the generator.

NOTING ACTIVITIES

1. Complete the listing of the issues and how they can be resolved.

2. How do you think the issues of energy supply in an MEDC are different from those in an LEDC? Write down some ideas before you read the next section.

CASE STUDY

Energy use in Africa

Africa has about 13 per cent of the world's population, yet accounts for only 2 per cent of world economic output. Energy production and consumption is very different to that in MEDCs such as the UK. For many Africans, the question is not which type of fuel to use, but whether there is any available at all.

Fuel consumption per person in Africa is less than half the world average. It is also very costly and inefficient, Africans spending a larger proportion of their GNP on energy than elsewhere. Nearly half of all energy used is by private households (see Figure 4A.23).

Africa is the world's largest consumer of **biomass** energy. This is the use of firewood, charcoal and animal waste for fuel (Figure 4A.24). For many people, particularly to the south of the Sahara desert, it is the only fuel available. It is also the most damaging to the environment. The clearing of trees to use for fuel is one of the main causes of **deforestation** in Africa.

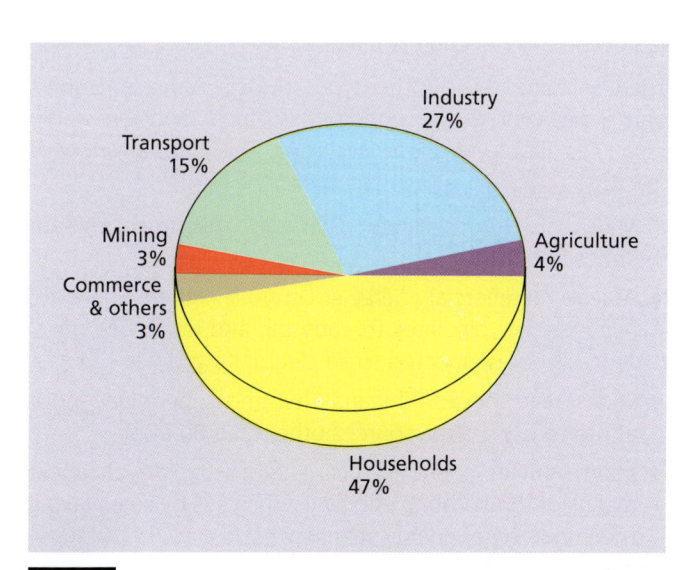

- Industry 27%
- Households 47%
- Transport 15%
- Agriculture 4%
- Mining 3%
- Commerce & others 3%

4A.23 *How energy is used in Africa*

Section 4 Using and Abusing the Environment

In Tanzania, for example, more than 90 per cent of the population depends upon firewood for energy. This is particularly the case in rural areas, where fewer than 1 per cent of the inhabitants have access to electricity. The forests of Tanzania are being destroyed for fuel at a rate of over 50 000 trees every day. The country has enormous potential for the development of renewable energy resources, yet they remain relatively untapped. Setting up these energy sources is very expensive, with the government increasing costs by adding taxes to them.

Many other African nations have lost over three-quarters of their natural forest. The loss of these forests may lead to soil erosion, eventually causing **desertification**. On a global scale, the burning of vast quantities of wood is one of the main human factors causing climate change.

4A.24 *Firewood is the principal use of biomass energy in Africa*

Wood is used throughout Africa as a fuel for cooking. It causes health problems because of the smoke generated, and is a very inefficient fuel. As the population of Africa increases and the forests are cleared for fuel, the shortage of firewood has become a major issue.

There is limited use of other types of fuels. Africa consumes only 3 per cent of the world's fossil fuels, and renewable resources are as yet underdeveloped. This is for a variety of reasons.

- Many of the continent's energy resources remain undeveloped.
- Africa's commercial energy structure is limited. There are relatively few pipelines to carry oil, and much of central Africa is not connected to an electricity grid.
- Widespread poverty means that most people cannot afford to use energy sources other than biomass.
- Many African countries are landlocked. The cheapest means of transporting energy resources is by sea, making the importing of energy very expensive.

Renewable energy

Renewable energy relies upon natural sources from the environment. These sources, such as wind, waves, and solar energy, are continually renewed and will not run out. The use of such sources of energy has obvious advantages over fossil fuels, which are predicted to become scarce in the near future. Renewable energy sources have become more important worldwide. They do not, however, contribute as much to global energy use as had been predicted. What are the advantages and problems of using renewable energy? How will the use of these sources develop in the future?

What sources of renewable energy are there?

Each of the most common forms of renewable energy has advantages and disadvantages.

1 Solar energy

This is energy that comes directly from the sun, and the form of renewable energy that has the greatest potential use. Trapping solar energy is not easy, and the amount of energy received depends on the season, cloud cover and distance from the equator. One main use of solar energy is for home heating, where a building has solar collectors to trap and distribute heat. This may then be used for central heating or providing hot water (Figure 4A.25). Solar energy may also be used to produce electricity. The most common form is where solar cells (also called **photovoltaic cells**) provide power for calculators, batteries and toys.

4A.25 *Solar energy is used to provide domestic hot water in Italy*

A Resources

Advantages of solar energy

- an unlimited supply of energy
- causes no pollution

Disadvantages of solar energy

- may be very expensive to use
- if energy has to be stored, this is very costly
- not always reliable: depends on availability of sunlight

2 Hydro-power

This is energy that comes from the force of moving water. Most hydro-power is used to generate electricity as water passes through turbines (Figure 4A.26). This form of power is widely used throughout the world, particularly in mountainous regions with a regular supply of snow and rainfall. Hydro-power also includes harnessing the power of waves and tides. These have enormous potential, but as yet are used relatively little.

- has other benefits: reservoirs often provide leisure facilities

Disadvantages of hydro-power

- can have an environmental impact. Large dams and reservoirs change the landscape, with many dams being built in spectacular mountain scenery. Roads often have to be built to provide access. River wildlife may also be affected, and large reservoirs create their own microclimate
- only effective where there is sufficient water supply
- many of the best and cheapest locations for dams have already been used

3 Wind energy

Huge wind turbines are used to produce electricity. Vertical 'windmills' are the most familiar (Figure 4A.27), although windmills with blades that turn horizontally near to the ground actually produce more electricity.

4A.27 *A wind farm*

Advantages of wind energy

- it is a free source of energy, available almost everywhere
- no pollution
- windmills are relatively cheap to build
- the land on which windmills stand can have other uses, for example grazing sheep

4A.26 *Hydro-power may be used on a small scale. Here, water from the steep slopes above Lake Garda in Italy is used to provide electricity for the town of Riva*

Advantages of hydro-power

- clean and readily available in most countries
- water may be stored in reservoirs so that its use can be controlled
- a cheap way to produce electricity

Disadvantages of wind energy

- requires constant and reasonably strong winds. Slight winds or breezes do not generate much electricity
- several windmills are required to produce enough electricity. This takes up a large area of land
- a 'wind farm' has a major impact on the landscape

Section 4 Using and Abusing the Environment

4 Geothermal energy

This comes from the heat stored within the Earth. The most commonly used form of geothermal energy is where water beneath the surface of the earth is naturally heated to produce steam. This may be harnessed and used to generate electricity. Geothermal energy is widely used in northern Europe, for example in Norway.

Advantages of geothermal energy

- an unlimited source of energy
- no pollution
- may be used for energy for individual homes as well as on a large scale

Disadvantages of geothermal energy

- expensive to set up. Trapping water and steam energy is difficult and costly
- expensive to run. People using geothermal energy have found that keeping the system running is very costly

5 Biomass

This refers to the use of organic substances (that are not fossil fuels) to provide energy. The most common fuels are wood and animal wastes. Biomass is classed as a renewable energy source because it can be replaced in a relatively short period of time. This form of energy is that most commonly used in Africa (see pages 101–102)

Advantages of biomass

- readily available, particularly in poorer parts of the world where there is often no other form of fuel available
- can make use of waste products

Disadvantages of biomass

- burning causes air pollution. The burning of biomass is a major cause of death in LEDCs
- a very inefficient method of providing energy

Why is renewable energy an important issue?

There was great interest in the development of renewable energy sources in the 1960s and 1970s. This was because people realised that fossil fuels would run out, and that alternative forms of energy had to be found. The oil producing countries (OPEC, see page 93) raised the cost of oil. By the 1980s, however, further supplies of oil had been discovered, and the cost of oil fell. Although it still varied, overall the price of oil had stabilised by the 1990s. Some renewable energy projects had been very costly to set up and run, and so interest in developing other forms of energy declined.

At the start of the 21st century, renewable energy supplies are once again an important issue. The concerns are now mainly environmental. The use of fossil fuels contributes to

---

NOTING ACTIVITIES

1 Complete a copy of the table below to show the main features of renewable energy.

TYPE	Main features	Advantages	Disadvantages
Solar			
Hydro-power			
Wind energy			
Geothermal			
Biomass			

4A.28 *Comparison of renewable energy sources*

2 What are the main advantages of renewable energy sources?

3 If renewable resources are 'free', why do you think that they are still used less than fossil fuels such as oil and gas?

4 Research solar energy. Find out how this form of power was used in the past, and its current uses. Prepare a report of your findings.

5 Undertake an energy survey in your home and at school. Write down ways in which energy is used, and include means by which you think better use could be made of energy.

acid rain and global warming. Governments have agreed to reduce the amount of pollution caused by the burning of fossil fuels, and alternative energy sources seem an ideal way of meeting ever-growing demands for energy.

Renewable resources remain relatively unpopular on a worldwide scale, despite many apparent advantages. There is still disagreement over exactly how much pollution is caused by the use of fossil fuels. The majority of gases in the atmosphere causing global warming, for example, are generated naturally. Fossil fuels remain relatively cheap, and their life expectancy is not currently reducing, as more reserves of oil and gas are being discovered. Making use of renewable resources is often very expensive, and many industries and national governments are not prepared to pay more than is necessary for their energy supplies.

STRUCTURED QUESTION

The United States government pays for research into and development of renewable energy sources. Figure 4A.29 shows the amount spent from 1974 to 1990.

1 Draw a line graph to show the information in the table. (5)
2 Describe the trends shown on your graph. (4)

Figure 4A.30 shows the average price of oil during the same period of time.

3 Draw a line graph to show the information in the table. (5)
4 Describe the trends in oil prices. (4)
5 What connection is there between the patterns on your two graphs? Give reasons for your answer. (5)
6 Explain why renewable energy resources are still less important on a world scale than fossil fuels. (7)

Year	Research and development funding ($ million)
1974	40
1975	132
1976	324
1977	513
1978	747
1979	875
1980	850
1981	759
1982	279
1983	244
1984	192
1985	181
1986	149
1987	123
1988	98
1989	88
1990	84

4A.29 *Investment in renewable energy 1974–1990*

Year	Average oil price ($US)
1974	3
1975	10
1976	11
1977	12
1978	13
1979	30
1980	36
1981	34
1982	32
1983	29
1984	28
1985	28
1986	13
1987	17
1988	13
1989	16
1990	22

4A.30 *Average oil prices 1974–1990*

Section 4 Using and Abusing the Environment

CASE STUDY

Renewable energy in the UK

The UK has relatively large reserves of fossil fuels, which provide most of the country's energy needs. Renewable resources remain relatively unimportant. There is huge potential for their development, particularly as fossil fuels become more scarce and environmental controls become tougher.

The UK is well placed for wind, wave and tidal energy. Wind turbines alone could generate up to 20 per cent of the country's electricity. A further 20 per cent could be provided by wave energy. Even solar power could make a significant contribution to the UK's energy requirements. The future of renewable energy in the UK depends upon a range of factors, including:

- **environmental** – is renewable energy in the UK really better for the environment than the fossil fuel alternatives? Most renewable energy also impacts upon the environment
- **technical** – generation of electricity on a large scale has proved to be difficult using renewable energy. In theory, wind power could generate most of the UK's electricity. Scotland is the windiest country in Europe, and has more wind power potential than the rest of the continent put together
- **economic** – the set-up and maintenance of renewable energy supplies has been very expensive
- **political** – the UK has a wide range of energy choices, and the eventual 'mix' of energy use is influenced by government decisions. Should nuclear power continue to provide energy? (It currently accounts for 20 per cent of electricity generation.) How important are environmental effects of energy use? How much energy is the UK prepared to import from abroad?

EXTENDED ACTIVITY

For the purpose of this activity, imagine that you are working for the British government. Your advisors have presented a report (below) about the present and future situation of energy supplies in the country. The government is unsure what to do. You need to present a written report of no more than one side of A4 summarising your recommendations.

What should the government do?

1 Help the producers of renewable energy by giving them subsidies, to make the cost of energy cheaper.
2 Put extra taxes on the cost of fossil fuels so that people use them less.
3 Do nothing and let the situation continue as it is.

The case of wind farms

Wind power could produce as much electricity for the UK as nuclear energy. It is safe and clean, and the cost of producing electricity through wind has dropped considerably in recent years. Why then has wind power failed to reach its potential for producing electricity?

1 The UK's thirty wind farms are concentrated in Cornwall, Wales, Yorkshire and Scotland. Many are located in popular tourist areas, and there is concern that visitors will be put off by the sight of ranks of huge windmills. To be exposed to the greatest wind, the farms have to be located on high land, making them visible for a great distance.
2 Local residents have complained of the noise made by the blades of the windmills. The blades operate whenever it is windy, and may keep local people awake at night.
3 In spite of decreasing costs, generating electricity using the wind is still expensive. The windmills need maintaining, and each windmill produces relatively little electricity.

To: HM Government Advisory Group on Energy

Subject: The future of energy supplies in the UK

The UK's dependence on imported fossil fuels is growing. Also, the environmental cost of these fuels is becoming less acceptable. Renewable energy is a realistic alternative in many parts of the country, but it has not become commercially successful. This is mainly because fossil fuels are relatively cheap. To help change this situation, one proposal is to help providers of renewable energy by giving money to help them set up and run their businesses.

This could meet with opposition from fossil fuel providers, who might feel that this gives their competitors an unfair advantage. It could also cost jobs in these industries. Renewable energy sources are never likely to create many jobs.

Another alternative would be to put higher taxes on to fossil fuels. If people have to pay more for products like petrol, they will use less. In industry, this would encourage companies to try harder than they have done to find other methods of buying and supplying energy. This solution could prove controversial, as there is little evidence to show that people actually do cut down their use when prices go up. They pay more, and cut back on other things. Many people depend upon fuel for transport, and would be hit hard.

We could leave things as they are. This would allow the free market to operate. If fossil fuels become scarce, the price will go up anyway. If people are going to buy renewable energy, it will have to be more competitive.

A Resources

Resource use in the future
- How will we be able to **sustain** our present quality of life?
- How will we **conserve** the environments we have so they are there for future generations?
- How will we travel in the future if oil runs out?
- How can we heat our homes if fossil fuels become too expensive?

These are all geographical questions and the issues can be studied at all scales. Figure 4A.31 shows two students discussing the future.

4A.31 *Future resource uses?*

Section 4 Using and Abusing the Environment

> **NOTING ACTIVITIES**
>
> 1 Give an example of a topic being discussed in Figure 4A.31 from each of the following scales: local, regional, national, continental and world.
>
> 2 Discuss with a partner another resource issue at the five scales stated in Question 1.

Before reading further answer the following questions about your lifestyle, or that of your family. Each question is about you as a global citizen.

DO YOU

A *Recycle waste?*

B *Walk to school?*

C *Grow fruit or vegetables?*

D *Have a garden pond?*

E *Feel safe when you go out at night?*

F *Intend to vote in elections when you are 18?*

G *Smoke?*

H *Live near shops and basic amenities?*

I *Turn lights off when you leave a room?*

J *Turn heaters down when windows are open?*

All these questions are based on **indicators of sustainability**. This is about sustaining and improving people's quality of life in a world where resources are running out.

Local Agenda 21

In 1992 world leaders met in Rio de Janeiro for the United Nations Earth Summit. Agenda 21 was an agreement on world action to achieve a sustainable pattern of development. Sustainable development means 'meeting the needs of the present without destroying the ability of future generations to meet their own needs' (see page 240).

Britain undertook to develop local plans for sustainability. These local strategies taken on by local authorities were known as **Local Agenda 21** programmes. If local environments could be improved then it was likely that the **quality of life** would improve.

Figure 4A.32 shows some of the features of the Local Agenda 21 Strategy for Richmond-on-Thames to the south-west of London.

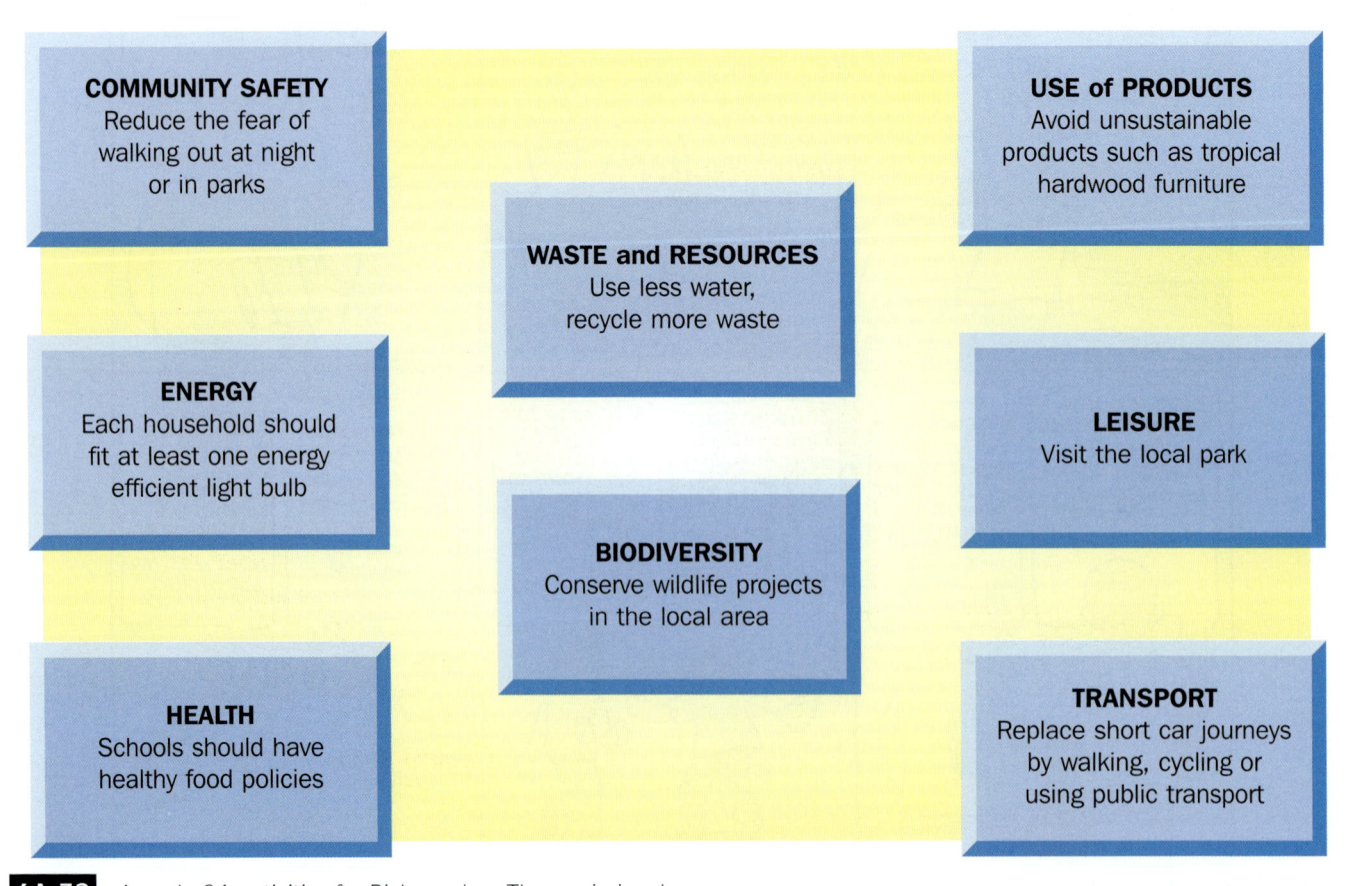

COMMUNITY SAFETY
Reduce the fear of walking out at night or in parks

USE of PRODUCTS
Avoid unsustainable products such as tropical hardwood furniture

WASTE and RESOURCES
Use less water, recycle more waste

ENERGY
Each household should fit at least one energy efficient light bulb

LEISURE
Visit the local park

BIODIVERSITY
Conserve wildlife projects in the local area

HEALTH
Schools should have healthy food policies

TRANSPORT
Replace short car journeys by walking, cycling or using public transport

4A.32 Agenda 21 activities for Richmond on Thames in London

A Resources

> **EXTENDED PRACTICAL ACTIVITY**
>
> Choose at least one local sustainability issue and research it. For example:
> - What your local area is doing as part of Local Agenda 21
> - Is the factory near you cutting down on packaging?
> - Does your school have an energy-saving policy?
> - To what extent you and your class recycle waste

Recycling: UK and Europe

It seems that the UK has a bad record in dealing with its rubbish. In the 1980s we were called the 'dirty man of Europe' because we dumped chemical and sewage waste directly into the North Sea. This has now stopped but the UK lags behind other European countries in how we deal with our waste (Figure 4A.33). The UK's high percentage of landfill leads to air pollution because CO_2, methane and CFCs escape from the ground. Over time there are also leakages of poisons to water sources.

Britain has set targets for improvement. By 2010 at least 45 per cent of waste must be recycled or converted into energy; this is still less than the Netherlands achieved at the turn of the century.

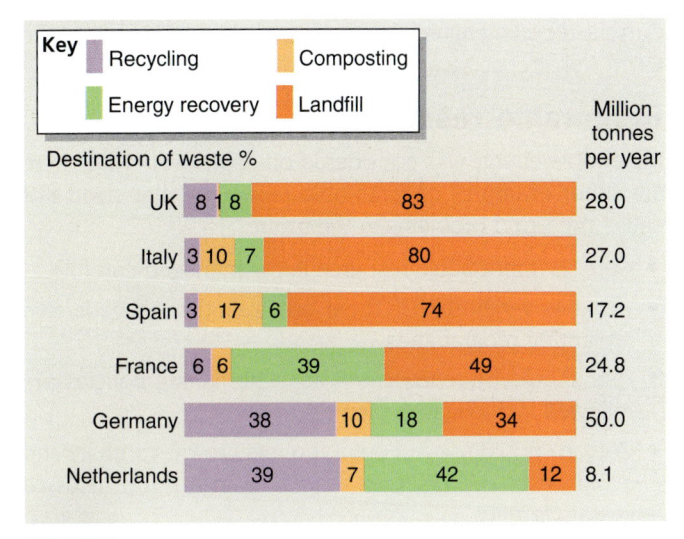

Key: Recycling | Composting | Energy recovery | Landfill

Destination of waste % | **Million tonnes per year**

Country	Recycling	Composting	Energy recovery	Landfill	Million tonnes per year
UK	8	1	8	83	28.0
Italy	3	10	7	80	27.0
Spain	3	17	6	74	17.2
France	6	6	39	49	24.8
Germany	38	10	18	34	50.0
Netherlands	39	7	42	12	8.1

4A.33 *European waste*

Figure 4A.34 shows the differing rates of recycling in Europe. The UK does not do very well. Recycling would be good for the UK, as it would save money and create jobs. If the UK reached 50 per cent recycling rates for newspapers and magazines 10 000 jobs would be created and £175 million saved on the cost of imports.

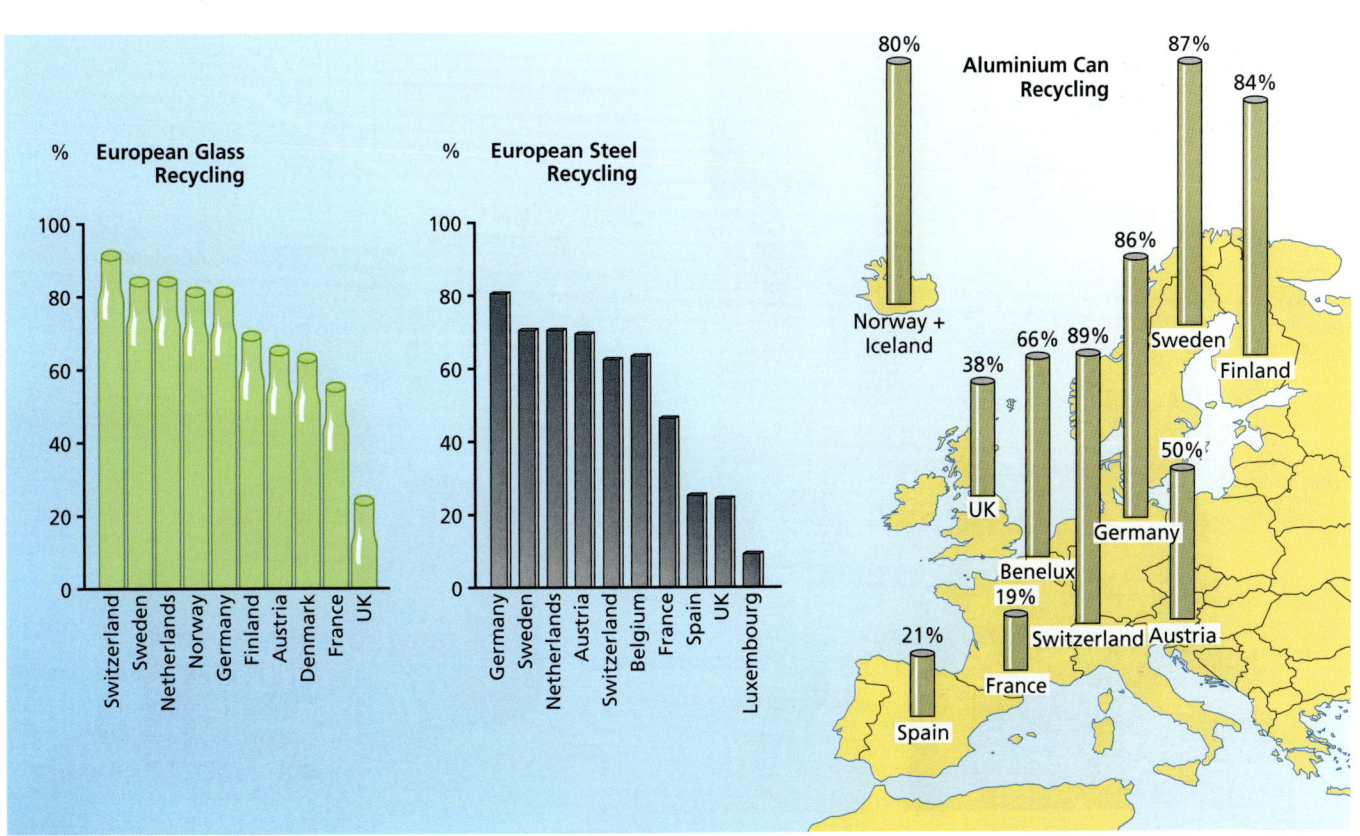

European Glass Recycling (%): Switzerland, Sweden, Netherlands, Norway, Germany, Finland, Austria, Denmark, France, UK

European Steel Recycling (%): Germany, Sweden, Netherlands, Austria, Switzerland, Belgium, France, Spain, UK, Luxembourg

Aluminium Can Recycling:
- Norway + Iceland: 80%
- Sweden: 87%
- Finland: 84%
- Germany: 86%
- UK: 38%
- Benelux: 66%
- Switzerland: 89%
- Austria: 50%
- France: 21%
- Spain: 19%

4A.34 *Recycling in Europe*

Section 4 Using and Abusing the Environment

Current recycling figures can be found on the Friends of the Earth website, at www.foe.co.uk

Renewable resources

Renewable energy was considered on pages 101–104. There are other examples of renewable resources that need not cause the world problems in the future.

- Water is a renewable resource if it is managed carefully.
- Wood is renewable if there are well thought out tree replanting programmes.
- Fish should be renewable if sensible fishing policies are followed including fish farming.
- Cotton should not run out if farmers grow it carefully and avoid pests and diseases as well as rotate the fields to sustain fertility.

But it is not guaranteed that the above resources will be infinitely renewable. Certainly there are serious problems conserving fish stocks. Cotton farmers use a very high input of pesticides and fertilisers and these are not renewable as they are made from artificial non-renewable chemicals.

Substitute products will have to be developed as non-renewable resources run out. We will not be able to wear clothes made from synthetic fibres derived from oil. We used to wear cotton and wool clothes; in the future other vegetable substitutes will be possible made from plants such as hemp, flax and maybe banana skins (see Figure 4A.35)

Personal energy consumption

If the world is to survive as resources run out we all have to play our part as global citizens. Figure 4A.31 gave examples of how we, personally, can reduce resource consumption. The issue is whether the people of the world will voluntarily cut down on energy consumption. Or will they need to be forced to do so?

The following proposals come from The Swedish Society for Nature Conservation (SNF). It has proposed the following energy taxes: carbon dioxide, nuclear power, electricity, diesel fuel, petrol, nitrogen oxides and sulphur. In addition the Society proposes aircraft landing fees, taxes on waste, agro-chemicals and tap water, plus taxes on phosphate and gravel (non-renewable resources). In Sweden a tax on sulphur emissions has already reduced the level to 40 per cent below the legal limit.

Studies have shown that environmental taxes generally have the desired effect, which is to change habits. In 2000 there was a mass protest by people in the UK and other countries in Europe. Will elected governments in the future be prepared to set very unpopular taxes that might lead them to be voted out of office?

4A.35 *Clothes made from vegetable fibres instead of wool and cotton*

4A.36 *Raising taxes to cut down energy consumption*

NOTING ACTIVITIES

1 Using the statistics shown in Figure 4A.34 describe the different rates of recycling throughout Europe.

2 a Make a list of four non-renewable resources and four renewable resources.

  b For each non-renewable resource write a sentence stating the consequences for the world as it runs out.

  c For each renewable resource write a sentence stating the problems of maintaining it as a renewable resource.

3 'The government should increase the amount of tax that people pay on using energy. This is the only way to conserve energy.'

'More money should be spent on research into alternatives to fossil fuels, for the long-term future.'

'There are plenty of oil and gas reserves left in the world, and probably many more that have yet to be discovered. These fuels won't run out in our lifetime.'

Write down your own opinion of each of these statements.

Section 4 Using and Abusing the Environment

B Water supply and management

Water is a resource that most of us take for granted. During the 20th century, the number of deaths caused by unclean water supplies decreased dramatically in MEDCs. For most people in these countries, fresh water is available at the turn of a tap.

Why, then, is the supply of water such an important issue in the 21st century that it has caused regional conflicts and even international wars? How can water supplies be increased? What effects does this increase have on the natural environment and on people?

Water is a **finite** resource. The total quantity of water available to the people of the world is limited. As the world's population continues to increase, so does the demand on this most precious natural resource. Agriculture accounts for most water consumption in developing countries, yet despite having a minority of the world's population it is the rich industrialised nations that are the greatest users of water.

Over 50 per cent of water used in MEDCs is consumed by industry. Although domestic water use is only a small part of the total, it is often the most costly to provide. The quality of water needed in the home is higher than that required for industry or farming, and the technology to keep drinking water clean is expensive.

A growing demand for water

Water demand and supply varies throughout the world. Unlike other resources, water cannot easily be transported from one part of the world to another. Reservoirs and pipelines are able to store and carry water over relatively long distances, but such transfer is costly and wasteful. Limited underground stores of water are often tapped instead; these are often being used up more quickly than natural processes are replacing them. Managing water supplies in the 21st century is a problem for both rich and poor countries alike, as shown by the following case studies.

CASE STUDY

Turkey's water scheme

Five thousand years ago the people of modern-day Iran and Iraq lived in an area known as the *fertile crescent*. The ancient people **irrigated** their farmland with water from the Tigris and Euphrates Rivers, which have their source in Turkey. Now Turkey wants to store and transfer water from these great rivers in order to irrigate dry lands in the poor southern part of the country.

4B.1 The main uses of water

112

B Water supply and management

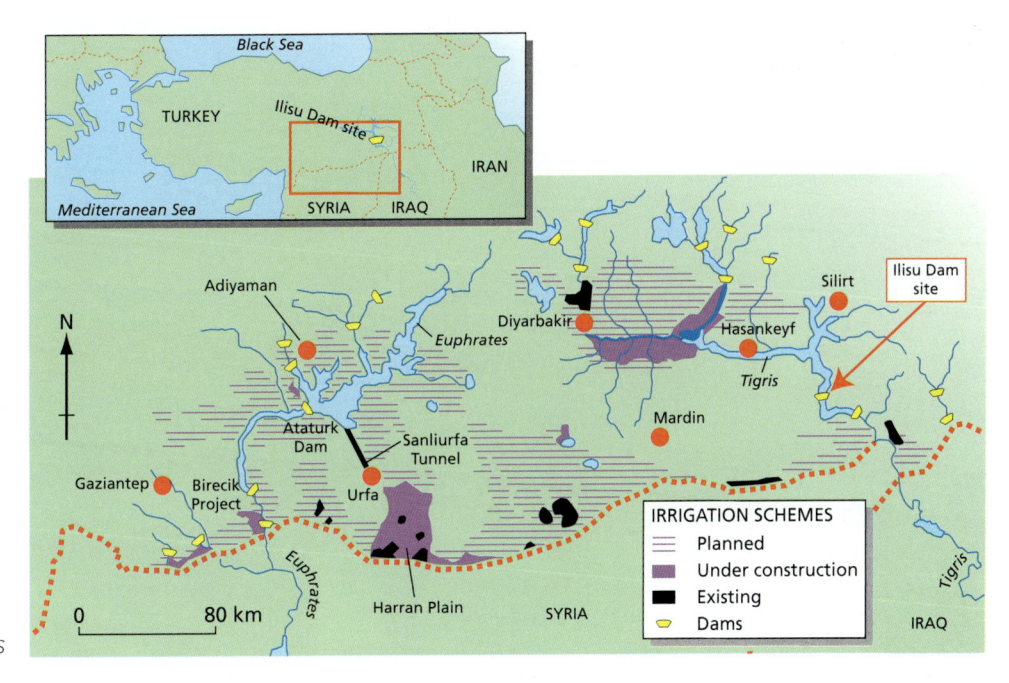

4B.2 *Turkey's irrigation schemes*

How will this benefit the people of Turkey? Figure 4B.2 shows the parts of southern Turkey that are already irrigated or it is planned to irrigate. The once arid Harran plain is now covered with green fields. Cotton is the most important crop and 25 per cent of Turkey's output came from this area in 1995. Cotton mills and textile factories are expanding, and farmers are becoming wealthier. Small companies are growing to provide services for the new farming industry, and banks are expanding and lending money. Southern Turkey is becoming an *agro-industrial* region, with very **intensive** farming, with the result that fewer people are migrating away from the area to towns and cities in the west of the country.

As well as irrigating farmland, the water management schemes will produce cheap hydro-electric power.

The Ilisu Dam Project

Located on the Tigris River 65 kilometres upstream from the Syrian and Iraqi borders is Turkey's largest planned water management scheme (Figure 4B.2). It will produce electricity from a 1200 MW power station which will cost $2 billion. The international consortium building the project is Swiss, although the British government is contributing $200 million.

What is the impact of the Ilisu Dam Project?

As with other schemes in southern Turkey, the Ilisu Dam is likely to bring both advantages and disadvantages. These are the main issues.

1 Who, if anybody, owns the water? Syria depends on water from the River Euphrates, and Iraq depends upon both the Tigris and Euphrates. This southern region of Turkey is home to Kurdish people, some of whom also live in northern Iraq. All claim the waters of the Tigris and Euphrates Rivers. There are already several dams on the Tigris in Turkey, reducing its flow to as little as one-sixth of its natural volume. Should Iraq have as much claim to the water as Turkey?

Does any one nation have the right to claim 'ownership' of a resource that passes through more than one country? Syria has complained that it is losing water from the Euphrates, and also that pesticides and fertilisers that Turks are using pollute the water that does reach their country. Does Syria have as much right to clean water from the Euphrates as Turkey?

2 Whose is the rivers' sediment? Sediment usually carried downstream by the rivers now becomes trapped behind dams in Turkey. It is this sediment, left behind after flooding, that used to form fertile farmland in Syria and Iraq.

3 Who owns the land? The Kurdish people who live in this part of Turkey have been threatened. It is claimed that some people have already been forced to leave villages at gunpoint. Local officials in some villages affected by the scheme did not even know that it had been approved by the Turkish government. Nearly fifty villages will be flooded. It is not yet known if there will be a plan to resettle people living in these villages.

Although no compensation plans have been revealed, Isa Parlak, the governor of Batman Province, insists that the state will take care of everything. 'Nobody will suffer as a result of this dam', he says. Those to be made homeless by the dam – estimates range from 16 000 to 45 000 – will either receive new homes from the state or be paid compensation for the loss of their property.' Parlak is keen to outline the advantages the dam will bring. Ilisu is part of the huge GAP water scheme (GAP are the Turkish initials of the South-

Section 4 Using and Abusing the Environment

4B.3 The historic town of Hasankeyf is threatened by the Ilisu project

Britain set to pull out of dam project

Patrick Wintour and Charlotte Denny

The government is about to withdraw its support for the Ilisu dam project in Turkey.

In a remarkable about-turn, ministers have agreed to publish new guidelines for export credit guarantees, taking account of the government's policies of sustainable development, human rights and good governance.

Cabinet level sources said the guidelines, once they are in force in a new mission statement, would debar export credits from being granted to the dam.

The $2bn hydro-electricity project, including construction work by Balfour Beatty, was expected to be funded with the help of $200m of British export credit guarantees. It has caused huge controversy amid concerns that the dam will require the enforced resettlement of thousands of villagers, despoil a beautiful environment and wreck sites of great architectural interest.

The all-party international development select committee has twice condemned the provision of any credits, saying the dam 'was from the outset conceived and planned in contravention of international standards.'

Turkey wants the dam, flooding large part of the Tigris Valley, to increase its power supply and feed its fast growing economy.

4B.4 *From the* Guardian, *26 July 2000*

eastern Anatolia Project) comprising 19 hydro-electric power stations and 22 dams.

4 Who owns historical treasures found in the area? The town of Hasankeyf has historical treasures going back 10,000 years. Figure 4B.3 and the comment from the town's mayor outline the historical losses that will follow flooding caused by construction of the reservoir. The mayor, Vahap Kusen, said 'If Hasankeyf goes it will be a great loss to humanity. This is especially true as we don't even know what lies under the ruins.'

5 Should Britain support such a large and potentially damaging scheme? Objections centre around arguments over sustainable development and human rights, as shown in the newspaper article Figure 4B.4.

6 Are there alternatives? Hydro-electric power is a *sunset* or declining form of technology. Perhaps Turkey should be considering developing *sunrise* technology such as small-scale irrigation or solar power. There is evidence from elsewhere in the GAP scheme that large-scale irrigation has not actually improved crop yields. Many farmers have not looked after the land, or grown only cotton which exhausts the soil. Powerful landowners do not live on or farm their own land, which is often left to poor and uneducated farmers who are unable to maintain the high quality of land provided by irrigation.

Using the water from rivers can bring a range of economic benefits, but such water is not always a national resource, as shown by this case study. It also belongs to the countries downstream and they must be a part of any plans to develop the water resources upstream. Local people have their own viewpoints about developing their local river water and these need to be taken into account. The actions being taken in Turkey could be very damaging to future relations with its neighbours as well as the local Kurdish people. Is a '**water war**' likely in this region in the future?

Where else is there conflict over water resources?

Nearly 40 per cent of the world's population live in river basins that cross national boundaries. There is no clear international treaty on water ownership, meaning that countries sharing river basins have to reach their own agreements. In Europe, the sharing of water is managed by nearly 200 international treaties, but elsewhere agreements are vague or non-existent.

Water resources play a crucial role in the politics of the Middle East, where population is growing at an average rate of 3 per cent per year. Water scarcity in Libya, Egypt, Israel, Jordan and Syria has increased the tension already existing between these countries. Israel and Jordan, for example, share water from the River Jordan, something that has caused continuous dispute since Israel's occupation of the west bank of the river in 1967. Over one-third of Israel's water came from these *Occupied Territories* until their withdrawal from the area.

Almost all Arab countries face increasing water shortages. By 2025, it is predicted that supply will be less than half the total quantity of water needed for farming alone. Arab countries will face increasing food shortages, together with the rising cost of importing food.

> **NOTING ACTIVITIES**
>
> 1 Write briefly about the GAP water scheme including the Ilisu Dam Project. What is it? Where is it? Why is it planned? Who is building it?
>
> 2 Summarise the advantages and disadvantages of the scheme.
>
> 3 a How do you think the problems created by the project could be solved?
>
>   b What could be the consequences of such problems if they are not solved?
>
> 4 What do you think should happen to the Ilisu Dam Project?
>
> 5 What alternatives do you think there are to the Ilisu Dam Project?

Water is a source of conflict elsewhere in the world.

- The Rio Grande River passes through Mexico and the USA. There has been conflict over who should pay to clean up pollution in the river.
- Proposed dams on the River Parana in South America have caused conflicts between Brazil and Argentina.
- Nine African countries depend upon water from the River Nile. The Nile Water Treaty, aimed at managing water in the river, has only been signed by Egypt and Sudan. Upstream, Ethiopia has planned to build a dam across the Blue Nile to store water. Most of Egypt's water comes from the Blue Nile, placing the country in a vulnerable position.
- Over 500 million people in Asia live in the catchment area of the Indus, Ganges and Brahmaputra Rivers. The irrigated area of the Indus is the largest in the world, and in 1947 it was split by the newly-formed border between India and Pakistan. The Indus Water Treaty took eight years to negotiate.
- In Europe, pollution is a major problem in the Rhine and Danube Rivers. Each flows through several countries, with the dumping of waste and sewage being a source of constant dispute.

> **NOTING ACTIVITIES**
>
> 1 Annotate an outline map of the world to show major areas of conflict over water resources. (An annotation is a label with descriptions or information.)
>
> 2 Carry out research into how water supplies are managed in your local area. Are there any disputes over water in the region where you live?
>
> 3 Look through recent newspapers and other media sources. Are any news stories linked to conflicts over the management of water resources?

Section 4 Using and Abusing the Environment

Water management in contrasting environments

During the 20th century the demand for water worldwide increased at twice the rate of population growth. Nearly one-third of the world's population lives in areas where there is a shortage of water. Other parts of the world have excess water. How is water managed in such contrasting environments? What are the issues that affect the management of water in Canada and Spain, two countries that have very different water supplies?

CASE STUDY

Canada

Canada is a country rich in water resources. There are more lakes in Canada than any other country in the world, and its rivers carry nearly 10 per cent of the world's fresh water. Canadians use more water per person than any other major industrialised nation, over twice as much as the average figure for Europeans. With such an abundance of fresh water, what issues are there related to the supply and management of Canada's water?

- Canada's population is approximately 30 million. Average population density is low, yet this hides great regional variations. Over 90 per cent of Canada's population lives in a narrow band within 300 kilometres of the southern border with the United States. Most rivers flow north to the Arctic Ocean and Hudson Bay (see Figure 4B.6). This means that there is a difference between the demand for water and its supply. The transfer of water over long distances is difficult and costly.

- The concentration of people in the south of Canada puts great pressure on local water supplies. It also leads to conflicts between users of water on different sections of

4B.5 *Water is an abundant resource in Canada. At an average of 326 litres per day, Canadians have the second highest water consumption rate in the world*

4B.6 *Water supply and demand in Canada*

rivers. Most of Canada's industry is located in the south. This greatly increases the demand there, as industry uses the greatest quantity of Canada's water.

- The price that Canadians pay for their water is very low. This means that people tend to over-use fresh water, and see no need to conserve supplies. The use of water in industry is very wasteful, and there are few schemes to recycle any water supplies.

- The use of water in Canada is increasing steadily (see Figure 4B.8). The greatest increase has been in water used by power stations, the majority of which are concentrated in the south. This further increases pressure on water resources there.

- Although the total quantity of water may be sufficient in many locations, it is unevenly distributed throughout the year. The greatest precipitation levels are in autumn and winter, while heaviest demand is in summer. Winter storms may also lead to flooding. The problem is in managing the supply of water, rather than needing to increase it.

- The quality of water supplies needs careful management. It is difficult to ensure that water supplies are high quality throughout a country as large as Canada.

Supplying water for Vancouver

Vancouver is Canada's third largest city, located on the Pacific coast just to the north of the border with the United States (see Figure 4B.7). The people of Vancouver use more water per person than anywhere else in Canada, and demand is rising rapidly (see Figure 4B.8). The local water authority estimates that, at current rates of increase, the demand for water will be greater than their ability to supply to the people of Vancouver by 2005. Maintaining the quality of water for drinking is also difficult. What is being done to ensure the future supplies of water to Vancouver?

Water is supplied to Vancouver from three catchment areas to the north of the city (see Figure 4B.9). These river basins, unlike others in Canada, are closed systems. This means that, except for water authority workers and people on guided tours, nobody is allowed within them. The water is transferred to the 1.6 million people of Vancouver through a series of dams, pumping stations and pipelines. Precipitation in the mountains above Vancouver is high, reaching 500 cm per year in some areas. The distribution of precipitation is very uneven, being concentrated in the autumn and winter. Severe storms make the water difficult to control and store. The fast-flowing mountain rivers become cloudy, creating problems for providing supplies of drinking water.

The people of Vancouver take their drinking water for granted, and so it came as a surprise in 1992 when the water authority restricted the amount of water that people were allowed to use during the summer months. In that year there had been very little precipitation, and an unusually warm spring. Demand was very high, and restrictions were brought in on the use of water for washing cars and sprinkling lawns. As the regulations decreased the amount of water used, they were made permanent the following year.

For the first time, the people of Vancouver were being told to conserve the water they used so freely. The water authority began a campaign designed to raise people's awareness of the importance of water as a resource (see

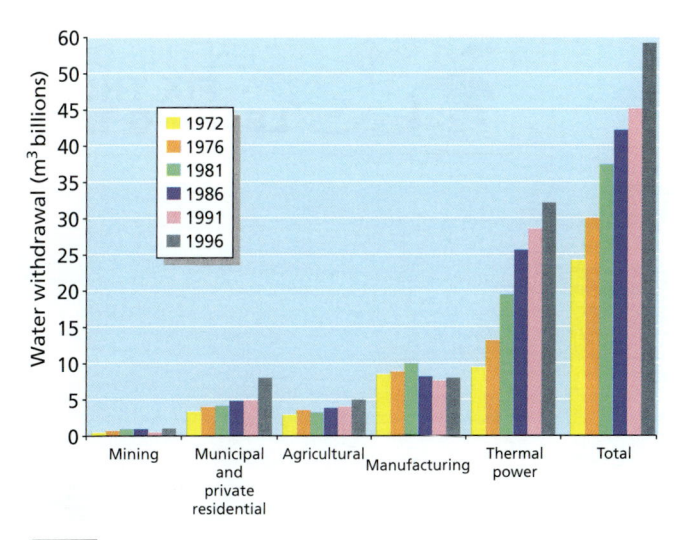

4B.7 The location of Vancouver

4B.8 Vancouver's increasing thirst for water

Section 4 Using and Abusing the Environment

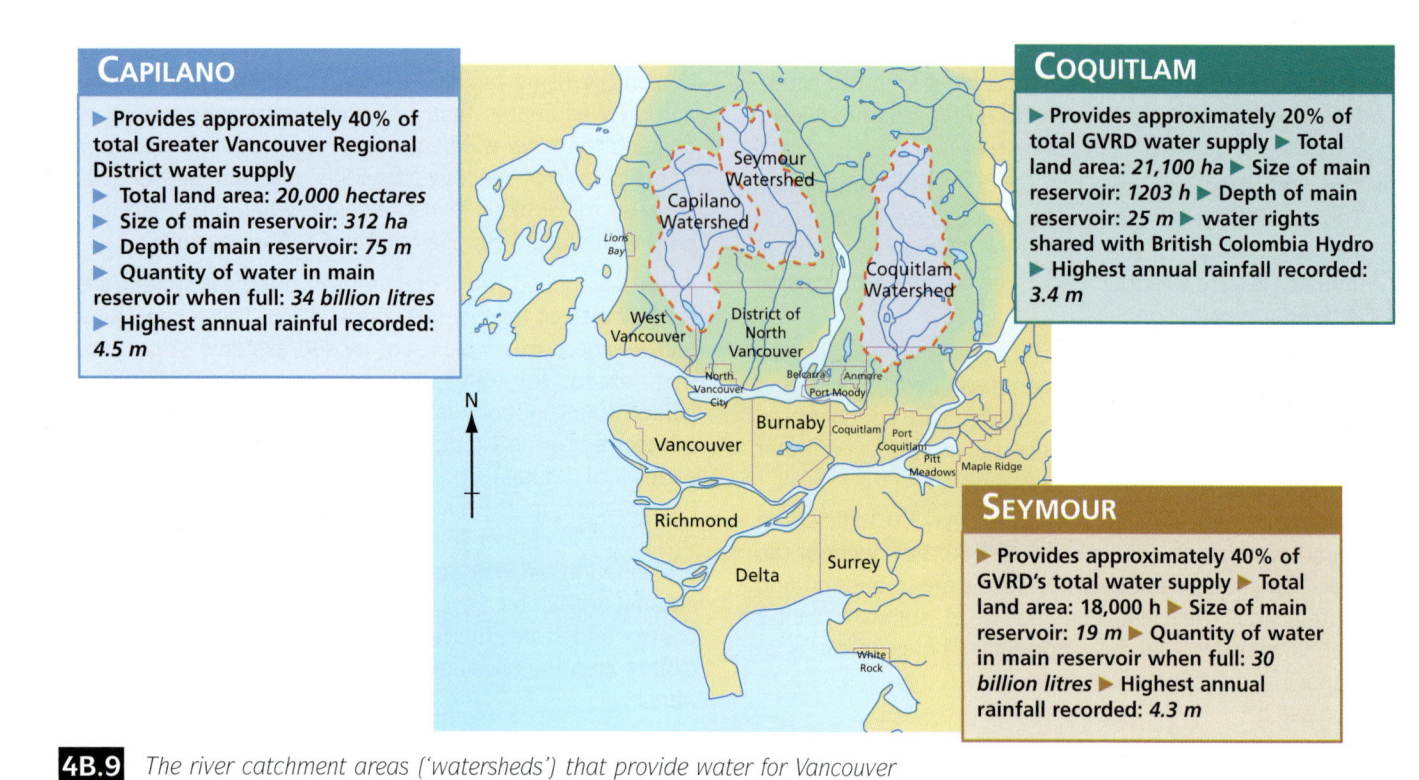

CAPILANO
- Provides approximately 40% of total Greater Vancouver Regional District water supply
- Total land area: 20,000 hectares
- Size of main reservoir: 312 ha
- Depth of main reservoir: 75 m
- Quantity of water in main reservoir when full: 34 billion litres
- Highest annual rainful recorded: 4.5 m

COQUITLAM
- Provides approximately 20% of total GVRD water supply
- Total land area: 21,100 ha
- Size of main reservoir: 1203 h
- Depth of main reservoir: 25 m
- water rights shared with British Colombia Hydro
- Highest annual rainfall recorded: 3.4 m

SEYMOUR
- Provides approximately 40% of GVRD's total water supply
- Total land area: 18,000 h
- Size of main reservoir: 19 m
- Quantity of water in main reservoir when full: 30 billion litres
- Highest annual rainfall recorded: 4.3 m

4B.9 *The river catchment areas ('watersheds') that provide water for Vancouver*

Figure 4B.10). Residents of the city were only allowed to water their lawns twice a week during the summer. The watering of gardens doubled the quantity of water used (see Figure 4B.11). All new homes in Vancouver were fitted with water-saving toilets and showers, which could cut domestic use by as much as half.

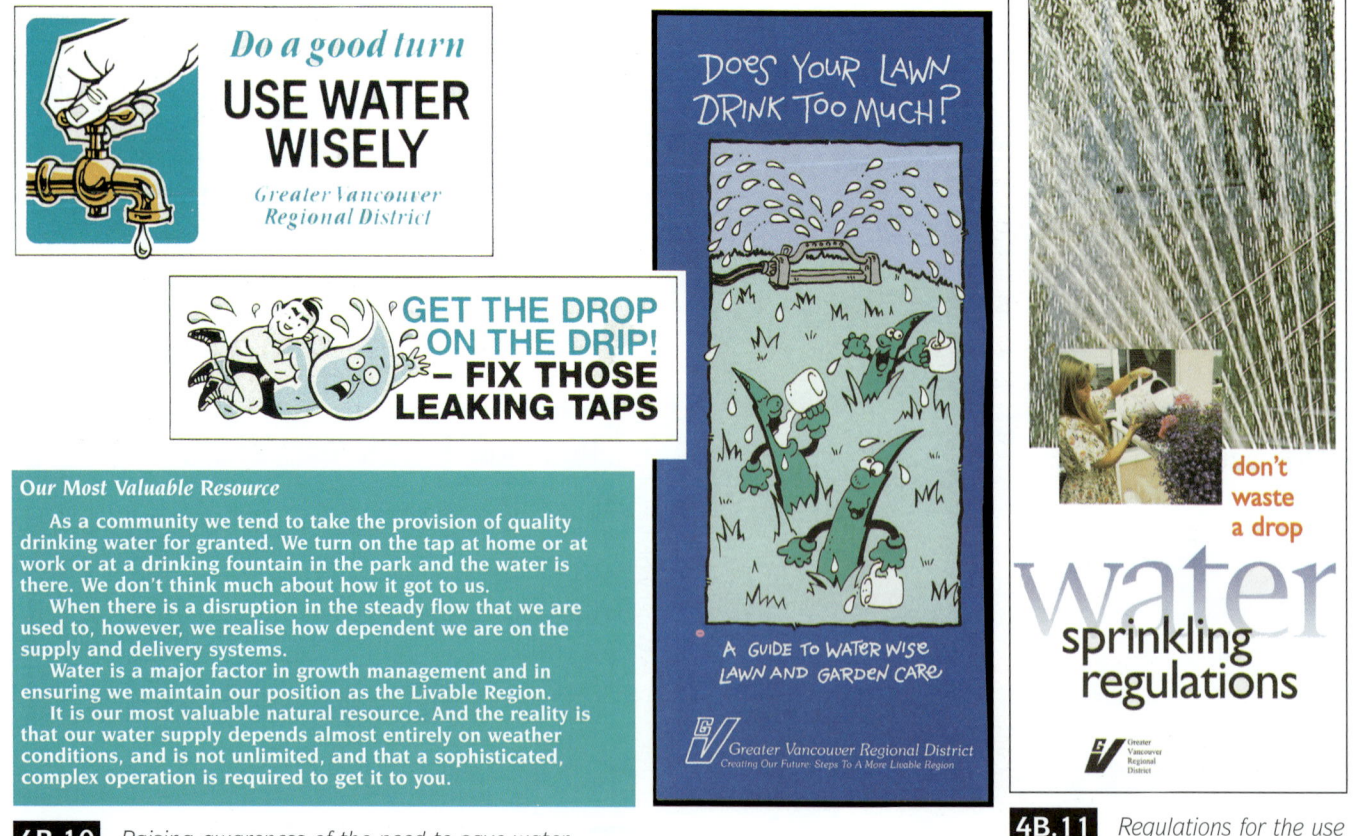

Do a good turn — USE WATER WISELY — *Greater Vancouver Regional District*

GET THE DROP ON THE DRIP! – FIX THOSE LEAKING TAPS

Our Most Valuable Resource

As a community we tend to take the provision of quality drinking water for granted. We turn on the tap at home or at work or at a drinking fountain in the park and the water is there. We don't think much about how it got to us.

When there is a disruption in the steady flow that we are used to, however, we realise how dependent we are on the supply and delivery systems.

Water is a major factor in growth management and in ensuring we maintain our position as the Livable Region.

It is our most valuable natural resource. And the reality is that our water supply depends almost entirely on weather conditions, and is not unlimited, and that a sophisticated, complex operation is required to get it to you.

DOES YOUR LAWN DRINK TOO MUCH?
A GUIDE TO WATER WISE LAWN AND GARDEN CARE
Greater Vancouver Regional District — *Creating Our Future: Steps To A More Livable Region*

don't waste a drop — water sprinkling regulations
Greater Vancouver Regional District

4B.10 *Raising awareness of the need to save water*

4B.11 *Regulations for the use of water*

B Water supply and management

The future management of Vancouver's water supplies aims to reduce the consumption of water per person, rather than increasing supplies. The building of new dams to collect water in the three catchment areas would be costly, with implications for the natural environment. Dams disrupt the ecosystem of rivers, and may affect local climates. They also have dramatic effects upon the scenery of upland regions. The greatest pressure is likely to come from the expansion of population in the region. There is growing demand for access to the catchment areas for recreation, housing and transport, pressures that are likely to increase in the future.

EXTENDED ACTIVITY

Your water supply

1. Which company manages water supply in the area where you live?
2. Where does your water supply come from?
3. What are the issues with water supply in the area where you live?
4. If there are any local issues, how are they being solved?
5. In what ways are you encouraged to save water?

NOTING ACTIVITIES

1. List the reasons why water management is an important issue in Canada.
2. Why are Canadians such high consumers of water?
3. What measures have the authorities in Vancouver taken to conserve water supplies?
4. What are the advantages and disadvantages of having 'closed' catchment areas, where there is no access to the public?
5. What other measures do you think could be taken to reduce water consumption in Vancouver?

CASE STUDY

Water supply in Spain

EXTENDED ACTIVITY

Look at Figure 4B.12. This shows the amount of water available in different parts of the world.

1. a Which two regions have the greatest potential amount of water available per person?
   b Which two regions have the least amount available?
2. Why is there so much difference in water availability between these regions?
3. List the regions according to the amount of potential water available per person, starting with the highest. (Use figures only for the regions, not whole continents.)
4. Draw a bar chart to show the potential water available for the world's regions. Plot the bars in order of water availability, starting with the highest on the left.
5. The Spanish government estimated recently that by 2010 average water demand would be 6000 m³ per person per year. Mark this amount on your graph by means of a vertical line.
6. Label all regions to the left of the line 'water surplus' and those to the right of the line 'water deficit'. Give your graph a title.
7. What does your completed graph suggest about the availability of water throughout the world?

As Figure 4B.12 shows, Canada has one of the highest levels of water per person. Spain is in southern Europe where water is more scarce, especially in the south of the country. What problems face Spain in managing its water supply? How successfully are the problems of water shortages being dealt with?

Shortage of water

The majority of the mainland of Spain suffers from a shortage of water. The problem does not affect the whole of the country. The north coast has heavy rainfall, towns such as Bilbāo and Santander receiving over 1200 mm per year. The situation is very different in southern Spain. Although Seville, for example, receives an average of 560 mm of rainfall per year, it is unreliable and unevenly distributed throughout the year (see Figure 4B.13).

Spain's water shortages are influenced by a variety of factors. Some of these are natural, and others (human factors) are caused by people.

Natural causes

- Average precipitation rates for Spain are low. Although the north coast has regular rainfall, most of central and southern Spain receives less than 600 mm per year. Almeria, a region in south-east Spain, has less than 160 mm of annual precipitation (see Figure 4B.14).

119

Section 4 Using and Abusing the Environment

Continent, region	Area (million km²)	Population (millions 1994)	Potential water availability (thous. m³/year) per person
Europe	10.46	684.7	4.24
Northern	1.32	23.2	30.4
Central	1.86	293	2.12
Southern	1.79	188	3.19
North of the European part of FSU	2.71	28.5	21.1
South of the European part of FSU	2.78	152	3.32
North America	24.3	453	17.4
Canada and Alaska	13.67	29	174
USA	7.84	261	7.03
Central America and Caribbean	2.74	163	6.82
Africa	30.1	708	5.72
Northern	8.78	157	0.71
Southern	5.11	83.5	5.29
East	5.17	193.5	3.94
West	6.96	211.3	5.22
Central	4.08	62.8	28.8
Asia	43.5	3445	3.92
North China and	8.29	482	2.13
Mongolia Southern	4.49	1214	1.76
Western	6.82	232	2.11
South-east	6.95	1404	4.78
Central and Kazakhstan	3.99	54	3.78
Siberia and Far east of Russia	12.76	42	76.7
Transcaucasia	0.19	16	4.63
South America	17.9	314.5	38.3
Northern	2.55	57.3	58.3
Eastern	8.51	159.1	45.1
Western	2.33	48.6	35.4
Central	4.46	49.4	22.5
Australia and Oceania	8.95	28.7	83.8
Australia	7.68	17.9	19.7
Oceania	1.27	10.8	190
The World	135	5634	7.59

4B.12 World availability of water

Seville (9 metres above sea level)	Jan	Feb	Mar	Apr	May	Jun	Jul	Aug	Sep	Oct	Nov	Dec
Temperature: max. (° C)	15	17	20	24	27	32	36	36	32	26	20	16
Temperature: min. (° C)	6	7	9	11	13	17	20	20	18	14	10	7
Rainfall (mm)	66	61	90	57	41	8	1	5	19	70	67	79

4B.13 Climate data for Seville, Spain

B Water supply and management

4B.14 *Almeria is one of the driest places in Europe*

- Temperatures are high, particularly in the summer months. Daytime temperatures in Seville frequently reach 40°C. Main streets in the city have canopies overhead to protect people from the sun. The heat causes high evaporation rates, leaving less rainfall actually available. The amount of usable water is called the **water balance** (see Figure 4B.15). It is clear from the map that most of Spain suffers from a water deficit. The south-east of the country has the most severe water deficit in Europe.
- Throughout much of Spain rainfall is seasonal and unreliable. Lowest rainfall figures are in the summer months, when temperatures and evaporation rates are greatest. Droughts are frequent.
- The distribution of rainfall in Spain is so uneven that some parts of the country have a water surplus while other parts suffer from a shortage. Water is a natural resource that is very costly and inefficient to transport over long distances. The regions of greatest surplus and shortage are at opposite ends of the Spanish mainland.

Human factors

- Demand is increasing. The Spanish government estimates that, by 2010, there could be severe water shortages in much of the mainland of Spain.
- Farmers use 80 per cent of available water, and the amount is growing. Many of the ways in which water is used is inefficient, with much being wasted.
- The demand for water by farmers is greatest in the summer months. This is when there is least rainfall.
- Reservoirs built to store water to supply dry regions have caused problems. The arid regions of Spain suffer from soil erosion. Much of this soil is washed in to rivers, but gets stuck behind dams. This reduces the amount of water that can be stored in reservoirs. Evaporation is also a problem. As well as wasting water, evaporation in reservoirs leads to a concentration of salts, which encourages the growth of algae. This process of **eutrophication** has become a problem in many dry parts of Spain.
- The amount of water lost through leakage in Spain is among the worst in Europe, with 28 per cent of water lost by leakage from pipes. In some of the poorer parts of the country this figure is as high as 50 per cent.
- Water conservation measures are unpopular and not generally followed by people. They are seen as unnecessary by many people.
- Tourism places the greatest strain on water usage in some parts of the country. The poorer south of Spain relies heavily on income from overseas tourists. Holidaymakers are heavy users of water, and the greatest demand is in the summer months when there is least rainfall. In 1998, 62 million visitors added to the Spanish population of 40 million. It is difficult to predict future numbers of tourists, and therefore planning future water demands is a problem.

Managing water supplies

Although water is in short supply in much of Spain, it is still relatively cheap for people to use. One of the biggest problems for managing the country's water supplies is that many Spanish people do not think there is a problem. Farmers pay less than 0.3 pence per cubic metre for their water. Although urban residents pay much more, it is still much less than people pay in the UK (about 80 pence per m^3). This means that there is relatively little money available to spend on improving water supplies in Spain. It costs more to supply water than people pay for it. For water supplies to improve, it is likely that people will have to be prepared to pay much more for their water.

To keep pace with increasing demand for water, more people have turned to using **underground supplies** to provide their water. Water that seeps down below the ground surface over a long period of time is stored there, and may be drawn up by means of pumps and wells. The advantages of using underground supplies are that the water is available all year round, and may be tapped from beneath even the driest parts of the country.

Using underground supplies of water has also created problems. The water has collected over a long period of time, often over many thousands of years. It is being extracted at a much faster rate than it is being replaced, using up a valuable resource. As more water is removed, so the upper level of water, or **water table**, is lowered. This makes it more difficult for plants to reach the water, and more costly for people to do so.

Section 4 Using and Abusing the Environment

In coastal regions, the over-use of underground water has caused further problems. As the water table is lowered, salt water from the sea seeps in. This then contaminates the drinking water and destroys crops (see Figure 4B.16). The lowering of the water table is also causing marsh regions to dry up. Using these supplies of water from beneath the surface is providing a short-term solution to Spain's water supply problem, but it is not sustainable in the long term.

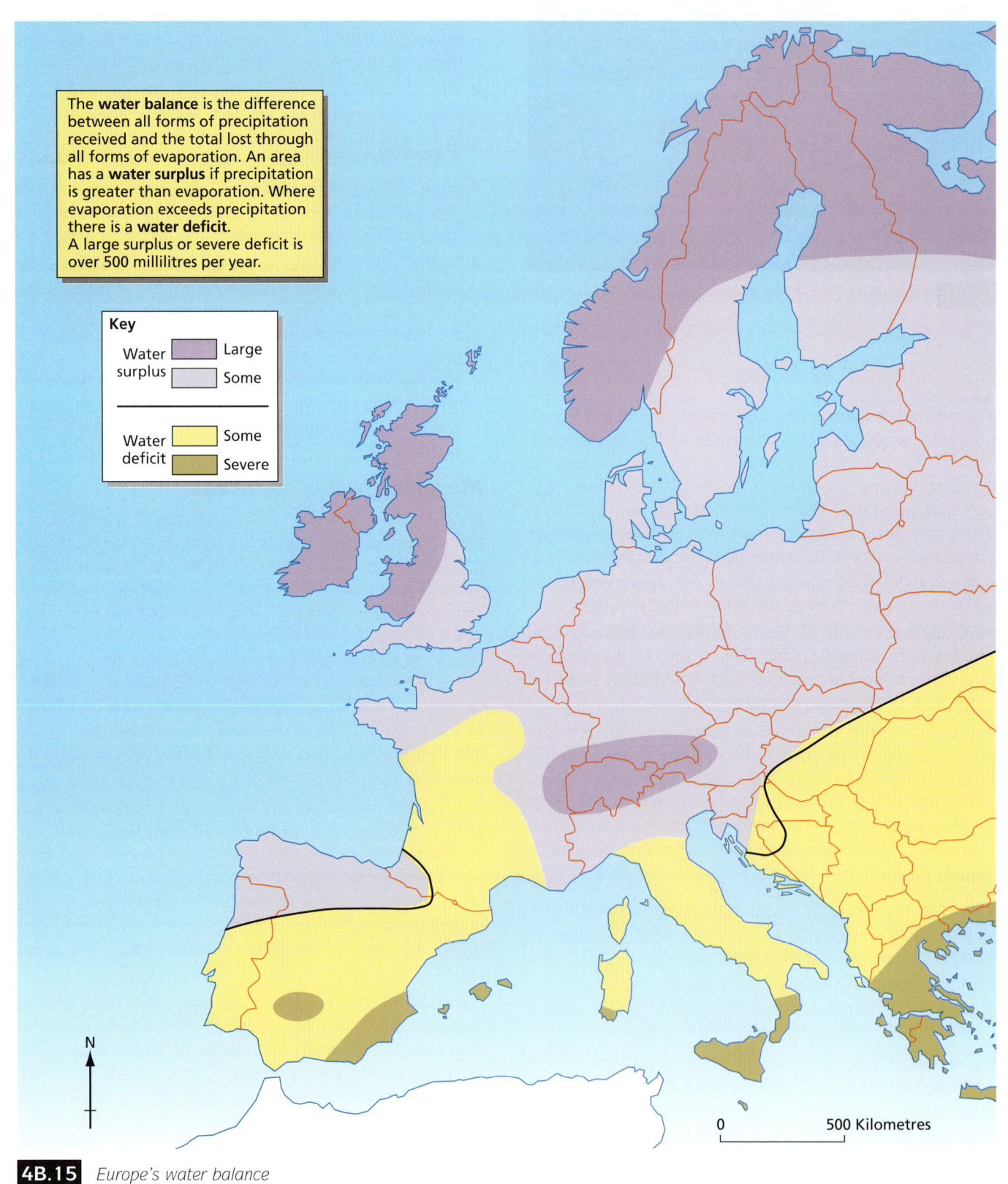

The **water balance** is the difference between all forms of precipitation received and the total lost through all forms of evaporation. An area has a **water surplus** if precipitation is greater than evaporation. Where evaporation exceeds precipitation there is a **water deficit**.
A large surplus or severe deficit is over 500 millilitres per year.

Key
Water surplus: Large / Some
Water deficit: Some / Severe

4B.15 *Europe's water balance*

B Water supply and management

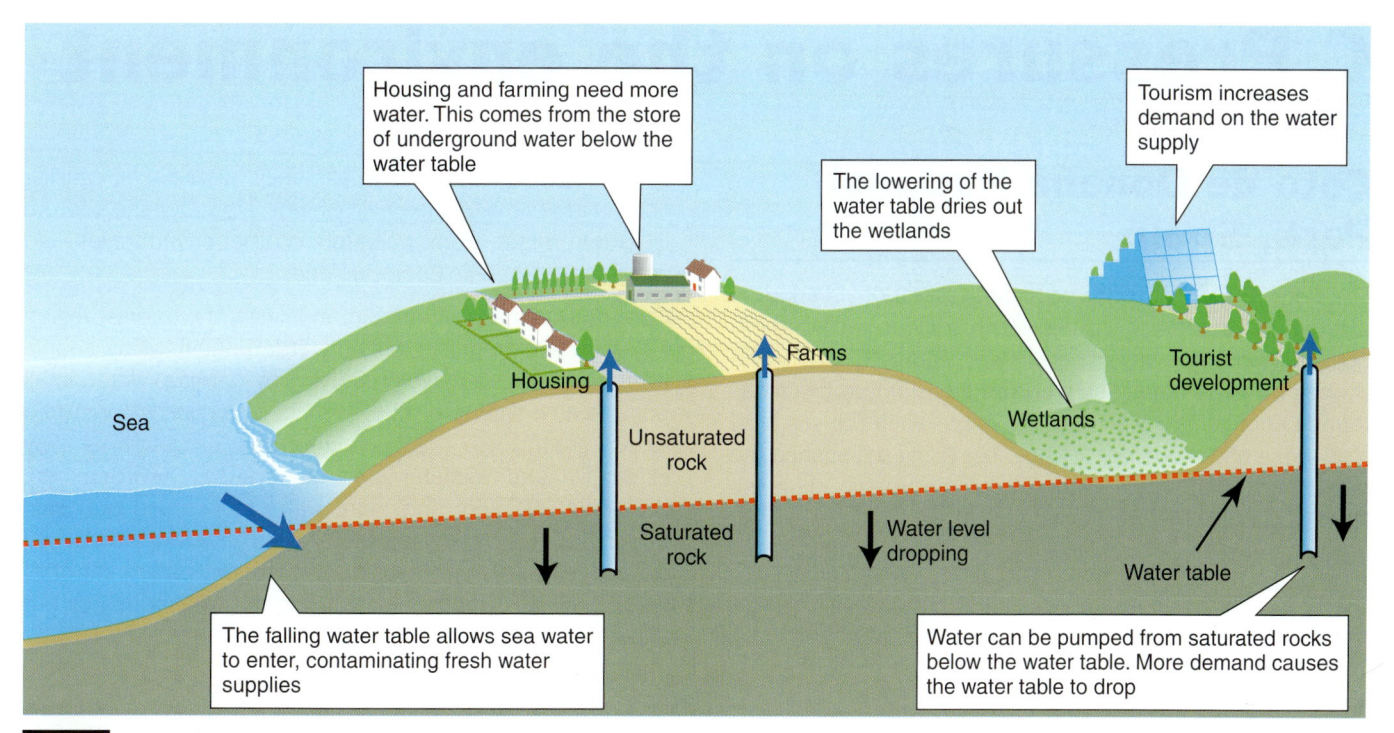

4B.16 *The use of underground water supplies has caused particular problems in coastal regions of Spain*

To manage water supplies longer term, the Spanish authorities have undertaken a large-scale programme of dam building to store water for use in times of greatest demand. Madrid, for example, is now circled by more than sixty reservoirs that provide the city with water. There have been attempts to conserve water in homes and businesses, but it is estimated that this will save less than 2 per cent of the total water consumption.

Farming remains the biggest user of water. More efficient irrigation methods have been tried, along with the possibility of growing crops which require less water. This could even enable the cultivation of crops which grow when rainfall levels are highest. While cities and industries have taken some measures to reduce water use, the demand for water by agriculture continues to grow. Without significant reductions in this sector of industry, Spain's water supply problems will increase in the future.

NOTING ACTIVITIES

1. Draw a climate graph to show the information in Figure 4B.13.

2. Find similar data for the region in which you live. Draw a graph to show this data.

3. What are the main similarities and differences between your two graphs? Give reasons for your answer.

4. Complete two case study cards on water management:

   a for Canada

   b for Spain.

Section 4 **Using and Abusing the Environment**

C Pressures on the environment

Coto de Doñana National Park, Spain

The Coto de Doñana is Europe's largest National Park. It is located on the estuary of the River Guadalquivir in southern Spain, south of the city of Seville (see Figure 4C.1). Doñana is one of the few remaining **wetland** areas in Europe. It was formed approximately 10 000 years ago, when the sea level rose at the end of the last Ice Age. The rising sea pushed the original coastline back nearly 20 kilometres, flooding the lower section of the River Guadalquivir.

The area is a fragile environment that is home to a wide variety of plants and animals, as well as a stopping point for migrating birds. It has always been used by people, for example for rearing cattle and hunting wild boar. Until recently this use of the land has been sustainable, causing little or no harm to the environment. Now Doñana's future is under threat from pollution of the environment and conflicting demands upon the land.

Coto de Doñana is situated in Andalusia, the poorest region in Spain. The area also has very little rainfall. Many people living in Andalusia make their living by farming. With rainfall being scarce and unreliable, farmers often use water stored under ground to irrigate their crops. Irrigation is very expensive and wasteful, and also causes environmental problems. As more and more water is pumped out from under ground, so the water table falls. This allows nearby sea water to enter, contaminating fresh water supplies (see Figure 4B.16). It is also causing the wetland to dry out (Figure 4C.3).

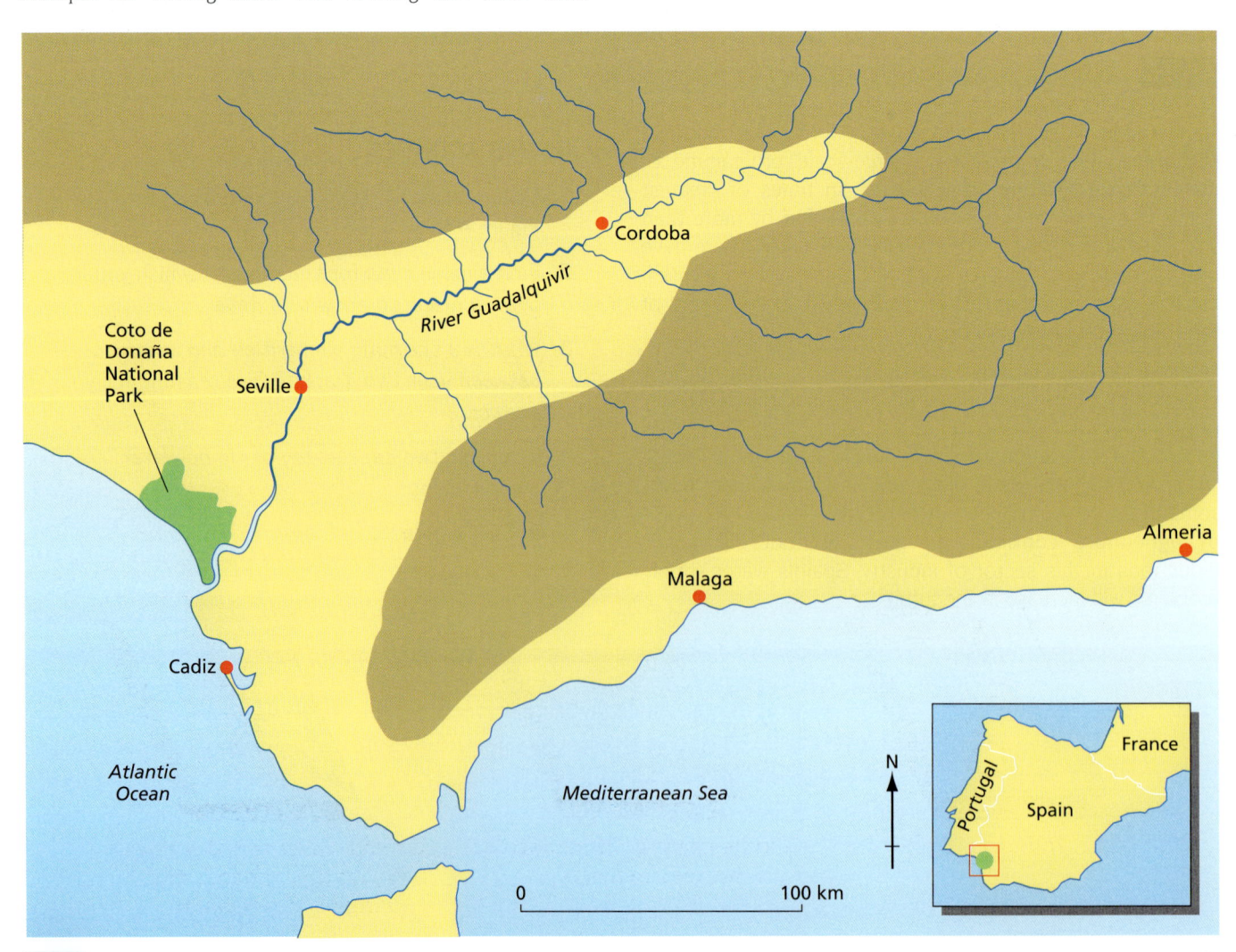

4C.1 *Location of the Coto de Doñana National Park*

C Pressures on the environment

In recent years the environment has come under increasing pressure from tourism. The hot Mediterranean climate and sandy beaches have made the southern coast of Spain a popular tourist destination for foreign visitors. The economy of Andalusia relies heavily upon money spent by these holidaymakers, and so the Spanish government encourages tourism.

The development of holiday resorts conflicts with the needs of farmers. People taking holidays use far more water than do the locals. Most people visit the Mediterranean in summer, at a time when water is at its most scarce. Many people have abandoned their farms to work in the tourist industry, but this generally offers only part-time and poorly paid jobs. Tourism also has a visual impact on the environment, for example with the building of large hotel complexes (see Figure 4C.4).

The region is also under threat from industrial development. In addition to the extraction of salt, there are valuable deposits of zinc, lead and silver that are mined. It was in response to increasing pressures on the environment that the Spanish government in 1969 designated Coto de Doñana as a National Park. Its worldwide importance as a natural environment was also recognised in 1994 when it became a United Nations *World Heritage Site*. These measures should have meant that the Park was safe from further

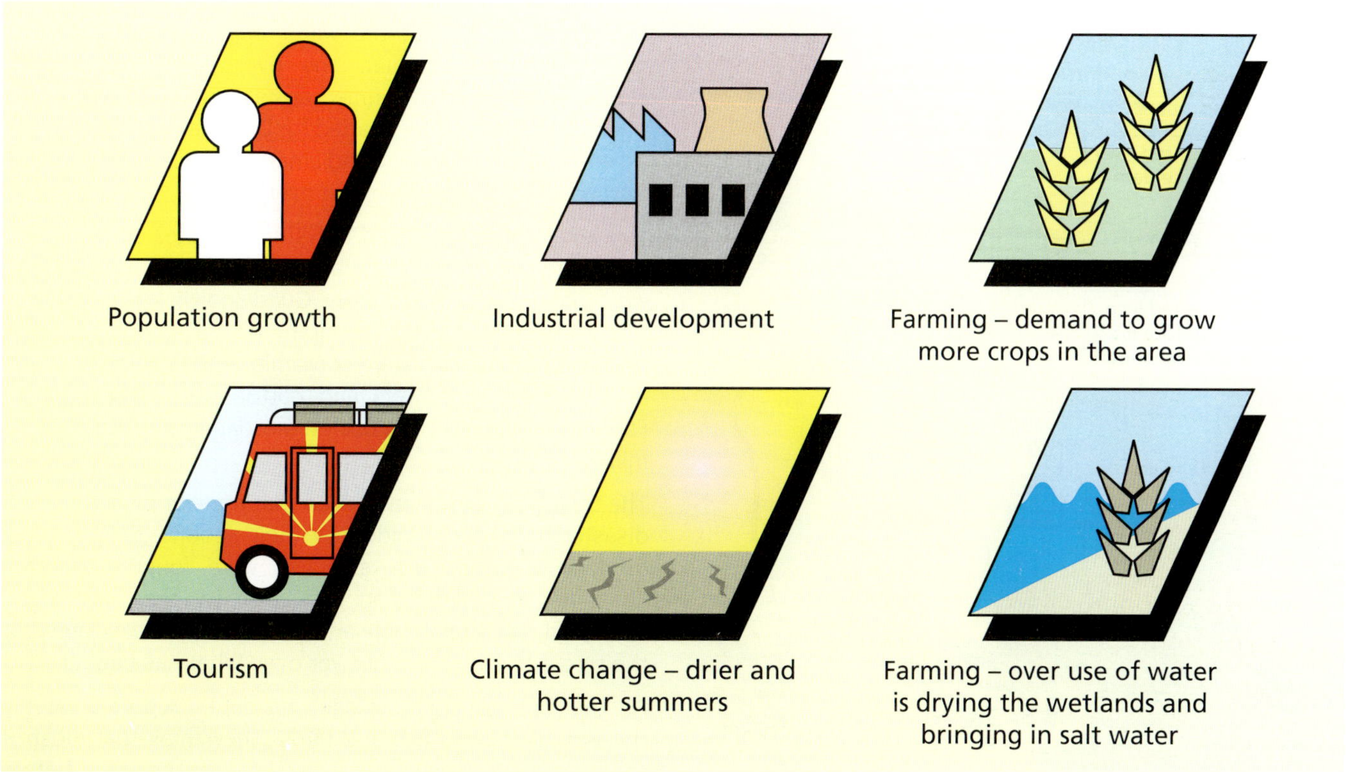

4C.2 Doñana is home to rare wildlife

4C.3 Pressures on the environment

Population growth

Industrial development

Farming – demand to grow more crops in the area

Tourism

Climate change – drier and hotter summers

Farming – over use of water is drying the wetlands and bringing in salt water

Section 4 Using and Abusing the Environment

4C.4 *Tourist developments often have a major impact on the local environment*

development. Unfortunately, the conflicting demands made upon the use of the land was soon to lead to a crisis for Doñana.

The Aznacollar disaster

The Aznacollar mine is located 25 kilometres to the north of Doñana National Park (see Figure 4C.5). Owned by a Canadian transnational company, the mine extracted zinc, copper, silver and lead. The mining of these metals produces poisonous waste water. This was stored behind a dam near to the mine before being treated to make it safe.

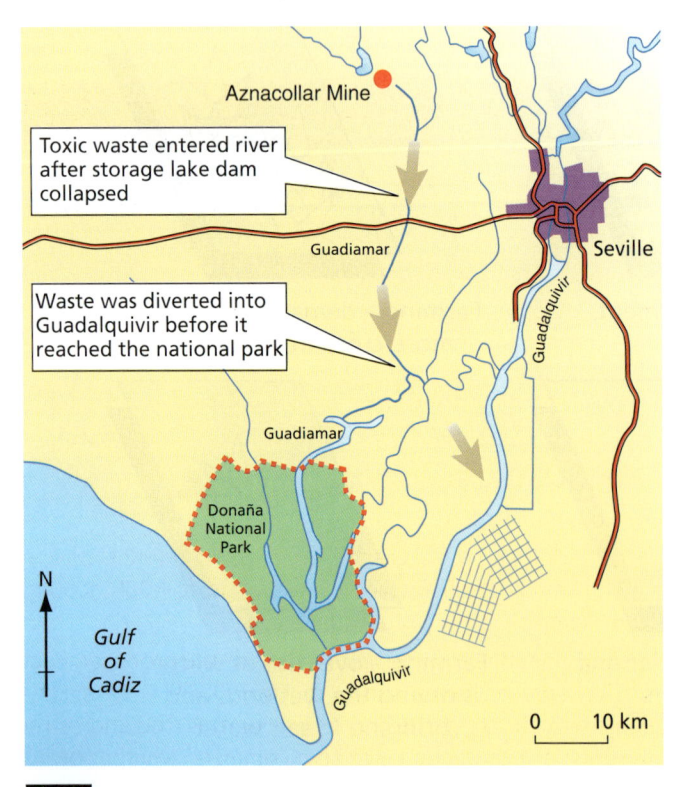

4C.5 *The location of the Aznacollar mine*

4C.6 *Lorries carry material to seal the dam in an attempt to halt the leak of toxic waste*

In April 1998 the dam broke, releasing 5 million cubic metres of waste water. Lorries tried to seal the dam with rocks and soil (Figure 4C.6), but the water began to flow into the nearby River Guadiamar. The river flows through the National Park, and environmentalists feared a disaster as the thick black waste water headed for Doñana. Residents of the seven towns along the Guadiamar and local farmers were warned to keep away from the river.

The local authorities used a system of gates and dams to divert the poisonous waste away from the National Park. It was channelled into the River Guadalquivir, and eventually out to sea. As a direct result of the disaster, over 5000 hectares of rice fields were contaminated. Other crops such as tomatoes, sunflowers and cotton were also affected. Farmers estimated the cost of the damage to be over £8 million.

The Spanish government stated that a major environmental disaster had been avoided by their actions. Only a small number of dead birds and fish were found along the coastline, and permission was given for the mine to be reopened. Yet local people and environmentalists claim that the threat to Doñana is not yet over. What has happened?

At the time of the spillage, residents reported seeing thousands of dead fish and birds. They think that most of these were removed by the local authorities before newspaper and television reporters arrived. This made the

C Pressures on the environment

problem appear to be less serious. Environmentalists said that as the poisonous waste was in the River Guadalquivir in the first place, some would be bound to seep into the National Park as the river flowed through. The waste was so poisonous that it would kill any plants and animals with which it came into contact. Once into the delicate ecosystem, the toxic waste could remain a danger for many years to come.

Environmentalists are worried about the effects on migrating birds which stop at Doñana. They think that birds could be poisoned, and could contaminate the areas to which they then fly. Figure 4C.7 is a press release that shows some of their concerns.

4C.8 *Plastic greenhouses are used to grow vegetables to sell throughout Europe*

Matalascas has grown up as a mass of concrete apartments for tourists, whose increasing numbers are damaging the fragile environment.

Local residents are angry at the way the government of Andalusia has given in to pressures to allow more building in the area. Under Spanish law, development is restricted if an area is classified as rural. The local government, despite the lack of population living near Doñana, has reclassified some of the region as urban. This then allows more development to take place. In particular, a local businessman plans to build two villages of 3000 homes, together with golf courses, country clubs and other leisure facilities. As urban areas, such developments do not have to conform to water restriction laws, as do other land users.

DOÑANA DISASTER NOT OVER

More than 70,000 birds, including thousands from the UK, have been heavily contaminated by the toxic sludge which spilled from the Aznacollar mine in Spain on 25 April 1998, say Spanish conservationists. Despite continuing environmental risks the Spanish authorities have authorised the re-opening of the mine. The Royal Society for the Protection of Birds (RSPB) believes that the Doñana disaster will have a long-term effect on wildlife that uses the area.

After the spill, fish were poisoned and small invertebrates and vegetation were contaminated by heavy metals. These were the foodstuff of many of the birds that overwinter in Doñana and which will be making their return journey to northern European breeding grounds.

4C.7 *The RSPB's concerns*

The future of the Park

Doñana is under extreme pressure for different kinds of land use. Mining and industrial development are not the only problems facing the National Park. To improve the Spanish economy, farmers have been encouraged to grow more crops. Many farmers have started to grow vegetables under huge plastic greenhouses (Figure 4C.8). With the help of money from the European Union, the region is also being opened up by a network of new roads. The town of

EXTENDED ACTIVITY

The local authorities have received an application for a development in an area known as Laiguel, on the outskirts of the village Sanlucar de Barrameda. This is just outside the Coto de Doñana National Park.

The proposed development is to include:

- a golf course
- two large luxury hotels
- a shopping centre
- two polo pitches
- a botanic garden
- a 'traditional Andalusian village' of self-catering holiday homes, capable of accommodating up to 3000 holiday-makers.

A public meeting is to be held to discuss the proposal. Each of the representatives shown in Figure 4C.9 is to make a short speech to put their own viewpoint. At the end of the meeting, a vote will be taken to recommend whether or not the development should take place.

Section 4 Using and Abusing the Environment

For this activity, you should work in a group of five people. Each person should adopt one of the roles shown in Figure 4C.9.

1 Prepare and give a short speech outlining your opinion in the role you have adopted. The speech should last for two to three minutes. One person should act as chairperson for the meeting, and allow time for questions.

2 At the end of the meeting, take a vote in role as to whether the development should take place.

3 Out of role, write about the main points that were raised at the meeting. What is your own opinion about the proposed development?

Mining engineer

Aznacollar was a 'one-off'. It won't happen again. Anyway, we provide more jobs in the area than any other industry except tourism. People say that we change the landscape with our mining. People have always changed Doñana. It has been used as an aristocratic hunting ground for centuries, and most of the vegetation has been planted by people. If the local economy is going to thrive, it needs industries like ours.

Property developer

New hotels and leisure facilities bring in more money to the area. This money can then be used to maintain the quality of the local environment. We also provide better quality roads and other facilities such as shops and restaurants. Surely it is better if development is planned, rather than just taking place anywhere. Our developments will also provide new homes and jobs for local people.

Local farmer

The increased demand for water from tourists, industry and housing has had a devastating effect on our livelihood. The authorities take too much water from under the ground, as there is not enough rainfall. This is drying out our fields, and drawing salt in from the coast. Tourists use so much more water than we do, and at a time of year when it is very scarce. Much more pressure and we will be driven out.

Conservationist

Any further developments in or near to the Park would be a disaster. Look at what happened at Aznacollar! The pollution is likely to carry on for years. There is a wider variety of wildlife in Doñana than anywhere else in Spain. Some species are under threat, such as the lynx. The government should give as much money for conservation as it is prepared to give to developers. There should be a zone of twenty kilometres around the Park where no more building is allowed.

Representative of tourist company

There is no need to make further restrictions on tourists. Visitors have to buy a pass which gives them access to a guided tour of the main features of Doñana. Trying to restrict numbers in the future is only likely to hurt the local economy: tourists bring money into the area, which after all is in one of Spain's poorest regions.

4C.9 *Some opinions of people affected by the proposed development*

C Pressures on the environment

Leisure and the environment

People in the United Kingdom are spending more time and money on leisure and recreation. Millions of people take their main holiday abroad, and spend time on short breaks or day visits within the UK. The development of the motorway network has made most parts of England, Wales and large areas of Scotland accessible by road for day visitors. Over 25 million people each year visit the Lake District for example, the largest proportion travelling from London. The increased use of the countryside puts pressure on the environment, which needs careful management (see Figure 4C.10).

4C.10 *Managing footpath erosion*

To understand the impact that people have upon the environment, it is helpful to define the term 'environment'. There are no entirely natural environments in the United Kingdom; all are to some extent the result of human action. An environment is a location with a certain set of features, which may cover only a few square kilometres, or many thousands. Within any environment, there are three different types of feature.

1 Natural (or physical) These are features that are entirely the result of natural processes, for example landforms that are the result of weathering and erosion.

2 Built This refers to anything in the environment that is constructed by people. Many environments in the United Kingdom are dominated by built features, such as roads and houses.

3 Managed These features result from people deliberately changing an environment. Farming is a good example of an environment that is managed.

Most environments are complex, and may contain elements of all these features. How easy is it to identify them in a landscape?

> **NOTING ACTIVITIES**
>
> 1 List the three components of environments, giving two examples of each.
>
>   Look at Figure 4C.11, which shows an environment in the Lake District National Park.
>
> 2 Draw an outline sketch to show the main features shown in the photograph.
>
> 3 Using three different colours, annotate your sketch to show the natural, built and managed features you have drawn.
>
> 4 Repeat this process for the area in which you live. Produce an annotated sketch to show your local environment.

4C.11 *An environment in the Lake District*

The National Parks

What issues face two contrasting National Parks in England, the Lake District and Dartmoor? How are these issues being dealt with?

The first National Parks of England and Wales were established in 1949. They were to be:

- areas of natural beauty, eg mountains, rivers and lakes
- places where people would have the opportunity for outdoor recreation, such as walking and pony trekking
- protected by law so that the natural beauty of the areas could be preserved.

Section 4 Using and Abusing the Environment

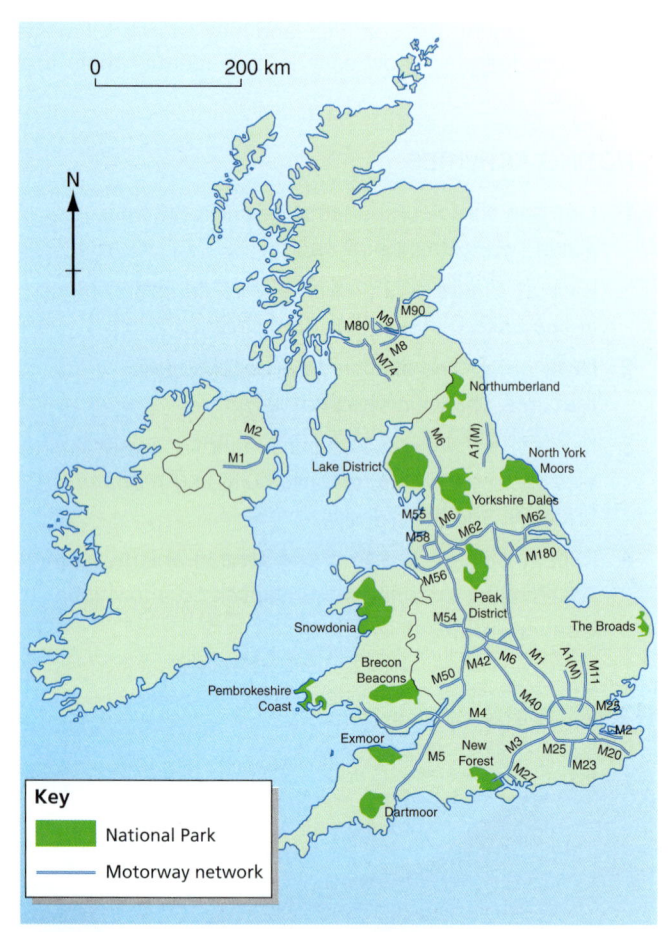

4C.12 *The National Parks*

The oldest National Parks are the Lake District, Snowdonia, the Peak District and Dartmoor. Six more areas have since been designated as National Parks (see Figure 4C.12). The Broads, occupying part of Norfolk and Suffolk, has similar status although not officially classified as a National Park. All of the Parks are in England and Wales, as there is no equivalent in Scotland or Northern Ireland. The National Parks occupy about 10 per cent of the total area of England and Wales.

The name 'National' Park is rather misleading. The Parks are not publicly owned, and people do not have unlimited access to all parts of them. Although there are National Park Authorities, the majority of land is privately owned. Farming remains an important land use, as well as the Forestry Commission and the Water Authorities. This situation is different from that in the United States and the mainland of Europe, where National Parks are government property.

The law covering management of the National Parks was changed in 1995. It was thought that the original laws were too much in favour of visitors, and ignored the views of people who lived in the Parks and the need to conserve the natural environment. As a result, the 1995 Environment Act stated that the National Parks should:

conserve and enhance natural beauty, wildlife and cultural heritage; and promote opportunities for the understanding of the special qualities of the Parks by the public.

CASE STUDY

Dartmoor

Dartmoor National Park occupies an area of nearly 1000 square kilometres in south-west England (see Figure 4C.13). Dartmoor is one of the less accessible National Parks from major urban areas, the majority of visitors travelling from elsewhere in the south-west of England. Despite this, it is located between two major roads (the A30 and A38) which link to the motorway system. Dartmoor receives over 10 million visitors per year, a number set to increase in the future.

Dartmoor is a mixture of steep wooded valleys, farmland, and wild open moorland. It is well known for its outcrops of granite called tors (see Figure 4C.14, bottom right). The environment of Dartmoor is under pressure from many different groups of people. What problems does this create, and what attempts have been made to solve them?

Pressures on Dartmoor

How is the land in Dartmoor used? The land uses in the National Park are not always to the benefit of the environment.

Farming

Approximately 10 per cent of the 30 000 people living in Dartmoor are farmers. The highest central areas of the Park are home to sheep and cattle, while sheltered valleys on the edges are used for both arable and pastoral farming. Much of the high land of Dartmoor is ancient *common land*. This is open moorland that farmers living in the area may use to graze cattle or sheep. More recently, it was agreed that members of the public should have free access to all common land for walking and pony trekking.

Farmers on Dartmoor receive grants from the government to encourage them to continue farming. In recent years, farm incomes in the area have fallen sharply, as elsewhere in the country. This has resulted in some farmers leaving the region or turning to other jobs. The government is prepared to give money to Dartmoor farmers to enable them to make a living, as farming is important for the creation and maintenance of landscapes in the National Park.

Military use

The Ministry of Defence owns much of the highest part of

C Pressures on the environment

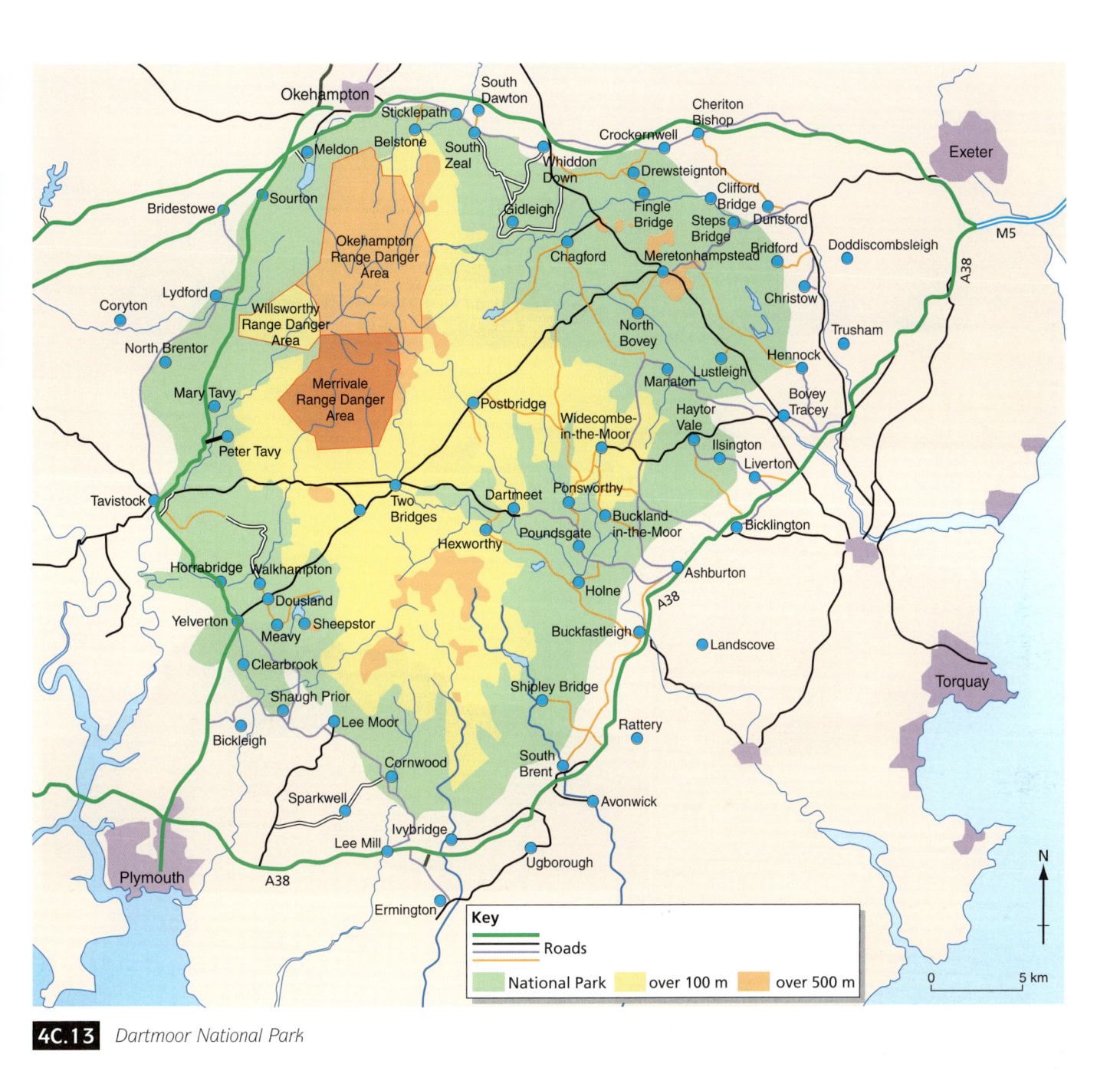

4C.13 Dartmoor National Park

central Dartmoor. This land is used for a range of military training exercises, some using live ammunition. Members of the public are warned in advance to keep away from the three firing ranges (see Figure 4C.15).

The National Park Authority and the Countryside Commission have both stated that military training is not suitable in a National Park. Live firing has damaged some of Dartmoor's ancient monuments, it disturbs wildlife, and also excludes the public from large areas of the Park. Despite these viewpoints, the government has recently extended the facilities in the Park at Willsworthy Camp.

Water supply

There are no natural lakes on Dartmoor, and so the storage of water for drinking supplies has to be by means of artificially created reservoirs. Demand for water is heaviest in surrounding urban areas such as Exeter and Plymouth, and also in the summer months because of tourism.

The south-west of England has regular water shortages. There are currently eight reservoirs on Dartmoor, with pressure to build more in the future. The National Park Authority has refused to give permission for more reservoirs to be created within the boundaries of Dartmoor.

Section 4 Using and Abusing the Environment

4C.14 *Landscapes of Dartmoor*

Mining

Minerals have been extracted from the rocks of Dartmoor for centuries. Until recently tin, silver, lead and copper were all mined. Although these are now no longer important, china clay is extracted from within the Park. China clay, or *kaolin*, is used in the manufacture of porcelain. It is removed from large open quarries, especially in the south of Dartmoor. The quarry at Lee Moor, for example, is one of the largest china clay mines in the world. It is nearly 100 metres deep, and covers over 40 hectares.

The mining of china clay produces large quantities of waste. This is very costly to remove, and so is dumped near to the quarries (see Figure 4C.16). It also has a major impact upon the scenery of the National Park. Regulations now require mining companies to landscape disused quarries, but it will be many years before they return to a natural landscape. Pressure from the National Park Authority has had limited success in altering the plans of mining companies regarding the dumping of waste within the Park.

C Pressures on the environment

1999
Live military firing ranges

THE MINISTRY of Defence has a large training area on the northern part of the moor within which are three live firing ranges. They are used for live firing on a limited number of days each year. At all other times, the public has access on these Range Danger Areas.

The boundaries of the three Range Danger Areas are marked on the ground by a series of red and white posts and information boards on most of the main approaches. When wishing to walk in these areas, **firing times must be checked and warning signals heeded.** Care must be taken when walking is permitted on ranges. **Do not pick up any metal objects on a range.**

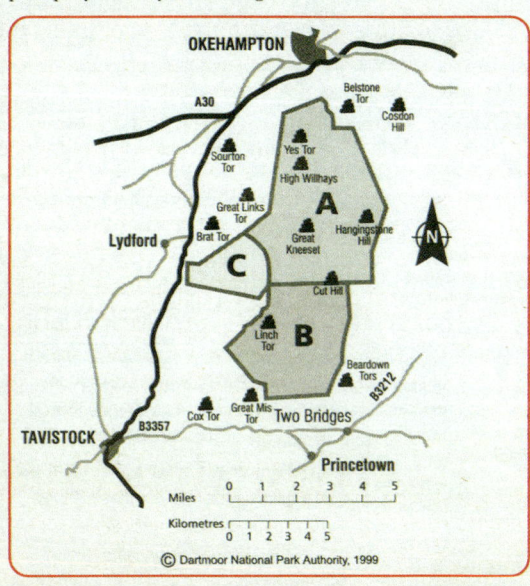

Specific non firing periods during 1999, when live firing does not take place on the Dartmoor Ranges and times when the public does have access are:

OKEHAMPTON RANGE (A)
There will be no firing:
- On any Saturday, Sunday, Monday and Public Holidays.
- During the months of April, May, July, August and the first 15 days of September 1999.
- From 9 November to 15 November 1999 inclusive.
- From 18 December to 3 January 2000 inclusive.

MERRIVALE RANGE (B)
There will be no firing:
- On any Saturday, Sunday, Monday and Public Holidays.
- From 1 April to 5 April 1999 inclusive (Easter).
- During the month of August.
- From 9 November to 15 November 1999 inclusive.
- From 21 December to 3 January 2000 inclusive.

WILLSWORTHY RANGE (C)
There will be no firing:
- On any Saturday or Sunday, except the weekend of each month containing the second Sunday.
- On public holidays.
- From 14 May to 16 May 1999 inclusive (Ten Tors Weekend).
- During the month of August.
- From 20 December to 3 January 2000 inclusive.

4C.15 *The firing of live ammunition takes place on three ranges on central Dartmoor*

4C.16 *China clay mining*

Forests

The river valleys around the edges of Dartmoor contain forests consisting mainly of oak trees. This is all that remains of extensive woodlands that used to cover all but the highest parts of the present day moorland.

The forests of Dartmoor are in decline. In all, 1000 hectares of woodland have preservation orders on them, but most are not managed in any way. There is pressure upon the remaining forests from farmers who want more land for sheep and cattle grazing. The National Park Authority will not allow the planting of trees on any areas of open moorland, aiming to preserve what is now seen as the traditional Dartmoor landscape.

Conservation

There is evidence that Dartmoor was inhabited as long ago as 3000 BC, when settlers began to clear woodland from the area. The National Park contains over 1000 ancient monuments, although others are continually being discovered. These ancient remains are under increasing pressure from farming, military activity and the growth of tourism.

Nearly 30 000 hectares of Dartmoor has been designated as *Sites of Special Scientific Interest* (SSSIs). This means that these areas have particular wildlife or landscape features that need to be preserved. The National Park Authority has monitored damage to the environment since 1977. There are now numerous projects aimed at maintaining the quality of the natural environment (see Figure 4C.17).

Tourism

Tourism puts the greatest pressure upon the environments of Dartmoor. Although less visited than some National Parks such as the Peak District, over 10 million people visit Dartmoor each year. Nearly half of these visitors travel from

133

Section 4 Using and Abusing the Environment

DART BIODIVERSITY PROJECT

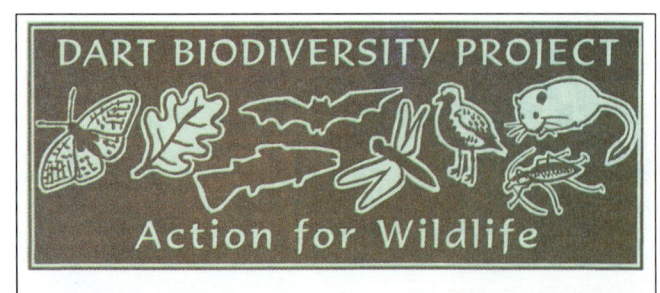

Action for Wildlife

The Dart Biodiversity Project is one of many schemes to protect wildlife. It aims to restore environments that have been altered by people, allowing a range of wildlife to thrive.

4C.17 *Five organisations have funded the Dart Biodiversity Project, including English Nature and the Environment Agency*

elsewhere in the south-west of England, particularly Plymouth and Torbay.

Most people travel to Dartmoor by car on day visits. There are few roads into the middle of the Park, so the majority of traffic is concentrated on the two main roads to the north and south of the Park boundary. Relatively few people travel to the centre of Dartmoor, and so one of the greatest pressures is on car park space and visitor facilities on the edges of the Park.

The National Park Authority has adopted a *Traffic Management Strategy* to cope with visitors arriving by car. Roads into Dartmoor are narrow and winding. There have been frequent accidents, involving both people and wildlife. A speed limit of 40 miles per hour is present on all roads. Routes are colour coded to advise drivers on the type of traffic they are able to carry (see Figure 4C.18).

Most people who visit the interior of Dartmoor leave their cars to walk or cycle. This has caused serious erosion of the land. Although erosion occurs naturally, it is made much worse by the actions of people who use the Park (see Figure 4C.19).

Green Routes ▶ Green routes are suitable for all vehicles and are national through routes.

Black Routes ▶ Black routes are A or B class roads, suitable for most types of traffic.

Blue Routes ▶ Blue routes are suitable for medium sized vehicles.

Brown Routes ▶ Brown routes are only suitable for cars and other small vehicles. Unsigned roads are only suitable for local access traffic.

FINGER POSTS ▶ Traditional finger signposts show roads which should only be used to local destinations.

4C.18 *Routes are graded for different types of traffic*

4C.19 *How the land is eroded in Dartmoor*

C Pressures on the environment

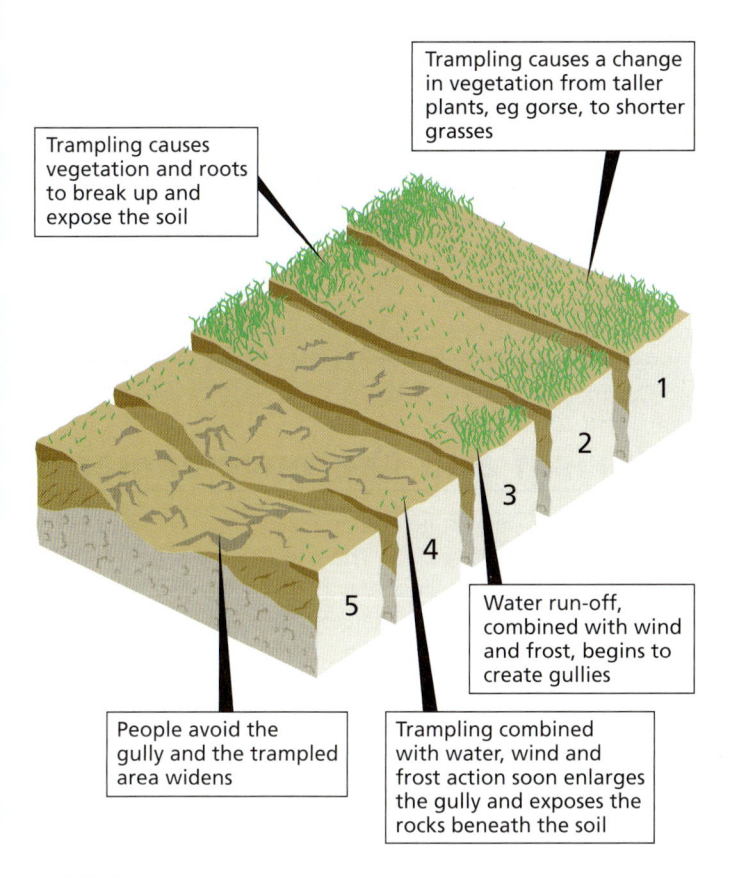

Figure 4C.20 labels:
- Trampling causes vegetation and roots to break up and expose the soil
- Trampling causes a change in vegetation from taller plants, eg gorse, to shorter grasses
- Water run-off, combined with wind and frost, begins to create gullies
- Trampling combined with water, wind and frost action soon enlarges the gully and exposes the rocks beneath the soil
- People avoid the gully and the trampled area widens

4C.20 *How footpaths are eroded*

Farmers, walkers, cyclists and pony trekkers all contribute to the erosion of the landscape. A narrow footpath, for example, may quickly be turned into a wide gash in the landscape by the trampling of visitors (Figure 4C.20).

To combat the problem, the National Park Authority has tried four different approaches.

1 Tell people about the damage they cause. The hope was that, if people know how much damage they may cause, they would be more careful. The National Park Authority introduced a publicity campaign called Moor Care to inform people of the damage caused by visitors (see Figure 4C.21).

2 Fine people who cause damage. If people knew they would be fined for causing damage to footpaths, they would take more care where they walked.

3 Fence off damaged areas. This would prevent people from walking on areas at greatest risk, allowing vegetation to recover.

4 Re-plant affected areas. Instead of allowing eroded paths to recover naturally, they could be repaired and re-planted.

How is Dartmoor managed?

The needs of many different groups of people will conflict. It is the job of the National Park Authority to manage the environments of the Park. Development within the boundaries of the National Park is strictly controlled. Any development has to have planning permission, agreed by the Park Authority. This is usually only allowed where a development is connected with farming or forestry, or is essential for the people who live and work in Dartmoor. Large areas of Dartmoor are conservation zones, including many villages. Within these areas, virtually no change is allowed, even to walls within a building. Over 1000 hectares of Dartmoor's trees are also protected.

Tread lightly on Dartmoor

We are asking YOU to act responsibly by taking MOOR CARE when spending time on Dartmoor. By doing this you will create LESS WEAR

4C.21 *Moor Care Less Wear*

Section 4 **Using and Abusing the Environment**

EXTENDED ACTIVITY

Moor Fun Holidays is an organisation that provides self-catering activity holidays in Britain and the rest of Europe. The company has put forward an application to build a new holiday centre inside the National Park, to the south of Okehampton (see Figure 4C.22).

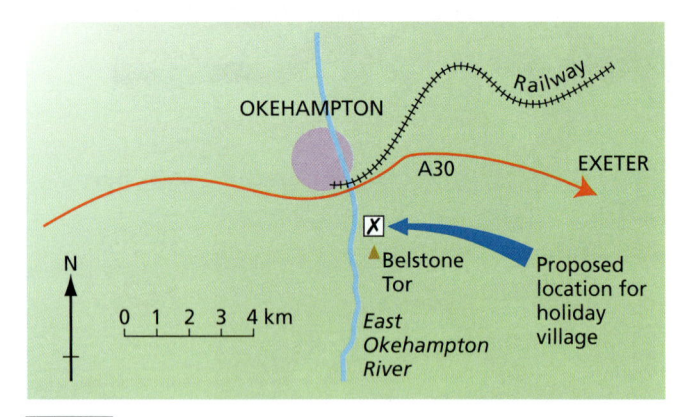

4C.22 *The proposed site for the new holiday village*

The plan involves the construction of accommodation for 1000 people, a water based activity centre, and a range of other indoor and outdoor facilities. The site would occupy about 500 hectares of low moorland near to the East Okehampton River and Belstone Tor. A new access road would have to be built to carry traffic to the centre from Okehampton. It is estimated that a new holiday village would create 500 jobs in an area of high unemployment, although half of these jobs would be seasonal.

ACTIVITY

1 What effects do each of the following have upon the environment in Dartmoor:
   a Farming
   b Military use
   c Water supply
   d Mining
   e Forestry
   f Conservation
   g Tourism?

2 For each of the following people, write down how you feel they would react to the proposal to locate a holiday village near Okehampton.
   a a member of the National Park Authority
   b a shopkeeper in Okehampton
   c a local farmer
   d a representative of the South-West England Tourist Board
   e a member of English Nature, a conservation organisation
   f an unemployed person living in Okehampton.

3 What is your opinion about the proposed development? Give reasons for your answer.

4 Imagine that you work for Moor Fun Holidays, and that your proposal has been accepted. Design a publicity leaflet to attract people to visit your new village in Dartmoor.

Tourism and the environment

Tourism is a major global industry and a source of employment worldwide. The most popular tourist destinations have traditionally been in Europe, although recently the pattern has changed (see Figure 4C.23). The greatest growth in tourism has been in LEDCs. This has involved people travelling within poorer parts of the world, and the growth of 'long haul' holidays from Europe and North America.

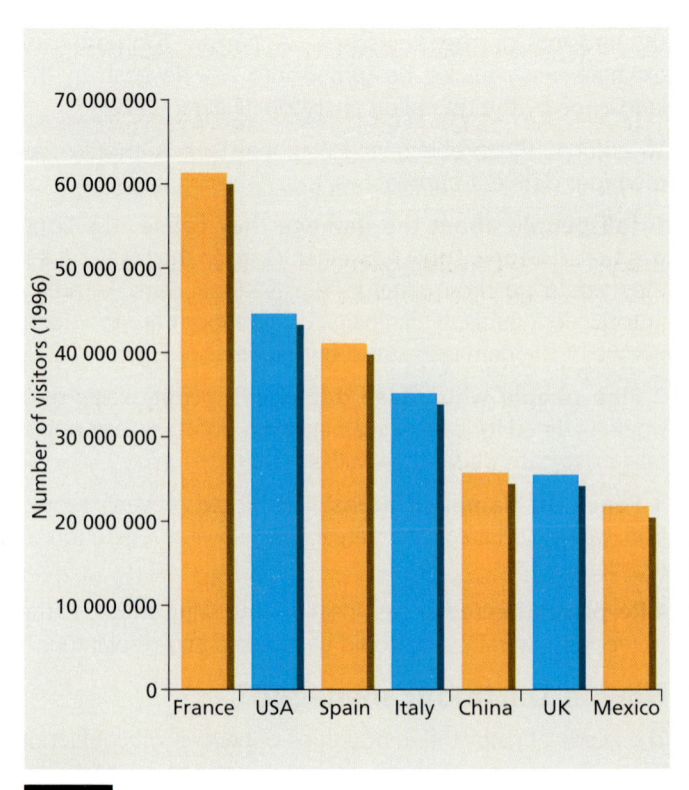

4C.23 *International tourist destinations*

C Pressures on the environment

4C.24 *The Seychelle Islands in the Indian Ocean*

The current expansion in tourism is due to a variety of factors.

1 Increased incomes People have more *disposable income*. This means that, after all regular bills and payments are made, more money is left to spend on other items such as holidays.

2 Longer paid holidays Annual paid holidays from work have increased, give people more opportunities to travel on holiday.

3 Package holidays The European holiday market remains the largest in the world, largely because of package holidays. Companies sell a holiday that includes transport, food and accommodation, often with extras like the cost of transfer to a hotel included.

4 Higher expectations The media, and people's own experiences, have led people to expect more from their holidays.

STRUCTURED QUESTION

Study the information in Figure 4C.25, which shows information about tourism in the United Kingdom.

1. a What was the total value of tourism to the United Kingdom in 1998? (2)
   b What proportion of this came from overseas visitors? (2)

2. a Describe the location of countries from which tourists travel to the UK. (2)
   b Calculate the average spending per visitor for each of the countries shown. What do your results show? (4)

3. a Make two copies of the map in Figure 4C.25. Use the information in the table to draw two choropleth maps. One map should show the trips taken by UK residents, the other by overseas visitors. (10)
   b Describe and explain the main similarities and differences between your two maps. (5)

Total 25 marks

Section 4 Using and Abusing the Environment

4C.25 *The United Kingdom tourist industry*

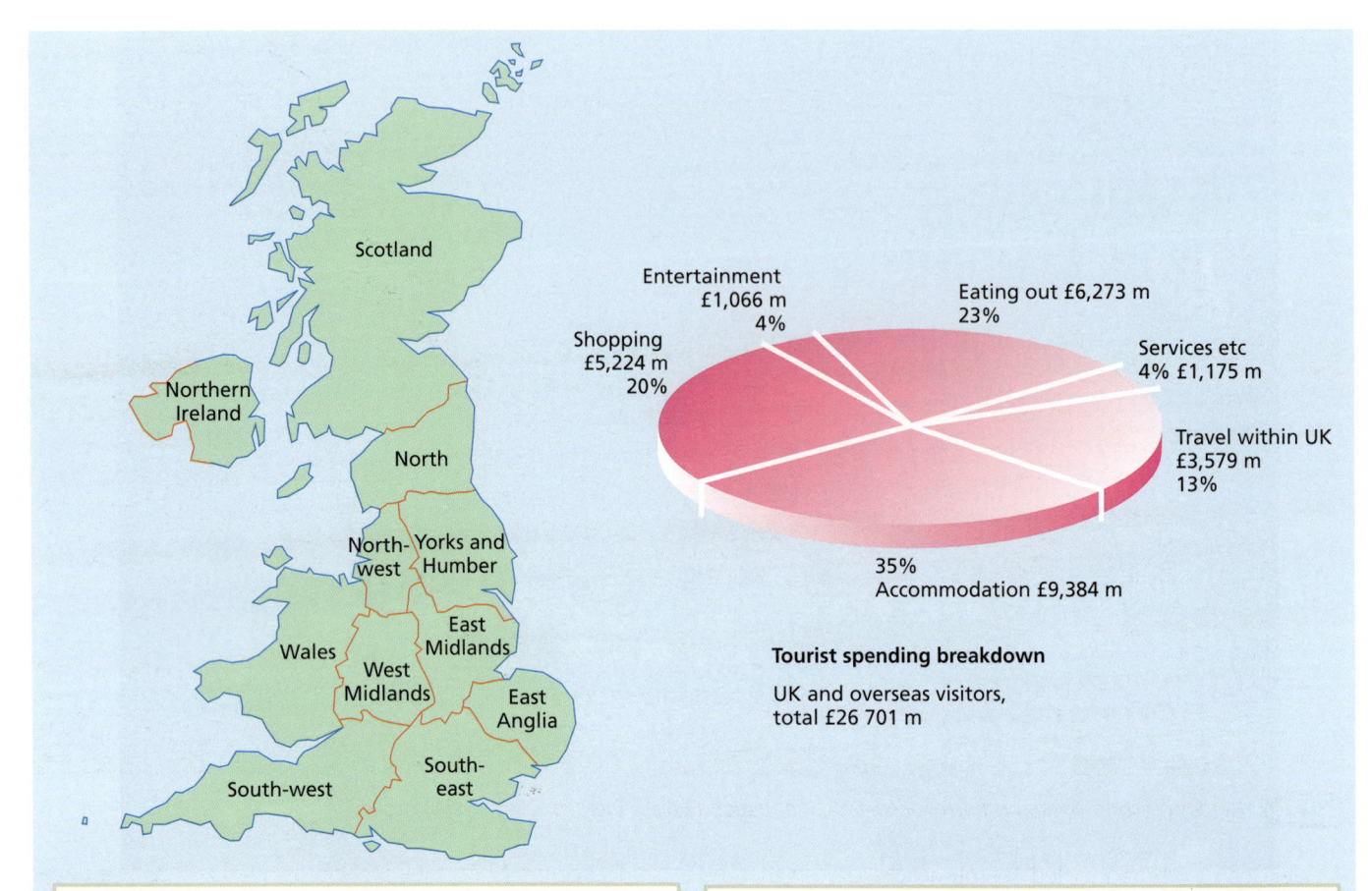

Tourist spending breakdown
UK and overseas visitors, total £26 701 m

- Entertainment £1,066 m — 4%
- Shopping £5,224 m — 20%
- Eating out £6,273 m — 23%
- Services etc 4% £1,175 m
- Travel within UK £3,579 m — 13%
- Accommodation £9,384 m — 35%

Origin of visitors	Visits (thousands)	Spending £ million
1 USA	3,880	2,482
2 France	3,274	750
3 Germany	2,830	882
4 Irish Republic	2,310	824
5 Netherlands	1,718	407
6 Belgium	1,183	225
7 Italy	1,090	555
8 Spain	900	396
9 Sweden	676	310
10 Canada	673	319

	UK residents' trips (millions)	Overseas visitors' trips (millions)
Cumbria	2.9	0.29
Northumbria	4.2	0.49
North West	8.4	1.28
Yorkshire	9.2	1.02
Heart of England	16.8	2.24
East of England	13.0	1.78
London	11.6	13.48
West Country	16.6	1.69
Southern	10.9	2.23
South East	10.5	2.54

The effects of tourism

What impact does tourism have upon the environment and the economy of countries and regions?

1 The Mediterranean

The Mediterranean coastline is the most popular tourist area in the world. Mass tourism developed in the 1950s and 1960s, especially in France, Spain and Italy. The effects of tourism here include the following.

- The transformation of quiet coastal villages into large purpose-built holiday complexes (see Figure 4C.26)
- Pollution of the coastline. Much waste is pumped untreated into the Mediterranean. This waste is not removed easily, as the Mediterranean is virtually tideless and there are few currents.
- Destruction of natural environments. This has included deforestation and the drying up of wetlands. This has endangered wildlife habitats.

C Pressures on the environment

4C.26 *Holiday resorts occupy a narrow coastal zone, beyond which there is little development*

- Over-fishing which has led to the stocks of fish in the Mediterranean being only 25 per cent of natural levels.
- Reliance on seasonal jobs, which has caused unemployment and underemployment in off-peak periods. The tourist boom is not providing long-term sustainable jobs for the Mediterranean areas.

2 Tourism in LEDCs

The growth of tourism in LEDCs has major environmental and economic impacts. For poorer nations, the natural environment is a vital resource, to be used to bring much needed foreign money into the country. Unlike MEDCs, poorer nations often do not have the range of industries necessary for economic growth. Many poorer countries have come to rely almost totally upon tourism. The benefits to LEDCs may be clear, but there are also disadvantages. Is tourism a good deal for poor countries?

Advantages

- Foreign tourists bring money into a country, an average of over £1000 per person for an overseas holiday.
- New roads are built to improve access. Local people benefit from these as well as tourists (see Figure 4C.27).
- Tourism creates jobs, for example in hotels and restaurants.
- Tourism creates a *multiplier effect* (see Figure 3A.13). Other jobs are created to service the tourist industry, such as providing entertainment or extra staff needed at airports.

- The country becomes more prosperous. It gains a better image worldwide, and more people want to visit. Tourism creates a *spiral of growth*.

4C.27 *New roads benefit the local community as well as tourists, but also bring extra traffic and pollution*

Disadvantages

- Much of the money from tourism goes to the transnational companies which organise the holidays or own the hotels. Relatively little money goes to the local people who actually work in the tourist industry.

139

Section 4 Using and Abusing the Environment

- Most jobs created are part-time or poorly paid. The best jobs are often given to people from abroad, brought in by the holiday companies.
- New roads bring more traffic and pollution.
- Tourists use more resources than do local people. The best supplies of food and water are often given to holidaymakers.
- Visitors change the culture of poorer countries. They have so much more money than local people, and can change the expectations of these people. There is often more crime in tourist areas, and locals are often treated badly by overseas visitors.

CASE STUDY

Tourism in Barbados

Barbados is one of the Caribbean Islands (see Figure 4C.28). The Caribbean is popular with tourists because of its sandy beaches, scenery and hot sunny weather (Figure 4C.29). Local people and international tourist organisations have developed a profitable tourist industry based on luxury holidays. In 1998, over 700 million people visited the Caribbean, spending more than $16 billion.

Tourism is the biggest industry in Barbados. The government has encouraged the growth of tourism, but has the industry really benefited the local people?

Advantages

- Tourism employs 20 000 people out of a total population of 260 000. It is easily the largest employer in Barbados.
- In 1999, a record number of 520 000 people visited Barbados. Tourism contributed $700 million to the island's economy, more than any other industry.
- Indirect employment in tourism is growing. There are now many jobs servicing the industry, evidence that the multiplier effect is taking place.
- The government has worked hard to maintain the island's luxury image. They have paid for *infrastructure* improvements such as to roads and sewerage. All islanders benefit from these improvements.

Disadvantages

- Barbados has relatively few natural resources. It is difficult for the island to cope with the arrival of 500 000 visitors per year, twice the permanent population of the island.
- Government money is spent providing holiday facilities for tourists that are not useful for local people, such as improving access routes to airports.
- Farmland has been used to build vast luxury holiday centres. As farming used to be the island's main industry, this has affected the economy of Barbados as well as its environment.
- Farmers used to grow food to sell to the local community. Much of this produce is now sold directly to hotels. This means that many locals have to buy their food from supermarkets. Most of these are foreign owned, and charge high prices.

4C.28 *The location of Barbados*

4C.29 *Barbados has a wealth of natural attractions for tourists*

C Pressures on the environment

- The natural environment is being changed by tourism. St James, for example, is an area of the island that was heavily wooded. The trees protected the surrounding area from all but the worst floods in periods of heavy rainfall, by absorbing and intercepting rain. The area has now been cleared to build a tourist complex and golf course. This increases the likelihood of flooding.
- Nearly 500 cruise ships dock each year at Bridgetown, the island's capital. Pollution caused by incoming shipping is an increasing problem.
- Sewage from coastal hotels is pumped straight into the sea. This is destroying the coral reef, one of the island's most important natural attractions.
- 77 per cent of money spent on overseas holidays to Barbados does not stay on the island, and therefore does not benefit the local economy.
- Most holidays to Barbados are 'all inclusive'. This means that tourists eat at their hotels, and do not spend money in the local community.

4C.30 *Large cruise ships contribute to the pollution of waters around Barbados*

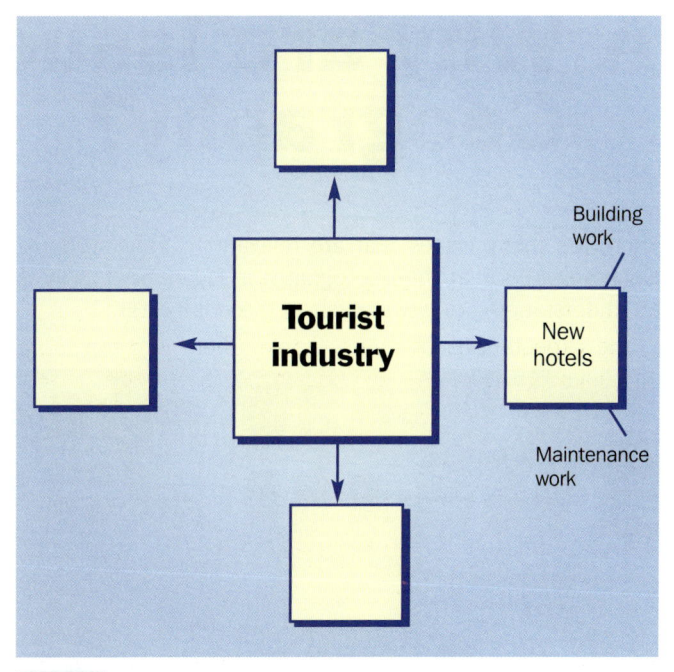

4C.31 *The benefits of tourism for an LEDC*

(Tourist industry → Building work, New hotels, Maintenance work)

NOTING ACTIVITIES

1. An LEDC has developed an international tourist industry. Using Figure 4C.31 to help you, complete a diagram to show how the multiplier effect might work for this country.

2. What are the disadvantages of tourism for LEDCs?

3. a Write a Fact File on Barbados.

   b Do you think that tourism has been good for Barbados? Give reasons for your answer.

Section 5 What You Need to Succeed

A Why are issues important in Geography?

There are many issues that are relevant to your study of Geography. Look at the photographs in Figure 5A.1. Why is an understanding of issues such as these important?

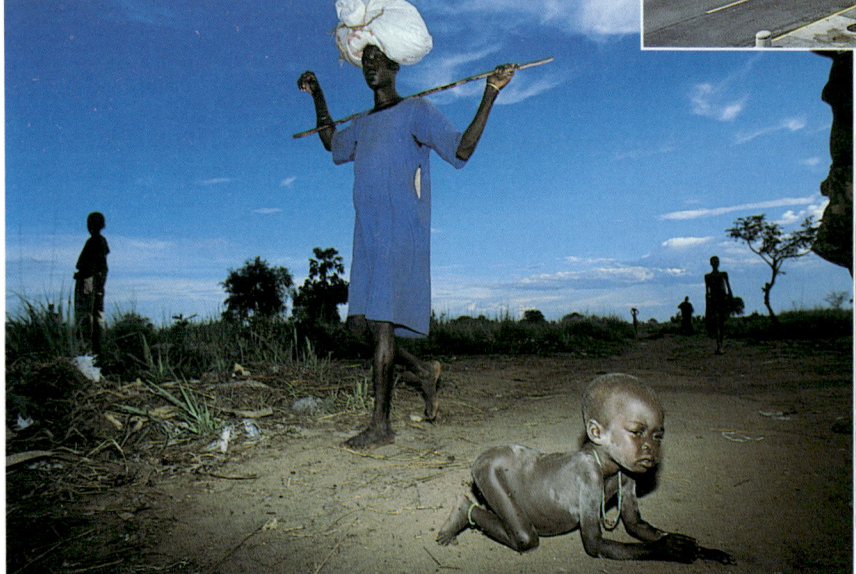

5A.1 *Issues in Geography*

A Why are issues important in Geography?

What is an issue?

Issues arise when individuals or groups of people cannot agree upon how resources or environments should be used. The resources in question may range from land to minerals or transport; environments include town centres and housing estates as well as natural ones such as wetlands and forests. Issues involve a *conflict of interest* but this does not necessarily mean conflict. Most issues are resolved through discussion, negotiation and compromise.

In this book, you are asked to consider a variety of issues related to your study of Geography. You will be examined on the content of some of these topics, but also need to understand the decision-making processes that lead to the solving of problems.

Some of the case studies involve attitudes, values and viewpoints. These are very important in your study of Geography. It is unlikely that an issue is clear-cut, with an obvious answer. There is usually more than one viewpoint, and you need to be able to *evaluate* different opinions and attitudes. This will eventually lead you to forming your own opinion about issues. As well as helping you to answer questions in your final examinations, a study of issues will be of value to you as a citizen in the democracy of the United Kingdom of the 21st century.

> In summary, when investigating an issue, you will usually go through the following stages:
>
> 1 Your initial awareness of the issue. What is the issue? Who is involved?
>
> 2 Definition and description. Why is the issue important?
>
> 3 Analysis and explanation. How does this affect different people? How could it be resolved?
>
> 4 Personal viewpoint. What do you think should happen? Why?

In addition to studying issues in Geography, you will meet *questions*, *problems* and *issues* in all aspects of your school life, and beyond. To gain a full understanding of resolving issues in Geography, it is important to have a clear understanding of how to use the **enquiry process**.

NOTING ACTIVITIES

1 For any *two* of the photographs in Figure 5A.1, say:

   a what is the issue

   b where this is taking place

   c who is affected

   d what the consequences could be for different groups of people

   e how this issue might be resolved

   f what you think should be done and why.

2 Choose two more photographs from this book and make the same notes for them.

3 Find a photograph from another source about a geographical issue. Make similar notes about this photograph.

Section 5 What You Need to Succeed

B Using and interpreting photographs

A photograph provides an accurate and **objective** record of human or physical features. The camera records a detailed and complete picture, and therefore provides a wealth of information that may be described and analysed.

Used in a textbook such as this, photographs are able to illustrate places or events in a different way from written text. They are particularly useful when relating to unfamiliar or unusual locations or events.

You are also likely to encounter photographs in your GCSE assessments. The written examination components often use photographs for data response questions. An apparently simple question such as 'describe what is in the photograph…' is often answered in insufficient detail, as candidates do not examine the contents of a photograph in sufficient depth. You may be required to draw a sketch map from a photograph, another skill that is often poorly undertaken in examinations.

Photographs may also be a valuable resource in coursework items. A study based on local fieldwork, for example, could incorporate a small number of photographs to illustrate the main features of different residential zones within an urban area. The photographs need to be used in the study, not included as an afterthought without reference made to them. They should also be *selected*; you may take several photographs of the same meander or oxbow lake but you do not have to include them all. Make sure that you **annotate** your photographs to highlight important information.

Using photographs also has some drawbacks. While a photograph is a different means of recording data to a fieldsketch, it does not replace a good sketch. The information shown by a photograph includes much that will not be relevant for your purpose; a fieldsketch may be used to select important features. But photographs can be selective in another way: it is possible to choose images to convey a particular viewpoint. Photographs may in this way carry **bias**.

How will you be able to use and analyse photographs? There are three main types of photograph that are generally used for geographical interpretation:

- ground level photographs
- aerial photographs
- satellite images.

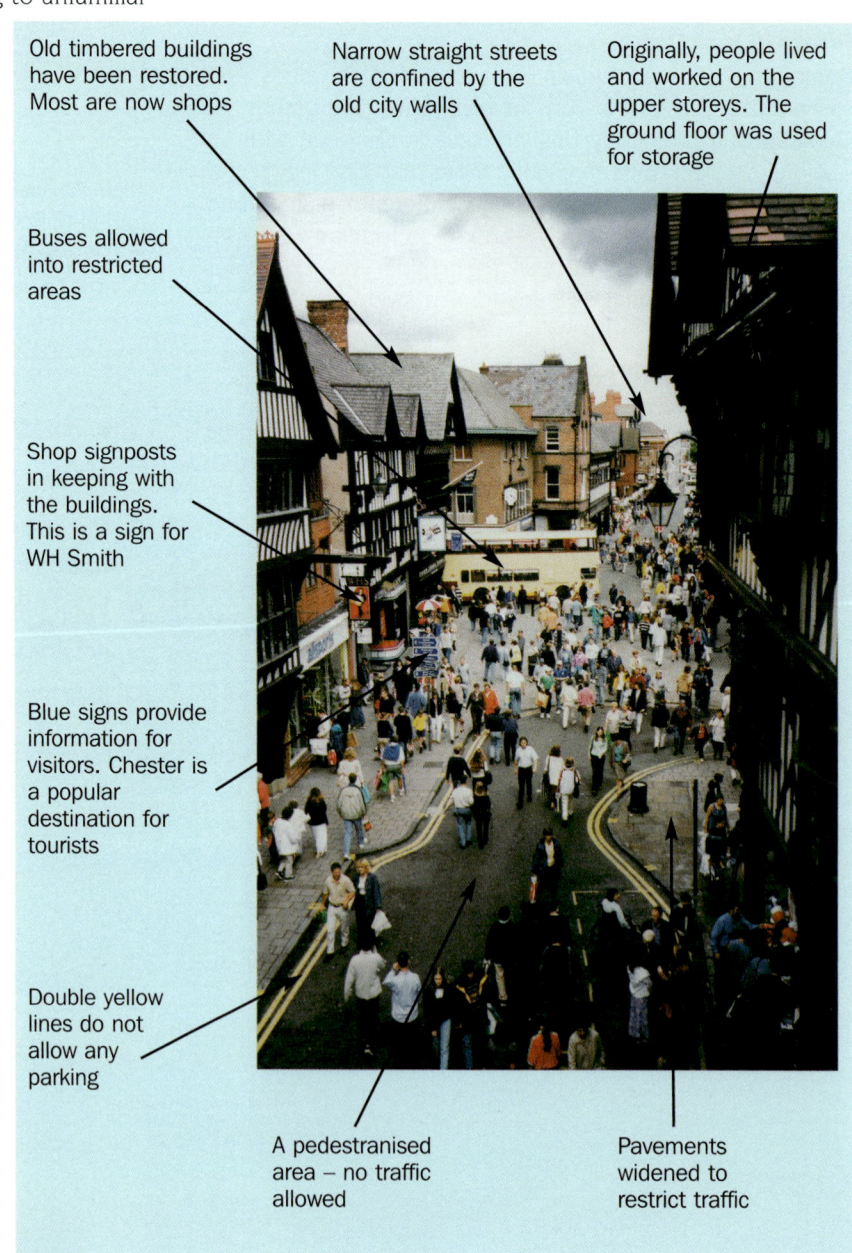

Annotations on photograph 5B.1:
- Old timbered buildings have been restored. Most are now shops
- Narrow straight streets are confined by the old city walls
- Originally, people lived and worked on the upper storeys. The ground floor was used for storage
- Buses allowed into restricted areas
- Shop signposts in keeping with the buildings. This is a sign for WH Smith
- Blue signs provide information for visitors. Chester is a popular destination for tourists
- Double yellow lines do not allow any parking
- A pedestranised area – no traffic allowed
- Pavements widened to restrict traffic

5B.1 *A street in the centre of Chester*

B Using and interpreting photographs

5B.2 *The Malvern Hills*

Ground level photographs

These are common in textbooks, easy to take, and the only type of photograph you will be able to include in coursework! A ground level photograph will show an enormous amount of detail, which is often not immediately apparent. With a trained eye, it is possible to spot patterns and features that may be annotated on the photograph. This is useful for coursework, and may gain you marks in your examinations.

Look at Figure 5B.1. This is a photograph of Chester. Examination of the photograph has enabled many features to be identified that illustrate the character of the city, and ways in which development of a historic city centre has been planned.

Now look at Figure 5B.2. This is a photograph of the Malvern Hills near Worcester. What **physical** and **human** features are there in this photograph?

ACTIVITY

1 Draw a sketch to show the main features in Figure 5B.2
2 Annotate your sketch to describe the features that you have drawn, using arrows to show relevant points on the sketch. Colour code your arrows to show physical and human features.
3 Choose a photograph from another source and repeat the above activities.

Aerial photographs

An aerial photograph is taken from the air. The amount of detail shown will vary according to how high above ground level it is taken. Aerial photographs are of two types: **oblique** and **vertical**. Each has its own advantages for geographical analysis.

An oblique aerial photograph is one that is taken looking down on the ground surface at an angle. Figure 5B.3 shows an oblique view of Eastbourne on the south coast of England. This type of photograph shows the three-dimensional nature of surface features, such as the buildings in Eastbourne and the cliffs at the bottom of the photograph. It is possible to pick out details such as footpaths and the groynes that are used to help prevent coastal erosion.

Figure 5B.4 shows a vertical aerial photograph. This is more like a map, as it shows the same view of the landscape. The three-dimensional nature is lost, but it is easier to spot patterns from a vertical photograph, such as the layout of streets in a settlement.

As aerial photographs usually show an extensive surface area, they are useful in recognising patterns, shapes and connections over a large area. Sketches from photographs are useful in analysing the geographical information on the photograph.

Section 5 What You Need to Succeed

5B.3 *An aerial view of Eastbourne*

ACTIVITY

Use Figure 5B.3 and the information on pages 201–205 to answer the following questions.

1 In which direction was the camera pointing when the photograph was taken?
2 Draw an outline sketch of the area shown on the photograph.
3 Label the following on your sketch. Use arrows to show the exact location.
   a Chalk Downs
   b English Channel
   c Groynes with material built up on south-west sides
   d Direction of longshore drift
   e Eastbourne Promenade
   f Pier
   g Langney Point
   h Sovereign Harbour
   i Pevensey Bay
   j Low lying Levels – flood risk area
   k Extensive new housing

B Using and interpreting photographs

5B.4 *A vertical aerial photograph provides a view similar to a map*

Section 5 What You Need to Succeed

Satellite photographs

Satellite **images**, like vertical aerial photographs, provide a **plan** view of a landscape. As they are taken from space, the area covered by a satellite photograph is much larger. This means that, while detail is lost, a wider and more general pattern is visible. Look at Figure 5B.5. This shows the Mississippi River in the USA, where it is joined by the Missouri River. The city of St Louis is in the bottom of the photograph. Notice how patterns of land use may be identified, which is not the case with other photographs.

Now look at Figure 5B.6. This shows the same area during the 1993 Mississippi floods. The area under water is clearly visible, showing the extent of the flooding. Much of the city of St Louis is covered by high cloud. Refer to the satellite images as you answer the questions which follow.

5B.5 *The Mississippi and Missouri Rivers near St Louis*

5B.7 *Sketch taken from the satellite photograph*

5B.6 *The 1993 floods*

B **Using and interpreting photographs**

ACTIVITY

Make a copy of Figure 5B.7, which shows the area covered by the satellite images.

1 Label the area covered by St Louis.
2 Mark the Mississippi River which flows from top left to bottom right. Label the direction of flow.
3 Show the Missouri which joins the Mississippi from the centre left. Label the **confluence** (where the two rivers join).
4 Annotate your sketch to show where the Missouri has been straightened. Label the grassland inside the meander that has been cut off.
5 Write on your sketch where there are large areas of fields and crops.
6 Shade your sketch to show where the flooding took place in 1993.
7 Next to your sketch, make a note of the types of problem and damage likely to be caused by the flooding.

EXTENDED ACTIVITY

Interpreting a vertical aerial photograph

The vertical aerial photograph has many uses. It can be the basis of map-making and is particularly useful when updating a map. Figures 5B.8 and 5B.9 have a similar scale. Figure 5B.8 comes from the 1998 *London A-Z* map and Figure

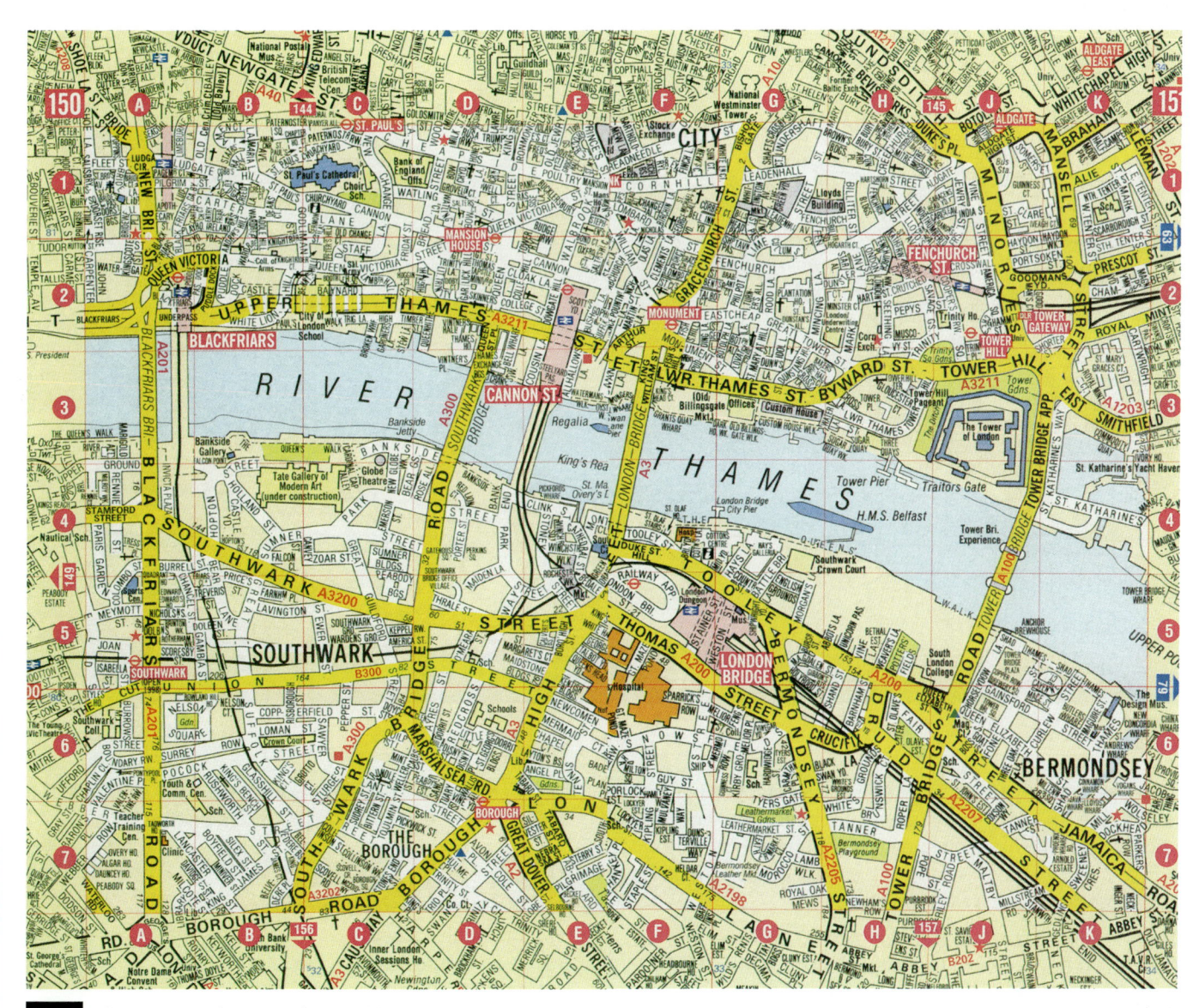

5B.8 *Street map of a part of central London*

Section 5 What You Need to Succeed

5B.9 *Vertical aerial photograph of the area shown on the street map (Figure 5B.8)*

5B.9 was taken in 1999. There are only a few buildings and land uses which are different on the map and the photograph. The Millennium pedestrian bridge is not shown on the map but the two ends of it are shown being built on the photograph (see west Thames).

The area shown is just to the east of the OXO Tower and the Coin Street development (see pages 28–29). It also shows St Katherine's Dock and the surrounding area (see pages 252–254).

1 Link the aerial photograph with the map and link the numbers 1–10 with the following landmarks:

Tower of London
London Bridge railway station
Canon Street railway station
St Katharine's Docks
St Paul's Cathedral
St Andrew's Wharf
HMS *Belfast*

B Using and interpreting photographs

What you need to succeed

5B.10 *Sketch taken from the aerial photograph*

The Monument (a tower near Monument station)
The Tate Britain Gallery
Tower Bridge

2 Describe and suggest the uses of the types of buildings in the areas of A and B on Figure 5B.9.

3 Where in the area shown are there parks and trees?

4 Look very carefully at the map details and locate where changes are being made in London eg new buildings being built and derelict land being developed.

5 Place the following characteristics of maps and photographs under the headings of:

Map characteristics or **vertical photograph characteristics**

Accurate scale
Accurate direction
Time of the year
Time of the day
Street names
Names of buildings
Individual trees
Names of parks
Boats, buses and cars
Heights of buildings
Width of roads

Section 5 What You Need to Succeed

C Using and drawing maps

Maps used in GCSE Geography

Maps are essential to the study of Geography. Most of the topics you study for GCSE will involve the use of some sort of map. A wide variety of maps are available, each serving a different and specific purpose. You will need to be able to read and interpret the following types of map:

- Ordnance Survey maps, which may be drawn at different scales

5C.1 *1:50,000 Ordnance Survey extract of Buxton, Derbyshire*

NOTING ACTIVITIES

1. Look through one section of one of your GCSE Geography textbooks. List the types of map used in this section, and the purpose for which they are used.

2. Are there any other subjects you study at school that make use of maps? If so, in what ways are maps used?

3. How do you use maps out of school? List three ways in which maps are useful to people in everyday life.

C Using and drawing maps

- Road maps and street plans
- Choropleth maps
- Topological maps
- Flow line maps.

Ordnance Survey maps

Maps drawn by the Ordnance Survey (OS) cover the whole of England, Scotland and Wales. They show an area in detail, and may be drawn at a variety of scales.

Scales

There are two common scales that you are likely to use.

1:50,000 On a 1:50,000 map, one centimetre represents 50,000 centimetres, or half of a kilometre. This means that two centimetres represents one kilometre. The gridlines

5C.2 *1:25,000 Ordnance Survey extract of part of the Peak District National Park*

Section 5 What You Need to Succeed

drawn on a map are two centimetres apart. This means that it is possible to estimate distances on a 1:50,000 map as each square represents one kilometre (see Figure 5C.1). Distance may be measured more accurately using the scale line and a ruler.

1:25,000 Every centimetre on a 1:25,000 map represents 25,000 centimetres. This means that four centimetres represent one kilometre. 1:25,000 maps show greater detail than 1:50,000 maps, but they cannot show such a large area. They have the same type of gridlines, again being the equivalent of one kilometre apart. This means that there are four centimetres between gridlines on a 1:25,000 map (see Figure 5C.2).

Grid references

Grid references locate positions on a map. There are two types of grid references.

Four-figure references give a location that is represented by the whole of a grid square. The first two figures (called *eastings*) are read from the bottom of the map. The third and fourth figures (or *northings*) are read from the side. In Figure 5C.1, for example, Lightwood reservoir is located in grid square 0575.

Six-figure references give a pinpoint location on a map. The first *three* figures are eastings, read from the bottom of the map. The first two refer to the main gridline, the third is an estimate of the distance across the grid square out of ten equal divisions. A reference of 345 for an easting, for example, means that the location is half way across from the main gridline 34. In the same way, the final *three figures* refer to the northings. Six-figure references are quite hard to locate accurately, as there are no gridlines on the map for the third and sixth figures. On Figure 5C.1, the railway station is located at 058738. (Notice that there is no separation of the figures by commas, etc.)

Direction

Ordnance Survey maps always have north at the top of the map. Direction from one location to another is expressed in terms of the sixteen compass points shown in Figure 5C.3.

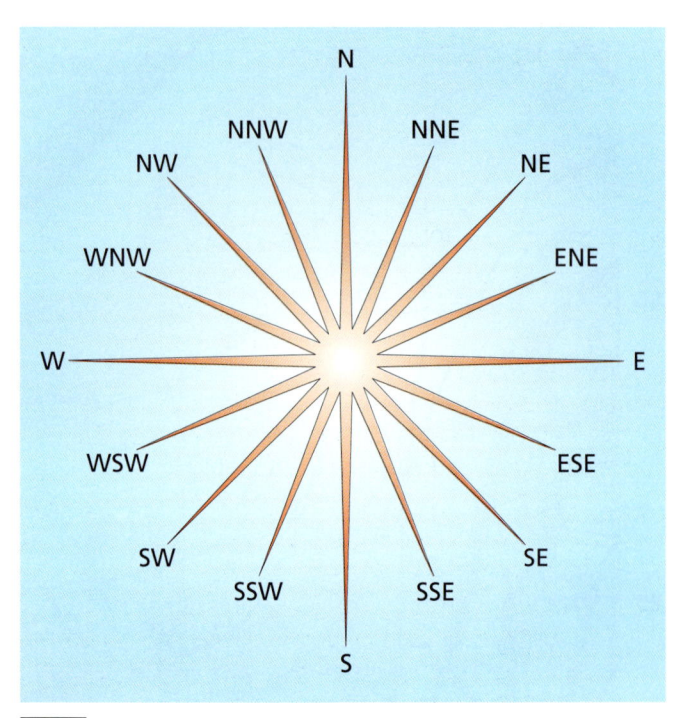

5C.3 *The points of the compass*

NOTING ACTIVITIES

Refer to Figure 5C.1.

1 In which grid square is each of the following?
   a Buxton railway station
   b The car park at Bibbington
   c Fairfield Common golf course
   d Buxton Country Park

2 Give a six-figure reference for each of the following:
   a Peak Rail Steam Centre
   b Stanley Moor Reservoir
   c Dove Holes railway station
   d Buxton Town Hall

3 Using map evidence, suggest three ways in which people have changed the landscape.

4 What evidence is there on the map to suggest that the area is an important tourist destination?

5 The boundary of the Peak District National Park goes round almost all of Buxton, keeping the town out of the Park. Why do you think this is?

Refer to Figure 5C.2.

6 Describe and give reasons for the types of land use in the area shown on the map.

7 Compare the two maps, both of which show a part of the Peak District National Park. What are the advantages and disadvantages of each type of map? Suggest one group of people who could use each map.

B Using and interpreting photographs

Signs and symbols

Maps use a range of symbols to represent features for the sake of simplicity and clarity, and to save space. The type of symbols used differs according to the scale of map. You should always be able to use a sheet of signs and symbols when reading a map; there is little point in memorising a long list of symbols, particularly when most of them will not be used very often. The more you use maps, the more symbols you will recognise and remember, especially those most regularly used. Remember, however, that even in an examination you will be provided with a sheet of signs and symbols to use with the map.

Road maps and street plans

Road maps are designed specifically to show information that will be useful for motorists. The whole of the United Kingdom is covered by many different road maps. Unlike with OS maps, there is no exclusive provider of such maps. Road maps clearly show routes from one location to another, often including the approximate distance taken. They do not, however, show much of the detail that is present on OS maps. There is no need, for example, for road maps to show footpaths, field boundaries or other features that might prove useful for users of OS maps.

Street plans provide detailed coverage of a small area, usually one settlement. The plan provides information that is useful for visitors to a town or city, for example the location of public buildings, or any traffic restrictions. Street plans are useful when used together with an OS map of the same area. The street plan shows information that is not present on the OS map, for example the names of streets. It is possible to trace the history and development of a settlement by finding old street maps.

Choropleth maps

A choropleth map is one that shows different values or categories by means of different types of shading. The highest figures, of greatest densities, are usually shown by the darkest shading. Figure 5C.4 is a choropleth map drawn to show GDP for countries in western Europe. A figure of 100 represents an average level of GDP, over 100 being above average. The darkest shading represents the wealthiest areas, the location of which may easily be identified through using a choropleth map.

Choropleth maps are quite easy to draw. Their main advantage is that they show a striking and immediate view of patterns and distributions. There are, however, disadvantages to them both in the way they are constructed and in the information they show.

When drawing a choropleth map, the data used must be grouped into a series of categories. It is important to bear in mind the following guidelines in order to make the completed map effective.

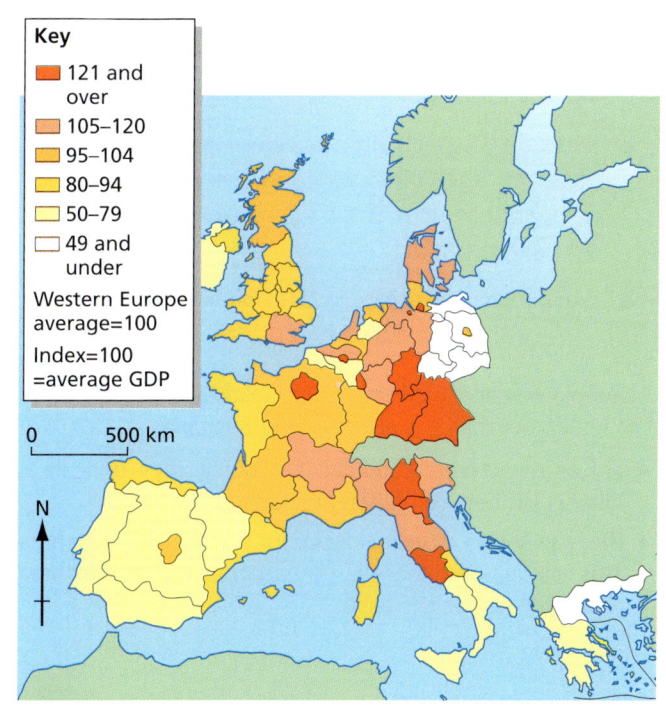

5C.4 *GDP values for western Europe 1998. A figure of 100 represents average GDP*

1 Choose the number of categories carefully. Too few groups will mean that there is no pattern apparent on your map. Too many will look messy, and again makes interpretation difficult. An ideal range is usually between four and six categories.

2 Make the categories equal in value, eg 0–2, 2.1–4, 4.1–6, etc. Make sure that your categories do not overlap; for example, if you make your groups 0–2, 2–4, 4–6, where would you fit a value of 2.0?

Although you need to make your categories equal, you can cope with some very high figures by making your final category larger, eg 10 and over.

3 When choosing the range of shades to use, make the lightest shading represent the lowest values, moving through to the darkest shading showing the highest. While it is common to use lines or dots for shading, block colours often show most clearly. It is often difficult to be consistent when drawing dots or lines over a large area on a map. Shadings that look very different in a key may not do so on a map. Practice before completing your map. Many choropleth maps are drawn using completely different colours for different categories, and they do not work. A clear choropleth may be drawn using one colour ranging from light to dark, or variations on one colour as used in Figure 5C.4.

Section 5 What You Need to Succeed

> **NOTING ACTIVITIES**
>
> 1 Describe the pattern shown on Figure 5C.4.
>
> 2 What do you think are the advantages and disadvantages of showing GNP as a value compared to an average figure, rather than the actual amount?
>
> 3 Explain the variations in GNP shown on the map.

A completed choropleth map may clearly show distribution, but remember that it is also has disadvantages:

- unless drawn very carefully, it is sometimes difficult to distinguish between different shadings on a map
- the map shows an *average* figure for a whole region or area. This implies that there is no variation within that area, which will not be the case.

Topological maps

Topological maps are not used often, but they serve a specific and useful purpose. A topological map shows connections between places and the routes taken to travel from one place to another. In so doing, both accurate measurements of distance and direction are lost. The most commonly used topological map is of the underground railway system in London (Figure 5C.5). A journey may be planned from one station to another, yet the distances and directions shown are not accurate.

Flow line maps

Flow line maps are used to show the quantity of movement from one place to another. They show volume of movement by means of variable thickness of lines. The direction of movement may be shown by an arrow or label in a key. A flow line map is often valuable in undertaking local fieldwork, for example for displaying the results of traffic counts (see Figure 5C.6). They may also be used to display information on maps of larger areas.

5C.5 *Part of the London underground railway system*

B Using and interpreting photographs

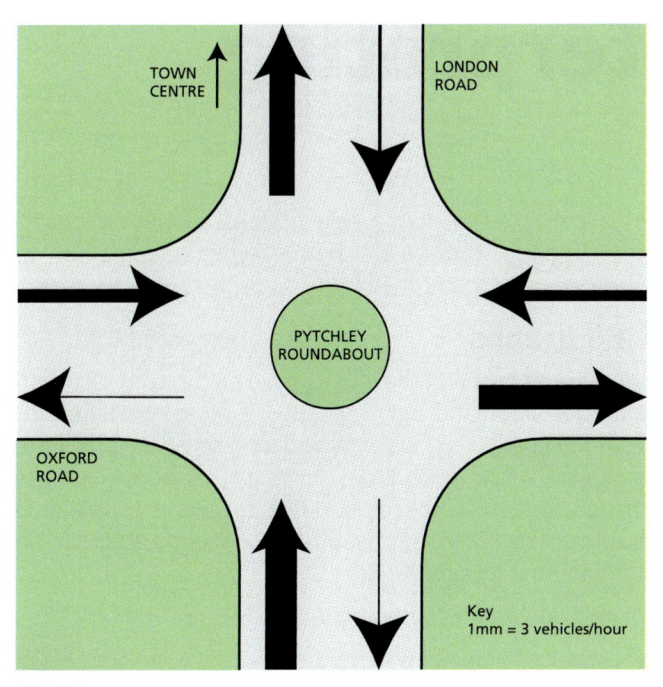

5C.6 *The results of traffic counts shown by means of a flow line map*

(Key: 1mm = 3 vehicles/hour; roads shown: Town Centre, London Road, Oxford Road, and southbound road around Pytchley Roundabout)

Country	Number of migrants
USA	110 000
UK	110 000
Poland	230 000
Austria	185 000
Yugoslavia	800 000
Greece	360 000
Italy	600 000
Spain	130 000
Portugal	125 000
Turkey	2 000 000

5C.7 *Migrants to Germany*

NOTING ACTIVITIES

1. Figure 5C.7 shows the number of people migrating to Germany from other parts of Europe. On a blank outline map of Europe, draw a flow line map to show the information in Figure 5C.7.

2. Use one other method to show the same information.

3. What are the advantages and disadvantages of the two methods of showing the data?

What you need to succeed

Section 5 What You Need to Succeed

D Drawing and interpreting graphs

Graphs are an important method of displaying data. In your study of GCSE Geography, you will need to be able to draw and to interpret a range of different types of graph. It is likely that graphs will be an element of both your coursework and the examination papers.

A graph is a visual means of showing data. The purpose of a graph is to organise and display information so that patterns are visible that may not be apparent from the original data. Look at Figure 5D.1. This shows two graphs that were used in a GCSE examination paper.

> **NOTING ACTIVITIES**
>
> 1. Why do the graphs in Figure 5D.1 show data more clearly than if the data were written as a list of figures?
> 2. Using the first graph in Figure 5D.1, compare the population change in the two cities shown.
> 3. Using the second graph in Figure 5D.1, describe the pattern of rainfall and temperature shown on the graph.

If you are asked to 'draw a graph', think carefully about what type of graph to draw. Is it better to use a line graph, bar graph, or some other method of showing the data?

Line graphs

A line graph is one of the most simple methods of displaying data, yet often the most effective. Line graphs show the relationship between two sets of data, using the x and y axes of a graph. The line drawn on a graph shows *continuous* change. In many cases, one of the data sets is constant; for example, the dates on a graph to show population change through time (Figure 5D.2).

Using a line graph it is possible to:

- estimate figures between those you have plotted
- predict figures for the future using current and past trends. For example, using Figure 5D.2, you can estimate the population of the UK in 1995.

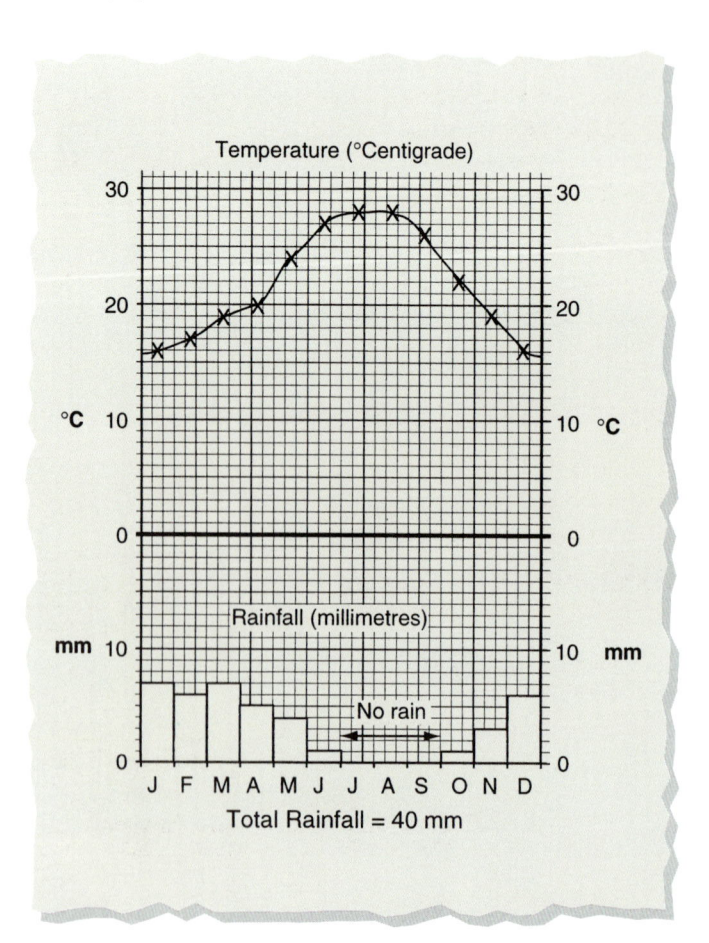

5D.1 *Graphs are often used in data response examination questions*

D Drawing and interpreting graphs

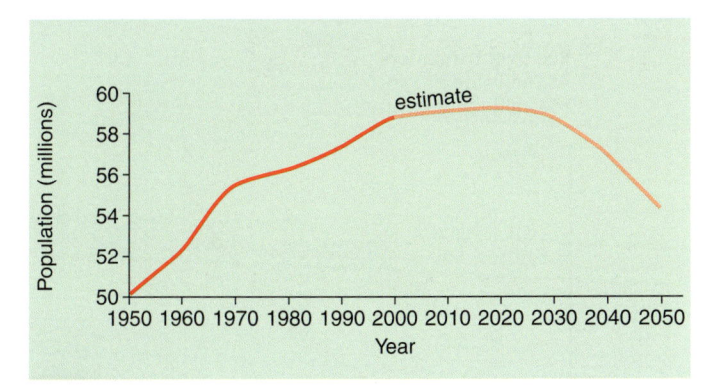

5D.2 *Population change in the United Kingdom*

Drawing line graphs

- When drawing any type of graph, choosing your scale is important. You will need to work out your scales before drawing your axes. Try planning these out in rough first.

When using a wide range of figures, consider breaking your scale.

- Join your points together using a smooth curve.
- Make sure your axes are clearly labelled and your graph has a title.

Bar graphs

The height of a bar shows the quantity it represents. Using a bar graph, it is possible to show data that is grouped together, for example over a period of time (1990–1995, 1996–2000, etc.)

Drawing bar graphs

Several groups of data may be shown using a bar graph. This is called a **stacked** bar graph (see Figure 5D.3). Using a stacked bar graph enables the trend in total figures to be seen, as well as differences within these totals.

NOTING ACTIVITIES

1. Use the data in Figure 5D.4 to draw a stacked bar graph.
2. Describe and explain the information shown on your graph.

Histograms

These are bar charts where the scale on the *x* axis is drawn proportional to the quantity it represents (Figure 5D.5). This enables the graph to show more clearly the value of data on this axis.

Date	Type of energy (million tonnes of oil equivalent)				
	oil	natural gas	nuclear	HEP	coal
1975	2800	950	100	100	1750
1980	2900	1000	150	110	1850
1985	2800	1100	220	105	2100
1990	3100	1200	320	110	2150
1995	3000	1400	400	120	2100
2000	3100	1550	520	120	2050

5D.4 *Trends in world energy consumption*

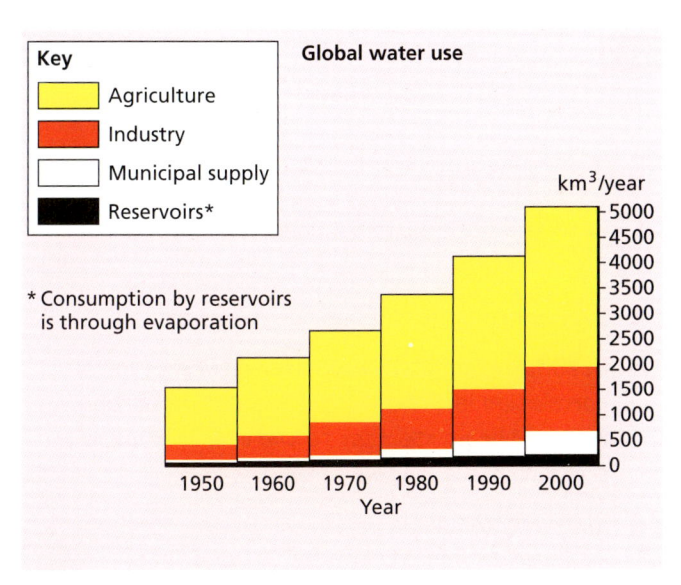

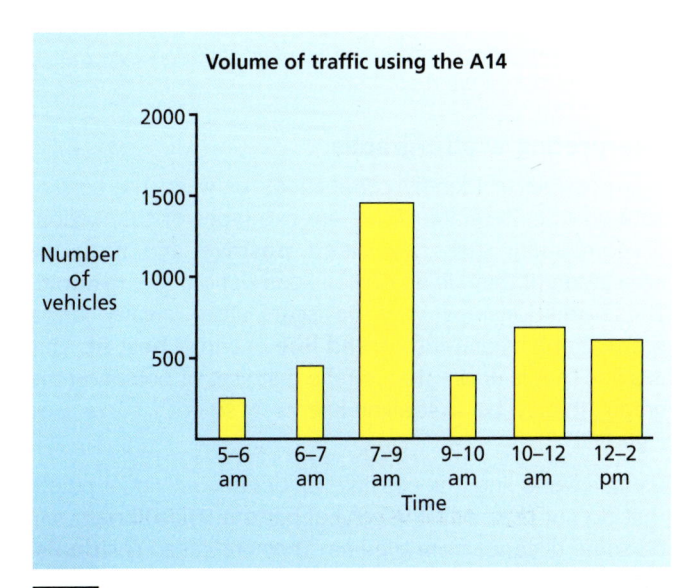

5D.3 *A stacked bar graph*

5D.5 *A histogram*

159

Section 5 **What You Need to Succeed**

Scattergraphs

Scattergraphs show the relationship or **correlation** between two sets of data. For example, a group of students undertook fieldwork in a National Park. They surveyed a busy car park, sampling the number of walkers passing survey points at different distances from the car park. The two sets of data in this example are:

- the number of visitors
- the distance of the survey point from the car park.

Drawing scattergraphs

Decide which set of data **depends** upon the other. The set of data which is **independent**, or influences the other set, will go on the *x* axis of the scattergraph. In this case, the number of people depends upon the distance from the car park, rather than the other way round. Distance from the car park will therefore be drawn on the *x* axis. Results plotted from the study are shown in Figure 5D.6.

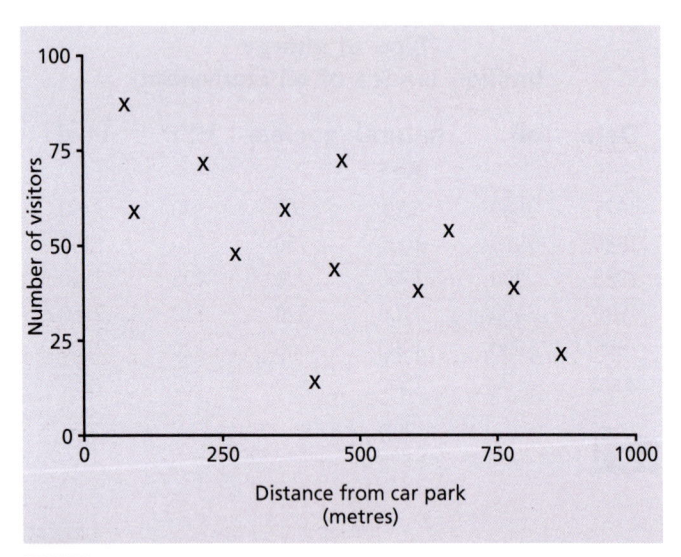

5D.6 *The relationship between number of visitors and the distance from a car park*

5D.7 *Correlation*

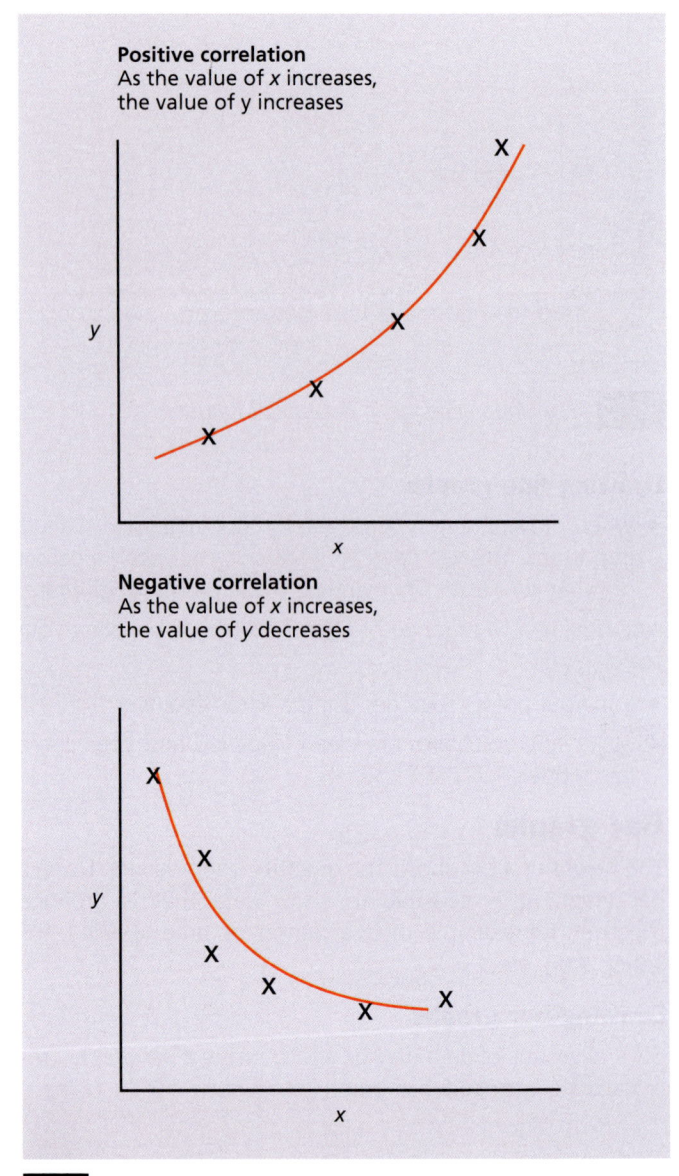

Positive correlation
As the value of *x* increases, the value of *y* increases

Negative correlation
As the value of *x* increases, the value of *y* decreases

Interpreting scattergraphs

It is possible to identify connections between the sets of data on a scattergraph. There are two types of connection, or correlation; these are called **positive** and **negative** correlation. If there is no obvious correlation, it is **random**. These relationships may be seen more clearly on a scattergraph by drawing a **trend line** or line of **best fit**. This is a line that is drawn through the main set of points on the graph. It may be a straight line or a smooth curve (see Figure 5D.7).

Using a trend line it is possible to identify individual points that do not fit in with the general pattern. These points will be some distance from the line. They are called **residuals**. It is possible then to look at reasons why a point does not fit the general pattern.

NOTING ACTIVITIES

1. Draw a scattergraph to show the information in Figure 5D.8.
2. Draw a line of best fit on to your graph.
3. Describe what your graph shows. What type of correlation is there? Is the correlation **strong**, with all the points near to the line, or **weak**, with some points a long way from the line?
4. Mark any residuals on to your graph. What explanation can you give for these points?

D Drawing and interpreting graphs

Country	GNP per person (US dollars)	% of workforce employed in agriculture
Argentina	8 330	12
Australia	18 720	5
Brazil	3 640	23
Canada	19 380	3
Denmark	29 890	6
Ethiopia	100	80
Germany	27 510	4
Hungary	4 120	15
India	340	64
Japan	39 640	7
Kenya	280	80
Nigeria	260	43
Russia	2 240	14
Thailand	2 740	64
UK	18 700	2
Venezuela	3 020	12

5D.8 *GNP and the workforce employed in agriculture for selected countries, 1998*

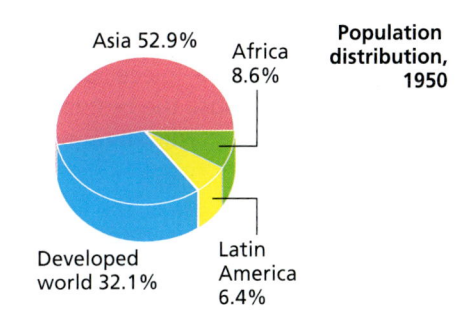

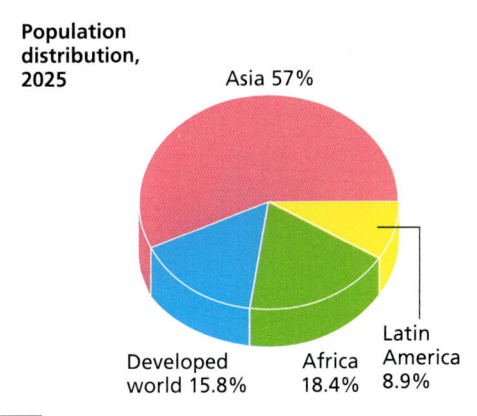

Population distribution, 1950
- Asia 52.9%
- Africa 8.6%
- Latin America 6.4%
- Developed world 32.1%

Population distribution, 2025
- Asia 57%
- Latin America 8.9%
- Africa 18.4%
- Developed world 15.8%

5D.9 *Distribution of the world's growing population*

Pie charts

Pie charts are useful to show data that may be divided into different groups or categories. A pie chart is divided into segments, each being proportional to the value that it represents.

Pie charts are a simple method of showing data in a very clear visual format. It is possible to show several pie charts together, for example located on a map. In this way comparison is possible between several sets of data. Pie charts may also be draw in different sizes, to make comparisons between two sets of data (see Figure 5D.9).

Drawing pie charts

Pie charts are easy to draw, especially if you use a pie chart measure to plot the angles for you. If you have to work them out, remember that the whole circle represents 360 degrees, and that your data need to be converted into this format before being plotted.

It is easiest to use figures that are in the form of percentages. This means that each figure will need to be multiplied by 3.6 to find its value on the pie chart. For example, if a figure is 40 per cent, this means that its value on the pie chart is 40 × 3.6, which equals 144. The value of this figure is 144 degrees on the pie chart.

There are drawbacks to using pie charts.

- They over-emphasize large values in a data set. It is very difficult to draw or to interpret small values on a pie chart.
- They work most effectively on a small number of categories. If a pie chart is drawn with many sections, it is difficult to identify any pattern in the sectors.
- As pie charts are relatively easy to draw and show information clearly, there is a tendency to use them too often. If you undertake a piece of research work, for example for coursework, make sure that you have a *variety* of methods of showing your data. Students' work that does not contain such a range is often dominated by pie charts.

EXTENDED ACTIVITY

For this activity, you will need to refer to any of your GCSE Geography textbooks.

1 Look through the book and find one place where the author has chosen to show information by means of one or more pie charts.

a Describe the information that is shown by the pie chart(s).

b What are the advantages in this case of using a pie chart?

c Suggest one other method of showing the same data.

Section 5 What You Need to Succeed

2 Look through your own GCSE Geography notes. In the same way, find a piece of work where you have drawn pie charts, if possible, in a piece of research work or coursework. Did you choose the best method to show your data? If not, how else could they have been displayed?

Triangular graphs

A triangular graph may be used to plot data that may be divided into three parts. The graph is usually set out in percentage sections, so the total figures represented must combine to equal 100 per cent. One example of data commonly plotted on triangular graphs is employment structure. This is divided into primary, secondary, and tertiary employment, and so may be shown using the three axes of a triangular graph (see Figure 5D.10). The example shown is blank, to show the way such a graph works.

Drawing triangular graphs

- When plotting figures on to a triangular graph, always read the value parallel to the line that represents zero for that group, as shown on Figure 5D.10.
- Triangular graphs may show clusters of points. It is possible to interpret these groupings, rather like in a scattergraph.

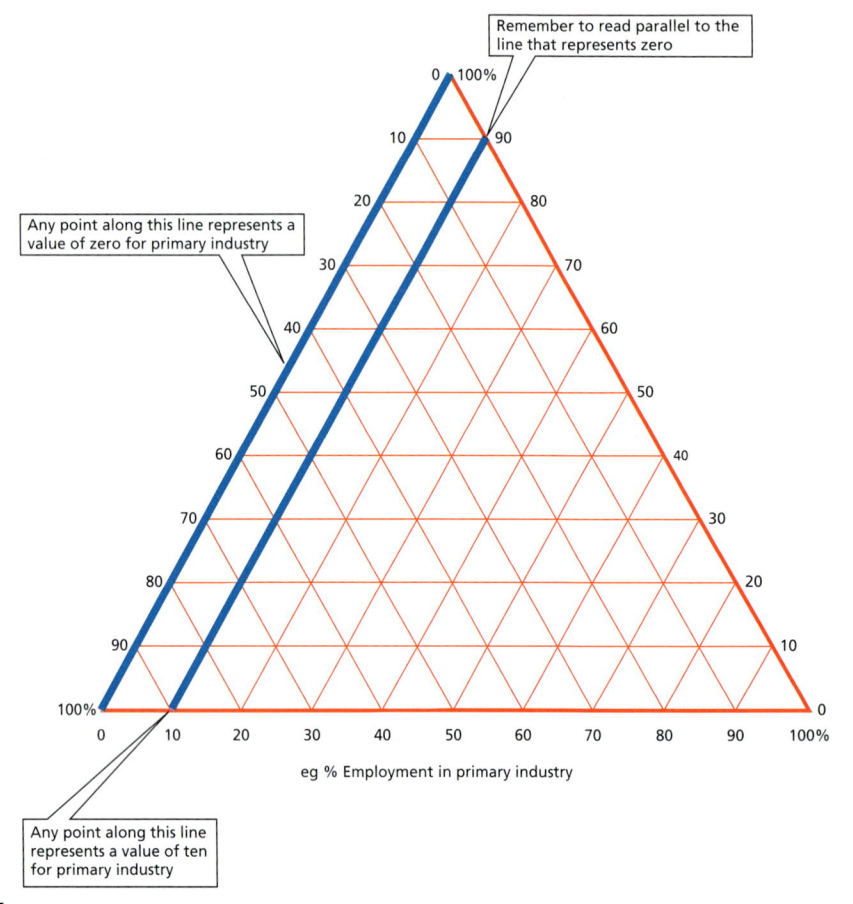

5D.10 *A triangular graph*

NOTING ACTIVITIES

1. Summarise the main characteristics of each type of graph outlined above.

2. For each type of graph, suggest one form of data that it may be used to represent.

3. Using a computer, describe how each form of graph may be drawn using ICT instead of being hand drawn. Name the software that could be used, and use the computer to produce a graph to show the data in Figure 5D.4.

Section 5 What You Need to Succeed

E Using ICT

There are many ways in which you can use Information and Communications Technology to help with your study of GCSE Geography. Some of these are mentioned elsewhere in this book. You are likely to encounter more in your other subjects, and find that skills learned elsewhere may be applied to your work in Geography.

5E.1 *Learn how to use all of the facilities offered by a search engine*

Section 5 **What You Need to Succeed**

Using computer technology is *one* method of collecting, analysing and interpreting information. It is not the only method, and should not be over-used. For every person who enjoys using computers, there is one who would rather avoid them at all costs. Remember that you should use computers *where appropriate*. You do not, for example, get extra marks for a piece of coursework simply because it is word processed. There are, however, advantages to this approach.

Computer technology is increasingly important in the world of work and in society in general, and so it is important that you attempt to use the technology at some stage of your course. You will probably find that your work in Geography builds on similar work covered elsewhere. You may even follow a specialist ICT course.

You should be aware of three major possible uses of ICT in Geography at GCSE.

Collecting information

It is possible to gain access to a wide range of material using ICT. Make sure that you are aware of the range of CD-ROMs available at your school. Learn to use the internet, if you do not already know how. The internet gives you access to information that is generally more up-to-date than through any other source.

Learn how to use a **search engine** effectively. Everyone's first experience of using the internet usually produces about a million results! Search engines have advanced facilities that may be used to narrow down your search and speed up the process.

Know how to cut and paste information from the internet to a word processing document. Internet material may be lengthy, and there is no need to save or to print whole documents. Whether on the school's system or on your own disk, have a separate folder to keep all of your internet files.

Make sure that you are able to use e-mail. Many internet documents contain e-mail contacts for further information. This is cheaper than writing letters, and much quicker.

Processing and analysing information

You may wish to process or *refine* some of your information. This generally involves converting information into graphs, diagrams or maps. A computer enables you to use a range of techniques, and to shift quickly from one means of presentation to another if the initial result is not satisfactory. Get to know how to use spreadsheets such as Excel. Within this software, you may easily produce a range of graphs to help with the processing of your figures. You may, for example, be able to input and graph the results of a questionnaire completed as a part of your coursework.

A **spreadsheet** or database is also a powerful tool in calculating and analysing data that you have collected. Make sure that you are familiar with all of the functions of these programs on your school computer.

Presenting coursework

A common reason for using ICT in GCSE Geography is to present coursework. Remember that a word processed piece of work is not automatically better than one that is handwritten. It may improve your presentation, however, and does have other advantages. You are able easily to edit and reorganise work held on computer, and to experiment with a variety of formats. It is possible to mix text and graphics effectively, for example, and to include scanned photographs and other material. Remember to use the **spellcheck** facility, but never rely on it. No spellcheck can reject 'there' wrongly used for 'their', for example; you need to read through your work carefully before handing it in.

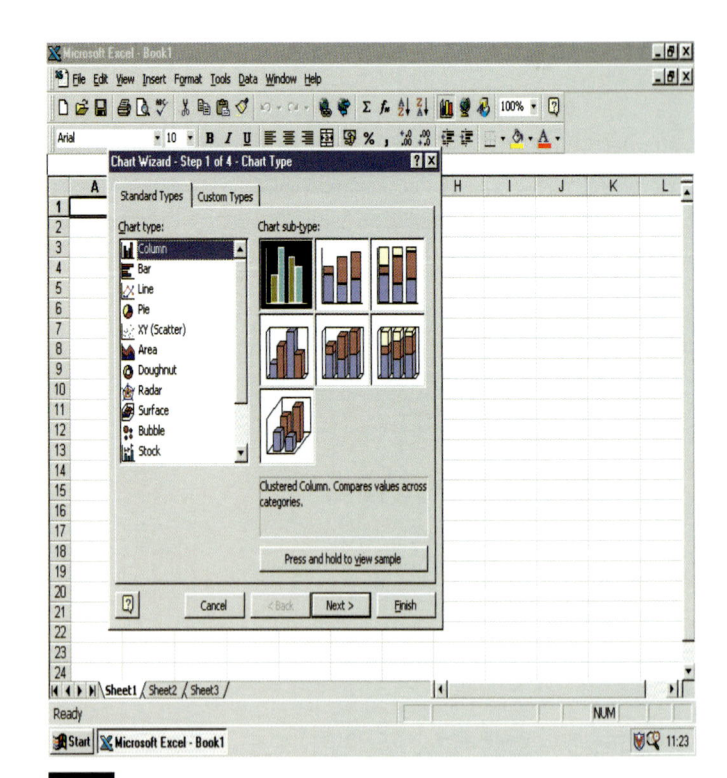

5E.2 *A spreadsheet has a range of functions to help with processing and presenting material*

Section 5 **What You Need to Succeed**

F Undertaking a coursework enquiry for GCSE

There is a **coursework** component of all GCSE syllabuses. This will be in the form of one or two pieces of work, depending on the syllabus you are following.

- The coursework component is approximately 25 per cent of the total assessment. Although this is less than the final examinations, coursework gives opportunities to be successful without the time pressures of the exam.
- Coursework requires you to complete an **enquiry** based on **primary** data collection. This will usually take the form of a fieldwork-based assignment, and involve the testing of an **hypothesis**.
- It will be assessed initially by your teachers. A sample of the work from your school will be sent to the exam board to check the standard of marking. This process is called **moderation**.

Why is coursework important?

The coursework component of the GCSE assesses your work in a different manner to the written examination papers. It is an important part of the assessment.

1 Coursework tests different elements of the syllabus to the written papers. It is not possible directly to test your ability to collect and analyse data over a period of time. The balance of assessment in coursework is on your understanding and application of knowledge. There is less weight given to factual recall, as there is in an exam. The ability to research, refine and analyse data is an important part of Geography that is best assessed over a period of time through coursework.

2 There is sufficient time available to revise and redraft your work. Many students do not produce their best work at the first attempt. The time allocated for coursework enables you to make mistakes, review what you have done, and improve it.

3 You have access to the expertise and guidance provided by your teachers. They are allowed to provide advice through the preliminary stages of coursework investigations, and should be seen as a valuable resource.

4 Many students improve their overall GCSE grade through high coursework marks. Continual assessment provides you with the opportunity to really show what you know, understand and can do.

5 You may receive the results of your coursework before sitting the final exams. In this way, you will already have a bench mark against which to measure the rest of your exam preparation.

6 Geography is about the world around you, and extends beyond the classroom and the exam room. Coursework gives you the opportunity to study a part of that world first hand.

Planning an enquiry

This piece of coursework requires primary data collection. This is very different from using textbooks or information from your teachers. Primary data is in essence information that you have collected yourself. It may be, for example, the data from questionnaires, traffic counts, or sketches and photographs. Primary data collection is often more challenging than **secondary** data, which is collected from books and other sources. You have to be organised, manage your time, and will probably need to design your own survey sheets and questionnaires.

5F.1 *Data collection*

Your enquiry will probably be based on your local area. Primary data is important because it is unlikely that there will be much information in textbooks about your topic.

Section 5 What You Need to Succeed

Your coursework will follow a series of stages, which are common to all geographical enquiries. The steps of a geographical investigation are shown in Figure 5F.2. Use the guidelines provided in the following sections to help you with your own enquiry. Throughout the stages, reference is made to an investigation made by students into the town of Kettering. This is used as an example; your enquiry topic will be different, but the steps taken will be the same.

your previous study for GCSE, and may involve reading, discussion or observation. The outcome of your enquiry needs to be an **extended piece of writing.** Although data collection is important, so too is the analysis and interpretation of that data.

Your topic for study will generally be phrased in the context of an **hypothesis**. This is an idea or question that you will use data to prove or disprove by means of your enquiry.

Kettering town investigation, Step 1

For the GCSE students in Kettering, Step 1 involved:

- Unit of study: People and Place
- Topic of study: Urban–rural interaction. This is related to a study of the ways in which urban areas have changed in the past, and are likely to develop in the future.
- The hypothesis which generated the enquiry was: *Urban environments in Kettering are changing as the town continues to expand.*

Step 2: Write about the hypothesis in more detail

Once the topic has been decided, you will need to complete a written introduction to your enquiry. This is where you will write about your hypothesis in more detail, but you need to keep the introduction quite brief. The majority of marks in the assessment of your enquiry will be allocated to data collection and data analysis. Do not, for example, undertake an extensive historical introduction to the location of your study.

You should think of your hypothesis as being broken down into smaller and more manageable sections. You will tackle a series of specific questions or problems in order to investigate your hypothesis.

5F.2 *The enquiry process*

(Ladder diagram, steps 1–8:
1. Decide upon a study topic
2. Write about the hypothesis in more detail
3. Decide what data to collect
4. Collect your data
5. Refine your data
6. Interpret and explain your results
7. Conclusion
8. Evaluation)

Kettering town investigation, Step 2

For the GCSE students in Kettering, Step 2 involved:

- Completing a title page and contents page
- A brief introduction to the ways in which Kettering has changed in the past and ways the town might develop in the future
- How the growth of the town could be related to models of urban growth (see Figure 5F.3).

Step 1: Decide upon a study topic

It is likely that the topic will be chosen by your teachers, or that you will be given a list to choose from. Deciding on a topic yourself is very difficult, but it is also a part of the enquiry process. Your topic for study will be connected to

F Undertaking a coursework enquiry for GCSE

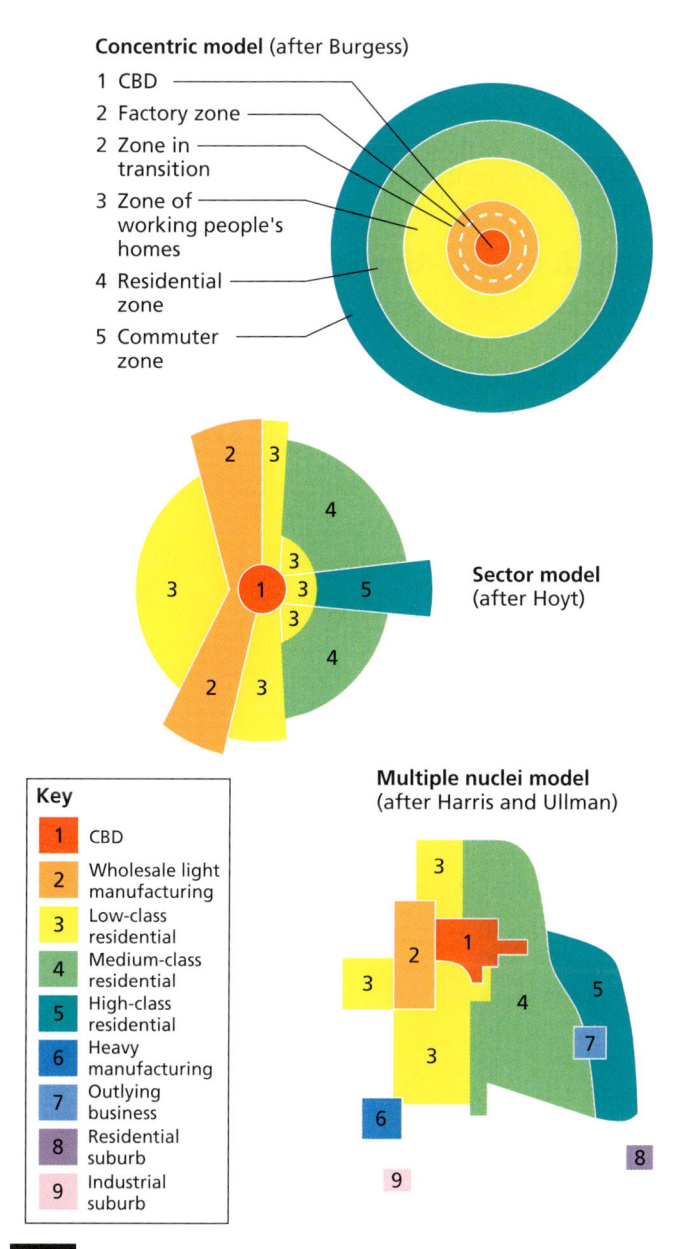

What you need to succeed

Concentric model (after Burgess)
1 CBD
2 Factory zone
2 Zone in transition
3 Zone of working people's homes
4 Residential zone
5 Commuter zone

Sector model (after Hoyt)

Multiple nuclei model (after Harris and Ullman)

Key
1 CBD
2 Wholesale light manufacturing
3 Low-class residential
4 Medium-class residential
5 High-class residential
6 Heavy manufacturing
7 Outlying business
8 Residential suburb
9 Industrial suburb

5F.3 *Comparing urban models to the growth of Kettering is one step in the enquiry process*

Bi-polar sheet

Date _____ Time _____
Location _____
Description of area _____

Circle one number for each of the descriptions below:

Unemotional	1	2	3	4	5	6	7	Emotional
Ugly	1	2	3	4	5	6	7	Beautiful
Obvious	1	2	3	4	5	6	7	Mysterious
Harmonious	1	2	3	4	5	6	7	Discordant
Cold	1	2	3	4	5	6	7	Warm
Soft	1	2	3	4	5	6	7	Hard
Frustrating	1	2	3	4	5	6	7	Satisfying
Private	1	2	3	4	5	6	7	Public
Dislike	1	2	3	4	5	6	7	Like
Unstimulating	1	2	3	4	5	6	7	Stimulating
Full	1	2	3	4	5	6	7	Empty
Pleasant	1	2	3	4	5	6	7	Unpleasant
Disruptive	1	2	3	4	5	6	7	Peaceful
Disordered	1	2	3	4	5	6	7	Ordered

Street survey

Date _____ Time _____ Street _____
Most common type of house, e.g. Terraced _____
Approximate height of house in metres/storeys: _____
Age of houses _____ House price _____

1 2 3 4 5 6

The pavement	Full of holes		No holes
Parked cars	Many cars		No cars
Litter	Lot of litter		No litter
Grass verges	None		Wide grass verges
Trees	No trees		Lots of trees
Air	Lot of fumes		No fumes
Buildings	Run down		In good condition
Noise	Lot of noise		Not noisy
Street lights	Badly lit		Well lit
Other			
Total			

5F.4 *Examples of data recording sheets*

Step 3: Decide what data to collect

For this section, you need to decide:

1 what data you need to collect
2 how to collect the data.

Remember that all data should be relevant to your enquiry. Before collecting any data, check this. If one or more methods of data collection are not relevant, leave them out. You will not gain credit, for example, for including questionnaires if they do not relate directly to your hypothesis.

You may need to design survey sheets or questionnaires. You will almost certainly need to plan when to visit particular locations. Even if taking part in group fieldwork, you are likely to be expected to organise some of your own data collection. Time will be limited, so make sure you are organised before you go.

Step 4: Collect your data

Ensure that you follow your plan for data collection. Record your information accurately. Remember that you do not need to interpret or analyse any results when doing fieldwork. You will have time to do this later. Make sure that you do not spend too long on your data collection, as the interpretation of data is also very important.

Section 5 What You Need to Succeed

> ### Kettering town investigation, Step 3
>
> The Kettering study involved visiting different areas of the town. These areas were selected by students to include the CBD, inner and outer suburbs, and areas undergoing development and expansion. Students worked in small groups, and decided upon a range of data collection that included various data recording sheets (Figure 5F.4). To follow the written introduction for Step 2, the final enquiry included:
>
> - a description of what data need to be collected
> - an explanation of why these types of data were relevant
> - a plan of how the data was to be collected.

> ### Kettering town investigation, Step 4
>
> For Kettering, the enquiry included:
>
> - a written description of the data collected
> - a sample of data recording sheets used
> - a description of problems encountered. Fieldwork never goes perfectly.

Step 5: Refine your data

The purpose of this step is to refine your data for interpretation and presentation. It is important that you do not simply copy out your results or include, for example, a batch of completed questionnaires (these may be placed in an Appendix, and referred to in your writing).

Refining data means presenting it in other, more useful, forms such as maps and diagrams. You may, for example, have completed traffic counts as part of your data collection. This information could be shown as a flow line map, with the width of the line being proportional to the amount of traffic. Questionnaire results could be shown by means of various graphs.

Step 6: Interpret and explain your results

At this stage you will begin to write in as much detail as possible. Look back at each of the questions or problems that you identified in Step 2 as part of the hypothesis. This will help you to analyse the data as it relates to the hypothesis. Compare what you *actually* found with what you *expected* to find when you started your enquiry.

Step 7: Conclusion

You need to relate your overall findings to the original hypothesis. This will involve bringing together your ideas. Try to write about general trends and patterns. If possible, refer to any models or theories that have been described earlier in your enquiry.

Step 8: Evaluation

It is important that you take time to look through your work, and to decide what went well and what did not go so well. This is your evaluation, which is a personal opinion of the work you have completed. Be honest with yourself.

- How well, overall, do you think your enquiry went?
- What problems did you have?
- What were the limitations of your enquiry?
- What do you think could have been improved?
- If you had more time, what else could be added to your enquiry?

You should also remember the following points before handing in your completed enquiry.

- At the end of your enquiry, include a bibliography. List all the resources that you used.
- Allow some time to read through your completed work. It is always possible that you have made some mistakes that could be corrected.
- Remember to carefully check your spelling, punctuation and grammar.
- Present your work clearly and organise it carefully. A completed enquiry is easier to read and to assess if it is well organised throughout. Include any extra information required by your exam board, for example your Centre or candidate number.
- Make sure that all diagrams and maps are labelled and titled. You should refer to these in your writing.
- Make sure your work is finished. You will not be able to gain high marks if some of your work is missing or incomplete.
- Meet the deadline set by your teacher. You need to remember that the amount of time allowed for the enquiry is set by the exam board, not your teacher. If you fail to meet the deadline, you run the risk of losing marks. See your teachers well in advance of the deadline to talk about any problems.

Section 5 What you need to succeed

G Taking notes and researching

Taking notes

Notes are your own personal record of the information you have recorded during your GCSE Geography course. As such, they are unique to you. Effective note-taking is essential to provide you with the basis for revision and success in your examinations. Photocopying or highlighting pages from a book are no substitutes for good notes.

Notes should be written 'in note form' which is not as continuous prose, which would be very difficult to revise from; your notes should ideally be ready to use for revision. Copying every detail from a source of information is not appropriate; you would not be able to remember it all. Make your notes reasonably brief, then, and to the point. Do not include irrelevant information.

Organise your notes effectively. Whether you use a folder or exercise book, keep an accurate and up-to-date list of the contents of your notes. Include all additional information such as worksheets, test results, etc. An accurate list is useful as a checklist from which to revise. If you have notes missing or incomplete, it is time consuming and difficult to catch up at the last moment. Your teachers will not have time to go through anything more than once.

Your notes will be more effective and easier to read if they include the following.

Key words These are the essential and basic pieces of information you need to know about a topic, eg factors affecting location of an industry, reasons for coastal erosion. Write these key words in a distinct way, for example by using different colours, block capitals, or leaving space around the words.

Bullet points These help you to write the main points as an orderly list of what you need to remember.

Diagrams A well-annotated diagram or sketch map includes a large amount of information in a format which is easy to learn.

Tables and charts These help you to organise your thoughts, and are easy to revise from. Fitting notes into boxes encourages you to keep to the point, as there is not enough room to write at length.

What should notes include?

Your notes are likely to be organised into sections and topics. You may, for example, have a section on urban geography, one topic within which may be *rural–urban interaction*. Make sure that you clearly title all sections and topics. For each topic, you should include information answering the following questions.

1 What? What is the topic or issue about? Are you studying a river landform, tropical storms, or transnational companies?

2 Why? What is the relevance of the topic to your study of Geography? Why is the topic important? Why, for example, is desertification an important issue? Why is acid rain a problem?

3 How? What are the processes that are taking place? How has the topic or issue developed over time? How, for example, has the gap between rich and poor countries become so great?

4 Where? You need to have specific case studies, and be able accurately to locate them. When studying the multiplier effect, for example, the NEC in Birmingham could be used as a case study to show what happens. For your revision, use **case study cards** (see Figure 5H.1).

> **NOTING ACTIVITIES**
>
> 1 Look at Figure 5G.1. Write down any points that you think make these good notes.
>
> 2 Take one topic in your GCSE notes. Organise them along the lines suggested above. Have you had to make many changes? Do you think your notes are now more effective?

Researching

Researching means finding information out for yourself. This will involve collecting information from a variety of sources. Researching is therefore very different from being given information in lessons by teachers. You may be given class time to research, but you will also need to use your own time to investigate a topic thoroughly. The aim of research is to gather information from more than just one source. In this way your knowledge and understanding of a topic will be more detailed, increasing your interest and improving your chances in the examinations. A question in an examination may ask for 'a named example of an ecosystem that has been changed by human impact'. As the question does not specify an ecosystem, you are free to choose any example to fit in with your interest and understanding.

Section 5 What You Need to Succeed

Two of the world's 10 largest cities are in Brazil
a) São Paulo
b) Rio de Janeiro

Many have moved to these cities and found:
- Favelas - slums on outside of city
- povety
- overcrowding
- few services
- high death rates

WHAT?

The growth of cities is called urbanisation. It is where an increasing proportion of people live in towns and cities. Urbanisation is a process which has affected all parts of the world.

WHY?

Urbanisation is an important issue in geography today. Cities are growing very quickly in LEDCs - not so fast now in MEDCs.

Predicted that by 2010, 8 out of 10 largest cities will be in LEDCs

1 = Mexico City 28 million
2 = São Paulo 24 million

Urbanisation causes problems:

- overcrowding
- pollution
- infrastructure (e.g. sewage, water, cannot cope)

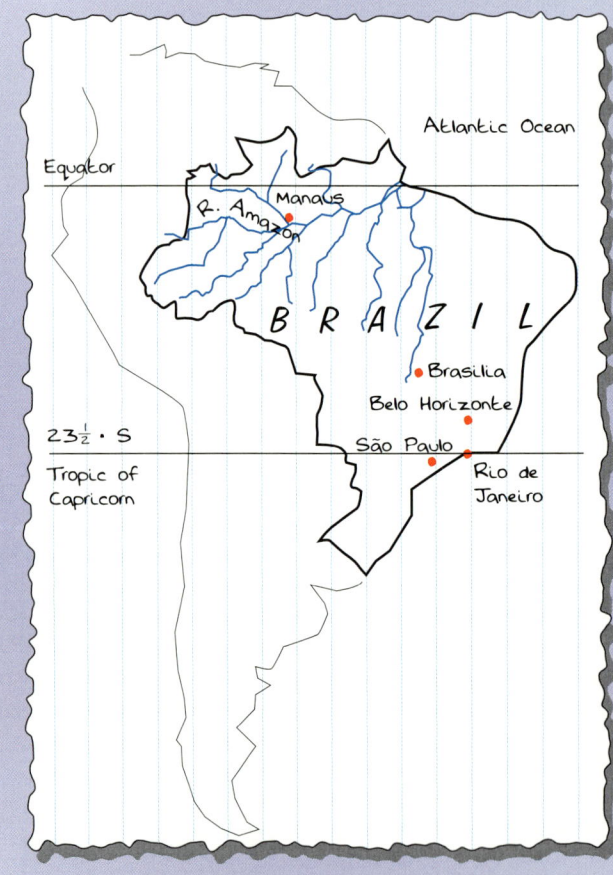

WHERE?

Case Study - Brazil
- 5th largest country in the world
- population 163 million (UK 58 million)
- urban population 78% (UK 91%)

Urbanisation:
- 1960, most people lived in villages
- 40 million people moved to cities in 30 years

Main reason = rural push. People know cities are not perfect, but life in the countryside is so hard.

HOW?

The process has happened because of:
Urban pull and rural push

Urban pull
- industrialisation in MEDCs
- attraction of better paid jobs
- services
- better housing
- "bright lights" - entertainment etc.

Rural push
- poor living conditions
- natural hazards - e.g. floods
- drought
- famine - poor crop yield
- pests and diseases
- conflicts

5G.1 *Notes on the topic of urbanisation*

G Taking notes and researching

Research requires the use of two types of material. The first is **primary** data. This is information that you collect through your own personal observations, such as street surveys or questionnaires. Primary data is very important in undertaking enquiries, especially as part of your coursework (see pages 165–168). In most of your class work, however, you will use the second type of data, which is **secondary** data. This involves the use of textbooks, the internet, newspapers and other media.

Collecting secondary data

You will use information within school in your research, and may also have access to materials at home. Alternatively, your local library may be a good source of information.

Get to know the sources available in your school library, if you are not already familiar with them. Make sure that you know what is available on your school's computer network, and are able to use the ICT facilities effectively. What sources of information should you look for when researching? Although it is not possible to give a complete list of all material suitable for GCSE Geography, you should make use of the following.

1 Textbooks You will probably use a core textbook in class, along with others for some sections of your course. In addition to these books, it is probable that your school library will have a range of books that provide useful background and extension material. These books are not bought in class sets, are sometimes very expensive, and are used less often than your core books. Use the classification system carefully, as some useful information will be stored in areas other than the Geography section of the library. You will need to look through the Science section, for example, to find information on earthquakes and volcanoes.

Textbooks provide specific information that you can quickly and easily add to your notes. Be careful with your choice of book to use. Is the book specific to the task in hand; is it geographical? Is the book up-to-date? Certain types of data become history very quickly. You do not, for example, want to write about the growing economies of south-east Asia from a book that was written before the problems of 1997 experienced by this region.

2 Reference books Your library will certainly contain encyclopaedias, atlases and other texts that may only be used in the library. These are useful sources of specific information, for example data relating to a named country or region. As with textbooks, reference material may date quickly. Encyclopaedias are so expensive to buy that it is not possible for them to be replaced regularly.

3 CD-ROMs Increasingly important as a source of research material, CDs are capable of holding a large quantity of material, and can store soundtracks and video footage as well as written text. They have the big advantage of inbuilt search facilities that allow you quickly to find and cross-reference information. You may then cut and paste material into a word processed document.

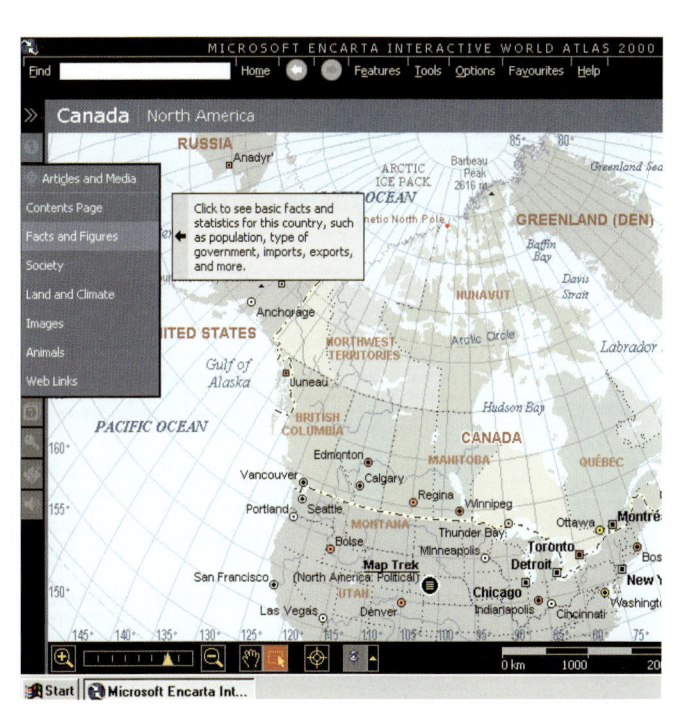

5G.2 *CD-ROMs provide detailed information that may easily be searched and cross-referenced*

4 Newspapers and magazines Your library probably takes at least one daily newspaper. The information provided by newspapers is up-to-date, and many articles provide web addresses and other useful links. Make sure that the information you use is relevant and geographical. Local newspapers often provide useful information about local issues.

There are also numerous magazines that provide information on geographical topics. Some of these are for the general reader, such as *The Geographical Magazine*. Others, such as *Wideworld*, are aimed specifically at students. Check to see if your library subscribes to any of these magazines.

5 The internet The internet gives you potential access to a vast range of information that would only have been available to academic researchers a few years ago. Using the internet you can obtain current information about almost any subject. You can download and print results, and often find e-mail contacts to develop your knowledge further.

Using the internet can be very frustrating at first. You can spend a long time 'surfing' without achieving anything useful. There is such a great deal available and the difficulty is finding your way to what you need. When searching for a topic such as tropical rainforests, for example, nearly one million references may appear. Advance search facilities are available, but they take time and practice to use well, so enlist help when you start your searches.

Section 5 **What You Need to Succeed**

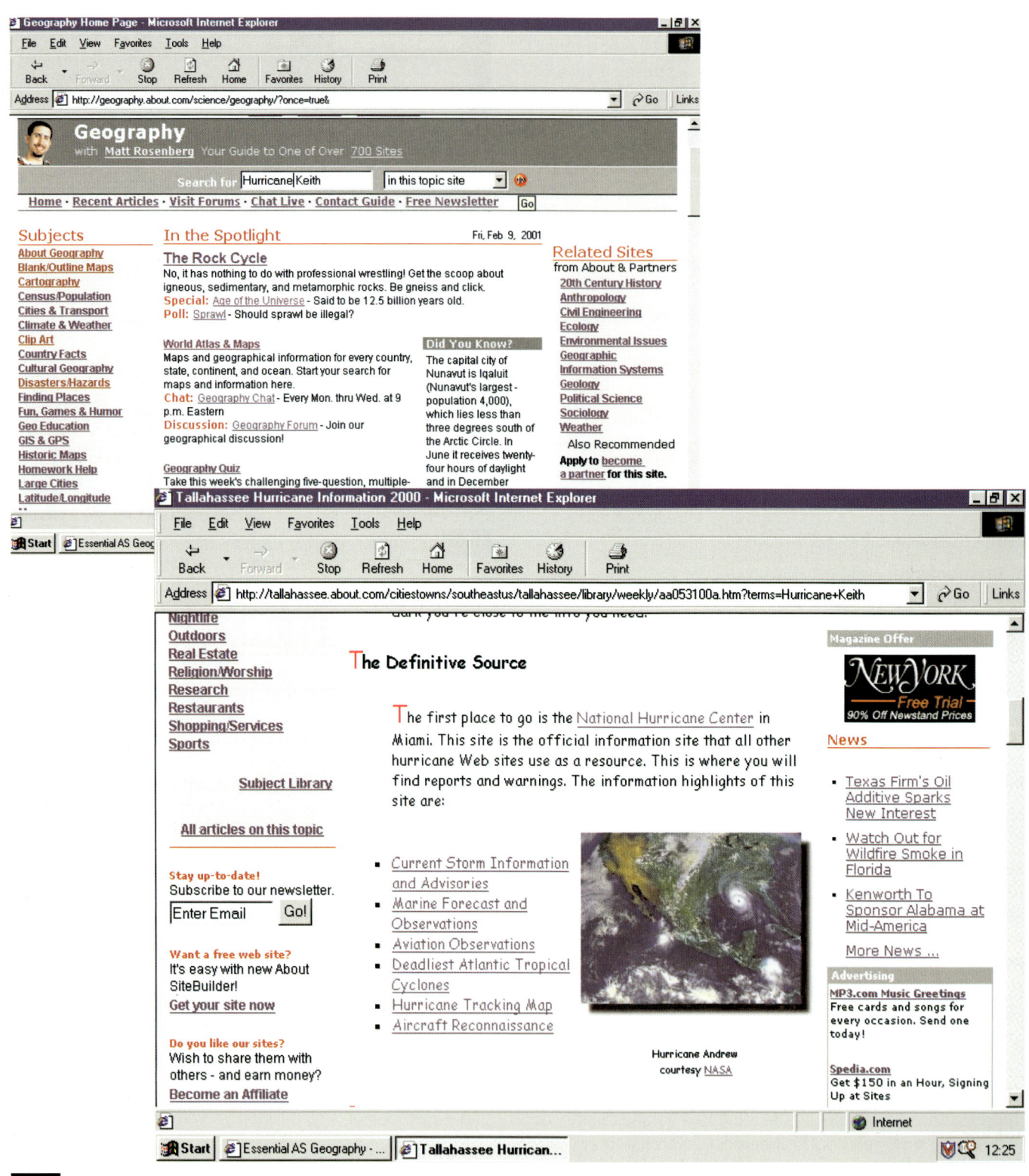

5G.3 *Using the internet (for more on Hurricane Keith see pages 224–225)*

Section 5 What You Need to Succeed

H Revision and exam preparation

The examinations that you sit at the end of your course form the major part of the GCSE assessment. Coursework is important, but your final grade will depend mainly upon how well you perform in the written examination papers. An exam paper lasting as little as 90 minutes, for example, is likely to be worth more towards your GCSE grade than all of your coursework.

It is impossible for the exam papers to assess absolutely everything you have learned during your course. Instead, the exams will:

- select material from elements of the syllabus
- test skills you have learned, as well as your knowledge and understanding.

To succeed, you must ensure that you have a complete set of notes from which to **revise**. There are numerous published materials to help you. While these are useful, the best source for revision is your folder or book of work completed in lessons. Your notes will be specific to your syllabus, and should also include feedback and advice from your teacher and extra material such as practice exam questions.

You will need to revise all of your work in preparation for the exams, and to practice past questions. This will greatly increase your chance of success in the exam. The following sections provide advice on how to revise, and give some tips on how to answer some written exam questions.

To be effective, revision should be a process that takes place throughout your course. It should not be something that is only undertaken in the last few weeks or days before the exam. You should revise a topic more than once, and revisit major sections as often as possible. This repetition helps to store information in your long-term memory. Your aim should be to turn up to the examination confident that you have covered everything thoroughly.

Revising case studies

Throughout your course, you will illustrate topics and issues with reference to named examples or case studies. These help to give meaning to and explain some of the theory covered in your Geography lessons. Case studies are also the single most important element of examination questions, and so must be revised thoroughly. You will probably choose your questions in the exams on the basis of the case studies required.

There are many different techniques for revision which apply to case studies. Revision is an individual process, and you must choose the method that best suits you. These are some popular revision techniques, which could be applied to most of your GCSE subjects.

1 Case study cards

One problem many students find when revising is the amount of written work that has built up during the course. After the GCSE exams, many students say that they struggled with the *quantity* of revision, rather than the level of difficulty. Revising from a large set of notes is difficult, and so it is useful to summarise your notes.

One way to do this is to write the important information relating to a case study onto a postcard-sized card. Restricting the information to two sides of a card gives you the opportunity to include the main points, without writing too much. This is what you will have to do in the exam.

What should case study cards contain?

Each card must be clearly **titled** (see Figure 5H.1). Start with the module or unit heading, then a sub-heading if appropriate. Colour coding your headings will help to organise your cards. You could even use different colour cards for each section.

Name your case study. You need to be precise. If an exam question requires information about rainforests, name countries such as Brazil and Cameroon. You will have to locate your case study. You will lose marks if you are unable accurately to locate your named examples; often a mark scheme restricts credit to half marks if this is missing. The information could be given either in written form or as a simple sketch map.

Key information Write the main points about your case study in note form. This is easier to learn than lengthy notes, and saves space. You will sometimes be able to use abbreviated forms of writing in the exam, particularly if you are running out of time (eg lists, bullet points).

Cross-referencing It is easy to regard case studies as only being relevant to one topic of work. Many named examples may be used in other parts of your syllabus. The ability to cross-reference in an examination answer is likely to gain you credit.

When should the cards be written?

The cards should ideally be written at the end of each module or topic of work. In this way, they are available for

173

Section 5 What You Need to Succeed

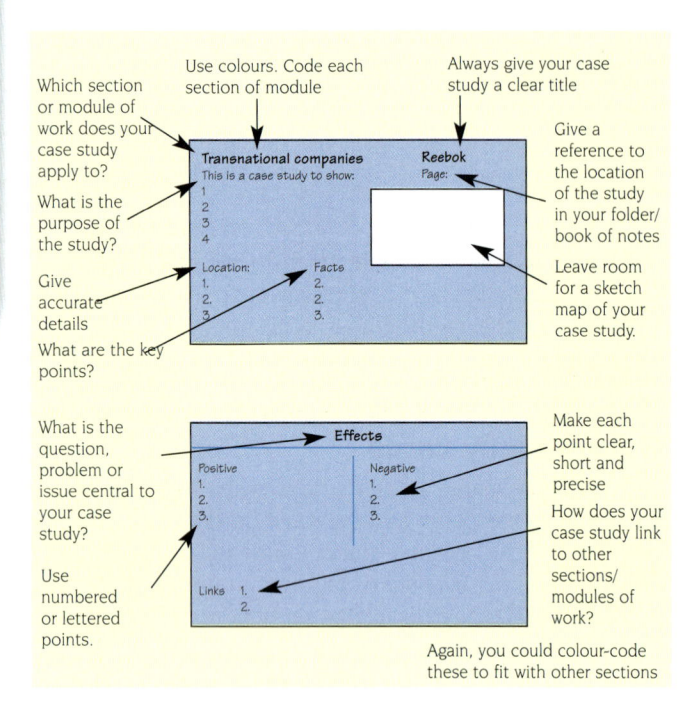

5H.1 *A case study card*

any assessments you may have, such as end of unit tests or mock exams. Writing cards throughout the course also spreads the workload, and enables you to revise over a longer period of time.

2 Revising with other people

Revision may be a lonely and repetitive task, and so many students find it easier to work with other people. Revising with friends enables the sharing of ideas, and informal testing of knowledge and understanding. Try to attend any revision sessions offered by your school. It is often not possible to ask for individual help with revision in lessons, while revision sessions allow greater flexibility.

3 Recording your notes

Some students find it useful to tape record their notes. Information is sometimes retained better when it is heard rather than read. Reviewing notes through a personal stereo provides the advantage that revision may take place almost anywhere, without reference to written notes.

4 Practice papers

It is essential to answer past exam questions if you are going to be fully prepared for your final examinations. It is useful to tackle individual questions, but it is only by working through a whole paper that you will gain a real understanding of the problems and the techniques needed to overcome them. It is likely that your school will give you formal mock exams, which provide practice under exam conditions. Make sure that you answer as many past questions as possible. Use mark schemes and examiners' reports, as well as feedback from your teachers.

To answer the questions accurately, you will need to have a clear understanding of **command** words. When marking your papers, examiners will look for your answers in response to these words. If asked to *explain* the pattern on a map, for example, is this what you do, or do you merely *describe* the pattern? Look at the key words in Figure 5H.2. Try to match each key word with its description, before looking at the answers on page 176.

Command word		Definition	
1	Compare	a	present in a brief, clear form
2	Describe	b	look for the similarities and differences between
3	Contrast	c	give a detailed account of
4	Outline	d	write about the main differences between
5	State	e	make a simple point
6	Comment on	f	make some simple points about
7	Interpret	g	give reasons for
8	What factors	h	state why
9	Assess	i	explain a graph or map
10	Explain	j	write about the main points only
11	Account for	k	give the influencing or main parts
12	Give your views	l	give the influencing arguments or factors
13	How might	m	choose or select
14	What considerations	n	state your opinions
15	Identify	o	in what ways could
16	Analyse	p	make a judgement on, often in relation to several points
17	Summarise	q	assess how well something has been done, or assess the success of something
18	Evaluate	r	examine carefully and find the main points
19	Justify	s	give reasons for your choice

5H.2 *Command words commonly used in examination questions*

H Revision and exam preparation

Now look at the extracts from examination questions shown in Figure 5H.3. Write out each question and highlight the command words contained in each of them. In the examination, use a highlighter pen to make it easy to pick out the command terms around which to base your answer. Many exam papers have the command words either in bold text or capital letters.

1. Describe the distribution of squatter settlements in the city.
2. Compare the two settlements under the following headings.
3. What, in your opinion, are the most important problems to solve in the settlements?
4. Summarise your recommendations, and justify your plan for the development of the settlements in the future.
5. For a named area outside the United Kingdom, describe how a natural landform is being managed by people.
6. For a named industrial or office development, describe the development and explain why the site was chosen.
7. With reference to the data, explain the differences in annual precipitation and temperature between Berlin and Shannon.
8. For either Japan or the USA, comment on any two of the following.
9. Using information in the table, identify the main reasons why people have moved.
10. With reference to a named ecosystem, assess the extent to which people have altered the natural environment.

5H.3 *Extracts from examination questions*

Examination tips

There are several tips to consider for when the day of your exam arrives.

- Arrive early. The last thing you want to do is to arrive in a panic, and to be agitated when you start your exam. Be at least fifteen minutes early.
- Relax before entering the exam room. Some people try deep breathing exercises, or thinking about another place or a person in order to take their mind off the exam. This helps to calm your nerves and to perform better in the exam.
- Arrive properly equipped. Have plenty of pens and pencils, a ruler, calculator, etc.
- Read the paper carefully. If there is a choice of questions, make sure you know exactly how many to answer.
- Read through each question before answering. Take your time before you start, rather than rushing to get going. A few minutes organising your thoughts before writing anything will help you later on.
- Make sure that you can answer every part of a question before starting. It is easy to begin a question with simple answers, only to find that you are unable to answer the final part of the question. This is the part that usually carries the greatest number of marks.
- Answer the question. Write about what the question is asking, not what you would like it to be asking. Do not simply write out everything you have learned about the topic; make your answers specific to the requirements of the question.
- Choose your named examples carefully. Your case study must be appropriate as well as accurate to gain high marks.
- Spend appropriate time on each question. Timing is likely to be a major pressure. Write the approximate timing for each question on your question paper.
- Finish the paper. It is no good leaving the exam room having needed five extra minutes to complete the exam. If you are under pressure towards the end of the exam, consider putting answers down as bullets, notes or a table. You are likely to gain some credit for this.
- Think of the exam as one task, rather than as a series of separate questions. You will only receive one grade at the end of it all.
- Read through your answers if you have time. It is surprising how many basic errors are made under the pressure of exams.
- Remember to check your spelling, punctuation and grammar. Your written English does not have to be perfect to gain full marks, but be aware that you will be assessed on geographical terminology as well as your general use of language.

Section 5 What You Need to Succeed

Command word		Definition	
1	Compare	b	look for the similarities and differences between
2	Describe	c	give a detailed account of
3	Contrast	d	write about the main differences between
4	Outline	a	present in a brief, clear form
5	State	e	make a simple point
6	Comment on	f	make some simple points about
7	Interpret	r	examine carefully and find the main points
8	What factors	l	give the influencing arguments or factors
9	Assess	p	make a judgement on, often in relation to several points
10	Explain	h	state why
11	Account for	g	give reasons for
12	Give your views	n	state your opinions
13	How might	o	in what ways could
14	What considerations	k	give the influencing or main parts
15	Identify	m	choose or select
16	Analyse	i	explain a graph or map
17	Summarise	j	write about the main points only
18	Evaluate	q	assess how well something has been done, or assess the success of something
19	Justify	s	give reasons for your choice

Section 6 Coping with Hazards

A What is a hazard?

A hazard is something that results from processes in the natural environment and that may be harmful to people. We are concerned here with **natural** hazards, rather than those caused by people. Acid rain may be a hazard in that it has the potential to harm both people and the environment. It is not natural, however, being caused by human activity. An earthquake is a natural process, but many are not actually classified as hazards. To be called a hazard, an earthquake has to have an impact upon people. Many natural processes such as volcanic eruptions and avalanches occur without affecting people, and therefore are not hazards.

There are two main types of hazard resulting from processes in the environment. Hazards are related either to the **climate** or to **landforms** (see Figure 6A.1). Why are hazards such an important issue in the study of Geography?

- Millions of people live in constant danger of hazards.
- In the last 30 years alone, hazards have killed millions of people throughout the world (Figure 6A.2)
- They do not occur at random, and may often be predicted. Although it is not possible to prevent hazards such as earthquakes, advance warning may reduce loss of life. Long term planning is able to reduce the amount of damage caused, for example by constructing earthquake proof buildings
- Many hazards attract people. A volcano may be as much a tourist attraction as a threat to local inhabitants.

The case studies in this section examine the effects of hazards upon people, and the different ways in which

6A.1 *Types of hazard*

Section 6 Coping with Hazards

people respond to hazards (see Figure 6A.3). Earthquakes and volcanoes are used as examples of landform-related hazards, fires and floods being associated with climate. Each study asks and answers the same questions.

- What was it?
- When was it?
- Where was it?
- Why did it happen?
- What impact did it have?
- Who did it affect?
- How were the problems solved?
- What could be done to prevent the hazard?

Landform hazards

Volcanoes and earthquakes are among the most common and destructive of hazards. They are responsible for a high death toll (Figure 6A.2) and for the destruction of property throughout the world. Volcanoes and earthquakes occur in regular patterns, linked to the boundaries of the Earth's **plates**. It is clear from Figure 6A.4 that they are likely to have a major impact on some countries, while others remain unaffected. It is possible for many earthquakes and volcanic eruptions to be predicted, although little can be done to prevent them happening.

Hazard	Number of people killed (approx.)
Earthquake	750 000
Volcanic eruption	3 000
Tsunami	8 000
Storms	1 000 000
Floods	350 000
Droughts	1 500 000
Extreme temperatures	5 000

6A.2 *The destruction caused by hazards since 1970*

Millions of people live in constant danger from earthquakes and volcanoes, yet many continue to live in danger zones even when there is the chance to move elsewhere. The damage and loss of life caused by earthquakes and volcanoes varies greatly throughout the world. The greatest destruction is usually in the poorer parts of the world. LEDCs often have poor early warning systems, and most buildings are not strong enough to withstand the effects of an earthquake.

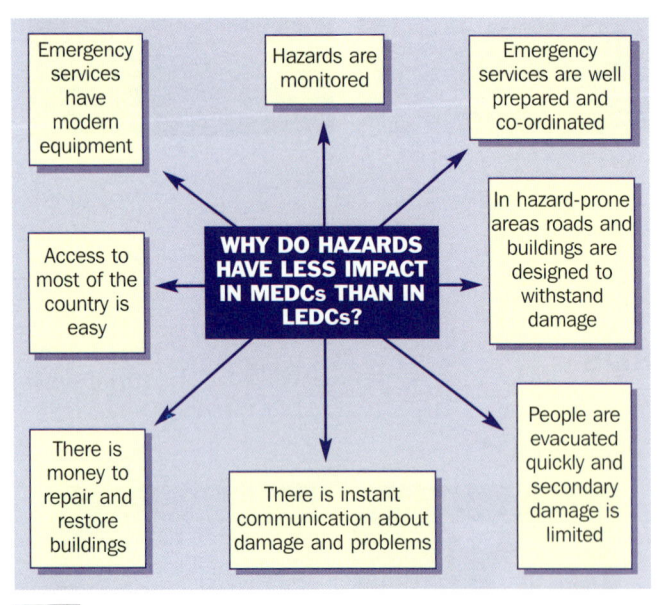

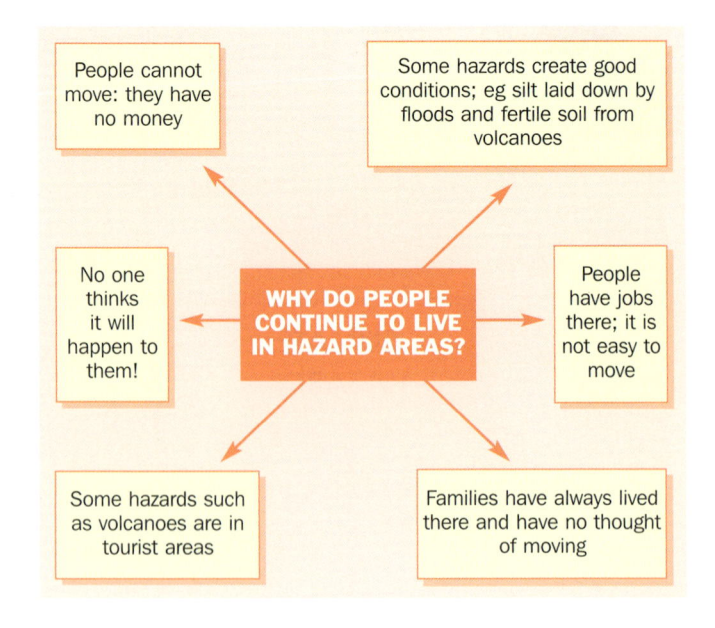

WHY DO HAZARDS HAVE LESS IMPACT IN MEDCs THAN IN LEDCs?
- Emergency services have modern equipment
- Hazards are monitored
- Emergency services are well prepared and co-ordinated
- In hazard-prone areas roads and buildings are designed to withstand damage
- People are evacuated quickly and secondary damage is limited
- There is instant communication about damage and problems
- There is money to repair and restore buildings
- Access to most of the country is easy

WHY DO PEOPLE CONTINUE TO LIVE IN HAZARD AREAS?
- People cannot move: they have no money
- Some hazards create good conditions; eg silt laid down by floods and fertile soil from volcanoes
- No one thinks it will happen to them!
- People have jobs there; it is not easy to move
- Some hazards such as volcanoes are in tourist areas
- Families have always lived there and have no thought of moving

6A.3 *Coping with hazards*

NOTING ACTIVITIES

1. List the hazards shown in Figure 6A.1.
2. Give a named example of each of these hazards. There is at least one example of each hazard in this book.
3. Locate each of your named examples on a map of the world.
4. Japan is a country of many hazards. Find out which hazards affect Japan, and give a named example of each.

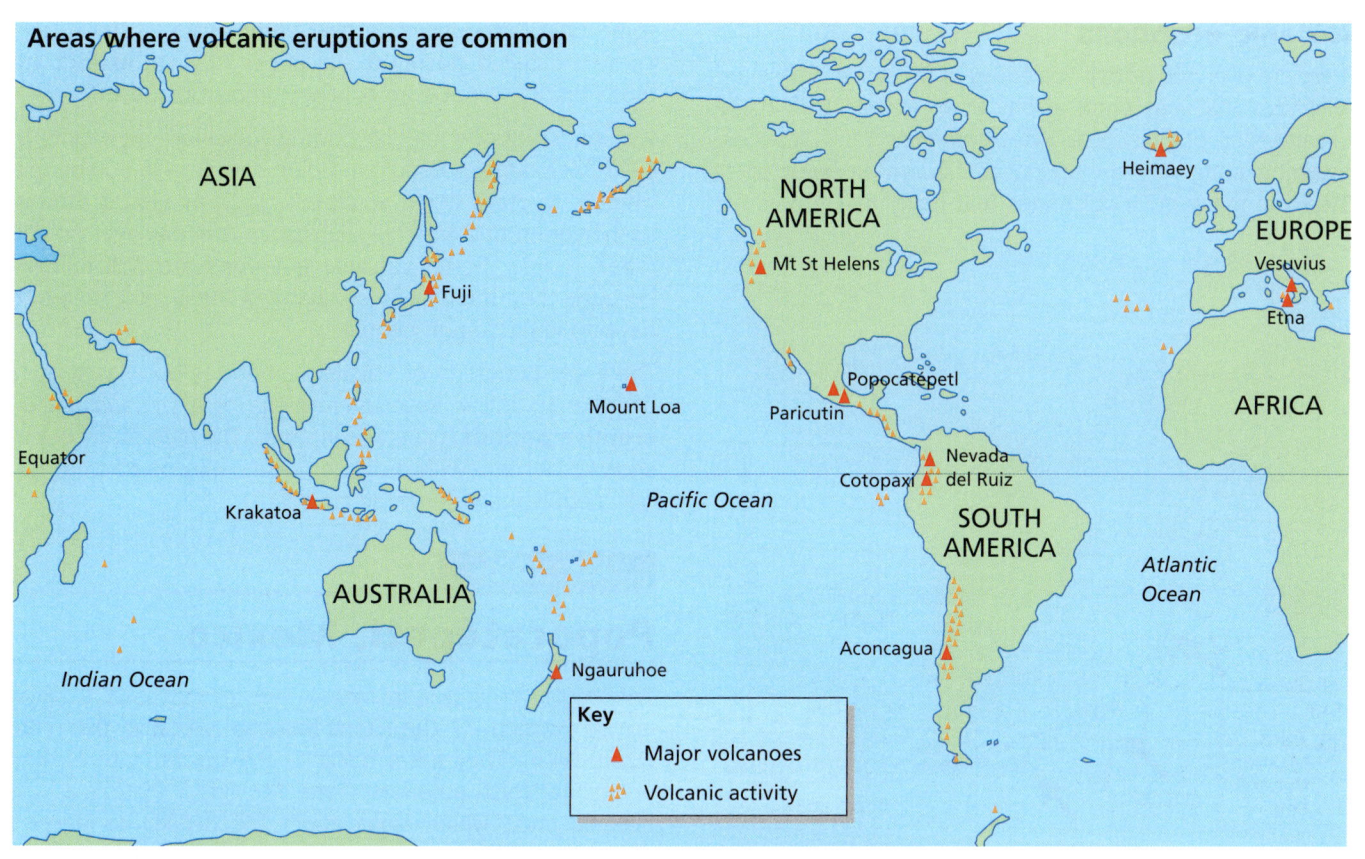

A What is a hazard?

Areas where volcanic eruptions are common

- Heimaey
- Fuji
- Mt St Helens
- Vesuvius
- Etna
- Mount Loa
- Popocatépetl
- Paricutin
- Cotopaxi
- Nevada del Ruiz
- Krakatoa
- Ngauruhoe
- Aconcagua

Key
- ▲ Major volcanoes
- Volcanic activity

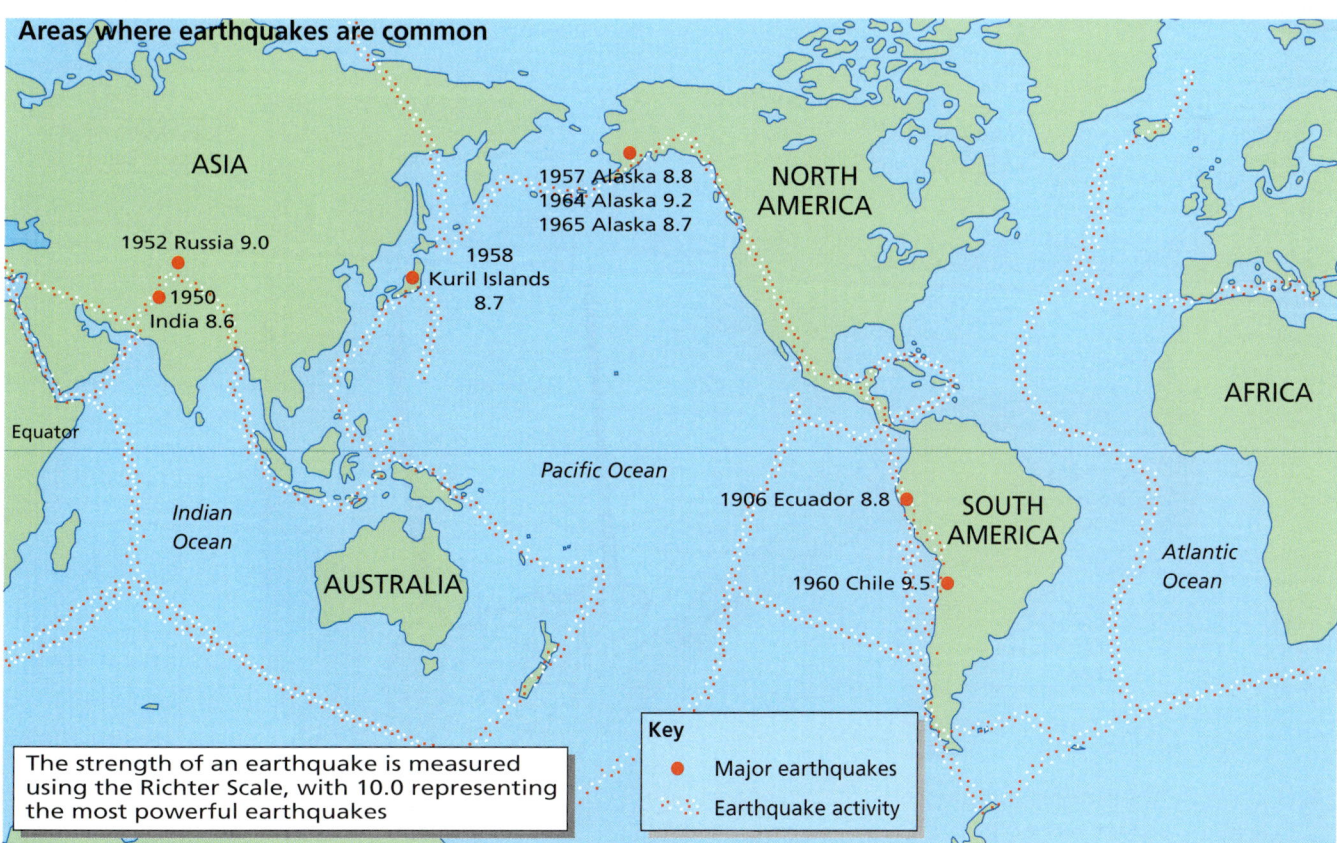

Areas where earthquakes are common

- 1952 Russia 9.0
- 1950 India 8.6
- 1958 Kuril Islands 8.7
- 1957 Alaska 8.8
- 1964 Alaska 9.2
- 1965 Alaska 8.7
- 1906 Ecuador 8.8
- 1960 Chile 9.5

The strength of an earthquake is measured using the Richter Scale, with 10.0 representing the most powerful earthquakes

Key
- ● Major earthquakes
- Earthquake activity

6A.4 *The occurrence of earthquakes and volcanic eruptions*

Section 6 Coping with Hazards

Volcanic eruptions

There are over 500 **active** volcanoes in the world. These are volcanoes that may erupt at any time. About 30 of these volcanoes erupt every year. Every continent has volcanoes, occurring along the plate boundaries shown on Figure 6B.1. There are many more volcanoes that have not erupted for some time, although they may erupt again in the future. These are called **dormant**. Volcanoes that are **extinct** are those that have not erupted since prehistoric times.

Volcanic eruptions may be both spectacular and deadly. In 1985, for example, Armero in Colombia killed 25 000 people when it erupted. Other volcanoes, such as Mount Etna in Italy, may erupt frequently but cause less damage and kill fewer people. Some volcanic eruptions are not hazards because they happen in uninhabited areas and therefore have no impact upon people.

There are hundreds of volcanic eruptions every year. It is possible to follow several eruptions of a volcano (called **eruptive periods**) using the internet. The case study below shows how the activities of one volcano may be studied, and how people respond to the hazard.

CASE STUDY

Popocatépetl, Mexico

The major volcanoes in Mexico are located east to west across Mexico in the Trans-Mexican Volcanic Belt (see Figure 6A.5). They are a result of the Cocos Plate moving under the North American Plate. The Cocos Plate is a light oceanic crust which sinks under the denser continental plate. Figure 6A.6 shows the two plates meeting at a zone known as the Mid-American Trench.

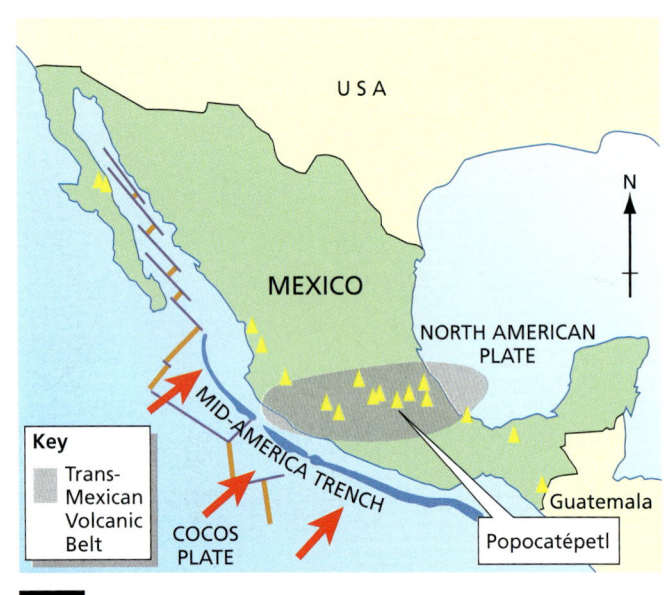

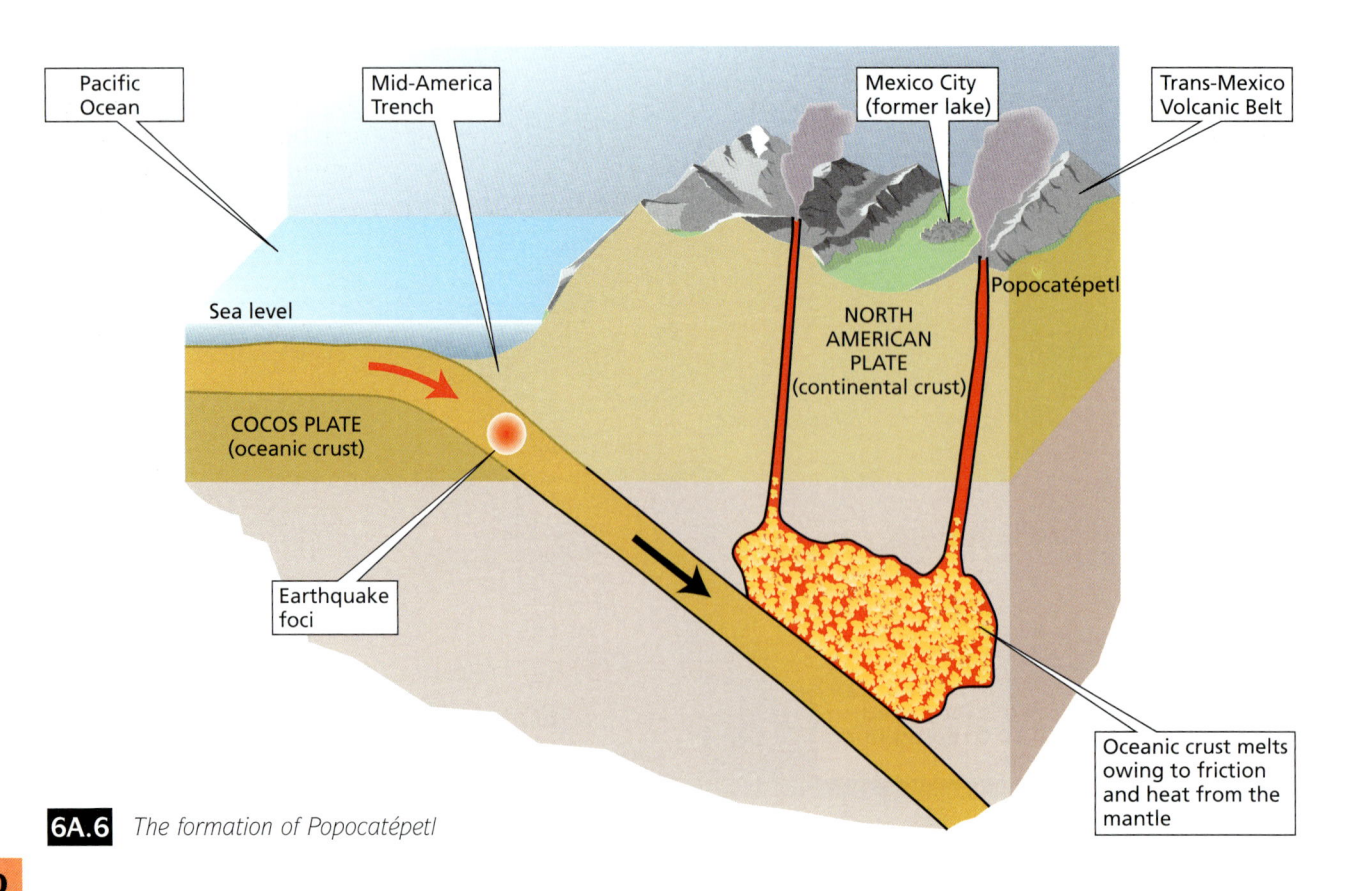

6A.5 The location of Popocatépetl

6A.6 The formation of Popocatépetl

A What is a hazard?

6A.7 *Popocatépetl*

The movement of these same two plates caused the Mexico City earthquake in 1985. Over 30 000 lives were lost and serious damage was widespread. The threat to central Mexico from earthquakes seems worse than the threat from Popocatépetl. However, authorities remain very worried that the volcano could have a very powerful eruption in the near future. There is a remote threat to Mexico City (population 18 million) which is only 72 kilometres from Popocatépetl.

Information about the volcano and its recent history are given below.

Popocatépetl

Location: 19.0N, 98.6W
Height above sea level: 5,465 m

History of eruptions: 14 eruptive periods since the Spanish arrived in 1519. None have caused a major loss of life

Monitoring activity: The National Disaster Centre keeps an eye on eruptions and seismic activity. Information on www.cenapred.unam.mx

Recent history:

22 December 1994

5000 tonnes of hot ash spewed from Popocatépetl; 16 nearby villages evacuated

Section 6 Coping with Hazards

Diary of events

24 May 1997

Two plumes of ash, sulphur, carbon dioxide and water vapour were emitted from Popocatépetl on 24 May. Ash and gas were thrown nearly 3000 m in the air over Popocatépetl on 27 May. It was the fourth such event this month.

30 June 1997

Popocatépetl threw ash 12 km into the air on Monday, June 30 during its largest eruption since 1925. Lava was also thrown 450 m into the air. This event led to the first ash fall in Mexico City, 72 km from the volcano, in over 70 years. Volcanic ash, water, boulders and trees mixed together to form a thick river on the flanks of Popocatépetl. This river measured 3 m deep around some mountain towns, but no casualties have been reported. The airport in Mexico City was closed on Monday due to this event, but reopened on Tuesday. At least 15 small towns are planned to be evacuated.

1 December 1998

The most powerful eruption at Popocatépetl in four years occurred on 1 December. An ash plume reached 10 km into the air.

21 December 1998

An eruption of Popocatépetl showered ash on Mexico City on 21 December, forcing the capital city's airport to close for two hours. This is only the second time since June 1997 that ash from Popocatépetl has fallen on Mexico City.

31 October 2000

On 30 October, the Popocatépetl volcano erupted and sent an impressive ash cloud skyward 3 km above the crater. Due to the vigorous eruption, the region is on yellow alert. New dome growth is occurring at the volcano. Popocatépetl was inactive for nearly 50 years, but has been active since 1995.

2 November 2000

It is recommended not to approach the volcano to less than 10 km from the crater after further tremors.

NOTING ACTIVITIES

Use the following questions to guide your notes.

1. What type of hazard is Popocatépetl?
2. Where is the volcano?
3. Why is the volcano there?
4. When has it erupted?
5. What damage has it caused?
6. How do the authorities monitor Popocatépetl?
7. How can people be protected from future eruptions?
8. Why do people continue to live near the volcano?

EXTENDED ACTIVITY

Montserrat volcano

Study the resources given below on the Montserrat volcano. Check on an internet site to find out if there is any current activity on Montserrat. You may gain access to the Volcano World website at: http://volcano.und.nodak.edu/

Answer the following questions.

1. Where is the volcano?
2. Why is the volcano there?
3. When did it erupt?
4. What damage did it cause?
5. What was done to help the local people?

Use the internet to research the activity of one other volcano. Use the same outline as that provided for Montserrat.

Montserrat

Location: 16.7N, 62.2W
Height above sea level: 915 m

Eruptions: 1995 to 2000 and beyond

Impact: 25 June 1997 most dangerous eruption when 19 people were killed. Later two-thirds of the island was destroyed along with Plymouth

Helping the people:

- monitoring devices set up
- emergency aid from Britain
- Cuba sent doctors and nurses
- new housing built
- infrastructure in the north improved
- families moved to Antigua, USA and Britain

Despite scientific monitoring, predicting activity has not been easy

A What is a hazard?

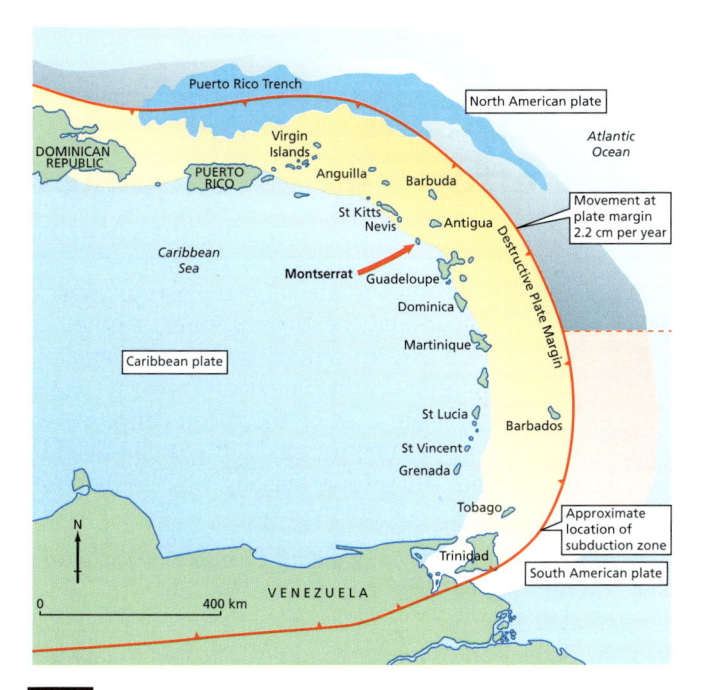

6A.8 The location of Montserrat

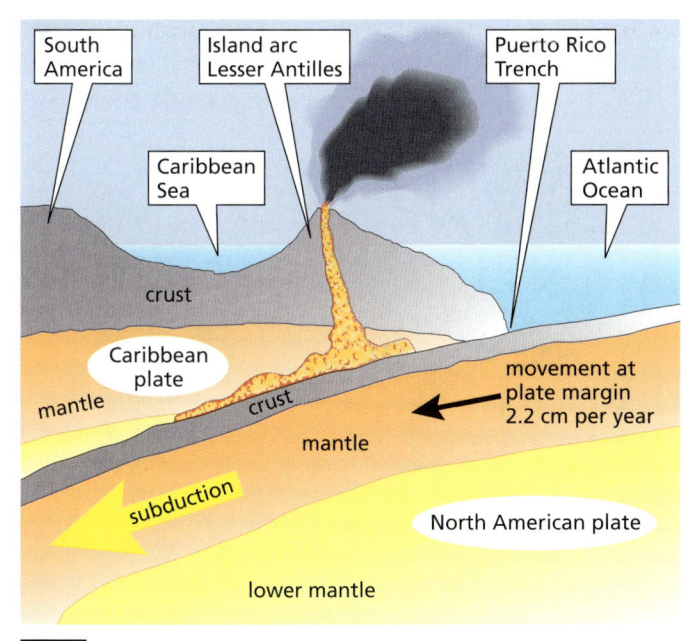

6A.9 The plate margin under Montserrat

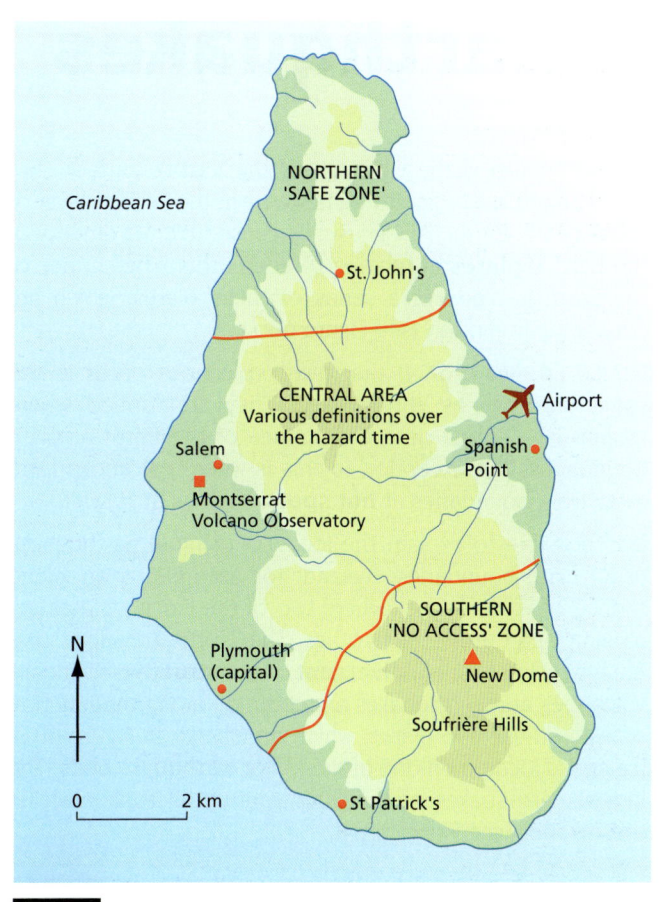

6A.10 Map of Montserrat showing zones

Section 6 Coping with Hazards

B Earthquakes

An earthquake is the vibration of the Earth's surface that follows a release of energy somewhere in the surface layer or **crust** of the Earth. This is usually caused by movements of the Earth's **plates** in relation to each other. The surface of the Earth is made of a series of these plates, which are constantly in motion (see Figure 6B.1).

Notice (in Figure 6A.4) that most volcanoes occur in the same locations as earthquakes. They are formed where molten lava erupts onto the surface of the Earth at plate boundaries. The exception to this is where volcanoes form away from boundaries at **hot spots**, such as at Hawaii.

It is possible to explain the location of most earthquakes using plate boundaries. Iceland, for example, is an island formed of volcanic rock where two of the Earth's plates are moving apart from each other. The North American and Eurasian plates form a **divergent** or **constructive** boundary. Volcanoes and earthquakes are common along the junction between these two plates, which are shown in Figure 6B.3. Iceland is located on one of the major earthquake belts. The largest earthquakes of the 20th century all took place in these zones (see Figure 6A.4).

What effects do earthquakes have?

It is possible for scientists to predict many earthquakes. In MEDCs such as Japan and the United States, earthquake warning systems are able to provide accurate information warning of future movements at plate boundaries. In spite of this, earthquakes remain one of the most dangerous of natural hazards. Over 25 000 people each year are killed by earthquakes. There are several reasons why earthquakes take so many lives.

1 Warning systems vary in standard throughout the world. The United States and Japan may be able to afford expensive high technology systems, but this is not the case in many of the world's poorer countries. The earthquake belt running through Iran and Pakistan is monitored less well than the one affecting the west coast of North America.

2 Warning systems are not perfect. Even the most sophisticated devices fail to predict some earthquakes. The Japanese earthquake that devastated the city of Kobe in

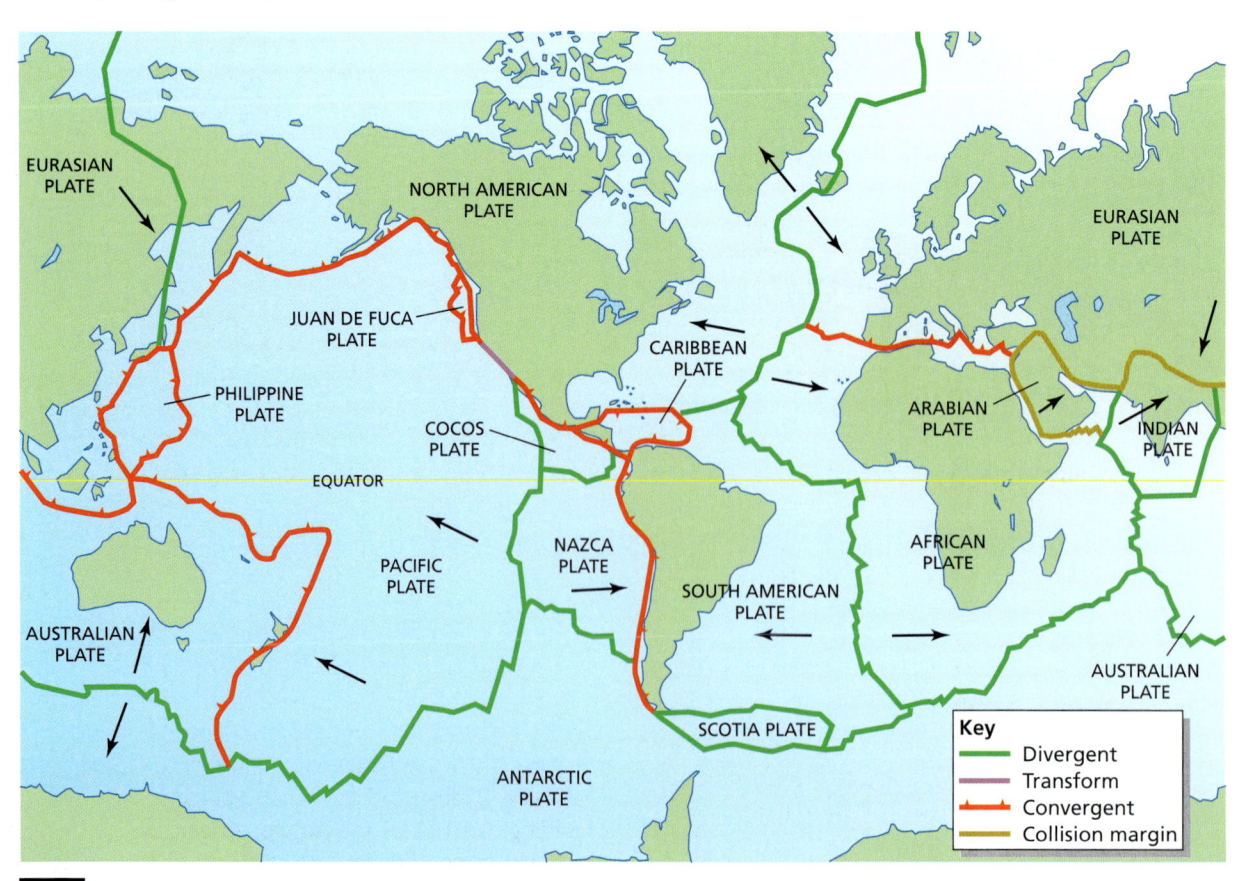

6B.1 *The Earth's plates*

B Earthquakes

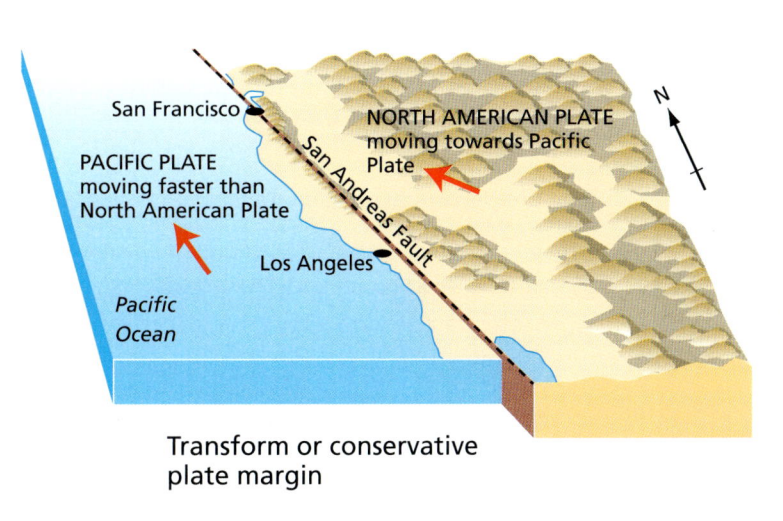

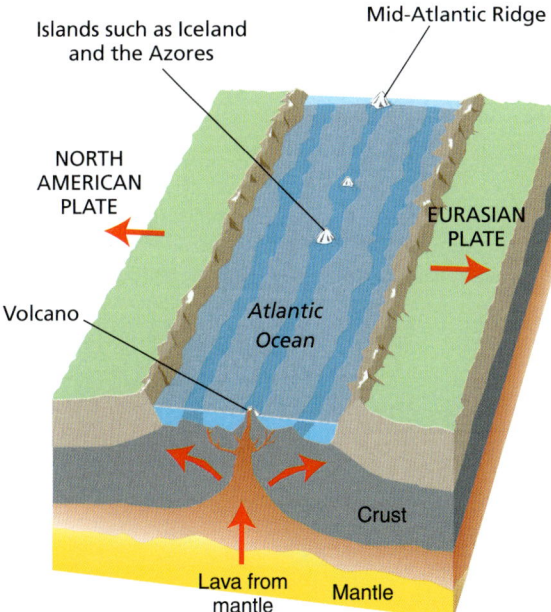

Transform or conservative plate margin
- San Francisco
- PACIFIC PLATE moving faster than North American Plate
- Pacific Ocean
- San Andreas Fault
- NORTH AMERICAN PLATE moving towards Pacific Plate
- Los Angeles

Divergent or constructive plate margin
- Islands such as Iceland and the Azores
- Mid-Atlantic Ridge
- NORTH AMERICAN PLATE
- EURASIAN PLATE
- Volcano
- Atlantic Ocean
- Lava from mantle
- Crust
- Mantle

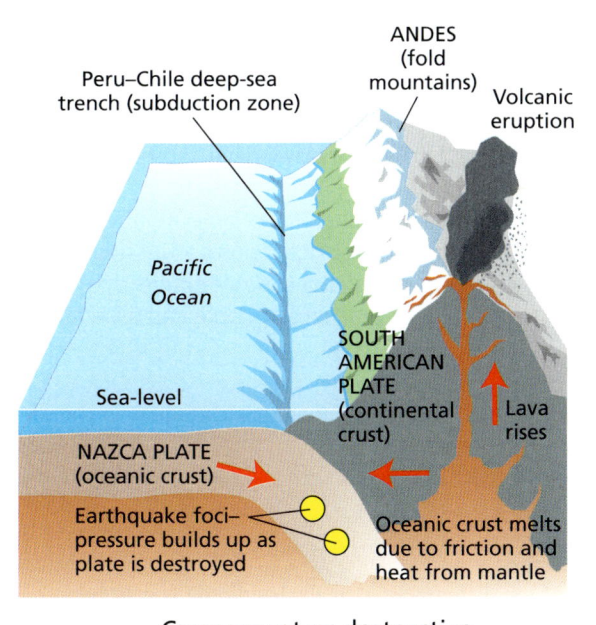

Convergent or destructive plate margin
- Peru–Chile deep-sea trench (subduction zone)
- ANDES (fold mountains)
- Volcanic eruption
- Pacific Ocean
- Sea-level
- NAZCA PLATE (oceanic crust)
- SOUTH AMERICAN PLATE (continental crust)
- Lava rises
- Earthquake foci – pressure builds up as plate is destroyed
- Oceanic crust melts due to friction and heat from mantle

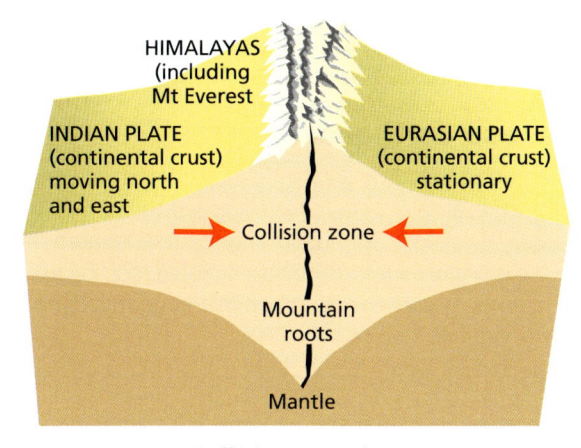

Collision margin
- HIMALAYAS (including Mt Everest)
- INDIAN PLATE (continental crust) moving north and east
- EURASIAN PLATE (continental crust) stationary
- Collision zone
- Mountain roots
- Mantle

6B.2 *Examples of the four types of plate margin*

1995 was not predicted. In that disaster 5 500 people were killed, and 300 000 lost their homes.

3 Even if warnings are given, they cannot prevent damage and loss of life. It is not possible to know exactly when an earthquake will happen, nor to prevent it from happening in the first place.

4 Most buildings are not able to withstand earthquakes. It is only in small areas of some MEDCs that buildings have been constructed to cope with earth movements. Other buildings in these areas are vulnerable. In most LEDCs, an earthquake will cause widespread destruction because of the collapse of buildings. In 1976, for example, an earthquake in Tangshan in China killed 250 000 people. Most of these deaths were caused by collapsing buildings and resulting fires.

Section 6 Coping with Hazards

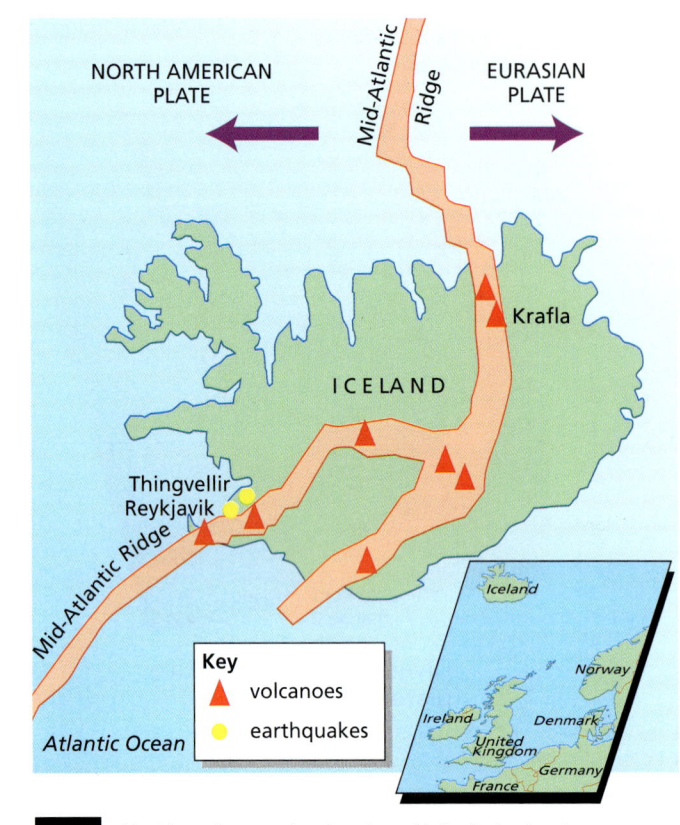

6B.3 *Earthquakes and volcanic activity in Iceland*

NOTING ACTIVITIES

1. Describe the location of the world's major earthquakes. Why are they located in these areas?
2. Why are earthquakes such dangerous hazards?
3. Why do you think the effectiveness of warning systems varies throughout the world?

Japanese earthquakes

The impact of earthquakes varies in different countries. In **Japan**, for example, people have learned to live with natural hazards. The main islands of Japan are located at the meeting point of four of the Earth's plates (see Figure 6B.4). Earthquakes and volcanoes happen frequently. Earthquake drills are as common in Japanese schools as fire drills are in the UK. The Japanese government spends nearly £75 million each year on earthquake prediction.

An English student spending a year in Kobe describes (below) her impressions of the university and its accommodation.

The Japanese have invested heavily in protection against earthquakes as well as in prediction. Modern high-rise buildings have a range of features designed to withstand earthquakes. Foundations are reinforced, and include a rubber buffer to let the building sway when the ground shakes. The main sections of buildings are strengthened with extra tension cables. Windows have shutters which are lowered automatically, to prevent people outside being showered with glass. Buildings have large numbers on the roof to allow identification by helicopters assessing damage after an earthquake. Regulations now require open areas around buildings where evacuated people can assemble.

Canada

In **Canada**, there were eight major earthquakes in the 20th century. Although few people were killed by these earthquakes, the Canadians take the risk of future tremors

---

The accommodation was very much like at home, but you notice some of the differences as well. Inside the wardrobe was a torch, first aid kit and list of earthquake regulations. We had a formal drill in the first week that I was there.

During my second month here, we had a real earthquake. I was woken by the sound of doors and windows rattling. Along with other people, I ran out of the building, thinking that it was going to collapse at any minute. It felt like an eternity, but apparently it only lasted for thirty seconds or so.

Anyway, we had an earthquake measuring over 5 on the Richter scale. Any more and we could have had serious structural damage. The really scary thing is the way the Japanese reacted to it all. They were so unemotional, so laid back about it.

One of my friends said, 'they have tremors like this all the time' (she meant at least once a year, apparently). If nobody gets killed, or no buildings are destroyed, it hardly makes the news at all. I understand that you did not hear much about it at home. The local people think of earthquakes as a part of their lives. They think little of the warning systems, believing that it will happen if it is going to – nothing can be done about it. Even though many know people who have been killed in earthquakes or have had their homes destroyed, nobody wants to move away.

B Earthquakes

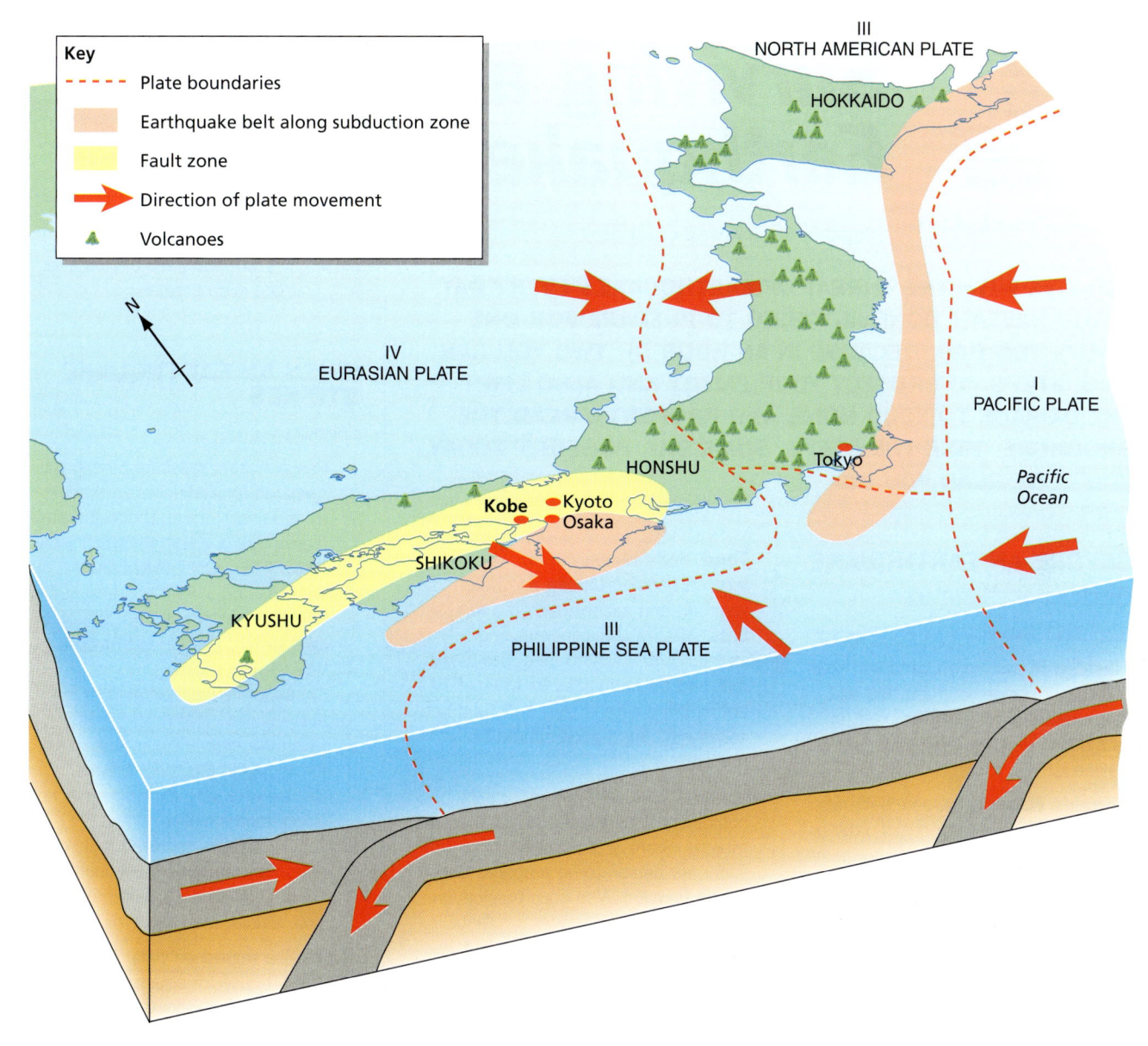

6B.4 *Japan lies at the junction of four plates*

very seriously. In order to warn people of the dangers of earthquakes, telephone directories have pages of advice on what to do before, during and after an earthquake. Many towns and cities have their own information in addition to this. The information in Figure 6B.5 shows how the people of Langley are advised to prepare for an earthquake.

Turkey

Turkey lies on the boundary of the Eurasian and African plates. The *North Anatolian Fault* runs right across Turkey, with the two plates moving in opposite directions. There have been nine major earthquakes along this line in only sixty years. This makes the region of northern Turkey one of the most active earthquake zones in the world (see Figure 6B.6).

Despite the frequency of earthquakes, Turkey remains poorly prepared. In 1999, the latest earthquake to strike the area hit the town of Izmit (see Figure 6B.7). It measured 7.4 on the Richter scale, and claimed at least 15 000 lives. After the initial tremor, there was another earthquake, called an **aftershock**. In large earthquakes, aftershocks may take place as much as a year after the original earthquake.

Why did the earthquake claim so many lives? It is estimated that the cost of repairing damage following the earthquake will be at least £10 billion.

187

Section 6 Coping with Hazards

Surviving an Earthquake

LANGLEY Printed by the Township of Langley

YOU LIVE WITH THE THREAT OF EARTHQUAKES EVERY DAY. IF YOU HAVEN'T DONE ANYTHING TO PREPARE FOR ONE THAT'S TOO BAD. BECAUSE IN AN HOUR OR TWO YOU CAN TAKE STEPS TO PROTECT YOUR FAMILY AND ALSO LIMIT THE DAMAGE TO YOUR HOME AND PROPERTY. READ THE BROCHURE. TAKE THE STEPS. SOME DAY, POSSIBLY TODAY, YOU'LL BE GLAD YOU DID.

BEFORE AN EARTHQUAKE
CHECKLIST OF ESSENTIALS
HAVE ON HAND FOR ANY EMERGENCY:

Flashlights with spare batteries. Keep a flashlight beside your bed. **Do not use matches or candles** after an earthquake until you are certain NO gas leaks exist.

Portable Radio with spare batteries. Most telephones will be out of order or used for emergency purposes so radios will be your best source of information.

First Aid Kit; first aid knowledge. Have a first aid book. Have members of your house-hold take basic first aid and CPR courses.

Fire Extinguisher. Keep a fire extinguisher handy for small fires. Some extinguishers are only good for certain types of fire: electrical, grease or gas. Class ABC extinguishers are designed to use safely on any type of fire. Your fire department can advise you.

Food. Keep a supply of non-perishable food on hand which can be rotated into your diet and replenished on a regular basis. Have a sufficient supply of canned or dehydrated food, powdered milk and canned juices for at least 72 hours. Dried cereals and fruits and non-salted nuts are a good source of nutrition.

Water should be stored in airtight containers and replaced about every six months. Store at least three gallons of water per person to be prepared for a 72-hour period. Also have purification tablets such as Halazone and Globaline, **but read the label on the bottle**.

Special Items. Have at least a week's supply of medications and special foods needed for infants or those on limited diets.

Tools. Pipe wrench and Crescent Wrench for turning off gas and water mains if necessary.

Clothing. You are going to need to move over broken glass and other debris. Keep a pair of thick-soled shoes and work gloves under your bed or nearby.

Electricity. If you are dependent on electrical power for life support or require an electric wheelchair, buy a small generator and keep extra fuel or fully charged extra batteries.

WHEN AN EARTHQUAKE STRIKES
Checklist

1. Remain calm; reassure others; be prepared for additional earthquakes.
2. If inside, stay there. If outside, stay there. TAKE COVER; PROTECT HEAD AND FACE; DON'T RUN DOWN STAIRS.
3. DO NOT light a match or turn on a light switch. USE A FLASHLIGHT.
4. Wear sturdy shoes.
5. Check for injuries; administer first aid.
6. Check for fires and gas leaks, and for damaged electrical fixtures.
7. Secure your safe drinking water and check food supplies.
8. Turn on battery operated radio or car radio for emergency bulletins.
9. Clean up hazardous materials.
10. Take routine medications.
11. Confine frightened pets.
12. Check house for structural damage.
13. Do not use telephone except in extreme emergency.
14. Stay out of danger area.
15. Respond to requests from Police, Fire Department or your Municipal/Provincial Emergency Response Agencies.

6B.5 *Langley's earthquake advice*

- Many buildings in Izmit and other towns were high-rise apartment blocks. They collapsed during the earthquake, killing people inside.
- The earthquake happened at 3 am, when most people were asleep.
- Turkey has regulations to make buildings withstand earthquakes. Despite this, most builders ignore the law, knowing they are unlikely to be caught. Many new buildings collapsed because they were built cheaply, using poor quality materials.

B Earthquakes

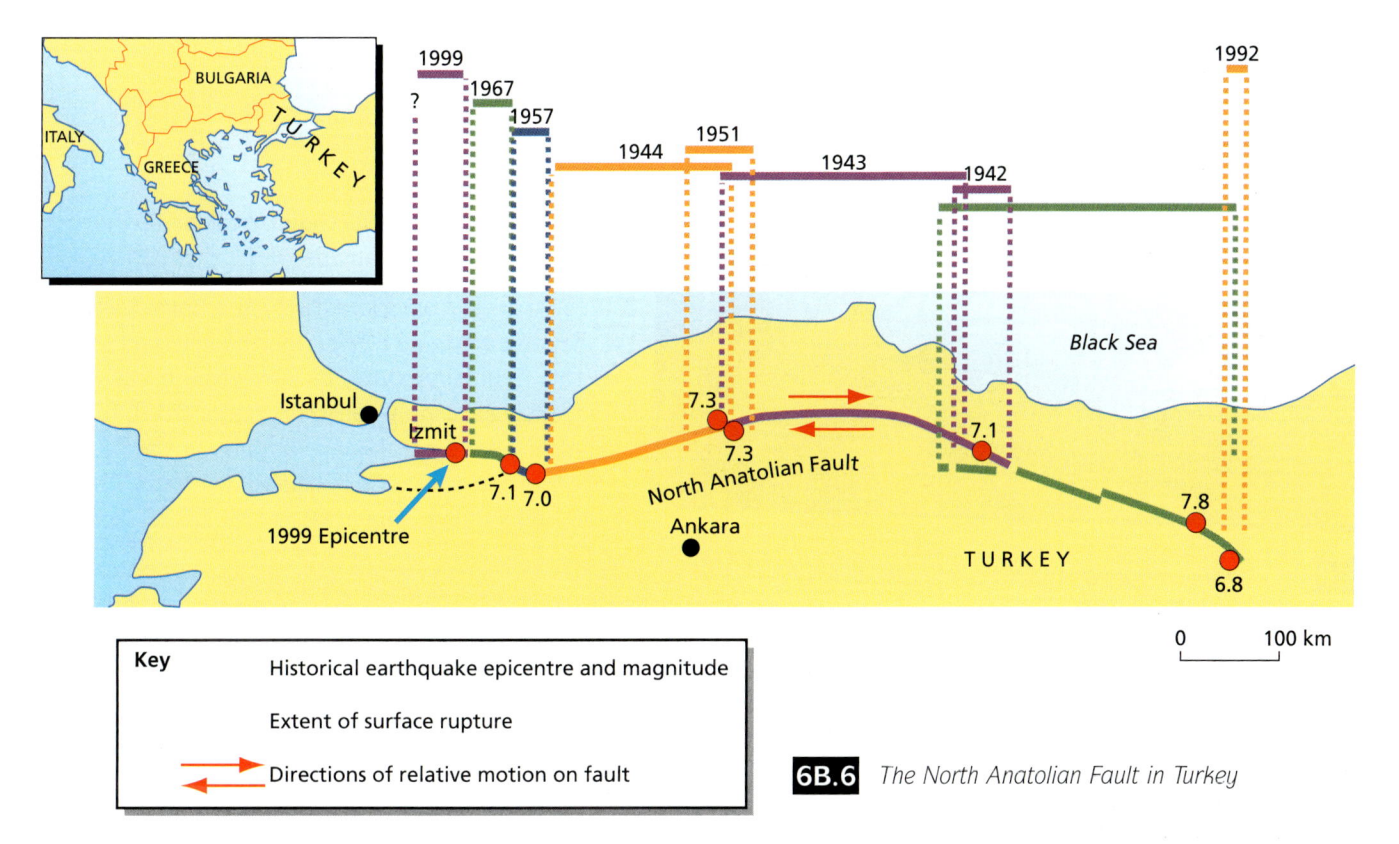

6B.6 *The North Anatolian Fault in Turkey*

Key:
- Historical earthquake epicentre and magnitude
- Extent of surface rupture
- Directions of relative motion on fault

- The authorities did not have many emergency supplies available, despite the fact that there had been earthquakes in the past.
- The emergency services were slow to respond to the disaster. This increased the number of lives lost.
- Turkey's largest oil refinery, near Izmit, was severely damaged. Experts had advised against industrial development in a region of such frequent earthquake activity.

THE LAND THAT IS A TOMB

At 3.02 am on 17 August 1999, disaster struck north-west Turkey. The epicentre of a massive earthquake was close to the town of Izmit, 95 km south-east of Istanbul. More than 10 000 people died and up to 35 000 were trapped under the rubble. Another 45 000 were hurt, with many having suffered serious injuries.

'Thousands of buildings are in ruins,' said Turkey's prime minister. 'It is not possible to reach all of them.' Roads were torn up and blocked, power-lines brought down and water and sewerage pipes broken. The country's largest oil refinery, the Tupras works outside Izmit, was also seriously damaged.

The earthquake caused tidal waves to smash boats and drown many tourists in the Izmit Bay area. The 2000 waves that struck the seaside resort of Degirmendere were over 6 metres high.

As temperatures reached 40°C, the risk of diseases like cholera and typhoid increased. Poor sanitation and a lack of clean water have made the problems worse. Children and the elderly are particularly at risk.

The clean-up operation is likely to take many months. The cost of damage could be as much as £10 billion.

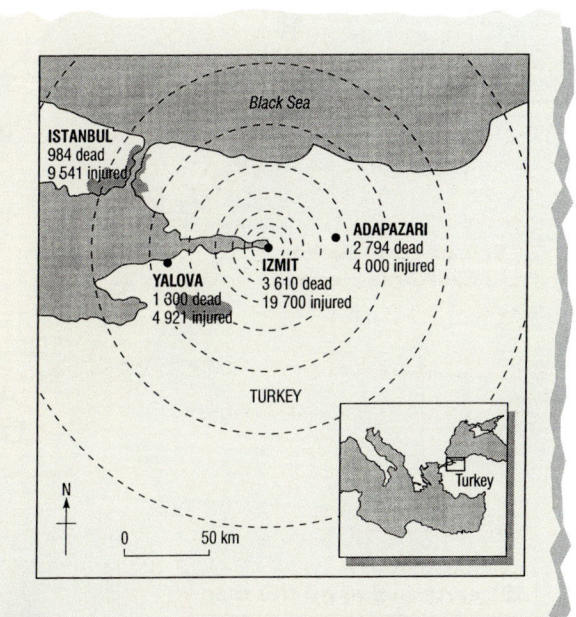

ISTANBUL 984 dead, 9 541 injured
ADAPAZARI 2 794 dead, 4 000 injured
IZMIT 3 610 dead, 19 700 injured
YALOVA 1 800 dead, 4 921 injured

6B.7 *Adapted from* The Times, *18 August, 1999*

Section 6 Coping with Hazards

6B.8 *The earthquake caused widespread destruction in Izmit and neighbouring towns*

NOTING ACTIVITIES

1. Describe measures that have been taken in Japan and Canada to reduce the impact of earthquakes.

2. Why did the Turkish earthquake cause so much damage and kill so many people?

3. Research earthquake activity in a named area within an earthquake belt. Use the internet to do this. You will probably be surprised at how frequently earthquakes occur. Figure 6B.9, for example, shows earthquake activity in the American states of California and Nevada. There were 301 earthquakes in December 2000 alone.

www.usgs.gov/ opens the home page of the United States Geological Survey. From here, you may search information about earthquake activity anywhere in the world.

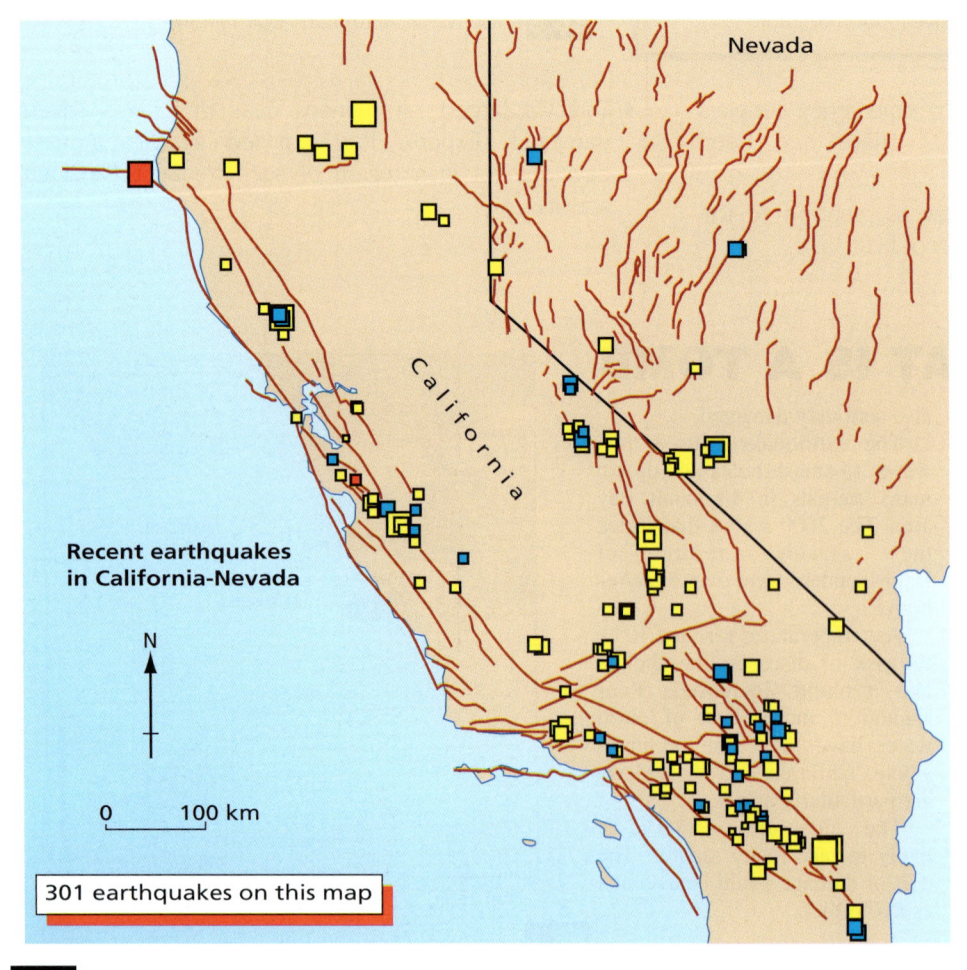

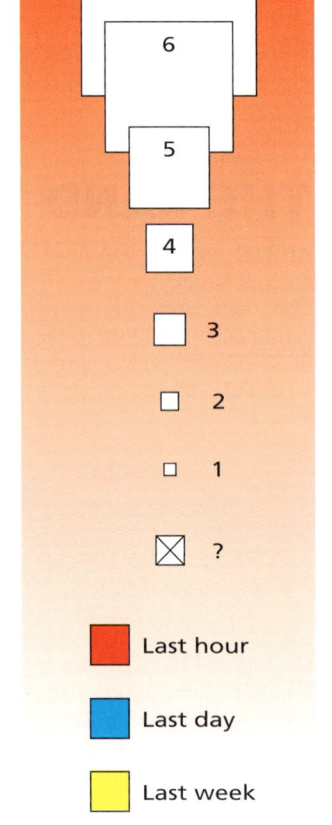

Recent earthquakes in California-Nevada

301 earthquakes on this map

MAGNITUDE
7
6
5
4
3
2
1
?

Last hour
Last day
Last week

6B.9 *Over 300 earthquakes were recorded in California and Nevada in December 2000*

190

Section 6 Coping with Hazards

C Floods

In April 1998, much of the English Midlands was affected by flooding. The amount of damage shocked local people, many of whom blamed the authorities for not giving them enough warning of the floods. They also said that not enough money had been spent on flood defences.

There were serious floods once again in October 2000. The autumn of that year was the wettest ever recorded, and some parts of Britain were flooded three times in little over a month. After the floods, experts suggested that four million houses were in fact built on floodplains. The amount of damage caused to property was as much the fault of poor planning and bad flood defences as it was due to very wet weather. It has also been suggested that another two million houses might be built on areas liable to flood in the near future. The Environment Agency said that flood reports had doubled in the last hundred years. Climate change and global warming in particular could lead to a warmer and wetter climate. This could result in the risk of flooding increasing tenfold during the 21st century.

The Environment Agency now advises householders in flood risk areas to make the following preparations.

- Keep a list of useful telephone numbers such as Flood Line.
- Have sandbags available to block up doorways and airbricks.
- Make up a flood kit including a torch, blankets and waterproof clothing.
- Make sure that important documents are kept away from flood risks.
- Switch off electricity and gas if flooded.
- Plan to have pets evacuated.
- Check for and report damage after a flood.

Park is shut for the first time
WICKSTEED Park in Kettering closed completely for the first time in history yesterday because of flooding.

Downpour ends caravan plans
A LEISURE park boss said the Easter holiday weekend was set to be a washout.

Woman feared drowned
A WOMAN is believed to have died when she fell into the swollen River Nene during a boating accident.

Residents face clean-up misery
RESIDENTS in Corby faced a weary day cleaning up their homes and assessing the damage caused by the floods.

Full to the brim!
PITSFORD Reservoir was full to the top today. Just last year, the reservoir was woefully short of water at just 51 per cent capacity. But now it stands at 100 per cent full, which makes this summer's water provision look healthy.

Clare Roberts, for Anglian Water, said 'This has done the situation no end of good.'

6C.1 *Effects of the 1998 floods on Northamptonshire, from the* Kettering Evening Telegraph, *11 April 1998*

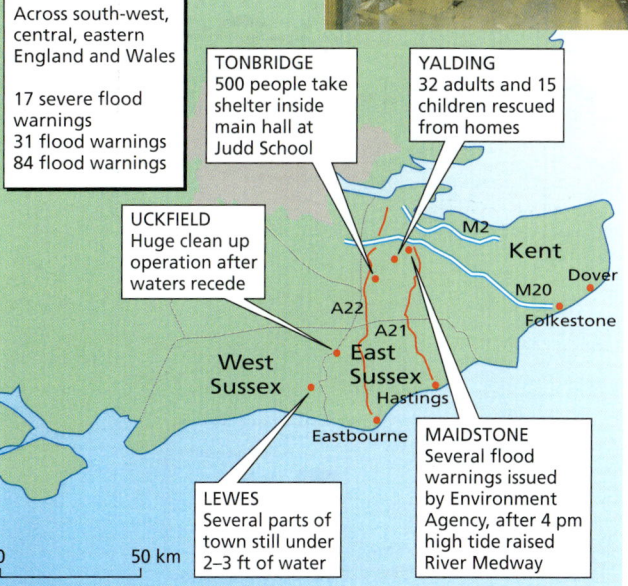

6C.2 *Much of the south-east of England was hit by the floods of 2000*

Across south-west, central, eastern England and Wales
17 severe flood warnings
31 flood warnings
84 flood warnings

TONBRIDGE 500 people take shelter inside main hall at Judd School

YALDING 32 adults and 15 children rescued from homes

UCKFIELD Huge clean up operation after waters recede

LEWES Several parts of town still under 2–3 ft of water

MAIDSTONE Several flood warnings issued by Environment Agency, after 4 pm high tide raised River Medway

Section 6 Coping with Hazards

> **NOTING ACTIVITIES**
>
> 1 What were the reasons for flooding in Britain in 1998 and 2000?
>
> 2 Using Figures 6C.1 and 6C.2, describe ways in which people were affected by the flooding.
>
> 3 Design a poster or leaflet advising people what to keep in a 'flood kit'.
>
> 4 Do you live on a flood plain or near to a river? How far is it to your nearest river?
>
> 5 Do you know if your house is in danger of flooding?
>
> 6 When buying a house in the future, do you think you would be aware if it was at risk of flooding? Is this something that you would consider important?

It is possible that global warming has led to an increase in flooding in Britain (see page 215). It is not only Britain that have seen severe floods in recent years. Much of Europe was also affected, for example parts of Italy.

CASE STUDY

The Italian floods of 2000

Italy is so mountainous that the valley of the River Po in the north of the country is the only large area of relatively flat land (Figure 6C.3). The river transports material that has been eroded from the Alps for over 600 kilometres from its source near Mount Viso near the French border. It has created a fertile valley in its lower course, eventually flowing into the Adriatic Sea. Almost every river in northern Italy is a tributary of the Po. Lakes Maggiore, Como, Lecco and Garda also empty their waters into the Po. The river is rapid in its upper course but becomes sluggish long before it reaches the sea.

The River Po has often caused floods. As long ago as 300BC the Etruscans built artificial embankments in an effort to control the waters. Flood prevention is not a new idea.

What was the hazard?

The river Po rose 10 metres above its normal level. In the upper reaches of the river there were landslides and mudflows as the water came down from the Alps. In the middle parts of the valley the Po overflowed its flood defence embankments. Farmland, industrial sites, roads, railways and homes were flooded. Lake Maggiore reached its highest level for 100 years.

When did this happen?

The floods occurred in the week beginning Saturday 14 October. It is possible to follow hazards such as this on websites, such as http://europe.cnn.com (see Figure 6C.4).

Why did it happen?

There were several days of very heavy rainfall in the Alps and the Po valley itself. There was low pressure over Europe and other parts of Europe, including south-east England, were experiencing flooding. Over 20 cm of rain had fallen in a few days. Figure 6C.5 explains what was happening in northern Italy.

Who was affected?

Farmers lost money from flooded crops, workers were laid off because of closed factories, schools were closed, 30 000 people lost electric power, and about 30 people were killed.

What was affected?

- A FIAT car factory north of Turin was flooded.
- Road and rail bridges were washed away.
- Water supplies were cut off and people were advised to boil their drinking water.

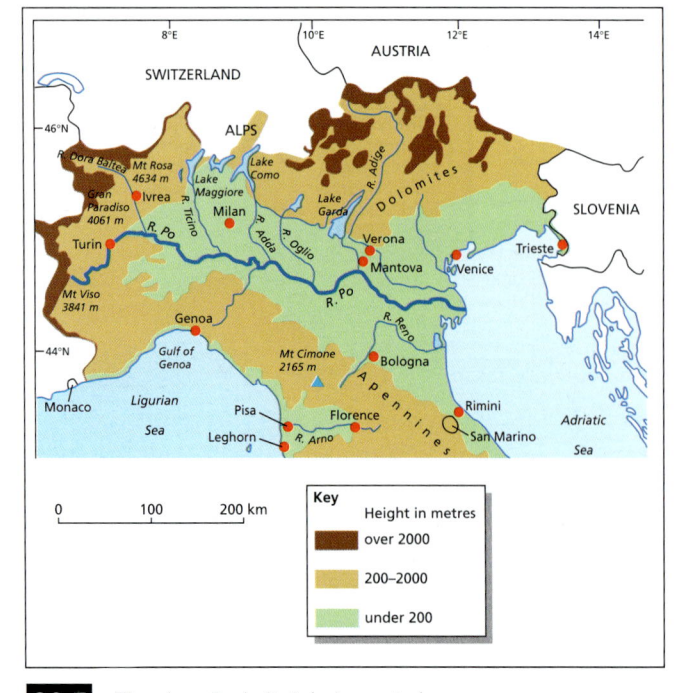

6C.3 *The river Po is Italy's largest river*

C Floods

- Maize, rice and soya bean crops were destroyed.
- Autumn planting of wheat and barley, the most important crops in the area, was made impossible.

How much damage was caused?

The cost of the damage was very high indeed. In Lombardy alone early estimates put the damage at $2.6 billion. The area around Mantova (Mantua), for example, was badly affected (see Figure 6C.6).

What was done to help?

At San Benedetto (see Figure 6C.6) the authorities used a controlled explosion to break the river banks to save inhabitants from being hit by a wall of water when the Po burst through its banks. Many farmers were very angry about this action because it flooded their farmland. On a different part of the river, volunteers were reinforcing the river banks to stop flooding. It seemed that in the emergency it was difficult to know exactly what to do.

In most places there was a well organized system of warnings. In the first few days of the flood 32 000 people were evacuated from their homes. Police closed transport routes and bridges. Many people had remembered earlier floods and had prepared themselves, for example by moving their possessions upstairs.

The Red Cross gave valuable assistance. Aid poured into northern Italy from other European countries, the USA and from the Italian government. Every family that lost their home was given $18 000.

Italy floodwaters force 12,000 to flee

17 October 2000

TURIN, Italy. Around 12,000 people are being evacuated from their homes in north-west Italy as rising flood waters threaten fresh devastation in the region.

The Po River, Italy's longest, is rising at a rate of nine centimetres per hour, threatening to flood the cities of Parma and Piacenza.

The death toll from days of floodwaters and mudslides in the country rose to 14 on Tuesday, after rescuers found two more bodies in the mountainous region of Valle d'Aosta.

Thousands of rescue workers searching through the mud, rocks and debris found the bodies of a one-year-old girl and an unidentified man, believed to be her father.

The government has already declared a state of emergency for Valle d'Aosta, Piedmont and the coastal region of Liguria, which includes part of Genoa.

Roads, railways and factories have been shut down in Turin where the Dora Baltea river burst its banks, flooding main streets with 50 cm of water and mud.

6C.4 *Report describing the floods in northern Italy*

Process diagram:

Intense rainfall → **Impermeable** rocks in the Alps → Water did not **infiltrate** the surface → High **surface run-off** → The Po valley became **saturated** → River waters rose, landslides were set off → Widespread flooding as rivers burst their banks

6C.5 *The process leading to the floods in northern Italy*

Section 6 Coping with Hazards

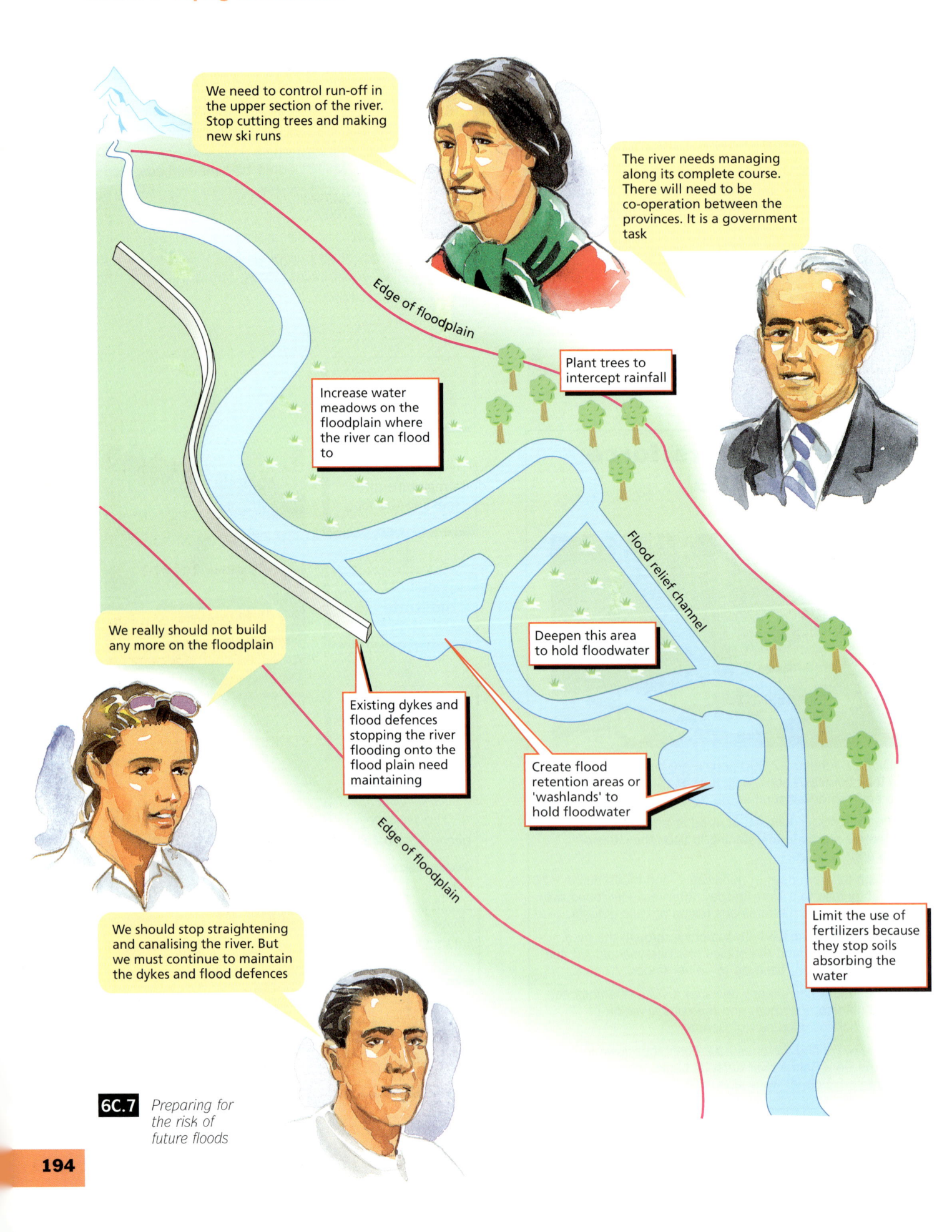

"We need to control run-off in the upper section of the river. Stop cutting trees and making new ski runs"

"The river needs managing along its complete course. There will need to be co-operation between the provinces. It is a government task"

Edge of floodplain

Plant trees to intercept rainfall

Increase water meadows on the floodplain where the river can flood to

Flood relief channel

"We really should not build any more on the floodplain"

Deepen this area to hold floodwater

Existing dykes and flood defences stopping the river flooding onto the flood plain need maintaining

Create flood retention areas or 'washlands' to hold floodwater

Edge of floodplain

Limit the use of fertilizers because they stop soils absorbing the water

"We should stop straightening and canalising the river. But we must continue to maintain the dykes and flood defences"

6C.7 *Preparing for the risk of future floods*

C Floods

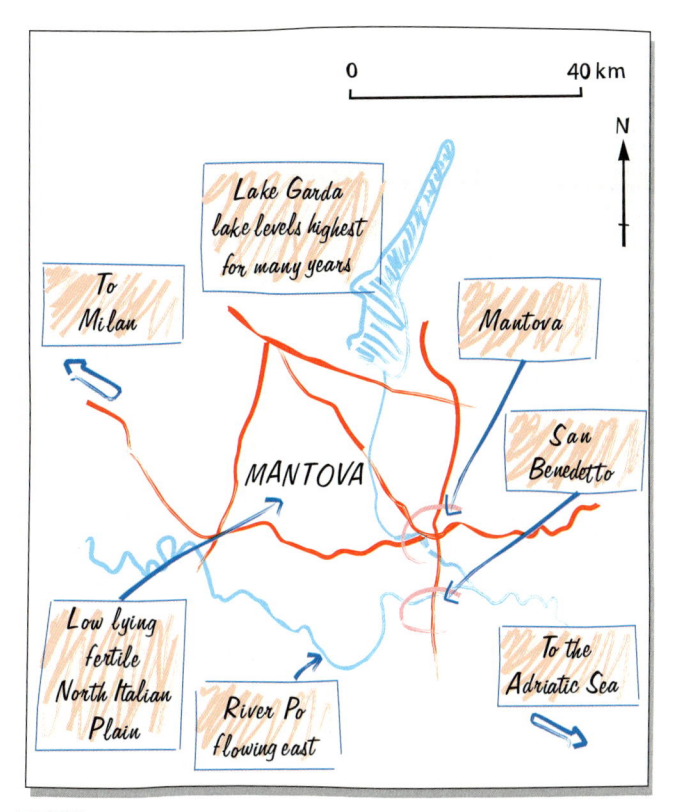

6C.6 *The location of Mantova*

1 **Run-off** is faster than it used to be because there are more buildings, roads and car parks in the Alpine areas. These impermeable surfaces cause more run-off.

2 **The cutting down of trees** and damaging of Alpine vegetation for ski slopes has also led to less interception of the rain. This has also increased surface run-off.

3 **The building of houses** and factories on the floodplain of the Po has meant there is more valuable property that may be damaged.

4 **Straightening the Po** for navigation and flood control in the past has meant the river flows faster and floodwaters are not retained.

5 **Building very high flood embankments** or artificial levees restricts the river too much and increases the danger when the waters eventually break them.

6 **Intensive farming methods** on the Po floodplain have damaged the soil structure and made the soil less permeable. Floodwaters do not infiltrate the soil so easily.

7 **Rising sea levels** may have increased flooding in the Po delta region.

8 Rainfall may have increased in some parts of Europe owing to global warming but there is no evidence yet for this.

Why do recent floods seem to be worse than in the past?

There do seem to be more floods in Italy and in Europe in general. Why might floods in Italy be more frequent and more serious than in the past?

What can be done to prevent future floods?

Figure 6C.7 shows some of the ways of coping with floods. These include **structural** and **engineering** solutions. These are answers not just for floods in the Po floodplain, but may be applied elsewhere. People may also change their attitudes and behaviour towards flooding.

NOTING ACTIVITIES

1 Draw a map of northern Italy and label the places mentioned in the text. Annotate your map to describe what happened at each place.

2 Make your own notes on what happened in the Italian floods. Use sub-headings, and limit your notes to two or three points for each sub-heading.

3 List some of the issues facing the Italian government concerning the future flooding of the Po and the bills that will have to be paid after the next big flood.

4 Why do different groups of people react differently to a serious flood such as that which occurred on the Po to the south of Mantova?

5 Why do you think it is difficult to manage the flooding of a large river such as the Po?

6 Why do MEDCs seem to cope with hazards such as flooding better than many LEDCs?

7 Research another major flood that has happened in recent years elsewhere in the world. Use an outline similar to that above. What similarities and differences are there between your chosen example and the floods in northern Italy?

Section 6 Coping with Hazards

D Fire

Fire is classified as a climate hazard. The most severe fires are brush fires that take hold of large areas of dry vegetation, such as in Australia or the western United States. It is possible that fire is becoming an increasing hazard, caused by a combination of natural and human factors. In recent fires in the USA, for example, some of the worst blazes were caused by high winds blowing trees onto power lines, which then set fire to surrounding vegetation.

As you read through this section, note down answers to the questions in the Noting Activities.

Finally, take note when you next hear about a large fire. Check up-to-date information about fires in the USA at www.nifc.gov and www.fs.fed.us/news/fire

What, where and why?

Major fires are occasionally in the news. Some are caused by people behaving carelessly and others are the result of natural causes such as lightning.

There are forest fires and grass fires; in some dry areas there are scrub fires whereas in some highland areas there are moorland fires. Naturally-occurring fires are more likely in semi-arid and savanna areas as well as in forests when there is a long dry spell.

NOTING ACTIVITIES

1. What different type of fires are there?
2. Why do they occur?
3. What damage can fires cause?
4. Are fires completely natural?
5. How do people's activities add to the causes of fires?
6. How do fires affect people in MEDCs compared to LEDCs?
7. Why do people continue to live in areas where there is a risk of fire?
8. How can people be protected from fires?
9. How can people be helped after fires?
10. Can fires be predicted?
11. Can fires be controlled?

CASE STUDY

USA fires 2000

In Europe natural causes are not very common but in the USA during the summer of 2000 natural fires were widespread. By August 2000 there had been twice the yearly average of wildfires in many western states (see Figure 6D.1). At one stage there were over 70 large wildfires burning over 375 000 hectares. These were the worst fires for over 50 years.

Lightning was the major reason for the fires. It was 'dry lightning' caused by high temperatures, low humidity and rainless thunderstorms. The very dry conditions had lasted for several weeks. The forests and the undergrowth were tinder dry. Linked to this natural cause were the activities of holidaymakers who light barbecues and sometimes drop cigarettes.

The oddest cause was one given by local officials: in Washington state a grasshopper was seen to jump onto an electric fence and burst into flames This set off a fire that eventually covered more than 1400 hectares in an Indian reservation.

What damage was done?

Figure 6D.2 shows a fire in California which burned everything in its path.

Damage was widespread and severe.

- **Ecosystems** The damage included forests and farmland. In Oregon there were fears that some endangered species of plants and animals would be seriously affected. Ecosystems can take many years to regenerate after damage by fire.
- **Tourism** In the Mesa Verde in Colorado tourist activities were restricted. This is a popular National Park with British visitors.

D Fire

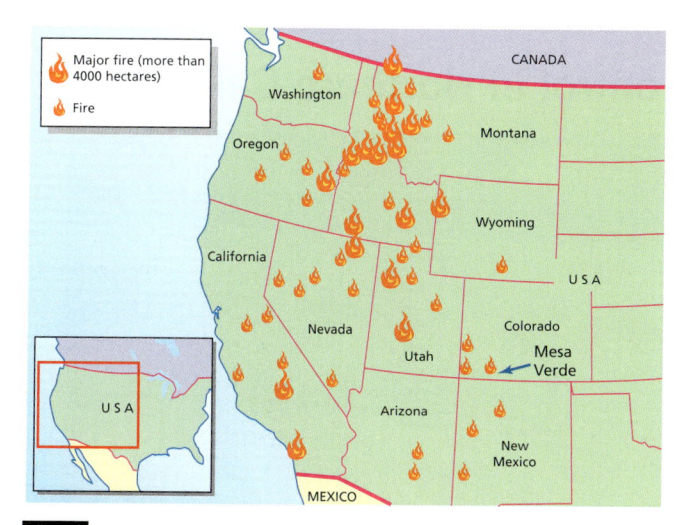

6D.1 *Fires burning in the USA in early August 2000*

- **Homes** Many people were evacuated after their homes burned down.

- **Smoke** Thick black smoke affected people's breathing and in Hamilton, Montana residents were warned to stay indoors.
- **Cost** The government were spending £10 million per day just supporting 20 000 civil and military fire-fighters. The costs of forest, farm and property damage was enormous.

Control and prevention

Fire-fighters controlled the fires with fire suppressants dropped from aircraft (see Figure 6D.3). 'Bombing' from flying water tankers was also used. Firebreaks were cut to stop fires spreading. This method of controlling the fires was in fact a prevention technique that can be used in many wild areas. If trees are felled in strips then fires will not be able to 'jump' the firebreak.

The Forestry Service tried to prevent more fires by educating people about being careful. Fires caused by lightning were more difficult to prevent.

How well did the USA cope?

This is another example of an MEDC being able to afford the resources needed to cope with a hazard. These resources in the richest country in world were used to fight the fires, evacuate the fire victims and compensate farmers. Where fires occur in the LEDCs there is no such quick response and compensation may not exist.

People will continue to live in those parts of the USA where fires are a hazard. Foresters make their living there, tourists will be catered for by local people who supplement their incomes from visitor income. National Park wardens, scientific researchers and farmers will live where their jobs are which may be in a fire hazard area. It is common for fires to spread to within a short distance of large urban areas, such as San José in California (see Figure 6D.4)

6D.2 *Raging fire in California, August 2000*

6D.3 *Fire attack from the air near Hamilton, Montana*

Section 6 **Coping with Hazards**

Wind-whipped grassfires under control in Northern California

23 October, 2000

SAN JOSE, California (AP) Fire crews have contained a number of blazes in Northern California, but the smoldering ashes represent an eerie reminder for residents who haven't forgotten what happened nine years ago.

A hillside fire in San Jose, one of at least five brushfires near the city Sunday, burned 25 acres, destroying one home and causing roof damage to five others. The fire began when a power line fell onto a pine tree.

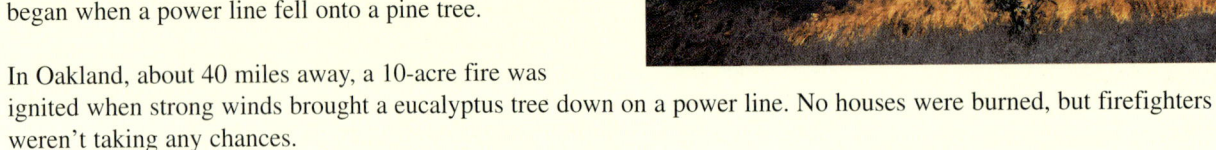

In Oakland, about 40 miles away, a 10-acre fire was ignited when strong winds brought a eucalyptus tree down on a power line. No houses were burned, but firefighters weren't taking any chances.

'I came outside and I saw smoke and I burst into tears. I said, "I've been there and done this"', said Adrienne Kohler, whose home was destroyed in 1991.

Nine years ago, gusty winds re-ignited a blaze firefighters thought they had under control in the Oakland hills, leading to a fire that destroyed 3000 homes and killed 25 people.

6D.4 *Report on the North American grassfires*

Section 7 **Changing Environments**

A Coastline management

The coast is the narrow zone that separates land from sea. It is a constantly changing physical environment; the nature of a beach or cliff can be transformed by a dramatic event within seconds. Coastal erosion and deposition are natural processes, affecting coastlines throughout the world. Why has the management of coastlines become such an important issue?

Natural change to the coastline is managed for several reasons.

- Coastlines are an important resource, as they are valuable to people.
- The coast is an attractive environment for people to live. Population density is often higher on the coast than inland. Many towns and cities have developed along coastlines, for example along the south coast of England.
- Coasts are an important destination for tourists throughout the world. They make an important contribution to national economies.
- With global warming predicted to cause a rise in sea level, coastal settlements in many parts of the world are under threat from flooding. It is important to protect people from this threat.
- Some coastal environments provide habitats for rare species of plants, animals and birds which need to be protected.

NOTING ACTIVITIES

1 List ways in which the area shown in Figure 7A.1 is a resource.

2 How might people damage resources in the area?

3 a Why is it important to conserve coastal areas?

  b Give two ways in which you think this could be done.

7A.1 *The coast is an important resource*

Section 7 Changing Environments

7A.2 *The management of coastlines does not always improve the quality of the environment*

Some people, such as conservationists and those who have to pay for management schemes, suggest that it is better to allow nature to take its course by not protecting the coastline. This view conflicts with those who live or work at the coast, and want to preserve their homes or businesses.

NOTING ACTIVITIES

Look at Figure 7A.3, which shows a coastal management issue to the east of Brighton on the south coast of England. What do you think?

1. Summarise arguments for and against protecting the cottages mentioned in Figure 7A.3.

2. In your opinion, should the cottages be preserved, or should coastal erosion be allowed to continue?

Managing natural processes is not straightforward: it is very costly, it may affect the appearance of the natural environment, and it may not work at all (see Figure 7A.2).

Publisher wins fight to save cliff cottages

A publisher has saved an historic row of cottages on one of Britain's most picturesque coastlines from tumbling into the sea despite a call from conservationists that nature be allowed to take its course.

Nigel Newton, who was born in San Francisco, said his family fell in love with the cottages as soon as they set foot in one of them. Mr Newton, 42, who bought the former coastguard's cottages as a holiday home, has been given permission to spend £25,000 to strengthen sea defences.

Mr Newton is the founder and managing director of Bloomsbury Publishing, whose authors include John Irving and Michael Ondaatje, has been at odds with conservationists for almost a year. Paul Walton, area manager of the Sussex Downs Conservation Board, said: "It is our view that the coastline is of such natural importance it should not be tampered with".

Mr Newton said: "When I bought the cottage I, along with my neighbours, were very aware that as custodians of these homes it was our duty to protect them for others to enjoy." They have already spent more than £20,000 and have just secured planning permission from Lewes District Council for a 75 ft rock revetment. Mr Newton has agreed to pay £25,000 for further work to be carried out.

He said yesterday: "I feel I have done my part in preserving the cliffs and these cottages for a few years."

7A.3 *From* The Times, *11 May 1998*

A Coastline management

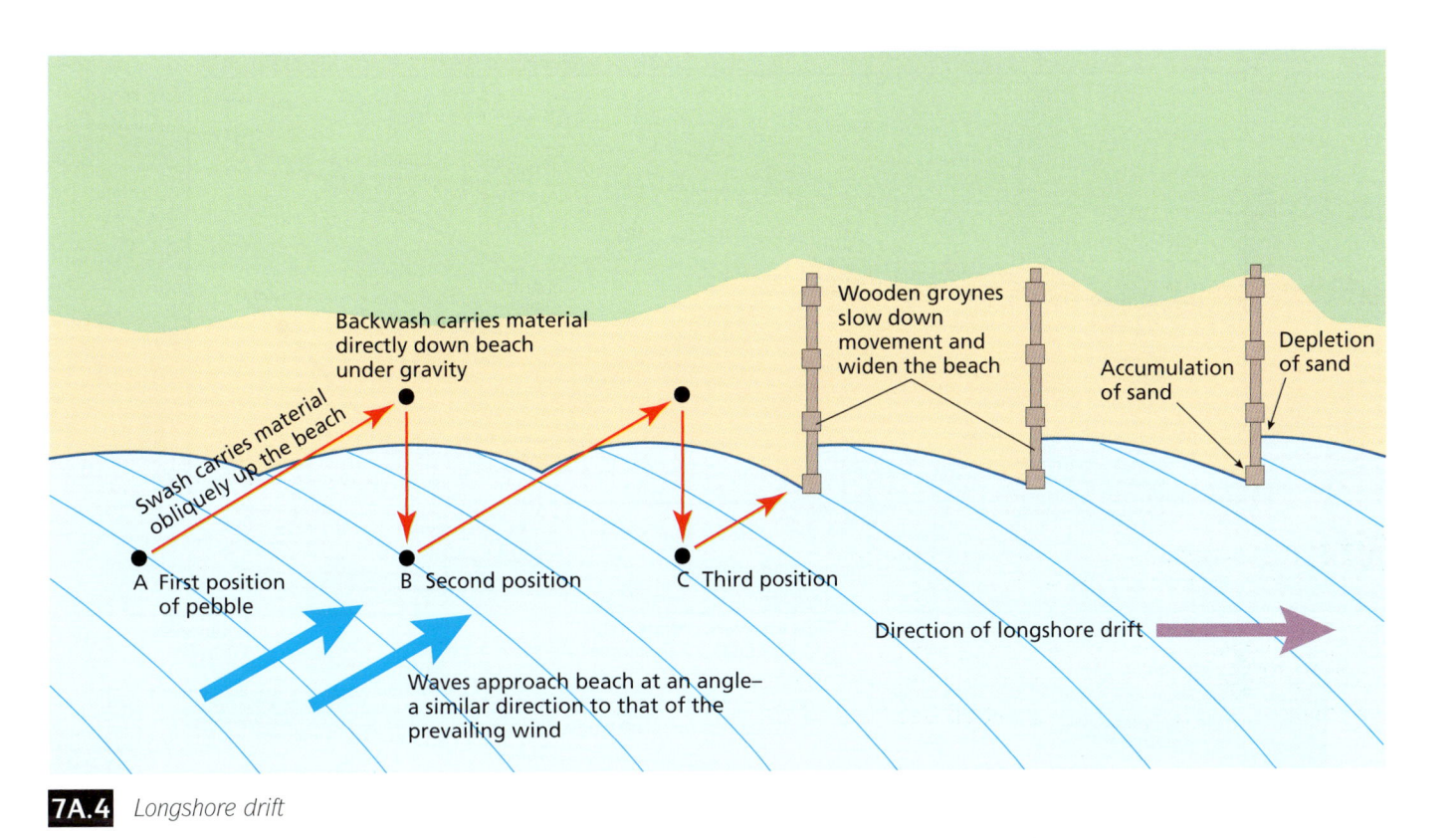

7A.4 Longshore drift

CASE STUDY

Eastbourne

The south coast of England is a popular location for residents and holiday-makers. Many settlements are built next to the sea to make the most of the natural scenery. While natural processes are responsible for changes to the coastline, the actions of people also have an impact. How has the coastline around Eastbourne been affected by both natural and human processes? Why is the coastline here so popular, and what is being done to prevent coastal erosion?

The coast is worn away by the action of waves. As with rivers, the processes of **corrasion**, **attrition**, **corrosion** and **hydraulic action** combine to erode the coastline. On the south coast of England, material is also removed from the shore by the process of **longshore drift** (see Figure 7A.4). The movement of material on this part of the coast is from west to east, as shown in Figure 7A.5.

Longshore drift has removed most of the large shingle pebbles from the beach at Eastbourne. The shingle acted as a protective barrier against the power of incoming waves. Without it, particularly in winter, waves crash over the town's promenade damaging many buildings. In 1997, in order to try to protect the seafront, the local council began to dump 330 000 tons of shingle on the beach. This was part of a £22 million plan to improve the town's sea defences, including 30-foot high wooden pillars built to prevent material being carried away by longshore drift.

The artificially built shingle beach will effectively bury the sandy part of the beach that had become exposed. Many people are worried that the wall of shingle will act not only as a deterrent to high seas, but also to holiday-makers. The 80 metres of sand exposed at low tide in recent years has become a major tourist attraction. Local hotel and restaurant owners fear that, with the sandy beach gone, tourists will go to one of the many other holiday destinations in the area instead.

7A.5 The direction of longshore drift on the south coast of England

Section 7 Changing Environments

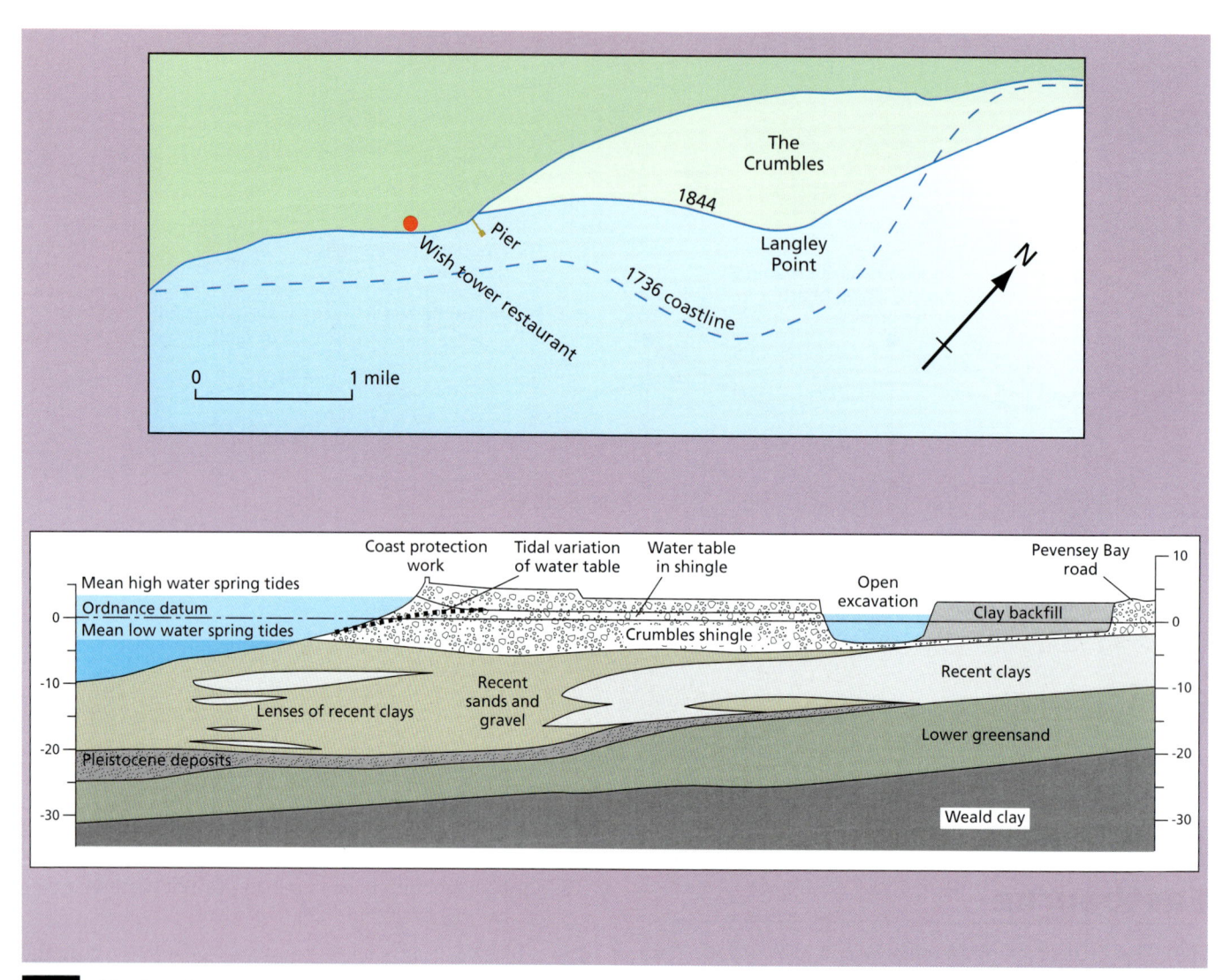

7A.6 *The Crumbles, to the east of Eastbourne*

Sovereign Harbour

The stretch of coastline to the east of Eastbourne has attracted people for settlement, industry and recreation. What has happened to this stretch of coastline? What impacts have human activities had on the natural environment?

Four kilometres to the north-east of Eastbourne is Langney Point, known locally as the Crumbles. This is an area of shingle which has built up over the last 800 years by longshore drift. Figure 7A.6 shows the location and geology of the Crumbles, and the way in which it is being eroded. Until recently, the area was an unspoilt and unique wildlife habitat. It was a stop-off point for migrating birds, and home to rare species of moths, crickets and wild flowers. Inland were low-lying levels at East Langney, at 6303 on Figure 7A.7.

The scenic attraction of Langney Point, together with its location near to settlements and tourist centres, put the area under increasing pressure. In 1971, planning permission was granted for a tidal harbour, a commercial centre, recreational facilities and for housing. The development was seen as vital for the future of the area. The County Planning Officer stated that developing the Crumbles 'is an essential strategic element in ensuring the future prosperity of the Eastbourne area. The creation of a high quality scheme, including a marina with associated commercial and residential developments, will bring significant benefits in terms of variety and quality of life and the strengthening of the economy.' Sovereign Harbour, shown in Figure 7A.8, was opened in 1993. It was still being developed in 2001.

A Coastline management

NOTING ACTIVITIES

1. Study the Ordnance Survey Map (Figure 7A.7).

   a Give three pieces of evidence from the map to suggest that the area is a popular holiday centre.

   b What method has been used along this stretch of coastline to stop longshore drift?

2. Draw a sketch map to show the following:

   a the coastline
   b the outline of urban areas
   c tourist facilities
   d Sovereign Harbour
   e the direction of longshore drift.

3. a Give the six-figure grid reference of the harbour entrance.

   b How does the OS map differ from the map produced by the Harbour Company (Figure 7A.8)?

   c Describe the land use in the area surrounding the harbour.

   d Why will the beaches to the north-east of the harbour start to be eroded?

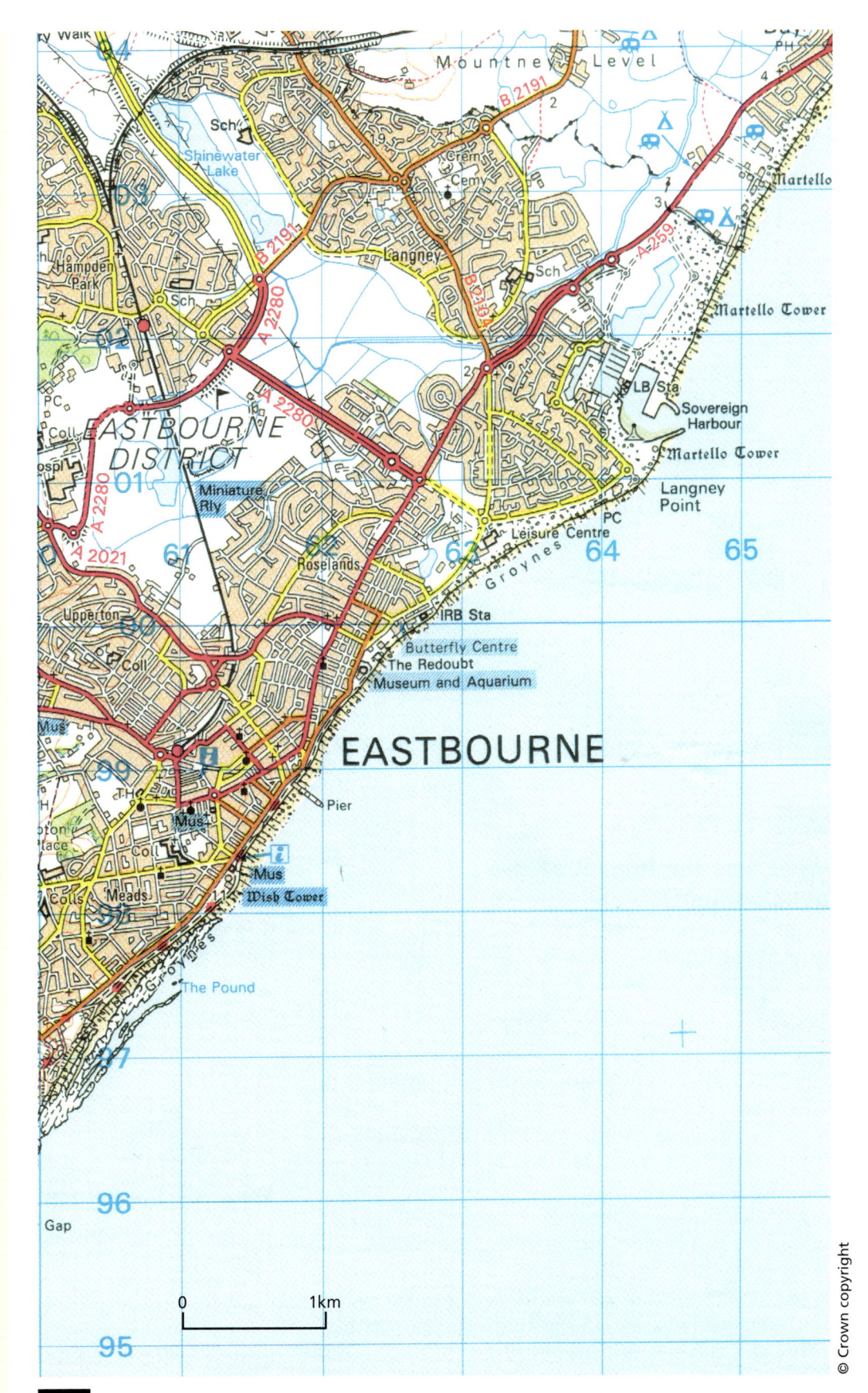

7A.7 1:25,000 OS map of Eastbourne and Langney, reduced in size

Section 7 Changing Environments

7A.8 *Sovereign Harbour*

What was the impact of the development?

As with the coastal defence work on Eastbourne beach, development at Langney Point has brought both benefits and problems to the area.

The local economy has gained in many ways.

- 38 commercial boats use the harbour. Half of these are fishing boats; others include sea angling boats on hire to tourists.
- Fishing boats and the lifeboat which used to operate from the steep beach now have a safe harbour. Fish catches have risen four-fold.
- Over 4000 boats visit the harbour each year, 60 per cent from the Netherlands. These tourists bring money to the local economy.
- In 2000, about 350 people were involved in building work. There are over 200 service jobs on the site, in shops and restaurants as well as in the boatyard.
- Between 1999 and 2006, over 2000 houses are to be built in the area. This represents 70 per cent of Eastbourne's housing needs during this time (see Figure 7A.9).

Losses were mainly environmental.

- Migrating birds were no longer attracted to the area. They used to inhabit old gravel pit workings which were incorporated into the harbour.
- The harbour site destroyed part of a coastal path, meaning that people could not walk along its length.
- Local residents were concerned about other changes to the natural environment (see Figure 7A.10).

What of the future?

In 1999 a row broke out concerning the possible risk of flooding to new homes in the harbour area. Without the sort of protection provided on the beaches at Eastbourne, longshore drift will simply carry shingle away from the harbour area, leaving housing on the low-lying areas at risk from being flooded by the sea. Local people feel that flood defences should have been provided – but who pays?

A Coastline management

> **Eastbourne councillor and member of the planning committee**
> We don't want to go down in folk history as the committee which approved the development which ended up in the sea.
>
> **Spokesperson for the Environment Agency**
> It is wrong to expect taxpayers to subsidise works to protect new developments.
>
> **Spokesperson for Sovereign Harbour Ltd**
> Sovereign Harbour will continue to ensure funds collected under the agreement are used in the appropriate and responsible manner.

HERITAGE Quay — An exclusive development of classically designed homes in the delightful setting of Sovereign Harbour, Eastbourne.

7A.9 *New homes for Sovereign Harbour*

STRUCTURED QUESTION

1. What developments have taken place at Langney Point? (2)
2. What are the economic gains and environmental losses caused by this development? (8)
3. What possible problems might this development have in the future? (6)
4. Can Sovereign Harbour be a sustainable development in the context of the Channel coastline? (4)

NOTING ACTIVITIES

1. In what ways might the harbour 'ensure the future prosperity of Eastbourne' and 'strengthen the economy'?
2. What has been lost with the building of Sovereign Harbour?
3. a Outline the reasons for possible erosion by the sea and flooding problems in the future.
   b Who do you think should pay for the long-term protection of Sovereign Harbour?
3. Do you think that Sovereign Harbour is a **sustainable** development?

Sad destruction on the Crumbles

I AM sure Graham Durey speaks for many in expressing his dismay at the wanton destruction of a unique wildlife habitat, the Crumbles, which is now lost to us, and to future generations, forever. And for what? Something so prestigiously banal as a marina.

It is indeed a sad fact of life that those with the power to effect such a change are also those with the least insight and imagination.

Just a small amount of intelligence might have shown them the long-term consequences of their 'exciting' (a word employed to justify any kind of destructive development) venture.

Name and address supplied.

IF only those who make so many decisions on our behalf could see the world through the eyes of my children, who love to watch the wild birds and look at the many photographs of the magnificent wild flowers I have taken down the Crumbles.

My children prefer conservation to concrete. Thank you Graham Durey for inspiring me to write this letter.

Name and address supplied.

7A.10 *Opposition to the Sovereign Harbour development*

Section 7 **Changing Environments**

Managing the shoreline zone

The south coast of England faces pressures caused by both natural and human processes. Elsewhere in the world, the same pressures extend beyond the immediate coastline, affecting ecosystems both inland and offshore. This wider area is called the **shoreline zone.** Management of this zone is an important issue in some of the world's most fragile and delicate natural environments. How has management of this zone been undertaken in two contrasting environments, The Great Barrier Reef, the world's largest coral reef, and in Canada, the country with the longest coastline in the world?

CASE STUDY

The Great Barrier Reef

This case study is in the form of an enquiry. Some of the analysis will be completed in the Extended Activity.

Aim

To answer the following questions:

1 Where is the Great Barrier Reef?
2 What exactly is it?
3 Why is it so important?
4 What are the threats to it?
5 How is it being managed?

Methods

- Read about holidays to the area from holiday brochures.
- If possible talk to tourists (friends or known people) about their experiences.
- Refer to books about coral reefs.
- Obtain information on the area from a travel guide.
- Investigate the reef using the internet.

Results

- Present the results in a variety of ways.
- Relate the results to the questions.
- Keep background information to a minimum.

1 Where is the Great Barrier Reef?

Figure 7A.11 is taken from a tourist brochure. The map shows that the reef is off Queensland in north-east Australia. Look at an atlas which will give the exact locations and latitudes eg Cairns is 16°50´ south. In this tropical area

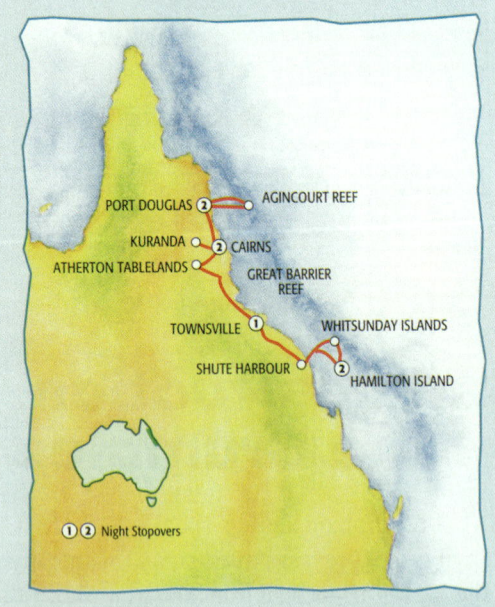

Tropics & Reef

PORT DOUGLAS ② — AGINCOURT REEF
KURANDA ○ ② CAIRNS
ATHERTON TABLELANDS — GREAT BARRIER REEF
TOWNSVILLE ① — WHITSUNDAY ISLANDS
SHUTE HARBOUR — ② HAMILTON ISLAND

① ② Night Stopovers

Spectacular Experiences
Best under the Australian sky

- Enjoy the renowned beaches of Queensland:
  - 2 nights Hamilton Island
  - 2 nights Port Douglas, Four Mile Beach
- 2 nights Cairns
- Skyrail Rainforest Cableway
- Scenic Kuranda Rail journey
- Tjapukai Aboriginal Experience
- Outer Barrier Reef Cruise
- Lake Barrine Wilderness Cruise
- Wildlife experience at the Billabong Sanctuary

Transportation
- Tour by luxury coach, air-conditioned, restroom equipped, reclining seats with seat belts & large panoramic tinted windows

Professionally Escorted
- Discover Queensland with our professional Tour Director & Tour Driver

Tour Features
- Welcome drink
- On-board reference library
- All purpose bag & map

7A.11 *A selection of information from a tourist catalogue*

A Coastline management

the reef stretches for 2300 kilometres and in places it is 70 kilometres wide. It is the largest reef in the world and is visible from space.

2 What exactly is it?

The reef has been built up slowly by the accumulation of the skeletal growth of millions of individual coral animals. Growth can be as much as 20–40 centimetres a century. Sea temperatures must be at least 18°C and the sea depth no more than 15 metres of clear unpolluted water. The Great Barrier Reef is an offshore linear reef in the shallow waters of a continental shelf. The reef off Belize in Central America is similar.

All reefs operate as open systems (see Figure 7A.12). From the air a reef looks like a small sandy island, called a **cay**, surrounded by a shallow lagoon, (see Figure 7A.13). A reef is a complex sensitive environment comprising several different habitats.

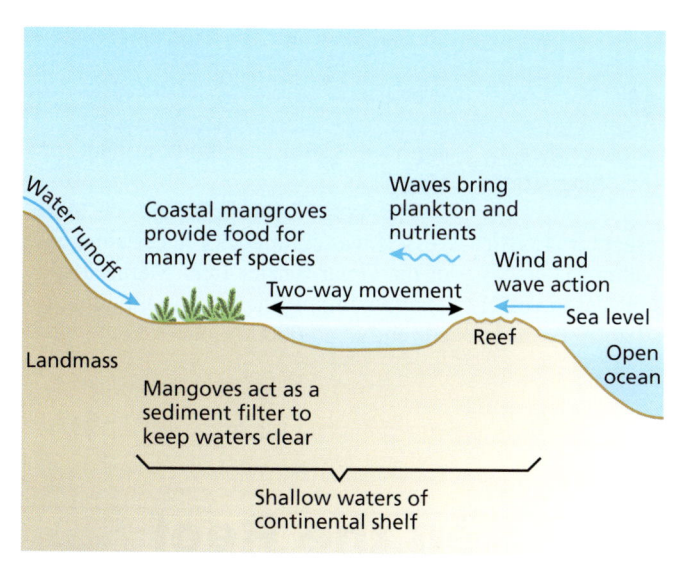

7A.12 *A coral reef as an open system*

7A.13 *A coral reef from the air*

3 Why is it so important?

The Great Barrier Reef is a World Heritage Area. This means that the United Nations has decided that it is somewhere so important that it must be protected for the benefit of people throughout the world. It is also the world's largest marine protected area. Its **biological diversity** includes:

- continental islands
- low wooded islands
- coral cays – small sandy islands
- bottom-dwelling communities
- deep ocean troughs
- mangrove estuaries – over half the of world's mangrove diversity
- algal and sponge gardens
- seagrass beds – over 3000 km^2
- over one-third of the world's soft coral species
- over 1500 species of fish
- 6 of the world's 7 species of marine turtle
- the world's largest breeding area for green turtles
- one of the world's most important dugong populations
- important seabird breeding islands
- breeding area for humpback and other whale species.

Tourism and fishing are important in the region of the reef. Tourism brings divers, cruise ships, helicopter flights and development of island resorts (see Figure 7A.11). The most highly used tourism areas are Cairns and Whitsunday.

4 What are the threats to it?

There are a variety of threats to the biological diversity of the reef. Some of these are shown as Figures 7A.14, 7A.15 and 7A.16.

There are other threats to the Great Barrier Reef including divers and snorkellers damaging to the coral. Recreational boats dropping anchor on the coral also damages it very easily.

Perhaps the biggest threat to the reef comes from global warming. A report by Sydney University Professor Ove Hoege-Guldberg warns that tropical marine environments are likely to be the first casualties of climate change. He predicts that reefs in the Central Pacific area may last until 2050, but that others have a far shorter life expectancy.

'Reefs around the West Indies in the Caribbean look as though they will be gone by 2020 while the Great Barrier Reef will probably last for just another three decades,' he warned.

1999 is thought to have been the warmest in terms of sea temperature for 400 years. If it is repeated the prospects look especially bleak.

Section 7 Changing Environments

> The dugong is a marine mammal that must surface every few minutes to breathe. Australia has the largest population of dugongs in the world but it is threatened with extinction. The threat to the dugong comes from the loss of the seagrass which it eats. Seagrass loss has occurred because of the dumping of waste and chemical run-off from farmland.
>
> There are also threats to the dugong from fishing nets as well as shark nets which are set up on tourist beaches to protect swimmers from sharks. Some animals are killed by collisions with boats and others are illegally hunted.

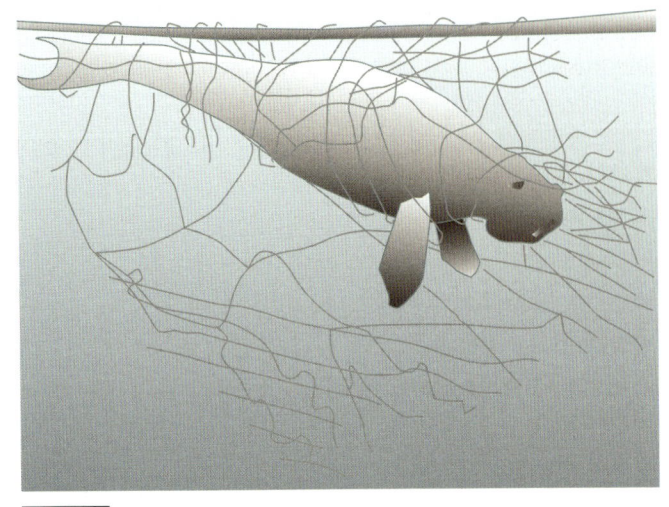

7A.14 *Nets are just one of the causes of the decline in dugong numbers*

Ship's Captain to Face Committal

Friday 9 June, 2000

A SHIP'S captain will face committal proceedings in October after being charged with sailing his vessel through part of the Great Barrier Reef without a pilot on board. The captain, age 40, was not required to enter a plea when he appeared at Townsville Magistrates Court today.

Commonwealth prosecutor Lousie Morse has alleged Adhikari, a Sri Lankan national, sailed the cargo vessel *Gazelle Coast* through Trinity Passage, north of Cairns, without a pilot on May 11.

The court heard pilotage of large vessels was compulsory in certain areas of the Great Barrier Reef Marine Park. The maximum fine for an individual is currently $55,000.

7A.15 *The threat to the reef from shipping*

Water Quality problems threaten the Reef

10 January, 2001

From our environmental correspondent

The ecosystems of the Great Barrier Reef owe their existence and continued health to suitable water quality environments. Most tropical marine ecosystems grow best in conditions in which plant nutrients, nitrogen and phosphorus, exist in low concentrations (excessive or changed nutrient state is known as *eutrophication*).

Change in the water quality of land run-off is one of the significant human impacts on the Great Barrier Reef. Sediment and nutrient input to the Reef from land run-off has increased fourfold in the last 150 years.

Much of the land on the catchment area has been cleared for agricultural purposes, primarily cropping and grazing. Sugar cane is now the largest crop and uses intensive fertilisers. Unfortunately the fertilisers and pesticides used by farmers end up in the offshore waters.

Beef grazing close to the Marine Park has involved extensive tree clearance and over-grazing during drought conditions. As a result, widespread soil erosion has occurred, 'exporting' the eroded material into the Great Barrier Reef.

7A.16 *Water quality is affected by farming methods*

A Coastline management

Australian Greenpeace spokesperson, Irwin Jackson, said that 'coral reefs are now in effect the canaries in the cage, warning the world that something must be done to limit carbon emissions and slow down global warming.'

It is more than just an environmental crisis, it is a human one as well. One-and-a-half million people visit Australia's Great Barrier Reef each year spawning a thriving local economy. If the reef dies, thousands face losing their livelihoods as the tourist industry crumbles.

5 How is it being managed?

The threats to the Great Barrier Reef are varied and the solutions to them complex. They involve many different initiatives from the Great Barrier Reef Marine Authority. Some of the management issues are shown in Figure 7A.17.

One of the effective ways of controlling the use of the Great Barrier Reef has been to divide it into thirteen zones of use. Examples of the zones are shown below. Designating zones is not enough: not everyone is prepared to follow the controls set out. Policing the zones is also necessary, and that is expensive.

Great Barrier Reef Zones

General use A zone
The least restrictive of the zones, this provides for all reasonable uses including shipping and trawling. Prohibited activities are mining, oil drilling and commercial spearfishing.

Buffer zone
This zone provides protected areas of Marine Parks and allows opportunities for their appreciation and enjoyment. Buffer zones allow mackerel fishing in areas adjacent to reefs zoned as National Park.

Preservation zone
This provides for the preservation of the area in an undisturbed state. All entry is prohibited, except in an emergency, with the exception of permitted scientific research.

7A.17 *Some of the management issues facing the authorities*

Section 7 **Changing Environments**

> **EXTENDED ACTIVITY**
>
> This activity asks you to analyse the threats and management issues presented as part of the enquiry.
>
> 1 In what ways are the following activities threatening the existence of the ecosystems of the Great Barrier Reef: intensive farming methods, dumping waste, fishing, shipping, tourist boats and snorkelling?
>
> 2 Why might global warming be the greatest threat to the reef?
>
> 3 How can zoning help to control activities in the area of the reef?
>
> 4 Why is it so difficult to control activities in the area of the reef?
>
> 5 Why will international activity be essential if the reef is to be conserved?
>
> 6 Write a brief summary of the Great Barrier Reef and its future.

> **EXAMINATION QUESTION**
>
> Marks
>
> 1 For a natural environment you have studied:
>
>   a State the nature of the environment and its location. *(2)*
>
>   b What are the human threats to this environment? *(7)*
>
>   c What has been done to reduce the threats to the environment? *(7)*
>
> 2 What other ways can you suggest to conserve this natural environment? *(4)*
>
> Total marks 20

Managing Canada's coastline

The need for management

Canada (Figure 7A.18) has the longest coastline in the world. As well as natural changes, the shoreline ecosystem is suffering from growing conflict among users causing damage to the natural environment (see Figure 7A.19). This also has harmful effects upon the people who live and work in the coastal zone. Global warming and consequent rising sea levels, for example, are predicted to have serious effects upon Canada's coastline. Threats include the flooding of property, coastal erosion and disruption to fisheries. Wildlife is threatened by pollution, such as that caused by major cities like Vancouver and Toronto. Pollutants that find their way into food webs also pose health hazards for people living in the area.

The need for management of Canada's coastline has long been recognised. The challenge has been to meet the needs of differing groups of people using the coastline, whose priorities often conflict. As in many other countries, there is no single authority responsible for managing the coastline in Canada. This means it is very difficult to make any policy actually work throughout Canada.

What options are available?

Management of the coastline in Canada aims to achieve the *conservation* and *sustainable use* of the coastal zone. In order to do this, the Canadian government looked at the four main types of strategy available.

1 Protect the current coastline. This usually involves building sea walls and other defences intended to prevent further coastal erosion. While having some success, such measures are often costly as well as unattractive. The sea often wins in the end, with few such coastal defence measures being permanent features of the coastline.

2 Build defences beyond the shoreline. In some cases, barriers have been built below the line of low tide, intended to absorb the energy of incoming waves so that they do not cause so much damage to the coastline. Again, such measures have met with limited success in the face of constant pounding from the sea.

3 Let nature take its course. Apart from ensuring the safety of people living in coastal areas, the sea is allowed to change the coastline naturally. This solution has become popular with some groups of people, for example conservationists and the authorities who have paid for expensive but failed defence schemes. It is not, however, favoured by the people whose lives and properties could be ruined by coastal erosion.

4 Managed retreat. This involves allowing the coastline to retreat, but in a controlled way. Any of the three strategies above may be used, making this the most *sustainable* method of coastal management.

What has the government done?

The Canadian government decided that if coastal management was to work properly, several points had to be agreed.

- No single group of people would be able to decide what happened to the coastline. This meant that the future of the coasts would not be in the hands of one interest group, for example industrialists or conservationists. These groups of people, who would probably want very

A Coastline management

7A.18 Canada

different solutions, would have to agree what was to happen.
- Protection of the coastline could only work by viewing the coast as part of a **shoreline zone system.** This extends inland with the catchment areas of rivers, and out to sea beyond low tide. All parts of this system affect what happens at the coastline.
- Management would have to be **integrated.** It would have to take into account the needs of all users of the coast, including humans, birds and plant life.
- Coastal management needed to be **sustainable.** Where erosion was taking place, it had to be accepted that it would continue, and the best that could be done was to manage the rate of erosion.
- The biggest problem was that current laws regarding use of the coastline did not work. They were too complicated, and easy for people to evade.

The government's solution: the CEPA

The Canadian government in 1988 passed the *Canadian Environmental Protection Act*. This was designed to meet the needs of coastline management in the future. The Act made 15 regulations about how the coast should be used. The problem remained, however, that it was very difficult to ensure that all groups of people obeyed what the law required.

In response to this, the government had three choices.

1 Keep the law as it is, but enforce it more strictly. This would involve employing more people to police the coasts of Canada, and imposing heavier penalties on people who break the law.

2 Change the law. This would lead to the development of a national coastal zone management policy, governed by one government department.

Section 7 Changing Environments

Plastics, which are not degradable, are polluting Canada's shores near to large towns and cities.

Pollutants found in marine wildlife transfer up the food chain. Concentrated amounts of pollutants are a danger to people.

Marine wildlife is under threat. This is due to pollution, and the unsustainable levels of fishing taking place.

Shellfish habitats have become so polluted that the fish are no longer fit for human consumption.

Rising sea levels predicted due to global warming threaten wetlands, industrial and other economic land uses. People will move elsewhere, putting increased pressure on other parts of Canada's coasts.

7A.19 *Pressures on Canada's shoreline zone*

3 Accept the present situation. With such a long coastline, it is impossible to ensure that the whole country is protected. It would cost too much. It is better to rely upon the good will of people, and to accept that the situation will never be perfect.

In the event, the CEPA decided to maintain present laws, and police them more vigorously, punishing offenders more severely. They also decided to make some enforceable new laws. They accepted that damage was likely to be caused, and that Canada has a long coastline that will last longer than people, and they could spend funds more usefully.

7A.20 *Much of Canada's extensive coastline is virtually uninhabited. Here erosion is a natural process rather than a problem. Should coasts like this be protected?*

A Coastline management

NOTING ACTIVITIES

1 Using an atlas, estimate the approximate length of Canada's coastline.

2 Repeat this exercise for the coastline of the British Isles. How do the two compare?

3 a Why is coastal management an important issue for Canada?

   b What options were available?

   c What do you understand by the sustainable development of Canada's coastline?

   d What is meant by the term shoreline zone? How does this differ from a coastline?

   e What purpose does the CEPA have?

   f What do you think are the advantages and disadvantages of each method of making the law work effectively?

Section 7 Changing Environments

B Weather and climate

Weather refers to daily conditions in the atmosphere. The weather is described in terms of sunshine, temperature, precipitation and so on. **Climate** describes conditions over a period of several years. Climate also describes conditions over a large area, while weather is more local. Geographers describe the climate of the British Isles, for example, as **temperate**. This means that it does not have great extremes of heat or cold. The weather today in the place where you live may be very different to the average suggested by Britain's climate.

Weather and climate are important issues in Geography because they affect people in many ways. The photographs in Figure 7B.1 show some of the different ways in which weather and climate are important for people.

> NOTING ACTIVITIES
>
> 1 For each of the photographs in Figure 7B.1, state how people are affected by weather and climate.
>
> 2 List ways in which the weather affected you for one day during this week.
>
> 3 Name three types of job that may be seriously affected by the weather.

How are people affected by weather and climate? Three examples are:

1 global warming, an issue affecting the world's climate;

2 tropical storms, severe weather conditions that affect over half of the Earth's surface; and

3 urban climates, an example of a **microclimate** created by people.

Global warming

The world's climate is changing. Global temperatures rose by an average of 0.6°C during the 20th century. Although this may not seem like a major change, if this rate of temperature increase continues, the world's climate zones will alter significantly. Scientists debate whether this change is entirely natural, or the result of human actions. Climate change is a natural process; 30 000 years ago, for example, much of Britain was covered in ice. There is evidence, however, that during the Ice Age temperatures varied dramatically. At some stages, temperatures were warm enough for elephants and rhinoceroses to live in what is now the British Isles.

The issue today is the speed at which temperatures are changing compared with changes in the past. The process of

7B.1 *Weather and climate affect people in many ways*

B Weather and climate

global warming is made much quicker by the **greenhouse gases** which are poured into the atmosphere (see Figure 7B.2). The main greenhouse gas is carbon dioxide, a result of the burning of fossil fuels such as oil and gas. As Figure 7B.3 shows, the United States is the key country in contributing to carbon dioxide in the atmosphere. Weather recording stations throughout the world report that levels of carbon dioxide in the atmosphere are continuing to increase.

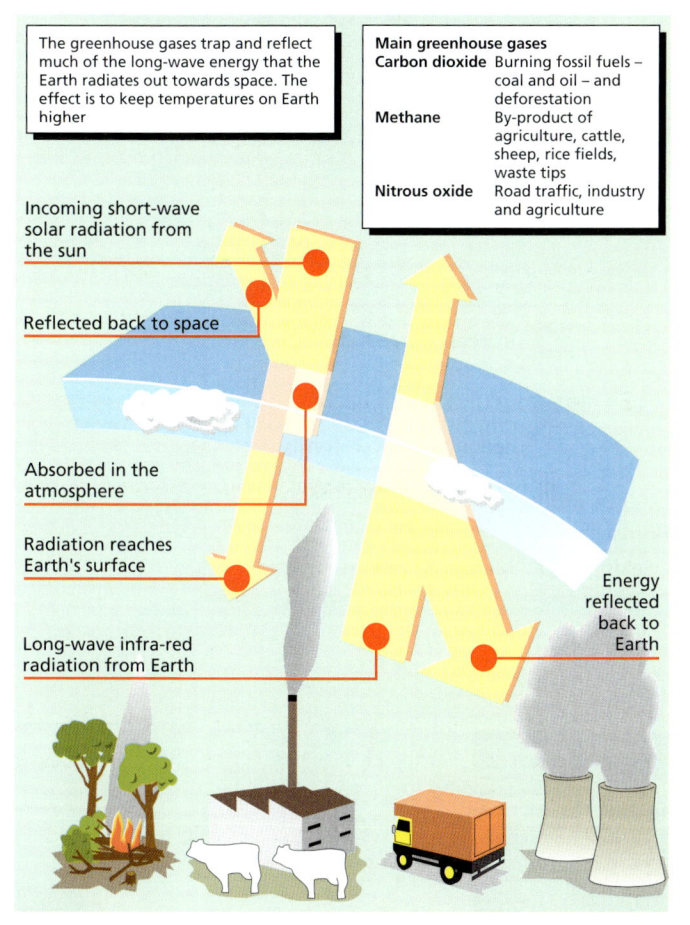

What are the effects of global warming?

Climate change is likely to affect all parts of the world in the 21st century and beyond. What changes might take place? The world could be a very different place by 2050, as shown in Figure 7B.4.

1 The British Isles

Britain will have warmer summer months, with more frequent droughts. Autumn and winter, on the other hand, will become wetter. This will cause more severe flooding in many parts of the country. The Environment Agency has published advice and maps on the internet. These tell people whether they are at risk of flooding where they live, and what to do in case of flooding (see Figure 7B.5).

Higher sea levels, as a result of the ice caps melting, could cause severe coastal flooding. In the north-west of England, for example, 100 000 people live and work on the coastal plain that could be in danger of flooding. This area also has much of the region's industry and tourism.

Milder weather will change the nature of Britain's plant and animal life. Crops such as soya, maize and sunflowers could become common. The British Isles could become one of Europe's main wine growing regions by the end of the 21st century (see Figure 7B.6).

2 The United States

Much of the east coast of the USA is under threat of flooding if temperatures continue to rise. An increase of 4°C, an average prediction, would see cities such as New York and Boston in danger.

Higher temperatures allow insects and rodents that would otherwise die to survive during the winter. There have already been cases of malaria in New York. Another disease carried by mosquitoes is West Nile disease, which has already affected parts of the country.

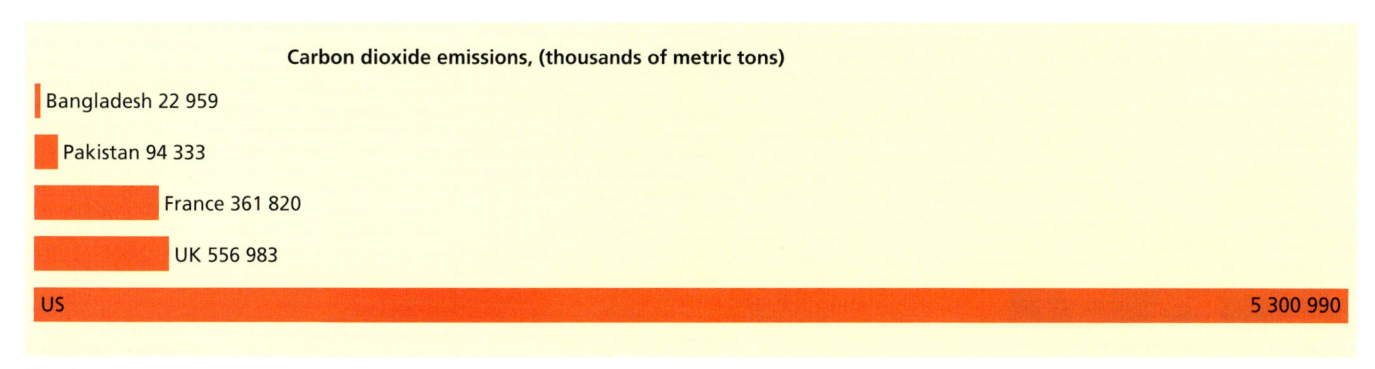

7B.2 *The greenhouse effect*

Main greenhouse gases
- Carbon dioxide: Burning fossil fuels – coal and oil – and deforestation
- Methane: By-product of agriculture, cattle, sheep, rice fields, waste tips
- Nitrous oxide: Road traffic, industry and agriculture

Carbon dioxide emissions, (thousands of metric tons)
- Bangladesh 22 959
- Pakistan 94 333
- France 361 820
- UK 556 983
- US 5 300 990

7B.3 *Carbon dioxide emissions, 1996*

Section 7 Changing Environments

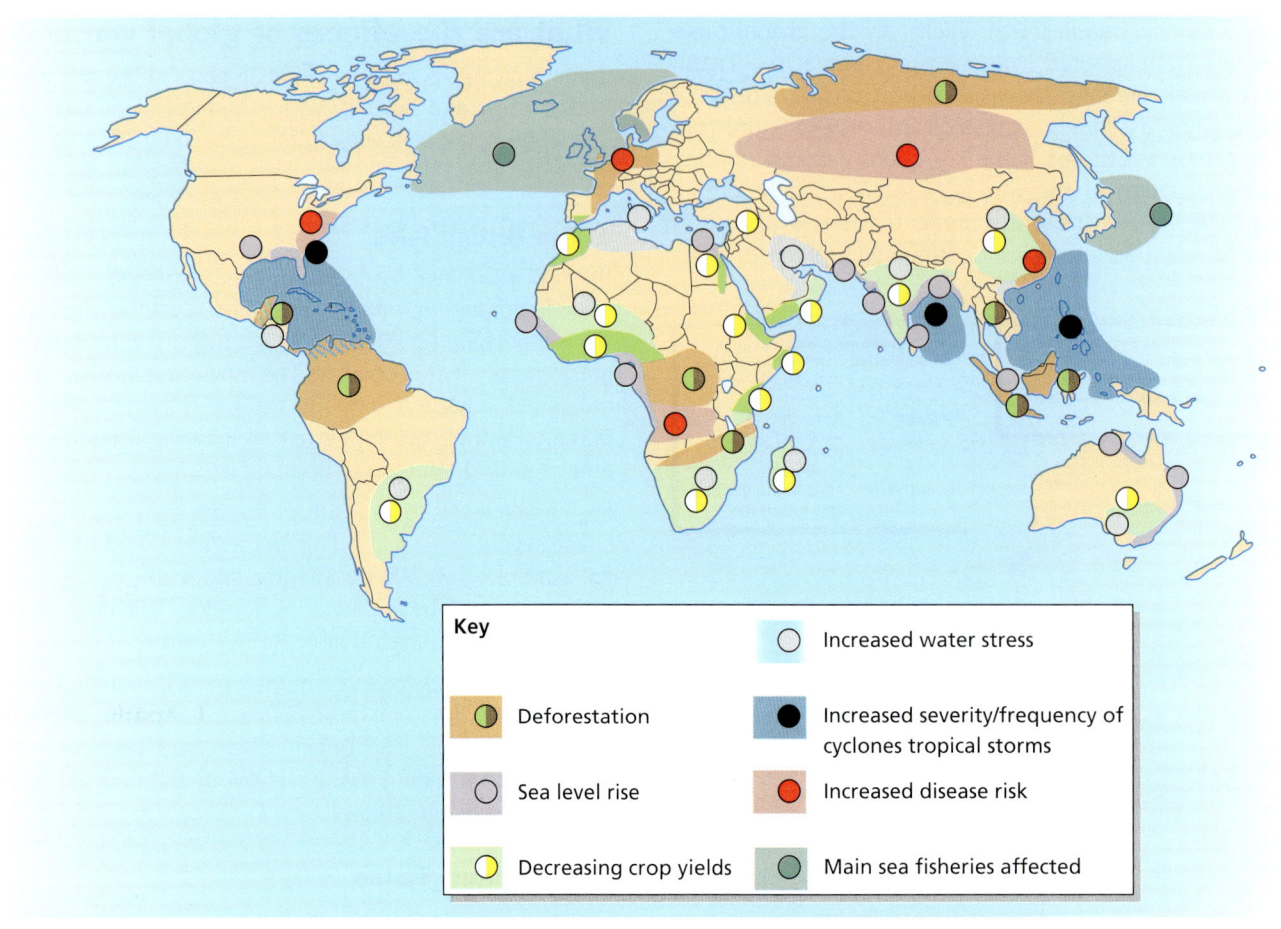

7B.4 *How climate change could change the world by 2050*

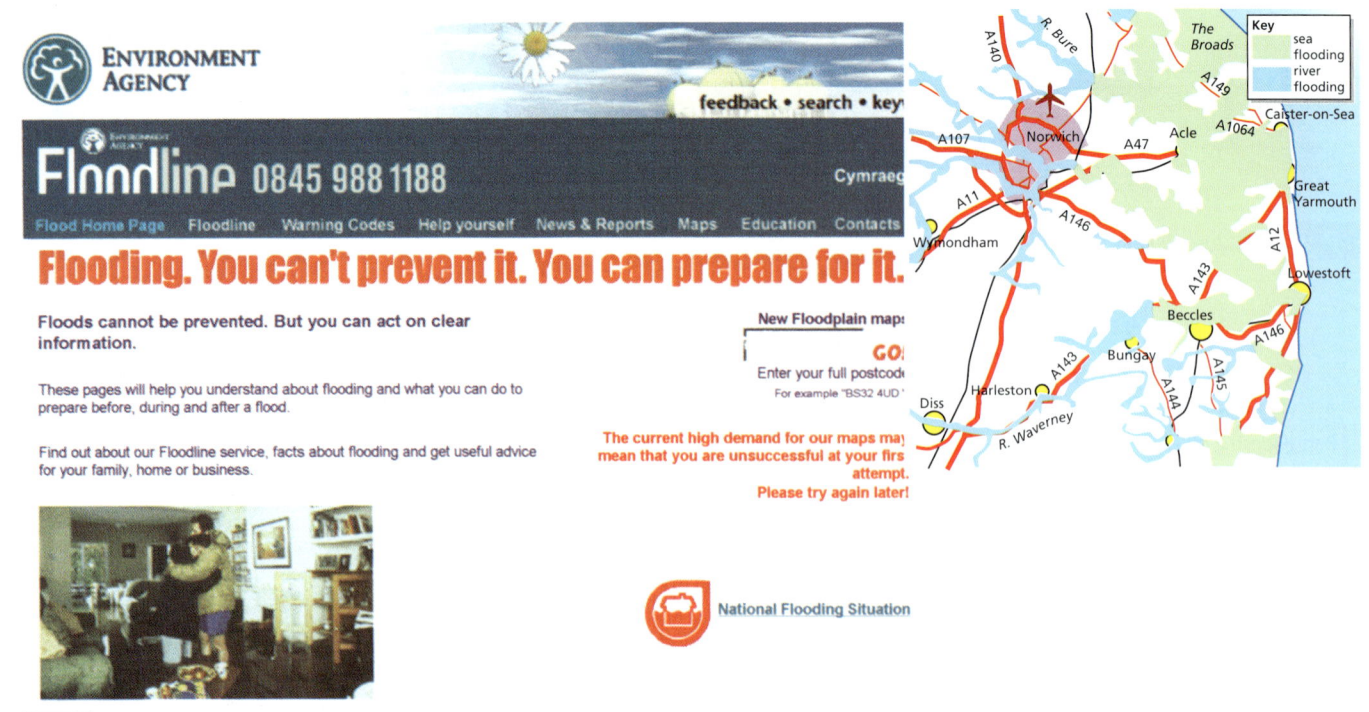

Key:
- Increased water stress
- Deforestation
- Increased severity/frequency of cyclones tropical storms
- Sea level rise
- Increased disease risk
- Decreasing crop yields
- Main sea fisheries affected

7B.5 *Advice published by the Environment Agency*

Flooding. You can't prevent it. You can prepare for it.

Floods cannot be prevented. But you can act on clear information.

These pages will help you understand about flooding and what you can do to prepare before, during and after a flood.

Find out about our Floodline service, facts about flooding and get useful advice for your family, home or business.

Floodline 0845 988 1188

216

Global warming makes case for Château Kintyre

BY NICK NUTTALL, ENVIRONMENT CORRESPONDENT

CHATEAU Dumfries and Château Gateshead could soon be the wines on connoisseurs' lips as global warming sends temperatures soaring in northern Britain.

Scientists charged with discovering how commercial wine-making in Europe will alter with climate change claim that areas currently too cold to support wine production, such as the very north of England and southern Scotland, will rival Alsace and the Rhineland for their superior crisp whites. The minimum temperature required to produce wine-making grapes is around 20° C.

7B.6 *From* The Times, *23 February 2000*

EXTENDED ACTIVITY

1 Find out about flood risks in the area in which you live using the internet.
   a Open up the home page of the Environment Agency, at www.environment-agency.gov.uk/
   b On the home page, click on Floodline.
   c Enter your postcode in the box under the section 'New Floodplain maps'.
2 Once the map is on screen, you may change the scale or move to view a different area.
3 Repeat the process for a part of the country that is at risk of flooding.

3 China

China faces the possibility of severe droughts. Over 400 million people live in areas of water shortage, particularly in the north of the country. In many major cities, people only have access to water for one hour each day. Marshlands are drying up, and every year over 2500 square kilometres of cultivated land is lost due to drought. The Chinese fear that, with an increase in annual temperatures, the droughts that affect the country will become worse.

4 Japan

Most of Japan's population and resources are concentrated on the narrow coastal strip between the cities of Tokyo and Osaka. A rise of one metre in sea level, quite modest by most predictions, would flood much of this coastal zone. As many as 15 million people could lose their homes.

5 Russia

Two-thirds of Russia is covered by **permafrost.** This is the name given to soil that is permanently frozen. Cities in permafrost regions have buildings on stilts that are driven into the frozen soil. Temperatures have increased so much in Russia that thousands of people have been evacuated because their homes have slid into melting soil. Transport and communications have been disrupted as roads and railways have slid away as the permafrost has melted.

What is being done about the problem?

Tackling the issue of global warming faces at least three problems.

1 Apathy Some people argue that there is not enough scientific evidence to prove that global warming is being caused by human action. The majority of carbon dioxide is produced by natural sources, and so temperature change would happen anyway. The timescale used to measure climate change is too short to state whether or not major changes are taking place. If temperature change is natural, why should it be seen as a problem? Some parts of the world could gain by having warmer temperatures.

2 Co-operation Global warming is an international issue. It is not possible to blame one country for all greenhouse gases. The United States may contribute most carbon dioxide, but rates of pollution are increasing rapidly in many LEDCs. Global warming affects all parts of the world, regardless of national boundaries.

3 Cost To cut down on greenhouse gases would be very expensive. Most carbon dioxide comes from industry. Should national governments pay to reduce emissions, or the industries that cause the pollution?

In 1997, world leaders met in the Japanese city of Kyoto to discuss the problems of climate change. It was agreed that all countries would reduce their greenhouse gases to 5 per cent lower than their level in 1990. At the same time, scientists stated that cuts would have to be as much as 80 per cent in order to have any real effect.

Since the Kyoto conference, few countries have kept to the agreement. The levels of greenhouses gases have actually gone up, at a rate of over 1 per cent per year. Many MEDCs have delayed measures to cut emissions. The United States increased carbon emissions by 10 per cent in the 1990s. With only 5 per cent of the world's population, the USA produces one-quarter of all greenhouse gases.

Section 7 Changing Environments

World leaders again met in 2000, this time in The Hague in the Netherlands. The conference faced the same problem, with many countries failing to reach an agreement on the main issues. Other **multinational** organisations, such as the United Nations, hold conferences to discuss the problems of climate change. In 1990, for example, a major conference was held to discuss the problems of desertification. Global warming is thought to be one cause of desertification, with increased droughts in northern Africa and southern Europe (see Figure 7B.7, and pages 227–230).

In addition to governments and multinational organisations, **pressure groups** try to force action on climate change. One of these groups is Greenpeace. Look at Figure 7B.8, which shows one of their posters. It is aimed at putting pressure on Coca-Cola to stop using HFCs. These are like chlorofluorocarbons (CFCs), which damage the ozone layer (see Figure 7B.9). Other pressure groups, such as Friends of the Earth, also campaign against climate change. Are these organisations likely to be effective, where national governments do not change their policies?

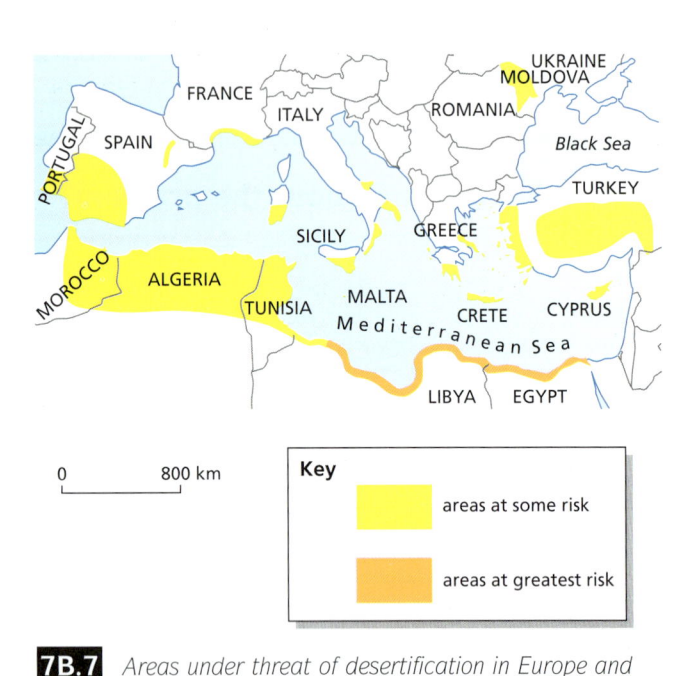

7B.7 Areas under threat of desertification in Europe and north Africa

7B.8 Greenpeace poster

7B.9 The growing hole in the ozone layer

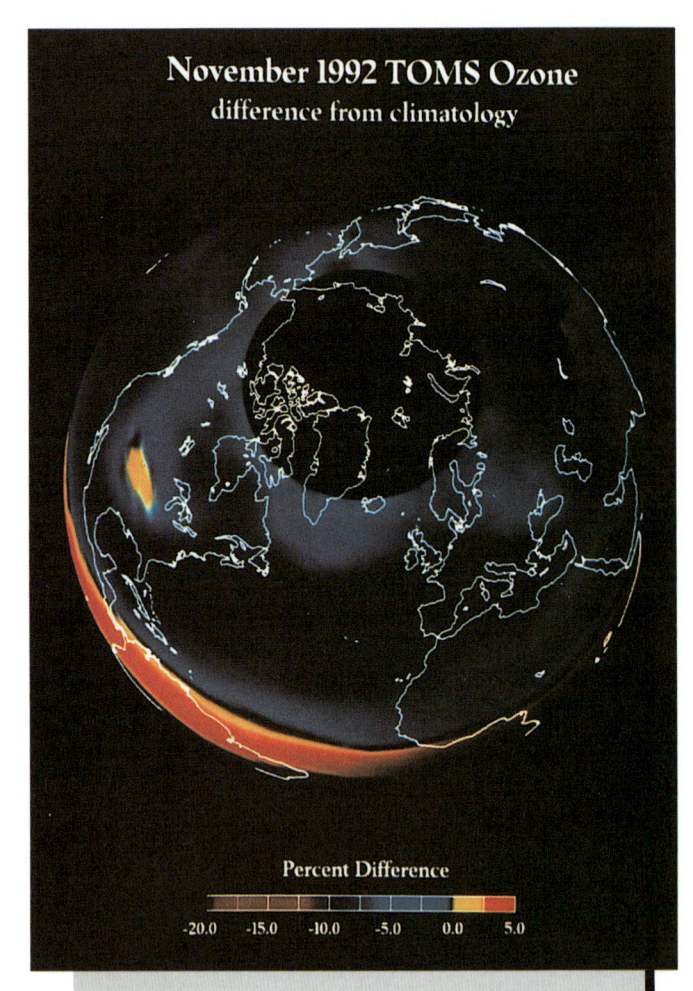

Ozone in the upper atmosphere blocks harmful radiation from the sun. This ultra-violet radiation causes skin cancer. Ozone is destroyed by chlorofluorocarbons (CFCs), which are released from aerosols and by cooling processes. CFCs were banned in 1987, but the hole in the ozone layer is continuing to grow. Some scientists predict that the hole will stop growing by 2010 if no more CFCs enter the atmosphere.

B Weather and climate

NOTING ACTIVITIES

1. Summarise the ways in which climate change is likely to affect the world in the 21st century.
2. What measures have been taken to deal with the problem?
3. Why do you think it is difficult for conferences such as Kyoto in 1997 to reach agreement on what to do about global warming?
4. Greenpeace chose to use polar bears for their poster because some Coca-Cola advertisements featured polar bears.
   a. What did you think when you first saw the Greenpeace poster?
   b. What messages is the Greenpeace poster trying to put across?
   c. Do you think the poster is very effective? Give reasons for your answer.
5. Do you think it is right that Greenpeace should focus in this way in one company, when many others contribute to climate change?

7B.10 *A typical multi-national product*

Tropical storms

What are tropical storms?

Tropical storms are intense low pressure systems which form over warm oceans in tropical areas. They occur when the oceans are at their warmest, up to 27°C and above. The season for tropical storms in the Atlantic and Caribbean is between June and November.

Warm moist air rises where trade winds meet. This is called the **Inter-Tropical Convergence Zone (ITCZ).** As the air rises the air pressure at sea level is reduced, which allows air from all around to rush in. Figure 7B.11 shows the weather conditions associated with a tropical storm.

Even though Atlantic Ocean **hurricanes** receive a lot of attention, only 12 per cent of the world's tropical storms happen there. These dangerous storms can be found in three of the four oceans, and in both hemispheres. Figure 7B.12 shows the regions of the Earth where tropical storms are hazards.

Nearly one hundred tropical storms are reported annually. Once the term 'storm' has been dropped it means that it has developed to a more serious level. In the Indian Ocean they are called **cyclones**, in the East Pacific and Atlantic **hurricanes**, in the western North Pacific Ocean **typhoons** and near Australasia **willy-willies.** In the western North Pacific there are an average of more than 25 typhoons each year. Another location with great activity is the Indian Ocean. No other part of the world has so much activity in such a small area.

The features of tropical storms are:
- very strong winds which can be in excess of 250 km per hour
- wind damage to overhead electricity lines, buildings and agricultural crops
- storm surges where the sea level rises because of the very strong winds. Surges can be over 5.5 metres in height
- flood damage from the sea inundating the low lying land
- heavy rainfall with over 200 mm per day
- flash floods from excessive rain
- landslides and mudflows.

Can tropical storms be predicted?

Unlike some natural hazards which only last for a short time, severe tropical storms can last for up to two weeks. As they develop they are tracked by satellite technology. In MEDCs storm 'Watch' and 'Warning' information services have been developed. Over the past few years the US hurricane warning systems have provided adequate time for people to move inland when hurricanes threaten. In Australia the Bureau of Meteorology runs a Tropical Cyclone Warning System which is communicated through TV, radio and newspapers.

Can people be prepared for storm disasters?

In MEDCs people have been trained to prepare for tropical storms. There are:
- well rehearsed evacuation plans
- community storm plans
- family and friends response systems
- prepared kits of disaster supplies
- property protection advice

Section 7 Changing Environments

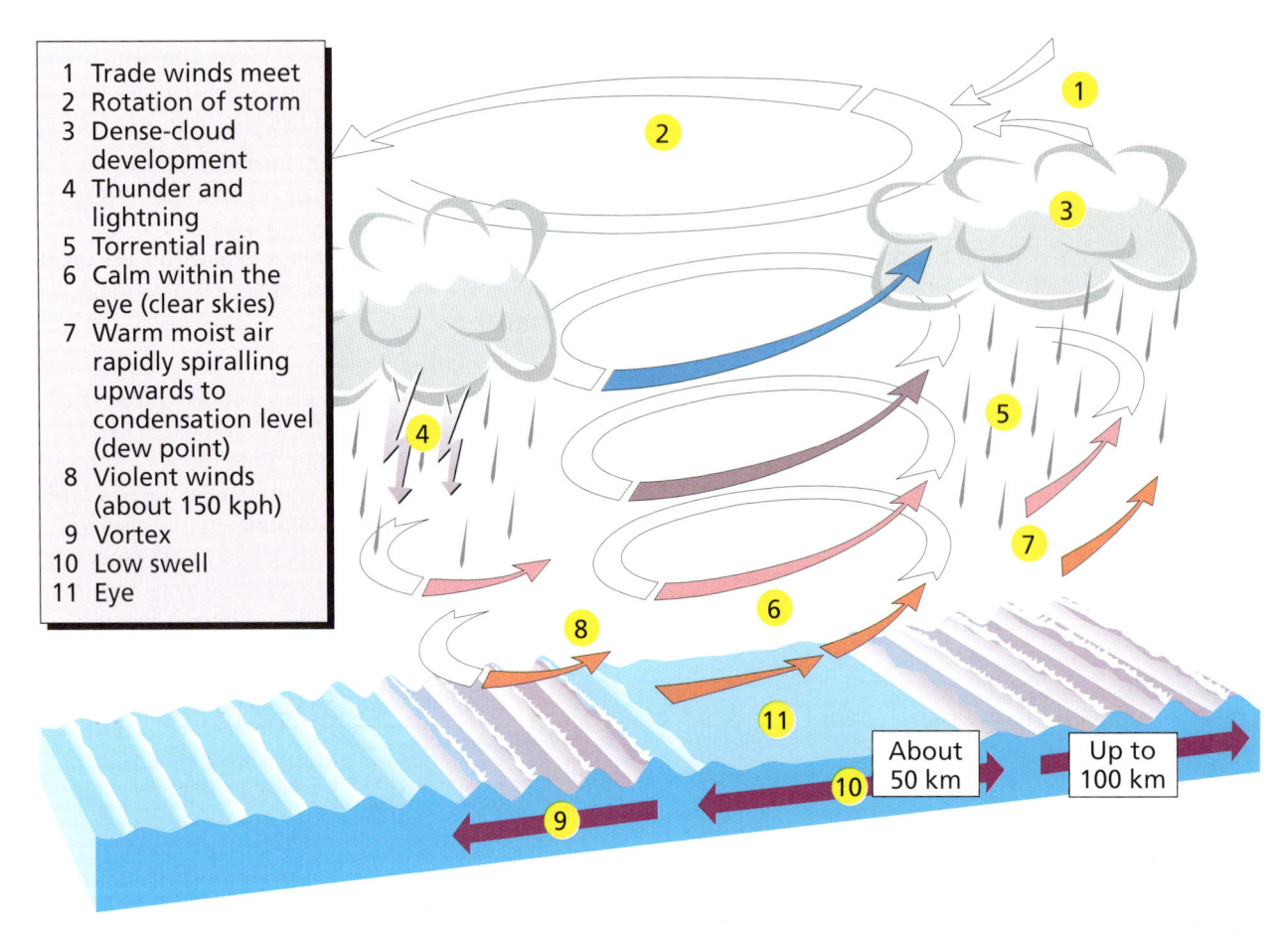

1. Trade winds meet
2. Rotation of storm
3. Dense-cloud development
4. Thunder and lightning
5. Torrential rain
6. Calm within the eye (clear skies)
7. Warm moist air rapidly spiralling upwards to condensation level (dew point)
8. Violent winds (about 150 kph)
9. Vortex
10. Low swell
11. Eye

About 50 km
Up to 100 km

7B.11 *A cross-section through a tropical storm*

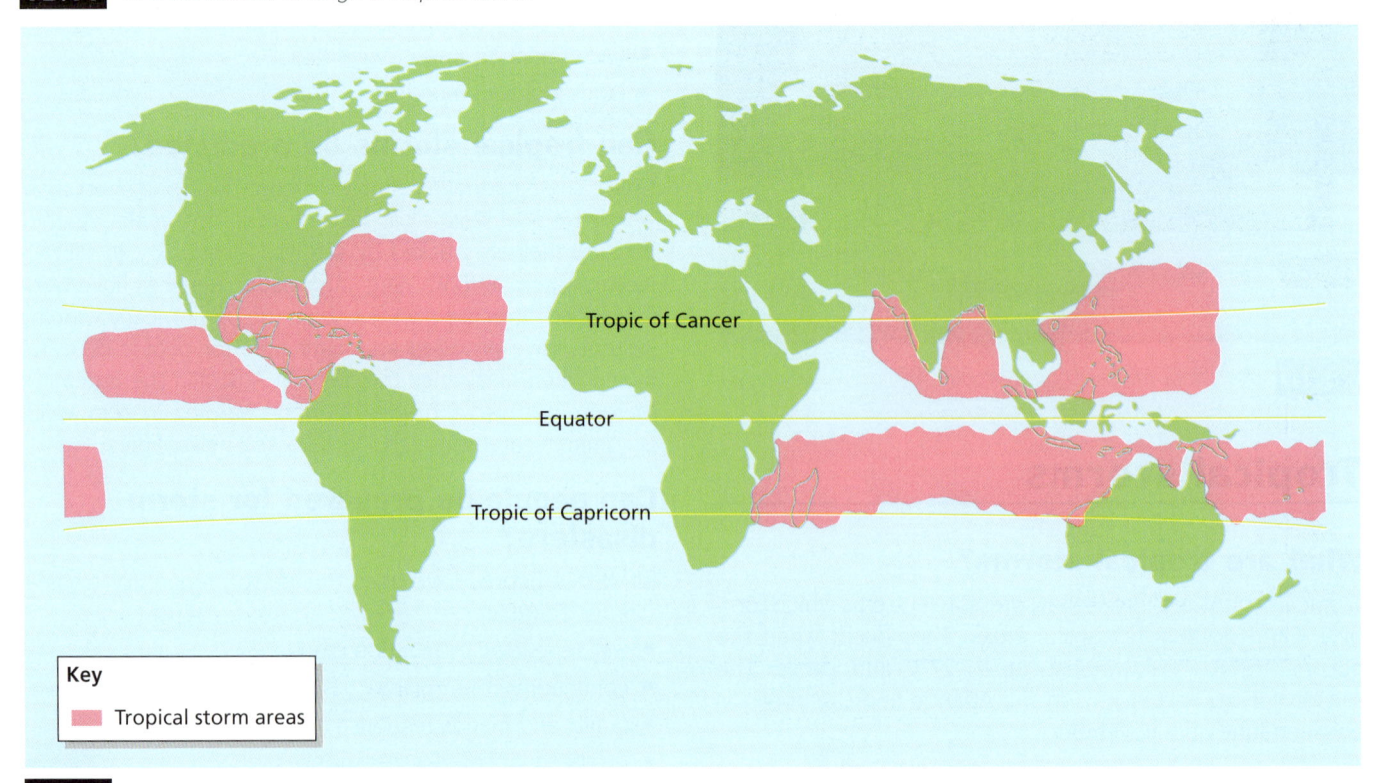

Tropic of Cancer
Equator
Tropic of Capricorn

Key
Tropical storm areas

7B.12 *World distribution of tropical storms*

B Weather and climate

- modern emergency services
- good coastal defences
- reinforced buildings
- cyclone shelters.

There is a large gap between the way people in MEDCs such as the USA and Australia are able to cope with storms and that of those living in LEDCs such as India and Bangladesh.

The advance planning for US Hurricanes can be read at www.disastercentre.com/guide/hurricane.html.

CASE STUDY

Cyclone in the Bay of Bengal

Figure 7B.13 gives a summary of a tropical storm that hit the east coast of India in 1999. The winds, rain and tidal surge caused massive flooding and loss of life. The last cyclone in the Bay of Bengal to have caused such destruction was in April 1991 when over 138 000 lives were lost in Bangladesh.

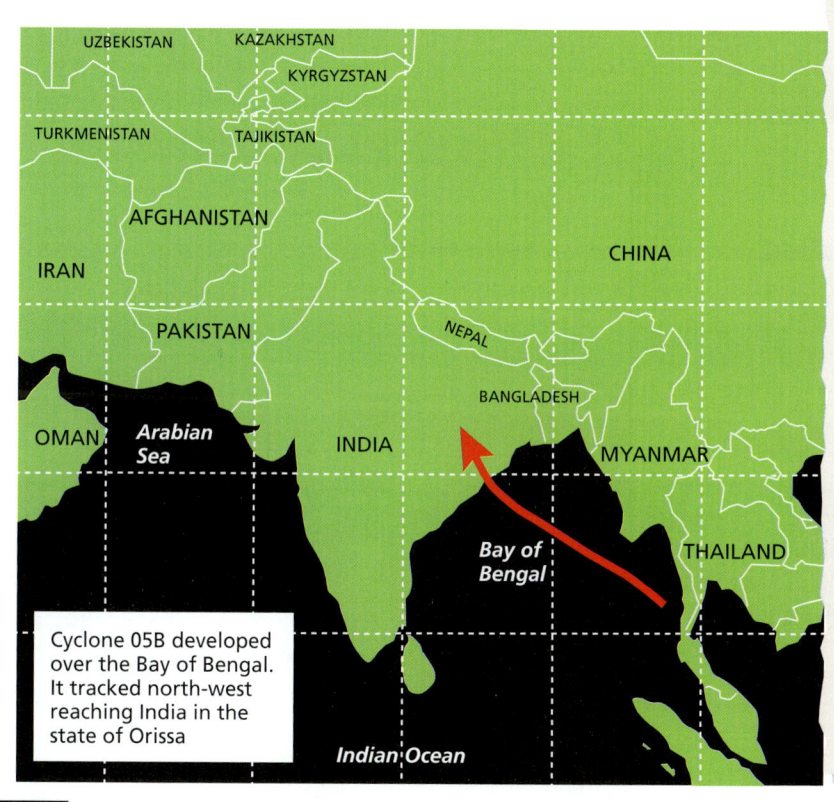

Cyclone 05B developed over the Bay of Bengal. It tracked north-west reaching India in the state of Orissa

Cyclone devastates Orissa

BHUBANESWAR, OCT 29, 1999: Several hundred people were feared killed and over 15 million affected as a super-cyclone, with a velocity of more than 260 km per hour, battered 10 coastal districts of Orissa for more than eight hours today. The Orissa government called in the Army and the Air Force to help the state carry out massive relief and rescue operations.

'You cannot imagine the devastation. The deaths will be not in tens but in hundreds,' Chief Minister Giridhar Gamang told UNI over the phone from his residence. Outside uprooted trees were blocking the gates of his house.

'The devastation is beyond imagination. More than 200 000 houses have been destroyed and vast tracts in the coastal areas submerged,' he said.

7B.13 *Newspaper report of the Bay of Bengal cyclone*

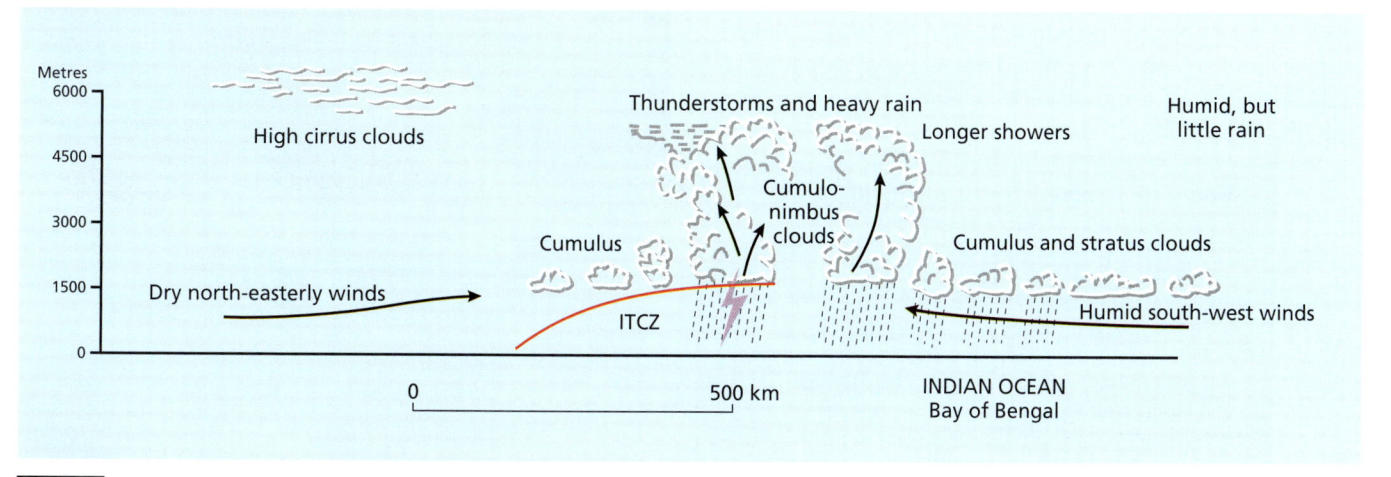

7B.14 *The meeting of the trade winds at the Inter-Tropical Convergence Zone*

221

Section 7 Changing Environments

Cyclones are not uncommon in the Bay of Bengal. This is because of the thunderstorms that develop in association with the nearby Inter-Tropical Convergence Zone and the very warm Indian Ocean (see Figure 7B.14).

For the people of Orissa the cyclone was devastating. This was not the USA or Australia where expensive preparations can minimise damage. Here people lost everything. Figure 7B.15 shows some of the intense wind damage.

Rebuilding after the cyclone

In Orissa rebuilding the livelihoods of the local people will go on for years. Unfortunately there is a high risk of damage from future storms and cyclones. Hurricane Mitch hit countries of Central America in 1998 when 20 000 were killed and two million left homeless. The UN estimated that development in the region was put back ten years.

7B.15 *Wind damage in Orissa*

Billions of dollars were sent to the Central America region after Hurricane Mitch. People form all around the world donated to charities. Unfortunately some years later a report told the world that much of the money had not found its way to people who desperately needed it. Money had been 'siphoned off' by corrupt officials and criminals. A few had become rich at the expense of the many. People who had donated to the charity effort were disillusioned and angry. What can be done to safeguard charity help? How can those who really need help be assured of receiving it?

CASE STUDY

Hurricane Keith in the Caribbean

In the autumn of 2000 Americans along the south and east coast of the USA were preparing for the hurricanes. Would one hit land in the USA? Would there be a repeat of a hurricane such as Hugo in 1989 or Andrew in 1992? The watches and warnings came as usual.

Some facts about Hurricane Keith
- Winds peaked at 216 km per hour
- Hurricane force winds extended 130 km from the hurricane's centre
- Slow moving as it drifted inland
- Heavy rain and flooding occurred (see Figure 7B.16)
- Wind damage: houses and shacks were toppled
- 5000 people evacuated from their homes
- Flash floods and mud slides
- Keith weakened rapidly once it hit land

7B.16 *Devastation in Mexico's Yucatan peninsula*

B Weather and climate

At the beginning of October Hurricane Keith developed over the Caribbean Sea and moved towards Mexico (Figure 7B.16). Coastal residents of Mexico's Yucatan peninsula and north-eastern Belize fled their homes as Hurricane Keith approached.

It was not a devastating hurricane but it made the Americans anxious. The US State Department urged US citizens living in Belize to consider leaving the country. People followed the hurricane to see if it would continue to develop and where it would track.

Hurricane Keith was another example of the changing natural environment. Each year there will be more hurricanes like Keith and some will be much worse. Some will cause a lot of damage and misery especially when they affect the poorer parts of Central America. When they affect the USA there will be more preparation for them and more money for people to rebuild and start again.

Categories of tropical storm

How severe was the Orissa cyclone and Hurricane Keith? Next time you read about a tropical storm check its severity (see Figure 7B.17).

Hurricane* Category	Wind speed (km. hour)	Storm surge (metres)	Typical damage
1	120–149	1.2–1.6	Minimal
2	150–179	1.7–2.5	Moderate
3	180–209	2.6–3.8	Extensive
4	210–249	3.9–5.5	Extreme
5	> 250	> 5.5	Catastrophic

* also applies to tropical cyclones and typhoons

7B.17 *Hurricane categories*

Urban climates

The impact of human activity upon climate is apparent in towns and cities. The **microclimate** of an urban area may be significantly different from that of rural environments. With about half of the world's population living in cities, a figure set to rise in the future, urban climates are an important issue for the 21st century. Why is the climate different in towns and cities? What effect does this have upon people? Is it possible to reduce the impact of urban climates?

What is an urban climate?

Climate is altered by towns and cities in a number of ways.

1 Temperature

Urban areas have higher temperatures. Cities can be very hot places in the summer. Temperatures may reach 5–6°C higher than the surrounding countryside. It is called an **urban heat island.** Higher temperatures occur because:

- there are fewer trees, shrubs and other plants to shade buildings and intercept solar radiation
- many buildings and pavements are made of dark materials. These absorb the sun's radiation raising their temperature and that of the air around them to rise
- cities are densely populated areas, full of homes and industries leaking heat into the atmosphere.

Figure 7B.18 shows how afternoon temperatures varied across the city of Los Angeles one summer day.

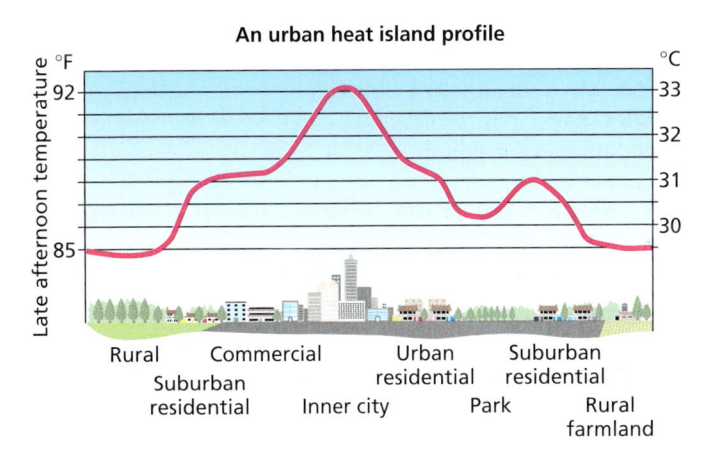

7B.18 *The effects of an urban area upon temperatures*

2 Air quality

Air quality is poorer in cities. Towns and cities are more polluted than the countryside. Motor vehicles, power stations, industry and domestic sources all produce pollution in urban areas. These pollutants rise into the lower atmosphere. The action of the sun's rays on them produces **photochemical smog** (a mixture of smoke and fog). These reactions are more noticeable in high temperatures, so smog is worst in summer months (see Figure 7B.19).

Poor air quality affects people's health, for example making asthma worse. It is estimated that 24 000 people each year in the UK die from the effects of air pollution.

3 Precipitation

Precipitation is greater. As cities are warmer than the countryside, there is likely to be more rising of warm air, condensation and precipitation. This is most pronounced in summer, leading to a greater number of thunderstorms.

Section 7 Changing Environments

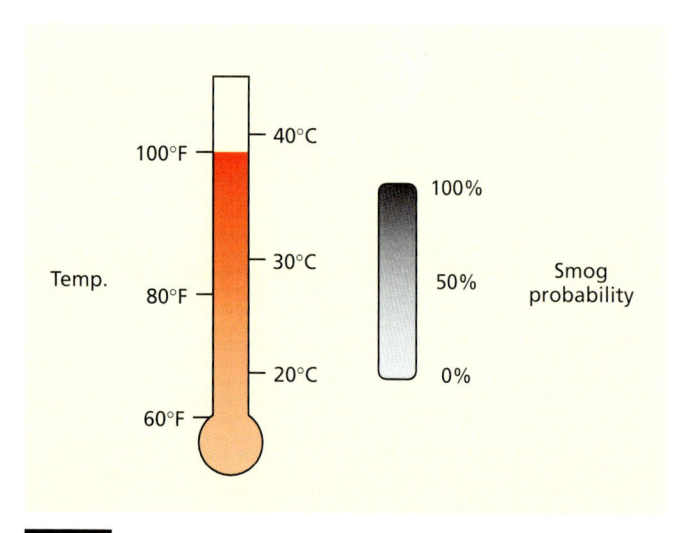

7B.19 Smog is more likely to occur on warm days

7B.20 Air pollution is a problem in cities throughout the world

4 Wind

Cities are windy. Although buildings may act as barriers to wind, air is channelled between buildings, often through narrow gaps. The result is that cities often have more gusty wind than in the country.

What can be done about urban climates?

Why is it an issue that urban areas have different microclimates? In the USA, it has been estimated that urban climates cost about $25 per household each year. This is because of the extra costs of air conditioning and purification. In addition to health probems, flooding is also an issue. The lack of vegetation in cities, together with increased precipitation, increases the likelihood of flooding.

The solutions to problems posed by urban climates are:

- plant more trees, which provide shade and lead to cooler ground surface conditions
- provide more open spaces such as parks. Open grass spaces are cooler than built-up areas, and allow for the more regular passage of wind

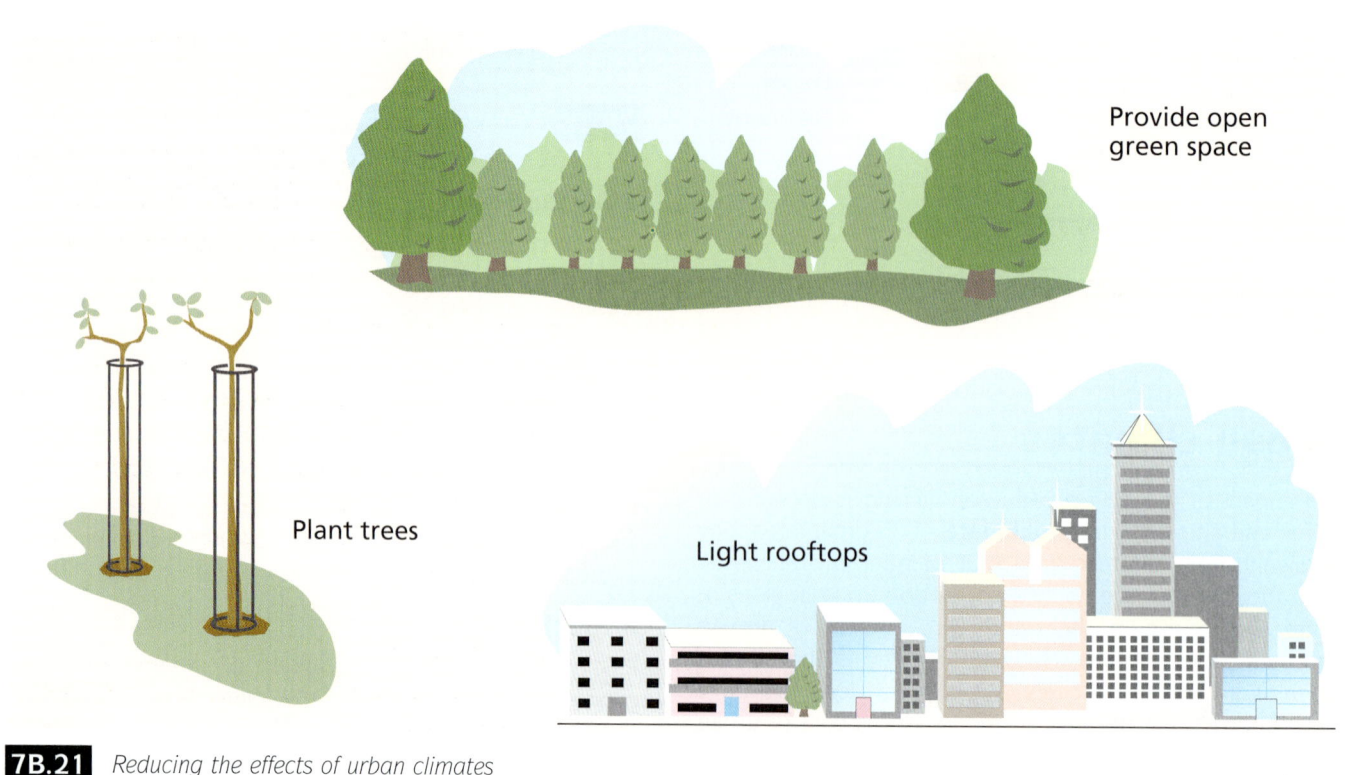

Provide open green space

Plant trees

Light rooftops

7B.21 Reducing the effects of urban climates

- using light surfaces where possible instead of dark. A light surface reflects more of the sun's energy, reducing heating. It is estimated that the population of Los Angeles would save nearly $60 million per year in reduced air conditioning costs if all homes had light coloured rooftops.

CASE STUDY

Urban climates of the USA

Urban areas throughout the world have their own climates. Cities in the USA have some of the most individual microclimates.

In **Los Angeles**, California, the relationship between urban growth and temperature increase has been apparent for many years (see Figure 7B.22). The decrease in temperature in the late 19th century followed the eruption of the Krakatoa volcano, the dust and ash from which temporarily obscured the sun throughout the world. In the early 20th century, much of the present day city of Los Angeles was covered by irrigated orchards. Rapid urbanisation took place from the 1940s, resulting in a steady rise in temperatures.

In **Atlanta**, Georgia, research has established that the city has changed the local climate. Atlanta is warmer than the surrounding countryside, which also brings air pollution problems (see Figure 7B.23).

A satellite image of part of **Washington DC** shows how different surfaces affect the temperature (see Figure 7B.24). Linking the photograph to the street map of the same area shown in Figure 7B.25 makes it possible to identify the areas that contribute most, and least, to the urban microclimate.

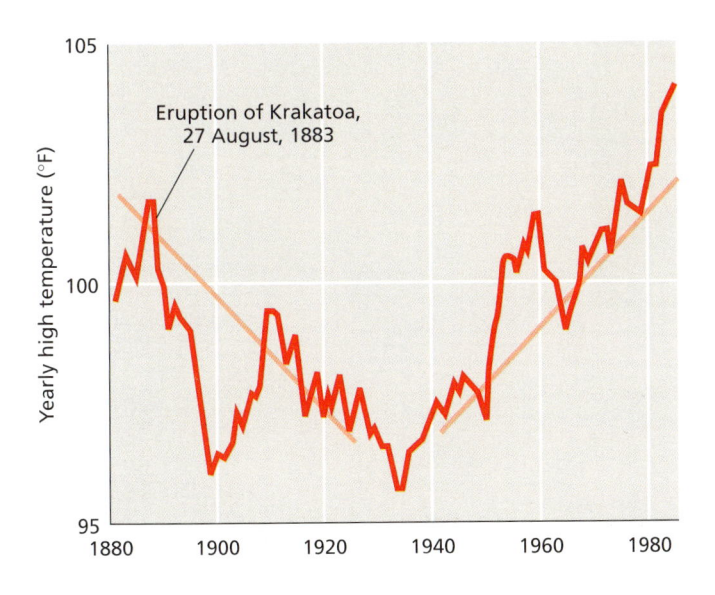

7B.22 *Rising temperatures in Los Angeles*

Team probes Atlanta heat island

24 March 2000

Web posted 1.45 EST

A hot time in the old town tonight is quite possible in Atlanta, Georgia, where the temperature is often 5 degrees Centigrade warmer than the surrounding area because of the urban heat island effect.

A National Aeronautics and Space Administration (NASA) sponsored study in Atlanta has found that the swapping of trees and other vegetation for heat-absorbing concrete and rooftops has created an urban heat island that can generate its own wind and thunderstorms, warm the city well into the night and dramatically increase the production of harmful ground-level ozone. The added heat has doubled the amount of pollution in the city.

7B.23 *Web page reporting on the Atlanta heat island*

NOTING ACTIVITIES

1 List the ways in which an urban area changes the climate.

2 What impacts do urban climates have upon people?

3 How is it possible to reduce the effects of climates?

EXTENDED ACTIVITY

1 Conduct an enquiry into a microclimate near where you live.
   a Name and locate the area.
   b Draw a sketch map to identify its main features.
   c Collect data to investigate the presence of a micro-climate, eg temperature readings in different locations.
   d Write up your results. Annotate your sketch map to summarise your findings.
   e Do your results support the suggestion that there is a microclimate in the area you have investigated?
   f What limitations do you think there were to your enquiry?
   g How could your enquiry be improved?

2 Research another type of microclimate, eg the effect of shelter, aspect, etc.

Section 7 **Changing Environments**

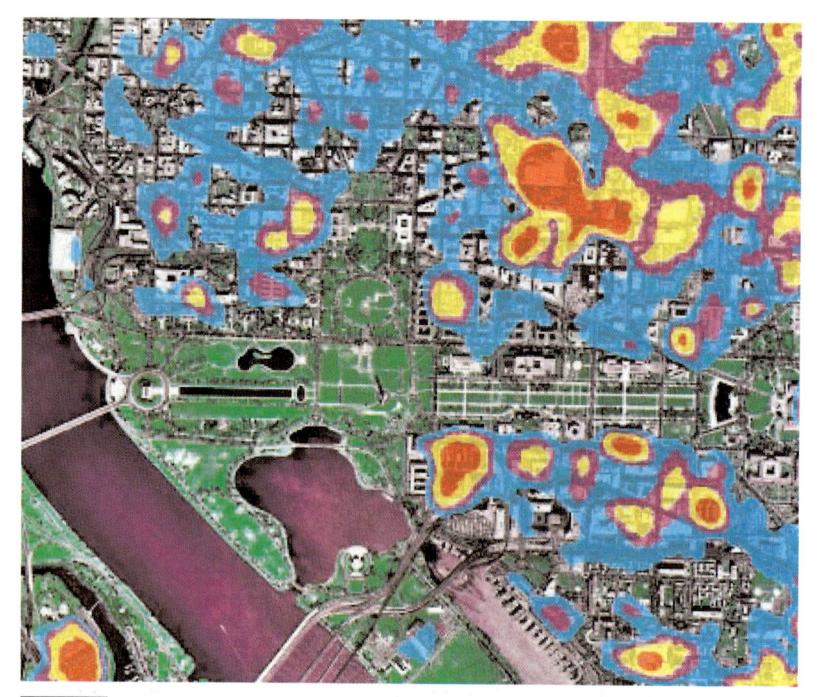

7B.24 *Satellite image of part of Washington DC*

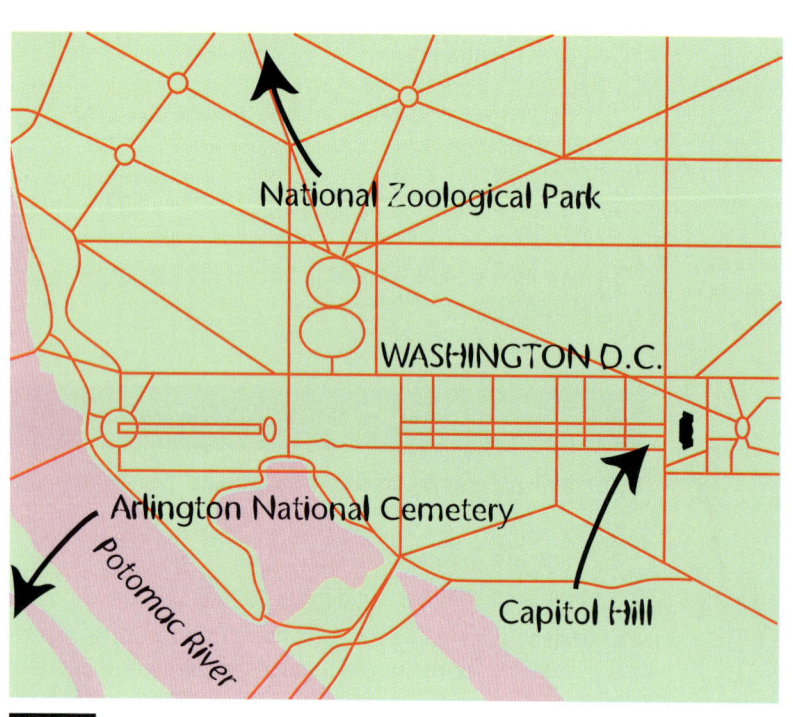

7B.25 *Street map of the area shown on the satellite photograph*

It's inevitable that towns and cities will have their own microclimates.

But there are some solutions to the problems of urban microclimates.

7B.26

Section 7 Changing Environments

C Environmental issues

Desertification

Hot deserts occupy about 10 per cent of the world's land surface. Some areas, like the middle of the Sahara desert in Africa, are virtually uninhabited. Elsewhere, many people live in or at the edge of deserts.

The world's deserts are expanding. Land that was once fertile and used for farming has become desert. This process is called **desertification**. Why is desertification taking place, and what effect is it having upon people? Can anything be done to stop the spread of the world's deserts?

CASE STUDY

The Sahel of West Africa

The Sahel is the region to the south of the Sahara desert (see Figure 7C.2). This is a region in which desertification is

7C.1 *Desertification causes a decline in the quality of land, making it unproductive*

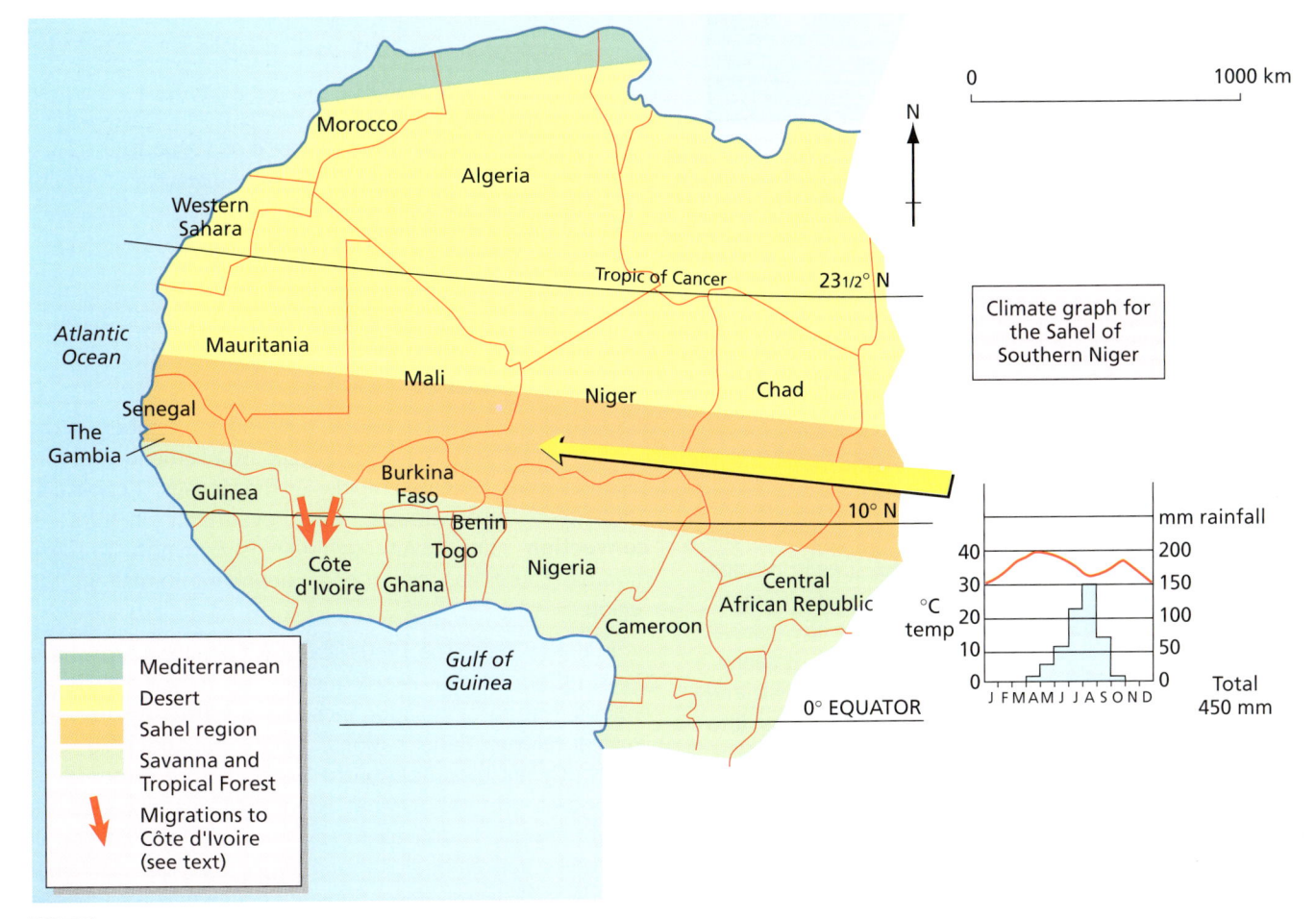

7C.2 *The location of the West African Sahel region*

227

Section 7 Changing Environments

taking place. The Sahara desert is gradually expanding to the south, at an average rate of three kilometres each year. Look at the satellite photograph of Africa (Figure 7C.3). The area of the Sahara desert may clearly be seen.

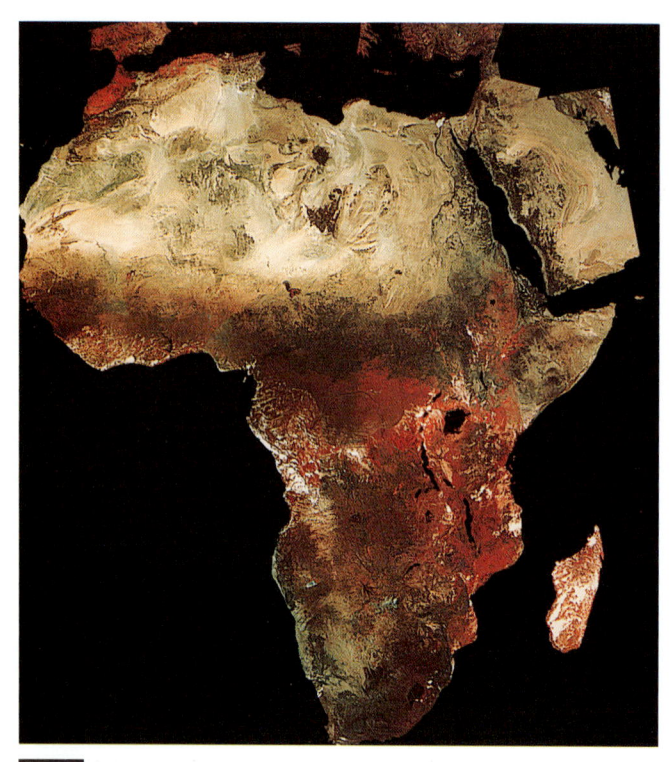

7C.3 *Satellite image of Africa*

Cote d'Ivoire (Ivory Coast) is a country on the southern edge of the Sahel. By 1999, over 3 million people had moved south into the forests of Cote d'Ivoire from the dry lands of Mali and Burkina Faso (see Figure 7C.2). This represents a population increase of over 30 per cent for Cote d'Ivoire.

The presidents of Mali and Burkina Faso have appealed for help in halting the mass migrations of their people. They see their countries losing their population as well as their semi-desert environment. The president of Mali spoke at the World Conservation Union conference near Paris in 1998. He said the rural population of his country depended on the environments that were being destroyed. Desertification was leading to fights for resources. He said, 'Climatic problems and repeated droughts have upset the natural balance of things. The desert is marching forward, it seems. Population increase, poverty, lack of education, slash and burn agriculture – these are all turning our forests into wastelands.'

What are the main causes of this problem? Desertification is probably the single greatest threat facing Africa. In the Sahel, the clearing of forests and the use of trees for firewood is one cause. While people may be responsible for desertification, there are also natural factors.

NOTING ACTIVITIES

1 Draw a sketch map of north Africa using the satellite photograph and Figure 7C.2. You may also need to refer to an atlas. Label the following on your map:
   - the Sahara desert
   - the Sahel
   - the equator
   - the Mediterranean Sea
   - the Red Sea
   - the Indian Ocean
   - the Atlantic Ocean
   - Lake Victoria.

2 Find out information about the climate of the following places:
   a Yaounde (Cameroon)
   b Abuja (Nigeria)
   c Khartoum (Sudan)
   d In Salah (Algeria).

Write a description of the climate of these four locations. How does the climate change with distance from the equator?

Climatic change

It usually only rains between May and September in the Sahel region. This is when the sun is overhead and the ground surface is heated rapidly. As the air rises, it cools and condenses into clouds. This eventually results in **convection** rainfall. Although rain is common in these months, there has never been abundant rainfall in the region.

From the 1920s to the 1960s seasonal rainfall extended into the southern Sahara. People moved into these semi-desert regions. Natural population increase was also high in these least developed Sahel nations. Throughout the 1970s and 1980s drought took hold of the Sahel and the wetter times have never returned. To what extent the climate change is a natural process is difficult to say. It does seem that one of the consequences of global warming is to reduce rainfall at the edges of desert areas. Climate change may also be the result of human activities in the dry areas.

C Environmental issues

Natural processes	Human processes			
Climatic change	Arable farming	Pastoral farming	Irrigated farming	Energy and building demands
Less rainfall, drought ↓	Cash crops grown for export ↓	Too many animals ↓	Poor irrigation practices ↓	Trees cut for fuel and building ↓
Fewer plants and trees ↓	Farmland is over-cultivated and yields fall ↓	Nomadic herders concentrated = overgrazing ↓	Soils become infertile or waterlogged and salty ↓	Less transpiration and evaporation ↓
Less evaporation and transpiration	Land is abandoned	Land becomes dry and dusty	Land is abandoned	Soil becomes degraded

7C.4 *The reasons for desertification*

"Just planting trees can hold the soil and reduce the impact of rainfall"

"In Niger and our neighbouring country Burkina Faso we have been building stone lines along the contours. By trapping the run-off we can hold on to water and allow it to run down to replenish the water table. We can also stop the soil being carried down the slopes. We locate the contours by finding the same level across the slope. To do this we use a levelling tube."

"We work for SOS Sahel, a British non-governmental organisation (NGO) working in Niger since 1995. We hope to help local people manage their dwinding forest resources better. The local people must participate"

"With the help of grants we are building shelter belts to protect our crop land from the strong Harmattan wind which blows from the Sahara in the dry season"

7C.5 *Solving the problem of desertification*

Section 7 Changing Environments

The contribution of human activities

Between 1934 and 1968 there was a six-fold increase in the area of groundnut (peanut) production in Niger in West Africa. This crop earned valuable money for Niger. The growing of the crops stopped nomadic herdsmen from using their traditional grazing lands. They were forced into small areas that became overgrazed, eventually leading to soil erosion. The growing of groundnuts takes nutrients from the soil, making it less fertile. Farmers ceased to use land once it had been used to grow groundnuts, with the result that many areas became disused and suffered from erosion.

In other parts of the West African Sahel people have moved away from their farmlands to nearby towns. Many have emigrated out of the region altogether. The **dry-farming** practices are no longer followed. In the past land was used sparingly and people travelled many kilometres to look after their dry land, only cropping it occasionally. With a lack of labour these conservation methods have stopped and fields close to where people live have become degraded and soil erosion has taken place, leading to desertification.

The causes of desertification are summarised in Figure 7C.4.

Can desertification be stopped?

The solutions to desertification involve stopping soil erosion. Figure 7C.5 shows examples of some of the successful methods used to battle with the advancing desert.

Drought is a problem in both rich and poor countries. In the Mojave Desert in the USA, development is taking place in a true desert (see pages 246–250). In Europe, the Almeria region of southern Spain is Europe's only desert region, having an average of less than 16 centimetres of rain each year (Figure 7C.6).

7C.6 *Almeria, Europe's only desert region*

In the poorer countries of the Sahel people are unable to cope so easily with drought. There are several reasons for this.

- Food cannot be stored so efficiently.
- People have to borrow money or sell their possessions to buy food.
- Animals are grazed in areas that are already exhausted.
- Animals are killed and eaten.
- The poor quality dry soils are over-cultivated.
- Seed grain is eaten and not planted.
- Family size is often large and the weakest die.
- People leave for the towns or emigrate.
- Sometimes people have to depend upon emergency food aid.

> **NOTING ACTIVITIES**
>
> 1 Why is desertification such a big issue in Africa?
>
> 2 Using Figure 7C.2,
>   - a name the countries of the Sahel region
>   - b link the map with the satellite image
>   - c describe how the Sahel may be picked out on the satellite image
>   - d describe how the southern coastal area of West Africa, shown on the satellite image, compares with the Sahel region
>   - e describe the rainfall distribution for southern Niger
>   - f explain why it only rains for a short period of time in the south of Niger.
>
> 3 Write a definition of each of the following terms: **desertification, deforestation, over-grazing, over-cultivation**.
>
> 4 Do you think desertification is caused mainly by climatic change, or by human activities?
>
> 5 How has the growing of groundnuts in Niger contributed to desertification?
>
> 6 How can the process of desertification be made worse by local people moving away from a farming area?
>
> 7 What can stop desertification? Why do you think that desertification is described as being an 'international problem'?
>
> 8 Why are rich countries more able to cope with drought than poorer parts of the world?

C Environmental issues

Deforestation

Deforestation is an important issue in Geography and is usually associated with the rainforests. But it is worth remembering that this destructive process of cutting down trees has occurred throughout most parts of the world, including Europe.

The United Kingdom is Europe's most **deforested** country. Wood has been continuously cut over the past 1000 years. People have used the wood of the British Isles for building ships, houses and furniture and for fuel. The forests were also cut down to make new farmland. In 1629 a Durham man was said to have cut down thirty thousand oak trees in his lifetime!

Figure 7C.7 shows a scene of past deforestation in France. Mount Ventoux is in Provence and is used as a climb in the Tour de France cycle race. It was deforested and its soil has since been washed away and vegetation has not been able to become established.

7C.7 *One of the Tour de France's toughest challenges is the climb up the deforested Mt Ventoux*

The rainforest

About 65 per cent of the natural rainforest area has been **deforested.** It is the rainforests of Asia that have been reduced most in percentage terms but the forests of South America have lost the largest area in terms of millions of hectares. Brazil lost an area of rainforest the size of Spain in the last 20 years of the 20th century.

Cutting down the Brazilian rainforest for cattle ranching has been a major reason for deforestation. Five years after the forest is cut down the land is useless and the ranchers move on to new forest areas. Figure 7C.8 gives further reasons for deforestation in Brazil; similar reasons apply in many other countries.

Building roads and railways

Logging for paper manufacture

Cattle ranching

Logging for hardwood sales

Establishing small farms

Building reservoirs for hydro-electricity

Mineral mining such as bauxite and iron ore

7C.8 *Reasons for deforestation in Brazil*

Section 7 Changing Environments

7C.10 *Rainforest plants that might provide medical cures for future generations*

Saving the forests

It is important to try to save the rainforests. One-third of the world's remaining rainforests are in the Amazon Basin. The biodiversity there is enormous: 10 million living species are found in them. Many useful drugs are derived from rainforest plants such as:

Curare the poison used by native Indians to tip their blowpipe darts, which is widely used in operating theatres as a muscle relaxant

Vinca rosea which has helped reduce the number of childhood leukaemia deaths.

Figures 7C.9, 7C.10 and 7C.11 show the characteristics of the rainforests and the effects of deforestation.

Governments, non-government organisations (NGOs) and individual people are trying to manage the Amazon rainforests.

- 91 areas have been designated for protection. These vary in size up to thousands of hectares. Most are in the Brazil, Peru and Bolivia border areas.

7C.9 *The Brazilian rainforest*

C Environmental issues

Effects of deforestation

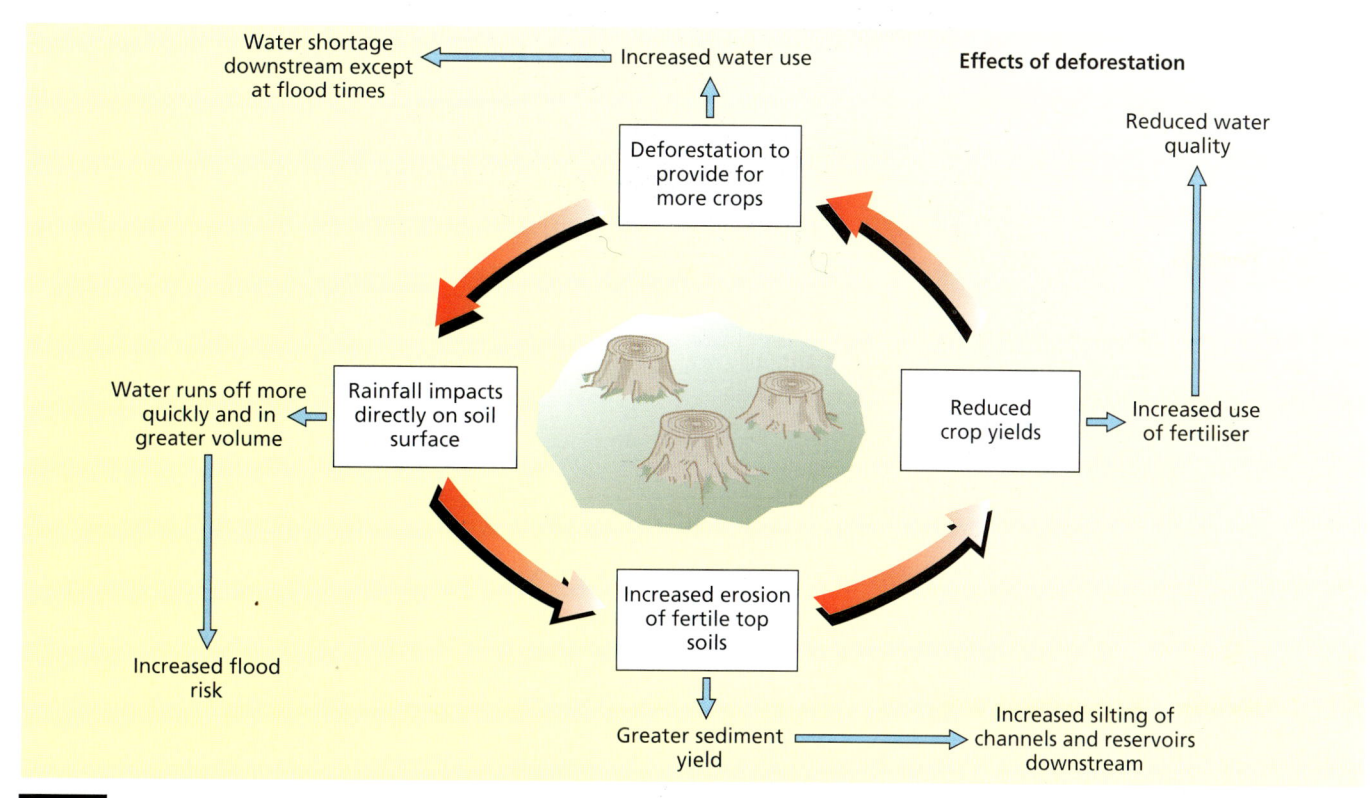

[Diagram showing cyclical effects of deforestation: Deforestation to provide for more crops → Rainfall impacts directly on soil surface → Increased erosion of fertile top soils → Reduced crop yields → back to Deforestation. Side effects include: Increased water use → Water shortage downstream except at flood times; Water runs off more quickly and in greater volume → Increased flood risk; Greater sediment yield → Increased silting of channels and reservoirs downstream; Increased use of fertiliser → Reduced water quality.]

7C.11 *It is essential to stop the spiralling effects of deforestation*

- The Brazilian government has promised to ban the extraction of mahogany from parts of the rainforest. It is difficult for a large country without resources to police the forests. Many large Asian transnational companies now work in the South American rainforests.
- International banks have started to negotiate with countries about debt repayments in terms of allowing them to forego debt repayments if they promise to protect their rainforests.
- Private individuals have set up parks such as the Ecopark outside Manaus. Here the non-profit Living Rainforest Foundation promotes conservation and education. This is a form of **eco-tourism** where visitors pay $25 for a half-day excursion. More general tourism to fragile areas could be controlled.
- The buying and selling of hardwoods such as mahogany can be controlled by worldwide organisations. Companies can agree only to buy mahogany from sustainable forests. Eastbourne Council have replaced the town's groynes using sustainable hardwood from Guyana. This decision was praised by many conservation bodies.
- Rainforest areas can be sustainably developed for the production of wood and wood products. **Agroforestry** imitates the canopy structure of the natural forest. Short-lived farm crops are grown and local farmers plant tree seeds for future tree seedlings.
- Local hunters and gatherers can be encouraged to collect tree products and are guaranteed a market for them.
- Individuals can refuse to purchase products from the rainforest but this is difficult as consumers do not know which products contain forest products.

Rainforest Action Network (RAN) campaigns to save the rainforest. It says 'Brazil is most at fault, but consumers and governments around the world have a role to play.' It seems everyone can help. Unfortunately little can be done to bring back the oak trees of Durham or the woodlands on Mt Ventoux.

NOTING ACTIVITIES

1 List the main characteristics of the Brazilian rainforest.
2 Why have large areas of Brazil been deforested?
3 How does large scale deforestation affect the soils?
4 Why is the rainforest worth saving?
5 In what ways can the rainforest be saved?
6 Look up the current activities of RAN on the internet at www.RAN.org

Section 7 **Changing Environments**

CASE STUDY

Deforestation in Nepal

Nepal is a very mountainous country on the southern edge of the Himalayas (Figure 7C.12). In Nepal, 96 per cent of population depend upon biomass energy for domestic purposes of which 76 per cent is provided by fuel wood alone. The country is facing a serious problem of deforestation. The population has increased to 18.5 million and continues to increase at the rate of 2 per cent annually. This puts even more pressure on the forest to provide energy, making deforestation more intense.

The forest cover in Nepal is estimated to be about 37 per cent of the total land area. The decrease in forested land is estimated to be equivalent to 100 000 hectares per year.

To combat this rate of deforestation, government, various NGOs and private agencies are planning and introducing different kinds of activities for reforestation and fuel wood saving programmes (Figure 7C.13, 7C.14 and 7C.15).

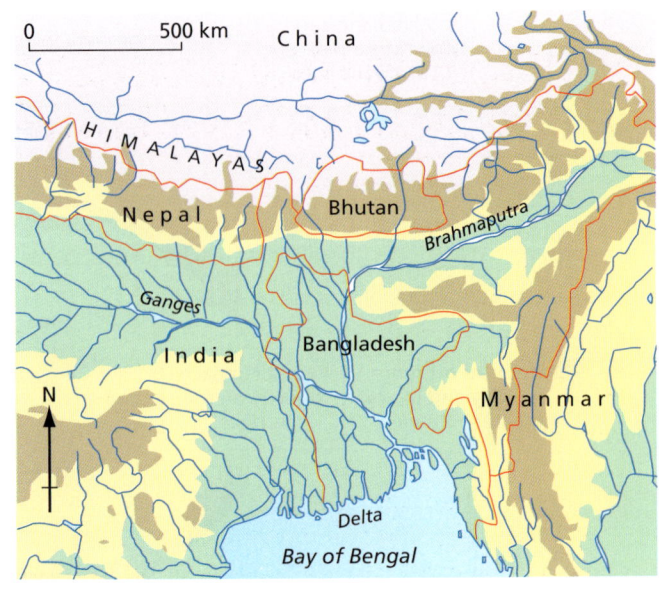

7C.12 *The location of Nepal and the Ganges delta*

Deforestation may ruin Nepal's future

**AGENCE FRANCE PRESSE
KATHMANDU, 10 OCT 1999**

The lush forests of Nepal, sheltering some of the world's rarest animals, are vanishing at a rate of 200 hectares a day, precipitating serious ecological and climatic change, conservation officials say.

The severe depletion has forced the government to use the Royal Nepal Army to guard national parks with 'shoot on sight' orders to counter a seemingly insatiable illicit logging demand for fuel and unauthorised settlement.

A system of community forests has also been introduced, with some success but not enough yet to reverse the decline of greenery. Demographers and agronomists warn that if rapid deforestation is not checked in Nepal, where more than two-thirds of the country's energy needs are met through wood burning, the remaining woodland could disappear completely in the next four to five decades.

7C.13 *The dangers of deforestation*

Saving forests for the future

Over half of Nepal's forests have been cut down in the last thirty years to make way for farming and to meet fuel wood, timber and fodder needs. Managing the remaining forests is one of the most urgent matters facing Nepal today.

To date, Nepal has developed an impressive network of protected areas as a means of conserving its biodiversity. The protected area network includes:
- eight National Parks
- four Wildlife Reserves
- two Conservation Areas
- one Hunting Reserve.

In all these conservation areas cover over 2 million hectares of the country's surface area.

7C.14 *Deforestation and conservation in Nepal*

C Environmental issues

PROMOTION OF SOLAR COOKING AS AN ALTERNATIVE SUPPLEMENTARY COOKING OPTION

From our Asia correspondent

In Nepal there are plans to introduce solar cookers. There is strong need for some alternative energy sources side by side with the reforestation activities. Solar cooking is one of the alternative technologies which helps reduce the pressure on the forest for cooking energy requirements. Everyone knows that sunlight gives heat but only a few are utilising it for cooking food in Nepal. Many people do not easily believe that solar energy can cook food but when seen with their own eyes, they become interested and not only cook food but also promote this pollution free, environment friendly option for cooking as well as for saving energy. Solar cooking has the following advantages for the benefit of developing countries like Nepal:

1 Solar cooking is an environment friendly technology as it uses solar energy which is not used up as any other conventional energy.

2 Solar energy is free of cost as is freely available to all.

3 It does not emit smoke and hence is pollution free.

4 It helps in pasteurising water to make it safe for drinking.

7C.15 *Plans to combat the problem of deforestation*

In the 1970s The Himalayan Degradation Theory was discussed. It described a *domino effect* beginning with human activities in the Himalayas, as shown in Figure 7C.16. People looking for reasons for severe flooding in Bangladesh started to blame deforestation in Nepal.

Population growth in the mountains of Nepal

⬇

increasing demand for fuel wood, fodder and timber

⬇

uncontrolled forest removal in more and more marginal areas

⬇

intensified erosion and higher peak flows in the rivers

⬇

severe flooding and siltation on the densely populated and cultivated plains of the Ganges and Brahmaputra Rivers

7C.16 *The Himalayan Degradation Theory*

Section 7 Changing Environments

7C.17 *Terrace farming on the higher slopes of Nepal*

Data collected on deforestation, rainfall and run-off did not support the theory. There is evidence, however, to show that people in Nepal should be careful to conserve their forests. Carefully managed forests will reduce run-off and stop topsoil being taken from the slopes to the rivers. Also the farmers of Nepal should avoid farming the highest and steepest slopes which are the most fragile (see Figure 7C.17).

NOTING ACTIVITIES

1 Write up the case study of deforestation in Nepal under the following headings using brief notes.

Questions	Details
Where is Nepal?	
What is the deforestation issue in Nepal?	
What could the long term problems be?	
How can conservation areas help the problem?	
How can solar cookers help slow down deforestation?	
Why has Nepal been linked with floods in Bangladesh?	
Why should the farmers of Nepal be aware of farming the very high slopes?	

7C.18

EXTENDED ACTIVITY

Soil erosion, desertification and global warming are linked to deforestation. Draw a diagram which helps to explain the links between these three environmental processes and deforestation. You should refer to other relevant sections in this book to help you.

Acid rain

What is acid rain?

Acid rain is a serious environmental issue that affects most of the world's industrialised countries. A more accurate term to describe the problem is *acid deposition*. This is because nearly half of the acid that falls from the atmosphere is in the form of gases and particles. This is called *dry deposition*. Acid rain, fog and snow is called *wet deposition*.

What causes acid rain?

Acid rain is caused by *sulphur dioxide* (SO_2) and nitrogen oxides (NO_2) in the atmosphere. Acid rain occurs when these chemicals react with water, oxygen and other chemicals to form various acid compounds. The result is that water in the atmosphere falling as rain is turned into dilute sulphuric acid or nitric acid. Sunlight dramatically increases the rate of these reactions. This is why acid rain is sometimes referred to as **photochemical pollution**.

The main cause of sulphur dioxide and nitrogen oxides in the atmosphere is the burning of fossil fuels, particularly coal and oil. Much of this is the responsibility of industry. In the United States, for example, two-thirds of sulphur dioxide comes from the burning of oil and gas to generate electric power.

7C.19 *The majority of sulphur dioxide comes from the burning of coal and gas*

C Environmental issues

How is acid rain measured?

The acidity of rainfall is measured using the pH scale (see Figure 7C.20). A value of 7.0 is represented by pure distilled water. A pH below 7.0 indicates acidity. Normal rainfall has a pH of about 5.5. Rainfall is normally slightly acidic, as it contains some natural carbon dioxide. Most acid rain that falls has a value of about 4.0.

What are the effects of acid rain?

Acid rain has a variety of effects. They include damage to forests and soils, fish, buildings, and human health (see Figure 7C.21).

1 Lakes and streams

The long term effects of acid rain are most clearly seen in freshwater ecosystems. Acid water kills many species of fish, as well as other plants and animals living in water environments. As Figure 7C.22 shows, some organisms are more tolerant of acid water. Frogs, for example, are able to survive in very acid water. They depend, however, upon other organisms for their survival. Their tolerance of acidic water is of no use if their food supply, such as the mayfly, cannot live in the same environment. A recent survey of large lakes in the USA found that over 75 per cent of lakes were acid, some having pH levels as low as 4.2.

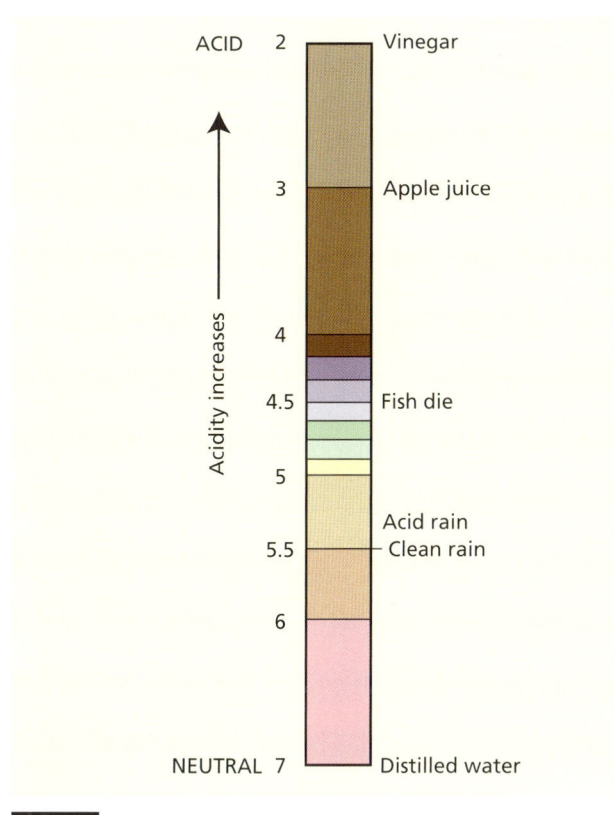

7C.20 *The pH scale used to measure acid rain*

7C.21 *The effects of acid rain*

Section 7 Changing Environments

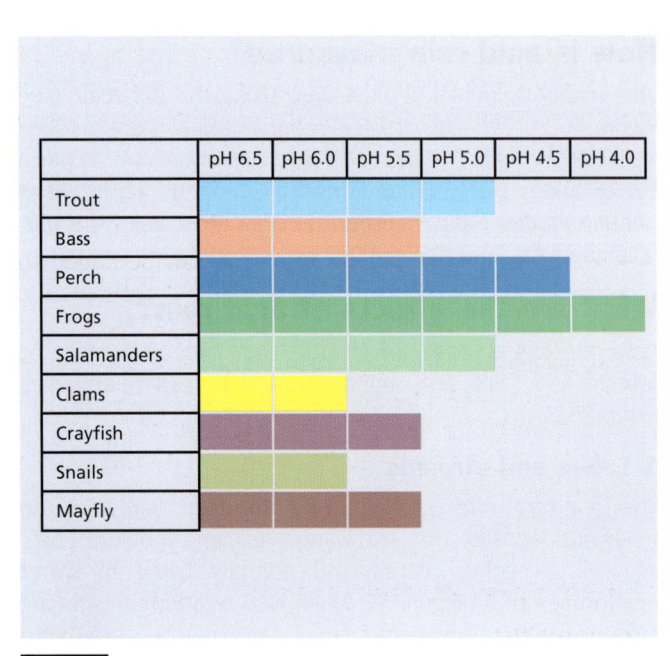

	pH 6.5	pH 6.0	pH 5.5	pH 5.0	pH 4.5	pH 4.0
Trout						
Bass						
Perch						
Frogs						
Salamanders						
Clams						
Crayfish						
Snails						
Mayfly						

7C.22 *Levels of tolerance of different organisms to acid water*

2 Forests

Acid rain is a problem that has affected many of the world's forests, not least in Europe (see Figure 7C.23). It does not usually kill trees directly, but damages leaves, limits the nutrients available and poisons roots. Trees are often killed by a mixture of acid rain and other environmental factors. Acid water dissolves nutrients and minerals in the soil and washes them away before trees and other plants can use them. At the same time, acid rain releases toxic chemicals into the soil, which are then taken up by tree roots.

3 Effects on people

People are affected by acid rain in many ways. The surfaces of buildings, for example, may be worn away by acidic water. People's health may also be affected by breathing in acid particles. There is evidence of links between high levels of acid in the air and increased rates of heart and lung disorders, such as asthma and bronchitis. The American government estimates that reducing acid rain would save the country $50 billion in reduced health care costs.

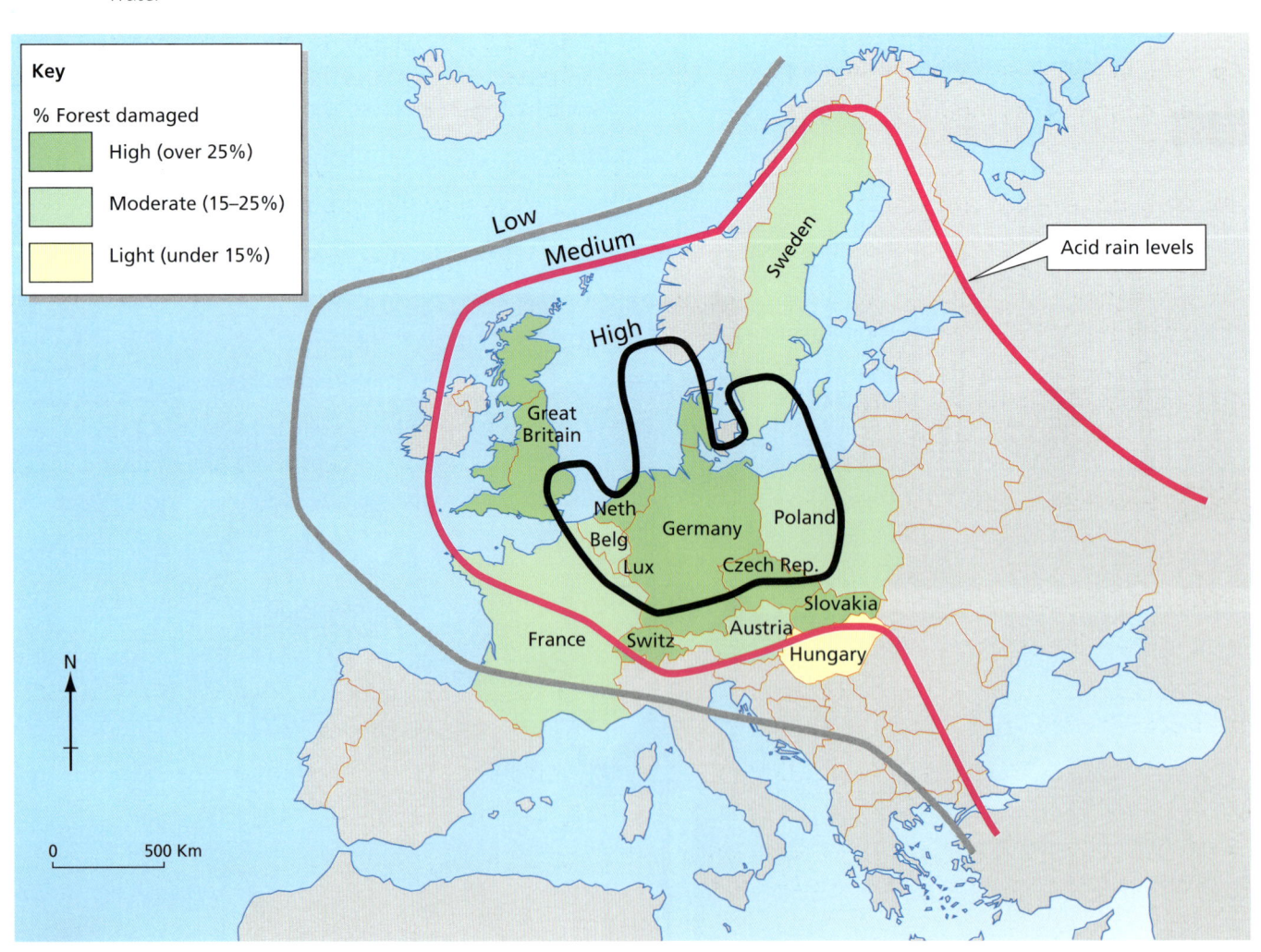

7C.23 *Levels of acid rain in Europe*

C Environmental issues

What can be done about acid rain?

The problem of acid rain may be reduced by cutting down on the amount of sulphur dioxide and nitrogen oxides that are released into the atmosphere. Many things could be done to achieve this.

- Burn cleaner coal. Sulphur is present in coal as an impurity. If it is removed before the coal is used, then the amount of sulphur gases released into the atmosphere will decrease.
- Remove the sulphur from smoke as it leaves factory chimneys, using devices called *scrubbers*.
- Change to gas power. This creates much less sulphur than burning either coal or oil.
- Use alternative or renewable sources of power. Nuclear and hydro-electric power are the most widely used at the moment. Solar, wind and geothermal energy could also be used instead of fossil fuels.
- Use other methods of powering vehicles. This includes battery powered cars and vehicles running on natural gas.
- Restore damaged environments. Lime can be added to acid rivers and lakes to cancel out the acidity. Vegetation and wildlife can be reintroduced to restored areas.
- Take action as individuals. Look at Figure 7C.24. This is an information poster suggesting ways in which people can reduce electricity consumption. This in turns leads to a reduction in demand, resulting in fewer greenhouse gases caused by the generation of electricity.

Individuals can contribute directly by conserving energy, since energy production causes the largest portion of the acid deposition problem.

- Turn off lights, computers, and other appliances when you're not using them
- Use energy efficient appliances: lighting, air conditioners, heaters, refrigerators, washing machines, etc.
- Only use electric appliances when you really need them.
- Keep your thermostat at 22°C in the winter and 22°C in the summer. You can turn it even lower in the winter and higher in the summer when you are away from home.
- Insulate your home as best you can.
- Use a car pool, use public transport, or better yet, walk or bicycle whenever possible.
- Buy vehicles with low NO_2 emissions, and maintain all vehicles well.
- Be well-informed.

7C.24 *How individuals can make a difference*

NOTING ACTIVITIES

1. List the main causes and effects of acid rain.
2. Why is acid rain described as an international problem?
3. What measures may be taken to reduce the effects of acid rain?
4. Who do you think should be responsible for taking action to reduce the problems caused by acid rain?

a national governments
b multinational organisations, such as the United Nations
c industries that cause the pollution
d individuals and communities

Give reasons for your answer.

Section 8 Towards a Sustainable Future

A What is sustainable development?

There are many definitions of **sustainable development**. The most commonly used definition is that:

sustainable development meets the needs of people at the present time, and allows for the needs of future generations to be met.

Development entails that the world's resources will continue to be used by people at the present time. To be sustainable, the use of these resources has to be possible in the future. **Energy resources** are a good example. Fossil fuels such as coal and oil are already becoming scarce; the current rate of use of these resources is not sustainable in the future. Even with more careful use of fossil energy resources, alternative sources of energy are likely to become increasingly important in years to come. Using the power of the sun, waves and wind, for example, is a sustainable way of providing energy.

The issue of sustainable development raises many questions. As with all the issues covered in this book, it is about how people can work together with the environment to create a sustainable future.

Needs and priorities

The definition above begins with present-day needs. What are these? What, for example, do you think are your needs, and those of your local community?

Do you think that any of the needs people have may conflict with one another? One environmental need might be to have clean air to breathe, free from pollution. Another could be to have transport, either for social purposes or for industry. These needs could conflict with one another, transport being one of the main causes of air pollution. Which should be given priority? Families living in tropical countries may chop down trees for firewood, having no other source of fuel. Yet this conflicts with the need to conserve forests to prevent soil erosion and desertification. Which need should be given priority? What happens when one country's need for electricity production leads to acid rain that damages another nation's forests and rivers? Who decides how these needs are met, especially when the needs of different people conflict with one another? Is it individuals, nations or organisations involving several countries?

The examples above show that sustainable development deals with different types of needs or priorities. Private car transport in a remote rural part of the United Kingdom is a **social** need. The use of transport in all types of industry and commercial is **economic**, while there are also **environmental** impacts of such use.

Figure 8A.1 shows some of these different aspects of sustainable development. Many of these may conflict with one another, for example the pressure for industrial growth and the need to conserve natural resources. For the

ECONOMIC
- maintaining economic growth
- efficient use of labour in agriculture in LEDCs

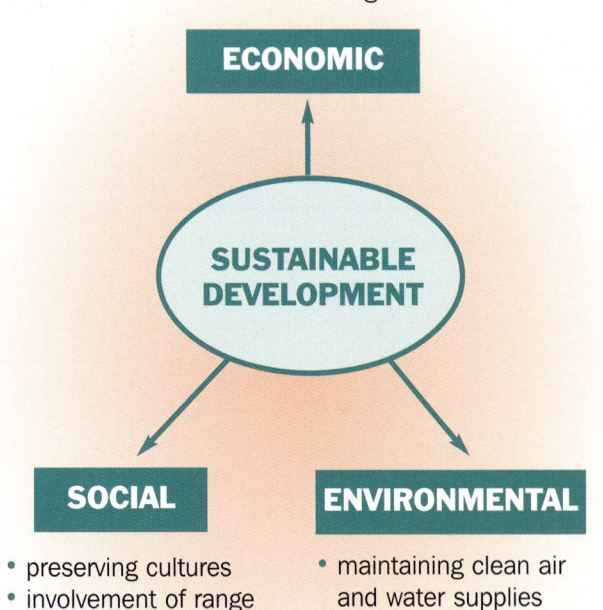

SOCIAL
- preserving cultures
- involvement of range of people and viewpoints in decision-making

ENVIRONMENTAL
- maintaining clean air and water supplies
- conserving natural resources

8A.1 *Sustainable development*

8A.2 *Uses of forests as a resource*

A What is sustainable development?

NOTING ACTIVITIES

1. What is meant by the term sustainable development?
2. Underneath a copy of Figure 8A.1, explain how some aspects of sustainable development could conflict with one another.
3. Who do you think should have the greatest responsibility for the sustainable use of the world's resources? What role should be played by individuals?
4. Make a list of the resources that you use in a day. Are there any that could be used in a more sustainable way?

sustainable development of our planet, these conflicts need to be solved in the long term, often by people taking decisions and making changes in the shorter term. Although governments and international organisations may make laws to enforce these changes, it is often the willingness of individuals to make changes that has the greatest effect.

How many people, driving a long distance to work each day, would be prepared to move or get a different job to reduce air pollution from their car exhaust? Should people living in a developing country without access to clean water worry about deforestation if they need wood to boil drinking water to make it safe for their children? The remainder of this section looks at case studies that develop issues introduced previously. How well do you think they meet the requirements of sustainable development?

Resource management

Sustainable development of forests

Forests have been used as a resource for thousands of years. Wood has long been used as a fuel, and is still important in many parts of the world, particularly LEDCs. Timber is used in the manufacture of furniture and other products. Forests are also a resource for leisure and recreation in some countries.

The world's forests are disappearing. In the last fifty years, over 10 per cent of the world's vegetation has been removed. Most of this has been forest clearance, particularly the tropical rainforests (see Figure 8A.3). The clearing of forests has also taken place in the past in MEDCs. Much of Europe was once covered by trees. Today, most of the land has been cleared for other uses, for example building or farming.

To preserve the world's remaining forests, their use needs to be sustainable. This could include:

- planting as many trees as are chopped down
- planting new forested areas
- providing alternative fuels to firewood in poor countries
- reducing the rate of rainforest clearance.

If forests are a valuable economic resource, and cleared forest land may be put to good use, why is it so important to preserve the world's remaining forest areas?

1. **Forests absorb rainwater**. Trees slow down the rate that water reaches streams and rivers. Flooding is a greater hazard where deforestation has taken place, for example in countries such as Nepal in the foothills of the Himalayan mountains.
2. **Forests help keep soil intact**, particularly fertile topsoil. Where trees have been cut down, soil is easily blown or

Section 8 Towards a Sustainable Future

8A.3

Deforestation taking place for farming in tropical areas, as it once did in Europe

washed away. Soil erosion is a problem in many African countries, for example Mali on the edge of the Sahara Desert.

3 **Forests have an impact upon the world's climate.** Where forests have been cleared by burning, for example in Indonesia, scientists believe that this has contributed to global warming.

Is it possible, or worthwhile, to save the world's forests by using them in a sustainable way? Management of forests is very expensive. People in South America and Africa say it is up to them how they use their forests, even if it means chopping them down to provide land to feed growing populations. This, after all, is what happened to the forests of Europe in the past. The rainforests also provide a vital source of income for poor countries.

Sweden: Factfile

Population	8 844 500
Area in square km	450 000
Population density	20 per square km
Population growth rate	0%
Life expectancy	79 years
Capital	Stockholm
% of 5–24 year olds in education	65%
GDP per head of population (US)	23 750
% annual growth of GDP (1998/97)	2.9%
Government	constitutional monarchy
Language(s)	Swedish
Main religion(s)	Protestant (Lutheran)

8A.4 *Sweden*

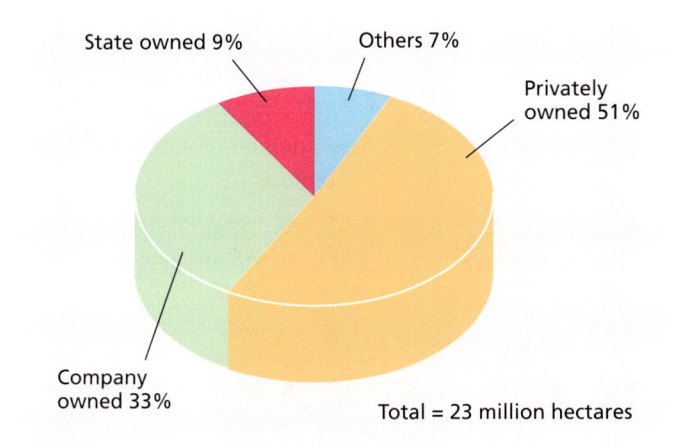

A What is sustainable development?

8A.5 *The ownership of Sweden's forests*

(Pie chart: State owned 9%, Others 7%, Privately owned 51%, Company owned 33%. Total = 23 million hectares)

The landscapes of Sweden are dominated by the effects of the last *Ice Age*. Scandinavia was covered by several kilometres of ice as recently as 10 000 years ago. After the ice melted, the landscape became a mixture of open mountains, lakes and forests. With population growth, much of the original forest cover was removed to make way for farmland, particularly for grazing cattle and sheep in the south of the country. By the mid-19th century, there was a shortage of forest in large parts of the country.

During the 20th century the forests of Sweden were restored, largely by private landowners. Just over half of the country's forests remain privately owned (see Figure 8A.5). More than half of Sweden is covered by forest. Deciduous trees such as birch are most common in the south of the country, while coniferous pines and spruce dominate the remote northern areas (Figure 8A.6).

The forests of Sweden are once again under threat. There are a variety of pressures.

- Forestry is Sweden's most important industry. Most wood is exported, timber being the country's main export. There is continued pressure from private companies to increase profits by felling and exporting more trees. Although many companies are now committed to replanting, even the fastest-growing trees take several years to grow.

- Where trees are removed, other plants and animals are affected. Many insects living in the forest need rotting wood from dead trees to live. These insects are eaten by birds and animals, which are also affected if there are fewer trees.

- Replanting of trees is a limited solution which does not maintain the forest in the long term. An old forest is a mixture of types and ages of trees. Newly planted trees are all of the same age, and are often limited in species. This means that a newly planted forest often lacks the variety of areas that have been cleared.

- The forests have become popular holiday destinations, both for people from Sweden and abroad. New roads have to be built to make the forests accessible, and accommodation provided. Tourists bring litter and pollution even though their money may boost the local economy. Activities such as pony trekking and mountain biking have become increasingly popular, leading to the erosion of footpaths and tracks through the forests.

- Some forests have also been cleared for other land uses, such as mining or farming.

CASE STUDY

Managing Sweden's forests

Only a few large forested areas remain in Europe, for example in Scandinavia. The forests of Sweden are under threat. How is this issue being managed? What is happening to Sweden's forests?

Sweden is Europe's third largest country, and one of the least densely populated. One-third of the country's nine million people live in the southern cities of Stockholm, Malmö and Göteborg. The northern two-thirds of the country has a population density of only 2 people per square kilometre. Much of this region, extending north into the Arctic Circle, is virtually uninhabited.

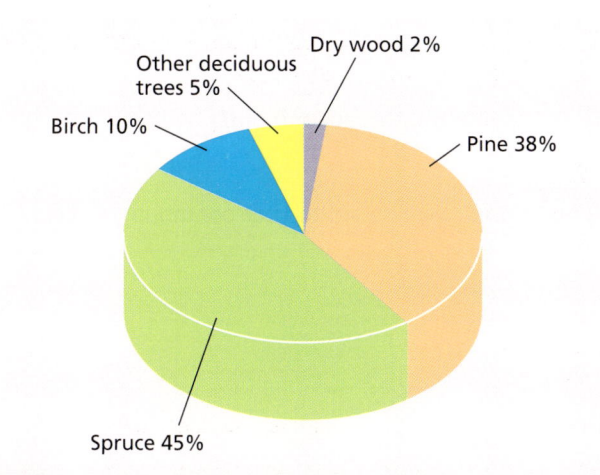

What is being done to manage the forests of Sweden, which are facing these pressures? The following activity looks at some of the main options for the management of the forests this century.

(Pie chart: Other deciduous trees 5%, Dry wood 2%, Birch 10%, Pine 38%, Spruce 45%)

8A.6 *Swedish timber by species of tree*

Section 8 Towards a Sustainable Future

EXTENDED ACTIVITY

For the purpose of this activity, imagine that as a student taking a course in Geography, part of your course involves working abroad. You have chosen to work in Sweden with a company advising the government on environmental issues.

Your department has been asked to prepare a report on the future management of Sweden's forests. You have been given some background information about the forests, together with some possible management options. You may, of course, decide not to choose one of these but to suggest your own plan instead.

Use all of the resources on pages 241–245 to help you to write your report. This should include the following sections.

1 The current forestry situation in Sweden
2 The problems facing the forests
3 A summary of the main points of each of the suggested management options
4 An evaluation of each of the options. This must include the advantages and disadvantages of each option
5 Your preferred option
6 A statement prepared to release to the press outlining why your chosen management plan is to take place. This should be no more than fifty words in length

---

Dear student

Welcome to Sweden. I hope that you enjoy your time working for our company. As you know, we provide advice to the Swedish government on matters connected to the environment. Forests are our greatest natural and economic resource. We are currently facing important decisions regarding the future of the country's forests. They are coming under increased pressure from the timber industry, from leisure and recreational users, and from conservationists.

In recent years, the Swedish government has encouraged the conservation of the nation's forests. It is important that, for the long term future of Sweden's ecosystems, we keep a significant part of the forests. We currently have about 23 million hectares that are forested, and our research shows that this should not decrease by more than 10%. If it does, the range of wildlife in the forests is likely to be reduced. One option for the management of our forests is to impose a limit of 200 000 hectares per year that may be cleared for the next ten years. In this way, most of the nation's forests will be saved, at least for the time being.

We realise that this is far less timber than is required by the timber industry. Timber is our greatest export earner. We sell most to Germany. In 1998, for example, 17% of all of Germany's timber was imported from Sweden. A second option is to allow for the clearance of forests at a rate no faster than they can be replaced. A problem with this is that so many different groups of people own and clear the forests.

Our third option is more radical, and involves conserving the forests completely. To preserve the natural ecosystem, we must leave the trees as they are. This may lose money for the forestry industries, but it is likely to bring in more money through our biggest growth industry – tourism. What we lose through timber, we gain through both Swedish and foreign holiday-makers.

We hope that you have the necessary information included here, and look forward to your contribution to our final report to the government.

Yours sincerely

Stefan Erikkson

Stefan Erikkson

8A.7 *Your task*

A What is sustainable development?

The suggested management options

1 Limit the number of trees cut down each year. A limit should be placed on the total number of trees felled in Sweden. Over ten years, the total area cleared will be less than 10 per cent of the nation's forested area. After this time, the situation could be reviewed.

2 A tree must be planted for each chopped down. Timber companies will have to plant trees in locations that would benefit from more forested area. They would have to plant a range of trees, and not just those types that will prove useful for the timber industry in the future. In this way, the forested area of Sweden will not decrease.

3 Conserve the forests. Over the next ten years, the number of trees felled should be steadily reduced, so that eventually no forests are destroyed. In this way, the present range of trees and wildlife will be preserved. There is evidence that tourism has the potential to earn Sweden more money than forestry. The natural forested areas of Sweden are already popular with visitors from all over the world: cleared forest areas and plantations are not.

8A.8 *Possible management options*

Manager of furniture manufacturer in England
We will only buy *FSC* wood to make our furniture. This is the Forest Stewardship Council, which checks that wood is grown in sustainable forests. About 45 per cent of Sweden's forests are FSC registered.

Manager of a forestry company
Forestry is an industry, just like any other. Thousands of jobs are created, not just in employment directly related to tree felling. There are distribution jobs, marketing, and then all of the jobs connected to manufacturing products made from the wood.

Government official
We must have a balance between the needs of different groups of people. The timber industry is important, but so is tourism; this will not grow if there are ugly bare areas where trees have been removed. We must also remember that people live in the forested areas.

National Park official
The clearance of forests must slow down. If we carry on chopping down trees at the current rate, many plants, animals and insects will disappear. This will affect all of us in the end.

Manager of large tourist company
There is a real growth in outward bound 'back to nature' holidays. People also go mountain biking and canoeing along the rivers. The real attraction is the natural environment. Forestry ruins this, not just by chopping down trees, but also by building roads, and providing places to live for the workers.

Conservationist
There are some areas of Sweden where so much tree felling has taken place that the existence of the forests is under threat. We are not saying that all forestry must stop, just in the worst affected areas. The companies make huge profits, and don't put enough back into their conservation.

8A.9 *The opinions of people affected*

Section 8 Towards a Sustainable Future

B Managing the desert environment

The Mojave Desert, USA

In the world's poorer countries, people are trying to stop the spread of deserts. There are deserts in MEDCs as well, and here the issues are often very different. There is pressure in some situations to preserve desert environments that are coming under threat from the actions of people. In the USA, for example, the **Mojave Desert** is more an area for recreation than for feeding or housing people. Managing desert environments does not mean the same in Africa and America. What is the environment of the Mojave Desert like? What pressures are there on the desert? Is it possible to meet the needs of different groups of people who use the desert, and to preserve the natural environment?

What is the Mojave Desert like?

The Mojave Desert is situated in the south-west of the United States (see Figure 8B.1). It covers 125 000 square kilometres of the states of Nevada, Arizona and Utah, and one-quarter of California. The Mojave is a mixture of mountains and plains, and is perhaps most famous for its Joshua trees (Figure 8B.2). These trees grow nowhere else in the world.

8B.2 *The Joshua tree*

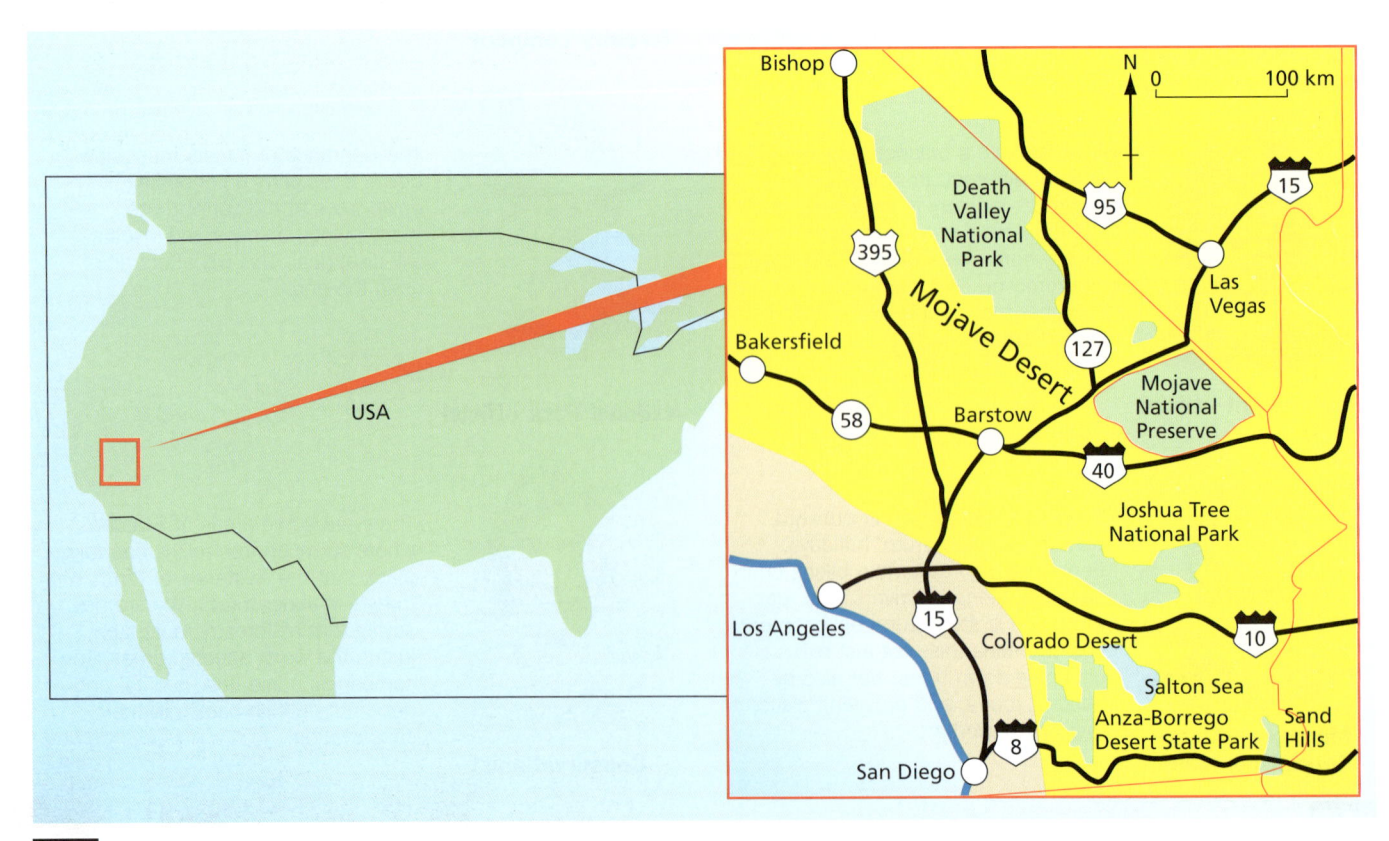

8B.1 *The location of the Mojave Desert*

B Managing the desert environment

	Year	Jan	Feb	Mar	Apr	May	Jun	Jul	Aug	Sep	Oct	Nov	Dec
Avg °C	16	5	8	9	14	19	24	27	26	23	17	10	6
Rain (mm)	100	13	15	8	11	5	5	5	5	6	4	12	11

8B.3 *Climate data for Beatty. The town is 150 km north-west of Las Vegas, and is the nearest settlement to Death Valley*

The Mojave is classified as a desert because of its low annual precipitation. The region receives on average about 10 cm of rain per year. The rainfall is also very unreliable. Although the winter months typically have most rainfall, it is not unusual for little or no rain to fall for several months at any time of year.

The desert is very hot during the summer months, but becomes much cooler in the winter (Figure 8B.3). Although still warm during the day, frosts are common at night in winter. In spite of its lack of rainfall and hot temperatures, the desert is home to a wide range of plant and animal life (Figure 8B.4).

What is the Mojave Desert used for?

The Mojave is surrounded by large urban areas. It is bordered by Los Angeles and Las Vegas, and is within reach for a day's visit by over 40 million people. The desert is crossed by major inter-state roads, and more than 42 000 km of minor roads and tracks lead to all parts of the Mojave. It is easily accessible to millions of wealthy Americans who have both the time and the money to use the desert as a resource for leisure and recreation. The Mojave is in danger of becoming little more than an enormous playground.

The Mojave has been used by people for many years. It has always been seen as a place where people could escape

> **NOTING ACTIVITIES**
>
> 1 Use the information in Figure 8B.3 to draw a climate graph for Beatty.
>
> 2 Describe and explain the pattern of temperature and rainfall shown on your graph.
>
> 3 Draw an annotated sketch map to show the main features of the Mojave Desert.
>
> 4 Research information about a desert in another continent. In what ways are the two desert areas similar and how are they different?

8B.4 *Desert life*

Section 8 Towards a Sustainable Future

from civilisation and the pressures of city life. Camping and back-packing in the desert are very popular. Because of its isolation, the Mojave has been used by the American military for most of its training exercises. The desert was seen as the last place in the United States where military training could take place without disturbing anybody.

Until recently human uses of the desert made little impact upon the environment. It is the urbanisation of the west coast of America, together with increased wealth and leisure time, that have led to growing pressures on the desert environment.

In addition to camping and back-packing, the Mojave is now a popular location for a variety of outdoor leisure activities. All have some impact upon the environment, and some conflict with one another. Much of the desert is now carefully mapped and laid out to provide areas organised for different leisure activities (see Figure 8B.5). What leisure activities taking place in the Mojave have an impact upon the environment?

- **Auto-touring and off-road vehicles** This is the biggest growth area, and the activity that probably has the greatest effect upon the environment. Special areas are set aside for 4-wheel drive vehicles, as shown on Figure 8B.5. There are now so many visitors, however, that many people ignore these tracks and drive their vehicles across the desert wherever they choose. These vehicles destroy plants and kill animals, and break the hard crust of the desert surface.
- **Mountain biking** The problems caused by cyclists are similar to those of off-road vehicles, though less severe. Cyclists cause less damage to the environment than cars, and to a smaller area.
- **Caving and climbing** The Mojave reaches almost 3000 metres above sea level at its highest point. Parts of the desert are very popular with climbers and cavers.
- **Horseback riding** Tracks left by horses have much the same type of impact upon the environment as cyclists and off-road vehicles.

In addition to leisure activities, the Mojave Desert is now used for the generation of electricity. The desert environment, with its unbroken sunshine throughout most days, is an ideal location for solar power plants. There are nine such plants spread across the desert, each containing thousands of solar panels, that provide electricity for the surrounding urban areas (see Figure 8B.7).

What is being done to protect the environment?

The American government has created four National Parks within the Mojave Desert. Each has its own characteristics, and is protected by law from development and over-use. The parks stretch across most of the expanse of the desert (see Figure 8B.1). The problem with the parks is that it is almost impossible to monitor what each visitor does in the desert. Many people ignore the rules, knowing they will probably not be caught.

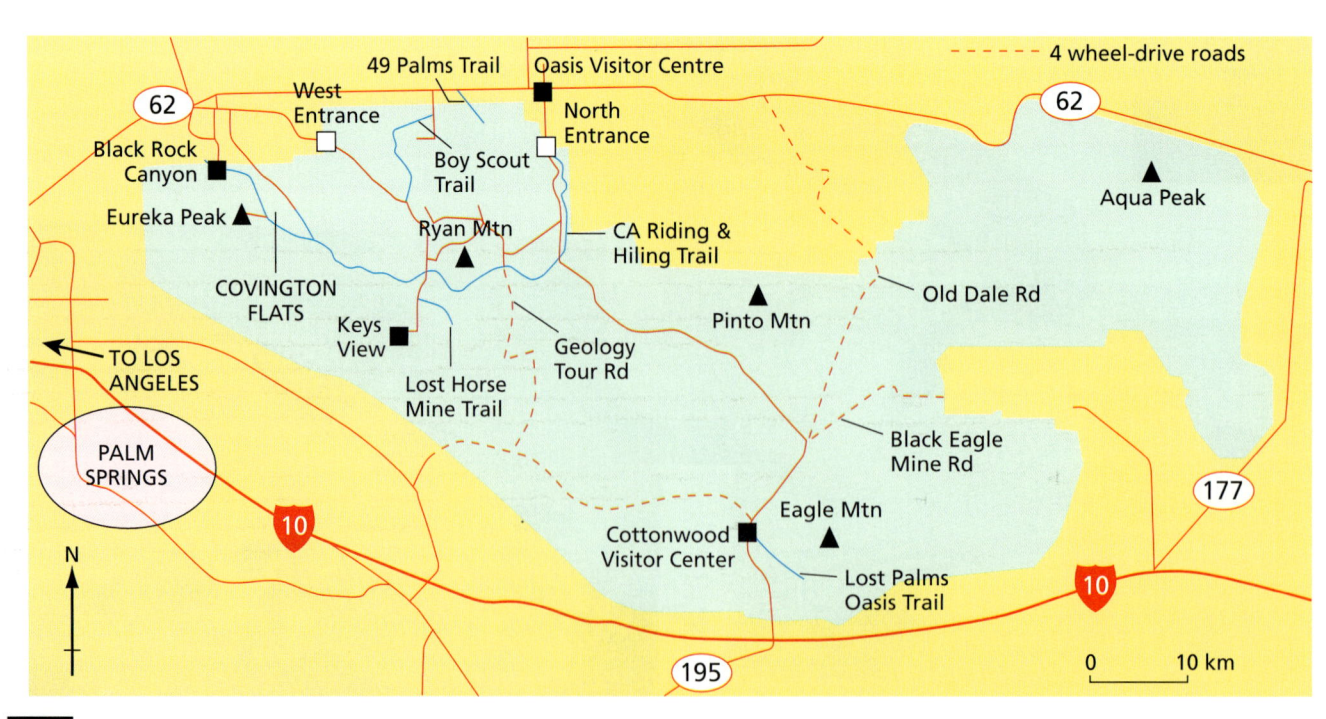

8B.5 *Detailed maps provide visitors with information about the leisure activities available in the Mojave*

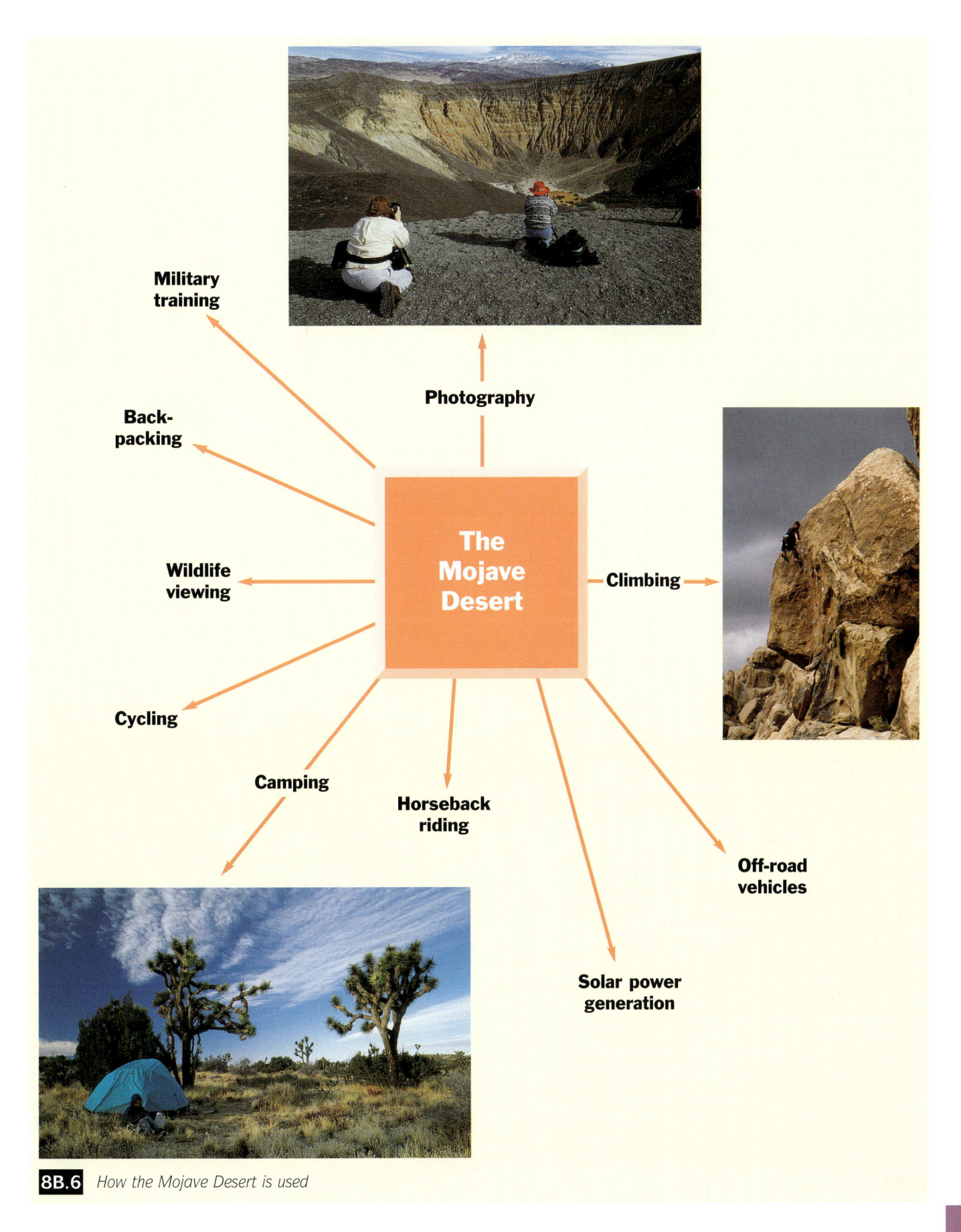

B Managing the desert environment

- Military training
- Back-packing
- Wildlife viewing
- Cycling
- Camping
- Photography
- Horseback riding
- Solar power generation
- Climbing
- Off-road vehicles

The Mojave Desert

8B.6 *How the Mojave Desert is used*

249

Section 8 Towards a Sustainable Future

8B.7 *Solar power generation in the Mojave Desert*

Several scientific studies have established exactly how much damage is being done to the desert. The US Geological Survey, for example, continually monitors the state of the desert using satellite photographs. It advises the local authorities on which activities should be allowed, and in which areas. They have concluded that the desert can recover if left untouched for several years. One solution suggested is to allow leisure activities in different parts of the desert every few years, giving the environment time to recover after it has been used by people.

There is an increasing number of companies that provide planned leisure activities, and many signposted footpaths and tracks. The aim is to ensure that people only visit certain areas of the Mojave. The most sensitive environments are advertised less, and public rights of way concentrate within the National Parks. Although this has encouraged more visitors, there are still many people who believe that the desert is a natural environment, and that they should have the right to go wherever they want.

EXTENDED ACTIVITY

Read the opinions shown in Figure 8B.8. Each is a suggestion about how the Mojave Desert could be managed in the future.

1 For each solution, give advantages and disadvantages for:
   a the natural environment
   b people who wish to use the desert for leisure activities.

> The desert is huge. All this talk of destroying the environment is nonsense. The scientists themselves admit that the desert is much stronger than us humans, and will recover as soon as we leave it alone! People should be allowed to go where they choose, as the Mojave is one of America's last great wilderness regions. And let's not forget all those millions of dollars that people spend on these leisure activities. It is, after all, the biggest growth industry in the region.

> We should have a 'soft' tourism approach. People should only be allowed into small parts of the desert, and their activities should be carefully regulated. Planned and guided tours should be given priority. If there is a conflict between leisure and preserving the environment, then the environment must come first.

> The desert is a natural environment, and it should be preserved. People should not be allowed to use the desert for leisure activities, as it is being destroyed. There are plenty of other places people can go for off-road racing or horse riding. There should be heavy fines for people who break these rules.

8B.8 *The future of the Mojave Desert?*

2 State which solution you prefer. Give reasons for your answer.

3 Suggest how your chosen solution could work. Give realistic ideas, and explain how you could deal with any problems that might be caused by the chosen plan.

Section 8 Towards a Sustainable Future

C The cleaned-up Thames

The River Thames flows for 346 km from the Cotswold Hills in the west to the Thames Estuary in the east (see Figure 8C.1). The river has been the lifeblood of London throughout history. Centuries ago the Thames was used as London's sewer and rubbish dump. The river was so polluted that it became almost lifeless and a danger to health. Now it is coming to life again after years of careful management. What has happened to improve the environment of the Thames? Are there still problems that remain to be solved?

Recent changes

The environment of the Thames has changed significantly in recent years.

Thames Barrier

The lower section of the Thames has always been at risk of flooding. The 150 km of the river from London to the sea is tidal. This means that the potential for flooding is from rising water coming from the estuary, rather than excess water from inland. In response to this threat, the Thames Barrier has been built across the river to the east of the city of London (see Figure 8C.2). This may be closed at times when there is a threat of a **tidal surge** that could flood London.

Wildlife encouraged

Wildlife now flourishes along the river. Cormorants and grebes now live beside the river, and winter wildfowl visit the mudbanks near to the site of the Millennium Dome and Thames Barrier. The Thames Wildlife Trust has taken over an island at Isleworth where herons breed and kingfishers can be seen. Salmon have returned to the river for the first time in 150 years. Some ecologists think that the Thames should be seen as a '**blue belt**'. This would mean that the area along the river would be protected, with nature reserves at selected points.

Waste management

Waste entering the Thames is now clean. At Mogden sewage works near Twickenham, waste methane is made into electricity. This provides enough power for 6000 homes.

Development

More people are prepared to live near the river now it is cleaner. This has encouraged a revival of life along the banks

8C.2 *The Thames Barrier*

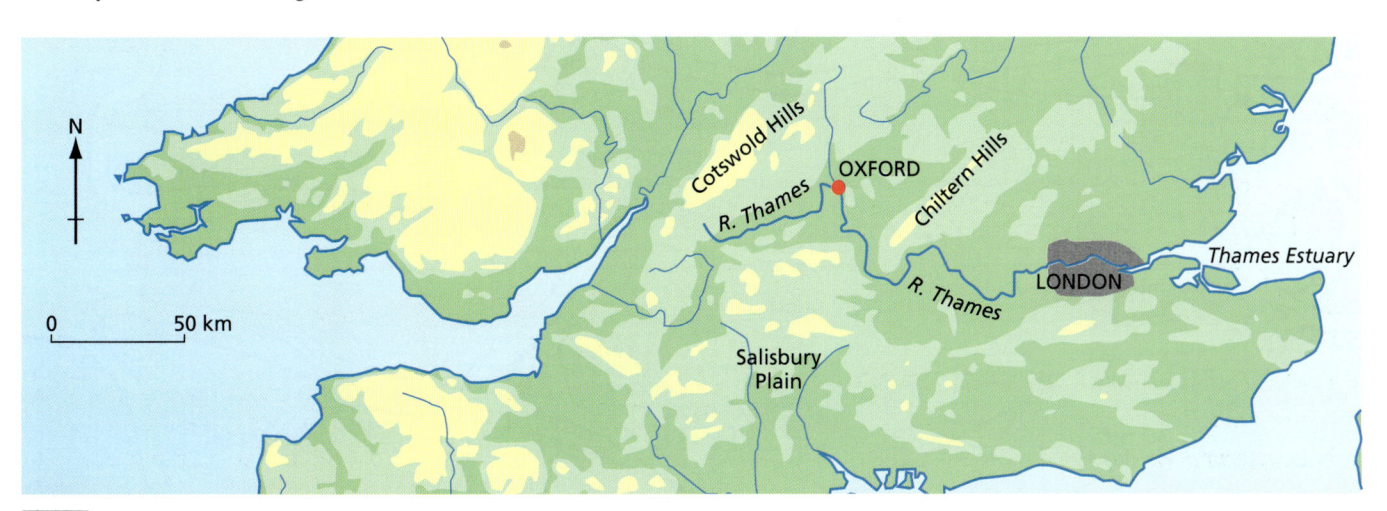

8C.1 *The course of the River Thames*

Section 8 Towards a Sustainable Future

such as the Thames Path, which extends from the source of the river in Gloucestershire to the Thames Barrier. To the south of the Thames in London there has been a growth of housing, offices and entertainment. The derelict dockland areas have been extensively renovated.

It is not all good news, however. Any pollution that enters the Thames along its course can end up in London. On 28 July 2000 over 1000 fish were killed in the Thames after a discharge of chlorine near Abingdon in Oxfordshire. In 1999 Thames Water had eight prosecutions for water pollution offences. Fines are often small in relation to the damage caused and magistrates were asked by pressure groups to take water pollution more seriously.

Changes to London's docklands

London was once the greatest port in the world. In the 19th century, many new docks were opened out beside the river as goods from the British Empire poured in and out of London. The docks were developed further downstream to cope with larger vessels (Figure 8C.3), but it was the lack of size and space of the docks that was a major contribution to their downfall.

- The collapse of the British Empire led to a reduction in imports from, and exports to, countries upon which Britain had relied for trade.
- Huge bulk carriers and container ships needed deeper water than was available in the Thames.
- New loading and unloading technology demanded more space than was available next to the Thames.
- The Second World War devastated the East End of London. In 1940, 25 000 bombs wrecked the docks in less than two months.

Already in decline, the docks could not recover from this bombing, despite attempts to continue after the war. In 1960, 50 000 people worked at the docks. This figure fell to just 3000 by 1980. Over 10 per cent of the total area of London became derelict.

Dockland regeneration

What has happened to improve the area? The **regeneration** of the docklands began in the 1980s. The government invested heavily in the area, providing new offices, leisure and recreation facilities, and riverside apartments. The Docklands Light Railway was built to connect the area to the rest of London (see Figure 8C.4). Regeneration completely transformed many of the old docks, such as St Katharine's Dock near Tower Bridge.

St Katharine's Dock is one of the oldest and smallest of London's docks (Figure 8C.5). It was cut out of the mud alongside the Thames in the early years of the 19th century. By modern standards it is very small, occupying a space little bigger than the nearby Tower of London.

The dock closed along with many others as it was no longer capable of handling the size of ships entering ports. St Katharine's is nearer to the city of London than other docks, and was the first to be regenerated. The once derelict buildings and frontages were quickly transformed into expensive accommodation, shops and restaurants. The St Katharine's of today bears little resemblance to how it was in the past (see Figure 8C.6).

Problems of regeneration

St Katharine's illustrates the problems as well as the benefits of the regeneration of the docklands. During the 1980s, redevelopment took place quickly and money poured into the area. Local people complained that there was little benefit for them. They were unable to afford the luxury

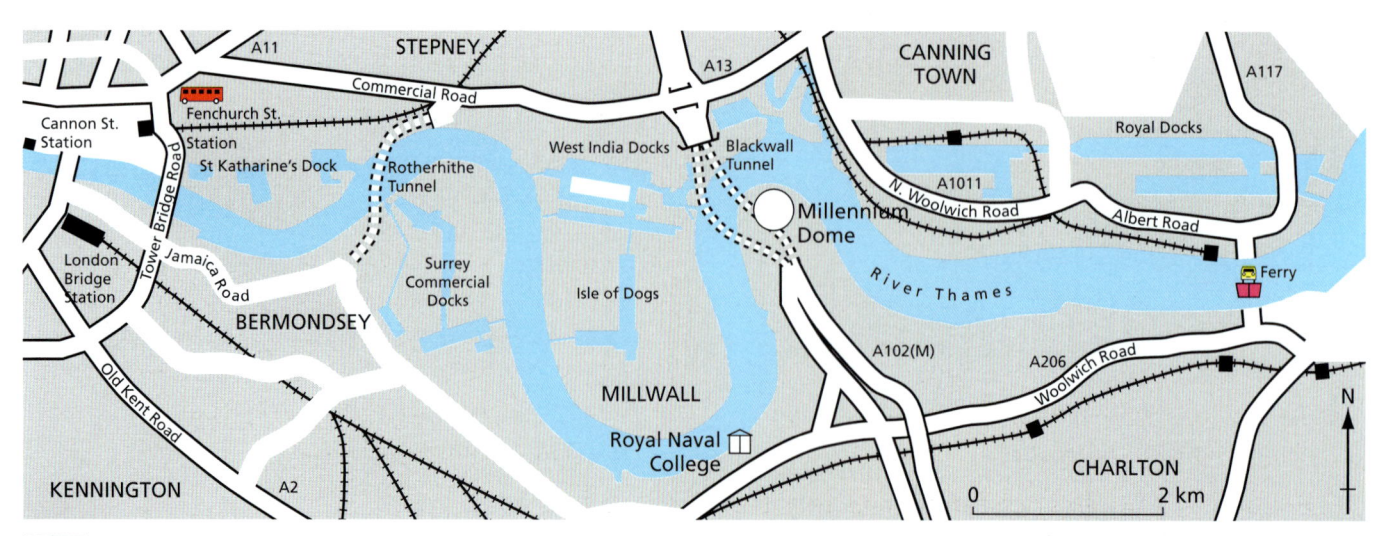

8C.3 *The docklands of London*

C The cleaned-up Thames

8C.4 *The Docklands Light Railway*

accommodation provided, and little of the money spent in the area went towards improving the environment for them. From the start, the docklands was seen as a 'showpiece' development that did nothing to solve the problems of the local community.

The re-growth of the docklands relied upon expanding companies working in a growing economy. In the early 1990s, Britain experienced an economic **recession**, where many jobs were lost and people generally had less money. The new dockland areas were hard hit. Many offices stood empty, people became unemployed, and costly apartments no longer sold.

Transport has also been a problem for development in the docklands. Separated from the city of London, the Docklands Light Railway provided only a partial solution. Extensions to the London Underground system have made access easier, but many people feel that providing public transport came second to building prestige developments. The *Lonely Planet* guide to London, for example, describes the docklands as 'restored with an eye as much to the tourist as to the workers.'

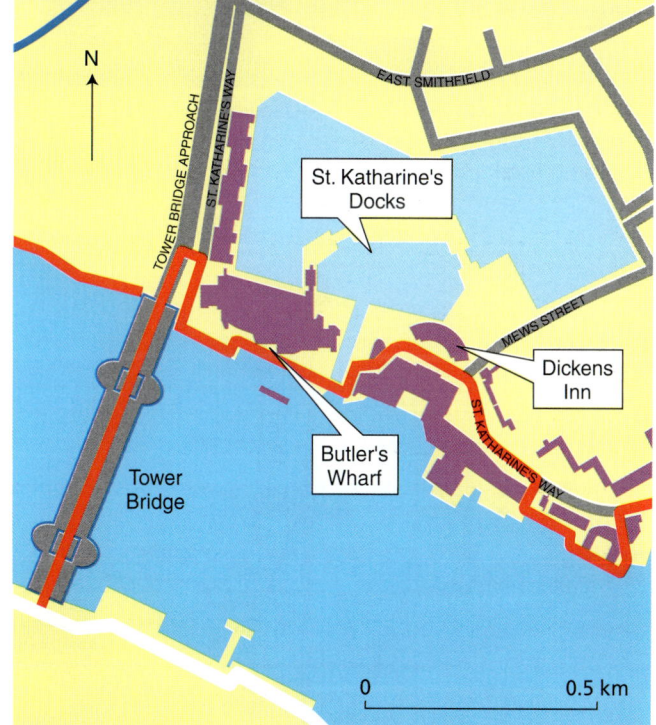

8C.5 *The location of St Katharine's Dock*

NOTING ACTIVITIES

1 Draw a spider diagram to show how the Thames has been cleaned up.

2 The regeneration of the docklands has brought advantages (benefits) and disadvantages (costs). Write a list of the main **costs** and **benefits** for different groups of people.

3 Do you think that the developments have been the best way to regenerate the area?

4 Look at the redevelopment of Coin Street (page 28). What similarities and differences are there between the redevelopment of Coin Street and St Katharine's Dock?

5 What else do you think could be done to improve the environment of the Thames?

Section 8 Towards a Sustainable Future

8C.6 *St Katharine's Dock today*

Section 8 Towards a Sustainable Future

D Managing fragile environments

The Camargue of southern France

Many of Europe's environments are **fragile**. They may be easily affected or damaged by the actions of people. What pressures face sensitive environments, such as the Camargue of southern France? How may the future of such areas be managed in a sustainable manner?

It is not accurate to call these environments *natural*, as most of the continent has at some time been altered by human impact. Much of Europe was, for example, once covered by forest. Many of Europe's forests today are relatively new plantations, containing a narrow range of species often grown for timber production.

Wetlands are among the most sensitive of Europe's environments. These are areas of fresh or saltwater marsh, peat bog and other environments where the soil is saturated and under water for at least part of the year. Although wetlands are located throughout Europe, many of the most important sites are coastal (see Figure 8D.1). Wetlands are home to many species of plants, animals and birds, many of which are rare. They are also often the site of human settlement and economic activity. This has resulted in pressure on the natural environment, with the result that wetlands are now rare. Those that remain are the scene of conflict between different groups of people including conservationists, farmers and developers.

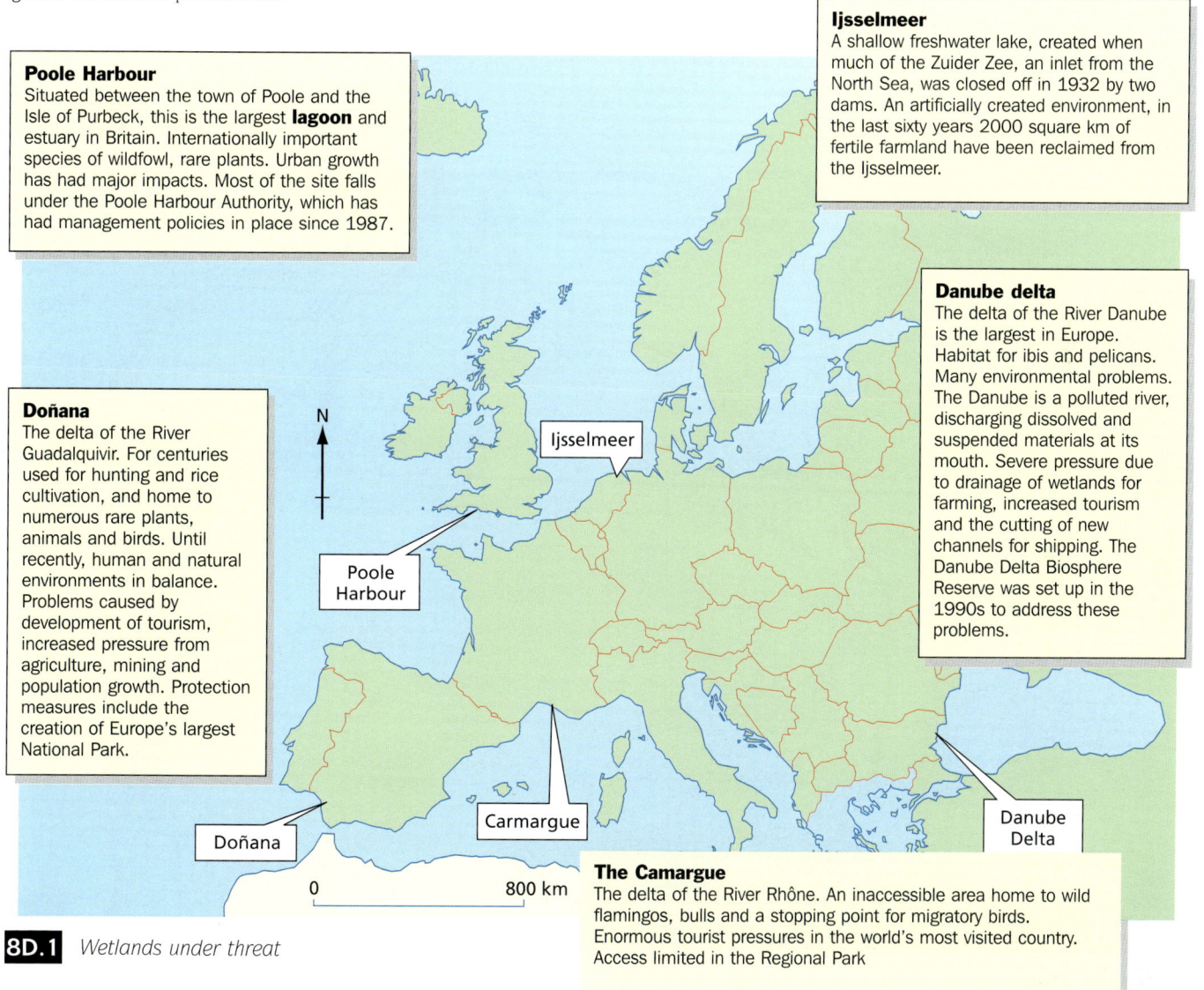

Poole Harbour
Situated between the town of Poole and the Isle of Purbeck, this is the largest **lagoon** and estuary in Britain. Internationally important species of wildfowl, rare plants. Urban growth has had major impacts. Most of the site falls under the Poole Harbour Authority, which has had management policies in place since 1987.

Ijsselmeer
A shallow freshwater lake, created when much of the Zuider Zee, an inlet from the North Sea, was closed off in 1932 by two dams. An artificially created environment, in the last sixty years 2000 square km of fertile farmland have been reclaimed from the Ijsselmeer.

Doñana
The delta of the River Guadalquivir. For centuries used for hunting and rice cultivation, and home to numerous rare plants, animals and birds. Until recently, human and natural environments in balance. Problems caused by development of tourism, increased pressure from agriculture, mining and population growth. Protection measures include the creation of Europe's largest National Park.

Danube delta
The delta of the River Danube is the largest in Europe. Habitat for ibis and pelicans. Many environmental problems. The Danube is a polluted river, discharging dissolved and suspended materials at its mouth. Severe pressure due to drainage of wetlands for farming, increased tourism and the cutting of new channels for shipping. The Danube Delta Biosphere Reserve was set up in the 1990s to address these problems.

The Camargue
The delta of the River Rhône. An inaccessible area home to wild flamingos, bulls and a stopping point for migratory birds. Enormous tourist pressures in the world's most visited country. Access limited in the Regional Park

8D.1 *Wetlands under threat*

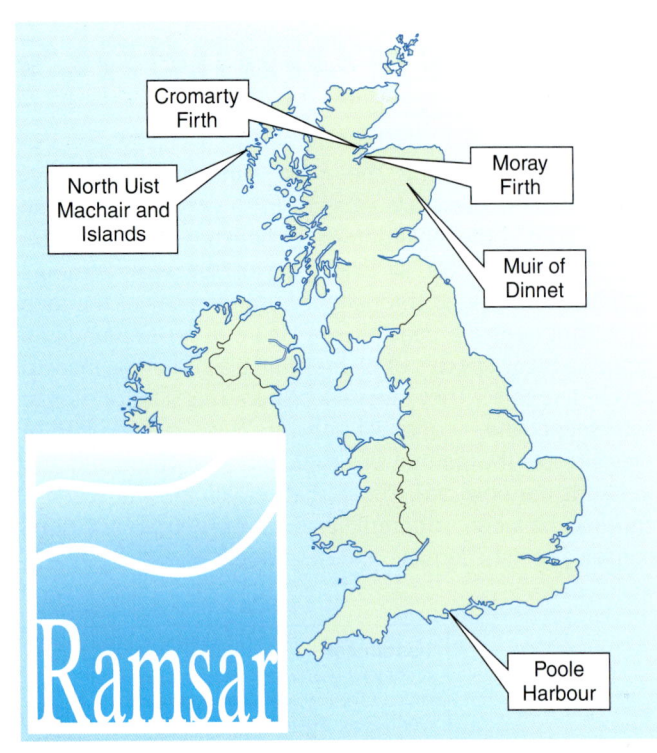

Section 8 Towards a Sustainable Future

8D.2 Britain's five new protected areas

The importance of these environments was recognised in 1971 by establishment of the *Ramsar Convention*. This was an agreement made by countries throughout Europe to:

- identify
- protect and
- manage

the remaining wetlands of Europe. There are 148 sites in the British Isles, including five new ones for 2000 (see Figure 8D.2).

CASE STUDY

The Camargue

The Camargue is one of Europe's largest remaining wetlands. It is the name given to the delta of the River Rhône in France where it enters the Mediterranean Sea (Figure 8D.3). The Camargue covers an area of more than 500 square km. It consists mostly of a network of small streams, lakes and marshland. The centre of the Camargue is a broad expanse of marshland that is virtually inaccessible (see Figure 8D.4).

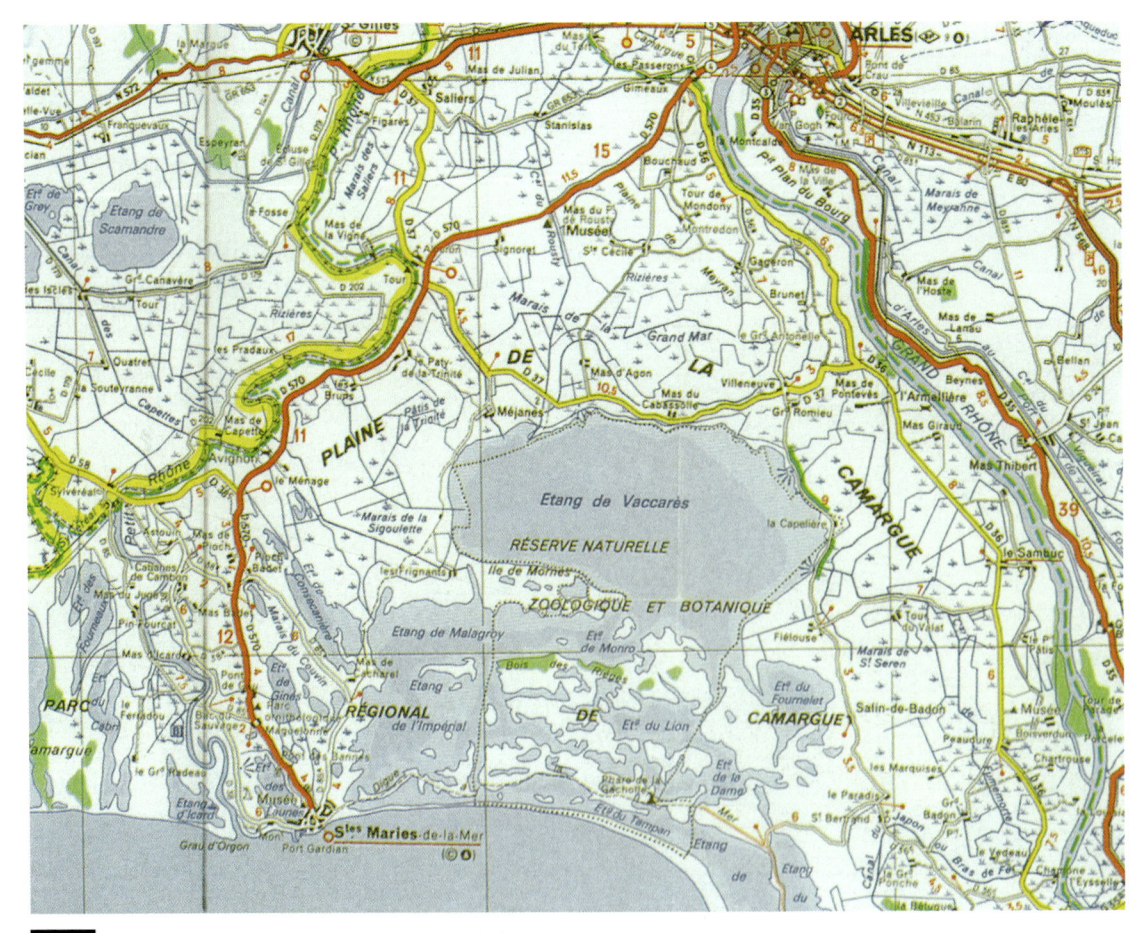

8D.3 The location of the Camargue

D Managing fragile environments

The Camargue has been home to wildlife longer than it has been a place for human settlement.

- The marshlands of the area are a stopping point for migratory birds on their way between northern Europe and Africa.
- Other birds, such as pink flamingos, live permanently in the Camargue.
- The area is well known for its horses and bulls.

Until the 19th century, the environments of the Camargue remained virtually unaltered by people. At this time, the population of the south of France was expanding, and more farmland was needed to feed the local people. In the 1850s, a sea dyke was built to prevent coastal flooding. This stopped salt water from encroaching on to farmland. This was soon followed by the building of embankments along the Rhône, to halt the flooding that sometimes affected the area. For the first time, it was possible to farm the land on a large scale. By the middle of the 20th century, vineyards and rice fields occupied over 40 per cent of the Camargue.

The Camague today: an environment under pressure

Why is the environment of the Camargue under such pressure today? What are the conflicting demands made upon the area? What are the possible solutions to these conflicts?

Farming

Although traditionally the main economic use of the land, farming is now placing an increasing stain on the environment of the Camargue. The flood defence measures of the mid-19th century were not without their problems. While embankments prevented fields from flooding, they also deprived the land of the rich silt that made it so fertile.

Since the Second World War, rice and vine cultivation has extended further into the Camargue. This has required more and more irrigation channels and other water control measures. Although these are well regulated, they place increasing pressure on the land.

8D.4 *The Plaine de la Camargue, between the main branches of the River Rhône*

8D.5 *Wildlife of the Camargue*

Section 8 Towards a Sustainable Future

8D.6 *Salt is farmed in the coastal areas of the Camargue*

Industry

The hot summers of southern France evaporate much of the marsh waters of the Camargue, leaving saltpans near to the coastal areas. These have long been worked through salt farms (see Figure 8D.6). Although these farms have an impact on the environment, modern industrial development has a greater impact.

The River Rhône carries pollution from industrial centres further upstream, together with fertilisers and pesticides that have been washed from farmland. This pollution is discharged into the sea at the delta of the river, the Camargue. The Mediterranean Sea is almost tideless; currents are slow and so pollutants are not washed away. High temperatures cause evaporation of water from the sea, concentrating pollutants. Many of these pollutants stay close to the shore in the calm, sheltered waters.

The industrial complex of Fos sur Mer lies just to the east of the delta (see Figure 8D.7). This is a centre for petrochemical and steelworks, located where there used to be only an isolated hamlet. The industrial development has been partly funded by the French government, keen to develop industry in the south of the country.

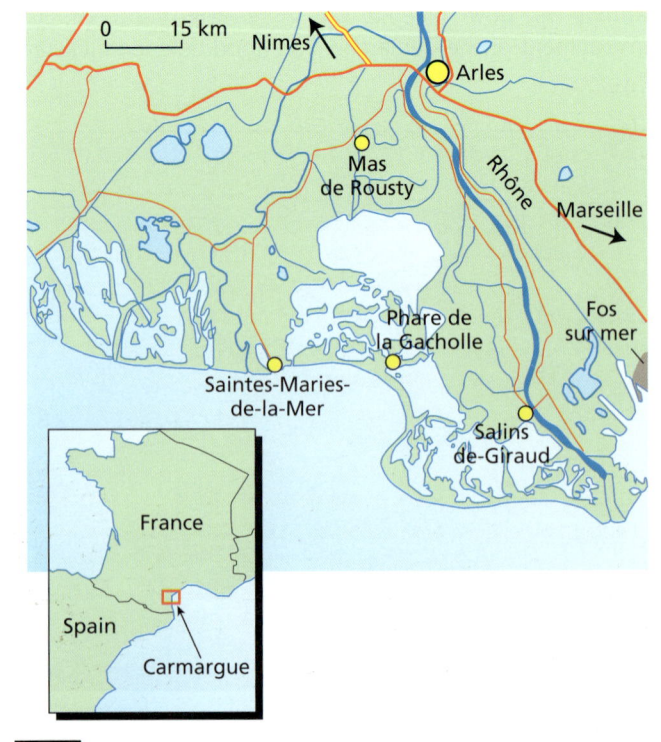

8D.7 *Settlements and industries ring the Camargue*

D Managing fragile environments

8D.8 *The port of Marseilles lies just to the east of the Camargue*

Pollution is made worse by the presence of Marseilles, France's largest port, just to the east of the Camargue. The Mediterranean Sea is the most polluted in the world.

Tourism

The growth of tourism has posed the greatest threat to the environment of the Camargue. The Mediterranean coastline of Europe is the most popular tourist destination in the world. Tourism is big business, and is encouraged by the French government. A series of 'New World' towns have been built along the coast, the largest being La Grande Motte. This resort is built along four kilometres of beach, and is capable of mooring 2000 ships and accommodating 15 000 people in its campsites alone.

Development has taken place within the Camargue itself, at Saintes-Maries-de-la-Mer (see Figure 8D.7).

Tourists use more resources than local people, particularly water. They create an enormous amount of waste, much of which is pumped into the nearby Mediterranean Sea. The *infrastructure* provided for tourism puts increased pressure on the environment, threatening to destroy what many people came to see in the first place.

The development of tourism has encouraged population growth in the region. Although there is employment in the industry, much is seasonal with relatively few jobs being available in the winter months. Many jobs are poorly paid, with most profits going to either the national government or international holiday organisations. The people of the Camargue have gained relatively little from tourism, while the growth of the industry has threatened to change their environment for the worse.

What is being done to protect the Camargue?

The Camargue is under pressure because there are many ways in which different people want to use the land. Some of these uses, for example tourism and conservation, may be in direct conflict. The sustainable development of the Camargue has to balance the needs of different groups of people at the same time as preserving the environment.

The need for protecting the environment was recognised as long ago as 1927, when the Camargue Nature Reserve was established. This was revised in 1970, and restricts areas that people are allowed to visit. There are also restrictions on the development that is allowed to take place, although tourist developments have gone ahead at Saintes-Maries-de-la-Mer. What other ways could the Camargue be managed in the future? Listed on page 260 are some possible alternatives.

Section 8 **Towards a Sustainable Future**

Managing the Carmargue

1 Encourage tourism

As tourism is the biggest growth industry in the area, everything should be done to develop the industry. This would involve opening up the Nature Reserve to the public. Access roads would be built into the centre of the Camargue, with new access roads being built where necessary. Money could be provided by the French government, as the economy of the whole country would benefit. Income from tourism could be put towards conservation measures to preserve the environment. Facilities provided for tourists would also benefit the local population, so there would be social as well as economic gains.

3 'Soft' tourism

This alternative allows for some visitors, but tourism has to take second place to the conservation of the environment. No special facilities would be provided, and tourists only allowed into the Camargue on guided tours or in strictly controlled zones.

2 Conserve the Camargue

Close the Camargue to tourists. Visitors to France would be actively encouraged to go elsewhere, where the environment is not so sensitive. The French government could provide support for the local community, by assisting the development of jobs in other industries. This would enable people to make a living without either relying on tourism or leaving the area. There are sufficient possibilities to develop the heavy industrial complex at Fos sur Mer, or to start other industrial developments.

4 Create a buffer zone

This would involve creating an area surrounding the Camargue that would be planted with natural vegetation. The buffer zone would be completely closed to visitors, and would make access to the Camargue itself more difficult, only being possible through a small number of strictly controlled entrances. This would restore much of what had been the original environment of the area. It would, however, greatly reduce the income from farming as well as tourism, because much of the interior would be inaccessible.

NOTING ACTIVITIES

1. What is a wetland?
2. Why are wetlands important environments to preserve?
3. Draw a sketch map to show the location of the Camargue.
4. What pressures are there on the environment of the Camargue?
5. Briefly outline the possible methods of future management of the Camargue.
6. Each of these methods will have advantages (benefits) and disadvantages (costs). There will be economic, environmental and social effects of each alternative. Complete a copy of the table below to summarise what you think will be the effects of each scheme.
7. Using your completed table, which alternative do you think is the best? Give reasons for your answer.

	Economic		Environmental		Social	
	costs	benefits	costs	benefits	costs	benefits
Encourage tourism						
Conserve the Camargue						
'Soft' tourism						
Create a buffer zone						

8D.9

Section 8 Towards a Sustainable Future

E Managing the coastline

The management of coastlines is an important issue for the British Isles.

1 Coastal erosion As islands, the British Isles are exposed to the sea from all directions. Coastal erosion is a continual process that affects all parts of the country.

2 Population The coast is a popular location for settlement. The population density of coastal regions is often higher than inland. Coastal erosion directly affects homes and businesses.

3 Tourism Coastlines are popular places for holidays. They are under pressure from many different land users. The needs of these different groups of people often conflict with one another, and there is no single organisation in charge of coastal management in Britain.

Most coastal management in the 20th century involved attempts to prevent coastal ersoion and flooding. Numerous schemes were built that involved the construction of sea walls, groynes and other *engineering* solutions (see Figure 8E.1).

These attempted solutions faced three main problems.

- Many sea defences are unsightly, affecting the visual appeal of a landscape. In popular tourist areas, this destroys the attraction which led many people to visit in the first place.
- The construction of sea defences simply moved the problem elsewhere. Although erosion may not take place at a particular location, the power of the waves may be transferred further along the coast.
- Many defences offer only temporary protection. Sea walls become broken, and groynes washed away. The sea always wins in the end.

8E.2 *Soft coastal defence measures: building a barrier of pebbles to reduce the impact of incoming waves*

By the end of the 20th century, opinions about how best to manage coastal erosion had changed. It was realised that, in most situations, 'hard' engineering solutions did not work. The advance of the sea could be managed by slowing it down, but it could not be halted. This approach is known as **managed retreat.** In some situations, the best solution was thought to be to use no defence at all against the sea, allowing land to be eroded naturally. Look at Figure 8E.3, which describes some attitudes towards coastal erosion in East Anglia. What do you think should happen?

The east Yorkshire coast

This is a stretch of coastline that extends from the estuary of the River Humber in the south to Flamborough Head in the north. This is a distance of approximately 60 kilometres of the Yorkshire coastline in northern England (see Figure 8E.4).

The coastline between Flamborough Head and the Humber estuary is suffering the most rapid erosion of any stretch of coastline in Europe. Some parts of this coast are being worn away at a rate of over two metres per year. Why is this happening, and what has been the effect upon the way people use the coastline? How is coastal erosion being managed?

8E.1 *Managing coastal erosion by building a sea wall*

Section 8 Towards a Sustainable Future

Resignation at call for retreat in face of sea

The north Norfolk village of Happisburgh has lived on a clifftop knife-edge for decades.

Large areas of cliff are claimed by the sea every year and in recent times villagers have seen homes tumble over the edge.

The Government has consistently refused pleas to grant aid to protect the area.

Now the recommendation by MPs to sacrifice low-lying farmland has left farmers resigned to a futile fight.

In 1953 serious flooding claimed dozens of lives in East Anglia, and damaged vast areas of coastal land. The disaster triggered a massive programme of defence building – much of which has now reached the end of its useful life and may never be replaced.

The local farm and residential land may be under immediate threat, but it seems likely that the sea will be allowed to advance unchecked. A recent government committee said that protecting land in the area was a pointless waste of money.

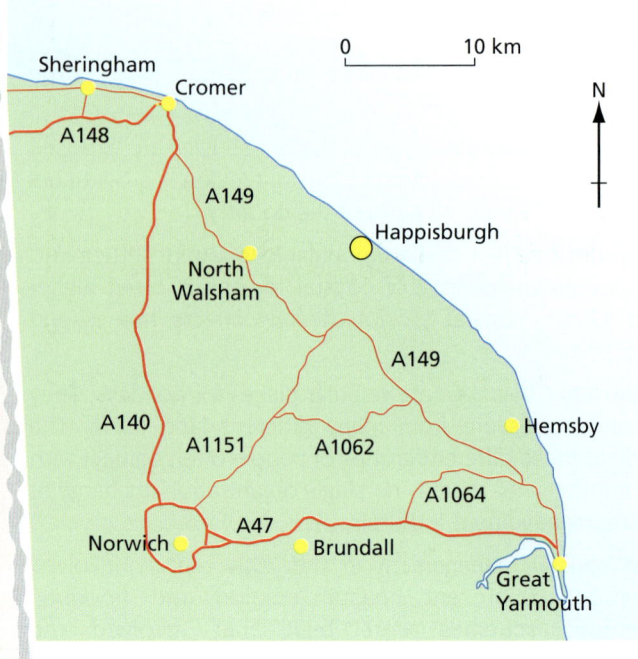

'Give up land to sea' – MPs

East Anglian farmers reacted with fury after MPs suggested abandoning their land to the sea.

Peter Luff, Tory MP said: 'We must work with nature and not against it – we must be a bit more humble.'

In parts of Lincolnshire, farmers would have to sacrifice most of their land. The County Council backed the plan, but said that they would have to receive compensation for their losses.

Martin Shaw, director of planning with Norfolk County Council, said: 'It's important that this is part of a planned strategy. It's unrealistic to defend all low-lying areas. A selective approach is the only realistic answer, and in some cases this means leaving the sea to do its work naturally.'

8E.3 *From the Eastern Daily Press, 6 August 1998*

It is estimated that the coastline has retreated by over 400 metres during the last 2000 years. During this time, more than thirty villages have disappeared. These settlements were lost to the sea before there were any coastal defence measures (see Figure 8E.5).

Erosion is taking place so quickly because of the nature of the rock on this stretch of coastline. The east Yorkshire coast consists of **boulder clay**. This material was eroded by glaciers during the last Ice Age and dumped on top of underlying rocks. Boulder clay is *unconsolidated*, having texture more like soil than solid rock. This soft material is easily eroded by the incoming waves. Before the beginning of the Ice Age, nearly a million years ago, the east coast of Yorkshire would have consisted of limestone cliffs, about thirty kilometres inland from the present coastline (see Figure 8E.6).

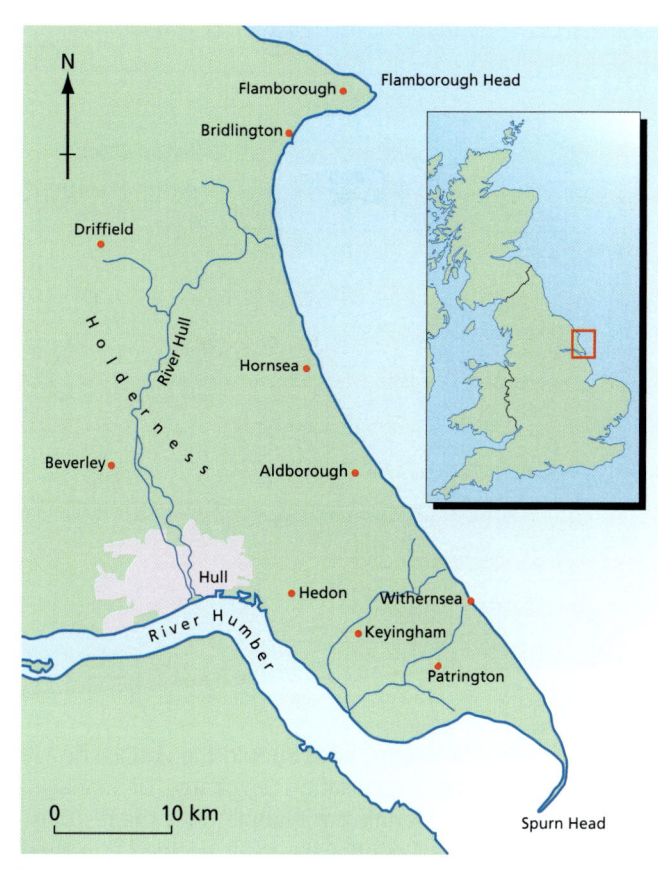

E Managing the coastline

8E.4 The location of the east Yorkshire coastline

8E.5 The lost villages of east Yorkshire

Investigating the coastline

Fieldwork at Mappleton

Mappleton is a small village located about four kilometres to the south-east of Hornsea. Coastal retreat is currently taking place at a rate of over two metres per year, threatening the existence of the village itself.

In response to the threat of coastal erosion, sea defences were put in place in 1991. Granite blocks were shipped from Sweden and unloaded on the sandy beach to create a boulder wall. At one location, a boulder groyne was built to stop longshore drift from taking place (see Figure 8E.7). The direction of longshore drift is from north to south (left to right on the photograph).

The local council have monitored erosion since 1951, at a series of points along the beach called **erosion posts**. The main sea defences are close to post 51. A group of students visited the area on two separate occasions to undertake fieldwork. They measured the distance from the post to the foot of the cliff in September 1997, and repeated the measurements in March 1998. These recordings were taken at erosion posts either side of the main sea defences. Their results are shown in Figure 8E.8.

> **STRUCTURED QUESTION**
>
> 1 Which part of the coastline was eroded most quickly? (2)
> 2 Which location did not erode during this time? (2)
> 3 Calculate the average rate of erosion (in metres per year) for this stretch of coastline. (3)
> 4 Draw a graph to show the amount of cliff lost along the coastline. (6)
> 5 Describe and explain the pattern of erosion of the coastline between South Hornsea and Cowden. (7)

What is being done to protect the coastline?

If left unprotected, the cliffs at Mappleton will continue to be eroded at over two metres per year. This is an average figure, based on measurements taken over several years. Although this gives a general indication of the rate of erosion, an average figure hides differences from one year to

263

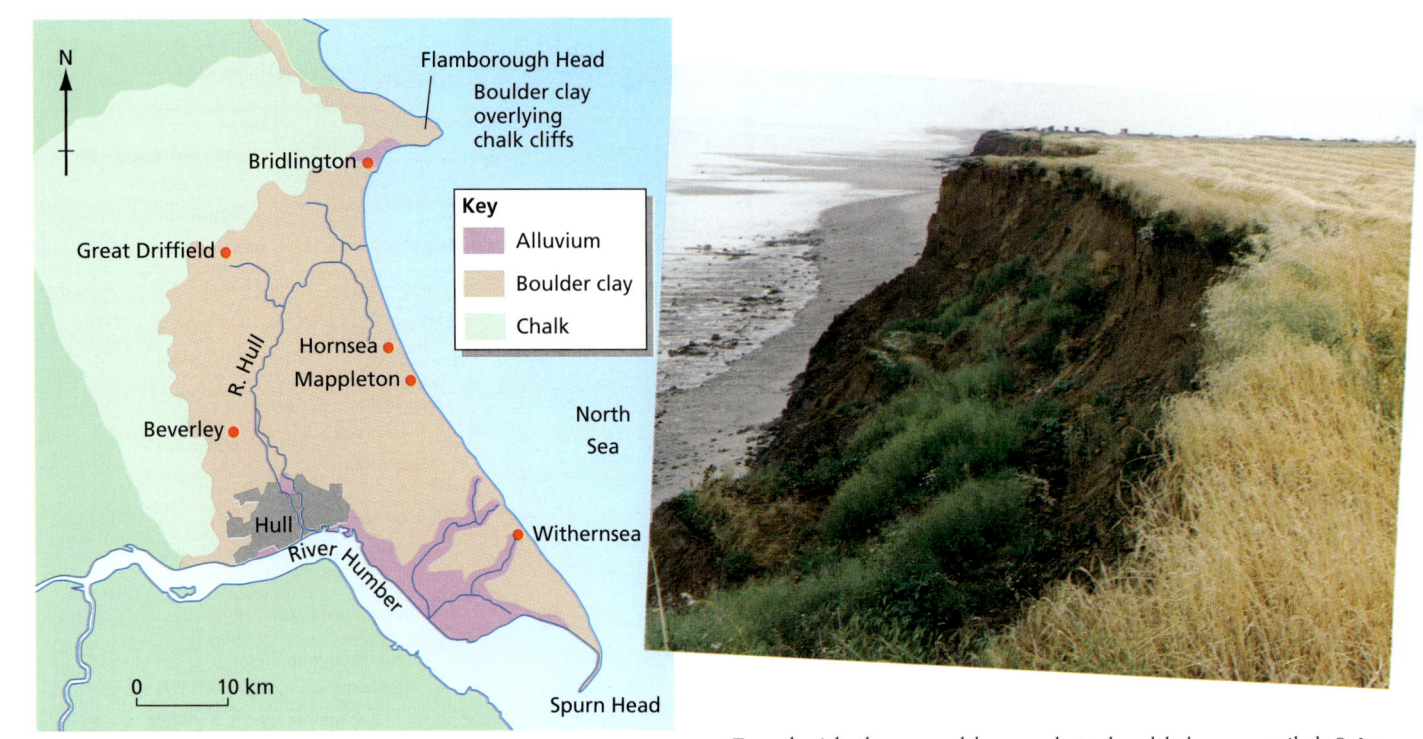

Section 8 Towards a Sustainable Future

8E.6 *Geology of the east Yorkshire coastline*

another. A severe storm, for example, is capable of removing as much cliff material as the average for an entire year. Storms wash away beach material, exposing the cliffs to further erosion. While the average rate of erosion is currently two metres per year, it might change. Land further inland is considered to be at immediate risk.

Figure 8E.9 shows that both land and buildings are under threat from collapse into the sea. There is a financial cost to this issue; in addition to the value of buildings, famland is expensive and roads have to be paid for out of public money.

Faced with these problems, what should the council do? As there is no national organisation in charge of managing coastlines in Britain, planning at Mappleton is the responsibility of the Yorkshire County Council. It decided that there were six options for future management of the coastline. Each was assessed for its possible costs, with the aim of providing sustainable management of the coast. Stopping the sea from advancing had to be seen as just one option. It might be decided to allow coastal erosion to take place, either in a managed way or totally naturally.

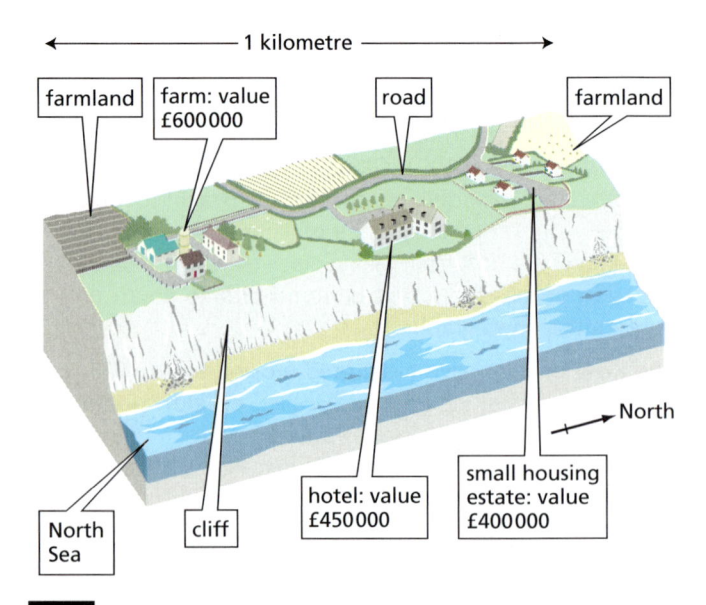

8E.7 *The boulder groyne on the beach near Mappleton*

8E.9 *The threatened coast at Mappleton*

E Managing the coastline

The Council's options

1 Groynes
Build a series of wood or boulder barriers in order to prevent longshore drift. The result of this type of management is that the beach at Mappleton is stabilised. Once the beach remains in place, the incoming waves lose power as they break on the beach, and so are less able to erode the cliffs behind.

Cost It is estimated that each groyne would cost £70 000. There would need to be five groynes every kilometre to stabilise the beach.

Advantages This would create a wider beach, and significantly reduce erosion. A stable and sandy beach is a tourist attraction, and it is likely that more tourists would visit, benefiting the local economy.

Disadvantages At the end of the protected are, waves **scour** the coastline. This causes greater erosion. Although the coast at Mappleton would be protected, the problem would be transferred further down the coast. This would also starve beaches to the south of material.

2 Revetments
It has been suggested that a boulder barrier could be built parallel to the shoreline along the beach. This would help to reduce the power of incoming waves, reducing erosion.

Cost £500 000 per kilometre.

Advantages As a *permeable* barrier, some water and material would pass through. This would maintain the current structure of the beach.

Disadvantages As the boulders are not cemented together, they could be moved by severe storms, making the revetment ineffective.

3 Breakwater
Building a barrier in shallow water, below low tide. The aim is to absorb the energy of incoming waves where they break, preventing erosion of the cliffs.

Cost At least £2 000 000 per kilometre.

Advantages A breakwater below low tide would create a calm inshore area. This would be popular with people visiting the area, particularly families with young children.

Disadvantages Breakwaters are ugly, and disrupt marine life.

4 Sea wall
Build a permanent and continuous wall of concrete to protect the cliffs behind.

Cost £1 000 000 per kilometre.

Advantages Potentially the longest term solution. A sea wall could protect the Mappleton cliffs for up to 50 years. There would be no erosion at all during this time, protecting building and farmland.

Disadvantages Very unsightly, and unpopular with visitors, possibly causing a reduction in numbers. Sea walls can fail dramatically, wrecking the protected cliff behind. Severe erosion takes place at the ends of the protected area.

5 Beach nourishment
Provide material to build up the beach, providing a buffer zone that then protects the cliffs from the incoming waves.

Cost £200 000 per year

Advantages Gives a more natural look to the beach, which is appealing to visitors. The most effective solution in the short term.

Disadvantages Unlikely to be sustainable in the long term. The beach can be rapidly lost in storms. The extraction of material to be used on the beach may cause environmental problems.

6 Do nothing
Let nature take its course, allow erosion to take place uncontrolled.

Cost Estimated to be about £100 000 per year in compensation for land and buildings lost to the sea. It is possible that some money for this could be available from the government.

Advantages A totally natural appearance to the coastline. No ugly coastal defences. It is what has always happened anyway.

Disadvantages Rapid erosion leading to significant and continuous loss of land. People will need to be evacuated and re-housed. Politically dangerous as it creates a bad feeling among local people who feel that something should be done to protect them.

Section 8 Towards a Sustainable Future

Erosion Post Details			Erosion Post Records				
Current Post No.	Original Post No. (all posts set up in 1951)		Latest cliff erosion measurement distance from post to cliff (m)			Total lost since post set up (m)	No. Annual records taken	Average erosion rate m/year
			Sept. 97	March 98	Cliff lost			
44	H7	Campsite, South Hornsea	–	48.00	–	54.30	43.5	1.25
45	H8	South Cliff, Hornsea	119.20	118.70	0.50	108.70	40.5	2.68
46	H9	South Cliff, Hornsea	38.80	37.50	1.30	126.32	38.5	3.28
47	9	Rolston Range	88.10	85.20	9.90	97.35	44	2.21
48	10	Opposite Rolston Cliffs	38.20	38.10	0.10	99.21	41.5	2.39
49	11	Old Campsite Rolston	–	33.20	–	121.31	42	2.89
50	12	North of Mappleton	135.00	134.50	0.50	59.50	21	2.83
51	13	Green Lane Mappleton	5.00	5.00	0.00	91.63	46.5	1.97
52	14	Car Park Mappleton	50.10	45.00	5.10	103.77	45.5	2.28
53	15	South of Mappleton	58.00	56.30	1.70	103.39	39.5	2.69
54	16	North of Cowden	19.20	19.10	0.10	142.56	45.5	3.13
55	17	Eelmere Land Cowden	27.20	23.80	3.40	112.17	44	2.55
56	18	Cliff House Cowden	25.80	23.70	2.10	121.23	44.5	2.72

8E.8 *The results of fieldwork at Mappleton*

The options for the council are listed below. No scheme is perfect – each had its advantages and disadvantages.

Decision making exercise

Imagine that you have been asked to work with the County Council to advise them on the best way to manage the coast at Mappleton.

Put the six management options in order of preference, starting with the scheme you consider the best. Give the advantages and disadvantages of each scheme, and justify your chosen option.

Do you think that your solution is sustainable in the long term? Give reasons for your answer.

Section 8 Towards a Sustainable Future

F Towards sustainable cities

Cities and citizens

A day in the life of Sarah

It had been a wet and windy Saturday in London where Sarah lives. She had been combining work and leisure with helping about the house. Look at the diary of Sarah's day below. How sustainable were her activities? What do you think of the comments made on them?

Sarah's day	Comments on the sustainability of Sarah's activities
7 am Got up and had breakfast: a bowl of cereal and orange juice	Healthy enough but the milk had been trucked from Poland and the cereals contained Californian raisins, Scottish oats and wheat from East Anglia. 80% of orange juice in Europe comes from Brazil. For every 1 kilogram of juice drunk at least 25 kilograms of materials are used. Why not try blackcurrant juice produced in Europe and save on the fuel and transport?
8 am Travelled to the shopping centre by bus to start work in the supermarket	The diesel-run bus was using up non-renewable hydrocarbons. Sarah doesn't like cycling in the city and there is nowhere to keep her bike safe at the shop.
8.30–1 pm At work on the till	The shop was hot and she had heard that the refrigerators were going to be turned up (turned down in temperature). More electricity being used from non-renewable sources.
Mid-morning break Apple	It came from South Africa. Importing apples from South Africa rather than buying them from Kent (50 km away) causes 600 times as much nitrogen oxide pollution.
1 pm Went to the large shopping complex at Brent Cross to meet friends. Bought a new top	More bus travel. The top was very smart; had been made in China. That's good for some Chinese people who helped to make it. But consider the resources used transporting it half way round the world. What about UK-made clothes? Should we not be buying these?
3 pm There was trouble at the centre with a burst water pipe	Most of the water companies have water loss through leaks and in the cities they are difficult to fix. About 20% of all water is lost between the source of supply and the consumer. In parts of Africa what was wasted at the shopping centre could supply a village for a week.
3.30 pm Bought kiwi fruit from market stall	Most kiwi fruit (Figure 8F.2) are grown in New Zealand and transported here by plane. For every 1 kg of fruit 5 kg of carbon dioxide is pumped into the atmosphere.
4 pm Went to the CD shop and then to the shoe shop	Sarah cannot make decisions on everything she buys. It is not up to Sarah alone to make the future cities sustainable, it is everyone's responsibility.
5 pm Home by bus. Caught up in traffic congestion with football and shoppers traffic	The UK has the lowest level of public transport use in Europe at 12%. Italy on the other hand has 24% public transport use. In some individual cities the use is much higher. In Amsterdam cars are banished from the city centre and there are cycleways and tram tracks (see Figure 8F.3).
6 pm Home and ate then got ready to go out to friend's house—no homework!	Italian pasta and a tomato sauce with a delicious cheesecake. It was worth pointing out that not that many years ago the British public ate more locally grown potatoes and home grown vegetables.
8 pm Met Suneet and Vaneeta and went out to a party	Suneet's mum drove them and they got a taxi back. It was within walking distance really but the girls never walk late on winter evenings, which is wise. It was easy travel from one warm home to another.

8F.1 How sustainable was Sarah's day?

Section 8 Towards a Sustainable Future

8F.2 *Fresh kiwi fruit for sale. We do not have to think about where they came from*

NOTING ACTIVITIES

1. In what ways does Sarah's lifestyle suggest that it is not a sustainable one which future young people will be able to enjoy?

2. Study Figures 8F.4 and 8F.5. Draw up two simple spray diagrams, one to show cities that are unsustainable and the other to show cities that are sustainable.

It is difficult to analyse the *sustainablity* of an individual's movements and activities in a day without sounding negative. But Sarah and her friends have a typical modern urban lifestyle. How long can a lifestyle like this continue? Are we not using up the Earth's resources so that future generations will have to change their lifestyles? We are not living *sustainably*; we are compromising the future of others.

Figure 8F.4 shows the cities the way they are today and Figure 8F.5 gives examples of changes in cities which are beginning to make them more sustainable.

8F.3 *Scene in central Amsterdam*

F Towards sustainable cities

Urban climates
Cities are hotter than surrounding areas because of the heat they give out from buildings and transport

Energy
Cities account for the use of 80 per cent of the world's fossil fuels As cities become richer so the consumption of electricity for heating and air conditioning increases

Transport and travel
Thousands of commuters travel into cities to work each morning and return to their homes in the evening.
The average speed of 'rush hour' traffic in London is 16 kph

Water
Every day water is supplied to cities from the surrounding countryside. Clean water is lost in the complex fabric of city water pipes

Food
Every day thousands of tonnes of food are transported into cities. One meat-eating city person in London or Sydney will need 1–2 hectares of land to support them

Crime
Street crime is high in some cities; residents perceive the city as unsafe

Parks and Open space
Most cities are overcrowded and lack trees, parks and open land

Housing
Old housing is often lacking modern amenities and may be overcrowded with poor people

Sewage
Urban sewage is 'flushed' away as quickly as possible and can be mixed up with toxic chemical waste

Rubbish
Refuse piles up each day and often is disposed of in incinerators and landfill sites.
New York produces more rubbish than any other city, 1.6kg per person: double that in an average European city

Sense of community
The sense of belonging to a community can be lost in very large urban areas. Homelessness and street children are a feature of some large cities

Air quality
Carbon dioxide, nitrogen oxide and sulphur emissions are all dangerous to people's health and the global environment
Ground level ozone can be dangerous in some cities such as Los Angeles and Atlanta in the hotter months

8F.4 *The city today: but for how much longer?*

Section 8 Towards a Sustainable Future

Water
Clean water is recycled and water leaks are cut to a minimum

Transport and travel
Cheap public transport reduces pollution
Electric trams and zero-emission public transport vehicles
Cycling encouraged

Energy
Cities use solar-electric roof tiles which were first used in Japan. Electricity consumption falls as people are educated about non-renewable fuels

Housing
People are encouraged back to the city as brownfield sites are built on

Food
The city grows much of its own food. Supermarkets are discouraged from buying foreign food

Sewage
Pipelines have been set up to transport urban sewage to farms and forest areas

Rubbish
Recycling schemes dominate refuse disposal. Cities in the Netherlands and Japan now recycle 50 per cent of their paper

Sense of community
People feel a part of their city and participate in decision-making. The city becomes a more caring community so there are fewer homeless people and street children

Crime
The city has been made safer as part of the plans to encourage people back to the city to live. As more people move back so the city feels safer

Parks and Open space
Trees are planted and existing parks are revitalised

Air quality
Air is fit to breathe. Pollution clean-up has provided clean air for urban dwellers

8F.5 *Towards a more sustainable city*

Examples of sustainable city developments

The examples given in this section are all European but there are similar places all over the world. Some schemes are sponsored by the United Nations under the **Sustainable Cities Programme**.

Throughout the United Kingdom new cycleways have been established in cities. The charity **Sustrans** has been raising money to enhance cycle tracks and to establish safe routes to and from schools (see Figure 8F.6).

In recent years UK cities have started to build homes in the city centres using brownfield sites.

8F.6 *Contrasts between a cycleway and an old street*

F Towards sustainable cities

The three photographs, Figures 8F.7, 8F.8 and 8F.9 show examples from Sheffield. When people are living in the city centre, it feels safer for everyone. Sheffield city councillors are attempting to establish their city centre as a '24-hour city' where a range of people are always welcome. They are trying to reverse the culture in Britain which believes that 'getting on is getting out'.

8F.7 *European money is helping to revitalise inner areas of Sheffield*

8F.9 *Former warehouse property in the Kelham Island area of Sheffield has been converted into homes*

One problem that towns and cities in the UK have suffered is the development of out-of-town shopping centres. From 2000 many projects have included the revitalising of town centre shopping. The new £250 million Oracle Centre in Reading in the M4 corridor was developed in the middle of the town. There are two large stores and 80 shops. It draws in half a million shoppers a week. Reading councillors hope they are more content than the millions travelling to the huge out-of-town complexes such as Meadowhall in Sheffield, the Metro Centre in Gateshead and Lakeside in Essex where there is traffic gridlock at weekends and in the evenings.

CASE STUDY

Leicester

Leicester is a city of almost 300 000 people, making it the ninth largest in the UK. It is located in the East Midlands and it has been pursuing an **Environmental City** programme which revolves around seven themes (Figure 8F.10).

The improvement of the social environment is as important as the improvement of the natural and the built environment. As Leicester has the largest community of people of ethnic Indian origin in Britain (25 per cent of the city's population), a special project called the Friends of Vrindavan has been established. This aims to inform the Hindu and Sikh community about environmental issues. Some temples have been renovated and the Vrindavan Garden has been set up as a new city park.

8F.8 *Victorian office buildings in Sheffield city centre being converted to luxury apartments*

Section 8 Towards a Sustainable Future

> **The following are some of the successful achievements of the programme**
> 1. Funding from the EU 'LIFE' programme
> 2. An EcoHouse which has been seen by 15 000 people a year
> 3. Increasing awareness of Local Agenda 21 processes
> 4. CO_2 emissions are to be reduced to half of their 1990 levels
> 5. The Riverside Park Project cleaned up the River Soar and the Grand Union Canal
> 6. Two new community forests were set up
> 7. Cycling in the city increased by 50 per cent between the 1985 and 1995

8F.10 *The seven themes of the Leicester 'Environment City' programme*

NOTING ACTIVITIES

1. Study the photograph of the new cycleway and old terraced housing street shown in Figure 8F.6. Head two columns: *The Cycleway* and *The Street* and make notes to contrast the provision for travel and recreation in this part of the city.
2. Study Figures 8F.7, 8F.8 and 8F.9 and write about the reasons why people wanted to leave the city centre in the past but are increasingly being encouraged to move back there.
3. In what ways has the city of Leicester tried to make its city greener and more sustainable?
4. Give examples from Sweden that show the cities are developing in a more sustainable way.

The Swedish cities of Göteborg (Gothenburg) and Stockholm have well-established transportation policies that favour the environment. In Göteborg heavy trucks and buses using diesel are banned from the city centre. Non-fossil fuelled vehicles using electric power, ethanol, natural gas and bio-gas fuel are allowed to park in the city centre at reduced rates. This makes the city cleaner and encourages people to buy clean vehicles. Volvo responded by making new trucks that use both electric and diesel power. The electric power can be used in the cities and the diesel outside.

In Stockholm commuting has been cut down by building new sub-centres around stations on the city's rapid transit system. There are high housing densities around the stations which cut down people's travel to the shops, their offices and factories and the rapid transit station.

EXTENDED ACTIVITY

Design a questionnaire, to use with a friend, that asks questions about the sustainability of their lifestyle and the environmental aspects of their home town or city. You might ask questions such as: Can you name a tree planting scheme in the local area? Is there a Park and Ride scheme nearby? Is there a Local Agenda 21 group?

Towards sustainable transport

CASE STUDY

Is transport in cities sustainable?

Road traffic is increasing throughout the world. The majority of road journeys are made either within or between cities. In the United Kingdom, traffic is growing at a rate of 3 per cent per year. What problems does this cause? What may be done to make transport in cities more sustainable?

Traffic congestion is getting worse in British cities. The majority of road journeys are made by commuters, leading to severe traffic problems in morning and evening peak periods (Figure 8F.11).

- It is estimated that people travelling to work in cities spend approximately 30 per cent of their journey time stationary. Commuting times are increasing.
- Slower average speeds, together with more 'stop-start' driving, causes more air and noise pollution.
- Traffic congestion makes deliveries to shops and businesses less reliable. This costs industry time and money.

F Towards sustainable cities

- Traffic congestion makes public transport less efficient. Buses are less likely to run on time. This causes more people to travel by car instead, making the situation worse.
- More drivers use 'rat runs' through residential areas to avoid the busiest and most congested routes.
- Increased stress from slow and difficult journeys has led to incidents of 'road rage', and it has been suggested that people work less effectively after a stressful journey to work.

What is being done?

How is it possible to make transport in cities more sustainable for the future? There are several schemes to reduce combat traffic congestion and reduce pollution in cities.

1 Emergency restrictions An increasing number of cities have emergency restrictions upon cars, usually when pollution levels are high. In Athens, for example, cars are only allowed to enter the city on alternate days according to the last digit of their registration number. Cars with even numbers enter one day, odd numbers the next. A similar scheme operates in Paris. The rule does not apply to drivers who have a *pastille verte*. This is a green disk that is displayed on cars that have a catalytic converter or run on electricity.

2 Park and Ride schemes (see Figure 8F.12). Motorists are encouraged to leave their cars on the outside of the city, where they travel by bus to and from the CBD. Park and ride schemes operate in many British cities, for example Oxford and Nottingham.

3 Charging Motorists can pay to enter cities. Electronically tagged cars can be charged automatically every time they enter the city.

4 Fines Motorists could be fined for driving cars that failed to meet pollution standards. Seven local authorities in London already operate this scheme. Westminster Council, in central London, has considered fining motorists who leave the engine running while their car is stationary.

5 New fuels Large organisations, such as Marks and Spencer, have turned to Liquid Petroleum Gas to power their vehicles instead of diesel. This causes less air pollution.

6 By-passes In 2000 the government gave the go-ahead for the construction of many more by-passes to reduce the amount of traffic in towns.

7 Public transport A longer term solution is to provide alternative means of public transport so that people do not take their cars. This is unlikely to happen in the short term because public transport systems in Britain are expensive to use and perceived as being unreliable.

8F.12 *A Park and Ride scheme*

8F.11 *Traffic congestion in London*

Section 8 Towards a Sustainable Future

G Towards sustainable industry

In Section 3, the Honda car manufacturing company was studied as an example of a transnational company. Transnationals are now responsible for the majority of manufacturing in the world. What responsibility does Honda have towards protecting the environment? Should transnationals such as Honda be working towards sustainable industry?

Honda is aware of the environmental impact of their activities. It follows a policy of 'Green Factories for a Green Planet' (see Figure 8G.1). Honda has been keen to introduce an environmental policy for its operations in Swindon. Figure 8G.3 has been adapted from information from Honda.

Figures 8G.2 and 8G.4 show returnable packaging at Honda. Most of the components are now received in returnable packaging or packaging that can be recycled. Honda aim to have zero waste being sent to landfill sites by 2010.

8G.2 *Minimising waste by using returnable packaging*

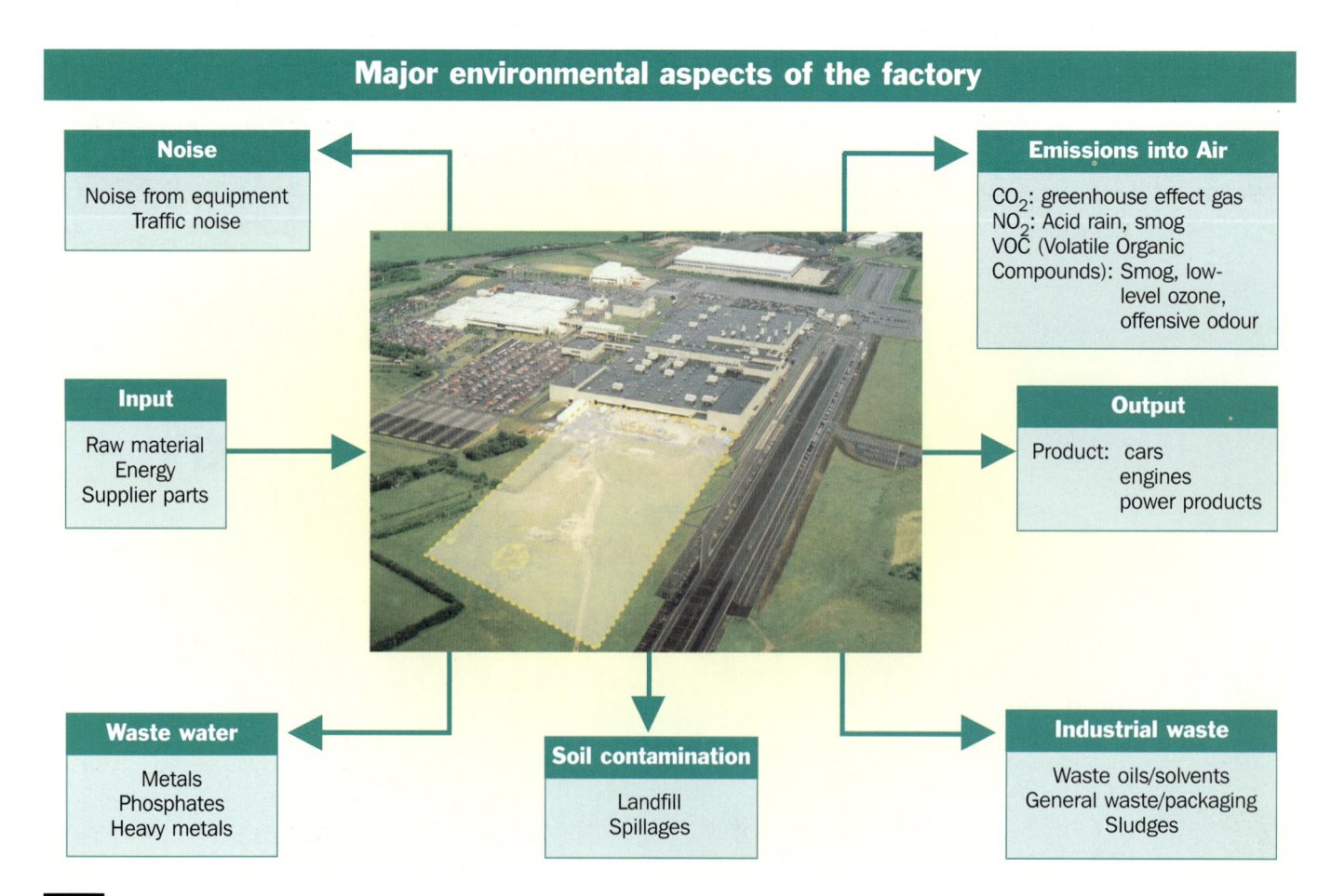

Major environmental aspects of the factory

Noise
Noise from equipment
Traffic noise

Emissions into Air
CO_2: greenhouse effect gas
NO_2: Acid rain, smog
VOC (Volatile Organic Compounds): Smog, low-level ozone, offensive odour

Input
Raw material
Energy
Supplier parts

Output
Product: cars
engines
power products

Waste water
Metals
Phosphates
Heavy metals

Soil contamination
Landfill
Spillages

Industrial waste
Waste oils/solvents
General waste/packaging
Sludges

8G.1 *The environmental aspects of the Honda factory at Swindon*

G Towards sustainable industry

HONDA OF THE UK MANUFACTURING LTD

ENVIRONMENT POLICY AND ACTION GUIDELINES

We will make every effort to protect the environment from the effects of our manufacturing operations and will achieve, by means of continuous improvement, the expectation of society and our Local Community.

Honda Motor Company is committed to being an industry leader in Environmental Excellence. In 1992, Honda Motor Company released an Environmental Declaration to formally state its position on this important issue. Honda has incorporated the principles of this Declaration into our Environmental Policy in order to meet and exceed our responsibility to preserve and protect people, property and the environment.

At Honda, our manufacturing business is conducted according to five environmental guidelines:

1 Manufacturing Environment
We minimise the environmental impact of our manufacturing operations by in-process controls for all emissions.

2 Corporate Citizen
As a corporate citizen of the UK, we minimise the environmental effects of our facilities.

3 Waste Management
We have a four-stage process for waste management which is applied on a strictly prioritised basis:

1 Minimise, and, where possible,
2 Re-use, or, failing that,
3 Recycle, but, if that is not an option, then
4 Dispose of the waste in a controlled manner.

4 Energy management
We manage the consumption of all sources of energy by:
1 Monitoring usage
2 Promoting maximum energy efficiency
3 Setting targets to reduce energy consumption

5 Suppliers
We support all our European suppliers in the quest for increased environmental awareness throughout their operations.

8G.3 *Policy statement from Honda*

8G.4 *Using returnable paint containers to minimise drum waste*

Towards a sustainable Europe

Europe and the European Union

At the end of the Second World War many cities in Europe lay in ruins. Thirty million people had been killed and 50 million had been made homeless. Industry, agriculture and transport needed help. In 1957 six countries formed the Common Market or European Economic Community (EEC). Later more countries joined the Community and it became known as the European Union (EU). At the beginning of the 21st century, the EU had 15 members and 12 countries in eastern Europe and the Mediterranean were preparing to join (see Figure 8G.5).

Section 8 Towards a Sustainable Future

EU members
Population, millions

Country	Population
Austria	8.08
Belgium	10.21
Denmark	5.31
Finland	5.16
France	58.96
Germany	82.03
Greece	10.53
Ireland	3.74
Italy	57.61
Luxembourg	0.42
Netherlands	15.76
Portugal	9.98
Spain	39.39
Sweden	8.85
UK	59.24

Prospective members under enlargement
Population, millions

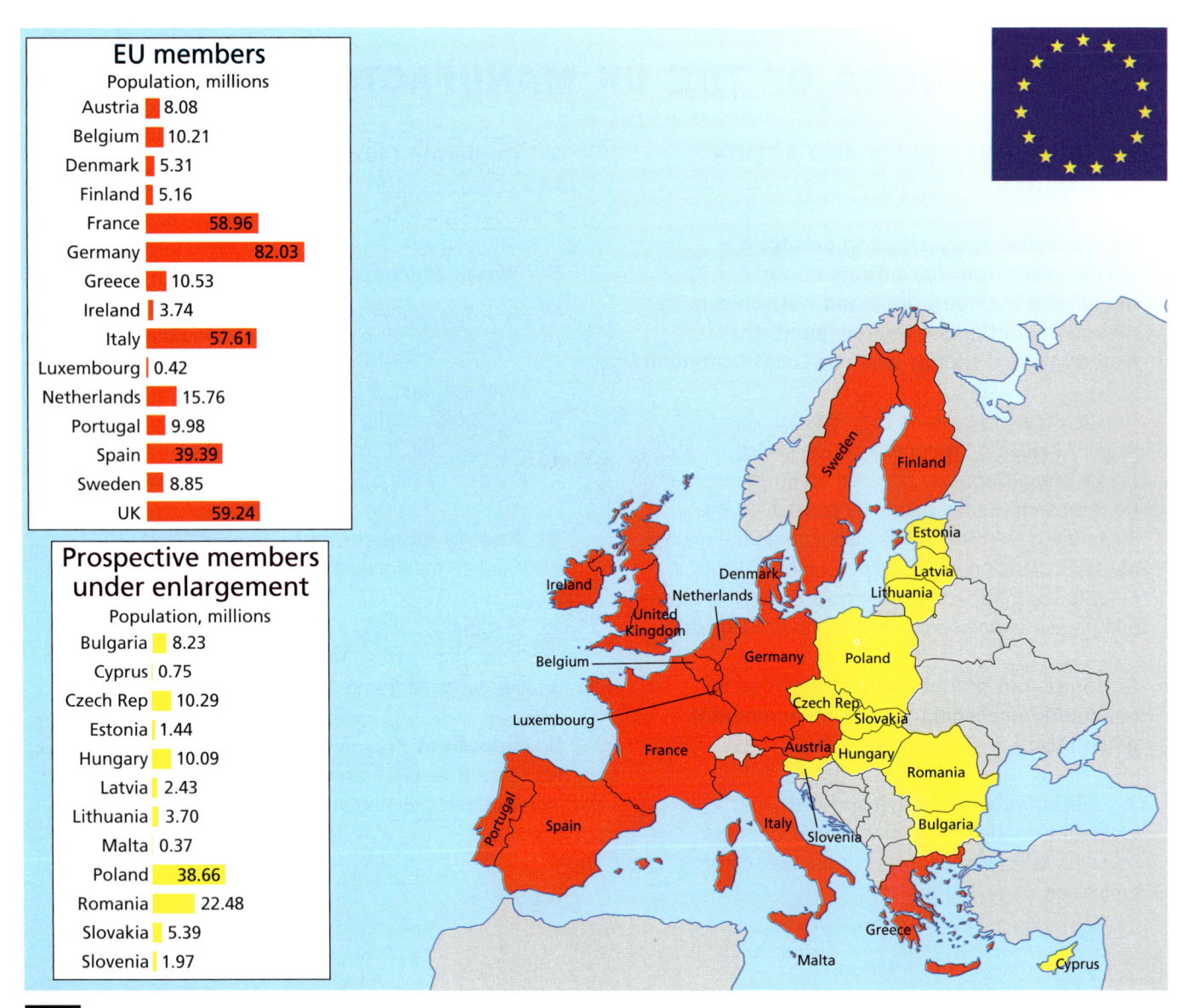

Country	Population
Bulgaria	8.23
Cyprus	0.75
Czech Rep	10.29
Estonia	1.44
Hungary	10.09
Latvia	2.43
Lithuania	3.70
Malta	0.37
Poland	38.66
Romania	22.48
Slovakia	5.39
Slovenia	1.97

8G.5 *The European Union and possible future members*

The economic advantages for those in the EU are enormous; they can trade freely with one another but countries outside who wish to export to the EU must pay **tariffs** (import taxes). The EU has been able to distribute wealth more evenly within the Union. Poorer regions have received assistance and agriculture has been helped substantially.

There has been much criticism of the Union from countries outside who sometimes see the Union as a 'rich countries' club'. There has also been criticism from countries within the Union. There has been an increase in bureaucracy and sometimes members fear they are losing their individual traditions and culture. There is a fear amongst some Europeans that the EU will become a 'superstate' – the United States of Europe – with a single currency and even a single official language. Some Europeans would welcome such a power base in Europe. Perhaps the majority would prefer the best of both worlds, where individuality is preserved alongside fuller co-operation.

An expanded EU

If more countries join the EU and the original aims are met, then the new EU could develop in a sustainable way:

- to give help to poor areas of the Union and to poor countries of the world
- to protect the environment
- to promote international trade
- to live in peace, and work for peace and international understanding.

G Towards sustainable industry

An Expanded EU — pros and cons

- More varied goods and services
- More trade, carried out more easily
- Eastern economies would be boosted and the people would be able to share in more wealth
- Pollution issues could be addressed on a European level
- Expansion with Turkey would 'widen' the horizons of Europe
- There is the possibility of corruption eg the spread of the Russian mafia into eastern countries in the EU
- Rivers such as the Danube could be better managed
- There would be free movement of labour in the EU
- Expansion with Turkey would 'stretch' the EU in terms of distance and culture
- An enlarged EU would become a very powerful world power
- Expansion with Norway and Switzerland would bring more wealth
- There are 'leaky' borders and there will be illegal immigrants
- The expansion of the EU to include poorer eastern countries would be a 'drain' on the richer west. Germany found the inclusion of East Germany 'expensive'
- More political stability
- More military stability
- There will be more investment and free movement of money (capital) for development

8G.6 *The pros and cons of an expanded EU*

As new countries join the EU there will be both advantages and disadvantages to existing members, some of which are shown in Figure 8G.6. If the two rich European countries not in the EU were to join, there would be big advantages to the EU but neither Norway not Switzerland plan to join. Turkey would like to join but is not being considered at present. The prospective members are less well off than the 15 members of 2001. Figure 8G.7 shows the comparison in GNP per capita of the 15 members and the 12 prospective ones.

Section 8 Towards a Sustainable Future

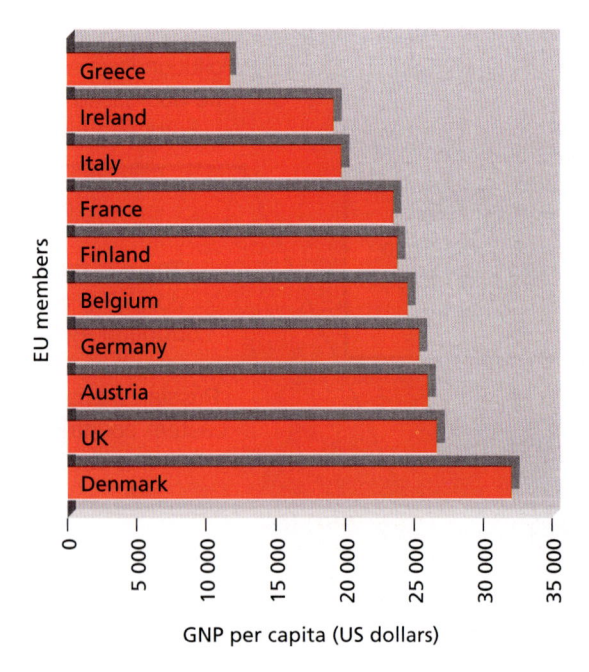

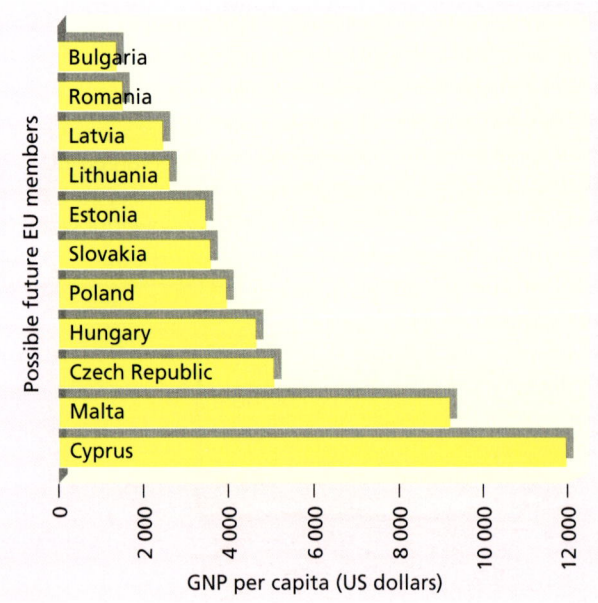

8G.7 *The distribution of wealth in the European Union*

NOTING ACTIVITIES

1. Name the 15 members of the EU.
2.
   a. How many more countries want to join?
   b. What is the total population of the countries that want to join?
   c. How does the GNP per capita of the possible future members differ from that of the present 15 members?
   d. Which country wanting to join is the richest? Which is the poorest?
   e. How poor is the poorest new country compared to the richest present member?
3. From the points of view of the present 15 members, what are the advantages and disadvantages of a future expanded Europe?
4. From the points of view of eastern European countries, what are the advantages and disadvantages of a future expanded Europe?

Quality of life can be defined as: how well off people are in terms of environment, pollution, energy supplies, diet and health. It can also include the social well-being of people and the lifestyle they are able to follow.

Standard of living can be defined as: how well off and comfortable people are. It depends on how much people have to spend on goods, clothes, housing, lighting, heating, travel to work, entertainment and holidays. It also depends on whether they have a good education, water supply and access to other amenities and services.

EXTENDED ACTIVITY

1. Write the case for Malta joining the EU.
2. Suggest why Turkey has not, as yet, been considered as a member.
3. Study the two photographs, 8G.9 and 8G.10. They show typical industrial characteristics of a rich EU country and a poorer eastern European one. Complete the table (Figure 8G.8). Remember this is a generalisation and there was bias in their choice.

Characteristics	Photo A	Photo B
Possible country where photo was taken		
Age of buildings		
Physical state of buildings		
Air quality		
Environmental landscaping		
Possible quality of life of workers		
Possible standard of living of workers		

8G.8

G Towards sustainable industry

8G.9 *Photograph A*

8G.10 *Photograph B*

Section 8 Towards a Sustainable Future

H Reducing world poverty

Eliminating poverty is one of the greatest challenges of the 21st century. Figure 8H.1 gives details about malnourished children and literacy. The differences among the richer and poorer regions of the world can clearly be seen.

Figures 8H.2 and 8H.3 show how the world would look if defined by two development indicators. To understand these maps you must realise that the countries have been redrawn on the basis of the indicators and not their actual size.

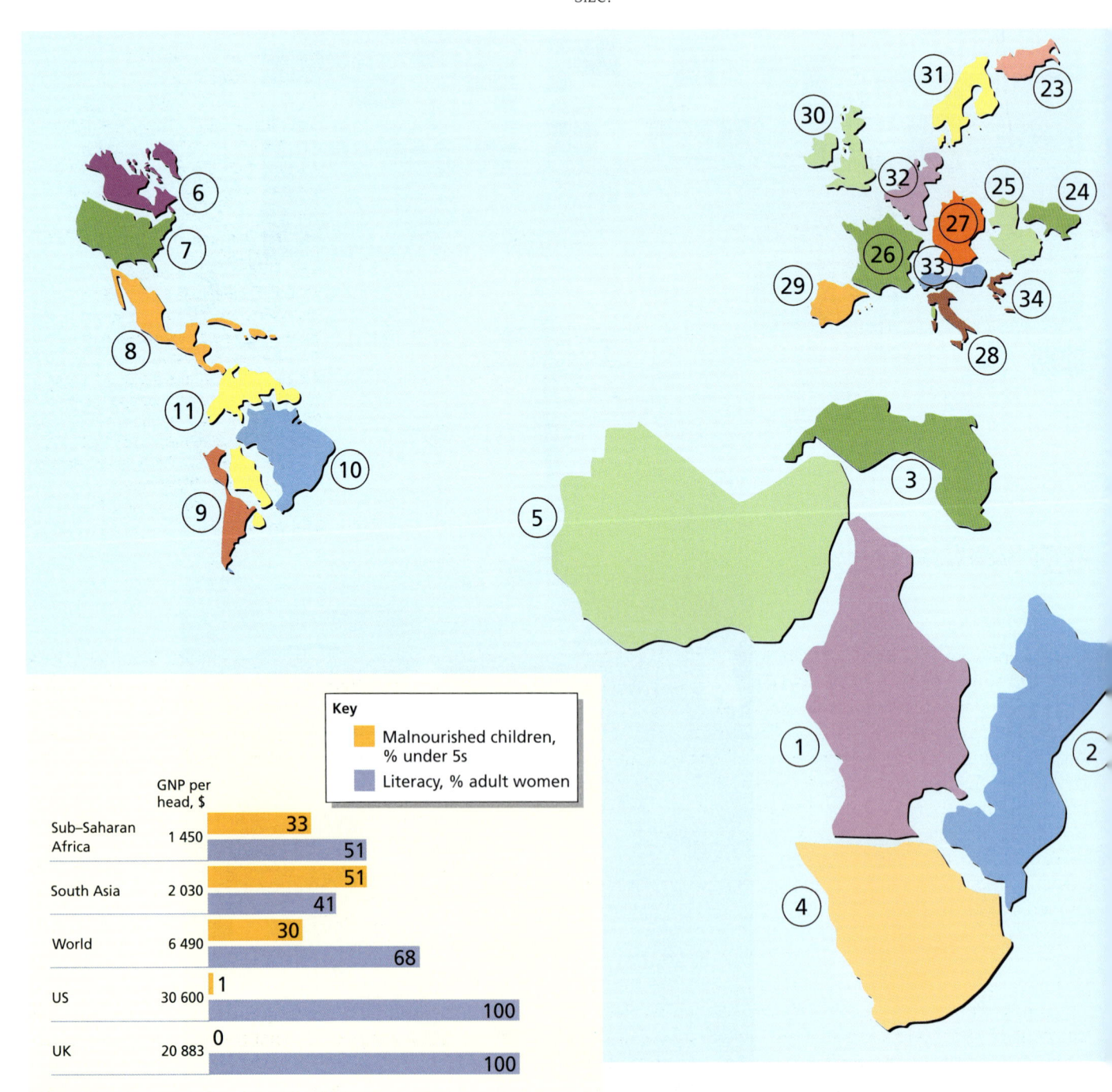

Key
- Malnourished children, % under 5s
- Literacy, % adult women

Region	GNP per head, $	Malnourished children	Literacy
Sub–Saharan Africa	1 450	33	51
South Asia	2 030	51	41
World	6 490	30	68
US	30 600	1	100
UK	20 883	0	100

8H.1 *Signs of poverty*

Reducing world poverty

Figure 8H.4 is a scattergraph to show the GNP per capita (per person) plotted against the percentage of children under 14 years.

Figure 8H.7 shows a new indicator of poverty. The overwhelming majority of people living with HIV/AIDS live in the LEDCs and 70 per cent of them in sub-Saharan Africa. In

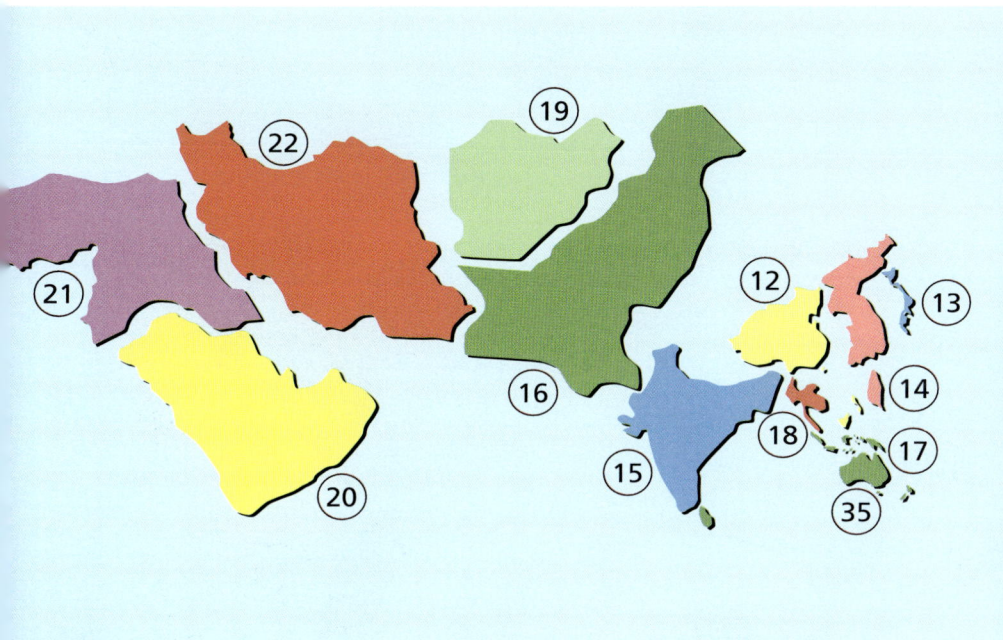

Number of births per childbearing woman

1 Central Africa 6.5 **2** East Africa
3 North Africa 6.06 **4** Southern Africa
4.5 **5** West Africa 5.98 **6** Canada 1.9
7 USA 2.1 **8** Caribbean, C America & Mexico 3.4 **9** Chile, Peru & Argentina
2.6 **10** Brazil 2.3 **11** Other South America 3.47 **12** China 1.8 **13** Japan
1.4 **14** Other Eastern Asia 2.0
15 India 3.2 **16** Pakistan 5.1
17 Other South Asia 3.45 **18** South East Asia 3.28 **19** Central Asia 3.1
20 Gulf Co-operation Council 4.26
21 Other South West Asia 4.9
22 Iran 4.7 **23** Russia 1.3 **24** Ukraine
1.2 **25** Other Eastern Europe 1.42
26 France 1.7 **27** Germany 1.5
28 Italy 1.2 **29** Spain & Portugal 1.35
30 British Isles 1.7 **31** Scandinavia 1.8
32 Benelux 1.6 **33** Austria & Switzerland 1.5 **34** Greece 1.4
35 Oceania 1.91

8H.2 *The world according to the number of births per childbearing woman (fertility rate)*

2000 there were 35 million people living in the world with HIV/AIDS and 19 million people had died since the epidemic began. The deaths from AIDS will continue to rise. But it is in the LEDCs where the deaths will be greatest. In some African countries up to 11 per cent of all children are now orphans as their parents have died from AIDS. In the richer countries there is much more knowledge of the infection and an understanding about how it can be prevented and dealt with. On the other hand the poorest people in the LEDCs do not have the knowledge nor the money for drugs or medical care.

What can the richer countries do?

Some statistics: 17 per cent the world's people produce 78 per cent of the world's goods and services and receive 78 per cent of the world's income: an average of $70 a day. Then 60 per cent of the world's people in the poorest 61 countries receive 6 per cent of the world's income: less than $2 a day. But their poverty goes beyond income. While 7 of every 1000 children die before age 5 in high-income countries, more than 90 die in low-income countries. How do we bridge these huge and growing income gaps, matched by similar gaps in social living standards? Can the nations of the world work together to reduce the numbers in extreme poverty? This is the fundamental challenge of the 21st century.

The UK is just one country that will play its part in reducing world poverty. The UK government has pledged to increase its assistance to developing countries from 0.26 per cent of GDP in 2000 to 0.33 per cent by 2004. This is still below the agreed 0.7 per cent UN target for assistance from the richer to the poorer nations.

The UK will:

- stop **tied aid** to developing countries because it stops them from buying exactly what they want from where they want
- speed up **debt relief** for the poorest countries that cannot pay off their debts

Section 8 Towards a Sustainable Future

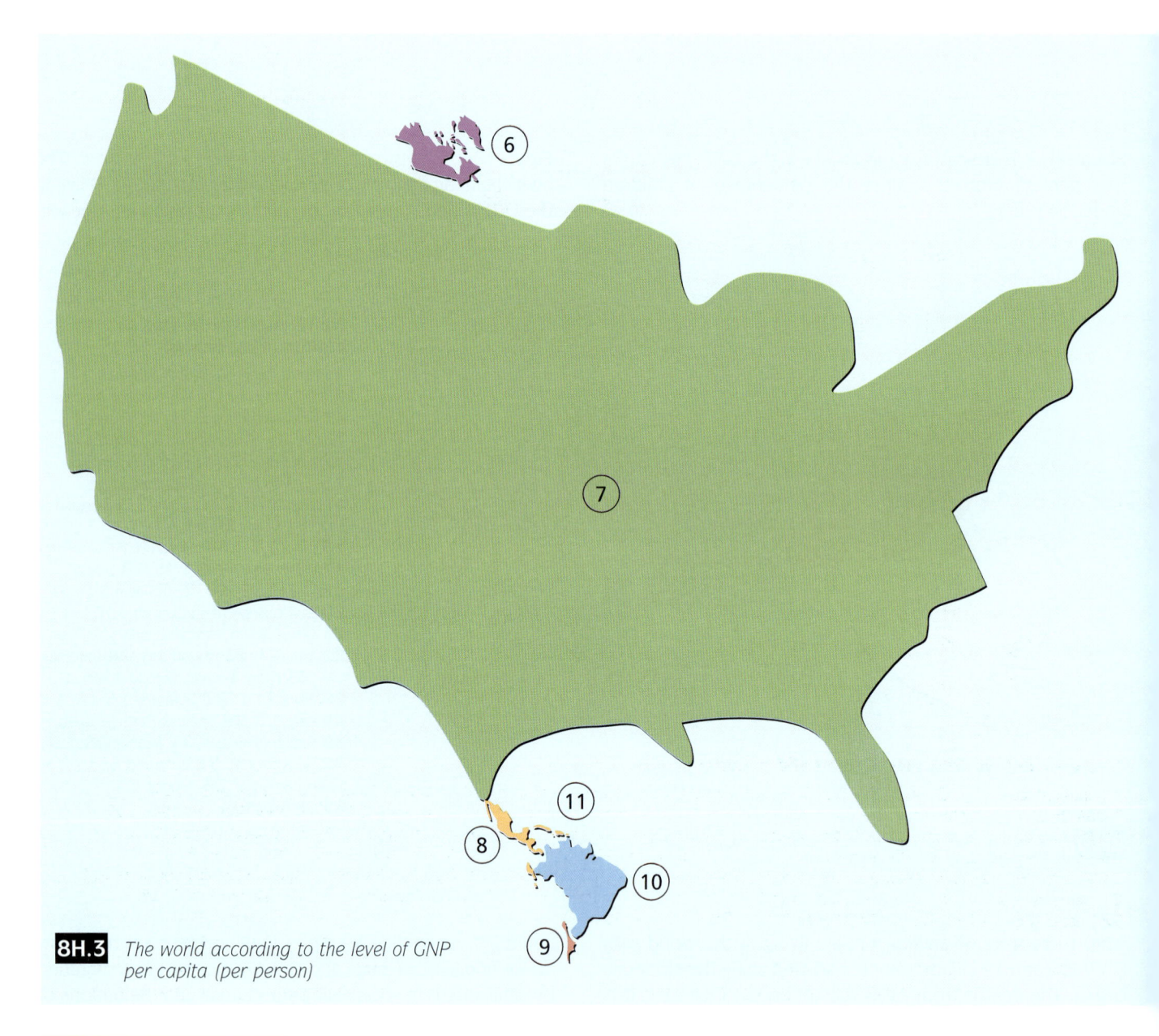

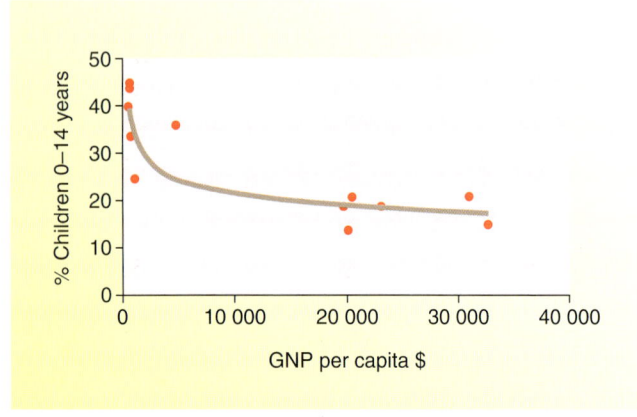

8H.3 *The world according to the level of GNP per capita (per person)*

8H.4 *Scattergraph showing a relationship between percentage of children under 14 years (y axis) and GNP per capita (x axis).*

- manage the process of **globalisation** as best it can and follow a pledge of 'Making Globalisation Work for the Poor'
- help reduce the proportion of people living in extreme poverty by 50 per cent by 2015
- give money to fight the disease polio
- help Africa to attract more investment for economic activities
- work to cut down trade barriers such as import duties and import tariffs.

H Reducing world poverty

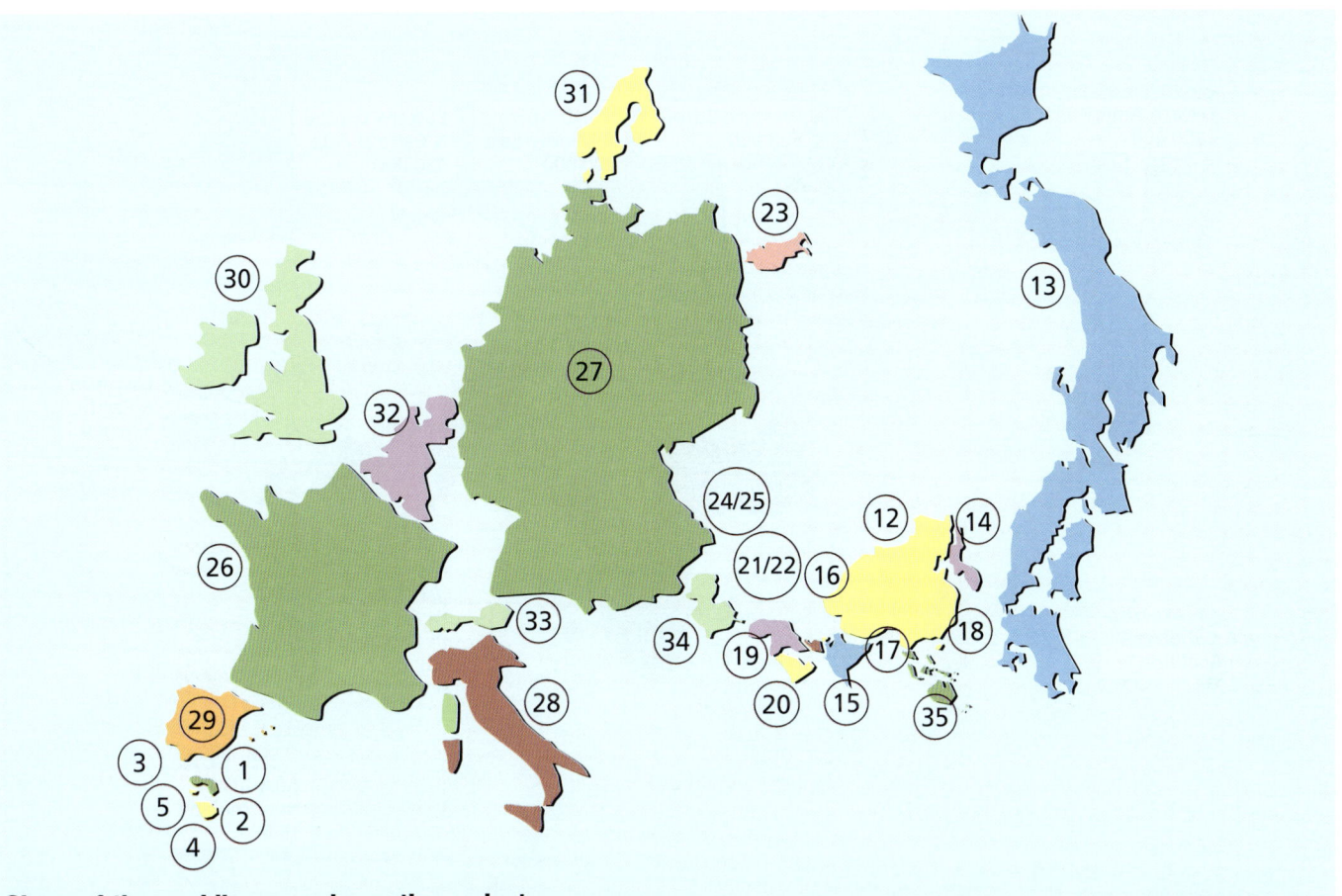

Share of the world's gross domestic product

1 Central Africa 0.09% **2** East Africa 0.19% **3** North Africa 0.68% **4** Southern Africa 0.48% **5** West Africa 0.22% **6** Canada 1.93%
7 USA 25.13% **8** Caribbean, C America & Mexico 1.63% **9** Chile, Peru & Argentina 1.01% **10** Brazil 2.4% **11** Other South America 1.1%
12 China 3.06% **13** Japan 17.41% **14** Other Eastern Asia 3.27% **15** India 1.21% **16** Pakistan 0.21% **17** Other South Asia 0.19%
18 South East Asia 2.74% **19** Central Asia 0.18% **20** Gulf Co-operation Council (Saudi, Bahrain, UAE, Kuwait, Oman, Qatar) 0.81%
21 Iran 0.44% **22** Other South West Asia 1.13% **23** Russia 1.20% **24** Ukraine 0.21% **25** Other Eastern Europe 1.31% **26** France 5.18%
27 Germany 8.00% **28** Italy 3.86% **29** Spain & Portugal 2.25% **30** British Isles 3.90% **31** Scandinavia 2.25% **32** Benelux 2.33%
33 Austria & Switzerland 1.83% **34** Greece 0.41% **35** Oceania 1.50%

Country	GNP, $ per capita	Under-5 mortality per 1000 live births
UK	22640	7
USA	30600	10
Japan	32230	6
China	780	43
Italy	19710	8
Gambia	340	213
India	450	119
Australia	20050	8
Canada	19320	8
Mexico	4400	32
Zimbabwe	520	81
Nigeria	310	191
Bangladesh	370	117

8H.5 *Data for Question 5*

Country	GNP, $ per capita	Cars (per thousand)
UK	22640	403
USA	30600	748
Japan	32230	520
China	780	8
Italy	19710	541
Gambia	340	n\a
India	450	6
Australia	20050	574
Canada	19320	630
Mexico	4400	131
Zimbabwe	520	33
Nigeria	310	n\a
Bangladesh	370	1

8H.6 *Data for Question 6*

Section 8 Towards a Sustainable Future

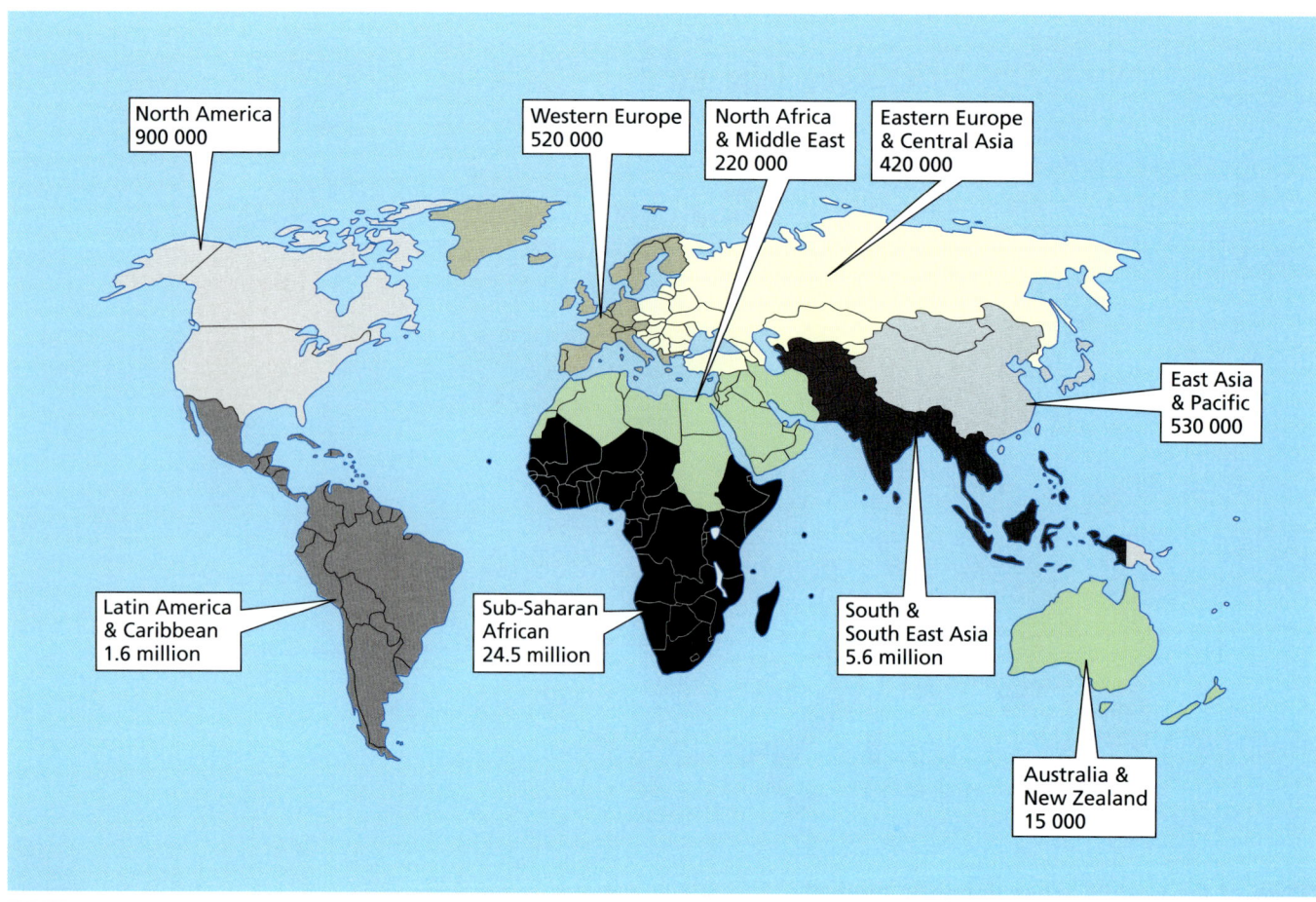

North America 900 000
Western Europe 520 000
North Africa & Middle East 220 000
Eastern Europe & Central Asia 420 000
East Asia & Pacific 530 000
Latin America & Caribbean 1.6 million
Sub-Saharan African 24.5 million
South & South East Asia 5.6 million
Australia & New Zealand 15 000

8H.7 *World distribution of HIV/AIDS*

NOTING ACTIVITIES

1. a Study Figure 8H.1. Describe how the two poor regions of the world compare with the USA and UK.

   b Why do you think these two indicators are useful in trying to define world poverty?

   c Name two other indicators that would show similar differences.

2. Study the proportional world 'maps' in Figures 8H.2 and 8H.3. Choose one country from each of the five main continents shown.

   a Write one sentence to describe that country in terms of the fertility rate and the GNP per capita. How effective do you think these indicators are in showing world poverty?

3. Study Figure 8H.4. Describe the information shown in the graph.

4. a Use an Excel spreadsheet to plot the data in Figure 8H.5 on a scattergraph similar to that in Figure 8H.4. (Plot the statistics in Figure 8H.5: under-5 mortality rate per 1000 live births (y axis) against GNP, $ per capita (x axis).

   b What type of relationship is this?

   c Describe the relationship between the richer and the poorer countries.

5. a In the same way as you answered Question 4, plot the data in Figure 8H.6 on a scattergraph.

   b What type of relationship is this?

   c Describe the relationship between the richer and the poorer countries.

6. Study Figure 8H.7 which shows the world distribution of HIV/AIDS. Describe the distribution and relate it to the distribution of world poverty.

H Reducing world poverty

The Oxfam Bucket Mark II

The tight-fitting lid prevents loss of water by spillage and keeps out dirt and germs

It has a built-in cap which never gets lost and helps to keep water safe and clean

They stack inside each other, which means they are easy and cheap to transport

Moulded from plastic that doesn't deteriorate in sunlight, Oxfam buckets last longer than other containers

The new design includes a tap (which can be removed for stacking) to dispense water more hygienically

8H.8 *The simple OXFAM bucket can help to improve hygiene and health*

Charity Aid is a small proportion of government aid but UK charities will continue to strive to bring more equality to the world. The Marlborough Brandt Group working with TARUD in Gambia (page 50) will continue to help the people of one village. There are thousands of other links between communities in the MEDCs and the LEDCs.

OXFAM is one of the UK's most important charities. Figure 8H.8 shows one of Oxfam's simple ideas that improve people's lives. It is not always the 'big projects' that have the greatest influence. Small-scale, appropriate aid can often have a very positive impact on people's lives.

The world is interdependent; the actions of one affect the lives of everyone else. If there is to be a more sustainable world, people will have to take more care with their actions so as to affect others in a more positive way.

EXTENDED ACTIVITY

There are many strategies that the richer countries (MEDCs) could use to improve the lives of people in the poorer LEDCs. There have been many references in this book to a future world where development and activities can be more sustainable.

1 From your point of view or that of a small group, list priorities for future actions by the MEDCs which will help the LEDCs and the world as a whole. You can group your priorities under the headings of:

   Environmental Issues

   Cities and Rural Settlement

   Leisure and Tourism

   Energy and Resources

   Aid, Trade and Debt

2 Finally choose your top priority from those presented by all the groups and write about how action from MEDCs can fundamentally influence the lives of people throughout the world.

Acknowledgements

The authors and publishers would like to thank the following for permission to reproduce copyright photographs and other illustrations in this book:

Abbey National – 3A.26; Art Director/Trip Photography – 1B.1, 1B.3, 1B.10, 2A.4, 2A.7, 2 (all), 2B.2, 2C.1, 3A.2 (all), 3A.6, 3A.12, 3D.1 (top), 4A.1 (all), 4A.12, 4A.15, 4B.1 (all), 4B.3, 4B.14, 4C.16, 4C.24, 4C.29, 4C.30, 5A.1(4), 6A.1 (top/bottom right), 7A.11 (right), 7B.9, 7B.24, 7C.17, 7C.20 (all), 8A.2, 8B.2, 8C.2, 8C.4, 8D.5 (x 2), 8E.1, 8F.11, 8F.12, 8G.8, 8G.9; Associated Press – 1B.1 (bottom), 1B.5, 4C.6, 5B.6, 6C.5 (x 2), 6D.2, 6D.3, 7B.15; Penni Bickle – 3A.4, 3D.2 (a and b), 5B.4; Blundell's – 8F.9; Christine Considine – 2C.12; James Davis Travel Photography – 4C.8; Environmental Images – 4A.8, 8D.6; Empics – 3E.4, 7C.7; Eye Ubiquitous – 1A.6(c), 4A.16, 4C.4, 4C.27; Fiat UK – 3A.1; Frank Lane Picture Agency – 3B.10, 3D.2 (c), 3D.7, 3E.15, 6A.1 (top and bottom left), 7A11 (left), 7A.20, 8E.2; Winston Fraser – 8B.6; Geophotos – 3D.1(b); Honda UK Ltd – 3C.1, 3C.6, 3C.8, 4C.3, 8G.3, 8G.4; The Hutchison Library – 1A.6 (a, b, d), 1A.8, 1B.2, 2B.1, 3E.5, 3E.8, 3E.9, 3E.14, 3E.18, 3E.19, 4A.27, 4B.5, 6A.1 (top middle left and right), 7A.3; Kettering Evening Post – 6C.1; Killingholme Power Station – 4A.18; London Aerial Photo Library – 2C.8 (x 2), 2C.11, 5B.3, 5B.9, 7A.1; Magnum Photos – 8D.8, 8G.10; Yiorgos Nikiteas – 2C.1(b); 3B.1, 3B.6; Northampton Newspapers Ltd – 6C.2; Oxford Scientific Films – 4C.2(b), 8B.4(d); Panos Pictures – 5A.1(3), 6A.1 (bottom middle right), 6A.7, 6B.9, 7A.13, 8F.2; Science Photo Library – 2C.5, 5B.5, 7C.3; Still Pictures – 3F.5, 4A.3, 4A.6, 4A.9, 4A.1, 4A.17, 4A.24, 4C.26, 5A.1(1 & 2), 7A.2, 7B.1 (all), 7B.16, 7B.20, 7C.1, 7C.8, 7C.10, 7C.18, 7C.20 (a & b), 8A.2 (a & b), 8A.3, 8B.4 (a, b, c), 8B.7, 8D.4, 8D.5, 8F.3, 8F.4; Sustrams – 8F.6; Topham Picturepoint – 4A.32, 7B.6; Simon Warner – 3A.24, 3A.25, 3B.5; Peter Webber – 3A.16, 3A.19, 3F.3, 3F.4, 4A.25, 4A.26, 4C.10, 4C.11, 4C.14, 5B.1, 5B.2, 5F.1, 8C.5, 8C.6, 8D.6, 8E.6, 8E.7, 8F.7, 8F.8.

Map extracts 5C.1, 5C.2 and 7A.7 are reproduced from 1:50,000 Ordnance Survey mapping with the permission of the Controller of Her Majesty's Stationery Office © Crown Copyright. Licence No. 07000U.

The authors and publishers are grateful to the following for permission to use copyright text material in this book:

Eastern Daily Press, Figure 8E.3; Environment Agency, Figure 7B.5; Geographers' A–Z Map Co Ltd, Figure 5B.8; Greenpeace, Figure 7B.8; London Transport, Figure 5C.5; Microsoft, Figure 5E.2; Oxfam, Figure 8H.8; Sunday Telegraph, Figure 3B.3; The Guardian, Figures 1B.4, 3A.5, 4B.4; The Times, Figures 6.B8, 7A.3, 7B.6; West Lodge Rural Centre, Figure 3B.9.

Every effort has been made to contact copyright holders. The publishers apologise to anyone whose rights have been inadvertently overlooked, and would be pleased to be advised of any errors or omissions so that these can be rectified.

Index

acid rain 99, 104–5, 177, 236–9
   effects on forests **237**, 238
   effects in lakes and streams 237
Action Aid 89
aerial photographs, interpretation 149–51
Africa, energy use in 101–2
aftershocks 187
agroforestry 233
aid 87–91, 281, 285
air pollution 109, **269**
Alaska, more oil from 96–7
annotation, of photographs **144**
Arctic National Wildlife Refuge, oil 96–7
Aspley Guise 40–1
Australia, aid from 89–90, **91**
Aznacollar disaster 126–7

Bangladesh 89, 235
Bengal, Bay of, cyclone 221–2
bias, in photographs 144
biodiversity 207–8, 232
biomass, for energy 101–2, 104
birth and death rates 4
boulder clay 262
Bradley Stoke 38, **40**, **41**
Brazil, loss of rainforests 231, **231**
brownfield sites 33, 35, **37–8**
BSE crisis and CJD 63

The Camargue 256–60
Canada 186–7
   coastline management 210–13
   water supply and management 116–19
Canadian Environmental Protection Act (1988) 211–12
carbon dioxide emissions 215
child labour 78, 85
China 6, 8–9, **9**, 217
cities
   British, traffic congestion 272–3
   citizens, and sustainability 267–8, **267**
   more sustainable 270–2, **270**
climate 214, **216**, 242
   and water shortage 119, **120**, 121
climate change 218, 228
coal, sulphur in 239
coastal erosion/deposition 199, 201, 261
   longshore drift 201, **201**, 202
coastline management 199–213
   Canadian coastline 210–13
   the east Yorkshire coast 261–6
   Eastbourne, coastal defences 201–4, **205**
   Great Barrier Reef 206–10
   managed retreat 210, 261, **262**
   sea defences **200**, 261
Colombia 81–2
conservation 107, 133, 260
core regions 16, 30
Cote d'Ivoire, refugees in 228
Coto de Donaña National Park 124–8
counter-urbanisation 32, **32**
countryside, who is it for? 66–8
cyclones 219, 221–2

Dartmoor National Park, pressures on 130–6
data, collection and analysis 164, 167–8
de-industrialisation 42–3, 58

debt for forest swaps 233
debt relief 83, **84**, 281
decentralisation 23, 26
deforestation 101–2, 231–5, **242**
demographic transition model 4–5, 58
desertification 6, 101–2, **218**, 227
   Sahel, West Africa 227–8, **229**, 230
deserts, managing the environment 246–50
diversification, by farmers 64, 66
drought 228, 230

earthquakes 24, 181–2, 184–90
east Yorkshire coast 261–6
   options for future management 264–5
Eastbourne, coastline management 201–5
   Sovereign Harbour 202, 204
   The Crumbles 202, **202**, **205**
eco-tourism 54–5, 76, 77, 233
economic development, stages of **43**
employment 43–4, 136, 140
   and development 78–92
employment structures, changing 42–62
   Gambia 49–50, **50–2**, 52–5
   regional, Yorkshire 56–61, **62**
   UK electronics economy 43–5
energy 92, 97–101, 110, 240, **269**
energy conservation 239
enquiry process 143, 165–8
environmental issues 227–39
environmental pressures 124–41
   the Camargue 257–9
environmental problems 75, 95–6, 204
environmental taxes 110
environments 107, 129, 141
   fragile, management of 255–60
erosion, on Dartmoor 134–5, **134**
Europe **238**
   changing employment in 45–8
   economic core and periphery **16**, 45, **47**
   and the European Union 275–7, **278**
   western, migration into 11–16
European Regional Development Fund 57
European Union 275, **276**
   expanded 276–8, **277**, **279**
eutrophication 121, 208
exports, using food-producing land 81–2

fair trade 82
family planning 7–9
farming 63–7, 113, 130, 257
fertility rate 17, **281**
fire 196–8
floods 6, 191–5, **216**
fossil fuels 99, 104–5
France 12, **12**, 45, 47–8
   the Camargue 256–60

Gambia, employment and development 49–50, **50–2**, 52–5
GDP, world shares **283**
genetically modified (GM) food 65
gentrification 28
geothermal energy 104
Germany, guest workers 11–12
global warming 104–5, 192, 199, 208, 214–19
globalisation 69, 78, 282
GNP per capita **46**, 282

Grameen Bank 89
graphs 158–62
   bar 159
   histograms 159–60
   line 158–9
   pie charts 161
   scattergraphs 160
   triangular 162
Great Barrier Reef 206–10
greenfield sites 33, 38
greenhouse gases 215, 217

hazards 177–90
   climate hazards 191–8
   landform hazards 178–90
hi-tech industries 38
Himalayan Degradation Theory 235–6
HIV/AIDS **284**
Honda, a transnational company 69–72
Honda UK 274, **274**
   car manufacturing, Swindon 70–2
hot spots 184
housing 28–9
   threat to the countryside 33–4, **33**
hurricanes
   cyclones, typhoons, willy-willies 219
   Keith, in the Caribbean 222–3
hydro-power 103, 114

Iceland, earthquake/volcanic activity **186**
ICT (Information and Communications Technology) 163–4
Ilisu Dam project 87, 113–15
illegal immigrants **13**
India 6, **20**
   see also Mumbai (Bombay)
Indus Water Treaty 115
industrial decline 56, 58
industry 24–5, 72, 258–9
   sustainable, moving towards 274–8, **279**
infant mortality rates 4
inner city decline 56
Inter-Tropical Convergence Zone (ITCZ) 219, **221**
intermediate/appropriate technology 88
Internet access 45, **172**
irrigation 112, 114, 124
Italy 17–18
   Po Valley floods, 2000 192–5

Japan 217
   earthquakes 24, 186
   see also Tokyo

Kainji Dam 87, **88**
Kurds, and the Ilisu Dam project 113–14
Kyoto agreement 217

labour, cheap in LEDCs 78–9
LEDCs 5, 6, 19–20, 42, 83, **84**
   tourism 74–5, **74**, **75**, 139–40
Leeds, an internet capital 45
Leicester, Environmental City programme 271, **272**
leisure activities 129, 130
Mojave Desert 248, **249**
Less Economically Developed Countries **see** LEDCs

Index

life expectancy, increasing 18
Liverpool, the electronics revolution 44–5
Local Agenda 21 109–10
London 32
   affordable housing, Coin Street 28–9
   changes to Docklands 252–3, **254**
London and the south-east 33–4
   Thames Gateway 35–6, **37–8**

M4 Corridor, electronics revolution 44
malnourishment **280**
maps 152–8
   chloropleth 155–6
   flow line 156, **157**
   Ordnance Survey 152–5
   topological 156, **156**
MEDCs (More Economically Developed Countries) 5, 94–5
Mediterranean region, tourism 138–9
mega-cities 19
Mexico City Earthquake (1985) 181–2
microclimates 214, 223
Middle East, oil producing regions 94
migration 6, 77, 112, 228
   into western Europe 11–14, **15**, **16**, 18
Milton Keynes (new city) 40–1
mining, Dartmoor National Park 132, **133**
Mojave Desert 246–50
   uses 247–8, **249**
Montserrat volcano 182–3
multinational organisations, and climate change 218
multiplier effect, tourism 48, **48**, 139
Mumbai (Bombay), an LEDC city 20–3

National Parks
   in England 129–36
   Spain, Coto de Doñana 124–8
natural gas 239
   UK's major fuel 100–1
Nepal, deforestation in 234–6
Nigeria, Abuja, new capital city 30, **31**
Nile Water Treaty 115
nitrogen oxides 236
North Anatolian Fault 187–9, **190**

oil 93–6, 97
   and gas 92, 100–1
   supply and demand 94, 95
oil pollution 95–6
OPEC 94
Ordnance Survey maps 152–5
   grid references 154
   scales 153–4
   signs and symbols 155
organic farming 65
out-of-town shopping centres 59, 271
OXFAM 285
ozone layer, hole in **218**

Papua New Guinea, use of aid 90
permafrost, affected by global warming 217
photochemical smog 223
photographs, use and interpretation 144–51
plate boundaries 184, **185**
plates
   and earthquakes 184–90
   and landform hazards 178, **179**, **180**
   and volcanoes 180–1, **180**, **183**
pollution, from tourism 138, 141
Popocatépetl volcano 180–2, **180**
population

ageing 6, 13, 17, 18, 25
   rising 4–10
population growth rates 5, **5**, 11–12
   controls on 7–9
poverty, worldwide, reduction of 280–5
power stations 97
primary data 61, 165, 171
primary industries **43**, 49–50, 63–7
Prudhoe Bay, oilfield extension 96

quality of life 20, 107, 108–9, 278
   improvements to 28–30, **31**
quaternary industries **43**

Rainforest Action Network (RAN) 233
rainforests, deforestation in 231–3
Ramsar Convention 256
recession 94–5, 253
recycling 92, 109–10
refugees 12, **13**, **14**, 228
renewable energy 92, 99, 102–6, 239
research 169–72
resources 92–111
   finite 92, 99, 112
   natural, limited 6
   renewable 92, 99, 102–6, 110
revision/exam preparation 173–6
river pollution 115
road maps and street plans 155
rural-to-urban migration 6, 19, **21**, **32**
rural-urban continuum 33, **33**

Sahara Desert, expanding 228
Sahel, West Africa, desertification 227–30
Scotland, Central, and the electronics revolution 44
search engines **163**, 164
secondary data 165, 171–2
secondary industries **43**, 69–72
set-aside land 66
Sheffield 56
   changing employment in 58–61, **62**
   city centre living 271, **271**
Sheffield Development Corporation **57**, 59
shoreline zone, management of 206, 206–13
Silicon Gorge (Swindon–Bristol) 38, **39–40**
social problems, from tourism 75
soil erosion 121
solar cookers **235**
solar energy 102–3, **249**, **250**
Spain **13**, 230
   Coto de Doñana National Park 124–8
   managing water supplies 121–3
   water shortage, factors in 119, **120**, 121
Special Enterprise Zones **57**
spiral of growth 139
spirals of decline 48, 56
squatter settlements 20, 21, **21**
standard of living 278
sulphur dioxide 236
supergrid electricity transmission 97
sustainability 108
Sustainable Cities Programme 270–2
sustainable development 233, 240–5
Sustrans 270
Sweden, managing the forests **242**, 243–5, **245**

tertiary industries **43**, 73–7
Thames, River, changed environment 251–4
Tigris and Euphrates rivers, waters a source of conflict 113–15
Tokyo: success and challenge 24–6, **27**

total fertility rates **17**
tourism 48, 73–7, 196, 199, 261
   Barbados, pros and cons 140–1
   the Camargue 160, 259
   and the Dartmoor environments 133–5
   and the environment 136–41
   Gambia 54–5, 76
   Spain 121, 125, 127
tourist environments 73, **73**
trade barriers, quotas and tariffs 81, 276
trade issues, imports and exports 80
transnational corporations (TNCs) 42, 69, 78–9, **81**, 274
transport, sustainable 272–3
tropical storms 219–23
Turkey 112–15
   earthquakes 187–9, **190**
   Ilisu Dam project, impact of 87, 113–15

UK **114**, **138**, 215, **217**, 231, **256**
   the cleaned-up Thames 251–4
   energy in 97–101
   farming industry 63–7
   floods 2000 191–2
   new electronics economy 43–5
UK Standard Economic Regions **56**
underemployment 50
underground water, use of 121–2, **123**, 124
unemployment 17, 25, 56
unfair trade 81–2
UNICEF, and child poverty 85
urban climates 223–6, **269**
   solutions to problems posed 224–5, **224**
urban heat islands 223, **225**
urban regeneration
   Coin Street 28–9
   London Docklands 252–3, **254**
   Thames Gateway 35–6, **37–8**
urban sprawl 33–4, 38, **39**
urban–rural interaction 32–41
urbanisation 19, 32
USA **190**, 215, **217**, 225, **226**
   fires 2000 196–8
   Mojave Desert 230, 246–50

Vancouver, water conservation 117–18
volcanoes 180–3

water 112–24
   conflicts over 112–15, 115
   management of 116–23
water balance, Spain 121, **122**
water pollution, from landfill 109
water quality, of Great Barrier Reef **108**
water shortages, south-west England 131
water table, lowered 121–2, **123**
wealth, cycle of 58
weather 214
West Lodge Farm 65–6
wetlands, under threat 255–60, **255**
   see also Coto de Doñana National Park
wildlife, and tourism, Zimbabwe 76–7
wind energy 103, 106

Yorkshire, changing regional employment structures 56–8

Zimbabwe, CAMPFIRE projects 76–7